Eschatology:

A History of the Global Future

Volume 2

Rochelle Ray

Spring Bud Media, 2025
1st edition
Paperback ISBN: 978-1-966579-04-5
Kindle ASIN: B0F1GGRR5Y

*To God the Father,
God the Son Jesus Christ,
and God the Holy Spirit,
for developing this perfect, awesome,
magnificent, cosmic and eternal plan
and for pouring out on me,
more love than I can possibly receive*

To my sister and friends for their encouragement

*To my husband who provided this opportunity
for researching and for writing*

Eschatology: A History of the Global Future Volume 2

A Biblical Chronology of Eschatology,
the Apocalypse, Last Things, and End of the Era Events:
What the Bible and the Prophets Said
About the Era of the Time of Jacob's Trouble,
Reestablishment of the Nation of Israel,
Prophecies of Daniel, John's Revelation,
Beasts, Seals, Trumpets, Bowls, Plagues, Battles, etc.
Ordered by Scripture, with Commentary

Book 1: Loss of the Perfection of the Original Creation, Era of the Time of Jacob's Trouble, Biblical Study Notes, God's Revelation and the Conflict of Revelation with Evolutionary Theory, This Cosmic Conflict's Beginning, The Author of Rebellion Against God the Creator, Deception of the First Woman and Rebellion of the First Man, God the Creator's First Covenant Agreements, Development and Growth of the Red Dragon / Serpent / Satan, Inc. and the Development of the Plan for Fully Establishing the Kingdom of Satan, Inc. / Kingdom of Man on Earth and in Heaven, The Problem of a Broken World and Broken Relationships, Corruption of the Human Lineage, Establishment of the Covenant Lineage, Plan for Redemption and Reclamation and Regeneration, Seasons to Mark Time, Fight Against Spiritual Force of Evil

Book 2: Major Prophecies of the Prophets of the Old Testament / Tanakh Concerning the Nation of Israel, Daniel's Four Beasts, Daniel's Seventy Sevens and the Seventieth Seven, Gospels' Presentation of Jesus Christ, Priest of the Order of Melchizedek, Two Messiahs or Two Visitations, Nation of Israel's Rejection of Jesus as Promised and Prophesied Messiah, Times of the Gentiles, Holy Spirit in the Book of Revelation, John's Book of Revelation, Jesus Christ's Message to the Angels of the Seven Churches, Other Messages Concerning This Historical Era

Book 3: God's Revelation for Our Generation, Jesus Christ's Revelation to John the Apostle, Responsibilities of the Followers of the Lamb During the Era of the Time of Jacob's Trouble, Purpose for this Era, The Red Dragon and the Three Predominate Beast and the Three Women of Revelation, Allies of the Rebellion /

Antichrist System / Unholy Trinity – Red Dragon and Beast of the Sea and Beast of the Earth

Book 4: Prophetic Importance of the Use of Specific Numbers, Problems with Rapture Theology, As It Was in the Days Before Noah, God's Plan for the Restoration of Nations and the Restoration of the Nation of Israel in Preparation for Jesus' Return, Sealing of the 144,000 Israelites and of the 144,000 Followers of the Lamb, Signs in the Heavens, Timeline Overview for the Era of the Time of Jacob's Trouble, Daniel's Seventieth Seven, First Half of the Era of the Time of Jacob's Trouble, Seven Seals, Seven Trumpets, Instructions of Three Angels, Events on the Temple Mount in Jerusalem Israel and the Resumption and Suspension of Animal Sacrifices

Book 5: Second Portion of the Era of the Time of Jacob's Trouble Begins, Red Dragon / Serpent / Satan, Inc. Hurled to Earth, War Against the People of Israel, Two Witnesses from Heaven, Abomination of Desolation Events, Activity of the Beast of the Sea and Beast of the Earth, Mark of the Beasts System, Miracles Performed Through the Followers of the Lamb / Jesus Christ

Book 6: Significance of Historical Events for the Second Portion of the Era of the Time of Jacob's Trouble and for the Finale for the Era of the Time of Jacob's Trouble, Ministry of the Two Witnesses, Third Heavenly Sign and Consecration of God's Temple in Heaven, Resumption of Animal Sacrifices, Israel's Rejection of Jesus Christ as the Promised and Prophesied Messiah, Flooding in the Land of Israel, People of Israel Recognize Jesus Christ as Promised and Prophesied Messiah, God Most High Remembers Israel and Fights on Israel's Side, Red Dragon / Serpent / Satan, Inc. Pursues the Followers of the Lamb, Three Nations Conquered, Assassination and Death of the Two Witnesses and the Commencement of the Events for the Finale for the Era of the Time of Jacob's Trouble – Final Seventy Five Days, Preparation for the Glorious Return of Jesus Christ, Preparation for the Destruction of the Allies of the Rebellion and the Full Establishment of the Kingdom of Heaven on Earth

Book 7: The Three Women of the Book of Revelation, Description of the Great Prostitute / Mystery Babylon the Great!, Description of the Scarlet Beast of Revelation 17, Relationship of the Great Prostitute / Mystery Babylon the Great! and the Scarlet Beast

Book 8: Scarlet Beast, The Abyss, Historical Development of the Scarlet Beast, Seven / Eight Pope Kings, Eighth King Beast, Relationships Between Prophetic Beasts and Heads and Horns

Book 9: Order of the Events for the Finale for the Era of the Time of Jacob's Trouble Required for the Destruction of the Allies of the Rebellion, Accomplishment of the Mystery of God and the Little Scroll, Sounding of the Seventh Trumpet / Pouring Out of the

Seven Bowls of God Most High's Wrath / Seven Last Plagues, Complete Union of the Great Prostitute / Mystery Babylon the Great! with the Scarlet Beast, Judgment and Destruction of Mystery Babylon the Great!, Ten Horns / Ten Kings Given Power for One Hour, Gathering of the Armies of the Nations of the Earth to Make War Against the Nation of Israel and Jesus Christ, Fall Feasts as Prophecy Documenting the Return of Jesus Christ, Necessity of the Practice of the Sacrificial System

Book 10: Order of the Events for the Finale for the Era of the Time of Jacob's Trouble Required for the Destruction of the Allies of the Rebellion, Immediate Events that Accompany the Return of Jesus Christ, Harvest of the Earth, Resurrection of God's Holy People, Reunion of the Kingdom of Heaven with Earth, Jesus Christ Prepares for the Final Battle of this Age, The Day of the Lord / Day of Atonement / Yom Kippur, Events for the Day of the Lord, Siege of Jerusalem, Jesus Christ Defeats the Enemies of God Most High, Destruction of Mystery Babylon the Great!, Gathering of the Grapes, Beast of the Earth and Beast of the Sea Captured, Books Opened and Closed, Cleanup of the Dead, Everlasting Kingdom of Heaven Permeates the Earth, Rewards for God's Holy People

Table of Contents

Table of Contents	6
Prophets of the Old Testament / Tanakh and the Writers of the New Testament	13
Exile and the Old Testament / Tanakh prophet Ezekiel's Vision of the Valley of Dry Bones	15
Nebuchadnezzar's Image of a Man – Daniel 2	**17**
Nebuchadnezzar's first three of four kingdoms – Daniel 2:31-33, 2:36-39	22
The end of the Babylonian empire and the handwriting on the wall: 'Mene, Mene, Tekel and Upharsin' / 'numbered, numbered, weighed and divided' – Daniel 5 (October 12, 539 BC – possibly the Day of Atonement / Yom Kippur)	22
Nebuchadnezzar's fourth kingdom in the image of a man – Daniel 2	26
Nebuchadnezzar's rock that shattered the feet and toes of Nebuchadnezzar's vision of the image of a man – Daniel 2	31
Daniel's Four Beasts – Daniel 7	**33**
A prophecy for the past, for history? Or a prophecy for the future era of the time of Jacob's Trouble?	36
A prophecy for the future, for the era of the time of Jacob's Trouble	37
The further context of Daniel's vision of the four beasts / four kingdoms – Daniel 7	39
The four winds of heaven – Daniel 7:2-3	39
The important work of the four winds of heaven in gathering the elect – Jeremiah 49:36, Ezekiel 37:8-10, Daniel 7:1-3, 8:7-9, 11:3-5, Zechariah 2:5-7, Matthew 24:30-32, Mark 13:26-28, Revelation 7:1-3	41
The work of the four winds, to scatter – Jeremiah 49:35-37	45
The great sea and the earth	46
The first three of four beasts / kingdoms – Daniel 7	53
The lion with wings like an eagle that were broken off, that stood like a man with the heart of a man – Daniel 7:4	59
The bear on its side with three ribs in its mouth between its teeth, that went to eat his fill of flesh – Daniel 7:5	59
The leopard with four wings of a bird and four heads given the authority to rule – Daniel 7:6	61
The fourth beast / fourth kingdom, with the ten horns / ten kings – global governance as the foundation for the little horn / eleventh king / king that will exalt himself / beast of the earth / final world ruler – Daniel 7	64

The biblical prophetic device of three parts – four parts, utilized in understanding the fourth beast / fourth kingdom of Daniel 7   68

The foundation of the fourth beast / fourth kingdom, as the source for the little horn / eleventh king that will rise from the ten horns / ten kings – Daniel 7   71

The destruction of the fourth beast / fourth kingdom – Daniel 7   72

Daniel's Seventy 'Sevens' / Weeks of Years – Daniel 9:20-27   74

Daniel's first sixty nine 'sevens' / weeks of years #1-69 - Daniel 9:20-27   75

The historical correlation between Daniel's prophecy of the seventy 'sevens,' the events that have taken place since then, and the events that must still take place.   81

The exile of the people of Israel into Assyria and Babylon, and their release from exile by the Medes and the Persians   86

The First Decree - King Cyrus of Persia 538 BC – Permission to return home and to rebuild the temple   89

The Second Decree - King Darius of Persia 520 BC – To continue the rebuilding of the temple   90

The Third Decree - King Artaxerxes 457 BC – Israel was officially released from Persian governance   91

The Fourth Decree - King Artaxerxes March 14, 444 BC – Persian support for work on the temple and the city walls of Jerusalem   92

Daniel's sixty-ninth 'seven' – the ministry years of messiah / the Lamb / Jesus Christ – Daniel 9:20-27   93

Daniel's seventieth 'seven' the prince / ruler who is to come – Daniel 9:20-27   95

Jesus Christ Fulfilled Messianic Prophecy and the Spring Feasts   98

Some of the typologies within the Old Testament / Tanakh, that identified the promised and prophesied messiah as coming twice in human history   102

Prophetic requirements for the promised messiah   103

The messianic fulfillment of the spring feasts by Jesus Christ during his earthly ministry (~4 BC to ~30 AD)   111

Lamb selection day – four days prior to Passover as a preparation for celebrating Passover – Nisan 10, (merely a preparation for observing the required feast of Passover)   117

Feast of Passover / Pesach – Nisan 14 – Exodus 12:1-30, 12:43-49, Leviticus 23:4-8, Numbers 9:9-14, Deuteronomy 16:1-8   118

Feast of unleavened bread, beginning the day after Passover – Nisan 15-21 – Exodus 12:1-30, 12:43-49, 34:18, Leviticus 23:4-8, Numbers 9:9-14, Deuteronomy 16:1-8   123

Feast of firstfruits / bikkurim – day after the Sabbath after Passover – first day of the week – Leviticus 23:9-14, and when coming into a new land – Deuteronomy 26   125

    Law of trees   132

Feast of weeks / Pentecost / Shavuot – Sivan 5 – Exodus 34:22-26, Leviticus 23:15-22, Deuteronomy 16:9-12   132

Messiah must be a descendant of Judah   141

Messiah / the Lamb / Jesus Christ, as the guardian / redeemer / goel   143

The Gospels' Presentation of Jesus   152
Jesus Christ's Own Message During His Earthly Ministry, Concerning His Return   153
Jesus Christ's Instruction to Watch!   154

Ezekiel's instruction to watch   162

Paul's emphasis on Jesus Christ's return – not to be a complete surprise / not a 'gotcha' event – 1 Thessalonians 5:1-6   162

Jesus Christ and the Religious Leaders Confrontation with Jesus Christ's Power and Authority to Provide Resurrection from Death   163
Jesus Christ as Priest of the Order of Melchizedek   167

Zechariah's vision of the kingdom of heaven's high priest, Joshua – Zechariah 3:1-10   169

The New Testament understanding of Jesus Christ as priest of the order of Melchizedek   172

Two Messiahs? or The Same Messiah with Two Works? – messiach ben Yosef / Ephraim and messiach ben David   177
Reasons Why the Nation of Israel Rejected Jesus Christ as the Promised and Prophesied Messiah, and God Most High's Response   181

God Most High's response to the people of Israel's rejection of Jesus Christ as the promised and prophesied messiah   187

God the Creator's knowledge from the time when they all lived together in the Garden of Eden / garden of God / paradise, that the promised and prophesied messiah would be rejected   194

The dynamics of the relationship of the people of Israel with God Most High, during the span of time between the people of Israel's rejection of Jesus Christ as messiah, and the return of messiah / the Lamb / Jesus Christ to the people of Israel   196

The Times of the Gentiles	**200**
Jesus Christ's understanding of the place of Gentiles within God Most High's redemption, reclamation and regeneration plan	200
The apostles' understanding of the times of the Gentiles	202
The duration of the times of the Gentiles	211
The Holy Spirit in the Book of Revelation	**216**
The sevenfold Spirit of God	220
Outline of John's Book of Revelation	**222**
The overall outlined for how Jesus Christ has planned to ready the bride / people of Israel who will receive Jesus Christ, and to ready the followers of the Lamb / Jesus Christ	224
Messiah / the Lamb / Jesus Christ's Message to the Seven Angels of the Seven Churches in Asia, as a Prophetic Historical Timeline for History between Messiah / the Lamb / Jesus Christ's Ascension into Heaven and His Return	**227**
Jesus Christ's message as a continual historical timeline	230
The Lamb / Jesus Christ's message to the seven churches, as a message for the era of the time of Jacob's Trouble	236
The role of women as influencers upon the events of the era of the time of Jacob's Trouble	245
Messiah / the Lamb / Jesus Christ's message provided to John the Revelator, using the term 'church' / ecclesia / εκκλεσια / 'called out ones'	251
The Lamb / Jesus Christ's message to the angels of the seven churches of Asia, as a reference to the historical work of Jesus Christ and of the church, within the seven thousand years plan of God Most High	257
Jesus Christ's message to the angels of the seven churches, as preparation for the events of the era of the time of Jacob's Trouble and the rest of the book of Revelation	260
Jesus Christ's message to the angel of the church at Ephesus: early apostolic church – Revelation 2:1-7	263
Historical message:	264
Historical timeline message to the historical era of the church of Ephesus:	267
The theology of the historical era of the church of Ephesus in the movement toward the theology of the historical era of the church of Laodicea	269
Jesus Christ's message for the era of the time of Jacob's Trouble from the message to the angel of the early apostolic church of Ephesus	269

Jesus Christ's message to the angel of the church at Smyrna: persecuted early church – Revelation 2:8-11	276
Historical message:	277
Historical timeline message to the historical era of the church of Smyrna:	279
The theology of the historical era of the church of Smyrna in the movement toward the theology of the historical era of the church of Laodicea	283
Jesus Christ's message for the era of the time of Jacob's Trouble from the message to the angel of the early persecuted church of Smyrna	284
Jesus Christ's message to the angel of the church at Pergamum: married church – Revelation 2:12-17	285
Historical message:	286
Basic information on the city of Pergamum	287
Pergamum, the home of the temple of Zeus / seat of Satan and the temple's Gigantomachy	288
The development of the college of pontiffs and the sovereign pontiff / Pontifex Maximus	289
Pergamum, the city of the serpent god Asclepius, the god of healing	292
The god Saturn and the transfer of the seat of Satan / the baal / mystery / mythology religion, from the Babylonian empire to Pergamum, and then to Rome	293
The martyrdom of Antipas in Pergamum	296
Balaam son of Beor and Balak of Moab – Numbers 22-25 and 31 (between 1446 and 1406 BC)	297
The Nicolaitans and their work in Pergamum	298
Historical timeline message to the historical era of the church of Pergamum:	302
The importance of receiving a new name	312
The theology of the historical era of the church of Pergamum in the movement toward the theology of historical era of the church of Laodicea	319
Mariology in conflict with the eschatological plan of God the Father, messiah / the Lamb / Jesus Christ / God the Son, and God the Holy Spirit	322
Other aspects of the historically developed doctrines of Mariology within the hierarchy of the Roman Catholic Church, and their conflicts with authentic biblical theology	331
Jesus 'the Christ' theology	338
Message for the era of the time of Jacob's Trouble from the message to the angel of the married church of Pergamum	341

Jesus Christ's message for the era of the time of Jacob's Trouble from the message to the angel of the married church of Pergamum — 344

Jesus Christ's message to the angel of the church at Thyatira: ruling church – Revelation 2:18-29 — 344

Historical message: — 346

   Thyatira's link to Semiramis and Nimrod — 348

   Thyatira's link to Jezebel and Ahab — 362

Historical timeline message to the historical era of the church of Thyatira: — 366

   The challenge of determining the 'birthdate' for the historical era of the church of Thyatira — 366

The theology of the historical era of the church of Thyatira in the movement toward the theology of the historical era of the church of Laodicea — 373

The dogmas, doctrines, theologies and practices of the historical era of the church of Thyatira, that distinguished it from other historical eras — 374

The repression of biblical authority and its impact upon human history to aid in the development of human culture during the era of the time of Jacob's Trouble — 399

Papal kingdom building and its foundation for the global religious community during the era of the time of Jacob's Trouble — 404

Preparatory work during the historical era of the church of Thyatira for the Renaissance, Protestant Reformation, and the historical era of the church of Sardis — 409

Jesus Christ's message for the era of the time of Jacob's Trouble from the message to the angel of the ruling church of Thyatira — 412

Jesus Christ's message to the angel of the church at Sardis: reformation church – Revelation 3:1-6 — 423

Historical message: — 423

Historical timeline message to the historical era of the church of Sardis: — 425

   Seeded and antagonized by the Roman Catholic Church — 427

   Seeded by the protestors against the Roman Catholic Church — 434

   The effect of the Protestant Reformation upon the Roman Catholic Church, and the Counter Reformation — 439

   The historical timeline and the historical era of the church of Sardis / Reformed tradition's incomplete theology — 443

The theology of the historical era of the church of Sardis in the movement toward the theology of the historical era of the church of Laodicea — 445

The influence of the historical era of the church of Sardis / Reformed tradition, upon the historical era of the church of Laodicea and the era of the time of Jacob's Trouble 447

Jesus Christ's message for the era of the time of Jacob's Trouble from the message to the angel of the reformation church of Sardis 458

Jesus Christ's message to the angel of the church at Philadelphia: holiness church – Revelation 3:7-13 463

Historical message: 466

Historical timeline message to the historical era of the church of Philadelphia: 467

The theology of the historical era of the church of Philadelphia in the movement toward the theology of the historical era of the church of Laodicea 473

Jesus Christ's message for the era of the time of Jacob's Trouble from the message to the angel of the holiness church of Philadelphia 476

Jesus Christ's message to the angel of the church at Laodicea: antagonistic apostate church – Revelation 3:14-22 482

Historical message: 483

Historical timeline message to the historical era of the church of Laodicea: 484

Laying the foundation for the global religious community – the great prostitute of Revelation 17 489

Scientism's modern evolutionary theory and its support from the church 490

The ecumenical movement as a precursor for the global religious community / great prostitute of Revelation 17 509

Various ecumenical movement historical events 510

The employment of the picker and chooser Bible study method in the development of the theology of the historical era of the church of Laodicea 514

World War II and the Holocaust / holy burning of 1938 to 1945, as a typology for the historical era of the church of Laodicea 518

The movement of Jesus Christ's foci from nations to individuals, and from churches to individuals 521

Jesus Christ's message for the era of the time of Jacob's Trouble from the message to the angel of the antagonistic apostate church of Laodicea, and the message to the followers of the Lamb / Jesus Christ: 526

The message to the overcomers / followers of the Lamb, concerning the antagonistic apostate church 527

The role of the antagonistic apostate church as it supports the red dragon / serpent / Satan, Inc. in the attempt to fully establish the kingdom of Satan, Inc. / kingdom of man, on earth 537

Messiah / the Lamb / Jesus Christ's role during the historical era of the church of Laodicean theology / era of the time of Jacob's Trouble 541

The Attempt to Disconnect the Message of the Lamb / Jesus Christ Given to the Angels of the Seven Churches, From the Rest of the Message Given Through John the Revelator as Recorded in the Book of Revelation 543

A Message 'Hidden in Plain Sight' From Paul to the Followers of the Lamb / Jesus Christ Who Live During the Era of the Time of Jacob's Trouble 545

Jesus Christ's message to those who will experience life during the era of the time of Jacob's Trouble 548

God Most High's Covenant with the Righteous, and with the Survivors of this Final Battle that Will Take Place with the Return of Messiah / the Lamb / Jesus Christ and the Full Establishment of the Kingdom of Heaven on Earth 556

Prophets of the Old Testament / Tanakh and the Writers of the New Testament

It is important in understanding the message of every written work, to understand who the author is, who the audience is, and what the personal agenda of the author is in writing.

The prophets whose recorded work was located within the Old Testament / Tanakh, were people of Israel who wrote God Most High's message from the perspective of how God Most High's activity would first impact the people and nation of Israel. Because the message belonged to God Most High, the impact of God Most High's activity through the people and the nation of Israel, would spill over into the rest of the world. But the people and the nation of Israel, were the covenant people that God Most High would first influence, and then use to influence the rest of the world. The people of the nation of Israel were designated to become the priests for God Most High, for the rest of the world. (Exodus 19:5-6, Isaiah 61:6, 1 Peter 2:9, etc.)

After the incarnate life of messiah / the Lamb / Jesus Christ, the books contained in the New Testament were written (35 to 99 AD). Every one of the New Testament writers was first of all an Israelite who observed the Jewish faith. But something changed between the events of the era of the Old Testament / Tanakh and the era of the writing of the books of the New Testament. The majority of the leaders of the nation of Israel, had adopted a track in their religious practice that would cause them to reject the promised and prophesied messiah when he came to them.

When the religious leaders of the nation of Israel and the majority of the people of Israel who followed their religious leaders, rejected Jesus Christ as their promised messiah, at that point the focus of God Most High turned to more fully include the Gentiles and the era of the times of the Gentiles officially began. The era of the times of the Gentiles has lasted almost two thousand years. As the era of the times of the Gentiles draws to a close, the era of the time of Jacob's Trouble will again focus God Most High's attention primarily upon the people of Israel, once again.

In understanding biblical prophecy, it is important to understand that the audience for the writers of the Old Testament / Tanakh focused first on the people and the nation of Israel. The writers of the Old Testament / Tanakh made their appeal to the people of Israel first. And they wrote from the context of how God Most High's message would first impact the people of Israel.

It is also important to understand that the audience for the writers of the New Testament focused upon the larger portion of the population, the Gentiles. Once the promised and prophesied messiah had physically come to the people of Israel, and had been rejected, the writers of the New Testament focused their message on what messiah / the Lamb / Jesus Christ had accomplished with his first coming, and what he will accomplish for both the people of Israel and for the Gentile followers of the Lamb / Jesus Christ, when he returns.

Exile and the Old Testament / Tanakh prophet Ezekiel's Vision of the Valley of Dry Bones

Israel entered the Promised Land of Israel (1406 BC) and experienced times of closeness in their relationship with God and times of distance from God. The united kingdom of Israel was initially led by judges, and then led by three kings; Saul, David and Solomon. Each of the three had their positive and negative characteristics. When King Solomon entered into the practice of killing his own children as sacrifices on the baal altars, God Most High decided to divide the nation of Israel into the northern ten tribes who took the name of Israel and the southern two tribes of Judah and Benjamin who took the name Judah (1 Kings 11:1-11, 11:31).

When the divided nations of Israel continued to refrain from honoring the Jubilee years, the Sabbatical years, the Sabbaths and the feast days, God Most High decided to place them into exile according to the number of years that they had neglected to honor God Most High's required holidays / holy days.

It was around the time of the exiles that the prophets of the biblical record received their visions and recorded them. The prophets of the Old Testament / Tanakh were active beginning with Elijah around 886 BC to Malachi around 430 BC).

Ezekiel (fl. 593 to 571 BC) - a prophet of Judah, provided prophesies for the people of Israel and for humanity in general, around 593 to 571 BC, beginning about seven years before the destruction of the temple on Av 9 / August 14, 586 BC. Ezekiel was given a vision of the Valley of Dry Bones, followed by the vision of a united kingdom of Israel and the people of Israel returning to the nation of Israel (Ezekiel 37). Following the vision of the Valley of Dry Bones and the vision of a united kingdom of Israel, Ezekiel had more visions that were set in the context of the era of the time of Jacob's Trouble; the battle against Gog (Ezekiel 38-39) and the vision given April 28, 573 BC of the new temple, the events of the new temple, the instructions for consecrating the new temple and its priests, the allotments of property, and the fulfillment of the kingdom of heaven being fully established on earth (Ezekiel 40-48).

While Ezekiel's visions in Ezekiel 40-48 were given to the people of Israel during the exile, those visions actually spoke of the ending of the second exile of Israel / the conclusion of the diaspora that began in 70 AD. The conclusion of the diaspora that began in 70 AD officially ended on May 14, 1948 when the people of Israel became the nation of Israel and the people of Israel officially again had a homeland. But the full conclusion of the diaspora will be experienced when messiah / the Lamb / Jesus Christ returns to fight on behalf of the people of Israel and to establish the nation of Israel as a nation that will never again experience the threat of annihilation.

Understanding that Ezekiel was written directly to the people of Israel, and that through the prophet Ezekiel, God Most High sent a message into the future for the people of Israel, Ezekiel chapters 37-48 acted for the people of Israel in a similar manner as John the Revelator's message of the book of Revelation acts for the followers of the Lamb / Jesus Christ.

Ezekiel's vision of the Valley of Dry Bones (Ezekiel 37) displayed a valley of bodies that were so decimated that there is no hope of resurrecting the bones again, let alone bringing life back to them. In the Israelite understanding of that time, a person's spirit hung around for three days after a person died. The fourth day, the spirit would finally depart from the body. When Jesus raised Lazarus from the dead, he waited until the fourth day to bring resurrection to Lazarus to demonstrate that God Most High has the power of resurrection no matter how many days a person's body lies in physical death (John 11).

The vision of the Valley of Dry Bones described dry lifeless bones coming together, obtaining flesh, and finally having new life breathed into them.

For the people of Israel, the vision of the Valley of Dry Bones was a vision whose fulfillment was realized beginning with the Holocaust / holy burning / holy sacrifice of the approximately six million Jews during World War II. Following the end of World War II, the nation of Israel was reestablished, May 14, 1948, breathing new life into the dead of the 'valley,' and into the Promised Land, and into the people of Israel who returned to live there.

In May, 2018, Israel celebrated its seventieth year as a reestablished nation. No other nation on earth has 'died' and been 'resurrected' after almost one thousand eight hundred seventy eight years. This fact alone should be recognized as only being able to be possible through the work of God Most High. The fact that the nation of Israel coming to life was prophesied almost two thousand four hundred seventy years prior to the birth of the nation is merely 'gravy' for those who believe that God Most High is the author of true miracles.

Nebuchadnezzar's Image of a Man – Daniel 2

During the time of the exile of Judah, the southern kingdom of the divided nation of Israel was taken into Babylon. (August 586 to 516 BC). It was while the Old Testament / Tanakh prophet Daniel (fl. 605 to 530 BC) - a prophet of Judah, was in exile that God Most High provided Daniel with several significant prophecies concerning the times to come.

Daniel received prophecies that were immediately fulfilled in his lifetime, and prophecies concerning the era of time from his lifetime until the first coming of messiah / Jesus Christ, and prophecies concerning the era of the time of Jacob's Trouble. Daniel received many of these visions personally. But some of the visions came through others.

King Nebuchadnezzar of Babylon had a dream, a vision set within the image of a man, which foretold the future history of the world, covering time, from the time of Nebuchadnezzar, through to the time of the conclusion of the era of the time of Jacob's Trouble. The image of a man was a historical timeline covering two thousand five hundred years of human history, illustrated in three dimensions.

There are those that view the Bible as having gaps where God Most High does not address human history. If this were true, then we would never know when God was present or when God was abandoning us.

But the biblical record documented God Most High as all knowing, ever present, and personally involved in human affairs. God Most High has never left a gap in time where God Most High did not tell us what to expect next, or where God Most High did not address time periods.

The biblical record identified God Most High's continuity throughout human history through:
- the lineage from Adam to Noah (Genesis 5),
- the table of nations (Genesis 10),
- the family of Jacob / Israel as they relocated into Egypt (Genesis 46),
- the lineage from Judah to David (1 Chronicles 2),
- the lineage from David (1 Chronicles 3),
- the descendants of Judah and his brothers, including Saul (1 Chronicles 4 through 8),
- Nebuchadnezzar's image of a man – covering history from Nebuchadnezzar's own lifetime, until the return of the promised and prophesied messiah to defeat the kingdoms of this world (Daniel 2),
- Daniel's prophecy of the kings of the north and the kings of the south that covered history from the time of the exile until the first abomination of desolation, followed by the king that will exalt himself during the era of the time of Jacob's Trouble (Daniel 11:1-35),
- Daniel's prophecy of the seventy sevens that covered history from the time of the return from exile, until the earthly lifetime of Jesus Christ, and then of the era of the time of Jacob's Trouble (Daniel 9:20-27),
- the genealogy of the people who returned from exile (1 Chronicles 9),
- the genealogy of Joseph the supposed father of Jesus Christ, through David and Bathsheba's second son Solomon (Matthew 1:1-17),

- the genealogy of Mary the mother of Jesus Christ dating from Adam, through David and Bathsheba's third son Nathan. Jesus Christ and Mary's genealogy was provided in reversed order, demonstrating that the God of heaven remains divine and sovereign over the future as much as the God of heaven has been divine and sovereign in the past (Luke 3:23-38), and
- the history of the church from the time of the apostles, through to the conclusion of the era of the time of Jacob (Revelation 2 and 3).

Every moment of the past six thousand years of human history, was accounted for within the biblical record. Every moment of the past six thousand years of human history has demonstrated God Most High's continuous interaction with humanity. The biblical record merely highlights some eras of time more than others.

The book of Daniel itself documented multiple messages of what would take place, beginning with the lifetime of Daniel, into our lifetime, and on until eternity officially begins. Nebuchadnezzar's image of a man was merely one of those prophecies.

Nebuchadnezzar's image of a man foretold of the various empires that would rule a significant portion of the world, and hold hegemony over the nation of Israel, starting with the golden head of the image of the man representing the Babylonian empire, and moving all the way down to the toes to the era of the time of Jacob's Trouble. Nebuchadnezzar's image was a vertical timeline, provided for us.

The fact that all this prophecy has found fulfillment so far, except for the prophecy concerning the feet and the toes that applied to the era of the time of Jacob's Trouble, added validity to the prophecy, and veracity to the potential for the prophecy to continue to be fulfilled. It is at the feet and toes, that our own current timeline is fully dramatized through the timeline of Nebuchadnezzar's image of a man.

Another similar vision, that portrayed the same message, was Daniel's image of the four beasts in Daniel 7. The four beasts nicely corresponded to the kingdoms that Nebuchadnezzar's image of a man portrayed.

There are many who claim that the two messages are exactly the same. On the surface, the two visions do convey similar messages. But both visions have multiple layers to their prophecies. And both prophecies hold both an initial fulfillment and then a later fulfillment. Both visions hold additional meaning specifically for our time. In order to understand the greater message of both visions, it is imperative to understand that they are separate visions with separate, but overlapping, messages.

Daniel wrote for the people of Israel / Judah of his time. So much of this may truly be boring ancient history for us. But the visions described in the book of Daniel foretold of the foundation for events that will take place during our time, during the era of the time of Jacob's Trouble. Even more, Daniel supplied probably the best biblically recorded description of the man who would like to establish himself permanently as the global ruler; the coming little horn / eleventh king / king that will exalt himself / prince who is to come / beast of the earth / final world ruler (Daniel 7, 8, 9:26b-27, 11:29-45). Daniel's multiple visions identified his character, some of the things that he will do, and described how we will be able to recognize him.

Daniel also offered timelines and dates. It was Daniel who precisely told of how long different aspects of the era of the time of Jacob's Trouble will last, measured in days. John the Revelator also provided the same kind of timelines and numbers of days, to a predominately Gentile audience.

Note in studying Daniel's prophecies, Daniel marked time in different ways including describing a time that he called 'distant time.' We are currently living in Daniel's 'distant time.' So, when studying Daniel, it is important to recognize the denotation of time, and to understand that Daniel was also writing for us who live in that 'distant time' era.

Daniel began to explain Nebuchadnezzar's vision to Nebuchadnezzar:

'Your thoughts, king, while you were lying on your bed, that came to your mind, were about what would come to pass after this. He who reveals mysteries, has made what will be, known to you. As for me, this mystery was not revealed to me because I have greater wisdom than anyone else alive. But this secret was revealed to me for our sakes, to make known the interpretation to the king and that you may know the thoughts of your heart.'

'You king, were watching, and you saw an image. This great image had great and excellent splendor and stood before you, with its awesome appearance. The head of the image was of fine gold. Its chest and arms were silver. Its belly and thighs were bronze. Its legs of iron. Its feet were partly iron and partly clay.' Daniel 2:29-33 translated

There were two kinds of mysteries referenced in the biblical record.

The mystery of God Most High was something hidden by God Most High that was disclosed to God's people. (Job 11:7, Daniel 2, Matthew 13:41, Luke 8:10, 1 Corinthians 2:7, 4:1, 14:2, Ephesians 3:8-9, Colossians 1:27, 2:2, 4:3, 1 Timothy 3:16, Revelation 10:7)

But the other kind of mystery referenced in the biblical record was the kind of mystery that the red dragon / serpent / Satan, Inc. provides. The mystery that the red dragon / serpent / Satan, Inc. has historically provided, has been an adulterated version of God Most High's mystery.

The red dragon / serpent / Satan, Inc. has capitalized on God Most High's standard of disclosing God Most High's mystery only to God's people, by selling the mysteries / 'deep secrets of God' (Revelation 2:24). But when the red dragon / serpent / Satan, Inc. sells the mysteries / deep secrets of God, the red dragon / serpent / Satan, Inc. changes the story before it is delivered. The first person that the serpent / Satan changed the message for was the first woman when the serpent deceived her. This act earned him the title 'father of lies.'

In order for Nebuchadnezzar to understand the vision / the mystery that he had received, Nebuchadnezzar needed a person who accurately

understood how God Most High communicated, in order to have the message 'translated' for him.

Nebuchadnezzar's first three of four kingdoms – Daniel 2:31-33, 2:36-39

'This was the dream and we will tell the interpretation before the king. You king, you are the king of kings. The God of the kingdom of heaven has given you power and strength and glory. Wherever the children of people dwell or livestock of the field and birds in the sky, God has given them into your hand and has made you ruler over them all. You are that head of gold.' Daniel 2:36-38 translated

The gold head represented the Babylonian empire as led by Nebuchadnezzar.

'After you will arise another kingdom, inferior to yours.' Daniel 2:39a translated

Notice that in this dream the arms of silver represented two empires: the Medes and the Persians. The Medes and Persians took the Babylonian empire from Belshazzar on October 12, 539 BC (Daniel 5).

'And then a third kingdom of bronze, will rule over all the earth.' Daniel 2:39b translated

The third kingdom represented the Greek Empire that conquered the Medes and the Persians around 331 BC.

The end of the Babylonian empire and the handwriting on the wall: 'Mene, Mene, Tekel and Upharsin' / 'numbered, numbered, weighed and divided' – Daniel 5 (October 12, 539 BC – possibly the Day of Atonement / Yom Kippur)

Daniel recorded God Most High's activity with the Babylonian empire as it related to the people of Israel living in exile there. And Daniel documented the events that took place when the Medes and the Persians conquered the Babylonian Empire in a single night.

It was the supernatural handwriting on the wall that caught the attention of Belshazzar.

Belshazzar had offended God Most High in multiple ways. But one of his final offenses was to go across the street from the palace to the place that stored the utensils that had been taken from the temple in Jerusalem during the Babylonian siege of Jerusalem Israel (Av 9, 586 BC), and to use the utensils as common meal service for Belshazzar's party dedicated to the baal / mystery / mythology gods.

If October 12, 539 BC was the Day of Atonement / Yom Kippur, the day of one of the highest and holiest feasts of the required feast days, then for Belshazzar to use the Jerusalem temple utensils in the worship of the baal / mystery / mythology gods, in the city of Babylon that was the center Nimrod had established for the tower of Babel empire and the baal / mystery / mythology religion, then God Most High would have been doubly offended. The Day of Atonement / Yom Kippur was the one day in the year when the high priest would traditionally enter into the Holy of Holies and personally communicate with God Most High face to face. The Day of Atonement / Yom Kippur was the one day in the year when the scapegoat that represented the red dragon / serpent / Satan, Inc. would be pushed off the cliff symbolizing the prophecy that the red dragon / serpent / Satan, Inc. would be defeated and incarcerated. To party in dedication to the baal / mystery / mythology religion gods, using the Jerusalem temple's utensils consecrated to God Most High, on the Day of Atonement / Yom Kippur, would have been extremely offensive to the God of the kingdom of heaven.

In response to Belshazzar's offense, God provided the handwriting on the wall that wrote 'Mene, Mene, Tekel and Upharsin.'

The four words on the wall were familiar to Belshazzar. The mene, tekel and peres were in fact Babylonian coins. The mene was worth approximately sixty shekels. The tekel was worth approximately a shekel. And the peres worth about half a mene or thirty shekels.

But Belshazzar did not understand the prophecy and meaning of the message. Hence the need to send for the prophet of the God who wrote the message, Daniel. Daniel explained to Belshazzar the message. 'Mene, Mene, Tekel and Upharsin' meant that Belshazzar had been 'numbered, weighed and divided.'

'Here is what these words mean:'

'*Mene*: God has numbered the days of your reign and brought it to an end.'

'Tekel: You have been weighed on the scales and found wanting.'
'Peres: Your kingdom is divided and given to the Medes and Persians.' Daniel 5:26-28

The statement on the wall; 'mene, mene, tekel and upharsin' *was in the format of a quad prophecy, a unique prophetic technic. The format of quad prophecy meant that three of the four parts were for immediate fulfillment ('...* mene, tekel, and upharsin'). *The first mene was ignored in the immediate fulfillment. That was reflected in Daniel's immediate interpretation for Belshazzar that omitted the first 'mene.'*

All four parts were to be reserved for a later fulfillment, a fulfillment for the era of the time of Jacob's Trouble.

On the night the prophecy was given, the first fulfillment was immediately filled.

Darrius the Mede conquered he Babylonian kingdom in a single night, October 12, 539 BC. Coincidently, on October 12, 539 BC, the sun was entering the constellation of Libra, the scales. This corresponded to Belshazzar also being weighed in the scales.

Darrius accomplished the capture of Babylon by stopping the river that came into Babylon and then using the riverbed for his troops to come into Babylon under the city walls. Conquering Babylon was such a surprise to the people of Babylon that many of the residents were not even aware that the city had been captured for the first few days after the capture.

That very night Belshazzar, king of the Babylonians (son of Nebuchadnezzar), was slain, and Darius the Mede took over the kingdom, at the age of sixty two. Daniel 5:30-31

Daniel also pointed out the generation gap between the young and arrogant Belshazzar the Babylonian, and the older and wiser Darius the Mede. One generation respected the sanctity of God Most High, and the other did not. Every generation must make its own discovery of who they will believe that God Most High is, and whether or not God is worthy of respect.

Read about the entire event with the writing on the wall, in Daniel 5.

In the original prophecy, 'mene' was stated twice implying that the verbs may also be interpreted as nouns. As a noun, a mene was 1000 garahs (a garah was a base unit of weight like our penny). A tekel was 20 garahs, and a peres was half a mene. ('upharsin' was the Hebrew way of saying 'and peres.') Adding the amounts together yielded 1000 + 1000 + 20 + 500 = 2,520 garahs.
2,520 is the number of days assigned for the era of the time of Jacob's Trouble if the second half of the era of the time of Jacob's Trouble is equal to the first half. The second half of the era of the time of Jacob's Trouble was documented to be one thousand two hundred sixty days (not including the seventy five days of the finale for the era of the time of Jacob's Trouble. (Daniel 12:11-12, Revelation 11:3, 12:6, etc.)

Av 9, 586 BC (~August 586 BC) was the date when the temple had been destroyed by the Babylonian king Nebuchadnezzar.
On the night that Belshazzar abused the temple vessels and lost the Babylonian empire to Darius the Mede (October 12, 539 BC), the control of the temple vessels began their return to the people of Israel. Later it would be the decrees of the kings of the Medes and the Persians that would return the people of Israel to return to their land, to rebuild the temple in Jerusalem, to regain real control over the temple mount and to again govern themselves as a nation.
Darius I (fl. September 29, 522 to October 486 BC) reigned over the Achaemenid empire. His son Xerxes I who would marry Hadassah / Esther, was born around 518 BC.
It was also in 518 BC that Darius I granted the people of Israel control over the temple mount. (Ezra 6:1-12). The Old Testament / Tanakh prophet Zechariah (fl. 520 to 480 BC), was also provided with prophetic visions around this time (Zechariah 1:1, 1:7, 7:1).

What was noteworthy concerning these dates, was that August 518 BC was approximately 2,520 years before June 7, 1967 AD. June 7, 1967 was when the people of Israel again gained control of the temple mount during the Six Day War. In this calculation of time, there needs to be noted that there was a one year conversion correction from BC to AD when no year existed, and the Jewish prophetic calendar was based upon a 360 day year.

There may be yet another layer of fulfillment to the prophecy of the handwriting on the wall, that is yet to take place during the era of the time of Jacob's Trouble. Daniel did not offer details for future fulfillments of this prophecy that will take place during our time.

Nebuchadnezzar's fourth kingdom in the image of a man – Daniel 2

Nebuchadnezzar's vision of the fourth kingdom in the image of a man, equated with Daniel's vision of the fourth beast / fourth kingdom from which the ten horns / ten kings and the little horn / eleventh king will rise.

(Notice the differences in the approaches for the interpretations of the original text.)

Finally, there will be a fourth kingdom, strong as iron — for iron breaks and smashes everything — and as iron breaks things to pieces, so it will crush and break all the others. Just as you saw that the feet and toes were partly of baked clay and partly of iron, so this will be a divided kingdom. Yet it will have some of the strength of iron in it, even as you saw iron mixed with clay. As the toes were partly iron and partly clay, so this kingdom will be partly strong and partly brittle. And just as you saw the iron mixed with baked clay, so the people will be a mixture and will not remain united, any more than iron mixes with clay.' Daniel 2:40-43 NIV

'This kingdom will be the result of a marriage between kingdoms, but it will crumble, just as iron and clay don't stick together.' Daniel 2:43 CEV

'You saw the iron mixed with clay, but iron and clay don't completely mix together. In the same way the people of the fourth kingdom will be a mixture. They will not be united as one people.' Daniel 2:43 ERV

'This mixture of iron with clay also shows that these kingdoms will try to strengthen themselves by forming alliances with each other through intermarriage of their rulers. But this will not succeed, for iron and clay don't mix.' Daniel 2:43 TLB

'As you saw the iron mixed with ceramic clay, they will mingle with the seed of humanity, but they will not adhere to one another, just as iron does not mix with clay.' Daniel 2:43 translated

Each interpretation brought unique nuances to the message provided by Daniel. What the iron and clay represented in this vision, were not definitively identified. But what was communicated that the alliances / marriage between the iron and clay will fail.

The legs of iron that stood above the feet of iron and clay, represented the Roman empire. The Roman empire was once the greatest empire on earth, unable to be defeated, able to break and smash everything. The Roman empire was known for its iron and the achievements that it was able to make using iron.

But in Nebuchadnezzar's image of a man, there were two legs that represented the Roman empire. The Roman empire was not conquered like the previous empires in Nebuchadnezzar's image of a man. Instead, the Roman empire was divided into two parts. And what came after the Roman empire was represented by two feet and ten toes, comprised of iron and clay.

The two legs / two parts of the Roman empire were the western leg and the eastern leg. It was Diocletian who divided the Roman empire into two parts around 284 AD. Diocletian determined that the western empire would be governed from Rome while the eastern empire would be governed from Constantinople. The western leg retained the Roman name. The eastern leg became the Byzantine empire.

Around 476 AD, the Roman empire was again divided, conquered through uprisings and barbarian tribes who would acquire land and people from the now weakened shell of what was once the Roman empire. These divisions resulted in the nations of Europe.

The Russian Revolution took place in 1917 and became the foundation for the development of the iron curtain that isolated the Soviet Union and its satellite states, from the nations of western Europe and the

Americas. It was a division that followed the religious boundary lines of the Orthodox Church of the east and the Roman Catholic Church of the west. But more importantly, the curtain that developed was described as iron, the material that constituted the two legs of Nebuchadnezzar's image of a man.

One possible fulfillment of the prophecy of the ten toes was the rough divisions caused by the various divisions that have been historically experienced on the European continent.

Note: iron and clay don't mix. Alliances of European kingdoms have consistently been unsuccessful in its goal of finding unity. Powerful leaders of Europe have attempted to revive the power and control that the Roman empire once held over people. There have been five major political attempts to reunite Europe. All have failed.

- Charlemagne (768 - 814 AD) - coronated by Leo III (fl. 795 to 816) as the first Holy Roman Emperor / Emperor of the Romans
- Charles V of Spain (1519 - 1556 AD) - held the office of Holy Roman Emperor / Emperor of the Romans
- Louis XIV of France (1643 - 1715 AD) - known as Louis the Great or the Sun King, modeled his seventy two year reign of absolutism, after Roman emperors
- Napoleon Bonaparte (1804 - 1814 AD) - modeled himself after Roman emperors ('I am a true Roman Emperor. I am the best race of the Caesars – those who are founders.')
- Adolf Hitler (1934 - 1945 AD) - Sought to revive the Roman empire ('The Fascist movement is a spontaneous return to the traditions of ancient Rome.' Hitler's Table Talk, Saturday, 5th July 1941)

But the pieces of the Roman empire have gone beyond influencing Europe, to permeate the entire world. The governments of all democracies were established from the foundation of the Roman empire's senate, and influenced by Roman law. Scientific names are usually Latin, the language of the Roman empire. And the Roman

Catholic Church has historically considered itself to be the extension of the Roman empire with the anticipation that the Roman Catholic Church will someday rule the world, establishing the global kingdom that Jesus Christ failed to establish during his earthly ministry.

It is possible, but not probable, that the ten toes corresponded to the beast with the ten horns in Daniel 7 and the beast with the ten horns in Revelation 12 and 13. This potential correspondence would be based solely upon the fact that the number of toes and the number of horns were both ten.

It is possible that the toes and the horns / ten kings, located on different ends of the bodies that they were connected to, will not share a connection with each other. Also, the ten toes were located on the image of a man. The ten horns / ten kings were also located on the heads of the red dragon / serpent / Satan, Inc. (Revelation 12), the beast of the sea / false prophet / eighth king beast (Revelation 13) and the scarlet beast with the seven / eight heads (Revelation 17).

In addition, the Roman empire would have only accounted for one of the two iron legs in Nebuchadnezzar's image of a man. The other leg would have included the descendants of the Byzantine empire, roughly the region of modern Turkey and other nations.

There have been multiple other possible interpretations presented for what the two feet and the ten toes represent in the future.

The two feet could represent:
- The necessary connection for the ten toes.
- Two aspects of rule (for example, religious and political, or religious and economic, or political and economic, etc.).
- Worldwide rule from two areas / continents / superpowers / ruling organizations (for example, United Nations and European Union?, United Nations and global elites?, United Nations and the global religious community?, etc.).

- *Another possible representation yet to be disclosed near the time of the complete fulfillment of the vision.*

The ten toes could represent:
- *The number ten symbolizes completeness. The meaning would be symbolic and the toes would represent all the nations of the world together.*
- *The transhumanist movement of the kingdom of Satan, Inc / kingdom of man. Iron does not mix with baked clay. Humanity was created by God the Creator, out of the dust of the earth. The iron could represent the kingdom of Satan, Inc. / kingdom of man's movement toward transforming humanity against bearing the image that God the Creator pressed into humanity.*
- *Ten of the common markets of the European Communities. The problem is that there are no longer just ten countries under the original Treaty of Rome that developed the original European Communities / EC / 1957 and subsequent development of the European Union through the Danish Maastricht Treaty / 1992, with amendments of treaties like the Amsterdam treaty / 1997, nice treaty / 2001, Lisbon Treaty /2009. Currently there are twenty seven nations within the European Union after Brexit / Britain's exit.*
- *Ten regions that the United Nations has decided to divide the world into after dispensing with the system of nations, national boundaries, national cultures, national economies, and nationhood that we currently enjoy.*
- *Ten nations, or more if the 'ten' here was symbolic, that will come together in the future and share a common political goal but still cannot agree together on how to proceed.*
- *Other possible representation to be disclosed near the time of its fulfillment.*

'And in the days of those kings, the God of heaven will establish a kingdom that will never be destroyed, ever. Nor will the kingdom be left to other people. It will break in pieces and consume all these kingdoms. And it will stand forever.'

'This is the meaning of the vision you saw. The rock that was cut from the mountain, without human hands, will break into pieces the iron, the bronze, the clay, the silver, and the gold. The great God has made this known to the king, to show what will take place in the future. The dream is certain and the interpretation is sure.' Daniel 2:44-45 translated

'In the time of those kings' referenced the era of the last world empire, the era of the time of Jacob's Trouble, the era that we are living in. This portion of the prophecy foretold that there will be a massive 'global governance' kingdom that will seek to control people for the advantage of those who consider themselves to be the elite and the elect. In the time of those kings, God Most High will no longer tolerate their rule which will seek to defy God Most High's intentions and God Most High's divinity and sovereignty.

When the 'rock from heaven' *arrives to smash the ten toes, the world government systems will fall and the global governance system will be destroyed. In its place, God Most High will act to set up God's kingdom. The Thousand Years Reign of Jesus Christ will begin.*

While the materials of gold, silver, bronze, iron and clay each have their own strength, it will be the rock that is cut by God Most High out of a mountain, that will break the feet and toes in this image into pieces. The prophecy communicated that the world's empires and kingdoms will ultimately be destroyed by God Most High through God's instrument, 'the rock.'

Jesus Christ was referred to throughout the Bible as 'the rock.' Jesus Christ is the only 'rock' that could originate from heaven.

Nebuchadnezzar's rock that shattered the feet and toes of Nebuchadnezzar's vision of the image of a man – Daniel 2

The vision

'While you were watching, a rock was cut out, but not with human hands; and it struck the image on its feet of iron and clay, and broke them into pieces. Then the iron, the clay, the bronze, the silver and the gold became like chaff on the summer threshing floors. And the wind carried them away, so that no trace of them was found. The rock that struck the image, became a great mountain and filled the whole earth.' Daniel 2:34-35 translated

The interpretation

'Just as you saw the feet and toes, partly of potter's clay and partly of iron, this kingdom will be a divided kingdom. And yet the strength of iron will be in it, even as you saw the iron mixed with ceramic clay. And as the toes of the feet were partly of iron and partly of clay, so this kingdom will be partly strong and partly fragile. As you saw the iron mixed with ceramic clay, they will mingle with the seed of humanity, but they will not adhere to one another, just as iron does not mix with clay.'

'And in the days of those kings, the God of heaven will establish a kingdom that will never be destroyed, ever. Nor will the kingdom be left to other people. It will break in pieces and consume all these kingdoms. And it will stand forever.'

'This is the meaning of the vision you saw. The rock that was cut from the mountain, without human hands, will break into pieces the iron, the bronze, the clay, the silver, and the gold.' Daniel 2:42-45a translated

In prophetic imagery, mountains represented kingdoms, empires and ruling bodies.

In Nebuchadnezzar's image of a man, the rock that shattered the feet and toes of iron and clay, was transformed into its own mountain / kingdom, and represented the kingdom of heaven that will take the place of all previous kingdoms, will overshadow all other kingdoms, and will provide sovereignty over all the earth. What the two beasts of Revelation 13 will have failed to accomplish in establishing global governance, the rock that will come from heaven, will achieve.

That rock that shattered Nebuchadnezzar's image of a man, would arrive incarnate approximately six hundred years later. And the actual shattering that this rock / man will accomplish will take place during the finale for the era of the time of Jacob's Trouble, approximately two thousand six hundred years after the prophecy was provided to Nebuchadnezzar.

In a sense, the rock that shattered the feet and toes of Nebuchadnezzar's image, has already begun to shatter kingdoms in the form of the spread of authentic

Christianity. The followers of the Lamb / Jesus Christ have shed the iron shackles of earthly kingdoms and the apostate church, in order to treasure human life as it was created by God the Creator.

Daniel's Four Beasts – Daniel 7

There are some who have interpreted Nebuchadnezzar's image of a man (Daniel 2) to share equivocacy with another vision also recorded by Daniel, the four beasts / four kingdoms (Daniel 7). But within the two visions, there were sharp distinctions that clearly indicated that the full meanings of the two visions were definitely not the same.

Nebuchadnezzar's image of man was a vision of four empires that were set squarely in the past on a historical timeline, comprised of components of ancient kingdoms, with the exception of the feet and toes made of iron and baked clay. (Daniel 2)

The vision that Daniel had of the four beasts / four kingdoms, depicted the first three beasts / three kingdoms as possibly having an ancient fulfillment. But the four beasts in Daniel's vision were all depicted as acting simultaneously during the era of the time of Jacob's Trouble. When reviewing the chapter as a whole, in connection with Revelation 12, 13 and 17, the final fulfillment of the prophetic four beasts / four kingdoms will consist of the components of all four beasts being present and needing to simultaneously work together as a whole to provide support to the rise of the beast of the sea (Revelation 13:1-10) the overall plan of the red dragon / serpent / Satan, Inc. (Revelation 12), the development of the ten horns / ten kings and the rise of the little horn / eleventh king (Revelation 13:11-18). (Daniel 7)

The timing of the interpretation of the four beasts / four kingdoms being set within the context of the era of the time of Jacob's Trouble, was also supported by the full description of the beast of the sea as the beast from the Abyss / eighth king beast of Revelation 13 and 17. (Daniel 7)

Daniel's vision of the four beasts / four kingdoms (Daniel 7):

Belshazzar (fl. 556-539 BC) was the prince under Nabonidus king of Babylon, and was possibly the grandson of Nebuchadnezzar II (fl. 605 to 562 BC) through his mother.

The vision

In the first year of Belshazzar, king of Babylon, Daniel had a dream and visions passed through his mind, while he was on his bed. Then he wrote the dream down, telling the main significant facts.

Daniel said, 'I was looking and behold in my vision at night, I saw the four winds of heaven were stirring up the great sea.'

'Four great beasts, each different, came up from this sea.'

'The first beast was like a lion, and had wings like an eagle. I watched until the wings were plucked off. This beast was lifted up from the earth, onto two feet like a man, and made to stand. A man's heart was given to it.'

'And suddenly, there was another beast, a second beast like a bear. It was raised up on one side, and had three ribs in its mouth, between its teeth. And they said to the bear, 'Arise, devour much flesh."

'After this I looked, and there was another beast like a leopard which had four wings of a bird on its back. And the beast had four heads. The authority to rule was given to the beast.'

'After this I saw in visions at night, a fourth dreadful and terrible and exceedingly strong beast with iron teeth. With its huge iron teeth, it was devouring and breaking into pieces. And the residue that was left, it trampled with its feet. It was different from all the other beasts before it. And it had ten horns.'

'As I was considering the horns, there was another little horn coming up among them. And three of the first horns were plucked out by the roots. The little horn had eyes like the eyes of a man, and a mouth that spoke pompous words.'

The Ancient of Days

'I watched until thrones were put in place and the Ancient of Days was seated. His garment was as white as snow and the hair of his head was like pure wool. His throne was a fiery flame, with its wheels a burning fire.'

'A river of fire was flowing, coming out before him. Thousands upon thousands came before him to minister to him. Ten thousand and ten thousand times ten thousand, stood before the court where he was seated. And the books were opened.'

'I watched then because of the sound of the pompous words which the little horn was speaking. I watched until the beast was slain, and its body destroyed and given to the burning flame. And as for the rest of the beasts, their dominion had been taken away, and yet their lives were extended for a prolonged season and a time.'

'I was watching in visions in the night and behold, with the clouds of heaven, came one like a son of man, coming to the Ancient of Days. He came and they brought him near before him.'

'To him was given dominion and glory and a kingdom that all peoples, nations, and languages should serve him. His dominion is an everlasting dominion which will not pass away. And his kingdom is the one kingdom that will not be destroyed.'

The interpretation
'I, Daniel, was grieved in my spirit, within my body. The visions in my head troubled me. I came near to the one who stood by, and asked him what the truth of all of this was. So he told me the interpretation, and made the things known to me.'

"There are four great beasts, which are four kings that will arise out of the earth."

"But the saints of God Most High will receive the kingdom and possess the everlasting kingdom forever and ever."

'Then I wished to know the truth about the fourth exceedingly dreadful beast which was different from all the others with its iron teeth and its bronze nails which devoured and broke into pieces, and trampled on what remained with its feet, and the ten horns that were on its head, and the other horn that came up from it, from which the three horns fell before it; specifically this horn which had eyes and a mouth which spoke pompous words, whose appearance was greater than his fellows.'

'As I was watching, this horn was making war against the saints and prevailing against them, until the Ancient of Days came and a judgment was made in favor of the saints of God Most High, and the time came for the saints of possess the kingdom.'

'He said, 'The fourth beast will be a fourth kingdom on earth, which will be different from all other kingdoms, and will devour the whole earth, and trample it and break it into pieces."

"The ten horns that will rise from this kingdom, will be ten kings. And another will rise after them. He will be different from the first kings, and three of the kings will be subdued. He will speak pompous words against God Most High, and against the saints of God Most High. He will persecute the saints and will intend to change the times and the law. The saints will be given into his hand for a time and times and half a time."

"But the court will be seated, and they will take away his dominion, to consume and destroy it forever."

"Then the dominion and greatness of his kingdom under the whole of heaven, will be given to the saints, the people of God Most High. His kingdom is an everlasting kingdom and all of his dominion will serve him and obey."

'This was the end of the matter. As for me, Daniel, my thoughts greatly troubled me. This changed my countenance. But in my heart, I kept this account.' Daniel 7:1-28 translated

A prophecy for the past, for history? Or a prophecy for the future era of the time of Jacob's Trouble?

There have been many interpretations of the Daniel's vision of the four beasts that either set the prophecy exclusively in the ancient past, or set the prophecy as having been fulfilled prior to the coming of Jesus Christ the first time, or as having been already fulfilled in human history since the first coming of Jesus Christ, or as mere allegory and without meaning. But all interpretations that set the fulfillment of this vision's message in the past, or that deny the validity of the prophecy for the era of the time of Jacob's Trouble, fall short of meeting the complete final fulfillment of the prophecy.

The Four Beasts of Daniel (Daniel 7)

beast	special features	first fulfillment (time of Nebuchadnezzar and Daniel)	second fulfillment (as preparation for the 'first era of Jacob's Trouble' / pre—WWII)	fulfillment during the era of the time of Jacob's Trouble
lion	wings like an eagle, stood like a man, given the heart of a man	Babylon	England with the wings plucked off being the United States	Great Britain with a dominate leader, speaking the dominate language of the world?
bear	raised up on one side, three ribs in its mouth between teeth, told to eat its fill of flesh	Medes and Persians	Russia	Russia and associated nations, allied with Russia?
leopard	four wings on back, four heads, given authority	Greeks	Germany	European nations?

terrifying and frightening and very powerful	large iron teeth, crushed and devoured its victims, trampled underfoot what was left, ten horns with a little horn with the eyes like a man and spoke boastfully	Romans	Allied powers / League of Nations / United Nations	global governance system

A prophecy for the future, for the era of the time of Jacob's Trouble

There were those who believed that Daniel's vision of the four beasts of Daniel 7 was a message for those who lived in the ancient past and that the prophecy was entirely fulfilled in the past. They equated the four beasts with previous kingdoms either in the ancient world or someplace in more modern history, but distant from current events.

But in the midst of the description of the four beasts, there were indicators that designated the vision of Daniel's four beasts as a message for people living during the era of the time of Jacob's Trouble.

One clue that Daniel's vision was primarily given for the people living during the era of the time of Jacob's Trouble was with the description of the Ancient of Days taking his seat and the opening of the books (Daniel 7:9-10). It was common practice that judges would be seated just before making their judgments. And the second judgment of the earth and its inhabitants, will take place in conjunction with the return of the promised and prophesied messiah.

Another clue in Daniel's vision placed the little horn that will arise from the ten horns / ten kings, that arise from the fourth terrifying beast / fourth kingdom, as being present at the time when the books are opened (Daniel 7:11), along with the four beasts / four kingdoms (Daniel 7:12).

According to Daniel, the fourth kingdom will rise and devour the whole earth (Daniel 7:23). This kind of event has yet to take place.

The one like a son of man came at that time with the clouds of heaven (Daniel 7:13), which was a reference to the glorious return of messiah / the Lamb / Jesus Christ who will come with the clouds of heaven. And at that time, Jesus Christ will take dominion over all the earth with his everlasting kingdom (Daniel 7:14).

Daniel documented that at the conclusion of these events, all earthly kingdoms will be placed under the hegemony of the everlasting kingdom of heaven (Daniel 7:14, 7:26-27). Historically there have been no kingdoms that have been stripped of their authority and then allowed to live on for a period of time (Daniel 7:12). And throughout human history, this kind of hegemony under the kingdom of heaven has yet to be established, and could not be established without the intervention of the God of heaven.

In addition to the internal evidence of Daniel 7 that placed these events to transpire during the era of the time of Jacob's Trouble, John the Revelator's vision also validated many of the details of Daniel 7, as taking place during this time period.

According to John the Revelator, the first three beasts / three kingdoms of Daniel 7, will be essential in supporting the rise of the beast of the sea (Revelation 13:2).

Also, according to John the Revelator, the ten horns / ten kings will actively participate at crucial points in the mission of attempting to fully establish the kingdom of Satan, Inc. / kingdom of man on earth. According to Daniel, the ten horns / ten kings will be essential for the rise of the little horn / eleventh king / beast of the earth. According to John the Revelator, the ten horns / ten kings will also hold relationship with the red dragon / serpent / Satan, Inc. (Revelation 12:3), the beast of the sea / beast from the Abyss / eighth king beast (Revelation 13:1, 17:3-18) and the beast of the earth (Revelation 17:12-17).

For all these reasons, the prophecy of the four beasts / four kingdoms, must be properly belongs set within the context of events that will take place during the era of the time of Jacob's Trouble.

The further context of Daniel's vision of the four beasts / four kingdoms – Daniel 7
Daniel's vision of the four beasts / four kingdoms contained some details of secondary elements, that further explained Daniel's vision of the four beasts / four kingdoms, and other visions recorded within the biblical record.

For example, Daniel described the origin of the four beasts / four kings as originating from the great sea. And the great sea was churned by the four winds of heaven, almost acting as a release mechanism for the four beasts / four kingdoms. But later within Daniel's description of the four beasts / four kingdoms, the fourth kingdom was described as rising from the earth.

The two beasts of Revelation 13 came separately from the sea and from the earth, and yet they were able to share their power and authority.

Within the biblical record, it was the Old Testament / Tanakh prophets like Daniel who first described these elements as affecting deeper descriptions of eschatological events. But it was the New Testament authors who described details that further connected the pieces.

The four winds of heaven – Daniel 7:2-3
In Daniel's vision of the four beasts / four kingdoms, Daniel said: 'I was looking and behold in my vision at night, I saw the <u>four winds of heaven</u> were stirring up the great sea. Four great beasts, each different, came up from this sea.' Daniel 7:2-3 translated
The four winds of heaven appeared to be the release mechanism for the development of the four beasts / four kingdoms and all that emerged from the four beasts / four kingdoms.

In Daniel's vision of the final horn from the shaggy goat, Daniel recorded that the first four horns grew up toward the four winds of heaven. It was from out of one of the four horns, that the final horn / beast of the earth, rose.

The male goat grew to be very great. When the male goat became strong, his large horn was broken off and four notable horns came up out of the large horn to take its place. The <u>four horns grew toward the four winds of heaven</u>.

Out of one of the four horns came a little horn that grew to be exceedingly great, growing toward the south and east and toward the Glorious (Land). It grew up to reach the host of heaven and to cast some of the host and some of the stars of heaven to the ground. And it trampled some of the host and some of the stars of heaven. He exalted himself as the Prince even as high as the host of heaven; and by him, the daily sacrifices were taken away. The place of the Lord's sanctuary was cast down. An army was given over to the horn to oppose the daily (sacrifices), because of rebellion. He cast truth down to the ground. In all that he did, he prospered. Daniel 8:8-12 translated

Daniel (fl. 605 to 530 BC) was a prophet of Judah, the southern kingdom of the people of Israel.

The great horn on the shaggy goat was later identified as representing Alexander the Great (356 to 323 BC), with the shaggy goat symbolizing Greece. Note that Alexander the Great was not actually Greek. Alexander was originally a Macedonian.

The Greek empire conquered the two horned ram / the Medes and the Persians.

After Alexander the Great died, the Greek empire was divided into four parts, by Alexander the Great's four generals. The four horns / four generals led their regions to become great. Two of the four horns / four generals' regions became the Ptolemy empire (generally Egypt) / 'kings of the south,' and the Seleucid empire (generally in the region of Syria) / 'kings of the north' (See also Daniel 11:1-35). From the Seleucid empire came Antiochus IV Epiphanes who established the first abomination of desolation event in the temple in Kiselev 167 BC, as a typology for the future abomination of desolation event (Daniel 8:23-25, 11:27-35, etc.).

The work of the four winds of heaven must have been an important detail in God Most High's communications with Daniel, because in the description of the kings of the north and the kings of the south, the four

winds of heaven were also essential (Daniel 11:1-35). The mighty king that arose and whose empire was uprooted and given to others, was also Alexander the Great.

Then a mighty king will arise, who will rule with great power and do as he pleases. After he has arisen, his empire will be broken up and <u>parceled out toward the four winds of heaven</u>. It will not go to his descendants, nor will it have the power he exercised, because his empire will be uprooted and given to others. Daniel 11:3-4

Alexander the Great had no heirs when he died, and so his empire was in fact parceled out to his four generals.

It was the growth of the four horns / four kingdoms, toward the four winds of heaven, that supplied the global dynamics necessary to establish the foundation for the four beasts, the four kingdoms, the four horns / four kingdoms, and the little horn / final horn on the shaggy goat, to be able to fulfill the rest of Daniel's prophecy. (Daniel 7, 8, 11)

Zechariah also provided an eschatological description of four chariots being released from heaven (Zechariah 6), with remarkable similarity to John the Revelator's four horses and their riders being released with the opening of the first four seals on the will of God Most High (Revelation 6:1-8).

I looked up again, and there before me were four chariots coming out from between two mountains — mountains of bronze. The first chariot had red horses, the second black, the third white, and the fourth dappled — all of them powerful. I asked the angel who was speaking to me, 'What are these, my lord?'

The angel answered me, 'These are the <u>four spirits of heaven</u>, going out from standing in the presence of the Lord of the whole world.' Zechariah 6:1-5

Zechariah's vision equated the four chariots with different colored horses, with four spirits of heaven that originally were in the presence of the Lord, and then commissioned to permeate the whole world.

The important work of the four winds of heaven in gathering the elect – Jeremiah 49:36, Ezekiel 37:8-10, Daniel 7:1-3, 8:7-9, 11:3-5, Zechariah 2:5-7, Matthew 24:30-32, Mark 13:26-28, Revelation 7:1-3

The four winds of heaven were referenced by prophets of the Old Testament / Tanakh, Jesus Christ during his earthly ministry, and by John the Revelator

(Jeremiah 49:36, Ezekiel 37:8-10, Daniel 7:1-3, 8:7-9, 11:3-5, Zechariah 2:5-7, Matthew 24:30-32, Mark 13:26-28, Revelation 7:1-3).

One responsibility of the four winds of heaven was to churn the great sea that provided for the rise of the four beasts / four kingdoms of Daniel 7. Another responsibility of the four winds was to scatter people, both the people of Israel and others designated by God Most High to be scattered.

But the most important work of the four winds of heaven, will be in the preparation for the gathering of the elect at just the right moment in history (Zechariah 2:6-13, Matthew 24:31, Mark 13:27, Revelation 7:1).

The Old Testament / Tanakh prophet Zechariah's vision of a man with a measuring line, detailed eschatological events (Zechariah 2). Zechariah described the city of Jerusalem being a city without walls because of the great number of people and animals in it (Zechariah 2:4).

While modern Jerusalem has walls that separate the Syrians / Palestinians from the people of Israel, the modern walls are not considered the same kind of military defensive walls that historically used to surround cities for protection and fortification. Modern military warfare can go through walls, over walls and under walls. City walls are no longer a barrier. Walls became somewhat superfluous. And Zechariah documented that instead of walls, there would be a day when Jerusalem would be protected by the Lord, who promised to be a fire around it (Zechariah 6:5).

In this context, Zechariah recorded:

'Come! Come! Flee from the land of the north,' says the Lord. 'For <u>like the four winds of heaven</u>, <u>I have spread you abroad</u>,' says the Lord.

'Come Zion! Escape, you who dwell with the daughter of Babylon. For this is what the Lord says, 'He sent the glorious one, to nations that plundered you; for whoever touches you, touches the apple of his eye. I will surely shake my hand against them and they will become spoil for their servants. Then you will know that the Lord of hosts has sent me.'

'Sing and rejoice, daughter of Zion, for behold I am coming, and I will dwell in your midst,' says the Lord.

Many nations will be joined with the Lord, and in that day, they will become my people. I will dwell with you and you will know that the Lord of hosts has sent me to you. And the Lord will take possession of Judah as his inheritance, in the holy land, and will choose Jerusalem again.

Be still all humanity, before the Lord, because he is aroused from his holy dwelling. Zechariah 2:6-13 translated

When the Roman empire destroyed the nation of Israel, destroyed Jerusalem and destroyed the temple (70 AD), the people of Israel entered into the diaspora. The majority of the survivors were taken away from Jerusalem, and dispersed throughout the world. They were literally scattered around the world.

But the instruction of Zechariah for the people of Israel for our time, was that there will be a Glorious One / messiah, who will finally avenge the hatred of the nations that the people of Israel have experienced for almost two millennia while they lived in exile from their homeland.

Because the four winds of heaven have scattered the people of Israel, the four winds of heaven should also be able to be employed with gathering the people of Israel.

I looked, and tendons and flesh appeared on them and skin covered them, but there was no breath in them.

Then he said to me, 'Prophesy to the breath; prophesy, son of man, and say to it, 'This is what the Sovereign Lord says: 'Come, breath, from the four winds and breathe into these slain, that they may live.'" So I prophesied as he commanded me, and breath entered them. They came to life and stood up on their feet — a vast army. Ezekiel 37:8-10

In the vision of the dry bones that came together, the dry bones gained flesh and then came to life. It was the four winds that were given the responsibility to breathe on the bodies and resurrect the bodies to life.

Ezekiel's vision of the valley of dry bones, prophetically foretold of the people of Israel returning to the land of Israel, with those who had been killed being raised from the dead, and the nation of Israel forming a vast army. With God Most High, a vast army will have an essential purpose.

In the first year of Belshazzar, king of Babylon, Daniel had a dream and visions passed through his mind, while he was on his bed. Then he wrote the dream down, telling the main significant facts.

Daniel said, 'I was looking and behold in my vision at night, I saw the <u>four winds of heaven</u> were stirring up the great sea. Four great beasts, each different, came up from this sea.' Daniel 7:1-3 translated

Prophetically, the sea represented the source of the baal / mystery / mythology religion, and the mass of people who embrace the baal / mystery / mythology religion (especially Revelation 17).

The god of the Philistines, Dagon, was a fish god that rose out of the sea, evolved to walk upon land like a man, and served as a typology of a creature changing into human-like form. The Hebrew word 'dag' means 'fish' and 'to twist.'

The activity of the four winds of heaven, churning up the great sea, was presented as a necessity for the development and evolution of the four beasts / four kingdoms.

Jesus Christ defined the four winds as being originally located in the heavens, active in the heavens, and holding the elect in trust until messiah / the Lamb / Jesus Christ gloriously returns with power and great glory.

'Then will appear the sign of the Son of Man in heaven. And then all the peoples of the earth will mourn. They will see the Son of Man coming on the clouds of heaven, with power and great glory. He will send his angels with a great trumpet call. They will gather together his elect <u>from the four winds, from one end of heaven to the other</u>.'

'Now learn the lesson from the fig tree. When its branch has become tender, and it puts forth leaves, then you know that summer is near. Matthew 24:30-32 translated

The fig tree was a prophetic representation of the nation of Israel. The lesson from the fig tree was a prophetic statement that identified the reestablishment of the nation of Israel. Jesus Christ provided the prophecy while the nation of Israel still was in existence, before the diaspora of 70 AD. The nation of Israel was reestablished May 14, 1948.

'Then they will see the Son of Man coming in the clouds with great power and glory. And then he will send the angels and they will gather his elect <u>from the four winds, from the end of the earth to the end of heaven</u>.'

'Now learn the parable of the fig tree. When the branch is already tender and it produces leaves, you know that summer is near. Mark 13:26-28 translated

In John the Revelator's description of the sealing of the one hundred forty four thousand people of Israel, John the Revelator noticed that the four winds can be held back by angels assigned for that purpose.

After this I saw four angels standing at the four corners of the earth, holding back <u>the four winds of the earth</u> to prevent any wind from blowing on the land or on the sea or on any tree.

Then I saw another angel coming up from the east, having the seal of the living God. He called out in a loud voice to the four angels who had been given power to harm the land and the sea: 'Do not harm the land or the sea or the trees until we put a seal on the foreheads of the servants of our God.' Revelation 7:1-3

It is possible that the four winds of heaven are not the same as the four winds of the earth.

What has been consistent throughout the descriptions of the four winds, was the fact that the four winds take their direction from God Most High through angels assigned for that purpose. And while the four winds are destructive against the rebellious enemies of the kingdom of heaven, the four winds provide protection to those who are servants of God Most High and have been sealed by God for God's purpose.

The work of the four winds, to scatter – Jeremiah 49:35-37

The prophecy provided to Jeremiah concerning Elam / Persia / southern Iran, promised that the Lord Almighty would break the bow of Elam.

During the exile of the people of Israel, Persia treated the people of Israel well. And in exchange, God Most High protected the Persian nation for over two thousand years.

In 1979, the Islamic Revolution ousted the Shah of Iran and brought home the exiled Ruhollah Khomeini to form a new Islamic government (April / December 1979). The Islamic Republic of Iran then purged the nation of non-Islamist political opposition, killing tens of thousands.

In the context of all human history, Persia / Iran's hatred against Israel is a relatively new development.

In the prophecy against Elam / southern Iran, instead of the four winds of heaven gathering the elect, the four winds of heaven will scatter the people of Elam, a mirror activity to the determination of Iran to scatter the people of Israel to the four winds.

> This is what the Lord Almighty says: 'See, I will break the bow of Elam, the mainstay of their might.'
> 'I will bring against Elam <u>the four winds from the four quarters of heaven</u>.'
> 'I will scatter them to <u>the four winds</u>, and there will not be a nation where Elam's exiles do not go.'
> 'I will shatter Elam before their foes, before those who want to kill them.'
> 'I will bring disaster on them, even my fierce anger,' declares the Lord.
> 'I will pursue them with the sword until I have made an end of them.'
> Jeremiah 49:35-37

According to this prophecy, the four winds cover the four quarters of heaven.

The four winds have been used as a tool of God Most High in the past and will be used in the future, to scatter people throughout the world.

The prophecy about scattering the people of Elam / Iran throughout the world, has yet to be fulfilled.

The great sea and the earth

From the visions provided to Daniel and to John the Revelator, and in other prophetic biblical recording, the great sea represented the spiritual or religious aspects of the world, and the earth / land represented the physical or political aspects of the world.

Within the logical framework of the baal / mystery / mythology religion, the religious aspects of life dynamics supported the political governance of monarchs. Historically, religion has been downplayed in order to elevate the power and authority of political leaders and the sovereignty of nations.

But the understanding within the authentic faith system is that it is God Most High who chooses who will govern. And all authority and power to rule is derived from the Law of God Most High. (Genesis 11:5-9, Deuteronomy 32:8, Job 12:23, Psalm 22:28, 33:12-19, 46:8-10, 66:7, 75:7, Isaiah 40:17-18, 41:2, 45:7, Jeremiah 30:8-9, Ezekiel 14:13-18, Daniel 2:21-22, Luke 1:51-52, Acts 17:24-28, etc.)

God Most High's understanding of 'religion' and politics has always been that the theocracy of God Most High is the only consistent divine and sovereign entity. Politics with governments and nations ruling over humanity, remain secondary to the rule of God Most High and of the kingdom of heaven.

The founders of the United States began their thoughts with an understanding that governments and nations were invented in order to ensure the rights that God the Creator endowed upon each individual human being. Governments govern at the pleasure of God the Creator. And when governments forget the divinity and sovereignty of God the Creator, they must be replaced with governments that remember and respect the divinity and sovereignty of God the Creator.

The beginning of the Declaration of Independence for the colonies that would become the United States of America:

'In Congress, July 4, 1776'

'The unanimous Declaration of the thirteen United States of America, when in the course of human events, it becomes necessary for one people to dissolve the political bands which have connected them with another, and to assume among the powers of the earth, the separate and equal station to which the Laws of Nature and of Nature's God entitle them, a decent respect to the opinions of mankind requires that they should declare the causes which impel them to the separation.'

'We hold these truths to be self-evident, that all men are created equal, that they are endowed by their Creator with certain unalienable Rights, that among these are Life, Liberty and the pursuit of Happiness. — That to secure these rights, Governments are instituted among Men, deriving their just powers from the consent of the governed, ...'

The understanding of the sea prophetically representing religion and the earth prophetically representing politics, was known to have been historically established at least by the time of the beginnings of the postdiluvian / postflood world's development of the baal / mystery / mythology religion.

The sea was the origin for the evolution of the Philistine baal / mystery / mythology religion's god Dagon. The story of Dagon was that Dagon was originally a fish that evolved into a man. Dagon in the form of a fish was able to survive the deluge / flood. In the form of a fish, Dagon was already considered to be a god. And then Dagon evolved into a creature of the land, a man. This evolution deemed the god Dagon to be worthy to possess authority to rule as a god.

During the battle of God Most High verses the gods of Egypt, the Red Sea was where God Most High deposited the locusts from the plague of locusts (Exodus 10:19). At the conclusion of the plagues, as the people of Israel exited Egypt, the people of Israel were led to the Red Sea. The Red Sea parted, and the people of Israel were baptized in their crossing through the Red Sea. The Egyptian military entered into the cavity created by the parting of the Red Sea, and were drown. (Exodus 13 through 15, Deuteronomy 11:1-7, Joshua 2:10, Isaiah 43:16-21, 51:10, 63:11-14, etc.).

The Red Sea acted as the waters for redemption and baptism for God Most High's nation of Israel. And the dry ground of the Red Sea acted as the strategy for removing the military might and political superpower status of the nation of Egypt.

And then God Most High promised the people of Israel that the Red Sea would one day be one of the borders of the nation of Israel (Exodus 23:31).

Daniel saw: the four winds of heaven stirring up the great sea. Four great beasts, each different from the others, came up from the sea. Daniel 7:2-3 translated

Daniel's four beasts with their spiritual / religious connection, provided a distinct contrast to the dynamics presented in Nebuchadnezzar's image of a man, whose elements were described as purely political and physical.

The four beasts / four kingdoms of Daniel 7, all originated from the sea. But in the course of Daniel's

description, the unique fourth beast / fourth kingdom was described specifically as appearing on earth, devouring the earth, trampling down the earth (Daniel 7:23). This was prophetic imagery that designated the fourth beast / fourth kingdom's self-image of having almost complete separation from any recognition of the religious influence of God Most High and of the kingdom of heaven upon the authority of the fourth beast / fourth kingdom.

Daniel's little horn / eleventh king / prince that is to come / beast of the earth was depicted as being most concerned with political matters and addressed religion when it hampered his political goals (Daniel 7, 8, 9:26b-27, 11:29-45).

For John the Revelator, the 'many waters' *were defined to be* 'peoples, multitudes, nations and languages' *(Revelation 17:1, 17:15), essentially the mass of humanity. Humanity received its humanness from God the Creator.*

In the vision that Jesus Christ provided for John the Revelator, there were two men that were described as different beasts, but they shared power and authority.

The first was the beast of the sea that heavily influenced world religion (Revelation 13:1-10). The beast of the sea / beast from the Abyss / eighth king beast will seek to rule over the 'many waters' / 'peoples, multitudes, nations and languages' *using religion (Revelation 13:1-10, 17). But his attempt to rule will not be complete without the beast of the earth bringing the political realm into the mix.*

The second beast of John the Revelator's vision, the beast of the earth, will be determined to rule the world through political structures. For both Daniel and for John the Revelator, the beast of the earth will provide the military and political leadership for the red dragon / serpent / Satan, Inc.'s attempt to fully establish global governance and the kingdom of Satan, Inc. / kingdom of man on earth. (Daniel 7, 8, 9:26b-27, 11:29-45, Revelation 13:11-18, 17:12-17, 19:20)

John the Revelator documented the beast of the sea and the beast of the earth, and their dependency upon each other (Revelation 13, 17, 19). The two beasts / men will work together and sometimes the power and actions of the two men will be indistinguishable.

While both beasts of Revelation 13 will address both religious and political issues, the beast of the sea was the beast most connected with religious matters and used religion to further his power (Revelation 13:1-10, 16:13, 17:3-11, 18, 19:20).

John the Revelator understood the beast of the earth to be most connected with political matters and as the leader in military battles. (Revelation 13:11-18, 17:12-17, 19:20).

In other prophetic writing, Isaiah recorded:
The Lord has stretched out his hand over the sea and made its kingdoms tremble. Isaiah 23:11

Kingdoms were generally located on land, not the sea. But Isaiah understood the connection between the prophetic imagery of the sea, and the existence of kingdoms.

Isaiah also included this in the description of the Day of the Lord:
In that day, the Lord will punish with the sword of the Lord, his fierce, great and powerful sword.
Leviathan the gliding serpent, Leviathan the coiling serpent, the Lord will slay the monster of the sea. Isaiah 27:1

The serpent within the Garden of Eden / garden of God / paradise, originally walked on legs. It was after the deception of the first woman and the rebellion of the first man that God the Creator altered the serpent to slither on the ground and eat dust (Genesis 3).

But Isaiah's depiction of the serpent, identified the serpent's abode as the sea.

In John the Revelator's description of the scheduled events of the era of the time of Jacob's Trouble, John recorded that the angel with the little scroll, will plant his right foot on the sea and his left foot on the land.
I saw another mighty angel coming out of heaven, clothed with a cloud, and a rainbow on his head. His face was like the sun and his feet were like pillars of fire. In his hand, he held a little scroll that was being opened.

He placed his right foot upon the sea and his left upon the earth. And he cried out in a loud voice as a lion roars. When he cried out, the seven thunders spoke with their own voice. And when the seven thunders had spoken, I was about to write. But I heard a voice out of heaven saying, 'Seal what the seven thunders have spoken, and do not write them.'

And the angel whom I saw standing on the sea and on the land, lifted up his right hand to heaven and he swore by the One living from age to age, who created heaven and the things in it, and the earth and the things in it, and the sea and the things in it, 'There will be no more delay! But in the days of the voice of the seventh angel when he is about to sound the trumpet, then will the mystery of God be completed, as God proclaimed through his servants, the prophets. Revelation 10:1-7 translated

How does one 'plant' one's foot and stand on the sea?

The angel in John the Revelator's vision, held authority over both the sea and the land.

In John the Revelator's description of the exile of the rebellious angels from heaven, initiated through the war in heaven of the rebellious angels against Michael and his angels, a voice from heaven will say:

'Because of this, rejoice Oh heavens and those dwelling there!'

'Woe to the earth and the sea because the devil has come down to you, having great fury, knowing that he has a short time.' Revelation 12:12 translated

This description of the exile of the rebellious angels from heaven, was placed as the precursor to the introduction of the beast of the sea and the beast of the earth (Revelation 13).

In John the Revelator's description of the destruction of the great prostitute / great city that rules over the kings of the earth, John recorded:

Then a mighty angel took a stone like a great millstone, and threw it into the sea saying,

> 'With such violence, the great city Babylon will be thrown down, never to be found again.' Revelation 18:21 translated

Generally, a stone being thrown into the sea does not render a city on earth to be destroyed and ruined. But this was the city that was defined as the city that 'sits by many waters' / 'peoples, multitudes, nations and languages' *(Revelation 17:1, 17:15-16).*

John the Revelator's vision also defined the great prostitute as Mystery Babylon the Great! The great prostitute represented all religion that is not the authentic faith system of God Most High (authentic Judaism / Christianity). The great prostitute / Mystery Babylon the Great! consists of all forms of the baal / mystery / mythology religion, that has located its headquarters in the city of the seven hills (Revelation 17:9).

Concerning the earth specifically, the biblical record repeatedly identified the kingdoms of the earth as being in contrast to the kingdom of heaven. And John the Revelator magnified this concept with identifying the classifications of humanity during the era of the time of Jacob's Trouble, as being those who are 'followers of the Lamb' *and those who are* '<u>inhabitants of the earth</u>' *(Revelation).*

The prophets Isaiah, Jeremiah and Ezekiel also utilized this classification system of identifying the inhabitants of the earth, *and the distinction between the kingdom of heaven and the kingdoms of the earth. (Isaiah 40:22-24, 45:8-9, 54:5, 55:8-11, 60:2, 66:1, Jeremiah 6:17-23, 15:4, 24:8-9, 25:29-33, Lamentations 4:12-13, Ezekiel 27:33, 31:12, Daniel 2:39, etc.)*

Fear and the pit and the snare are upon you, O <u>inhabitant of the earth</u>. Isaiah 24:17

In that day, the Lord will punish the hose of exalted ones in the heavens above, and <u>the kings on the earth below</u>. Isaiah 24:21 translated

Daniel's four beasts / four kingdoms of Daniel 7, originated from the great sea that was churned by the four winds of heaven. But the first beast / first kingdom like a lion was <u>lifted up from the earth</u> *in order to stand like a man (Daniel 7:4). The fourth beast / fourth kingdom was described as being* <u>located on earth</u> *(Daniel 7:23). And all four kingdoms were designated as kingdoms that* <u>arise from earth</u> *(Daniel 7:17).*

Within the biblical record, the prophetic imagery of the 'sea,' represented the religious attitudes and beliefs of the inhabitants of the earth who have embraced the various forms of the baal / mystery / mythology religion.

And within the biblical record, the prophetic imagery of the 'earth,' represented the various forms of governance employed by the kingdom of Satan, Inc. / kingdom of man, as an effort of separating God the Creator's religious divinity and sovereignty from influencing the power of the kingdom of Satan, Inc. / kingdom of man.

The first three of four beasts / kingdoms – Daniel 7

Both Daniel and John the Revelator, established the first three beasts / three kingdoms, as being separate from the fourth unique beast / fourth kingdom.

In Daniel's vision, the distinction was specifically articulated and documented in the description of the fourth beast / fourth kingdom.

'After this I saw in visions at night, a fourth dreadful and terrible and exceedingly strong beast with iron teeth. With its huge iron teeth, it was devouring and breaking into pieces. And the residue that was left, it trampled with its feet. <u>It was different from all the other beasts before it</u>. And it had ten horns.' Daniel 7:7 translated

Daniel's descriptions of the first three beasts / three kingdoms were associated with the sea, while the fourth beast / fourth kingdom was unconnected with the sea.

Daniel's descriptions of the first three beasts / three kingdoms were also associated with living creatures: a lion, a bear and a leopard. But the fourth beast was defined using the imagery of metal; iron and bronze.

'Then I wished to know the truth about <u>the fourth exceedingly dreadful beast which was different from all the others</u> with its iron teeth and its bronze nails which devoured and broke into pieces, and trampled on what remained with its feet, and the ten horns that were on its head, and the other horn that came up from it, from which the three horns fell before it; specifically this horn which had eyes and a mouth which spoke pompous words, whose appearance was greater than his fellows.' Daniel 7:19-20 translated

The uniqueness of the fourth beast / fourth kingdom was significant enough that Daniel explicitly noted it in his request for the interpretation of the vision.

And again in the interpretation, the fourth beast / fourth kingdom was noted to be unique from all other kingdoms.

The interpreter said, 'The fourth beast will be a fourth kingdom on earth, <u>which will be different from all other kingdoms</u>, and will devour the whole earth, and trample it and break it into pieces.' Daniel 7:23 translated

Notice that the domain of the fourth beast / fourth kingdom will be only the whole earth, and not the entire sea. The fourth beast / fourth kingdom will also not have authority in heaven where the Ancient of Days has established his abode.

John the Revelator also separated the first three kingdoms from the fourth kingdom of Daniel's vision, in the description of the beast of the sea.

And I saw a beast rising out of the sea, having ten horns, and seven heads. And on its horns, there were ten royal crowns (diademata / διαδηματα). And upon its heads were names of blasphemy.

And the beast that I saw was like a leopard, and its feet like a bear, and its mouth like the mouth of a lion. And the dragon gave to the beast, his power and his throne and great authority. Revelation 13:1-2 translated

It was John the Revelator who identified Daniel's first three beasts / three kingdoms as the foundation for the rise of the beast of the sea.

Both Daniel and John the Revelator identified all these beasts / kingdoms as all working together. But it was Daniel who best identified the fourth beast / fourth kingdom as being the foundation for the ten horns / ten kings and for the little horn / eleventh king that John the Revelator identified as the beast of the earth (Revelation 13:11-18).

For Daniel, the first three beasts / three kingdoms, were associated with the fourth beast / fourth kingdom, and yet the fourth beast / fourth kingdom was unique in its scope of covering the whole world, and in its protege of the ten horns / ten kings and the little horn / eleventh king.

Understanding that the fourth beast / fourth kingdom will be unique from the first three, allows for the

first three beasts / three kingdoms to be assigned an interpretation from among the kingdoms that already exist on earth.

However, the fourth beast / fourth kingdom must be assigned an interpretation that is not like the first three. The fourth beast / fourth kingdom must be a relatively new manifestation of governance set in the context of six thousand years of human history.

The Old Testament / Tanakh prophet Hosea also prophesied that there will be a time when the manner in which God Most High will approach the people of Israel will be like a wild animal in the form of a lion, a leopard and a bear.

'I cared you in the wilderness, in the land of great drought. When they had pasture and they were satisfied, they were satisfied and became proud. And so they forgot me.'

'So I will be like a lion to them; like a leopard by the road, I will lurk. I will meet them like a bear deprived of her cubs, and I will tear open their rib cage. And there I will devour them like a lion. The wild animal will tear them apart.' Hosea 13:5-8 translated

This was God Most High's description of what God Most High planned to do with the rebellious nation of Israel. This was fulfilled via the exiles and diaspora of 70 AD.

If Hosea's prophecy has a second fulfillment scheduled, then the people of Israel should expect that the nations represented by the lion, the leopard and the bear, will attack Israel sometime during the era of the time of Jacob's Trouble.

And I saw a beast rising out of the sea, having ten horns, and seven heads. And on its horns, there were ten royal crowns (diademata / διαδηματα). And upon its heads were names of blasphemy.

And the beast that I saw was like a leopard, and its feet like a bear, and its mouth like the mouth of a lion. And the dragon gave to the beast, his power and his throne and great authority. Revelation 13:1-2 translated

Revelation 13:1-10 was the record of John's vision of the beast of the sea during the era of the time of Jacob's Trouble. By the time that the future abomination of desolation event takes place half way through the seven

years of Israel's covenant peace treaty agreement, the beast of the sea's authority and power will have become completely developed. John the Revelator described Daniel's first three beasts, without their extra heads or wings of a fowl - leopard, ribs -bear, and wings of an eagle- lion.

    One of the best interpretations for the first three beasts / three kingdoms, assigned the lion to be the kingdom of Great Britain, the bear to be Russia with or without an association with Asians nations, and the leopard to be Germany or European nations. Currently, all three empires / nations have pursued the dream of establishing global governance.

    Great Britain has been a worldwide empire and is currently led by those who continue to desire to establish global governance.

    Russia has for centuries, held a dream of ruling the world. Even now Vladimir Putin works to reestablish the greatness that Russia once held.

    Hitler called his reign over Germany, the Third Reich, as a reference to Germany's third attempt in its history, to establish political supremacy throughout the world. The Third Reich was also associated as the third head of the prophecy of the four heads of the leopard. And the goal of Adolf Hitler's Third Reich, was to establish global governance that would reign for a thousand years, which would have been Adolf Hitler's fulfillment of the Roman Catholic Church's understanding of the promised Thousand Years Reign of Jesus Christ.

    All three of these empires / nations, have been essential in the rise of the Roman Catholic Church and in the now common practice of churches around the world, to accept under the umbrella of the church, all religions and theologies that are enemies of the biblically defined authentic faith system of God Most High.

    All three of these empires / nations represented by the lion, the leopard and the bear, also share another commonality. Since the origination of the diaspora (70

AD), all three have been a host empire / nation for the people of Israel. Sometimes their hospitality has been gracious. Other times their hospitality has been adversarial, dangerous and destructive against the people of Israel.

      The first Jewish communities of significant size came to England with William the Conqueror in 1066, when William issued an invitation to the Jews of Rouen to move to England. The unique ability of the Jewish community to use currency, aided William in his establishment of a feudal system, the model government of choice for the Roman Catholic Church. In 1218, Henry III proclaimed the Edict of the Badge that required Jews to wear a marking badge, and the following years, taxes on Jewish people were significantly increased. England experienced growth while they provided hospitality for the people of Israel. But on July 18, 1290, Edward I issued a royal decree expelling all Jews from the kingdom of England by November 1st of that year. Later in 1656, people of Israel were again invited to live in England. In 1914, the Balfour Declaration that initiated the formation of a homeland for the people of Israel was signed. During the World War II era, the people of Israel were given verbal support, but in reality, Great Britain did not fully deliver on its promises of support for the people of Israel.

      The people of Israel living in Russia once constituted the largest population of the people of Israel in the world. But the bloody Russian pogroms and persecution that were later hurled upon the people of Israel, decreased their population in Russia. For example, in 1827 Tsar Nicholas ordered the conscription of all male Jews into the Imperial Russian Army beginning at the age of 12, and then forbade Jews from being officers. In 1844 Nicholas officially classified all Jews into two categories, 'useful' and 'non-useful.' It was a Russian intelligence agent in Paris who wrote *The Protocols of the Elders of Zion* (1903) that claimed a secret Jewish cabal was taking over the world. (In the United States, Henry Ford sponsored the publication's circulation.) Initially in 1939, Stalin cooperated with Nazi Germany and advanced *antisemitism further within Russia. And after World War II, Stalin continued his repressive policies impacting the people of Israel. With the establishment of the nation of Israel in 1948, the population of the people of Israel formerly located withing the Soviet bloc nations, has dramatically declined as they have emigrated to the land of Israel.*

The people of Israel living in Germany have historically been treated according to the financial benefits they have offered to the emperors / monarchs that ruled. When they provided economic benefit, they were protected and when they no longer provided benefits or their presence threatened the power and authority of Germany's rulers, the treatment of the people of Israel living among the German people deteriorated. The Judensteirer / Jewish tax at one point comprised the largest share of revenue for the crown, while the population of the Jewish people within Germany, remained quite small. Initially in exchange for paying the Judensteirer / Jewish tax, the people of Israel would receive protection from the crown. But by the late fourteenth century, Charles VI negotiated treaties that allowed for the killing of Jews as long as he received compensation for his loss. The people of Israel were relegated to live in walled ghettos. This collective isolation led to the rise of Yiddish that later incorporated elements of Hebrew. By the end of the fifteenth century, many Jewish communities were expelled from Germany. During the Reformation era, the people of Israel continued to be physically and economically oppressed. Martin Luther, a leader in the Reformation, failed to convert the Jews to Protestantism and then denounced them, which led to more religiously inspired violence against them. In the eighteenth century, the people of Israel were readmitted to Germany and were granted rights more similar to natural born citizens. During the 1860s, all restrictions on the right of residence, acquisition of real estate, and choice of profession, were abolished in various states within the region of Germany. It was in the late nineteenth and early twentieth centuries that antisemitism manifested itself in politics and society within Germany, and then in the aftermath of World War I, became extremely pronounced. In 1933, the legal discrimination and violence against the people of Israel, accelerated, coming to a climax with the Holocaust / holy burning. In Berlin, only about one thousand five hundred people of Israel survived the Holocaust, by hiding.

Currently only about 9% of the global population of the people of Israel, now live in Europe, compared with nearly 90% in the late nineteenth century. This fact also supported Daniel's first three beasts / three kingdoms as being the foundation for the beast of the sea. And it supports the beast of the sea as being a Gentile.

The lion with wings like an eagle that were broken off, that stood like a man with the heart of a man – Daniel 7:4

'The first beast was like a lion, and had wings like an eagle. I watched until the wings were plucked off. This beast was lifted up from the earth, onto two feet like a man, and made to stand. A man's heart was given to it.' Daniel 7:4 translated

In Nebuchadnezzar's image of a man's the head of gold which represented Babylonian empire, was depicted as a lion.

But there are other modern interpretations which identified this lion beast of Daniel 7 to be a different empire. And because Daniel's vision of the four beasts / four kingdoms was a prophecy to coincide with the coming of messiah, all the four beasts / four kingdoms must have a modern interpretation.

One interpretation identified the lion as a representation of the nation of Great Britain. And the wings of the eagle that were torn off, represented the United States which received its independence from Great Britain on 7/4. (Note that this verse reference is Daniel 7:4.)

Or the wings of the eagle may represent Ireland, Scotland, Whales, the rest of the British empire, etc.

The bear on its side with three ribs in its mouth between its teeth, that went to eat his fill of flesh – Daniel 7:5

'And suddenly, there was another beast, a second beast like a bear. It was raised up on one side, and had three ribs in its mouth, between its teeth. And they said to the bear, 'Arise, devour much flesh.'" Daniel 7:5 translated

In Nebuchadnezzar's image of a man's the arms of silver which represented Medo Persian empire, was depicted as a bear. The Medo Persian empire took over three continents.

Most modern interpretations have identified that this bear beast represented the nation of Russia.

The bear was noted as being lopsided, raised up on one of its sides. It is difficult to determine what being 'raised up on one of its sides' *means.*

One possibility would be the Russian relationship with Ukraine. Ukraine is the second largest nation in Europe, after Russia. In the past four hundred years, Ukraine has experienced a fluid relationship with Russia regarding national borders. At one point, the land of Ukraine had even been partitioned between Russia, Poland and other nations.

Another possibility for the description of being raised up on one of its sides, could be Russia's relationship with Crimea, or with China.

Another possibility for the description of being raised up on one of its sides, could be Russia's governmental corruption and its issuance of propaganda / fake news that continues to be used to manipulate and govern the people of Russia.

The bear itself had three ribs in its mouth, between its teeth. Several possibilities also exist for what the three ribs in the mouth mean. The three ribs could be a literal three ribs, or it could be representative.

The ribs could represent nations that Russia has devastated in the past. Or the three ribs could be nations that Russia currently devastates. Or the three ribs could represent a future action of Russia, controlling three related nations or holding alliance with three other nations.

During World War II, the United Soviet Socialist Republic / USSR had annexed several countries.

The Yalta Conference that took place in 1945 at the close of World War II was one of the most important events in modern history. Held on the southern side of Russia, the Yalta Conference was the meeting of Joseph Stalin the Czar of Russia, Winston Churchill the Prime Minister of Britain, and Franklin D. Roosevelt the President of the United States.

In order to bring World War II to a close, the three superpowers agreed to relinquish some of the nations that the Soviets had recently annexed in war. The eastern bloc countries of eastern Poland, Hungary, Czechoslovakia, Romania, Albania and East Germany, became part of the United Soviet Socialist Republic / USSR.

The annexation of the eastern bloc nations could have been the fulfillment of the depiction of the bear raised up on one side. Or it could have been the fulfillment of the three ribs in the bear's teeth.

At the same time as the Yalta Conference, Alger Hiss drafted the charter for the United Nations. Just months later, Alger Hiss was accused and convicted of being a Russian spy. The nature of the United Nations' ties to Russia have highly influenced the thinking of the United Nations, and the culture of the United Nations. The lopsidedness of the bear may be a reference to Russia's influence over the United Nations.

While these are possibilities for the fulfillment of the prophecy of the lopsided bear, they remain only possibilities until the actual fulfillment takes place.

As the scheduled events of the era of the time of Jacob's Trouble take place, the prophecy of the raised up bear with the three ribs in its teeth, will solidify and become apparent.

The leopard with four wings of a bird and four heads given the authority to rule – Daniel 7:6

'After this I looked, and there was another beast like a leopard which had four wings of a bird on its back. And the beast had four heads. The authority to rule was given to the beast.' Daniel 7:6 translated

In Nebuchadnezzar's image of a man, the man's belly and thighs of bronze represented the Greek empire. The Greek empire was traditionally depicted as a leopard.

When Alexander the Great died, his kingdom went to four different generals who divided the Alexander the Great's empire roughly into the regions of Turkey, Greece, Syria, and Egypt. Many interpreters have noted the four wings and the four heads of Daniel's leopard, and the coincidence that the Greek empire was divided by Alexander the Great's four generals.

Many modern interpretations indicated that this leopard beast represented the nation of Germany and the four heads represent the four Reichs of Germany.

Germany became the embodiment of the four-headed leopard. One definition for the four reichs of Germany included:

1. *The Holy Roman empire (800-1806) which began with the crowning of Charlemagne as the first Holy Roman emperor. Holy Roman emperors and some monarchs, were generally crowned by the pope.*
2. *The German Empire (1870-1919) which began under the diplomatic statesmanship of Otto Von Bismarck / the 'iron chancellor.' From the unification of Germany following the Franco-Prussian War, to the German defeat of the First World War. Bismarck attempted to stop Roman Catholic Church political control over Germany, but failed. The Reichstag (Parliament) was established.*
3. *Adolf Hitler's Third Reich / 'Third Reign' (1933-1945). After a brief interim called the Weimar Republic, Adolf Hitler rose quickly to power. After World War II, Germany became divided into East and West Germany, to prevent it from again rising to a superpower. It was a 'deadly wound.' But when the United States President*

Ronald Reagan stood in the Brandenburg Gate (1989), and challenged Mikhail Gorbachev to 'Tear down this wall,' *the deadly wound was healed, and Germany was made whole again. (But this was not the deadly wound that was healed on the beast of the sea (Revelation 13:3), because this event was not contemporary with the era of the time of Jacob's Trouble.)*

4. *Possibly, the European Union (1951 / 1958 to present), which is an entity largely held and controlled by Germany (leopard) and France (fowl). The original European Coal and Steel Community, evolved into the present-day European Union / EU. The Euro is now the common currency, and Germany is still the dominating nation in the EU. This is one possibility for the fulfillment of the fourth reich / fourth head on the leopard with the wings of a fowl. But the fulfillment of the fourth head of the leopard, may be defined differently.*

The four wings like a bird, have frequently been interpreted to mean the nation of France that has been represented by its wings of a bird. Historically, France has held a tight historical connection with Germany.

The Holy Roman empire was also depicted as a leopard with the wings of a fowl.

From the region of Germany, Charlemagne birthed the Holy Roman empire (800 AD). Charlemagne was a strong Germanic leader. From his German base, Charlemagne was able to develop his further empire over Europe. One of his leading accomplishments was the unification of France.

Historians have identified that the Holy Roman empire was the incubator for both modern Germany and modern France. The Franco-German Alliance remains at the heart of the European Union to this day.

Daniel's prophecy said that the leopard had great dominion. Eventually, (from the 16th Century forward), the German empire was called the Holy Roman empire of the

German Nation. Germany so influenced the global environment that Germany has historically been recognized as the seedbed for the aggression of World War II.

Newsweek magazine, April 9, 1984 published, 'Since the time of Charlemagne, the area that is now Germany has been the pivot of European history. In the past 120 years, the Germans have dominated Europe; intellectually and militarily.'

'Reich' is the German word for kingdom. In all the history of the Holy Roman empire, the German parliament was known as the Reichstag. 'Reich' meaning 'empire' and '-stag' meaning 'assembly'. The modern nation of Germany evolved from Charlemagne's Reichstag. As far back as 919 AD, the Reichstag elected the first king of the Germans, and in 1871 the Reichstag became the parliament of the German empire.

The fourth beast / fourth kingdom, with the ten horns / ten kings – global governance as the foundation for the little horn / eleventh king / king that will exalt himself / beast of the earth / final world ruler – Daniel 7

One of the main features of the first three beasts / three kingdoms depicted in Daniel's vision, was that each of the three kingdoms represented kingdoms with defined regions and boundaries. They were represented by living creatures that were contained within the confines of their flesh. The power and authority of the first three beasts / three kingdoms had borders. The power and authority that the first three beasts / three kingdoms enjoyed, was initially at the pleasure of the citizens of those kingdoms.

One of the main differences of the fourth beast / fourth kingdom, from the first three, was that this kingdom filled the whole earth. This kingdom will have a relationship with the world that will be depicted as this kingdom devouring the whole earth. This kingdom will not be accountable to any group of people. Instead, this kingdom will trample the earth and leave devastation in its wake.

'The angel said, 'The fourth beast will be a fourth kingdom on earth, which will be different from all other kingdoms, and will devour the whole earth, and trample it and break it into pieces." Daniel 7:23 translated

It will be the fourth beast / fourth kingdom that will achieve the greatest advances in its attempt to establish global governance. And the fourth beast / fourth kingdom will attempt to establish global governance through ten horns / ten kings that will rise from its midst. Out of the ten horns / ten kings will arise a little horn / eleventh king that will serve to advance the mission of the fourth beast / fourth kingdom in establishing global governance. (Daniel 7:7-8, 7:11-27)

According to John the Revelator's description of the beast of the earth, Daniel's little horn / eleventh king will need to rely upon the power and authority of the beast of the sea in order to finally enjoy his global dominance and his authority over the temple mount.

And I saw another beast rising out of the earth. And the beast of the earth had two horns like a lamb, and it was speaking like a dragon.

And the beast of the earth exercises all of the authority of the first beast, on behalf of the first beast. The beast of the earth causes the earth and those dwelling in it, to worship the first beast of whom had its fatal wound healed.

And the beast of the earth works great signs so that it should even cause fire to come down out of heaven to the earth, in the presence of humanity.

And the beast of the earth deceives those dwelling on the earth by reason of the signs that it was given to perform before the beast, telling those dwelling on the earth to make an image to the beast that was wounded by the sword and has lived.

And the beast was given the ability to give breath to the image of the beast, so that the image of the beast should also speak. And the image of the beast should cause as many as would not worship the image of the beast, would be killed. Revelation 13:11-15 translated

Daniel who wrote for the people of Israel as his first audience, did not include the partnership that the little horn / eleventh king / ruler who is to come, will share with John's beast of the sea.

After the sixty two weeks, messiah will be cut off, and will have nothing. The people of the prince / ruler who is to come, will destroy the city and the sanctuary. And the end of it shall come with a flood. War will continue until the end and desolations are determined.

The prince / ruler will confirm a covenant with many, for one 'seven' / 'week.' But in the middle of the 'seven' / 'week,' the prince / ruler will bring an end to the sacrifice and offering. On the wing (of the temple), the prince / ruler will establish abominations that will cause desolation, even until the consumption which has been determined is poured out on the desolate / the one who destroys. Daniel 9:26-27 from the original text

The entity that will fulfill the prophecy of the fourth beast / fourth kingdom, must:
- *be capable of taking dominion over the entire earth,*
- *must be at least loosely connected with the first three beasts / three kingdoms, in order to be the fourth beast / fourth kingdom in this conglomeration of kingdoms,*
- *must be a source for the ten horns / ten kings that will rise from the fourth beast / fourth kingdom, and that will support the rise of the little horn / eleventh king,*
- *must share a connection with the global religious entity that will be headed by one man, the beast of the sea / false prophet / beast from the Abyss / eighth king beast, and*
- *must be the source for the rise of the little horn / eleventh king.*

These facts dramatically limit the candidates for the fourth beast / fourth kingdom.

There currently is only one entity that has the capability of fulfilling the prophecy of the fourth beast / fourth kingdom, and it has only been in existence for a relatively short period of time, since just before the establishment of the nation of Israel on May 14, 1948.

It is interesting that the United Nations was a development out of the League of Nations that was a development of the First World War. With the failure of achieving world peace, and the action of World War II, the League of Nations morphed into the United Nations. A case could be made that the United Nations was a result of Daniel's first three beasts / three kingdoms; Great Britain and the United States / lion with its wings, Russia /

lopsided bear with its three ribs, and Germany and France / four headed leopard with its four wings of a foul.

Officially the United Nations began on October 24, 1945. The foundation of the United Nations was most heavily influenced by the empires / nations that were described by Daniel's first three beasts, Great Britain, Russia and Germany, with the eagles' wings that had been plucked off / the United States.

The Roman Catholic Church was granted status within the United Nations as a permanent observer state on April 6, 1964, as the Holy See. In that capacity, The Roman Catholic Church Holy See has the right to attend meetings of the agencies of the United Nations, and to influence the decisions and recommendations of the United Nations.

The most recent global publicity event between the Roman Catholic Church and the United Nations, took place September 23, 2017 when Francis addressed the United Nations to bless the United Nations Agenda 2030, a global religious organization, addressing the entity whose mission is to establish global governance.

It has been agencies sourced by the United Nations, that have sectioned the globe into ten regions. And the goal of adopting those global regional boundaries is to remove national boundaries for the purpose of weakening the authority of nations in order for the United Nations to absorb the authority once held by nations. The designated regions have already been utilized by the United Nations agencies of the International Monetary Fund and World Bank Group, in the establishment of global banking.

The United Nations has an agency or organization that addresses almost every aspect of human life, culture, religion, economy, law, etc.

For a more detailed list of United Nations Organizations, see websites like Wikipedia's List of United Nations Organizations, https://en.wikipedia.org/wiki/List_of_United_Nations_organizations .

It is possible that the ten horns / ten kings will not be responsible for physical regions, but instead be responsible for ten cultural aspects of global dynamics.

The mission and policies of the United Nations have predominately been opposed to the existence and prosperity of the nation of Israel. In that mission, the permanent partitioning of the land of Israel continues to be a goal of the United Nations.

The United Nations unsuccessfully attempted to influence the establishment of the nation of Israel with United Nations Resolution 181, on November 29, 1947. If the resolution would have been successful at that time, the land of Israel would have been partitioned between the Syrian / 'Palestinian' Arabs and the Jewish state. Permanent partitioning of the land of Israel, would have established the Syrians / Palestinians rule over the people of Israel living in the region. One of the stated goals of Islam since its inception in 610 AD, has been to eliminate all people of Israel, as a form of spiritually cleansing the earth.

The United Nations will support a global leader who will advance the mission of the United Nations of establishing global governance, and of destroying the people and nation of Israel.

The biblical prophetic device of three parts – four parts, utilized in understanding the fourth beast / fourth kingdom of Daniel 7

In the prophecies of the Old Testament / Tankah prophet Daniel, there was utilized the prophetic device of three parts – four parts. The most dramatic three parts – four parts prophecy that Daniel recorded was with the handwriting on the wall's message to Belshazzar on October 12, 539 BC, giving notification that the Babylonian empire was to be defeated that day. Three parts of the prophecy were fulfilled that night. The fourth part of the prophecy will be fulfilled with the scheduled events of the era of the time of Jacob's Trouble.

The three part – four part prophetic device was also a part of Nebuchadnezzar's image of a man. The first three parts (head – gold, arms and chest – silver, belly and thighs – bronze), were finished with the legs of iron and the feet and toes of iron and clay (Daniel 2). The first three empires, and even the fourth empire, were all established prior to the arrival of Jesus Christ for his earthly ministry. But the second portion of the fourth part, the feet and toes of iron and baked clay, have a future fulfillment.

In Daniel's vision of the four beasts / four kingdoms, the first three beasts / three kingdoms, shared similarities to Nebuchadnezzar's image of a man's empires from a distant history. But the fourth beast / fourth kingdom was a relatively new development in the context of human history. And further utilizing the three part – four part prophetic device, the fourth beast / fourth kingdom naturally will be a result of the foundation established by the first three parts / three beasts / three kingdoms. But the fourth beast / fourth kingdom will be unique during the time of its prophetic fulfillment.

Daniel did not miss the importance that this fourth beast / fourth kingdom will have upon the events of the era of the time of Jacob's Trouble and the importance of the necessity of the followers of the Lamb / Jesus Christ to be aware of this fourth beast / fourth kingdom and its influence upon the world.

For almost two thousand five hundred years people have sought to find an interpretation of Daniel's four beasts that was completely satisfactory to events of the era of the time of Jacob's Trouble.

Following the pattern of the three parts – four parts prophetic device, the iron mixed with baked clay of the feet and toes of Nebuchadnezzar's image of a man (Daniel 2), and the deviation from living creatures to the use of iron and bronze (and teeth) to describe the terrible fourth beast / fourth kingdom, Daniel's prophecy depicted something akin to the current global movement toward transhumanism.

In biblical imagery, clay represented humanity who was formed from the dust of the earth (Genesis 2:7). Iron was material utilized by those who chose rebellion against God Most High (first book of Enoch, Genesis 4:22, Numbers 35:16, Deuteronomy 3:11, 4:20, 27:5, 28:48, Joshua 8:31, 2 Samuel 23:7, etc.). The mixture of clay (human life form), with iron, would yield the prophetic imagery of modern transhumanism, a mixture of biological human life with technology and inert materials.

Transhumanism will be best demonstrated with the image of the first beast / beast of the sea, being brought to life on the temple mount, through the breath of the man who would like to be recognized as greater than God Most High (Daniel 7:25, Revelation 13:15, etc.). The image of the beast of the sea, being brought to life, would be the full representation of the kingdom of Satan, Inc. / kingdom of man's vision for merging biological human life with technology and inert materials.

Consequently, the fourth beast / fourth kingdom cannot exist without the foundation of the first three beasts / three kingdoms that will be essential for the rise of the beast of the sea (Revelation 13:1-2). And yet the fourth beast / fourth kingdom will be so unique from the first three beasts / three kingdoms, that it will have developed its own unique character. And the fourth beast / fourth kingdom will act in a manner that will also be unique from the traditional methods of action employed by the first three beasts / three kingdoms. Historically, every kingdom has been accountable to the people of that kingdom. But this fourth global kingdom, will not be accountable to anyone or anything.

'After this I saw in visions at night, a fourth dreadful and terrible and exceedingly strong beast with iron teeth. With its huge iron teeth, it was devouring and breaking into pieces. And the residue that was left, it trampled with its feet. It was different from all the other beasts before it. And it had ten horns.'

'As I was considering the horns, there was another little horn coming up among them. And three of the first horns were plucked out by the roots. The little horn had eyes like the eyes of a man, and a mouth that spoke pompous words.' Daniel 7:7-8 translated

The foundation of the fourth beast / fourth kingdom, as the source for the little horn / eleventh king that will rise from the ten horns / ten kings – Daniel 7

'Then I wished to know the truth about the fourth exceedingly dreadful beast which was different from all the others with its iron teeth and its bronze nails which devoured and broke into pieces, and trampled on what remained with its feet, and the ten horns that were on its head, and the other horn that came up from it, from which the three horns fell before it; specifically this horn which had eyes and a mouth which spoke pompous words, whose appearance was greater than his fellows.'

'As I was watching, this horn was making war against the saints and prevailing against them, until the Ancient of Days came and a judgment was made in favor of the saints of God Most High, and the time came for the saints to possess the kingdom.'

'He said, 'The fourth beast will be a fourth kingdom on earth, which will be different from all other kingdoms, and will devour the whole earth, and trample it and break it into pieces."

"The ten horns that will rise from this kingdom, will be ten kings. And another will rise after them. He will be different from the first kings, and three of the kings will be subdued."

"He will speak pompous words against God Most High, and against the saints of God Most High. He will persecute the saints and will intend to change the times and the law. The saints will be given into his hand for a time and times and half a time." Daniel 7:19-25 translated

Because of the fourth beast / fourth kingdom's global influence that will be unique from all other government styles, the little horn / eleventh king from the fourth beast / fourth kingdom of Daniel's vision will:

- *have global authority.*
- *not be accountable to any group or body of citizenry. The concept of government ruled by the people and for the people will not exist within the four beast / fourth kingdom's ideology and the little horn / eleventh king's practice.*
- *have ten horns / kings that will relinquish their rule to the little horn / eleventh king.*
- *rule based on blasphemy and other lies, as he redefines messiah / the Lamb / Jesus Christ; denying Jesus Christ's inherent divinity and sovereignty. Denying the divinity and sovereignty of God Most High, will leave a void in the minds and hearts of the adherents of the*

red dragon / serpent / Satan, Inc. that the little horn / eleventh king and the beast of the sea will seek to fill.
- create an environment of 'lawlessness' with a set of governmental rules for the privileged elite, ruling class and a different set of governmental rules for those who are to be ruled.
- experience authority to rule with full power and authority granted through the red dragon / serpent / Satan, Inc., and shared with his partner, the beast of the sea / false prophet / beast from the Abyss / eighth king beast, for only three and a half years (Revelation 13).

As terrifying and as powerful as the fourth beast / fourth kingdom will be, its terror and power will pale in comparison to the one man, the little horn / eleventh king, that will be able to subdue three of the ten horns / ten kings, and will assume the role of supreme leader within the global governance system. But it will be the fourth beast / fourth kingdom that will be essential for establishing the foundation for the ten horns / ten kings and the little horn / eleventh king to operate from.

The destruction of the fourth beast / fourth kingdom – Daniel 7

Each of the participants in this rebellion against God Most High and against the kingdom of heaven, has their own distinctive destruction planned for them.

The kings of the earth and their armies will be destroyed by messiah / the Lamb / Jesus Christ and his armies collected from heaven and earth.

The first three beasts / three kingdoms of Daniel 7 will be defeated, but allowed to live on for a while afterward.

The great prostitute / Mystery Babylon the Great! / great city that rules over the kings of the earth, will be destroyed by the beast of the earth and the ten horns / ten kings. The ruins of the great city will remain as a reminder of the history of the mighty acts of God during the finale of this era.

The two beasts of Revelation 13 will be defeated and incarcerated by messiah / the Lamb / Jesus Christ when he leads in the final battle of this age.

But the Ancient of Days / God Most High has determined that this fourth beast / fourth kingdom will be utterly destroyed and its remnants will not be retained. This decision was supported by the court of heaven. In fact, this fourth beast / fourth kingdom will be replaced by the fully established kingdom of heaven on earth.

'I watched until thrones were put in place and the Ancient of Days was seated. His garment was as white as snow and the hair of his head was like pure wool. His throne was a fiery flame, with its wheels a burning fire. A river of fire was flowing, coming out before him. Thousands upon thousands came before him to minister to him. Ten thousand and ten thousand times ten thousand, stood before the court where he was seated. And the books were opened.' Daniel 7:9-10 translated

Ezekiel 1:26-28 also described his vision of God in a similar manner to Daniel's
'Ancient of Days.'

'Then I wished to know the truth about the fourth exceedingly dreadful beast which was different from all the others with its iron teeth and its bronze nails which devoured and broke into pieces, and trampled on what remained with its feet, and the ten horns that were on its head, and the other horn that came up from it, from which the three horns fell before it; specifically this horn which had eyes and a mouth which spoke pompous words, whose appearance was greater than his fellows.'

'As I was watching, this horn was making war against the saints and prevailing against them, until the Ancient of Days came and a judgment was made in favor of the saints of God Most High, and the time came for the saints to possess the kingdom.'

'He said, 'The fourth beast will be a fourth kingdom on earth, which will be different from all other kingdoms, and will devour the whole earth, and trample it and break it into pieces."

"The ten horns that will rise from this kingdom, will be ten kings. And another will rise after them. He will be different from the first kings, and three of the kings will be subdued."

"He will speak pompous words against God Most High, and against the saints of God Most High. He will persecute the saints and will intend to change the times and the law. The saints will be given into his hand for a time and times and half a time."

"But the court will be seated, and they will take away his dominion, to consume and destroy it forever."

"Then the dominion and greatness of his kingdom under the whole of heaven, will be given to the saints, the people of God Most High. His kingdom is an everlasting kingdom and all his dominion will serve him and obey." Daniel 7:19-27 translated

Daniel's Seventy 'Sevens' / Weeks of Years – Daniel 9:20-27

During the first year of the reign of the Mede / Persian Darius, son of Xerxes (539 BC), the Old Testament / Tanakh prophet Daniel (fl. 605 to 530 BC) – a prophet of Judah, was praying. During his prayer time, Daniel received the vision of the seventy 'sevens.'

The vision of the seventy 'sevens' was divided into three parts with the first part of seven 'sevens' correlating with the Jubilee Year that followed 7 X 7 (49) years. The second part, added to the first part, provided sixty nine 'sevens' and resulted in the execution of messiah. A gap of time followed the first sixty nine 'sevens,' that concluded with the events designated to take place during the seventieth 'seven.'

The seventieth 'seven' was also recognized as the era of the time of Jacob's Trouble. It was Daniel and John the Revelator who provided the definition of the era of the time of Jacob's Trouble to be seven years. (Jeremiah 30:7, Daniel 8:13-14, 9:20-27, 12:11-12, Revelation 11:1-14, 12, 13, 17)

Seventy weeks are determined for your people, for your holy city, to finish the transgression – to make an end of sins, and to make reconciliation for iniquity and to bring in everlasting righteousness; and to seal up vision and prophecy, and to anoint the Most Holy.

Therefore, know and understand, that from the going forth of the command to restore and build Jerusalem, until messiah the prince, there will be seven weeks, and sixty two weeks.

The street and the wall will be built, but in troublesome times.

After the sixty two weeks, messiah will be cut off, and will have nothing.

The people of the prince / ruler who is to come, will destroy the city and the sanctuary.

And the end of it shall come with a flood. War will continue until the end and desolations are determined.

The prince / ruler will confirm a covenant with many, for one 'seven' / 'week.' But in the middle of the 'seven' / 'week,' the prince / ruler will bring an end to the sacrifice and offering. On the wing (of the temple), the prince / ruler will establish abominations that will cause desolation, even until the consumption which has been determined is poured out on the desolate / the one who destroys. Daniel 9:24-27 from the Hebrew text

Daniel's first sixty nine 'sevens' / weeks of years #1-69 - Daniel 9:20-27

The biblical record presented numerous examples of God Most High's use of exile in a variety of forms, as a means of rescuing God's holy people while simultaneously destroying the enemies of God Most High and of the kingdom of heaven.

The deluge / flood was the venue for rescuing Noah, Noah's family, and living creatures, while simultaneously bringing the destruction of the enemies of God the Creator and of the kingdom of heaven.

The passing of the people of Israel through the Red Sea provided salvation for the people of Israel as they fled Egyptian bondage, while simultaneously bringing destruction to the Egyptian military and ending Egyptian global dominance. As the people of Israel passed through the Red Sea, the nation of Israel was baptized into new life. But for the army of the Egyptians that represented an unholy nation, baptism brought death.

Only what is holy and dedicated to God Most High survives baptism. What is unholy is destroyed through baptism. The same principle applies to God Most High's judgment.

The psalmist claimed that, the stone the builders rejected, has become the chief cornerstone (Psalm 118:22 translated).

Jesus Christ described himself as that unique rock, that if a person falls upon Jesus, they will be broken into pieces that can be restored. But anyone on whom this stone falls upon, will be crushed, from which there can be no restoration (Matthew 21:44).

Following this pattern, God Most High's message to the people of Israel, who were enveloped in despair as they sojourned in exile (722 to 516 BC), was God Most High's message to Daniel that spoke of the promise of God Most High to fully establish the kingdom of heaven at a future specified date, through the work of the promised and prophesied messiah.

In the midst of the bleakest darkness, God Most High makes provision for the establishment of the greatest light. God Most High's pattern of activity continues to proclaim that even when it appears that God Most High has abandoned the situation or seems to have been defeated, and when other peoples with pagan gods rule over God Most High's people, that God Most High does not consent to this kind of ending. God Most High authored happy endings.

Daniel was given a vision from God Most High describing the timing of the coming of the promised and prophesied messiah, both the first coming of messiah as the sacrificial Lamb (sixty nine sevens) and the second coming of messiah as the triumphant victor over the enemies of God Most High and of the kingdom of heaven (the seventieth seven). This 'era' was measured in 'seventy 'sevens." (Daniel 9:20-27)

The conversion into human years was seventy weeks of years. 70 x 7 days in a week yielded 490 years, until the coming of Messiah as the victor over the enemies of God Most High and of the kingdom of heaven.

When Jesus Christ was asked how many times we are to forgive, Jesus' answer was seventy times seven. This may have been a reference to God Most High forgiving Israel seventy times seven, and why the period of seventy sevens was used to mark the time of the coming of messiah to fully rescue the people of Israel.

The people and nation of Israel had the greatest God of all on their side and they turned their backs to that God. According to human standards, they did not deserve redemption.

But while the people of Israel were in exile for their idolatry, for their nonobservance of the Sabbatical and Jubilee Years, for their sacrificing to idols and foreign gods including their human sacrifice to the gods, and for a variety of other offenses, God Most High spoke to Daniel a message of redemption, reclamation and regeneration.

The people of Israel had abandoned their relationship with God Most High. They deserved exile.

But God... God Most High must be true to God's word. There is nothing that God Most High cannot redeem except a heart and soul that does not desire to be redeemed. God must be faithful to the covenant agreement that God Most High made with Adam and Eve, with Noah, with Abraham, Isaac, and Jacob, with Moses and the people of Israel, with David, etc. God Most High must provide a messiah that worships and fulfills the law in the temple in Jerusalem. God Most High needed to bring the people of Israel back to their homeland and to a state of forgiveness and right relationship with God.

So, God Most High told Daniel the plan for how to know when the promised and prophesied messiah would come. And also in this prophecy, were clues on how to know when the messiah will come again.

One must read carefully, because the transition between the description of the first coming of messiah and the second coming of messiah is seamless.

Seventy weeks are determined for your people, for your holy city, to finish the transgression – to make an end of sins, and to make reconciliation for iniquity and to bring in everlasting righteousness; and to seal up vision and prophecy, and to anoint the Most Holy.

Therefore, know and understand, that from the going forth of the command to restore and build Jerusalem, until messiah the prince, there will be seven weeks, and sixty two weeks.

The street and the wall will be built, but in troublesome times.

After the sixty two weeks, messiah will be cut off, and will have nothing.

<u>The people of the prince / ruler who is to come, will destroy the city and the sanctuary</u>.

And the end of it shall come with a flood.

War will continue until the end and desolations are determined.

<u>The prince / ruler will confirm a covenant with many, for one 'seven' / 'week</u>.' But in the middle of the 'seven' / 'week,' the prince /

ruler will bring an end to the sacrifice and offering. On the wing (of the temple), the prince / ruler will establish abominations that will cause desolation, even until the consumption which has been determined is poured out on the desolate / the one who destroys. Daniel 9:24-27 from the Hebrew text (Daniel 9:20-27)

Daniel's vision of the seventy 'sevens' was the prophecy that determined the time for the first coming of the promised and prophesied messiah for Israel, his ministry, crucifixion and resurrection.

And then abruptly, the second half of the message of the seventy sevens, described events surrounding the little horn / eleventh king / prince who is to come / beast of the earth that will come during the era of the time of Jacob's Trouble. It was almost as if the greater message was not the coming of the promised and prophesied messiah and his redemptive work, but of the prince / ruler that will commit the future abomination of desolation event. Daniel's presentation of this prophecy almost hinted that the future abomination of desolation event will be the attempt to totally undo all that was accomplished through the sacrifice that messiah / the Lamb / Jesus Christ made as the Passover / Pascal Lamb. Daniel's vision even stressed the importance of the consumption / destruction of the prince / ruler that is to come, as almost equal in significance to the work that messiah / the Lamb / Jesus Christ accomplished with his first coming.

The fact that this prophecy had two parts, separated in time, meant that there must also be two partial fulfillments of this prophecy, separated in time.

The first part fulfillment:

The first sixty nine 'sevens' were divided into two sections:

The first seven 'sevens' or the first forty nine years (7 x 7) began with the decree to rebuild Jerusalem and ended with the people of Israel having restored Jerusalem and their right to self-rule also restored. The decree to both restore <u>and</u> to rebuild Jerusalem set the 'timer' for dating the coming of the messiah. During the conclusion of the people of Israel's exile in Assyria, Babylon, and Persia, there were a total of four decrees. But only one of the four *decrees was a decree to both <u>restore</u> <u>and</u> to <u>rebuild</u> Jerusalem.*

The next sixty two 'sevens' or 434 years (62 x 7) spanned time from the restoration of the nation of Israel, to the beginning of Jesus' ministry. Knowing this, Israel should have been prepared for the coming of the promised and prophesied messiah. Jesus Christ even referenced the expectation of God that the people of Israel should have known when the promised and prophesied messiah would come, when Jesus Christ said during his last week prior to his crucifixion, 'For the days will come upon you that your enemies will build an encampment around you, barricading you. And they will surround you and close you in on every side. And they will level you to the ground and your children within you. They will not leave a stone upon a stone within you. <u>For you did not recognize the season of your visitation</u>.' Luke 19:42-44 translated

The last 'seven' of the sixty nine 'sevens,' represented the seven years of Jesus' ministry. But, in the middle of the seven years, after three and a half years of ministry, the people of Israel rejected Jesus Christ as messiah. Jesus Christ was crucified / 'cut off,' without heir.

The later portion fulfillment:
At the end of the sixty ninth 'seven' there was a gap between the death of the promised and prophesied messiah, when messiah was 'cut off,' to the final seventieth 'seven.'

This period of time, beginning with the cutting off of messiah and ending sometime around the era of the time of Jacob's Trouble was called in other biblical references the times of the Gentiles. Daniel's prophecies focused upon their effect upon the people of Israel. Consequently, the almost two thousand years that filled in that gap, were not the focus of Daniel's vision.

The seventieth 'seven' identified by Daniel, was known by the prophet Jeremiah as the era of Jacob's Trouble / 'a time of trouble for Jacob' (Jeremiah 30:7).

Daniel (fl. 605 to 530 BC) and Jeremiah (fl. 626 to 585 BC) were prophets of Judah. Both survived the siege of Jerusalem that cemented the exile of Judah into the Babylonian empire.

Daniel's vision of the seventy 'sevens' indicated that the seventieth 'seven' will prepare Israel to come to the place where Israel will once again call upon God and finally realize and accept Jesus Christ as their promised and prophesied messiah.

Until Israel accepts Jesus Christ as messiah, Jesus Christ will not be able to fight on the side of the people and nation of Israel, defeating their enemies and establishing his kingdom forever. In a sense, Jesus Christ was also exiled, when the people of Israel rejected him as their promised and prophesied messiah. Until the people of Israel are willing to welcome him back, Jesus Christ remains in his own form of 'exile' in heaven.

Until Israel recognizes and accepts Jesus Christ as messiah, Jesus Christ will not come to establish his reign.

Until Israel recognizes and accepts Jesus Christ as their messiah, Israel will not be qualified to become the nation of priests that God Most High has designated Israel to be.

Side note: Seven days of consecration were required before a person could become an Israelite priest. The seven year era of the time of Jacob's Trouble is required of Israel before they will be qualified to be a nation of priests.

Daniel's vision also communicated that the end will come like a flood, quickly, catching many unprepared. During this era of the time of Jacob's Trouble, the prince who is to come / beast of the earth / final world ruler will establish a seven year treaty for Israel. This will set the timer for the beast of the earth's own term of power and authority (Revelation 13), and also set the timer for determining the date for Jesus Christ's return. Although no one will know the day nor the hour that Jesus Christ will actually return, we will be able to zoom in on the year, the season, the month and maybe even the week. For a prophecy that was established in the Garden of Eden / garden of God / paradise six thousand years ago, the kind of precision in dating that will provide the year, season, month and possibly even the week, should be considered to be quite precise.

Midway through this seven year covenant peace treaty agreement between Israel and many nations, that the prince who is to come / beast of the earth / final world ruler will confirm, the prince who is to come will break the covenant peace treaty agreement. He will desecrate the temple mount through his abomination of desolation event, and this desecration will render sacrifice on the temple mount to be unacceptable to God Most High. In this way he will discontinue the temple sacrificial system once more.

In order for Daniel's prophecy to be fulfilled, there must be a temple, and a functioning temple sacrificial system in place. The covenant peace treaty agreement was already established September 15, 2020.

The historical correlation between Daniel's prophecy of the seventy 'sevens,' the events that have taken place since then, and the events that must still take place.

The Old Testament / Tanakh prophet Daniel (fl. 605 to 530 BC) was exiled into Babylon while he was a teenager. It was when Daniel was living under the reign of Darius, during the first year of the reign of Darius (539 BC), that Daniel received the vision of the seventy 'sevens.'

Seventy weeks are determined for your people, for your holy city, to finish the transgression – to make an end of sins, and to make reconciliation for iniquity and to bring in everlasting righteousness; and to seal up vision and prophecy, and to anoint the Most Holy.

Therefore, know and understand, that from the going forth of the command to restore and build Jerusalem, until messiah the prince, there will be seven weeks, and sixty two weeks.

The street and the wall will be built, but in troublesome times.

After the sixty two weeks, messiah will be cut off, and will have nothing.

The people of the prince / ruler who is to come, will destroy the city and the sanctuary.

And the end of it shall come with a flood.

War will continue until the end and desolations are determined.

The prince / ruler will confirm a covenant with many, for one 'seven' / 'week.' But in the middle of the 'seven' / 'week,' the prince / ruler will bring an end to the sacrifice and offering. On the wing (of the temple), the prince / ruler will establish abominations that will cause desolation, even until the consumption which has been determined is poured out on the desolate / the one who destroys. Daniel 9:24-27 from the Hebrew text

The time required for the fulfillment of this vision spanned the time from the issuance of the decree for the people of Israel to restore and build Jerusalem, until the future abomination of desolation event; approximately two thousand four hundred sixty six years. Within Daniel's prophecy there were some significant notations of events that marked time.

The beginning of the 'seventy sevens,' was marked by the command to restore and build Jerusalem.

After the seven 'sevens' and the sixty two 'sevens,' or during the sixty ninth 'seven,' messiah was cut off, crucified.

Then the people of the prince / ruler who came to destroy the city and the sanctuary, were the Romans. On the 9th of Av / August 30, 70 AD, the city of Jerusalem and the temple were destroyed.

The destruction of the temple was followed by a period of almost two thousand years. Currently we wait for the rest of the prophecy to be fulfilled. The next event will be the prince / ruler will confirm a covenant with many, for one 'seven' / 'week' / seven years. And halfway through the seven years, the prince / rule will bring an end to the sacrifice and offering in the temple, by desecrating the temple. The manner in which he will desecrate the temple will be to establish abominations that will cause the temple to no longer be acceptable for presenting sacrifice and offering to God Most High.

In Israel's history, there have been a number of times when the temples have been desolated or destroyed.

Solomon's temple was destroyed on August 10, 586 BC when the Babylonian empire destroyed the temple and the people of Israel from the kingdom of Judah were taken into exile. The temple was rebuilt under the management of Zerubbabel in 516 BC.

In 167 BC, Antiochus IV Epiphanes / Mithradates, king of the Seleucid empire, desecrated the temple with the first abomination of desolation event. Antiochus IV Epiphanes authorized the sacrificing of a pig on the altar that he had set up to honor Zeus on the temple mount. Pigs were declared unclean animals. To sacrifice a pig on the altar was considered to be a desecration of the altar and caused the sacrifices on the desecrated altar to be unacceptable. Three years later, the temple was reconsecrated.

Herod the Great (fl. ~36 to 1 BC) took on the task of enlarging the temple and making the temple into an impressive building, in time for earthly ministry of messiah / the Lamb / Jesus Christ.

On the 9th of Av / August 30, 70 AD, the people who came to destroy the temple and the city of Jerusalem Israel, were the Romans during the First Jewish Roman War.

But it was during the reign of Antiochus IV Epiphanes that the first abomination of desolation event took place (167 BC). This fact made Antiochus IV Epiphanes the typology for the man who will commit the future abomination of desolation.

Antiochus IV Epiphanes was the first Seleucid king to use divine epithets on coins referring to himself as 'manifest god' for example. As the supreme world ruler of the time, he sought to Hellenize the world; to cause the world to live with one language, one religion, one government, etc. He outlawed Jewish religious rites and traditions. He forbade the reading and possession of the Jewish scriptures, making the possession of the Jewish scriptures, punishable by death. He ordered the worship of Zeus as the supreme god.

In response, the Israelites renamed Epiphanes ('the illustrious one'), Epimanes ('the mad one') as a word play on his name.

According to a letter recorded in the book of Maccabees 1, Antiochus IV Epiphanes: took away the temple vessels, temple treasures, temple utensils, temple precious metals; shed much blood and spoke with great arrogance; forbade offerings and sacrifices; required the Israelites to profane the Sabbaths and feast days, built pagan altars, temples and shrines; sacrificed swine and unclean animals; required the Israelite sons to remain uncircumcised and to defile themselves with impurity and abomination, etc. Whoever refused to honor the command of Epiphanes was to be put to death. Any scrolls of the law that they found they tore up and burned. Whoever was found with a scroll of the covenant or observed the law was condemned to death by royal decree. On the twenty-fifth day of each month, sacrifice was offered on the pagan altar that was placed over the temple altar of burnt offerings. They put to death women who had their children circumcised, hung their babies from their necks, and had their families also killed.

The Israelite response to the desecration of the temple was the Maccabean revolt which ended in the rededication of the temple and is today celebrated as the eight day feast of Dedication / feast of Hanukah.

Because of the connection between the recognition of the destruction of the city of Jerusalem and its temple, with the future abomination of desolation event, there are those that interpreted Daniel's vision as having already been fulfilled with a 'second abomination of desolation' event when the Romans destroyed the city of Jerusalem and its temple in 70 AD under the leadership of the Roman general Titus.

Following the Jerusalem riots of 66 AD, there was a Judean Free Government in Jerusalem. The Romans would not allow the Israelites' rebellion to stand and so they sieged Jerusalem, not allowing people to enter or leave. Finally, on August 30, 70 AD, the siege ended with the burning and destruction of the temple. Josephus, an immediate witness, claimed that 1.1 million people were killed during the siege.

But the rest of the prophecy was not fulfilled. Titus did not confirm a covenant for seven years. Titus did not break the covenant halfway through and suspend sacrifice and offering. Titus did not cause the temple to become desolate because the temple was completely destroyed. The altar was not desecrated because the altar was completely removed. Etc.

The Romans did construct a temple for Jupiter on the temple mount and placed a giant statue in front of it. They also placed a huge statue of Jupiter inside the temple of Jupiter. There were some that determined that Titus sacrificed a pig on the altar of the Israelite temple because the Romans sacrificed pigs before their deities. But the historians that witnessed the events claimed that Titus did not even enter into Jerusalem until after the temple had been set on fire and destroyed, and therefore Titus did not offer a desecrated offering on the temple altar.

Like Antiochus IV Epiphanes, the Romans prohibited circumcision. Circumcision represented to the people of Israel, their covenant with God Most High that was first established with Abraham and Isaac. Prohibiting circumcision was symbolic of cutting off the people of Israel from their God in the same way that messiah / the Lamb / Jesus Christ was cut off from Israel.

The Arch of Titus, celebrating the Roman sacking of Jerusalem and the temple, still stands in Rome complete with the story carved within its features.

The Israelite response to the destruction of the temple in 70 AD was a series of revolts. After the third revolt failed, Rome forbade all Israelites to enter Jerusalem.

But with all the similarities to the first abomination of desolation event, there were too many differences and unfulfilled pieces of Daniel's vision to interpret the destruction of the city of Jerusalem and the temple in 70 AD, as the abomination of desolation that was described by Daniel. Possibly one of the greatest unfulfilled pieces of Daniel's vision was the description of the consumption that has been determined to be poured out on the one who commits the abomination of desolation. Titus was not destroyed but went on to enjoy a greater military and political career.

This means that there will be a future abomination of desolation event that will take place during the era of the time of Jacob's Trouble. The future abomination of desolation event will follow the pattern of the first abomination of desolation event. The temple altar will be desecrated, possibly through the sacrifice of pigs, but probably through the murder of human beings on the temple mount (Revelation 13:14-15). Worshipers will be marked as belonging to the system established by the two beasts instead of as belonging to God Most High.

The exile of the people of Israel into Assyria and Babylon, and their release from exile by the Medes and the Persians

The timing of the exiles of Israel and Judah, along with the return of the people of Israel from exile, consisted of a set of events that demonstrated the precise timing of God Most High's prophecies and activities.

The Old Testament / Tanakh prophet Jeremiah (fl. 626 to 585 BC) of Judah was assigned with communicating God Most High's displeasure with the people of Israel, for their turning away from God Most High to do things like worship the Queen of Heaven / Ishtar / Astarte / Semiramis / etc. and other gods, as well as ignoring the Sabbath years which were intended to renew the covenant between the Israelites and God Most High (Jeremiah 7:12-19).

(Also see Jeremiah 25:11-12 and Jeremiah 19:10.)

Jeremiah instructed the Israelites that they would be in exile for seventy years.

Because the people of Israel did not honor the Sabbath years nor the Jubilee Years for four hundred ninety years beginning with the destruction of Shiloh in 1094 BC, God Most High's response was for the people of Israel to experience exile under the rule of those who honored the gods of the baal / mystery / mythology religion. For the people of the southern kingdom of Judah, that captivity lasted for seventy years, one year of captivity for every Sabbatical year the people of Israel had ignored. At the end of their seventy years of exile and captivity.

The Lord said: 'Say to them, 'This is what the Lord says: If you do not listen to me and follow my law, which I have set before you, and if you do not listen to the words of my servants the prophets, whom I have sent to you again and again (though you have not listened), then

I will make this house like Shiloh and this city (Jerusalem) an object of cursing among all the nations of the earth. Jeremiah 26:4-9

Shiloh was King David's first location for the home of the Ark of the Covenant. The city of Shiloh was later destroyed because of its apostasy.

God Most High's word was true and fulfilled. From 722 BC to 717 BC the Assyrians held siege, captured and finally took into exile, the northern kingdom of the ten tribes of Israel.

In 605 BC the Babylonian King Nebuchadnezzar completed the capture of the Assyrians and absorbed the Assyrian empire into the Babylonian empire. So, it was King Nebuchadnezzar who led in the battle to capture and exile the southern two tribes of Judah and Benjamin. The task of exiling all the people of Israel was concluded on Av 9 / August 10, 586 BC when Nebuchadnezzar captured and destroyed Jerusalem and the first temple. Nebuchadnezzar also took possession of the temple ware.

In 539BC, King Cyrus of the Persians crushed the Babylonians. King Cyrus the Persian king dried up the Euphrates River by diverting the water. Then the Persians traveled through the riverbed, slipped under the city walls, and took the city in a single night on October 16, 539 BC (Daniel 5:30), without resistance. The Medes and the Persians were now the new rulers of Babylon and consequently, all the Assyrian / Babylonian captives.

The kings of Persia that reigned during the time of the exile of the people of Israel and afterward:

- *Cyrus (539-530 BC) (Ezra 1);*
- *Cambyses, Cyrus' son (530-522 BC) (Ezra 4:6);*
- *Darius I Hystaspes (522-466 BC),*
- *Xerxes, Darius' son (486-465 BC) and husband of Esther (Purim was established),*
- *Artaxerxes Longimanus, Xerxes son (465-423 BC).*

In Daniel's prophecy of the seventy 'sevens', Daniel identified that there would be a specific decree that would be issued after the time of Daniel that would signal the beginning of the seventy 'sevens'. There were four decrees which commentators believe were the candidates for the starting of the clock for the prophecy of the seventy 'sevens.' Depending upon which decree is used to begin the timing, determines the ending date and the fulfillment of the prophecy.

In the calculations, there must be an allowance made of the lack of a year in the changeover from BC to AD. From the year 1 BC to the year 1 AD, there was no year 'zero.'

For the people of Israel, the existence of a physical temple with a functioning sacrificial system, always been a precondition for the arrival of the promised and prophesied messiah.

So, the completion of the temple's rebuilding would have been a natural choice for setting the timer for the coming of the messiah.

The four decrees for consideration as the possible decree that began the timer, were:

1) *Cyrus the Persian who issued the first decree allowing the Israelites to return to their homeland and provided for the funding of the building of the temple (Ezra 1:1-4). Zerubbabel was the priest who oversaw the temple building project. So, the second temple was called Zerubbabel's temple. Later Zerubbabel's temple was built over when Herod the Great built what was called Herod's temple. Among scholars both Zerubbabel's temple and Herod's temple were referred to as the second temple primarily because the schedule of temple sacrifice continued uninterrupted in the transition.*
2) *Darius was a Mede (who married into the Persian royal family, marrying two of the daughters of Cyrus as well as other daughters of Persian rulers, effectively making a claim for the Persian throne as well as the throne of the Medes). Darius issued a decree to allow the temple building to continue (Ezra 6:8). The*

temple of Zerubbabel was completed in 517-516 BC which was seventy years after the southern kingdom of Judah entered into captivity.
3) *Xerxes I / Ahasuerus succeeded his father Darius and was the husband of Queen Esther / Hadassah. Artaxerxes Longimanus / Artaxerxes was the son of Xerxes and succeeded his father. Artaxerxes Longimanus issued the decree allowing the Israelites to fully return to Jerusalem to build the wall and to reestablish self-governance for the people of Israel (Ezra 7:11; 9:9).*
4) *Artaxerxes Longimanus also issued a letter to Nehemiah allowing the work to continue (Nehemiah 2:7-9).*

Marking off sixty nine 'sevens' from any of these starting points leads to significant events taking place that were favorable to Israel.

Other information that aids in understanding the return of the people of Israel to the land of Israel following the exile:

Ezra was responsible for governing the people of Israel as they returned to the land of Israel. Ezra and Zerubbabel were responsible for the building of Zerubbabel's temple.

Nehemiah was responsible for the building of the walls around Jerusalem.

Ezra, Zerubbabel and Nehemiah needed to work together to accomplish the institution of stability for the city of Jerusalem, the rebuilding of the temple and the reestablishment of the nation of Israel.

The First Decree - King Cyrus of Persia 538 BC – Permission to return home and to rebuild the temple
In the first year of Cyrus king of Persia (538 BC), in order to fulfill the word of the Lord spoken by Jeremiah, the Lord moved the heart of Cyrus king of Persia to make a proclamation throughout his realm and to put it in writing: 'This is what Cyrus king of Persia says: 'The Lord the God of heaven has given me all the kingdoms of the earth and God has appointed me to build a temple for God at Jerusalem in Judah. Anyone of God's people among you – may the

Lord their God be with them, and let them go up." 2 Chronicles 36:22-23

Cyrus, king of Persia, issued the decree in 539-538 BC which allowed the Israelites to return to Israel and to begin work on rebuilding the temple. Isaiah had prophesied approximately one hundred years before the birth of Cyrus (Isaiah 44:28, 45:1) that Cyrus would decree that Jerusalem would be rebuilt and the temple foundations would be laid.

Notice that Isaiah's prophecy, given one hundred fifty years earlier, actually referred to Cyrus by name. Isaiah 44 - 45 foretold with detail even what Cyrus would do and indicated that God would bless Cyrus.

In 537 BC, the evening and morning sacrifices began again with the feast of trumpets / Rosh Hashanah / New Year, and the New Moon sacrifices, along with the feast of ingathering / feast of tabernacles / feast of booths / Sukkot (Ezra 3:3-6).

Ezra also documented the decree of Cyrus.

In the first year of Cyrus king of Persia (538 BC), in order to fulfill the word of the Lord spoken by Jeremiah, the Lord moved the heart of Cyrus king of Persia to make a proclamation throughout his realm and to put it in writing: 'This is what Cyrus king of Persia says: 'The Lord, the God of heaven, has given me all the kingdoms of the earth and God has appointed me to build a temple for God at Jerusalem in Judah. Anyone of God's people among you – may their God be with them, and let them go up to Jerusalem in Judah and build the temple of the Lord, the God of Israel, the God who is in Jerusalem. And the people of any place where survivors may now be living are to provide God with silver and gold, with goods and livestock, and with freewill offerings for the temple of God in Jerusalem." Ezra 1:1-4

The Second Decree - King Darius of Persia 520 BC – To continue the rebuilding of the temple

Concerning Darius' renewal of the temple work in Jerusalem: 'Moreover, I hereby decree what you are to do for these elders of the Jews in the construction of this house of God: The expenses of these people are to be fully paid out of the royal treasury, from the revenues of Trans-Euphrates, so that the work will not stop. Ezra 6:8 (6:3-12)

Darius the Persian in 520-521 BC issued a decree which allowed the temple building to continue.

So the elders of the Jews continued to build and prosper under the preaching of Haggai the prophet and Zechariah, a descendant of

Iddo. They finished building the temple according to the command of the God of Israel and decrees of Cyrus, Darius and Artaxerxes, kings of Persia. The temple was completed on the third day of the month of Adar, in the sixth year of the reign of King Darius. Ezra 6:14-15

In 516 BC the temple was completed, seventy years after the temple and the city of Jerusalem were destroyed, and the southern kingdom was taken into exile. The temple was completed and rededicated March 12, 516 BC (Ezra 6:13-15) in time for Passover, almost seventy years after the temple had been destroyed (August 10, 586 BC) and the series of exile events had been completed.

Artaxerxes was not yet a king of Persia, but was given credit for his later support of reestablishing Jerusalem and for his later declaration of the nation of Israel's independence.

The Third Decree - King Artaxerxes 457 BC – Israel was officially released from Persian governance

This is a copy of the letter King Artaxerxes had given to Ezra the priest and teacher, a man learned in matters concerning the commands and decrees of the Lord for Israel: Ezra 7:11

A copy of the actual letter was included in the book of Ezra.

This letter to Ezra was given in 457 BC. This was the decree that issued authority to the Israelites to reestablish their own government. This was the decree that recognized the nation of Israel's independence.

The fact that this third decree marked the date of Israel's independence was why many believe that this date should be the beginning point of Daniel's seventy 'sevens'.

Ezra indicated that all four of the decrees, were actually one decree reinforced by three kings (Ezra 6:14) and used as his 'anchor in time date' the completion of the temple in 516 BC. For Ezra, the building of the physical building was a visible indicator of the time of the fulfillment of this prophecy.

Using the solar calendar to mark time, beginning with 457 BC, adding four hundred eighty three years (69 x 7 = 483), and adding one year for BC to AD conversion, concluded with 27 AD. The year 27 AD marked the beginning of Jesus Christ's ministry and the year of Jubilee according to Luke 4:14-21.

It is amazing that applying sixty nine 'seven's to the third decree concluded with the beginning of Jesus' ministry. But it was not amazing to the disciples of messiah / the Lamb / Jesus Christ who were looking for the promised and prophesied messiah at the appropriate time in order to become his followers.

The Fourth Decree - King Artaxerxes March 14, 444 BC – Persian support for work on the temple and the city walls of Jerusalem

In the month of Nisan in the twentieth year of King Artaxerxes … (Nehemiah requested a decree and a letter for the purpose of reinvigorating and completing the work on the city wall of Jerusalem.) (Nehemiah 2:1-8)

The commission for Nehemiah was provided on March 14, 444 BC. The Persian king, Artaxerxes Longimanus, began his rule in July 465 BC after the murder of his father Xerxes, husband of Esther, and of Artaxerxes' older brother. Artaxerxes' twentieth year began July, 445 BC.

On March 14, 444 BC, which was also during the month of Nisan, the month of Passover, Artaxerxes issued a decree which reinvigorated the rebuilding of Jerusalem's wall.

One proposal for calculating time, using the 'Fourth' Decree as the beginning point for Daniel's seventy 'sevens', provided this reasoning:

7 x 7 = 49 years for the first portion of the seventy 'sevens' (one year short of a Jubilee cycle);
plus 62 x 7 = 434 years
totaling 483 prophetic years;

or 69 x 7 = 483 prophetic years;

483 years x 360 days per Jewish lunar calendar year = 173,880 days;
173,880 days / 365.25 days per solar year = 476 solar years;
Beginning with the decree that was given on March 14, 445 BC, adding one year for the lack of year in the

conversion from BC to AD plus one conversion year, yields the date of March 31 AD.

March 24, 31 AD would have possibly been the fourteenth day of the month of Nisan / Passover. This was a possible date for the death of Jesus Christ.

For those who were watching the timeclock of heaven, they knew when the promised and prophesied messiah would have begun his ministry, and when he would have been cut off / crucified, according to Daniel's prophecy.

Jesus Christ was a student of the Old Testament / Tanakh and its prophets. Jesus Christ was fully aware of God Most High's timing.

During Jesus Christ's last week, Jesus taught, 'For the days will come upon you that your enemies will build an encampment around you, barricading you. And they will surround you and close you in on every side. And they will level you to the ground and your children within you. They will not leave a stone upon a stone within you. <u>For you did not recognize the season of your visitation</u>.' Luke 19:42-44 translated

The high priest of the Sanhedrin, the seventy one elders of the Sanhedrin had a responsibility to understand the prophecies of Daniel and to teach them to the people.

But the religious leaders of Israel did not fulfill their responsibilities, nor did they desire to share their power with the messiah. Jesus issued seven woes against the religious leaders and teachers that were recorded by Matthew ... 'because they did not recognize the time of their messiah's coming.' *(Matthew 23)*

Daniel's sixty-ninth 'seven' – the ministry years of messiah / the Lamb / Jesus Christ – Daniel 9:20-27

Seventy weeks are determined for your people, for your holy city, to finish the transgression – to make an end of sins, and to make reconciliation for iniquity and to bring in everlasting righteousness; and to seal up vision and prophecy, and to anoint the Most Holy. Daniel 9:24 translated (9:20-27)

The language of this prophecy indicated that these seventy 'sevens' were essential to anointing the most holy place. The 'most holy place' was usually a reference to the temple on the temple mount.

Because the anointed one / messiah / Christ was cut off midway during the sixty ninth 'seven,' and seventy 'sevens' are required for the anointing of the people of Israel to become holy, when Israel cut off their messiah, they also cut themselves off from the opportunity to be anointed as holy and to finish the time of their transgression. The nation of Israel cut themselves off a mere three and a half years plus the last seventieth 'seven,' from becoming the nation of priests that God Most High determined that they should be.

The beginning of Jesus Christ's earthly ministry marked the beginning of the sixty ninth 'seven.' The stoning of Stephen took place around the time of what would have been the end of the sixty ninth 'seven.'

The time required to complete the process of consecrating the people of Israel as a nation of priests will resume during the era of the time of Jacob's Trouble. The people of Israel must atone for their wickedness in order to proceed in the consecration process as required for God Most High's priesthood. The events scheduled for the era of the time of Jacob's Trouble will be substantial in the process of the atonement process for the people of Israel. And the era of the time of Jacob's Trouble was designated to be seven years.

Notice that at the end of the seventieth 'seven,' there will be everlasting righteousness. And everlasting righteousness accompanies the kingdom of heaven being fully established on earth. With the fullness of the kingdom of heaven comes what is holy.

After the sixty-two 'sevens,' messiah will be cut off and will have nothing.

The people of the prince / ruler who is to come, will destroy the city and the sanctuary.

And the end of it shall come with a flood. War will continue until the end and desolations are determined.

The prince / ruler will confirm a covenant with many, for one 'seven' / 'week.' But in the middle of the 'seven' / 'week,' the prince / ruler will bring an end to the sacrifice and offering. On the wing (of the temple), the prince / ruler will establish abominations that will cause desolation, even until the consumption which has been determined is poured out on the desolate / the one who destroys. Daniel 9:26-27 translated (9:20-27)

The word that was translated 'cut off' was also translated as 'executed.'

Daniel's vision was abrupt in moving from 'the Anointed One will be cut off and will have nothing,' to 'The end will come like a flood.' But the time for the fulfillment of the two statements has been about two thousand solar calendar years.

Then Daniel returned to fill in the time gap: 'War will continue until the end.'
'Desolations have been decreed / determined.' etc.

The rest of the message was entirely focused upon the activity of the prince / ruler that is to come who will be the main actor, the star attraction for committing the future abomination of desolation event.

If during Jesus Christ's earthly ministry, he would have been accepted by the people of Israel as the promised and prophesied messiah, there would have been no further need to audition other candidates for the role.

Daniel's seventieth 'seven' the prince / ruler who is to come – Daniel 9:20-27

The focus of Daniel's seventy 'sevens' identified two major events; the execution of messiah, and the events surrounding the prince / ruler that is to come.

After the sixty-two 'sevens,' messiah will be cut off and will have nothing.
The people of the prince / ruler who is to come, will destroy the city and the sanctuary.
And the end of it shall come with a flood. War will continue until the end and desolations are determined.
The prince / ruler will confirm a covenant with many, for one 'seven' / 'week.' But in the middle of the 'seven' / 'week,' the prince / ruler will bring an end to the sacrifice and offering. On the wing (of the temple), the prince / ruler will establish abominations that will cause desolation, even until the consumption which has been determined is poured out on the desolate / the one who destroys. Daniel 9:26-27 translated (9:20-27)

The prince / ruler that is to come / beast of the earth will first confirm a covenant with many for one 'seven.' This ruler that is to come / beast of the earth / final world ruler will come as a 'friend' of Israel, confirming the covenant peace treaty agreement and even providing miraculous signs that will serve to 'validate' himself as an 'anointed one.' (Revelation 13:13-14).

It was interesting that Daniel described the prince / ruler that is to come as confirming a covenant instead of establishing a covenant. Confirming a covenant implies that the covenant will already have been established and that the prince / ruler that is to come will merely place his approval upon the covenant. Possibly because the prince / ruler that is to come will not necessarily be an active participant in the establishment of the covenant, he will not be personally invested enough in the covenant to have the fortitude to uphold the covenant, even though he will at one point have personally approved the covenant.

It is possible that the confirmation of the covenant may serve merely as a path for establishing a functioning sacrificial system on the temple mount as part of the ritual for establishing the prince / ruler that is to come's power and authority over the temple mount, over the people of Israel, as the aspiring global ruler, etc.

Once his confirmation of the covenant peace treaty agreement has fulfilled its purpose of elevating the prince / ruler that is to come to his role as global leader, he will then choose not to honor the covenant.

In all of Daniel's various presentations of the little horn / eleventh king / final horn on the shaggy goat / prince who is to come / king that will exalt himself (Daniel 7, 8, 9:26b-27, 11:29-45), the ruler that is to come must initially offer himself as a friend to the people and nation of Israel in order for the people of Israel to consider him as a viable candidate for fulfilling their long awaited promised and prophesied messiah. As the king that will exalt himself and as the beast of the earth, he will convince many that he is qualified to be their messiah.

But, midway through the seven years of the covenant peace treaty agreement the prince / ruler that is to come will need to break the covenant peace treaty agreement in order to advance his own personal agenda.

At the foundation of the covenant peace treaty agreement will be the understanding that the people of Israel are the formulation for the nation of Israel. The entire reason for the people of Israel to exist as a special entity, according to God Most High, was for the people of Israel to become a nation of priests for God Most High. But the goal of the little horn / eleventh king / ruler that is to come / king that will exalt himself / beast of the earth, will be to establish himself as greater than God Most High. With the goal of establishing himself as greater than God Most High, having a nation of priests dedicated and consecrated to God Most High will be unacceptable and intolerable.

In addition, the ruler that is to come, can only make his proposal to the people of Israel as a result of the events of the sixty ninth 'seven' with the execution of messiah / the Lamb / Jesus Christ.

Once the ruler that is to come / beast of the earth has established himself as a global leader, the purge of anything to do with validating the divinity and sovereignty of God Most High will begin.

Daniel identified the ruler that is to come / king that will exalt himself as committing the future abomination of desolation event that will render the temple sacrificial system deconsecrated and ineffectual.

John the Revelator identified the beast of the earth as committing the future abomination of desolation event. And John the Revelator identified the beast of the earth's determination to destroy the religion of Judaism, and to mold Christianity to serve his own interests.

Another important detail of Daniel's seventieth seven concerned the identification of the ruler that is to come. Daniel, John the Revelator, and other biblical authors, presented that the ruler who is to come / king that will exalt himself / man of lawlessness / beast of the earth will not make himself known as this global leader until midway through Daniel's seventieth 'seven.' (Daniel 7, 8,

9:26b-27, 11:29-45, Revelation 13:11-18, 17:12-17, 19:20, 20:10) (king of Assyria - Isaiah 10:5-7, 10:12-14, 14:24-27, arrogant and greedy and plunderer of nations - Habakkuk 2:2-20, man of lawlessness - 2 Thessalonians 2:1-12)

Jesus Christ Fulfilled Messianic Prophecy and the Spring Feasts

The historical question to be answered is, 'Who is the promised and prophesied messiah?'

Who is God the Creator's person that was promised to the first man and first woman in the Garden of Eden / garden of God / paradise, to be the savior offered for humanity, that would be the means for God the Creator to provide redemption, reclamation and regeneration?

Who will be the means for God the Creator in the restoration process, for both human life and for life within earth's biome?

Who will be the means for restoring God the Creator's perfection and order, in the midst of the evil and chaos of the evil one / serpent / Satan, and what the red dragon / serpent / Satan, Inc. has brought to the earth?

Who is God Most High's messiah that was promised to the people of Israel, to lead the nation of Israel into global prominence and who will lead in the defeat of the enemies of the people of Israel?

Humanity's next question that needs to be answered will be, 'How will we know or recognize this messiah?'

To answer the significant questions concerning the identity and role of messiah, God Most High instructed God's people to celebrate seven feasts annually. When God Most High provided the Law to Moses and the people of Israel (1446 BC), God Most High required that the people of Israel observe the seven feasts as an annual dramatization and reminder of the various aspects of messiah in God Most High's redemption, reclamation and regeneration plan. (details of the required feasts - Exodus 12:1-30, 12:43-

49, 34:18, 34:22-24, Leviticus 23:4-43, Numbers 9:9-14, Deuteronomy 16:1-17)

The intrinsic message of the required feasts, duplicated God Most High's plan of redemption that was written in the message in the stars. But after the interpretation of the message in the stars was altered by the baal / mystery / mythology religion, it became necessary to find a new mode of communicating the plan for redemption message.

The feasts were intended to be a pre-reenactment of what the promised and prophesied messiah would do and accomplish, so that the people of Israel would be able to recognize the promised and prophesied messiah, as he accomplished and will accomplish the prophesied activities required for the role of messiah.

The required feasts were typologies, exclusively for representing the activity of the promised and prophesied messiah. A biblical typology uses a current type or symbol to communicate a message concerning what is to come. Jonah was a type for Jesus Christ when he spent three days inside the whale, and then Jonah was resurrected, in a manner similar to Jesus Christ who spent three days in the tomb. Isaac was a type for Jesus Christ when Isaac's father Abraham was instructed to sacrifice Isaac on the altar as a message that God would offer his only begotten son Jesus Christ as a sacrifice.

Typologies were intended to provide an impression stamped upon the audience, to be a pattern, model, or mold, that would be able to identify the later fulfillment of God Most High's prophecy.

The required feasts were also typologies, for the purpose of communicating the promised and prophesied messiah's work on behalf of humanity. The feasts themselves are prophecy, placed in a dramatic setting, so that the message was not merely the telling of a narrative, but were experiential.

When Jesus Christ, the second member of the office of God, became fully human, Jesus' life, crucifixion, death and resurrection, fulfilled all the typologies of the first four of the required feasts, the spring feasts.

When messiah / the Lamb / Jesus Christ returns, he will fulfill the requirements of the typology of the remaining feasts, the fall feasts.

Abraham was instructed by God Most High to offer his son Isaac on the altar as a typology for when God Most High would offer God's Son Jesus Christ as a sacrifice, on the tree through crucifixion. When Abraham built the altar for offering Isaac, God Most High gave instructions as to the place for the altar, which was where Jerusalem Israel came to be located. And when God Most High stopped Abraham from actually sacrificing Isaac, God Most High supplied a ram for replacing Isaac as the sacrifice. Abraham understood that God Most High's redemption, reclamation and regeneration plan, included resurrection and that if Isaac died, Isaac would be resurrected. Isaac had to be alive in order to be the child of the covenant that God Most High promised would be in the messianic lineage. The ram that was substituted that day, was provided by God Most High, as a typology that God Most High would supply his own sacrifice to fulfill the prophecy in the altar typology, and God Most High's sacrifice was messiah / the Lamb / Jesus Christ.

Abraham and Isaac's sacrificial experience, identified the place that messiah / the Lamb / Jesus Christ would be sacrificed approximately two thousand years later.

The Old Testament / Tanakh prophet Daniel, was given a vision of seventy 'sevens' that would mark the time before messiah would arrive. Daniel's prophecy established that during the sixty ninth 'seven,' messiah would be cut off / executed.

The vision of seventy 'sevens' that was supplied to Daniel, provided the time that the promised and prophesied messiah, would be sacrificed. (Daniel 9:26-27)

Jesus Christ's earthly ministry merely laid the foundation for the future full transition from the kingdom of Satan, Inc. / kingdom of man's dominion over the earth, to the fully established kingdom of heaven on earth that will be accomplished when Jesus Christ returns. Through Jesus Christ's earthly life, he was able to fulfill the requirements of the first four required feasts, and to establish the foundational work for total transition of kingdoms to take place.

When messiah / the Lamb / Jesus Christ returns, it will be to finish what was begun in the Garden of Eden / garden of God / paradise, and what was further established through Jesus Christ's fulfillment of the Law, in fulfilling the prophecy of the first four required feasts, spring feasts.

Jesus Christ must return to finish fulfilling the Law through meeting the requirements of the remaining required fall feasts.

The prophets and Jesus Christ were given many details that needed to be met, concerning the return of Jesus Christ, and the climate of the culture of the earth before his return. The meaning of the impact of Jesus Christ's second coming, was given to Moses in the message of the fall feasts, and then repeated through the prophets in their visions.

The prophets of the Old Testament / Tanakh were provided the time of messiah / the Lamb / Jesus Christ's return through the pattern of the seven days of creation, and through other details of prophecy.

Daniel's visions identified the seven year covenant peace treaty agreement established with Israel and many nations, as providing the time framework for the era that will prepare the earth to be ready for messiah's arrival to defeat the enemies of God Most High and of the kingdom of heaven.

During the earthly ministry of Jesus Christ, Jesus provided further understanding to the prophecy of the required feasts, and how he fulfilled the required spring feasts. And Jesus Christ also provided further understanding for how he will fulfill the required fall feasts with his return.

The apostles and disciples who witnessed the ascension of the resurrected messiah / the Lamb / Jesus Christ, were told that Jesus Christ would return in the same way that he ascended into heaven (Acts 1:1-11).

And then John the Revelator, an apostle of Jesus Christ, received the visions through the resurrected and ascended Jesus Christ, that John recorded as the book of Revelation. The entire focus of the book of Revelation was concerned with the global preparation necessary for the return of messiah / the Lamb / Jesus Christ in order to fully establish the kingdom of heaven on earth / fulfilling all inherent prophecy of the fall feasts.

There were many other prophecies that foretold the characteristics and activities of the second coming of messiah. There were too many prophecies from the Old Testament / Tanakh to include them all in this work. The prophecies selected for inclusion in this timeline, provide direction as to how God Most High has worked in the past, in order to lay the foundation for the future of what the promised and prophesied messiah still must fulfill.

Some of the typologies within the Old Testament / Tanakh, that identified the promised and prophesied messiah as coming twice in human history

There were multiple typologies within the Old Testament / Tanakh, that provided information for the people of Israel, that their promised and prophesied messiah would come two times in the context of human history.

Throughout the history of the people of Israel, there were multiple times when the leaders of the people of Israel, were rejected and then later they were received. This pattern was itself a typology of Jesus Christ coming the first time and meeting rejection, followed by the future second coming of Jesus Christ when he will be received.

Joseph was rejected by his brothers until decades later when the brothers who were starving, went to Egypt and accepted him (Genesis 37, 42 to 47).

Moses was rejected the first time he came to his people, and the people of Israel asked him, 'Who made you leader over us?' Forty years later, Moses came again and led the people of Israel out of Egypt. (Exodus 2:11-14, 3 to 4, ff)

David was rejected when he was first anointed to be king, and was forced to live among the Philistines until he was able to come the second time and receive the throne.

Notice that when the people of Israel rejected their leaders, their leaders went to live with the Gentiles. During Joseph's rejection by his family, Joseph lived with the Egyptians. During the forty years prior to becoming leader of the nation of Israel, Moses lived with the Midianites. And when Saul and Saul's followers rejected David, David lived with the Philistines.

These accounts laid the typology that when the promised and prophesied messiah would come to the people of Israel, that the people of Israel would initially reject their messiah, and their messiah would be accepted by the Gentile nations. When messiah / the Lamb / Jesus Christ returns, then the people of Israel will accept him.

Prophetic requirements for the promised messiah

There were at least seventy prophecies that identified the coming of the promised messiah / anointed one / God incarnate / Jesus Christ.

1. *The promised messiah must be a descendent of Abram / Abraham (Genesis 12:1-3, 18:1-5, 18:17-19, 22:15-18, Matthew 1:1-17, Luke 3:21-38, Galatians 3:8-9, 3:16).*
2. *The promised messiah must be a descendent from the tribe of Judah. Judah was the third son of Jacob / Israel. Jacob was the second twin of Isaac and Rebecca. Isaac was the son of Abraham and Sarah. (Genesis 49:8-12, Matthew 1:1-17, Luke 3:21-38, Hebrews 7:14, Revelation 5:5)*
3. *The promised messiah must be a descendant of David (2 Samuel 7:4-5, 7:12-16, 1 Chronicles 17:3-4, 17:11-14, Psalm 132:11-12, Isaiah 11, Jeremiah 23:5-6,*

Matthew 1:1-17, Luke 1:26-33, 1:67-70, Luke 3:21-38, Acts 2:29-36, 15:15-18, Romans 1:1-6).

4. The promised messiah must be born in Bethlehem (Micah 5:2-6, Matthew 2:1-12, John 7:40-42).
5. The promised messiah must be from Nazareth and be called a Nazarene (Matthew 2:19-23, 21:11, 26:71, Mark 1:9, 1:24, 16:6, Luke 1:26-38, 2:4, 2:39, 2:51, etc. (Judges 13:5-7)).
6. The promised messiah would be born at the right time, reach the age of ministry, thirty years of age, at the right time, and be crucified as the paschal / Passover lamb at exactly the right time. Time would be marked from the decree issued during the exile to both build the temple and to establish a governor over the land from the people of Israel, until the crucifixion, death, resurrection and ascension of messiah / the Lamb / Jesus Christ, as the fulfillment of the prophecy of the first sixty nine 'sevens.' (Daniel 9:20-27)
7. The promised messiah must be born of a virgin (Genesis 3:15, Isaiah 7:14, Matthew 1:18-25, Luke 1:26-38, Galatians 4:4).
8. The name of the promised messiah would be 'Immanuel' (Hebrew), which means 'God is with us' (Isaiah 7:14, Matthew 1:21-23).
9. The name of the promised messiah would be Yeshua (Hebrew) / Joshua (Hebrew) / Jesus (Greek). The name Jesus means, 'savior' or 'salvation.' The origin of the name Jesus was Yashah in Hebrew, which means 'to save, deliver, preserve, bring salvation, obtain victory.' (Zechariah 3, 6:9-15 – the name of the high priest that served as a typology for the role that messiah / the Lamb / Jesus Christ would fulfill was named Joshua, Matthew 1:20-21 – the name of messiah was provided by God Most High as Jesus. When the father named the child, the father was recognizing the child as his own.)

10. The promised messiah would assume the title of messiah. 'Mashiach' (Hebrew) / 'Christos' (Greek) means anointed one. (Matthew 1:16-18, 2:4, 16:13-20, 22:41-42, 24, Mark 8:27-29, Luke 2:1-12, 2:22-32, 4:40-41, 9:18-20, 22:66-71, 23:1-2, 24:4-6, John 1:40-42, 4:1-26, 7:25-44, 11:17-27, 12:34-36, 20:30-31, Acts 2:29-36, 3:11-23, 5:42, 17:1-4, Revelation 11:15, 12:10, etc.)
11. There would be only one promised messiah, who would fulfill both roles as the provider of salvation for humanity and for the earth, and as the King of kings and Lord of lords, who will rule over the fully established kingdom of heaven on earth (Psalm 2:1-9, John 1:14, 3:10-16, Acts 13:32-33, 1 Timothy 6:13-16, Hebrews 1, Revelation 17:14, 19:16, etc.)
12. The promised messiah would be identified as the Son of God and would call God Most High his father (Psalm 89:26-29, 1 Chronicles 22:9-10, Hebrews 1, Mark 14:32-36, John 20:30-31, etc.).
13. The promised messiah must be circumcised when he would be eight days old, according to the covenant promise agreement established with Abram / Abraham, Isaac and Jacob / Israel. Isaac was the first child born under the covenant promise agreement. Messiah / Jesus Christ was the fulfillment of the promise of the circumcision covenant promise agreement. (Genesis 17, 21:1-7, Leviticus 12:1-2, Jeremiah 4:4, 9:25, Luke 2:21-24, Acts 7:8, Romans 2:25-29, 4:1-12, etc.)
14. The promised messiah must go into Egypt and then return to the land of Israel. (The typology for this was established with Abram / Abraham's time spent in Egypt, and with the family of Jacob / Israel entering and then returning from the land of Egypt; Nisan 14, 1876 BC to Nisan 14, 1446 BC). (Exodus 4:22, Hosea 11:1, Matthew 2:13-15, etc.)

15. The birth of the promised messiah would be associated with the killing of babies in Bethlehem (Jeremiah 31:11, 31:15, Matthew 2:1-18).
16. The promised messiah must be preceded by a messenger after the pattern of the Old Testament / Tanakh prophet Elijah. This forerunner was John the Baptist (2 Kings 2:1-18, Isaiah 40:3-5, Malachi 3:1, 4:5, Matthew 3:1-6, 11:10-13, Luke 1:17 (1:5-25), 1:76-80).
17. The messenger that would precede the coming of the promised messiah, would be preaching in the wilderness (Isaiah 40:3-5, Luke 1:80, 3:1-6).
18. The promised messiah must be a prophet like Moses (Deuteronomy 18:15, John 1:45, Acts 3:20-23)
19. The promised messiah must be anointed by the Holy Spirit (Isaiah 11:1-3, 42:1, Matthew 3:16-17, Mark 1:9-11, Luke 3:21-22, John 1:29-34).
20. The promised messiah would preach and teach in the temple (Malachi 3:1, Matthew 26:55, John 7:28-29, 8:1-2, etc.).
21. The promised messiah would come specifically to the people of Israel first, and then send the message to Gentiles ((Jeremiah 50:6) Ezekiel 34:23-24, Micah 5:4-5, Matthew 10:1-8, 15:21-28, John 10:11-16, Galatians 4:4-5, Romans 1:16, Revelation 7:17, etc.).
22. The promised messiah would initially be rejected by his own people, the leaders of the people of Israel, and those who followed their Israelite leaders. Even Jesus' own brothers did not initially believe Jesus' messiahship until after Jesus' resurrection. (Psalm 118:22, Isaiah 52:13-15, 53, John 1:11, 7:5, 12:37-38, etc.)
23. The promised messiah would be generally received by Gentiles (Isaiah 11:10, 42:1-7, 49:1-7, 49:22-23, 60:1-16 (for the nation of Israel, but also applied to messiah), Luke 2:25-32, Acts 28:28, etc.).

24. The promised messiah would utilize parables within his teaching techniques (Psalm 78:1-4, Matthew 13:34-35).
25. The promised messiah would minister from Galilee (Isaiah 9:1-2, Matthew 4:12-16, 4:23).
26. The promised messiah would proclaim freedom for captives and vengeance of our God (Isaiah 61:1-2, Luke 4:16-19, Matthew 4:23, 9:35, Acts 2:22, 10:34-38, etc.).
27. The promised messiah would become the shepherd of Israel, a leader to a nation without a leader (Genesis 49:22-25, Psalm 23:1, 28:8-9, 80:1-3, Isaiah 40:10-11, Ezekiel 34:1-24, 37:24, Micah 5:2-4, Matthew 2:6, 26:31, Mark 14:27, John 10:1-16, Hebrews 13:20, 1 Peter 2:25, 5:4, Revelation 7:17, etc.).
28. The promised messiah would teach a message that would not be believed (Isaiah 53:1-3, John 12:37-46).
29. The promised messiah would provide miracles – the blind would see, the deaf would hear (Isaiah 35:5, Matthew 12:22, 15:31, Luke 7:22, etc.)
30. The promised messiah would be praised by children (Psalm 8:1-2 (Septuagint), Matthew 21:14-16).
31. The promised messiah would establish the temple as a house of prayer (Psalm 69:8-9, Isaiah 56:6-7, Jeremiah 7:9-11, Matthew 21:1-16, John 2:13-17).
32. The promised messiah would be hated (Psalm (35:17-21), 69:4, 109:1-5, 119:161, John 15:24-25, etc.).
33. The promised messiah would receive insults because of his relationship with God the Father (Psalm 35:19-21, 69:8-9, 89:50-51, John 15:23-25, Romans 15:3).
34. The promised messiah would not seek publicity (Isaiah 42:1-2, Matthew 8:1-4, 9:29-30, 12:15-21, etc.).
35. The promised messiah would be compassionate (Isaiah 42:1-4, Matthew 12:17-21 (12:1-21), etc.).

36. *The promised messiah would live a sinless life and not be deceitful (Isaiah 53:9, Luke 23:26-41, John 1:47, 1 Peter 2:21-22, 2 Corinthians 5:21, etc.).*
37. *Many of the disciples of messiah would scatter (Zechariah 13:7, Matthew 26:31-35, 26:55-56, 26:69-75, etc.).*
38. *The promised messiah would not be physically attractive ((1 Samuel 16:7), Isaiah 53:2).*
39. *The promised messiah would set aside his sovereignty in heaven to assume the confines of human life on earth / kenosis / εκενωσεν (Isaiah 7:14, 42:1-4, 52:13-15, Matthew 1:23, 2 Corinthians 8:9, Philippians 2:5-8, Colossians 2:9-10, etc.).*
40. *The promised messiah would enter Jerusalem riding on a donkey (Zechariah 9:9, Matthew 21:1-5).*
41. *The promised messiah would be sold for thirty pieces of silver (Zechariah 11:7-13, Matthew 26:14-16, 27:1-10).*
42. *The same thirty pieces of silver used for betraying messiah, would be used to purchase a potter's field (Zechariah 11:7-13, Matthew 26:14-16, 27:1-10).*
43. *Messiah would be betrayed by a friend (Psalm 41:9, Matthew 27:1-4, John 13:18, etc.).*
44. *The promised messiah would be crucified through the efforts of both the people of Israel and Gentiles (Psalm 2:1-2, Matthew 26:3-5, 27:1-2, 27:11-26, John 19:16-18, Acts 4:25-28).*
45. *The promised messiah would endure the cursed death on a tree (Deuteronomy 21:22-23, Psalm 22:16-18 (pierced hands and feet, bones on display, and naked – described a death by crucifixion), Matthew 27:32-33, Mark 15:22-23, Luke 23:33, John 19:16-18, 20:24-28).*
46. *The promised messiah would be a suffering servant on behalf of others (Isaiah 53:4-6, 53:12, Matthew 20:25-28, 1 Peter 2:23-25, etc.).*
47. *The promised messiah would die for the sins of humanity to provide atonement with God Most*

High and restore relationship with God Most High (Isaiah 53:4-6, 53:12, John 3:16-18, 1 Corinthians 15:3-4, 1 Peter 2:23-25, etc.).
48. The promised messiah would be mocked (Psalm 22:7-8, Isaiah 50:5-6, Matthew 27:27-31, 27:39-44, Mark 15:27-32, Luke 23:8-11).
49. The promised messiah would die among criminals (Isaiah 53:12, Matthew 27:38, Mark 15:27-28, Luke 23:32-33)
50. The promised messiah would pray for his murderers (Isaiah 53:12, Luke 23:34).
51. The promised messiah would be struck on the cheek (Isaiah 50:6, Micah 5:1, Matthew 26:57-67, 27:27-30).
52. The promised messiah would be spit upon (Isaiah 50:6, Matthew 26:57-67, 27:27-30).
53. While being crucified, the promised messiah would be temporarily forsaken by God / separated from the other two persons called 'God' (Psalm 22:1, Matthew 27:46).
54. While being crucified, the promised messiah would be offered gall and vinegar (Psalm 69:21, Matthew 27:33-34, 27:48).
55. The promised messiah would not open his mouth to defend himself when accused by those who would murder him (Isaiah 53:7, Matthew 26:57-63, 27:11-14, Luke 23:8-9, Acts 8:32).
56. The promised messiah would have his garments parted, and they would cast lots to determine who would receive them (Psalm 22:16-18, Matthew 27:35, Mark 15:24, Luke 23:34, John 19:23-24).
57. The crucified messiah would not have any bones broken (Exodus 12:46, Psalm 34:19-20, John 19:31-36).
58. In the crucifixion process, the promised messiah would be pierced (Isaiah 53:5, Zechariah 12:10, John 19:31-37).

59. As the paschal / Passover lamb, the promised messiah would be like a lamb going to slaughter (Isaiah 53:7-8, Acts 8:32).
60. It was determined by God Most High, that the promised messiah would be a willing sacrifice, and that his death would have a purpose (Isaiah 53:10-12, Matthew 27:50, Mark 15:37-39).
61. The promised messiah would be buried with the wealthy (Isaiah 53:9, Matthew 57-60, Mark 15:42-46, Luke 23:50-53, John 19:38-42).
62. The body of the promised messiah would not be abandoned with the dead (Psalm 16:8-11, Acts 2:25-28, 2:31-32).
63. The promised messiah would be resurrected from death (Psalm 16:8-11, Matthew 28:1-10, Mark 16:1-8, Luke 24:1-48, Acts 2:22-33, etc.).
64. The promised messiah would rise three days after his crucifixion and death (Jonah 1:17, Matthew 12:40, Luke 24:45-48, 1 Corinthians 15:3-8).
65. Following his resurrection, the promised messiah would ascend into heaven (Psalm 68:18, Luke 24:50-51, Acts 1:6-11).
66. The resurrected messiah would sit at the right hand of God the Father (Psalm 110:1, Hebrews 1:1-4, Ephesians 1:15-23, 1 Peter 3:18-22).
67. The promised messiah would establish a new covenant (Jeremiah 31:31-34, Matthew 26:26-30, Mark 14:12-26, Luke 22:20, 1 Corinthians 11:25, 2 Corinthians 3:6-8, Hebrews 8:13, 9:15, etc.).
68. The promised messiah would be the cornerstone for the authentic faith system of God Most High (Psalm 118:22-23, Isaiah 28:16-19, Matthew 21:42, Mark 12:10-11, Luke 20:17, Acts 4:11-12, 1 Peter 2:4-8).
69. The promised messiah would be / will be King of the Jews (Psalm 2:1-6, Matthew 2:1-2, 27:11, 27:27-29, 27:35-37, Mark 15:1-2, 15:6-13, 15:16-18, 15:22-26, Luke 23:1-3, 23:33-38, John 18:28-37, 19:1-3, 19:13-16, 19:17-22).

70. The promised messiah would be of the order of Melchizedek (Psalm 110:4, Hebrews 5:5-10, 6:19-20, 7).

It is a wonder as to how it could ever be possible for one single and solitary man, to be able to fulfill all these prophecies that were established many centuries before his birth. And yet, one single and solitary man did fulfill all these requirements of the role of messiah.

When the one man comes who is not messiah, but who desires to fulfill the role of messiah (beast of the earth), he will not be able to meet the requirements of these prophecies. Out of frustration in not being able to meet the requirements of these prophecies, he will reject the Law that was given to Moses and the people of Israel (1446 BC), and all that has been associated with the Torah / Pentateuch / five books of Moses, including the reality of the biblical account of creation and the inherent prophecy of the required feasts.

The messianic fulfillment of the spring feasts by Jesus Christ during his earthly ministry (~4 BC to ~30 AD)

Within the Law that God Most High provided for Moses and for the people of Israel as they left Egypt (1446 BC), was the instruction to observe seven required feasts. Observing the required feasts acted as a continual renewal of the covenant between God Most High and the people.

The required feasts were to be a reminder for both the people of Israel and for God Most High of the relationship that God desired to restore with humanity. To not observe the feasts was a decision to opt out of the offer to have one's relationship with God Most High restored.

So, for example, to refuse to observe the first required feast, the feast of Passover, was understood by God Most High as a person's statement that they did not desire to belong to God Most High and did not desire to be a citizen of the kingdom of heaven.

Consequently, the penalty for not observing Passover required that person to be cut off from their people, and not being forgiven for their sin (Numbers 9:13).

Because Passover dramatized the sacrifice of messiah / the Lamb / Jesus Christ and the shedding of his blood that covers sin, to neglect to celebrate Passover represented a person's lack of desire to have their sin covered, and to be in right relationship with God Most High.

(Exodus 12:1-30, 12:43-49, 34:18, 34:22-24, <u>Leviticus 23:4-43</u>, Numbers 9:9-14, <u>Deuteronomy 16:1-17</u>)

Before the crucifixion, death, resurrection and ascension of messiah / the Lamb / Jesus Christ, observing the required feasts was the only path for restoring one's right relationship with God Most High and for becoming a citizen of the kingdom of heaven.

When messiah / the Lamb / Jesus Christ became incarnate / dwelling in human form, in order to provide a new path for humanity to have their relationship restored with God Most High, a new covenant, Jesus Christ first was required to fulfill all the requirements of the old covenant. That meant that Jesus Christ was required to observe all the required feasts just as it was required of everyone else that desired to enter into a right relationship with God Most High.

But because the required feasts were the dramatization of what the promised and prophesied messiah would accomplish in restoring the relationship of God and humanity, Jesus Christ actually became the center of the dramatization. As the divine and sovereign messiah / anointed one, Jesus Christ became the sacrifice in the required feast of the Passover. Jesus Christ lived the sinless life for the feast of unleavened bread. Jesus Christ became the firstfruit of the resurrected in the feast of firstfruits. And Jesus Christ sent the Holy Spirit that was the seal of the new covenant between God and humanity for the feast of Pentecost.

In this way, Jesus Christ fulfilled the required spring feasts. And what remains in order to complete the restoration of the relationship between God Most High and humanity, is Jesus Christ's fulfillment of the required fall feasts.

There were 72 annually required Jewish holy days / holidays in a year defined in the Law God gave through Moses (Exodus 12:1-30, 12:43-49, 34:18, 34:22-24, <u>Leviticus 23:4-43</u>, Numbers 9:9-14, <u>Deuteronomy 16:1-17</u>):

- 52 Sabbaths; A sabbath takes place every seventh day and relates the six thousand years that God's Holy Spirit will contend with humanity's rebellion before the seventh thousand years when messiah / the Lamb / Jesus Christ will reign and there will be peace between God, humanity and creation.
- 12 new moon festivals; The new moon festivals were required to annually mark the progression of time so that the people would know when to celebrate the required feasts. In addition, the twelve new moon festivals corresponded to the message in the stars / Way of Salvation / Mazzaroth that communicated the first coming of messiah / the Lamb / Jesus Christ, the work that messiah / the Lamb / Jesus Christ would accomplish for the purpose of providing a saving path for humanity, and the work that messiah / the Lamb / Jesus Christ would accomplish with his second coming.
- 8 feasts for gathering:
  - feast of Passover / Pesach – Nisan 14,
  - feast of unleavened bread (seven days) – Nisan 15-21,
  - feast of firstfruits / Bikkurim (barley harvest) – Nisan 16,
  - feast of weeks / Pentecost / Shavuot – Sivan 5 or fifty days after the first sabbath after Passover (early wheat harvest),
  - feast of trumpets / Yom Teruah / Rosh Hashanah / New Year / day of remembrance / Yom HaZikaron / day of judgment / Yom HaDin / day of concealment / Yom HaKeseh / coronation of the king / Melech – Tishri 1-2
  - Day of Atonement / Yom Kippur (fast day)– Tishri 10,

- feast of ingathering / feast of tabernacles / feast of booths / Sukkot (seven days) (fruit / grape harvest) – Tishri 15-21,
- eighth day assembly / Shemini Atzeret / eighth festival, that follows the week long feast of ingathering / feast of tabernacles / Sukkot – Tishri 22.

Each one of the required Jewish feasts, told of a portion of the redemption, reclamation and regeneration plan established by God Most High. Each feast was an annual dramatization of some aspect of the plan. But only when the messages of all the feasts were told together, could the larger message actually be recognized and understood.

The purpose of Jesus Christ's earthly ministry was to fulfill the Law; specifically, the Law that was intrinsic within the spring feasts.

The official spring feasts consisted of the feasts of Passover, Unleavened Bread, Firstfruits and Pentecost. Within the required spring feasts was the message of redemption / atonement / the process for becoming right in one's relationship with God Most High / at-one-ment.

The purpose of Jesus Christ's return will be to also fulfill the Law; specifically, the Law that was intrinsic within the fall feasts.

The official fall feasts consisted of the feasts of trumpets, Day of Atonement, and tabernacles. Within these feasts was the message of reclamation. The fall feasts dramatized that with his glorious return (feast of trumpets), messiah / the Lamb / Jesus Christ will defeat the enemies of God Most High and of the kingdom of heaven (Day of Atonement / Yom Kippur), and will fully establish his kingdom of heaven on earth (feast of tabernacles).

The eighth day feast that follows the seven days of the feast of tabernacles, marked the promise of the Thousand Years Reign of Jesus Christ, and the everlasting life that will follow. During the Thousand Years Reign of Jesus Christ, the earth will experience regeneration.

Following the Thousand Years Reign of Jesus Christ, the earth will be made new.

Note that while all the required feasts possessed their own history, definition, ceremonies and meanings, each of the required feasts were interrelated and dependent upon the rest of the required feasts in order for their full fulfillment to be realized. None of the required feasts had meaning or significance without the context of the rest of the required feasts. If any of the required feasts were to be omitted, the entire required feast system would have lost its ability to complete its mission of restoring the right relationship between God Most High and humanity.

Without Passover, there would be no feast of unleavened bread. Without the meaning of the feast of unleavened bread, there would be no firstfruits, no resurrection from death. Without the firstfruits of resurrection, there would be no need for the Law / new covenant, of the feast of weeks / Pentecost. And without the Law / new covenant provided with the feast of weeks / Pentecost, there would be no recognition of the need for Passover.

The required fall feasts shared a similar interconnection. Without the return of messiah (feast of trumpets), there can be no defeat of the enemies of God Most High and of the kingdom of heaven (Day of Atonement / Yom Kippur). Without the defeat of the enemies of God Most High and of the kingdom of heaven, there can be no rescuing of the bride, marrying the bride and the ending where 'they lived happily ever after' (feast of tabernacles).

In addition, there was a connection that tied the required fall feasts with the required spring feasts.

Without the fulfillment of the feast of firstfruits, there would have been no messiah / the Lamb / Jesus Christ who fulfilled the feast of firstfruits through his resurrection from death, to provide the existence of the opportunity for second fruits / the resurrection of believers in messiah (BC) and followers of the Lamb (AD) that is scheduled to take place with the first fall feast / feast of trumpets / Yom Teruah, when messiah / the Lamb / Jesus Christ returns.

And that connection between the required spring feasts and the required fall feasts was reiterated in the timing of the required fall feasts in relationship with the timing of the required spring feasts.

Every year, the number of days between the required spring feasts and fall feasts remained exactly the same. The time between the required spring feasts and the fall feasts never varied.

Any variance in the number of days for a year, were adjusted for in the time between the required fall feasts and the spring feasts.

But between the required spring feasts and the fall feasts, the time was always determined to be set without alteration.

Fifty days following the first Passover as the plague of death passed over the homes of the people of Israel whose doorframes were covered with the blood of their sacrificial lambs, Moses and the people of Israel were provided with the Law of God Most High (1446 BC). Within that approximately fifty day period, the people of Israel experienced the foundation for all the inherent prophecy of the required spring feasts: the salvation from the death of the firstborn, the living of a life of purity with partaking of unleavened bread, the 'resurrection' of a nation through the crossing through the Red Sea, and meeting with God Most High on the mountain in order to receive the covenant of the Law of Moses.

During the approximately fifty days at the conclusion of the earthly ministry of messiah / the Lamb / Jesus Christ, the people of Israel, and all of humanity, experienced the entire fulfillment of the promise of God Most High's covenant, inherent within the required spring feasts. Jesus Christ became the Paschal Lamb of Passover. The sinless life of messiah / the Lamb / Jesus Christ fulfilled the requirements of the feast of unleavened bread, which qualified Jesus Christ to become the first to be resurrected with the feast of firstfruits. And with the gift of the presence of the Holy Spirit to every follower of the Lamb, the new covenant / feast of Pentecost was fulfilled.

Messiah / the Lamb / Jesus Christ fulfilled all the requirements inherent within the spring feasts.

What remains to be accomplished is the fulfillment of all the requirements inherent within the fall feasts. But to understand the work that will be accomplished with messiah / the Lamb / Jesus Christ's return to fulfill the prophecy of the fall feasts, it is essential to understand the inherent prophecy of the spring feasts and exactly how Jesus Christ fulfilled that prophecy.

Lamb selection day – four days prior to Passover as a preparation for celebrating Passover – Nisan 10, (merely a preparation for observing the required feast of Passover)

Four days prior to Passover, it was a requirement that every family would select the lamb that they would offer as their Passover lamb sacrifice. This lamb would be taken into the house and loved. The lamb would become like a pet and would share life with the family. And symbolically, because the lamb would become part of the family, the sins of the family would be placed on the Lamb.

In the bless that Jacob / Israel gave to his son Judah before Jacob died, Jacob detailed the arrival of the promised and prophesied messiah who would be a descendant of Jacob and Judah. And that detail prophesied that the promised and prophesied messiah / possessor of the scepter and staff / future ruler of nations, would come to the people of Israel, riding on a donkey.

The scepter will not depart from Judah, nor the ruler's staff from between his feet, until he comes to whom it belongs and the obedience of the nations is his.

He will tether his donkey to a vine, his colt to the choicest branch.

He will wash his garments in wine, his robes in the blood of grapes. Genesis 49:10-11

Jacob / Israel's prophecy given in 1859 BC (Genesis 47:28, Exodus 12:40-41), foretold of a messiah that did not come for another approximately one thousand eight hundred fifty five years. And this messiah will not wash his garments in wine and his robes in the blood of grapes, until he returns to battle the enemies of God Most High and of the kingdom of heaven, approximately three thousand eight hundred and eighty five years after Jacob / Israel's prophecy for Judah.

Jesus Christ honored Lamb selection day by riding into Jerusalem on a donkey and hearing the praise from the people that identified him as the king and messiah / Son of David, that they had been looking for (Zechariah 9:9, Matthew 21:1-11).

Jesus Christ must return with his garments washed in wine and his robes in the blood of grapes, during the era of the time of Jacob's Trouble (Revelation 19:11-13).

Feast of Passover / Pesach – Nisan 14 – Exodus 12:1-30, 12:43-49, Leviticus 23:4-8, Numbers 9:9-14, Deuteronomy 16:1-8

According to the biblical record, the first time Nisan 17 was a notable historical date, was when the ark came to rest on the mountain top (Genesis 8:3-4).

The first time Nisan 14 was a notable date in the biblical record was in 1876 BC when Jacob / Israel moved his family into Egypt on that day (Genesis 45:16-47:10).

It was possible that when Abraham was called to sacrifice his son Isaac, that the event also took place on Nisan 14. But there was no scriptural evidence to support this supposition.

The day that the people of Israel left Egypt was the anniversary of the day that Jacob / Israel took his family to live in Egypt, Nisan 14.

Now the length of time the Israelite people lived in Egypt was 430 years. At the end of the 430 years, to the very day, all the Lord's divisions left Egypt. Exodus 12:40-41 *(Exodus 12:29-40)*.

The celebration of Passover marked the conclusion of the war that God Most High declared upon the gods of Egypt with the ten plagues. The celebration of Passover also marked the consecration of the firstborn. It was on the day of Passover, after the plague of death had killed the firstborn of every house not marked by the blood of the Lamb on its doorposts, that the people of Israel left Egypt (1446 BC). The people of Israel were considered to be God

Most High's firstborn, and were a target of slavery, control and genocide for the Egyptians (Exodus 4:22-23).

God Most High's plan for redemption, reclamation and regeneration was entirely set in place in order to redeem all of God's people from the slavery, control and genocide of sin and death and the kingdom of Satan, Inc. / kingdom of man.

Within the typology of the nation of Israel's exodus from Egypt, were many details of the prophecy of the promised messiah:
- For the blood of the Paschal lamb to be effective, both God Most High and the people who sacrificed their lambs needed to act. The people of Israel were required to select their lamb, place their trust on the lamb that the lamb was able to carry their sin, sacrifice their lamb, place the blood of the lamb on their doorposts, and then eat all the lamb, that night. Then God Most High needed to honor the sacrifice and allow the plague of the death of the firstborn, to passover their homes.
    Messiah / the Lamb / Jesus Christ was the necessary willing and believing sacrifice that lived a perfect life and willingly allowed the sin of the world to be placed upon him. Jesus Christ's action and faith in God Most High was honored when Jesus Christ was resurrected from death, in a sense having the effects of death 'passover' being able to hold Jesus Christ.
- In the process of preparing for the Passover of the plague of death, each family was required to make their choice for the perfect sacrificial lamb / Paschal lamb, a lamb that was without spot or blemish, a lamb that was perfect, a lamb that the family would depend upon to offer blood that was pure enough to provide a cover of protection from the plague of death.

Messiah / the Lamb / Jesus Christ provided the perfect blood through the perfect sacrifice, that covers the sins of all who have chosen to become believers in messiah (BC) or followers of the Lamb (AD). But each person must make messiah / the Lamb / Jesus Christ their own personal selection.

- *In choosing their Paschal lamb, the people chose to trust in God Most High and to reject the gods of the nation of Egypt.*

   In choosing to be a believer in messiah (BC) or be a follower of the Lamb (AD), one must choose to reject all other gods.

- *The Paschal lamb was required to be hidden within the home for four days.*

   Messiah / the Lamb / Jesus Christ became the Paschal lamb at the four thousand years mark of human history (One God day = a thousand human years (Psalm 90:4, 2 Peter 3:8). During the four days between lamb selection day and Passover, Jesus Christ taught in the house of God / the temple on the temple mount. During the first four thousand years of human history, messiah / the Lamb / Jesus Christ was hidden from humanity.

- *The Paschal lambs were to be inspected to ensure that each Paschal lamb was perfect, without spot or blemish.*

   Before the crucifixion of Jesus Christ, he was examined by the chief priests and elders, by Pilate who was the Roman governor, by Herod who was the Roman ruler, by Ananias and Caiaphas the high priests of the temple, by Judas, by the centurion, and by the repentant thief that was crucified next to Jesus Christ. All these inspectors were unable to find fault with Jesus Christ. Jesus Christ was accused by compensated liars to be a blasphemer / person who lied about his divinity, and then Jesus Christ was found

guilty by the hyped emotions of those who felt threatened by the power of his inherent authority. But Jesus Christ was determined to be a man without sin by all those who inspected him.
- The bones of the paschal lamb were not to be broken (Exodus 12:46).
    Messiah / the Lamb / Jesus Christ was crucified without breaking any of his bones.
- The Passover lamb was required to be eaten with unleavened bread / Matzah. Leavening represented sin. Unleavened bread represented the desire to live a sinless life.
    Messiah / the Lamb / Jesus Christ lived a continuously sinless life. No sin was found in him. And Jesus Christ's sacrificial blood was able to wash away the sin of all who have chosen to become believers in messiah (BC) or followers of the Lamb (AD).
- Traditionally, three wafers of unleavened bread are used within the family ceremony of the observation of Passover. The middle layer was broken and hidden for the children to find.
    Messiah / the Lamb / Jesus Christ is one of three persons that comprise the office of the God of heaven: God the Father, God the Son / messiah / the Lamb / Jesus Christ, and God the Holy Spirit. For three days, the crucified body of Jesus Christ laid hidden in the tomb, waiting for the followers of Jesus Christ to find him resurrected on the third day.
- In leaving Egypt, the people of Israel left their bondage and slavery that they had experienced for centuries while they lived in Egypt.
    Messiah / the Lamb / Jesus Christ provided the opportunity for believers to experience freedom from bondage, slavery, sin and death. With release from slavery, believers are able to be adopted as people fully

belonging to God Most High and to become inheritors within the kingdom of heaven.
- The Egyptian nation was spoiled as the people of Israel left Egypt. The people of Israel were given the spoils of war / the wealth of the nation of Egypt, prior to the exodus. After the exodus, the Egyptian military was defeated by God Most High through its drowning in the Red Sea.

    When messiah / the Lamb / Jesus Christ was crucified, died and resurrected, the red dragon / serpent / Satan, Inc. could not hold him. Like the people of Israel escaping from the land of Egypt, messiah / the Lamb / Jesus Christ won the victory over death and escaped death. The spoils of the sacrifice of Jesus Christ included the resurrected Jesus Christ ascending into heaven and sitting at the right hand of God Most High, a position of ultimate power. And the spoils of this cosmic war for all believers in messiah (BC) and followers of the Lamb (AD) will be eternal life dwelling in a regenerated earth and a new heaven, with all the benefits of Garden of Eden / garden of God / paradise living.

There were multiple other details that were included within the observance of the first Passover of 1446 BC, that acted as prophecy that was fulfilled through the crucifixion and death of messiah / the Lamb / Jesus Christ. But what has been listed here were the most significant aspects contained within the observance of the feast of Passover.

Jesus Christ's observance of Passover by becoming the Paschal Lamb, served to demonstrate that messiah / the Lamb / Jesus Christ came to completely fulfill the Law that God Most High provided to Moses and the people of Israel.

Feast of unleavened bread, beginning the day after Passover – Nisan 15-21 – Exodus 12:1-30, 12:43-49, 34:18, Leviticus 23:4-8, Numbers 9:9-14, Deuteronomy 16:1-8

Even though the people of Israel ate unleavened bread with their Passover meal, the traditional observance of the feast of unleavened bread did not begin until the day following the feast of Passover. The feast of unleavened bread, like the fall feast of tabernacles, lasted for seven days. For seven days, the people of Israel were to eat unleavened bread.

The unleavened bread / matzah resembled a cracker. Generally, the matzah bread was a flat bread with stripping.

The reason for the unleavened bread was twofold.

First the people of Israel left Egypt with haste. There was not enough time to allow bread to rise while they were traveling to the Red Sea, and then passing through the Red Sea to escape the Egyptians.

Second, leavening represented sin. As the people of Israel were leaving Egypt, they were considered by God Most High to be leaving the slavery of sin behind. The new nation of Israel experienced a process of baptism while traveling through the Red Sea (1 Corinthians 10:1-5) and were considered in that moment to be sinless for the purpose of advancing the six thousand / seven thousand year plan for redemption, reclamation and regeneration (1446 BC). This baptism of the nation occurred again as the nation of Israel crossed the Jordan River to enter the Promised Land (1406 BC).

The feast of Passover and the feast of unleavened bread were inextricably linked. One feast could not be celebrated without the other.

The consequences of sin have always led to death in some form (Romans 6:23, etc.). Lying destroys relationships by stealing trust or stealing something else from someone else that could not be gained with telling the truth, and then lying attempts to cover up the truth. Murder steals life from someone else, but also steals life from the person that commits the murder. Sex that has not been freely given by both parties with the blessing of God Most High, is stealing a form of life and trust from the sexual partner, stealing from that sexual partner's future or current spouse, and most importantly stealing from oneself. The act of sex requires one's covenant commitment to another, and if that covenant commitment is not offered under the blessing of God Most High, by default that covenant commitment is offered to the forces of rebellion against the order created by God the Creator and offered to the gods of the kingdom of Satan, Inc. / kingdom of man.

Since the time of the Garden of Eden / garden of God / paradise event when the first man rebelled against God the Creator and the first woman was deceived, sin has been an unescapable dynamic of human life. With the first woman's act of being deceived and the first man's act of rebellion, sin actually became a portion of every human being's genetic code. Sin cannot be purged. Sin can only be removed through the one sinless human being, offering his own blood, for a spiritual blood transfusion into the lives of those who have sinned and request salvation from sin and its effects.

The feast of unleavened bread dramatized the promised and prophesied messiah / the Lamb / Jesus Christ offering his sinless life as the payment demanded for redemption according to the justice system agreement established with the serpent / Satan in the Garden of Eden / garden of God / paradise (Genesis 3:15).

Because of this one man's sacrifice, the full penalty for sin has been paid for whomever chooses to become a believer in messiah (BC) or a follower of the Lamb (AD).

The apostles and disciples invested a great deal of ink in explaining the dynamics of what messiah / the Lamb / Jesus Christ accomplished through living a sinless life and then becoming an acceptable sacrifice in order to remove sin. It may be that the feast of unleavened bread lasts for a full seven days because of the weight of the significance of what Jesus Christ was able to accomplish by living a sinless life. (John 1:26-27, 1:29, 2 Corinthians 5:21, Hebrews 1:1-4, 9:22, 1 Peter 2:21-25 (Isaiah 53:4-9), 1 Peter 3:18-22, 2 Peter 1:5-9, 1 John 1:7, 1 John 3:4-6, etc.)

As a side note: The name 'Bethlehem' means 'house of bread.' The significance of Jesus Christ having been born in Bethlehem defined Jesus Christ as the ultimate 'house of bread.' So when the followers of the Lamb (AD) participate in eating the bread of communion, they are spiritually receiving bread from the house of bread, into their being. Spiritually, the lives of the followers of the Lamb / Jesus Christ are intended to be the manifestation of the house of God upon the earth. Leaven / sin is to be cleaned out of our house, as a prerequisite for the Spirit of Jesus Christ to be able to take up residence within us. (Matthew 26:26, 1 Corinthians 3:16-17, 6:19-20, 2 Corinthians 6:15-18, Hebrews 3:6, 1 Peter 2:5, 1 Timothy 3:14-15, Ephesians 2:19-22, etc.)

Feast of firstfruits / bikkurim – day after the Sabbath after Passover – first day of the week – Leviticus 23:9-14, and when coming into a new land – Deuteronomy 26

The feast of firstfruits was celebrated with the barley harvest, the first grain to be harvested in the season. The time of the celebration was based upon the date established for the celebration of the feast of Passover.

The feast of firstfruits followed the seven days of the feast of unleavened bread.

The pattern of the seven days of the feast of unleavened bread followed by the one day feast of firstfruits, was repeated with the fall feast of tabernacles followed by the eighth day assembly / Shemini Atzeret.

The year that messiah / the Lamb / Jesus Christ fulfilled the prophecy of the feast of firstfruits, the feast day fell on the 'seventeenth day of the seventh month' according to the civil calendar or the seventeenth day of the first month according to the religious calendar. It was the seventeenth day of the month of Nisan.

The 'seventeenth day of the seventh month' was the anniversary of the day when Noah's ark came to rest on the mountains of Ararat (Genesis 4:3-5). The waters did not recede enough to be able to leave the ark for another few months. But when the ark came to rest on the mountains of Ararat, it was the promise to Noah and his family, that *there would come a day when they would be able to emerge from the ark. (~2458 BC)*

It was the seventeenth day of Nisan that the people of Israel crossed through the Red Sea (1446 BC). (Exodus 3:18, 5:3, 14). That was also the day when God Most High provided manna from heaven to feed the people of Israel for forty years. At the end of the forty years, the people of Israel ate the firstfruits of the food of the Promised Land (Joshua 5:10-12).

The thirteenth of Nisan was when Haman was able to accomplish the decree to be sent out throughout Persia that all the people of Israel living in exile in Persia, would be killed (Esther 3:1-6, 3:12). Upon hearing the news, Esther proclaimed a three day fast for her people / the people of Israel, which would have taken place on Nisan 14-16 (Esther 4:15-16). Esther then risked her own life and invited the king of Persia, Xerxes to come to a banquet on Nisan 16 and then again on Nisan 17 (Esther 5). During the day in between Esther's two banquets, Esther's uncle Mordecai was honored (Esther 6). The banquet on Nisan 17 was when Haman's plot to genocide the people of Israel was exposed and Haman was hanged with his ten sons, and Haman's estate was given to Esther (Esther 7, 8). (474 BC)

It was Nisan 17, ~30 AD that was the date when messiah / the Lamb / Jesus Christ fulfilled the prophecy of the feast of firstfruits through his resurrection from death (Matthew 27:52b-53, 1 Corinthians 15:12-58).

During the era of the time of Jacob's Trouble, there will be another group of people who will be specifically designated as firstfruits. The one hundred forty four thousand that were described by John the Revelator as standing on Mount Zion with the Lamb, who had also been redeemed from the earth as followers of the Lamb, were designated as firstfruits to God and the Lamb (Revelation 14:1-5).

Before he was crucified, Jesus Christ understood that he was to be the firstfruits of the resurrection.

Then the Jews demanded of Jesus, 'What miraculous sign can you show us to prove your authority to do all this?'

Jesus answered them, 'Destroy this temple, and I will raise it again in three days.'

The Jews replied, 'It has taken forty-six years to build this temple, and you are going to raise it in three days?'

But the temple Jesus had spoken of was his body. After Jesus Christ was raised from the dead, his disciples recalled what he had said. Then they believed the Scripture and the words that Jesus had spoken.

Now while Jesus was in Jerusalem at the Passover Feast, many people saw the miraculous signs Jesus was doing and believed in his name. But Jesus would not entrust himself to them for Jesus knew all people. Jesus did not need humanity's testimony about a person, for Jesus knew wat was in a person. John 2:18-25

And Jesus Christ understood what was required of him to endure before fulfilling the resurrection prophesied within the required feast of firstfruits. After his resurrection, Jesus Christ again taught his disciples.

Jesus said to them, 'How foolish you are, and how slow of heart to believe all that the prophets have spoken! Did not the Christ have to suffer these things and then enter his glory?'

And beginning with Moses and all the Prophets, he explained to them what was said in all the Scriptures concerning himself. Luke 24:25-27

Jesus Christ was recognized as the firstfruit of resurrection by the apostles and disciples (Acts 26:23, Romans 8:29 1 Corinthians 15:12-58, 1 Thessalonians 4:13-17). But the resurrected and ascended Jesus Christ also described himself as the firstfruit of resurrection (Revelation 1:5).

Being the firstborn from the dead, defined Jesus Christ. Without the resurrection of Jesus Christ, Jesus would have been merely just another man who had been crucified / executed / murdered. And the fulfillment of the feast of firstfruits would not have been fulfilled. And the promise covenant agreement that God Most High established with Abram / Abraham, Isaac and Jacob / Israel would have not had the opportunity to be fully realized.

  For the followers of the Lamb / Jesus Christ, it was Jesus Christ's crucifixion and death that remains preeminent and the pivotal point for faith.
  If the resurrection of messiah / the Lamb / Jesus Christ was a faked event, then the entire rest of God Most High's redemption, reclamation and regeneration plan has no foundation for further fulfillment. If the resurrection of Jesus Christ was a false narrative, then the entire biblical record must be considered to be inaccurate and a huge hoax thrusted upon humanity's hopes and dreams for a better living experience; and the biblical record must be relegated to the category of being a historical mythological novel epic, best used as fodder for entertainment.
  But if the resurrection of messiah / the Lamb / Jesus Christ was a true and actual event, then the rest of the biblical record must also be considered to be factual. This would mean that Jesus Christ will return as promised and prophesied, will defeat the enemies of God Most High and of the kingdom of heaven, and will fully establish the kingdom of heaven on earth. It also means that human life does not cease with the death of the physical body, but extends into everlasting life (or everlasting death / permanent separation from God Most High).
  For those who are truly followers of the Lamb, the resurrection of Jesus Christ as the firstfruits of all resurrections that follow, remains the foundation and central focus for faith and hope.

  When the serpent / Satan seduced the first woman and man, the serpent / Satan instigated their deaths, and then took dominion. The serpent / Satan rejoiced.
  When the red dragon / serpent / Satan, Inc. caused the death of messiah / the Lamb / Jesus Christ, again there was rejoicing by the red dragon / serpent /Satan, Inc.
  But in causing the death of messiah / the Lamb / Jesus Christ, the red dragon / serpent / Satan, Inc. also provided the path for the resurrection of messiah / the Lamb / Jesus Christ. The resurrection of Jesus Christ provided the opportunity for all who were believers in messiah (BC) or who would become followers of the Lamb

(AD) to experience God Most High's plan for redemption, reclamation and regeneration. And those who accepted God Most High's offer, were lost to the red dragon / serpent / Satan, Inc.

In conspiring to cause the death of messiah / the Lamb / Jesus Christ, the serpent / Satan also triggered the resurrection of messiah / the Lamb / Jesus Christ. The resurrected Jesus Christ cannot be held by the bonds of death, rendering the resurrected Jesus Christ to be invincible, indestructible and unable to be defeated in his mission. And the mission of Jesus Christ is to reclaim dominion over the earth on behalf of humanity. So, when the red dragon / serpent / Satan, Inc. orchestrated the crucifixion of Jesus Christ, the events were set into motion that caused the red dragon / serpent / Satan, Inc. to lose his opportunity to hold permanent dominion over the earth.

While the red dragon / serpent / Satan, Inc. believed that they were fully in control of death, they missed the law of death which stated that a perfectly lived life in accordance with the laws of heaven, and without the seed of Adam as the father, will be able to conquer death and will be able to share the effects of that victory over death, with whomever the conqueror chooses to share the life giving effects with.

Jesus Christ fulfilled the feast of firstfruits by being resurrected from death. First Jesus Christ lived a perfect life and fulfilled the Law given to Moses and the people of Israel in every way. And then messiah / the Lamb / Jesus Christ willingly offered himself as the perfect sacrifice. The perfect life of Jesus Christ needed to be offered willingly, without compulsion. All work of the kingdom of heaven in every human being must be accomplished through love and not through force, power, compulsion, etc. Only a willing sacrifice from the heart affects the development of the right relationship between a human being, the God of the kingdom of heaven, and the kingdom of heaven itself. The economy of heaven is love, not the trade of power or coercion or force.

Having met these requirements of living a sinless life, messiah / the Lamb / Jesus Christ could not be held by death. The kingdom of death cannot hold a true citizen of the kingdom of heaven who belongs to heaven. Because Jesus Christ belonged to the kingdom of the living, Jesus Christ was resurrected from death by the Holy Spirit as the firstfruits of all believers in messiah (BC) and followers of the Lamb (AD), who will also be resurrected in that moment when messiah / the Lamb / Jesus Christ returns to earth to reclaim what belongs to God Most High and to the kingdom of heaven.

When the people of Israel left Egypt as the first nation that would enter into God Most High's holy covenant, it was the first fulfillment of the feast of firstfruits (1446 BC) (Jeremiah 2:3).

When messiah / the Lamb / Jesus Christ was resurrected from death, it was the second fulfillment of the feast of firstfruits (~30 AD).

When messiah / the Lamb / Jesus Christ returns to resurrect the believers in messiah (BC) and followers of the Lamb (AD), it will be the completion of what began with the observance of the feast of firstfruits. But it will take place with the feast of trumpets (the first fall feast), providing continuity of the fulfillment of the fall feasts with the foundation established with the spring feasts. This event has been scheduled to take place within just a few years.

The interconnectedness of the required feasts, demonstrated that to participate in the resurrection that will accompany the return of messiah / the Lamb / Jesus Christ, a person must choose to honor the full requirements of the meaning of the feasts. And to participate in the inherent prophecy of the feast of firstfruits (and feast of trumpets) through resurrection, means that all the rest of the inherent prophecy of all the rest of the required feasts, must also be experienced.

Messiah / the Lamb / Jesus Christ fulfilled the required spring feasts, acting alone. But the inherent prophecy of the required fall feasts will require the *participation of all believers in messiah (BC) and followers of the Lamb (AD).*

Because messiah / the Lamb / Jesus Christ was resurrected with the feast of firstfruits ~30 AD, when he returns with the feast of trumpets to resurrect all believers in messiah (BC) and followers of the Lamb (AD), the inherent prophesy of the required fall feasts will be experienced. The Day of Atonement / Yom Kippur will be the day for the final battle of this age and all resurrected believers in messiah (BC) and followers of the Lamb (AD) will share in this experience. Following the Day of Atonement / Yom Kippur, will be the feast of tabernacles when all citizens of the kingdom of heaven will celebrate the fully established kingdom of heaven on earth. It will no longer be messiah / the Lamb / Jesus Christ experiencing the effects of the inherent prophecy of the required feasts alone, but all citizens of the kingdom of heaven will become the intrinsically active participants of the observations of the feasts.

Because messiah / the Lamb / Jesus Christ was resurrected with the feast of firstfruits and lives (feast of firstfruits - spring), we who are believers in messiah (BC) and followers of the Lamb (AD) will also be resurrected (feast of tabernacles - fall). Because Jesus Christ defeated the enemies of the kingdom of life, we who are believers in messiah (BC) and followers of the Lamb (AD) will also be participants in defeating the enemies of God Most High and of the kingdom of heaven (Day of Atonement / Yom Kippur - fall). Because messiah / the Lamb / Jesus Christ lives in the presence of God Most High through his ascension into heaven, all believers in messiah (BC) and followers of the Lamb (AD) will live eternally in the presence of God (feast of tabernacles - fall).

After messiah / the Lamb / Jesus Christ was crucified, dead, resurrected and ascended into heaven, the requirement to practice the full details of the required feasts, was no longer mandated. In 70 AD, the temple in Jerusalem Israel was destroyed, rendering it impossible to participate in the required sacrificial system. The requirement to literally practice the required feasts was relinquished during the era of the early apostolic church (see the book of Acts). The reason that the practice of observing the required feasts was relaxed was because of the work accomplished by messiah / the Lamb / Jesus Christ in fully fulfilling the inherent prophecy of the required spring feasts. (See the epistles of the New Testament, especially the book of Romans.)

But what remained a requirement for those seeking to experience the benefits of God Most High's plan that was dramatized within the required feasts, was to acknowledge that messiah / the Lamb / Jesus Christ will provide the fulfillment of all inherent prophecy within the required feasts, on our behalf.

Law of trees

In Leviticus, God Most High included through Moses, the Law of the Trees.

'When you enter the land and plant any kind of fruit tree, regard its fruit as forbidden. For three years you are to consider it forbidden. It must not be eaten. In the fourth year all its fruit will be holy, an offering of praise to the Lord. But in the fifth year you may eat its fruit. In this way your harvest will be increased. I am the Lord your God.' Leviticus 19:23-25

The concept of spiritual firstfruits was tied to the firstfruits of the harvest.

Notice that only in the fourth year, was the fruit to be holy, an offering of praise to the Lord. It was the fourth year of Jesus Christ's ministry, that Jesus Christ became the willing sacrifice. Jesus Christ's earthly ministry was three and a half years. It was approximately four thousand years after the creation of the first man and first woman, that Jesus Christ became the willing sacrifice that could be considered to be holy / dedicated to the Lord.

Feast of weeks / Pentecost / Shavuot – Sivan 5 – Exodus 34:22-26, Leviticus 23:15-22, Deuteronomy 16:9-12

One Jewish tradition also holds that Enoch was taken to heaven on his birthday which was celebrated at the time of Pentecost ~ Sivan 5. Another Jewish tradition proposed that Enoch was born on the feast of trumpets – Tishri 1.

Pentecost was the last of the required spring feasts. The required feast of Pentecost was celebrated with the firstfruits of the wheat harvest, mainly the second harvest of the agricultural year.

The history of Pentecost began with the people of Israel exiting Egypt in 1446 BC. Fifty days after Passover, the people of Israel met with God Most High at the foot of Mount Sinai while Moses ascended the mountain with his brother Aaron and the seventy elders, to receive the Law from God Most High. Moses stayed upon the mountain for forty days, conversing with God Most High and receiving instruction from God Most High. And then Moses spent another forty days with God Most High on the mountain. (Exodus 19f).

The Lord's instructions to Moses and to the people of Israel concerning the observance of the feast of Pentecost:
'You will count for yourselves from the day after the sabbath, from the day that you brought the sheaf of the wave offering; seven sabbaths will be completed. Count fifty days to the day after the seventh sabbath. Then you will offer a new grain offering to the Lord.' Leviticus 23:15-16 translated (from Leviticus 23:15-22)

Traditionally the book of Ruth was read at the time of Pentecost. In the account of Ruth, Boaz was traditionally viewed as the typology for messiah as the kinsman redeemer. Boaz was also a farmer who gave instruction to the reapers to reserve some of the harvest for Ruth to gather for herself.

After Jesus Christ was resurrected, Jesus spent forty days with his apostles and disciples prior to ascending into heaven. Ten days later, on the Day of Pentecost, the Holy Spirit came upon all the disciples gathered in the upper room in Jerusalem Israel. They experienced the filling of the Holy Spirit and the new covenant that was established between God Most High and humanity through the crucifixion, death, resurrection and ascension of messiah / the Lamb / Jesus Christ. (Luke 24:13-53, Acts 1:1-3).

Another place where Jesus Christ observed a devoted forty day period was prior to the feast of trumpets – fall, as Jesus Christ prepared for his earthly ministry.

In preparation for Jesus Christ's earthly ministry, Jesus Christ was baptized by John the Baptist and then spent the next forty days alone with God and with Satan in the wilderness. During his time in the wilderness, Jesus was propositioned by Satan to switch sides, to acknowledge Satan as supreme over God Most High and in exchange, Satan promised to make Jesus Christ a leader in the kingdom of Satan, Inc / kingdom of man. (Matthew 4:1-11, Mark 1:12-13, Luke 4:1-13)

(This proposed arrangement was similar to the Islamic eschatological stance concerning the Islamic version of Jesus / Isa.)

In exchange for Jesus Christ's allegiance, Satan promised to give Jesus vast lands to rule over, a portion of Satan's proposed realized kingdom of Satan, Inc. / kingdom of man. If Jesus would have accepted Satan's offer, Jesus would have been able to have skipped the entire crucifixion experience. But as a fully human being, accepting Satan's offer would have resulted in Jesus' eventual death anyway. And Jesus' separation from God Most High in order to join the kingdom of Satan, Inc. / kingdom of man, would have made the resurrection of Jesus from death, an impossibility.

Accepting Satan's offer to become a prince in the kingdom of Satan, Inc. / kingdom of man, would have also required Jesus Christ to relinquish his role in the future defeat of the kingdom of Satan, Inc. / kingdom of man, and to relinquish his divine and sovereign position in the future establishment of the kingdom of heaven on earth where Jesus Christ has been appointed to be the King of kings and Lord of lords. Jesus Christ turned down Satan's offer.

After his forty days in the wilderness, Jesus Christ blessed the wedding in Cana of Galilee by turning water into wine. The wedding probably took place in relationship with the feast of trumpets, as the first day of Tishri has traditionally been recognized as the day the first man and first woman were created and married. Consequently, Tishri 1 has been a favored wedding day.

Ten days after the feast of trumpets, on Tishri 10, was the Day of Atonement / Yom Kippur. Every fifty years the Day of Atonement / Yom Kippur served to usher in the year of Jubilee / the year of the Lord's favor. A Jubilee year would begin at the end of the Day of Atonement and would extend until the next year's Day of Atonement / Yom Kippur.

Having reached the required age of thirty years old in order to be a teacher in the temple / synagogue system, Jesus Christ was given the opportunity to lead Sabbath worship. Isaiah 61 was traditionally read in the synagogue on the Day of Atonement / Yom Kippur to usher in the Jubilee year. When Jesus read this passage in the synagogue, Jesus Christ officially ushered in that Jubilee Year. But Jesus also took the opportunity to officially proclaim his own earthly ministry.

Jesus went to Nazareth, where he had been brought up, and on the Sabbath day Jesus went into the synagogue, as was his custom. And he stood up to read.

The scroll of the prophet Isaiah was handed to him. Unrolling it, Jesus found the place where it is written: **'The Spirit of the Lord is on me, because he has anointed me to preach good news to the poor. He has sent me to proclaim freedom for the prisoners and recovery of sight for the blind, to release the oppressed, to proclaim the year of the Lord's favor.'**

Then Jesus rolled up the scroll, gave it back to the attendant and sat down. The eyes of everyone in the synagogue were fastened on him, and he began by saying to them, 'Today this scripture is fulfilled in your hearing.' Luke 4:16-20

Jesus read only the first part of the Isaiah 61 passage. The full passage read:

The Spirit of the Sovereign Lord is on me, because the Lord has anointed me to proclaim good news to the poor. He has sent me to bind up the brokenhearted, to proclaim freedom for the captives and release from darkness for the prisoners, to proclaim the year of the Lord's favor and the <u>day of vengeance of our God</u>, to comfort all who mourn, and provide for those who grieve in Zion — to bestow on them a crown of beauty instead of ashes, the oil of joy instead of mourning, and a garment of praise instead of a spirit of despair. They will be called oaks of righteousness, a planting of the Lord for the display of his splendor.

They will rebuild the ancient ruins and restore the places long devastated. They will renew the ruined cities that have been devastated for generations. Strangers will shepherd your flocks. Foreigners will work your fields and vineyards. And you will be called priests of the Lord, you will be named ministers of our God. You will feed on the wealth of nations, and in their riches you will boast.

Instead of your shame you will receive a double portion, and instead of disgrace you will rejoice in your inheritance. And so you will inherit a double portion in your land, and everlasting joy will be yours.

'For I, the Lord, love justice. I hate robbery and wrongdoing. In my faithfulness I will reward my people and make an everlasting covenant with them. Their descendants will be known among the nations and their offspring among the peoples. All who see them will acknowledge that they are a people the Lord has blessed.'

I delight greatly in the Lord. My soul rejoices in my God. For my God has clothed me with garments of salvation and arrayed me in a robe of his righteousness, as a bridegroom adorns his head like a priest, and as a bride adorns herself with her jewels. For as the soil makes the sprout come up and a garden causes seeds to grow, so the Sovereign Lord will make righteousness and praise spring up before all nations. Isaiah 61:1-11

Jesus stopped his reading with proclaiming the year of the Lord's favor, ending before the mention of the '<u>day of vengeance of our God</u>,' because the purpose of Jesus Christ's earthly ministry was to fulfill only the first portion of Isaiah's prophecy. The rest of the Isaiah prophecy referenced the day of vengeance that has been reserved for the era of the time of Jacob's Trouble.

By claiming that the Spirit of the Lord was upon him, Jesus indicated not only that he was the anointed one / messiah, but that he had the authority to bring to humanity, accessibility to the Holy Spirit. By sending the Holy Spirit on the Day of Pentecost following his resurrection and ascension into heaven, Jesus Christ and the Holy Spirit fulfilled prophecy of the feast of Pentecost.

There were fifty days between the feast of firstfruits – spring, and Pentecost - spring. For Jesus Christ, forty of those days after the resurrection were invested in updating the apostles and disciples so that they could understand the prophecies concerning the kingdom of heaven and exactly how Jesus Christ fulfilled those prophecies. But then there remained another ten days before the day of Pentecost would arrive. During those ten days, the apostles and disciples waited... and waited for the coming of the Holy Spirit.

The ten days immediately prior to the day of Pentecost (~30 AD), shared similarities to the Ten Days of Awe that span the time from the required fall feast of trumpets / Yom Teruah / day of concealment that begins on the first day of the month of Tishri, until the required fall observance of the Day of Atonement / Yom Kippur that takes place on the tenth day of the month of Tishri.

During his earthly ministry, Jesus had taught his followers:

'When the Counselor (Holy Spirit) comes, whom I will send to you from the Father, the Counselor will testify about me. And you also must testify for you have been with me from the beginning.' Luke 15:26-27

The Holy Spirit has always been with the people of Israel. Sometimes the Holy Spirit dwelt with the people of Israel in the tabernacle / temple. Sometimes the Holy Spirit has resided with only a few individuals. Other times, the Holy Spirit's presence has been undeniable, such as the forty years when the Holy Spirit was a pillar of fire by night and a cloud by day, camping with the people of Israel as they wandered in the wilderness.

In the wilderness, the Holy Spirit's presence was made known in a variety of methods including the cloud / fire pillar. But after the ascension of Jesus Christ, the Holy Spirit became more than a protector of the people of God Most High. After the Holy Spirit was given at Pentecost, the Holy Spirit now dwells with each individual who has been redeemed and reconciled to God Most High and is a follower of the Lamb.

When the day of Pentecost came, the group of about 120 was all together in one place. Suddenly a sound like the blowing of a violent wind came from heaven and filled the whole house where they were sitting. They saw what seemed to be tongues of fire that separated and came to rest on each of them. All of them were filled with the Holy Spirit and began to speak in other tongues as the Spirit enabled them. Acts 2:1-4

The first Pentecost recognized the people of Israel as being the people responsible for the dissemination of God Most High's message (1446 BC).

The Pentecost that followed the resurrection and ascension of Jesus Christ, recognized the followers of the Lamb who would later be comprised mostly of Gentiles, as being the people responsible for the dissemination of God Most High's message. (~30 AD)

Concerning the future fulfillment of the fall feasts when messiah / the Lamb / Jesus Christ returns, there will again be approximately ten days between his return with the feast of trumpets / Yom Teruah - fall, and the Day of Atonement / Yom Kippur - fall. On the Day of Atonement / Yom Kippur, God Most High's rejection of the people and nation of Israel, will be fully reversed to become the blessing of the remnant of the people and nation of Israel.

Most importantly, the feast of Pentecost - spring, served as a betrothal contract between God the Father and God's people. The first Pentecost was a marriage betrothal with the people of Israel (1446 BC). The Pentecost that Jesus Christ promised, acted as a marriage betrothal between messiah / the Lamb / Jesus Christ and the followers of the Lamb (~30 AD).

The Old Testament / Tanakh prophet Jeremiah (fl. 626 to 585 BC) documented what the ultimate goal of the total fulfillment of the inherent prophecy of Pentecost will be.

'Behold the days are coming,' says the Lord, 'when I will make a new covenant with the house of Israel and the house of Judah.'

'It will not be according to the covenant that I made with their fathers when I took them by the hand to lead them out of the land of Egypt; my covenant which they broke when I was a husband to them,' says the Lord.

'But this is the covenant that I will make with the house of Israel after those days,' says the Lord.

'I will put my law in their minds and write it on their hearts.'

'I will be their God, and they will be my people.'

'No more will every person teach their neighbor and every person teach their siblings, 'Know the Lord,' for they will all know me, from the least of them to the greatest of them,' says the Lord.

'For I will forgive their wickedness and their sin, and I will remember it no more.' Jeremiah 31:31-34 translated

Comparison of the original covenant that God Most High made with the people of Israel after they left Egypt (1446 BC), and the covenant that was established with the work of messiah / the Lamb / Jesus Christ

Exodus 19f - original covenant	Jeremiah 31:31-34 - new messianic covenant
The covenant was provided through a dense cloud and with the mountain to provide a safe distance between God Most High and the people of Israel, with Moses representing the people of Israel (Exodus 19:9)	The Law of God will be written into the minds and hearts of humanity instead of on stone tablets. And God Most High will dwell with humanity. No intermediary necessary.
Provided the opportunity for the people of Israel to choose to accept or reject God Most High	Only those that have already chosen God Most High to be their God, will be included within this covenant.
Commandments of God Most High written on tablets of stone (Exodus 24:12)	Commandments of God Most High known in minds and written on hearts (Jeremiah 31:33-34)
While Moses was receiving the Law on the mountain, the people of Israel constructed a golden calf to worship. In the course of God Most High dealing with the idol worship, three thousand people of Israel were killed (Exodus 32:28 (32)).	On the day of Pentecost following the resurrection and ascension of Jesus Christ, three thousand people chose to become followers of the Lamb / Jesus Christ, received Jesus Christ's forgiveness of sins, were baptized and received the internal presence of the Holy Spirit (Acts 2:38-41).

The feast of weeks / Pentecost / Shavuot that followed the resurrection and ascension of Jesus Christ into heaven (~30 AD), was fulfilled by Jesus Christ through the sending of the Holy Spirit as a gift to seal the new relationship established between the follower of the Lamb and God Most High (Acts 2).

In the traditional Jewish marriage protocol, the betrothal process would include the exchange of gifts to seal the covenant agreement. Gifts would be given by the family of the bridegroom to the bride and her family. The bridegroom in this particular scenario is messiah / the Lamb / Jesus Christ. The bride consists of every person who has chosen to be a follower of the Lamb / Jesus Christ. The gift that was given to seal the betrothal of every follower of the Lamb / Jesus Christ, has been the presence of the Holy Spirit to dwell within them.

In addition to the significance of the feast of weeks / Pentecost / Shavuot being the recognition of the giving of the Holy Spirit, the feast of weeks / Pentecost Shavuot was also marked by the sounding of the first of three primary trumpets that marked major events in God Most High's redemption, reclamation and regeneration plan.

The three trumpet soundings of major significance, associated with the required feasts, were known as the first trump, the last trump and the great trump.

The first trump was sounded at the conclusion of the observance of the Day of Pentecost. It was reminiscent of the trumpet sounds associated with Moses' meeting with God Most High on the mountain in 1446 BC when Moses and the people of Israel received the Law on the first day of Pentecost. (Exodus 19:19)

The last trump was sounded at the conclusion of the continuous sounding of the trumpets at the feast of trumpets. It signaled the conclusion of the day of trumpets / Yom Teruah – Tishri 1 or 2. But the last trump will also signal the return of messiah / the Lamb / Jesus Christ. (Matthew 24:30-31, 1 Corinthians 15:51-56)

The great trump was sounded on the Day of Atonement / Yom Kippur – Tishri 10. The sounding of the great trump was associated with the closing of the books at the end of the Day of Atonement / Yom Kippur.

The first trumpet of Pentecost concluded the spring feasts. But the sounding of the first trump also provided a connection of the spring feasts to the fall feasts where greater significant events will be marked by the soundings of the trumpet. The first trumpet of Pentecost served to provide a continuity between messiah / the Lamb / Jesus Christ's fulfillment of the spring feasts almost two thousand years ago, with the scheduled events of the era of the time of Jacob's Trouble when messiah / the Lamb / Jesus Christ will return to fulfill the fall feasts.

The first trumpet that concluded the feast of Pentecost, was sounded to mark the conclusion of the spring feasts. And yet the first trumpet signified that there was more that is yet to come.

Messiah must be a descendant of Judah

A shoot will come up from the stump of Jesse. From his roots a Branch will bear fruit. The Spirit of the Lord will rest on him – the Spirit of wisdom and of understanding, the Spirit of counsel and of power, the Spirit of knowledge and of the fear of the Lord – and he will delight in the fear of the Lord. Isaiah 11:1-3a

Genesis 38 told of the relationship of Judah and his daughter-in-law Tamar.

Judah had given his oldest son Er to Tamar to marry. But Er was wicked in the Lord's sight so God put Er to death without leaving an heir.

Judah's next son Onan was unwilling to provide an heir that would be assigned to his brother's inheritance, and so Onan spilt his seed on the ground to keep from providing offspring for his brother. God Most High considered this to be wicked and put Onan to death, also.

Judah promised Tamar his third son Shelah. But Shelah was young when the promise was made. When Shelah became old enough to marry, Judah gave Shelah to another.

This situation left Tamar without prospects. So Tamar disguised herself as a prostitute and camped on the

road that she knew Judah traveled. She enticed Judah to come into her tent. As payment, Judah left Tamar with his seal and its cord, and the staff in his hand.

When it was discovered that Tamar was pregnant, Tamar was brought to her father-in-law for judgment. But Judah also wanted to know who she had slept with in order to also pass judgment against him. When Tamar produced the seal and its cord, and the staff in his hand, Judah recognized them as his own.

According to the law given to Moses, a child with an illegitimate parent could not sit upon the throne of Israel for ten generations (Deuteronomy 23:2). Because Tamar's twin sons were denied legitimacy by Judah, it was ten generations between Judah and the acceptable person for reigning over the people of Israel, David. Nine generations after Judah, Jesse was the father of David who became king of the nation of Israel. David was the tenth generation, and was of the tribe of Judah.

In the original text of Genesis 38 that related the account of Judah and Tamar, there was a unique phenomenon of a message within the message. Using equidistant lettering at 49 letter intervals of the Hebrew text, Genesis 38 spelled out in order: Boaz, Ruth, Obed, Jesse, and David.

Boaz was the son of Rahab who was rescued out of the battle of Jericho for her assistance to the spies from the people of Israel. Ruth was the Moabitess who married Boaz and together Boaz and Ruth produced Obed. Obed was the father of Jesse. Jesse was the father of David. David became the king of the united nation of Israel.

Jesus Christ's parents, Mary and Joseph both were descendants of David through two different sons of David and Bathsheba; Solomon and Nathan. Joseph was descended through David and Bathsheba's son Solomon. And Mary was descended through Solomon's younger brother, David and Bathsheba's son Nathan.

This was just one of many Old Testament / Tanakh messianic prophecies that Jesus Christ fulfilled. The New Testament fulfillment of this prophecy that messiah would be a descendant of Judah, was recorded in Matthew 1:1-17 (Joseph) and Luke 3:23-38 (Mary).

Messiah / the Lamb / Jesus Christ, as the guardian / redeemer / goel

The Old Testament / Tankah book of Ruth documented the life of Ruth, Naomi and Boaz. Ruth and Boaz were in the messianic lineage of Jesus Christ. In addition, the account of Ruth, Naomi and Boaz, acted as a typology for the work that messiah / the Lamb / Jesus Christ would accomplish as the guardian / redeemer / goel for all of God's holy people. And it served as a typology for the role that the nation of Israel would fulfill in bringing Gentiles into the community of God's holy people. (Ruth – entire book)

The first eleven chapters of the book of Genesis, along with the book of Job and the book of Ruth, were entirely centered around the lives of Gentiles. Included within the Old Testament / Tanakh, was the first evidence that God Most High made provision for Gentiles within the kingdom of heaven, from the beginning.

The time setting of Ruth, Naomi and Boaz's account was 'in the days that the judges ruled.' The time of the judges followed the era of Joshua's leadership of the people of Israel, which was immediately after the people of Israel entered into the land that would become the nation of Israel. In fact, Boaz's mother was Rahab the harlot who assisted the people of Israel to conquer Jericho. Jericho was the first city that the people of Israel captured upon entering the promised land (1406 BC). (Joshua 2, 5:13-15, 6).

The story began when Naomi traveled from Bethlehem / Ephrath in the region of Judah in the land of Israel, into the land of Moab, with her husband Elimelek and their two sons. The name Bethlehem means 'house of bread.' The name Ephrath means 'fruitful.' But Elimelek, Naomi and their two sons, left Bethlehem because of a famine in the land.

The family traveled to the land of Moab, occupied by Gentiles. Moab was the son of Lot with one of his two daughters conceived after Sodom and Gomorrah were destroyed (Genesis 19).

While living in the land of Moab, Elimelek and Naomi's two sons married Moabite women. After they had lived in the land of Moab for a time, Naomi's husband and their two sons died. One daughter-in-law, Orpah, remained in Moab. But the other Moabite daughter-in-law Ruth, determined that she would return with her mother-in-law Naomi, to Bethlehem Israel.

In Bethlehem Israel, Ruth caught the eye of Boaz. Boaz was a kinsman who was second in relationship to Naomi and able to act as a kinsman redeemer. Boaz went on to redeem the land of Ruth's father-in-law and mother-in-law Elimelek and Naomi. In the process of redemption, Ruth became the bride for Boaz the bridegroom.

Boaz's father was Salmon who was of the tribe of Judah. Boaz's mother was Rahab, the Canaanite prostitute living in Jericho, who aided the spies as they spied out the city of Jericho, and then defeated Jericho upon entering the Promised Land (1406 BC). (Joshua 2, 6:17, 6:23-25, Matthew 1:5, James 2:25) (Note: Rahab was also a place and should not be confused to be the woman.)

Within the account of Ruth, Naomi and Boaz: both Orpah and Ruth were Moabites. Orpah represented Gentiles who reject the authentic faith system of God Most High. But Ruth represented Gentiles who would become believers in messiah (BC) and followers of the Lamb (AD). Naomi served to represent the people of Israel. And Boaz served to represent the guardian / redeemer / goel role that will be entirely fulfilled with messiah / the Lamb / Jesus Christ.

Ruth was a Moabitess, a Gentile. The land of Moab provided a great view of the land of Israel (Deuteronomy 34:1).

But it violated Jewish law, for the people of Israel to marry Moabites because of the Moabites and Midianites' opposition and seduction to the people of Israel after the people of Israel exited Egypt (Numbers 22 through 25,

Deuteronomy 23:3-4). The Moabites also worshiped in the baal / mystery / mythology religion.

    Naomi represented the people of Israel. During the time that Naomi lived in Moab, she represented the people of Israel living in exile. When safety and food were reestablished in the land of Israel, Naomi returned to her homeland, the land of Israel. Naomi's return to Bethlehem represented the people of Israel returning to the land of Israel.
    In order to bring Ruth to the land of Israel, Naomi had to be exiled from the land, and then return.
    When Naomi returned to the land of Israel, one Moabite daughter-in-law Orpah, remained in Moab. But the other daughter-in-law Ruth insisted upon moving with her mother-in-law, to the land of Israel. Ruth denounced her Moabite citizenship in order to become a citizen of God Most High's people. Ruth also denounced the baal / mystery / mythology religion of her people in order to belong to the God of Israel.
    Ruth replied (to Naomi), 'Don't urge me to leave you or to turn back from you. Where you go, I will go, and where you stay, I will stay. Your people will be my people and your God my God. Where you die, I will die, and there I will be buried. May the Lord deal with me, be it ever so severely, if even death separates you and me.' Ruth 1:16-17
    Ruth did not replace Naomi. In fact, Ruth needed Naomi's relationship with her homeland to remain intact in order for Ruth to receive benefit.
    When they arrived home, Naomi asked the people of Bethlehem to call her Mara / bitter, because she went away full and returned empty (Ruth 1:20-21).

    Boaz had remained in the land of Bethlehem Israel. As the kinsman redeemer / goel, Boaz provided the typology that the promised and prophesied messiah always belonged to Israel and originated from the people of Israel.
    Boaz would become the father of Obed, grandfather of Jesse, and great grandfather of David, which was part of the heritage for why Bethlehem Israel was recognized as the 'city of David.' It would be in the 'city of David' that the promised messiah would be born over a millennia later.

The account of Naomi and Ruth arriving in Bethlehem Israel, documented that they returned just as the barley harvest was beginning (Ruth 1:22).

The barley harvest coincided with the required feast of firstfruits - spring, immediately following the feast of Passover in the month of Nisan. The required feast of firstfruits was fulfilled by the resurrection of messiah / the Lamb / Jesus Christ, over a thousand years later.

Ruth worked the fields after the harvesters had already gathered their harvest (Ruth 2:2-3). The nation of Israel was considered by God Most High to be the initial harvest, with the Gentiles receiving the benefit / gleanings (Jeremiah 2:3). Boaz acted as the typology for the promised and prophesied messiah in the role of the lord of the harvest (Matthew 9:38, Luke 10:2). Ruth's harvesting acted as the typology for the Gentiles also receiving benefit from the generosity of the lord of the harvest.

There were multiple other facets to the typology of the account of Ruth, Boaz and Naomi, with Ruth representing Gentiles, Boaz representing the future promised and prophesied messiah as guardian / redeemer / goel, and Naomi representing the people of Israel.

Ruth and Boaz met through the overseer of Boaz's harvesters (Ruth 2:5-7). Isaac and Rebecca were introduced through Isaac's father's servant Eleazar (Genesis 24). The followers of the Lamb / Jesus Christ are also introduced to the redeemer Jesus Christ through a third party, the Holy Spirit (Romans 8:16, Hebrews 10:15, 1 John 5:6).

Ruth was invited to stay and work the fields, by Boaz (Ruth 2:8-9). And Boaz fulfilled the laws as established by God Most High through Moses. The law of gleaning was recorded in Leviticus 19:9-10 and 23:22.

Ruth experienced the protection of Boaz (Ruth 2).

Ruth was also known for the great care that she had provided for Naomi (Ruth 2:11-12).

Boaz provided bread and wine to Ruth (Ruth 2:14).

Boaz made provision for Ruth's needs, and for Naomi's needs (Ruth 2:14-18).

Naomi recognized Boaz as the guardian / redeemer / goel who could provide Ruth with a home (Ruth 2:19-20, 3:1-2).

Ruth was expected to stay with Boaz's workers, until they finished harvesting all the grain (Ruth 2:21).

Ruth learned Boaz's ways through Naomi. But Naomi met Boaz through Ruth.

In chapter 3, the focus of the story shifted from Naomi and Ruth's activity, to laying the foundation for Boaz to assume the role of guardian / redeemer / goel.

Boaz was Naomi's husband's second nearest cousin (Ruth 2:1, 3:2, 3:12-13).

When the harvest time had come to its end, Ruth washed, perfumed and dressed in her best clothes, and then attended the harvest party (Ruth 3:3).

At the conclusion of the harvest party, Ruth lied down at Boaz's feet. Lying down at Boaz's feet was Ruth's recognition that Boaz was her family's guardian / redeemer / goel. (Ruth 3:1-10)

And Boaz spread his garment over Ruth. With the act of spreading his garment over her, Boaz recognized his relationship to Ruth as her family's guardian / redeemer / goel. (Ruth 3:1-10)

Traditionally, the hem of one's garment was where the rank or authority of a person, was recorded. It was much like the stripes of a naval officer or pilot, on the sleeve of a uniform. Later, David cut the corner off Saul's robe as a symbolic gesture of cutting off Saul's authority to rule over the nation of Israel as king (1 Samuel 24). The woman who touched the edge of Jesus' cloak, understood that merely touching the authority of Jesus Christ would bring her healing (Matthew 9:20-22, Mark 5:25-34, Luke 8:42-48). Others also understood that just touching the edge of Jesus Christ's cloak would bring healing (Matthew 14:35-36, Mark 6:54-56).

Boaz blessed Ruth for her kindness in recognizing Boaz as her guardian / redeemer / goel (Ruth 3:10). It was amazing that Boaz would supply the greatest amount of benefit to this relationship, and yet Boaz blessed Ruth for her comparatively miniscule kindness in recognizing Boaz.

No matter how much Boaz loved Ruth, Boaz had to wait for Ruth to act. Love does not force, nor steal. Love gives. Love is patient.

With Ruth's recognition of Boaz as her guardian / redeemer / goel, the real work of redeeming Ruth began.

The guardian / redeemer / goel was a legal position. According to the Law provided to Moses and to the people of Israel, the guardian / redeemer / goel was obligated to redeem a relative who was experiencing serious difficulty. (Leviticus 25:25-55)

To act as a guardian / redeemer / goel, the person must be a close relative, able to perform the redemptive act, and willing to voluntarily perform the redemptive act. The guardian / redeemer / goel was charged with the duty of restoring the redeemed person's rights and avenging the wrongs done to that person. One duty of the goel was to redeem / purchase a relative that was sold into slavery. Another duty of the goel was to avenge the death of a relative who had been wrongly killed. Also, the guardian / redeemer / goel would then assume all the obligations of the beneficiary.

In the same manner that Boaz acted as Ruth's guardian / redeemer / goel, God Most High acted as the people of Israel's guardian / redeemer / goel (Isaiah 41:14, 43:14, 44:6, 44:24, 47:4, 48:17, 49:7, 49:26, 54:5, 54:8, 60:16, 63:16, Jeremiah 50:34). And messiah / the Lamb / Jesus Christ acted as the guardian / redeemer / goel for all believers in messiah (BC) and followers of the Lamb (AD) (Isaiah 59:20, Luke 1:68, 24:13-21, Galatians 3:13-14, 4:1-7, Titus 2:11-14, 1 Peter 1:17-25, Revelation 14:3).

It is vital to remember that God Most High's redemptive acts are not confined by time. God the Creator created time, and therefore holds authority over time. Time does not hold authority over God the Creator.

It is within God Most High's prerogative to apply future events to past history, as well as applying past history to future events. Isn't that ability to apply future *decisions to past actions, intrinsic within the act of forgiveness? In relationship to the earthly ministry of messiah / the Lamb / Jesus Christ, we live in the future. And yet the redemptive work of messiah / the Lamb / Jesus Christ that took place in the past, reached into the future to be able to be applied to us. Limitations based upon history remain under the scrutiny of God Most High.*

According to God Most High's understanding of property, a property belongs to a family and is intended to be inherited by family members. The law of redemption required that land would not be sold permanently, because the land ultimately belongs to God Most High who created heaven and earth. (Leviticus 25:23-55, see also Jeremiah 32:6-44, Revelation 5, etc.)

With this understanding of property rights, because humanity was created by God the Creator, God the Creator is ultimately the first owner of every human being. This relationship between God the Creator and humanity meant that every person has been endowed with inalienable rights that cannot be removed by anyone other than God the Creator. (See the United States Declaration of Independence, July 4, 1776.)

Dominion over the earth, and consequently dominion over one's own personal being, was granted to the first man and first woman by God the Creator. The first man and first woman then transferred that dominion to the serpent / Satan who ultimately had no right to be granted dominion. The red dragon / serpent / Satan, Inc. has invested all human history in the goal of separating humanity from their inalienable rights.

Because the serpent / Satan stole dominion over the earth that did not belong to him, God the Creator rendered the serpent / Satan's dominion to be subservient to God the Creator's original claim upon humanity. God the Creator legally provided the opportunity for God the Creator to provide a redemption plan for redeeming, reclaiming and regenerating humanity. In this way, messiah / the Lamb / Jesus Christ acts as the guardian / redeemer / goel for all who choose to meet the requirements of redemption.

Through the Levitical law, the responsibilities of the guardian / redeemer / goel, were to redeem the relative from slavery, to repurchase a relative's property when it had been sold because of poverty, to avenge the improper death of a relative, to marry the widow of a relative in order to provide an heir for the relative and provide a lineage for the name of the relative, etc. (Leviticus 25:23-55, Deuteronomy 25:5-10, Numbers 5:5-8)

Ruth needed to act of her own freewill. And then the redemption process began with the actions of Ruth. ('When Ruth came to her mother-in-law...' Ruth 3:16-18, 4:1-12)

Once Ruth had recognized Boaz as her guardian / redeemer / goel (because she was a widow of Boaz's relative), it became Boaz's responsibility to supply all the rest of what was required for redeeming Ruth.

Boaz confronted the man who had a closer kinsman relationship claim to Ruth and to Elimelek's estate, than Boaz's claim. And then Boaz negotiated the transaction. (Ruth 4:1-8)

The finalization of the transaction was sealed with the closer relative relinquishing his sandal to Boaz (Ruth 4:7-10). For Boaz and Ruth, that sandal became their marriage license.

The elders' concluding statement was also prophetic: 'May you have standing in Ephrathah and be famous in Bethlehem. Through the offspring the Lord gives you by this young woman, may your family be like that of Perez, whom Tamar bore to Judah.' Ruth 4:11c-12

Centuries before (~1500 BC), Tamar took the initiative to fulfill the law in providing the heir of the messianic lineage through Perez (Genesis 38).

Over a millennium later, Bethlehem Israel became the birthplace of messiah / the Lamb / Jesus Christ (~4 BC), through Ruth (Matthew 1:1-17 – Joseph, Luke 3:23-38 – Mary).

Ruth would become the Gentile bride of Boaz in the same manner as the church eventually filled the role as the Gentile bride for the bridegroom Jesus Christ (John 10:16).

Boaz and Ruth shared a love story where the depth of their love soaked through the pages that recorded it, and through history to reach every person who reads it.

But another reason that Boaz chose to marry Ruth was to provide Elimelek, and his sons Kilion and Mahlon, the continuation of their name and property, so that their names would not disappear from among the family or hometown (Ruth 4:9-10). Boaz's motivation to preserve the Hebrew family, even though it was through a Gentile wife, foretold of the times of the Gentiles when the preservation of both the people of Israel and the authentic faith system established through the people of Israel, would come through Gentiles.

Boaz and Ruth had a son Obed. Obed had a son Jesse. Jesse was the father of David who became the great king of the nation of Israel, and the carrier of the messianic lineage. (Ruth 4:17-22)

Boaz and Ruth's son Obed was a child that was considered legally to be both Gentile and fully Jewish. All three Gentile women within the lineage of messiah / the Lamb / Jesus Christ, Ruth, Boaz's mother Rahab, and Tamar who was the mother of Perez, were all Gentiles. These three women provided the typology for the Gentiles to be effectively grafted into God Most High's authentic faith system that was first given to the people of Israel.

Even though Boaz and Ruth's son Obed shared Israelite and Gentile genealogy, Obed was considered to also be fully an Israelite. This was accomplished through the Israelite Naomi's 'adoption' of Obed as her own natural descendant. Naomi had already raised two sons. But when Naomi considered Obed as her own son, Obed became the recipient of Elimelek's inheritance. (Ruth 4:13-17)

Naomi's adoption of Obed served as a typology for Joseph's adoption of Jesus as his own son. While Mary's genealogy through Solomon's son Nathan and as a Levite, brought to Jesus the authority to sit upon the throne of Israel and to become the effective high priest for Israel, Joseph brought to Jesus the recognition of Solomon's political greatness.

Naomi's adoption of Obed also served as a typology for the people of Israel receiving the male child born to the people of Israel (Revelation 12:5, 12:13, etc.), as their promised and prophesied messiah, after Jesus Christ was received as the promised and prophesied messiah by the Gentiles (Zechariah 12:10, John 19:31-37, Revelation 1:7).

The Gospels' Presentation of Jesus

The New Testament began with four gospel presentations about Jesus Christ. Each of the four authors wrote for different audiences. Each audience had a different focus of interest in Jesus Christ. Consequently, while the gospel messages centered on the same message, the nuances of the various gospels added detailed information that was not necessarily contained within the other gospel messages.

Gospel author:	Matthew	Mark	Luke	John
Presentation of Jesus Christ as:	messiah	servant	Son of Man	Son of God
Provided his genealogy from the point of:	Abraham / according to Jewish Law (Matthew 1:1-17)	(A servant's genealogy is unimportant)	Adam / according to the messianic blood line (Luke 3:23-38)	The beginning of creation: Jesus Christ is eternal and preexistent / because Jesus is God / divine (John 1)
Focused on what Jesus:	said	did	felt	was, his nature and character
The first miracle provided in the gospel that Jesus performed:	Leper cleansed / sin removed	Demon expelled / slavery removed	Demon expelled / spiritual healing	Water into wine / demonstration of divine power over all creation
Gospel ending focused upon:	Resurrection / fulfillment of God's Law's promise for life over death	Ascension	Promise of the Holy Spirit == (Luke wrote the book of Acts)	Promise of Jesus Christ's return == (John wrote the book of Revelation)
Jesus was symbolically represented by:	Lion / king of Judah	Ox / beast of burden	Man / humanity's divinity restored	Eagle (frequently the eagle holds the

				snake in his mouth) / indicated God's defeat of rebellion

Jesus Christ's Own Message During His Earthly Ministry, Concerning His Return

When Jesus Christ came the first time, Jesus provided details within his teaching that documented that he fully understood God Most High's plan for the redemption, reclamation and regeneration of the earth and of the believers in messiah / followers of the Lamb / Jesus Christ.

When the first man and the first woman surrendered their dominion of the earth to the serpent / Satan, through the serpent / Satan's illegal trade, the serpent / Satan was informed that God the Creator would not allow the transaction to stand forever. God the Creator made it clear that the serpent / Satan's deal would be challenged and that the serpent / Satan's acquired dominion over the earth would be only temporary. (Genesis 3:15)

During his earthly ministry, Jesus Christ understood his mission as the promised and prophesied messiah, to provide a path for God Most High's plan for reacquiring dominion of the earth and for returning that dominion to humanity. And Jesus Christ repeatedly taught that this plan would require that Jesus Christ would come to dwell with humanity twice as the promised and prophesied messiah (Hebrew) / anointed one / Christ (Greek).

God had already covenanted with the people of Israel to send the promised and prophesied messiah to redeem, reclaim and regenerate the earth and the people of God. For two thousand years from Abram / Abraham until the arrival of Jesus Christ, the people of Israel had time to prepare to receive their promised and prophesied messiah.

But when their promised and prophesied messiah came to dwell on earth, the religious leadership at that time, believed that their promised and prophesied messiah would fulfill all prophecy with only one trip. And they rejected Jesus Christ as the one selected to fill that role.

There were however, many that understood that Jesus Christ filled the entire role as promised and prophesied messiah. Twelve of those many were specifically chosen by Jesus Christ to receive special teaching and to share a major portion of his ministry. And then there were an additional initial seven hundred who all carried the message that the promised and prophesied messiah had come, and would be returning. (Matthew 10:1-5, 19:28, 20:17-19, Mark 3:13-19, 6:6b-13, Luke 6:12-16, 9:1-6, John 6:66-71, Acts 2, etc.)

The entire job description for promised and prophesied messiah included being prophet, priest, suffering servant / messiah ben Joseph, righteous branch, son of David / messiah ben David, etc. The problem that the religious leaders of Israel had at the time, was that they could not grasp that the complete filling of the messianic job description would require time. (prophet - Deuteronomy 18:15-18 and Acts 7:37, priest - 1 Samuel 2:35, king - 1 Kings 14:14, suffering servant - Isaiah 52:13, righteous branch - Jeremiah 23:5, son of David - Jeremiah 30:9, etc.)

Jesus Christ's Instruction to Watch!

Some who have claimed to believe in the redemptive plan of God Most High through Jesus Christ, have also denied that Jesus Christ will return in order to fulfill all that the redemptive plan of God Most High requires.

Others have continued to insist that Jesus Christ did not intend for humanity to know the signs, the season, the time when Jesus Christ will return. They have cited Matthew 24 and 25 where Jesus said, 'No one knows the day nor the hour that the Son of Man will come.'

But for those who have interpreted Jesus Christ's teaching that 'No one knows the day nor the hour…' as an instruction to mean that we are not to be watching the signs that will surround his return, required them to take Jesus Christ's instruction out of context. Removing just the *statement,* 'No one knows the day nor the hour that the Son of Man will come,' *from its context, totally adulterates Jesus Christ's message. Providing only half of the message imparts the opportunity for the communicator to manipulate their listeners away from Jesus Christ's full message.*

The purpose in adulterating the message of Jesus Christ that 'No one knows the day nor the hour...,' *has been to either deny the factuality of the return of Jesus Christ, or to justify the marketing of rapture theology, or to disregard the responsibility assigned to followers of the Lamb / Jesus Christ in the activity of preparing for the return of Jesus Christ. More importantly, the adulteration of the entire message of Jesus Christ, allows for the communicator to elevate their own message and mission, over and above the original message that Jesus Christ taught.*

Reading Jesus' words in context, Matthew provided instruction in three portions concerning Jesus Christ's statement, 'you will not know the day nor the hour':

1. Matthew 24:34-39 Truly I say to you; this generation will not pass away until all these things have taken place. Heaven and earth will pass away, but my words will not pass away.'
'<u>Concerning that day and hour, no one knows, not even the angels in heaven, nor the Son; only the Father.</u>'
'As it was in the days of Noah, so it will be with the coming of the Son of Man. For in those days before the flood, people were eating and drinking, marrying and giving in marriage, until the day Noah entered into the ark. <u>And they did not know until the flood came and took them all away</u>. It will also be like that with the coming of the Son of Man. translated

2. Matthew 24:42-51 '<u>Therefore, keep watch! For you do not know on what day the Lord comes to you.</u>'
'Understand this, if the master of the house had known at what time of night the thief was coming, <u>he would have watched, and not have allowed his house to be broken into. You also must be ready</u>, because the Son of Man will come at an hour you do not expect him.'
'Who then is the faithful and wise servant, whom the master has set in charge of the servants of his household, to give them the food at the proper time? Blessed is the

servant that when his master comes, will find him doing so. Truly I say to you that the master will put him in charge over all his possessions.'

'If, however, the servant is evil and says in his heart, 'My master is delayed,' and he begins to beat his fellow servants, and to eat and drink with those who are drunkards, the master will come and find that servant on a day that the servant does not expect, and at an hour which he is not aware. The master will cut the servant in pieces and place him with the hypocrites, where there will be weeping and gnashing of teeth.' translated

3. Matthew 25:1-12 'At that time, the kingdom of heaven will be like ten virgins, who took their lamps with them and went out to meet the bridegroom. Now five of them were foolish and five were wise. The foolish did not take their lamps with them. And they did not take oil with them.'
'But the wise took oil in jars and took their oil and their lamps with them.'
'When the bridegroom tarried, they became drowsy and all fell asleep.
'In the middle of the night, there was a cry, 'Behold the bridegroom! Go to meet him!' Then all the virgins woke up and trimmed their lamps.'
'The foolish virgins said to the wise, 'Give us some of your oil, because our lamps are going out.'
'But the wise answered them saying, 'No. Our oil may not be enough for both us and for you. Instead, go to those who sell oil and buy oil for yourselves.''
'While they were going away to buy oil, the bridegroom came, and those who were ready went in with him to the wedding feast. And the door was shut.'
'Afterward, the other virgins came and said, 'Lord, Lord, open the door to us!''
'And answering he said, 'Truly I say to you; I do not know you.''
'Watch therefore, for you know neither the day, or the hour, in which the Son of Man comes.' translated

When the biblical record used women to communicate a prophecy and the women were either prostitutes or virgins, the condition of the women equated to represent the condition of their spiritual lives. The prostitute was an idolater like Jezebel / Semiramis. The virgin

represented believers in God's promised messiah / followers of the Lamb / Jesus Christ.
Because this prophecy was definitely established for its fulfillment during the era of the time of Jacob's Trouble, there was no use of the word 'church' in this parable of the ten virgins. In fact, the word 'church' / ecclesia / ecclesia / called out ones, was not commonly used until after the crucifixion, death, resurrection and ascension of Jesus Christ. And Jesus Christ knew that during the era of the time of Jacob's Trouble, the 'church' would have already been divided to include both those who embraced the baal / mystery / mythology religion / Mystery Babylon the Great! and those who were dedicated to being followers of the Lamb / Jesus Christ. To utilize the word 'church' in the description of events that will take place during the era of the time of Jacob's Trouble, would only add confusion to the description of the actors in the scheduled events. The ten virgins of this parable were all 'church' members. But Jesus foretold that five would be wise, watching and prepared to persist to the end. And five would be foolish, not taking seriously the environmental conditions that surround the events of the coming of the bridegroom. The five that came without oil represented those that will miss the coming of the bridegroom / Jesus Christ. The door / entrance into heaven will be shut against them. Jesus Christ expects that belief in Jesus Christ is not enough to enter into the kingdom of heaven. Even the demons believe that Jesus Christ is messiah, and they are not allowed entrance into the kingdom of heaven. James said that faith without works is dead (James 2:14-26). Instead of actionless faith, Jesus Christ is seeking followers of the Lamb / Jesus Christ who also have developed a personal relationship knowing and following Jesus Christ. They will hear his voice,

and then respond. They will be the salt of the earth. They will be the recipients of the outpouring of the Holy Spirit in the last days. They will be active ambassadors on the earth, etc.

For humanity, life on earth is a courting period, a time to choose whether to enter into a covenant 'marriage' relationship with the bridegroom / messiah / the Lamb / Jesus Christ, or to remain unmarried and owned by default to the baal / mystery / mythology religion established through the serpent / Satan.

The earthly life of messiah / the Lamb / Jesus Christ acted as God Most High's love letter and offer of marriage. With Jesus Christ's willing sacrifice through crucifixion, Jesus Christ provided the marriage proposal and the sealing of the betrothal contract.

While Jesus Christ then left to prepare a place for the followers of the Lamb / Jesus Christ, the bride has been instructed to wait without leaving, waiting for the coming of the bridegroom to present himself in person again, for the wedding that can only take place after Jesus Christ has truly claimed (the second coming) what he has purchased / redeemed (the first coming).

The parable of the ten virgins also demonstrated the dynamic that belonging to an organization or institution does not translate into an automatic acceptance of the foundational concepts that the organization or institution advocates. In the parable of the ten virgins, five were fully devoted to understanding and embracing the plan of God Most High. But the other five had embraced a comfortable doctrine and theology of Christianity that was devoid of a willingness to commit to actually preparing for entering into a covenant 'marriage' with Jesus Christ. They were brides that did not bother to show up for their wedding.

The message of the five virgins, placed in the context of the era of the time of Jacob's Trouble, demonstrated that some people depend upon the church for their salvation (the five virgins who were members of the church, but without oil), while other people depend upon their relationship with the Lamb / Jesus Christ for their salvation and act upon their faith (the five virgins that came prepared and determined to meet with the bridegroom).

3. *In Matthew's account, the third time the statement of not knowing the day nor hour of Jesus Christ's return was recorded, was immediately following the parable of the virgins.*
Matthew 25:13 'Watch therefore, for you know neither the day, or the hour, in which the Son of Man comes.' translated
Jesus Christ also immediately followed the parable of the ten virgins, with the parable of the master sharing three bags of money with his servants to invest. Two invested their bags of money. One buried his bag. The first two were told they were good servants. The one who buried what was given to him, had what was given to him taken away and that servant was thrown out into the darkness where there will be weeping and gnashing of teeth. (Notice the two thirds – one third theme that was used.)
Then Jesus followed up with a third parable, the parable of the sheep and the goats. The parable of the sheep and the goats detailed the separation of the sheep for protection and care, from the goats who will depart into eternal fire prepared for the devil and his angels, and eternal punishment.
All three parables, the parable of the ten virgins, the parable of the unfaithful servant and the parable of the separation of the sheep and the goats, demonstrated the same message; that not being prepared will not be recognized as an

acceptable excuse for being unprepared for the return of messiah, that being an unfaithful member of the household of the master will not be an acceptable excuse for being unprepared for the return of messiah, and that to be unprepared for the return of messiah will warrant being classified as a goat and unacceptable for being included as a sheep.

Reading all of Matthew's account of Jesus Christ's instruction 'to watch' *in context, one cannot miss the* 'weeping and gnashing of teeth' *references along with the references to being stripped of one's resources and experiencing* 'utter darkness,' 'eternal fire' *and* 'eternal punishment.' *These three parables demonstrated Jesus Christ's seriousness concerning the responses of people living during the era of time prior to his return.*

Jesus Christ has clear expectations for those of us who seek to obtain eternal life and avoid eternal punishment. The followers of the Lamb / Jesus Christ do not have the option of ignoring the signs that God has instructed us to be watching for. The followers of the Lamb / Jesus Christ do not have the option of ignoring the responsibilities given to them to invest the treasure of knowledge that God has provided. And to ignore or shirk those responsibilities, warrants the ignorer and shirker to be placed in the category of being merely an 'inhabitant of the earth.'

When Jesus Christ's statements are read in context, the statements that 'no one will know the day or the hour,' *no longer can be considered to be a viable rationale for being uninformed. The context of Jesus Christ's statements provided the opposite message. The prudent person will be on alert because of Jesus Christ's imperative notice. And for those many preachers who present a God who intends that Jesus Christ's coming is supposed to be a complete surprise, they will be caught completely off guard, and fine themselves needing to go into town to purchase their oil.*

The biblical record stressed the importance of the context of the message, in understanding biblical instructions.

All Scripture is God-breathed and is useful for teaching, rebuking, correcting and training in righteousness, so that the servant of God may be thoroughly equipped for every good work. 2 Timothy 3:16-17

Jesus Christ did not want us to be ignorant. In fact, Jesus Christ's teaching stressed the importance of understanding the signs that would be present that would indicate his eminent return. And this fact was highlighted by all the gospel writers and throughout the epistles.

'Now learn the lesson from the fig tree. When its branch has become tender, and it puts forth leaves, then you know that summer is near. So you also know that when you see all these things, that he is near, right at the door. Truly I say to you, this generation will not pass away until all these things have taken place. Heaven and earth will pass away, but my words will not pass away.' Matthew 24:32-35 translated

'If anyone says, 'Look, here is the messiah!' or 'Look, there he is!' Do not believe it. False messiahs and false prophets will appear, and will provide signs and wonders to deceive the elect, if that is possible.'
'You however, need to be on your guard. I have told you everything ahead of time.' Mark 13:21-23 translated

'Concerning that day and that hour, no one knows; not even the angels in heaven, nor the Son; only the Father.'
'Be on guard! Watch! For you do not know when the time is. It is like a man going on a journey, having left his house and having given his servants authority; each with their assigned task. And the man assigns the doorkeeper that he should keep watch.'
'Therefore, watch! For you do not know when the master of the house comes, at evening or at midnight or when the rooster crows or morning.'
'If he comes suddenly, do not let him find you sleeping. What I now say to you, I say to all. I say, 'Watch!'' Mark 13:32-37 translated

'And there will be signs in the sun and moon and stars; and upon the earth, the nations will be distressed with the perplexity of the roaring of the sea and the rolling surge. Humanity will faint from fear and expectation of what will be coming on the earth. For the powers of the heavens will be shaken. And then will they see the Son of Man coming in a cloud with power and great glory.'

'When these things begin to take place, look up and lift up your heads, because your redemption is coming.'

Jesus spoke a parable to them: 'Behold the fig tree and all the trees. When they are already budding, you look at them and know for yourselves that already summer is near.'

'So you also, when you see these things happening, know that the kingdom of God is near.' Luke 21:25-31 translated

Ezekiel's instruction to watch

The prophet Ezekiel recorded this message from the Lord:

The word of the Lord came to me again, saying, 'Son of man / son of humanity / son of Adam, speak to the descendants of your people. Say to them, 'When I bring the sword against a land, and the people of the land choose one of their men and appoint him their watchman, and he sees the sword coming against the land and blows the trumpet (shofar) to warn the people; then whoever hears the sound of the trumpet and does not take warning, if the sword comes and takes away someone who heard the sound of the trumpet, but paid no attention to it, that person's blood is on their own head.''

''That person heard the sound of the trumpet, but did not respond to the warning. That person's blood will be upon that person. But the one who responds to the warning will save their life.''

''But if the watchman sees the sword coming and does not blow the trumpet, and the people are not warned; and then the sword comes and takes any one of them, that person's life will be taken away because of their sin, but I will require the watchman to be accountable for their blood.''

'So you, Son of man, I have made you a watchman for the people of Israel. Therefore, you will hear the word from my mouth and warn them for me. When I say to the wicked, 'You are a wicked person, you will surely die,' and you do not speak to warn the wicked to leave their way, then that wicked person will die in their iniquity, but that person's blood I will require at your hand.'

'Nevertheless, if you warn the wicked person to turn from their way, and that person does not turn from their way, then that person will still die in their iniquity, but your soul will have been delivered.' Ezekiel 33:1-9 translated

Paul's emphasis on Jesus Christ's return – not to be a complete surprise / not a 'gotcha' event – 1 Thessalonians 5:1-6

Paul stressed that the return of Jesus Christ was not intended to be a complete surprise, a 'gotcha' event.

Now brothers and sisters, concerning the times and the seasons that this will happen, we do not need to write to you. For you know very well that the day of the Lord will come like a thief in the night.

For when they say, 'Peace and security,' then suddenly destruction comes upon them; destruction like the labor pains of a pregnant woman. And they will not escape.

However, you brothers and sisters, are not in darkness so that the day will surprise you like a thief. For all of you are descendants of the light. We do not belong to the night or to the darkness.

So then, we should not sleep / be unaware, as others. But we should watch and be sober. 1 Thessalonians 5:1-6 translated

Jesus Christ and the Religious Leaders Confrontation with Jesus Christ's Power and Authority to Provide Resurrection from Death

Just days before Jesus Christ was crucified, Jesus was called by Mary and Martha to come and heal their brother Lazarus. But Jesus delayed his coming and during the time that Jesus tarried, Lazarus died.

The people of Israel who believed in the message of Abraham, Isaac, Jacob, Moses, etc. traditionally believed that the soul and spirit of a person could linger for three days after death.

In order to prove that the promised messiah has the power over death, Jesus Christ waited until Lazarus had been dead for four days before calling Lazarus out from the tomb and restoring Lazarus' life.

In response to Jesus Christ's raising Lazarus from death, the Pharisees and the chief priests of the temple, called an emergency meeting of the Sanhedrin.

'What are we accomplishing?' they asked. 'Here is this man performing many signs. If we let him go on like this, everyone will believe in him, and then the Romans will come and take away both our temple and our nation.'

Then one of them, named Caiaphas, who was high priest that year, spoke up, 'You know nothing at all! You do not realize that it is better for you that one man dies for the people than that the whole nation perish.'

He did not say this on his own, but as high priest that year he prophesied that Jesus would die for the Jewish nation, and not only for that nation but also for the scattered children of God, to bring them together and make them one. So, from that day on they plotted to take his life. John 11:47b-53

Notice that the motivation of the Pharisees and chief priests was to maintain their supremacy and authority in Israel. They chose to stand in opposition of the man who had the power to bring life out of death, in the vain hope of sustaining their own power.

Jesus Christ's response was to withdraw from public events. Instead, Jesus went to a region near the wilderness, to Ephraim, where he stayed with his disciples and waited until it was time to attend Passover and experience his own crucifixion.

Raising Lazarus from the dead was a pivotal point in Jesus Christ's ministry. For many who heard of the restoration of Lazarus, there was a cementing in their belief that Jesus was the promised and prophesied messiah of God Most High. There was also a renewed belief in the possibility of the resurrection and eternal life promised to the first woman in the Garden of Eden / garden of God / paradise; the same promise that was provided throughout the messianic lineage and to the people of Israel: Enoch, Methuselah, Noah, Shem, Abram / Abraham, Isaac, Jacob / Israel, Moses, David, etc.

For those who chose not to believe that Jesus Christ was the promised and prophesied messiah sent by God Most High, the restoration of Lazarus was a crisis point. For the Sadducees who had embraced the Hellenization of culture and the baal / mystery / mythology religion, the resurrection of Lazarus proved that there is an afterlife and shattered a major piece of the theology of the Sadducees that claimed that there was no eternal life after death.

The resurrection of Lazarus from death, provided one more opportunity for the religious leaders to recognize the true identity of Jesus Christ as the promised and prophesied and prophesied messiah. Instead, the religious leaders of Israel designated the resurrection of Lazarus as an upset to the entire power structure of Caiaphas and the Sanhedrin. As a response, they plotted to kill the resurrected Lazarus with the idea that people who die, need to stay dead. (as if causing Lazarus to die a second time could ensure that Lazarus could not be restored again?)

Most importantly for all who heard of the event in Israel, the restoration of Lazarus was a compulsory decision point where people were required to choose what they were going to believe about Jesus, about the kingdom of heaven, about life after death, and about which kingdom they were going to choose to be a part of. In this way, the restoration of Lazarus poignantly offered information to the people of Israel, in preparation for lamb selection day prior to Passover.

Six days before Passover / the day before lamb selection day, it was Mary in the presence of Lazarus and Martha who poured out expensive perfume upon Jesus' feet and wiped his feet with her hair during a dinner they gave in Jesus Christ's honor. Mary anointed Jesus for burial. The next day, four days before Passover, on lamb selection day, Jesus entered Jerusalem riding on the donkey and was greeted by the people with acclamation as the Son of David.

Meanwhile, the Pharisees, chief priests and the Sanhedrin / Israel's religious court and leaders of the aristocracy of Israel, continued with their plot to have Jesus crucified. A person who could raise someone from death had power beyond their own power and was to be considered a contender for the titles of both King of Israel and High Priest.

As the high priest, Caiaphas engaged his visioning for the future, the scenario with Jesus Christ as a leader, led him to believe that there would be an insurrection in Israel. Or at least Caiaphas presented the danger of a possible insurrection as a further reason to rid Israel of the source of their potential insurrection.

In Caiaphas' imaginary scenario, Rome's response would be to send legions to crush the rebellion. Then Rome also would threaten Caiaphas' own position as the current high priest.

Caiaphas knew about Jesus. Caiaphas had conducted espionage to gather information concerning Jesus. Caiaphas was briefed daily through the news of the nation.

Caiaphas should have known who Jesus really was. Caiaphas had knowledge of Jesus' work. But the Pharisees, chief priests and the Sanhedrin were more interested in privilege than they were in truth. Not willing to accept the little truths of what motivated Jesus to do what he did, they missed the larger truth of the plan of God Most High who had sent Jesus for the purpose of making God Most High's redemption, reclamation and regeneration plan into reality.

Because the Pharisees, chief priests and the Sanhedrin were the leaders of the people of Israel, they spoke for the people of Israel and made decisions on behalf of the people of Israel. And the majority of the people of Israel at that time, listened to and believed the fake news of the Pharisees, chief priests and the Sanhedrin. Because of the leaders of Israel's decisions, their followers within Israel were subjected to share in the consequences of those decisions.

John the gospel writer, who was also John the Revelator, noted the irony in Caiaphas' words. Unwittingly Caiaphas, a totally ungodly person, had prophesied correctly that Jesus would be dying for the benefit of all of humanity. Jesus Christ's death would offer to all who would receive the offer, the opportunity to also be resurrected and experience eternal life. While Caiaphas believed that sacrificing Jesus would ensure that the elite of Israel would not lose their privileges and positions, Caiaphas was actually and unconsciously summarizing the message of Jesus, 'One person should die for the people, so that the whole nation (and whole nations) should not perish.'

It was because of Jesus Christ's crucifixion, death and resurrection, that the nation of Israel has not permanently been ordained to remain in a perished state.

During the era of the time of Jacob's Trouble, the people of Israel will have the opportunity to finally know and understand the work of their promised and prophesied messiah, and to avoid the track that leads to perishing. In a sense, Caiaphas' statement was a veiled way of saying, 'Behold, the Lamb that will take away the sin of the world.'

Caiaphas also prophesied correctly that there would be rebellion in the nation of Israel, a revolt, and a war with Rome. That war took place forty years later and led to the diaspora of the nation of Israel (70 AD). But the question of whether or not Jesus Christ was the promised and prophesied messiah, was not the core reason for the First Jewish Roman War.

Jesus Christ as Priest of the Order of Melchizedek

Within the Jewish tradition, there have been a number of orders that designated the various statuses of Jewish priests. The various orders of priesthood were named and identified by the first priests in their respective orders. For example, there are Levitical priests that are the descendants of Levi. Aaronic priests are descendants of Aaron. Etc.

But before the people of Israel were forged into a nation (1446 BC), there was a priest recognized as Melchizedek (2458 BC). Because Melchizedek lived before the forging of the nation of Israel, and because of the position that Melchizedek held in blessing Abram / Abraham, the order of the priesthood of Melchizedek was considered to be higher than any other form of priesthood.

In addition, Jesus Christ was a descendant of both the tribe of Judah (the royal lineage) and of the tribe of Levi (the priestly lineage), through his mother's family. Both Judah and Levi were distant descendants of Melchizedek.

God Most High designated the promised and prophesied messiah, to be a priest of the order of Melchizedek. The promise was included in the psalms of David. (~1000 BC)

<u>A Psalm of David</u>
The Lord said to my lord, 'Sit at my right hand until I make your enemies your footstool.'
The Lord will extend your mighty scepter from Zion.
Rule in the midst of your enemies!
Your people will be volunteers in the day of your power.

> In the beauties of holiness, from the womb of the morning, you have the dew of your youth.
> The Lord has sworn and will not relent,
> 'You are a priest forever according to the order of Melchizedek.'
> The Lord is at your right hand.
> The Lord will execute kings in the day of the Lord's wrath.
> The Lord will judge among the nations.
> The Lord will fill the places with dead bodies.
> The Lord will execute the heads of many countries.
> The Lord will drink of the brook by the wayside.
> Therefore, the Lord will hold his head high. Psalm 110:1-7 translated

While this was a prophecy for the promised and prophesied messiah, only part of this prophecy was fulfilled with Jesus Christ's prior earthly ministry. When Jesus Christ defeated death and ascended into heaven, he took up his place at the right hand of God the Father and because Jesus Christ defeated death, his priesthood will forever be indefinite.

The rest of this prophecy, the portion where the Lord is able to make the enemies of God a footstool for the promised and prophesied messiah's feet, has yet to take place.

There was a rite of passage in the Jewish tradition for the passing of the priesthood from the aged priest to the designated younger priest. First the chosen younger priest was taken through a ritual bath in the mitzvah / ritual bath. Next, the young priest was anointed as the designated person to fill the role. And last, the aged priest announced, 'This is my son in whom I am well pleased.'

When John the Baptist baptized Jesus Christ in the Jordan River before Jesus began his ministry, Jesus fulfilled the requirements for receiving the designation of the Priest of the Order of Melchizedek. The Jordan River acted as the mitzvah. The Holy Spirit came upon Jesus Christ in the form of a dove, anointing him. And the voice from heaven spoke and said, 'This is my Son, whom I love; with him I am well pleased.' *Matthew 3:13-17*

Jesus Christ did not seek baptism for the purpose of having his sins forgiven, because Jesus had no sin. But

Jesus did seek to fulfill all righteousness after the Order of the Priest of Righteousness / Priest of the Order of Melchizedek.

Zechariah's vision of the kingdom of heaven's high priest, Joshua – Zechariah 3:1-10

The Old Testament / Tanakh prophet Zechariah (520 to 480 BC), also described the role of priest that the promised and prophesied messiah would fulfill. (Note, the name 'Joshua' (Hebrew) translated into the Greek name 'Jesus.')

Then he showed me Joshua the high priest, standing before the angel of the Lord. And Satan was standing at his right hand to accuse him. The Lord said to Satan, 'The Lord rebukes you Satan! And the Lord who has chosen Jerusalem, rebukes you. Is this not the man a burning stick plucked from the fire?'

Now Joshua was dressed in filthy clothes, as he stood before the angel. The angel spoke to those who stood before him, 'Take away his filthy clothes.' Then he said to Joshua, 'See I have removed your sin from you and I will clothe you with rich robes.'

Then I said, 'Let them put a clean turban on his head.' So they put a clean turban on his head when they clothed him. And the angel of the Lord stood by.

The angel of the Lord directed Joshua saying, 'This is what the Lord of hosts says, 'If you walk in my ways and keep my command, then you will also govern my house and have charge of my courts, and I will give you places to walk among these standing here.''

'Listen, Joshua the high priest, you and your companions who sit before you, they are a wondrous sign of things to come. Behold I am bringing forth my servant, the Branch. See the stone that I have laid before Joshua! Upon the stone are seven eyes. Behold I will engrave an inscription on it,' says the Lord of hosts. 'And I will remove the sin of the land in a single day.'

'In that day, says the Lord of hosts, 'each of you will invite your neighbor under your vine and under your fig tree.' Zechariah 3:1-10 translated

Zechariah's vision was rich with detail, and held multiple layers of prophecy within the vision.

The role of high priest was intended to provide a conduit between God Most High and God's people. The pattern of God Most High communicating through a high priest, was established in 1446 BC as the people of Israel exited Egypt and were at the mountain of God when God Most High provided the Law to Moses and to the people of

Israel. The people of Israel were overwhelmed by the voice of God and begged God to speak through Moses instead (Exodus 20:18-19).

Within Zechariah's vision were multiple messages to multiple audiences.

To the people living at the time of Zechariah, there was the contemporary prophetic message to the high priest Joshua, son of Jozadak (fl. ~515 to 490 BC). And there was a message to the nation of Israel concerning their coming messiah, identifying the promised and prophesied messiah as the highest and holiest high priest.

For the promised and prophesied messiah, the message to Jesus Christ directly, identified his relationship with God the Father and his eternal role.

And imbedded in Zechariahs' vision was also a prophetic message to the people of earth concerning the future coming of messiah / 'Joshua' / 'Jesus,' who will come as the conquering king.

In Zechariah's vision, the promised and prophesied messiah was represented by the high priest of Israel, the actual Joshua son of Jozadak. But as the high priest, Joshua did not just represent the authentic faith system established within Judaism. The high priest Joshua that Zechariah knew at that time, also represented the nation of Israel, wearing the names of the twelve tribes of Israel on his shoulders and the stones that represented the twelve tribes of Israel on the breastpiece / ephod. Joshua stood in front of the throne of God and in front of Satan the accuser / 'satanizer,' not as a private person, but as a representative of the nation designated to be holy, Israel. In all of these ways, the Joshua who lived at the time of Zechariah, served as a typology for the coming messiah / the Lamb / Joshua (Hebrew) / Jesus (Greek).

Throughout the biblical record, 'the angel of the Lord' was recognized as the preincarnate messiah / Jesus Christ. In Zechariah's vision, the angel of the Lord that served as high priest, also represented the preincarnate messiah / the Lamb / Jesus Christ. The preincarnate messiah / the Lamb / Jesus Christ considered Joshua the son of Jozadak, to be a *typology for himself / messiah / the Lamb / Jesus Christ. So the preincarnate messiah / the Lamb / Jesus Christ, provided a message to the future incarnate messiah / the Lamb / Jesus Christ, to walk blamelessly in order to be given the opportunity to govern the house of Israel, to have charge in the courts, and to hold a place in heaven.*

Zechariah amazingly told us the name of the messiah who is able to stand before Satan his accuser. 'Joshua' is the Hebrew form of the Greek name 'Jesus.'

The further message through Zechariah was that Joshua / Jesus would be snatched from the fire (of hell). Joshua / Jesus would come dressed in filthy clothes (bearing the sins of the nation of Israel, and by extension, the sins of the world). And then Joshua / Jesus would be redressed in rich garments. While the highest of high priests would have no sin of his own, Joshua / Jesus would bear the sin of the world.

Zechariah continued to describe the consecration of Joshua / Jesus, as he would become God's high priest. He would be dressed in the clothing of the high priest (with the high priest's turban, not a crown), and dressed by God's angel.

Joshua / Jesus would become the fulfiller of God Most High's Law, governor of God Most High's house / King over creation, eternal judge of God Most High's courts, and hold position as royalty. The high priest's clean turban would come first, then the king's crown would be added.

God Most High's plan included raising up a nation of priests that would serve under this high priest, priests who must go through the process of consecration in order to become priests worthy to serve under the high priest Joshua / Jesus.

God Most High's message through Zechariah also told that this high priest and king Joshua / Jesus would be known as the 'branch.' In Greek, the word 'branch' became 'nazarene' / nazoraios / ναζωραιος. Messiah would be called,

'Joshua / Jesus the high priest and king, the Branch / Nazarene.'

The message of Zechariah continued. 'See, the stone I have set in front of Joshua! There are seven eyes on that one stone, and I will engrave an inscription on it, and I will remove the sin of this land in a single day.' Zechariah 3:9

When Jesus Christ asked his disciples, 'Who do you say that I am?' *Peter finally answered,* 'You are the Christ, the Son of the Living God.'

Jesus answered to Peter, 'On this rock I will build my church, and the gates of Hades will not overcome it.' *(Matthew 16:13-20) It was also the first time that Jesus used the word 'church' / ecclesia /* εκκλεσια.

In Jesus Christ's depiction of himself to John the Revelator, and Jesus Christ's message to the seven churches in Revelation 1-3, the seven eyes on that one stone portrayed the image of the church with seven eras of seven dominant theological positions. The effects of the 'stone' / 'rock' began with the first coming of Jesus Christ. But the full effects of the 'stone' / 'rock' will not end until the second coming of Jesus Christ when Jerusalem Israel will finally embrace that stone and provide a setting for that stone so that Jerusalem Israel will not be able to be moved.

'On that day, when all the nations of the earth are gathered against Jerusalem, I will make Jerusalem an immovable rock for all the nations. All who try to move it will injure themselves.' Zechariah 12:3.

Zechariah's prophecy also provided a picture of the effects of the work of the promised and prophesied messiah. The promised and prophesied messiah will bring to every single person who was a believer in messiah (BC) or a follower of the Lamb (AD), the opportunity to invite neighbors to sit under their own vine and fig tree. It was a picture of the fully established kingdom of heaven on earth.

The New Testament understanding of Jesus Christ as priest of the order of Melchizedek

After the crucifixion, death, resurrection and ascension of Jesus Christ, the writer to the Hebrews identified the promised and prophesied messiah as being of the order of Melchizedek, and provided an explanation for why this distinction was necessary.

If perfection could have been attained through the Levitical priesthood (for on the basis of it the law was given to the people), why was there still need for another priest to come – one of the order of Melchizedek, not in the order of Aaron?

For when there is a change of the priesthood, there must also be a change of the law. The one of whom these things are said belonged to a different tribe, and no one from that tribe has ever served at the altar.

For it is clear that our Lord descended from Judah, and in regard to that tribe, Moses said nothing about priests. And what we have said is even more clear if another priest like Melchizedek appears, one who has become a priest not on the basis of a regulation as to his ancestry but on the basis of the power of an indestructible life. For it is declared: 'You are a priest forever, in the order of Melchizedek.'

The former regulation is set aside because it was weak and useless (for the law made nothing perfect), and a better hope is introduced, by which we draw near to God. Hebrews 7:12-19

Jesus Christ came as the one authentic prophesied and promised messiah. Unique from and higher than other orders of priests, the prophesied and promised messiah was to be of the order of the first Melchizedek who was originally prophet, priest and king of Salem; three roles in one person. Having three roles in one person was a status that was higher than a single position as a prophet, or priest, or king.

Melchizedek / Shem was the covenant bearer of the messianic lineage and held the position of 'King of Righteousness.' Shem was the first to hold the position after Noah and Noah's family exited the antediluvian / preflood world and the ark. Melchizedek / Shem, approximately four hundred sixty years old at the time, was the person who confirmed the call of Abram / Abraham to be the lineage bearer for the promised and prophesied messiah, and also confirmed the covenant of God Most High with humanity through the descendants of Abram / Abraham (Genesis 14:18).

Shem was the <u>person</u>. Melchizedek is the <u>title</u> ('Malek' means king. 'Zedek' means righteousness.). Shem was altogether prophet, priest and king. Melchizedek was the <u>King</u> of Salem, later known as Jerusalem. The title of righteousness qualified Shem as <u>priest</u> and as a priest, Shem provided Abram / Abraham with the communion elements of bread and wine. The communion elements would not be instituted again until Jesus Christ offered them to the disciples gathered in the Upper Room on the night before his crucifixion. Shem's act of confirming the call of Abram / Abraham was a result of his role as <u>prophet</u> of Most High God.

Nowhere in the lineage of Abram / Abraham, with the exception of Shem, was there any mention of a single person holding all three roles of prophet, priest, and king. In fact, there was no other record of anyone else in the world having simultaneously held the roles of prophet, priest, and king. But the promised and prophesied messiah must hold all three roles of prophet, priest and king after the order of Melchizedek.

The nation of Israel was designated by God Most High to be an entire nation of priests.

The Levitical priesthood, established as the people of Israel exited Egypt (1446 BC) were comprised of descendants of Levi, Jacob / Israel's third son with Leah, and Abraham's great grandson. Only descendants of one of the twelve tribes of Israel were Levitical priests.

But Shem who was one of the three sons of Noah that entered the postdiluvian / postflood world via the ark, represented all the people of the earth that were dedicated to God Most High. To live under the priesthood of the priest of the order of Melchizedek would mean that all who were dedicated to God Most High would be beneficiaries of this priest's work.

The writer to the Hebrew followers of the Lamb / Jesus Christ, further described the dynamics of the promised and prophesied messiah being a priest of the of the order of Melchizedek.

And it was not without an oath! Others became priests without any oath, but Jesus became a priest with an oath when God said to Jesus: 'The Lord has sworn and will not change his mind; 'You are a priest forever."

Because of this oath, Jesus has become the guarantee of a better covenant. Now there have been many of those priests, since death prevented them from continuing in office. But because Jesus lives forever, Jesus has a permanent priesthood. Therefore, Jesus is able to save completely those who come to God through Jesus Christ, because Jesus Christ always lives to intercede for them. Hebrews 7:20-25

When Jesus Christ died and rose again, a number of events happened.

- *The temple veil that covered the holy of holies was rent in two.*
- *Hundreds of people who had previously died and were buried, experienced their graves opened and they rose from death.*
- *The room in the temple where the court of the Sanhedrin met was totally destroyed and the Sanhedrin would not meet in that room again.*

From the point of Jesus Christ's resurrection onward, Jesus Christ would effectively fulfill the combined roles of prophet, priest and king for Israel; and provide the same service for the followers of the Lamb throughout the world.

All other priests have their priesthood ended with their death. But the priest of the order of Melchizedek is a priest forever. Therefore, in order for the new order of the law of Melchizedek to be established, there must be a prophet, priest and king who experiences death and yet lives forever. Only a priest that is able to live forever can establish and enforce his roles as prophet, priest and king, forever.

The Israelites who accepted Jesus Christ as Lord became known as 'followers of the Way' / 'Christians.' The Israelites who did not accept Jesus Christ as Lord became known as the remnant of Judah or Jews. Those who did not accept Jesus Christ as Lord remained the nation of Israel.

Near the end of the times of the Gentiles, God Most High's focus will return to the remnant of Israel that descended from those who rejected Jesus Christ as their promised and prophesied messiah. In preparation for the return of messiah / the Lamb / Jesus Christ, God Most High will prepare a remnant from the people of Israel to finally recognize Jesus Christ as their promised and prophesied messiah. Once the remnant of the people of Israel have recognized Jesus Christ as their promised and prophesied messiah, the remnant of the people of Israel will then be qualified to become priests of God Most High in the fully established kingdom of heaven on earth.

Such a high priest meets our need – one who is holy, blameless, pure, set apart from sinners, exalted above the heavens. Unlike the other high priests, this one does not need to offer sacrifices day after day, first for his own sins, and then for the sins of the people. He sacrificed for their sins once for all when he offered himself. For the law appoints as high priests, men who are weak. But the oath, which came after the law, appointed the Son, who has been made perfect forever. Hebrews 7:26-28

It was a requirement of the Law given to Moses that before the priests could offer sacrifices to cover the sins of the people, the priests must first offer sacrifices to cover their own sins.

Jesus Christ knew no sin. But when he was crucified, he took upon himself the sins of the world. In this way, the sacrifice of Jesus Christ provided the covering for all sins, and provided a way for all believers in messiah (BC) and followers of the Lamb (AD) to become qualified to serve as priests.

The point of what we are saying is this: We do have such a high priest, who sat down at the right hand of the throne of the Majesty in heaven, and who serves in the sanctuary, the true tabernacle set up by the Lord, not by humans. Hebrews 8:1-2

In order to fulfill the requirements of what it is to be God Most High, God Most High's plan for redeeming the world needed to have some kind of finality, a finality of sacrifice, a sacrifice that would be so complete that no other sacrifice would be needed to cover the comprehensive sin of the world. It has been God Most High's prerogative to institute the same person of God to be both the sacrifice and the high priest to fulfill the role of bringing complete propitiation.

Only with a priest that is divine, and a sanctuary that is established by God Most High, can humanity have any hope of receiving a perfect righteousness that is required for an eternity defined as perfection.

The promised and prophesied messiah became that high priest, able to fulfill the requirement of being fully human and fully divine, possessing two natures, the divine nature of God Most High and the perfection that humanity was created to possess. This kind of high priest would not be limited by imperfection or the finiteness of human earthly living, and therefore would also be qualified to also hold the position of king, possessing the throne of the Majesty in heaven and fulfilling all that the first man and the first woman were originally created to be.

When Christ came as high priest of the good things that are already here, Christ went through the greater and more perfect tabernacle that is not made with human hands, that is to say, not a part of this creation. Christ did not enter by means of the blood of goats and calves; but Christ entered the Most Holy Place once for all by his own blood, having obtained eternal redemption. Hebrews 9:11-12

How much more, then, will the blood of Christ, who through the eternal Spirit offered himself unblemished to God, cleanse our consciences from acts that lead to death, so that we may serve the living God! Hebrews 9:14

All of the blood sacrifices of the world, provided only partial cleansing because there was and is no sinless blood available that could actually remove all the stain of sin... except the perfect blood from a life perfectly lived without sin.

Only the blood of the perfect fully divine and fully human messiah was able to meet the requirement of being the perfect sacrifice, and providing what is necessary to fully fulfill the role of God's highest priest.

Two Messiahs? or The Same Messiah with Two Works? – messiach ben Yosef / Ephraim and messiach ben David

Some students of the biblical record, claim that the biblical record prophesied two messiahs. Others claim that the prophecies pointed to one messiah who accents two distinctly different roles.

The 'two messiahs' tradition came out of the recognition that in describing the prophesied messiah, there were conflicts. For example, does the promised and prophesied messiah bring peace? Or does the promised and prophesied messiah bring war because he will battle and defeat the enemies of God Most High and of the kingdom of heaven?

The messiah was to come riding on a donkey. And the messiah is to come with the clouds of heaven, to gather his armies for battle.

The messiah was to come in peace as a suffering servant (Isaiah 53). And the messiah was to come as a conqueror to defeat the enemies of the people of Israel.

The two messianic titles were messiach ben Yosef / Ephraim as the king of peace (Zechariah 9:9-10), and messiach ben David as the conquering king (Zechariah 13:2-4 and 14).

Messiach ben Yosef / Ephraim would come and suffer just as Joseph suffered because of his brothers, and for his brothers. Just as Joseph redeemed his brothers and brought salvation in the midst of famine, the messiach ben Yosef would also redeem and bring salvation. Joseph was placed in a position to save the physical bodies of the people of Israel. Through his own suffering, the messiah ben Joseph was to be placed in a position to also save the physical bodies of God Most High's people through the initiation of resurrection. The suffering servant messiah was best described in Isaiah 53.

Messiach ben David / Son of David, is to come as the kingly messiah to assume reigning on the throne of God and to rule as earth's king, forever, over all the nations of the earth. It was the promise that God Most High made with David, that one of his descendants would rule Israel, and that one day, Israel would rule the world. The Son of David will come fulfilling the title of King of kings and Lord of lords. In order to accomplish this great feat of being King of kings over all the nations, the hearts and minds of the people of the nations will need to be changed in order to even recognize the authority of the King of kings. Messiach ben David / Son of David, will come in the clouds, displaying his glory. The promised and prophesied messiah coming in the clouds was best described after Daniel described the four beasts; lion, bear, leopard, and terrifying beast (Daniel 7:13). Isaiah also described the conquering messiah in Isaiah 2.

When Joseph's brothers went to Egypt during the worldwide famine, they stood before Joseph and did not recognize him. When they returned to Egypt again for more food, they ate with Joseph and they did not recognize him… until Joseph told them who he was.

The people of Israel did not recognize Jesus Christ as their messiah when he came the first time. Even Jesus Christ's disciples did not recognize the resurrected Jesus until he stood among them and told them who he was. Messiah / the Lamb / Jesus Christ will not return for the second time until the remnant of the people of Israel that remain, are able to willingly recognize him as their promised and prophesied messiah.

The view of many rabbis has been that Jesus Christ did not bring peace to the world when he came. Therefore, Jesus Christ could not be recognized in any form as messiah. For those who embraced this belief, the prophecies that Jesus Christ fulfilled during his earthly ministry, were nullified in their minds.

In reality, Jesus Christ fulfilled many of the prophecies that applied to messiah, the first time he came. Jesus Christ's fulfillment of so many of the prophecies documented in the Old Testament / Tanakh provided reason to trust that the rest of the promises and prophecies concerning messiah, will be fulfilled when he returns.

For those who have chosen to be followers of the Lamb / Jesus Christ, it is obvious that Jesus Christ fulfilled the first role of messiach ben Yosef / Ephraim during his earthly ministry. And he will return to fulfill the second role of messiach ben David / Son of David when he returns.

But the idea that there must be two men to fill the two roles, still lingers today. For those who rejected Jesus

Christ as the promised and prophesied messiah, but who understood the prophecies of Daniel who told of the time when messiah would arrive, and of Isaiah who described the suffering servant, etc., the explanations for not recognizing Jesus Christ as messiah two thousand years ago, consisted of rationalizations and denials.

If God Most High would not have been faithful to the people of Israel by sending messiach ben Yosef / Ephraim at the prophesied time the first time, then how could the same people trust that God Most High would be faithful in fulfilling the second role of messiach ben David / Son of David?

The red dragon / serpent / Satan, Inc. will be taking advantage of the confusion concerning the biblical descriptions of the two roles of messiah when he supplies the world with the two beasts of Revelation 13.

The beast of the sea / false prophet / eighth king beast will appear to be the suffering servant and will experience a near fatal injury. His recovery will be utilized as 'proof' that he is messianic in nature.

The little horn / eleventh king / final horn on the shaggy goat / prince who is to come / king that will exalt himself / beast of the earth / final world ruler, will prove himself to be superior in battle.

These two men will comprehensively mimic the fulfillment of the prophecies that described Jesus Christ's earthly ministry as messiah ben Yosef / Ephraim, and the prophecies that described the work that Jesus Christ will accomplish when he returns as messiach ben David / Son of David.

The Old Testament / Tanakh prophet Zechariah portrayed the Lord as rebuking Satan and then rebuking Satan again (Zechariah 3:2). In the context of this portrayal of Joshua the high priest, as a typology for Jesus Christ, the fact that the Lord rebuked Satan twice, was interpreted as a precursor for the two workings of Jesus Christ. Joshua the high priest must first deal with personal sin and set the course for walking in obedience to God Most High. The second work portrayed Joshua in association with the seven eyes on the stone, removing sin of the land of in a single day which depicted the promised and prophesied messiah as defeating the enemies of God Most High and of the kingdom of heaven on the Day of Atonement / Yom Kippur – fall feast.

Jesus Christ's first coming accomplished work that was focused upon the redemption of individuals and humanity. Jesus Christ came the first time to bring a path for salvation and redemption.

The second coming of Jesus Christ will focus on the defeat of nations that continue their stance in rebellion against God Most High and against the kingdom of heaven. Jesus Christ will provide reclamation of the earth and fully establish the kingdom of heaven on earth, assuming the throne of God Most High over all nations, that will be eternally secured.

Reasons Why the Nation of Israel Rejected Jesus Christ as the Promised and Prophesied Messiah, and God Most High's Response

The title 'messiah' / 'messiach' is Hebrew. The title 'Christ' / 'Christos' is Greek. They both mean, 'the anointed one' and designated a unique position that could only be filled by one individual in all the world and throughout all time, sent and anointed by God Most High.

During Jesus Christ's earthly ministry, there were some in Israel who accepted Jesus Christ as the promised and prophesied messiah; beginning with his mother, and then his cousin John the Baptist, the twelve apostles, the disciples who were both men and women, and those that believed Jesus Christ's teachings or were healed or experienced some other kind of miracle because of Jesus Christ. Those who were believers in Jesus Christ as the promised and prophesied messiah and chose to be followers of the Lamb, were the first to be called 'Christians.'

But the nation of Israel's religious ruling body at the time, the Sanhedrin (with the exception of Nicodemus), *believed and taught, that Jesus was a false prophet, a blasphemer, and a false messiah / someone posing as messiah.*

The religious leaders and elders in the nation of Israel, compiled a list of rationales for why they rejected Jesus Christ as the promised and prophesied messiah. But all their rationales were based upon rejecting the message of God Most High that was provided through Moses and the prophets, or based upon lies that they concocted and then perpetrated.

The religious leaders and elders taught the people that Jesus of Nazareth was an illegitimate child which would have disqualified him for sitting on the throne of Israel and for filling the position of messiah, and a blasphemer which would have also rendered Jesus to be ineligible to be able to be considered for the role of messiah.

The people who supported the religious leaders and elders, followed in the path which the religious leaders and elders led them in.

The culture that was embraced at that time, was established by the teachings and practices of the religious leaders and elders that created an environment for the people of Israel to easily reject Jesus Christ as the promised and prophesied messiah.

First, the leaders and the people of the nation of Israel had grown accustomed to rejecting the commands of the kingdom of heaven.

And Jesus said to them: 'You have a fine way of setting aside the commands of God in order to observe your own traditions! For Moses said, 'Honor your father and your mother,' and, 'Anyone who curses his father or mother must be put to death.' But you say that if a man says to his father or mother; 'Whatever help you might otherwise have received from me is Corban' (that is, a gift devoted to God), then you no longer let him do anything for his father or mother. Thus, you nullify the word of God by your tradition that you have handed down. And you do many things like that.' Mark 7:9-13

The ten commandments had caused Judaism to be unique among the religious options available during ancient times. There was a purpose for each of the ten commandments. Each commandment was based upon the character and nature of God Most High, and upon how

God Most High envisioned healthy relationships between God and humanity, and also for how God Most high envisioned healthy human relationships to be expressed. In order to understand God Most High's character and nature, it was important to practice the rules that God Most High established. To break a commandment was to violate the principles of the kingdom of heaven, the kingdom of life. To break a commandment was an act of rebellion against the created order that God the Creator had established. To break a commandment was an act of aggression against God Most High and against the kingdom of heaven.

Each act of aggression against the kingdom of heaven moves the kingdom of heaven further away. The kingdom of rebellion and the kingdom of heaven cannot coexist. These kingdoms are such opposites that they seek to destroy each other.

The fifth of the ten commandments, was a command to honor your father and your mother. The fifth commandment was an instruction to care for parents instead of casting parents aside as they aged. Wisdom comes with age. But if a person is not willing to hear wisdom, then parents may be viewed as merely weak and useless organisms that consume limited resources, and therefore worthy of being cast aside or euthanized.

The Lord taught that all human life has been created as a result of creation, and is a treasure of God the Creator who created it. All human life is valued in God Most High's eyes. God Most High's offer of eternal life began with simple human life created at the beginning of this seven thousand years era. God Most High's vision for life has always been that human life is precious and humanity's best experiences for living, will come in the future, not in the past. God the Creator's entire creative mission has been to preserve human life and to fully transform human life into a magnificent treasure.

God Most High has provided the opportunity for human life to experience redemption, along with a process of baptism, cleansing, perfection, and sealing by God Most High, for the purpose of receiving promises and blessing.

When life is measured on the scale of eternity, then the helpless young and weary aged have value, unmeasurable value. Life at all stages has always been valued by God the Creator. To be valued by God the Creator causes what God the Creator values, to be more valuable than any finite human being can even imagine.

The commandment to honor one's father and mother was a requirement to take care of them in their old age, as the parents cared for the child in the child's young age. It was an act that was intended to mirror God Most High's provisions made for us. God Most High cares for us when we are unable to care for ourselves.

What Jesus Christ referred to in this message that identified their failure to honor their fathers and mothers, was the custom that some people would practice in diverting the funds that should have gone to the care of parents, into the coffers of the synagogue. The thought behind this activity was to give a gift to the religious organization while simultaneously denying parents the funds that they needed for living. The rationale was that if the funds were diverted to God Most High / 'corban' then there would be nothing to forgive.

The practice of diverting funds into the synagogue / 'corban,' was a source of revenue for the temple / synagogue system. So, when Jesus Christ spoke against this practice, the religious leaders and elders recognized an attack upon their source of wealth and power. This was just one of many things that Jesus Christ taught that offended the religious leaders and elders, and that the religious leaders and elders believed threatened their own wealth and power. And the response of the leaders and elders of the people of Israel, to the perceived attack upon their personal wealth and power, was to reject Jesus Christ as the promised and prophesied messiah.

Another reason for rejecting Jesus Christ as the promised and prophesied messiah was that the leaders and the nation of Israel had become accustomed to rejecting the prophets of God Most High, for centuries. Consequently, when Jesus Christ appeared among them, they were already skilled in how to dispose of true prophets of God Most High. Jesus Christ understood that ultimately, the leaders of the nation of Israel along with their followers, would reject him as the prophetic promised and prophesied messiah, and dispose of him as well (Matthew 21:33-46, Mark 12:1-12, Luke 20:9-19, etc.).

But Jesus Christ was a product of Israel. God Most High's entire purpose for creating and fostering the nation of Israel, was so that God Most High could produce a messiah through the nation of Israel. That message was inherent within the covenant promise agreement of circumcision, first provided to Abram / Abraham, Isaac, and Jacob / Israel. That message was foundational as the purpose for the seven required feasts and the Law given through Moses to the people of Israel. That message was amplified through the nation spending forty years in the wilderness as a preparation for them to enter the Promised Land. It was within God Most High's promise to David that his descendant, messiach ben David / Son of David, would one day rule over Israel with a kingdom that would reign forever. Etc.

But the leaders of the nation of Israel, set aside their previous two thousand years of covenantal history aside that had begun with Abram / Abraham, in order to reject Jesus Christ as their promised and prophesied messiah.

Jesus Christ's teachings were abhorrent to the leaders of the nation of Israel.

For example, Jesus said: 'I have come to bring fire on the earth, and how I wish it were already kindled!'

'Do you think I came to bring peace on earth? No, I tell you, but division. From now on there will be five in one family divided against each other, three against two and two against three. They will be divided, father against son and son against father, mother against daughter and daughter against mother, mother-in-law against daughter-in-law and daughter-in-law against mother-in-law.' Luke 12:49

Even in the synagogue of his hometown, the people took offense against what Jesus Christ taught.

Jesus said to them, 'Only in his hometown, among his relatives and in his own house is a prophet without honor.' He could not do any miracles there, except lay his hands on a few sick people and heal them. And he was amazed at their lack of faith. Mark 6:1-6

Notice that a lack of faith has the power to stifle the will of God Most High for individuals as well as stifling an individual's ability to experience miracles.

There were many reasons why the leaders of the nation of Israel rejected Jesus Christ as messiah: belief in the fake news of the day, the expectation that becoming a follower of Jesus Christ required an internal dedication to set aside one's favorite sins and seek to become holy, the expectation that being a follower of Jesus Christ required practicing honesty and compassion, the assessment that what Jesus Christ taught was deplorable, the expectation that wealth and prestige and power were considered by the kingdom of heaven to be of lesser value than engaging in integrity and practicing love, the expectation that one's power was to be used to advance the kingdom of heaven and its citizens instead of advancing one's own ability to control and experience personal comfort at the expense of others, etc.

What Jesus Christ taught and did, was mightily offensive and threatening to the leaders of the nation of Israel. All four of the gospel writers of the New Testament, documented the opposition that the leaders of the nation of Israel engaged in against Jesus Christ. The leaders of the nation of Israel, opted to protect their personal power and positions, rejecting the man they perceived to be a threat to their personal power and positions, and trading away their opportunity to experience eternal life in the kingdom of heaven.

And the leaders of the nation of Israel led the people of Israel to also embrace their position of rejecting Jesus Christ as the promised and prophesied messiah.

Because the leaders of the nation of Israel rejected Jesus Christ as the promised and prophesied messiah, Jesus needed to be promoted as a fake, a liar / blasphemer concerning his claim to be divine and sovereign.

The religious leaders and elders sought to use the clause in the Law of Moses that condemns a false prophet to death. They used this clause to justify putting Jesus Christ to death. It was this motivation that set the crucifixion of Jesus Christ into action.

Jesus then began to teach them that the Son of Man must suffer many things and be rejected by the elders, chief priests and teachers of the law, and that he must be killed and after three days rise again. Mark 8:31

Jesus even knew that he would die on the cross, and that only three days later he would be resurrected.

When the majority of the people of the nation of Israel rejected Jesus Christ as messiah, they added their support to the crucifixion of Jesus Christ.

And after the resurrection of Jesus Christ, the majority of the people of the nation of Israel, chose to believe the false story that the leaders of the nation of Israel perpetrated, that instead of being resurrected, the disciples stole his body and hid it (Matthew 28:11-15).

After Jesus' death and resurrection: While the women who had discovered the empty tomb were on their way, behold, some of the guard came into the city to report to the chief priests all the things that had happened. When the chief priests had consulted with the elders and devised a plan, they gave the soldiers many pieces of silver to the soldiers saying, 'Say that his disciples came at night and stole him while we were asleep.' If the governor were to hear about this, we will persuade him and will keep you secure.'

So they took the money. They did as they were instructed. And spread this report among the Jews. It remains widely circulated to this day. Matthew 28:11-15 translated

Note, the body of Jesus was never discovered. If it had been discovered, the entire Christian movement would have been quashed.

God Most High's response to the people of Israel's rejection of Jesus Christ as the promised and prophesied messiah

The people of Israel missed it! And it was a big miss! Humungous!!!

The people of Israel missed their promised and prophesied messiah's coming when Jesus Christ was among

them. And missing that one event, put all of what was promised to them, in jeopardy.

In cutting off their relationship with their promised and prophesied messiah, they also cut off their relationship with God Most High.

But God Most High never ever reneges on a covenantal promise. God Most High covenanted with Abram / Abraham, Isaac, Jacob / Israel, Moses and the people of Israel / David, etc. that there would be a time when they would all share resurrected and regenerated live dwelling with God on earth.

With the rejection of Jesus Christ as the promised and prophesied messiah, what was God Most High to do?

To incorporate the rebellious people of Israel into God Most High's redemption, reclamation and regeneration plan, would be to bring that rebellion back into the perfect environment that God Most High is striving to achieve.

To totally and forever reject the people of Israel, in the manner that they rejected God Most High, would cause God Most High to become a liar and if God Most High were to become a liar, it would rip into the cosmic fabric of eternity's stability.

The Old Testament / Tanakh prophets Jeremiah and Isaiah had documented that God Most High would respond to the rejection of messiah, by causing the people of Israel who rejected messiah, to become people with eyes that would not be able to see and ears that would not be able to hear.

The prophet Jeremiah, around 626 to 585 BC, documented the era when the people of Israel would experience the era of 'blindness,' (Jeremiah 5:20-22). That blindness came approximately six hundred years later.

Isaiah (fl. 740 to 681 BC) also documented that God Most High foreknew that the people of Israel would reject the promised and prophesied messiah when he came.

In Isaiah 29, God Most High spoke of the city of Jerusalem / 'Ariel' that would experience the removal of God Most High's protection after rejecting God Most High's *plan. Jerusalem / Ariel would experience years of cycles of festivals that would be fruitless.*

With Jesus Christ's crucifixion and fulfillment of the prophecies of the spring feasts, the feasts that the Jewish people observed, began their years of fruitlessness. And yet the people of Israel continued to attempt to celebrate their fruitless required feasts as if nothing happened.

During the era of the time of Jacob's Trouble, the people of Israel will again attempt to celebrate the required feasts, as their desperate hope to connect with God Most High. Their observances of the required feasts will again be fruitless (possibly another source of motivation for the beast of the earth to discontinue the temple sacrificial system). Their attempt to celebrate the required feasts will be necessary in establishing the foundation for the future abomination of desolation event. And the future abomination of desolation event will be necessary in order for messiah / the Lamb / Jesus Christ to fulfill the prophecies of the fall feasts.

The prophet Isaiah detailed the separation from God Most High that the people of Israel would experience after rejecting their promised and prophesied messiah. And Isaiah described the end of that period of estrangement. But Isaiah began with the description of the conclusion of the estrangement period, and then explained the condition of the people of Israel who would reject Jesus Christ.

According to Isaiah's record, this estrangement between the people of Israel and God Most High, will conclude with many enemies becoming like fine dust. Also associated with their enemies becoming like fine dust,
Moreover, the multitude of your enemies will be like fine dust. And like chaff, the multitude of ruthless hordes will blow away; and yes, it will be suddenly in an instant. Isaiah 29:5 translated

While this description clearly described the return of messiah / the Lamb / Jesus Christ, the fact that Jesus Christ did not fight against the enemies of the nation of Israel during his earthly ministry, was just another reason for the leaders of the nation of Israel to reject Jesus as the promised and prophesied messiah.

Isaiah's description also identified the period of time when the people of Israel would not recognize their messiah, as beginning with their rejection of their promised and prophesied messiah.

For the Lord has poured out on you, the spirit of deep sleep, And has closed your eyes to the prophets, and covered your heads from understanding the seers. Isaiah 29:10 translated

According to Isaiah, the 'blindness' will be relieved with the events surrounding the arrival of messiah:

In that day, the deaf will hear the words of the book, and out of the darkness and out of the obscurity of darkness, the eyes of the blind will see. Isaiah 29:18 translated

Isaiah also described the king who will reign in righteousness. And with the king who will reign in righteousness, the eyes of those who see will no longer be closed, and the ears of those who hear will listen (Isaiah 32:3 (32)).

When Jesus Christ came the first time, and Jesus' cousin John the Baptist asked him if he was the one they were looking for or should they expect someone else? Jesus' answer was, 'The blind receive sight, the lame walk, those who have leprosy are cleansed, the deaf hear, the dead are raised, and the good news is proclaimed to the poor' (Matthew 11:2-6).

This was a reference to Jesus Christ fulfilling the prophecy given to Isaiah (Isaiah 9:1-3). But it was also a confirmation offered to his cousin John the Baptist, that Jesus Christ was the promised and prophesied messiah.

Jesus Christ's providing sight to the blind and hearing to the deaf, acted as a typology for his power and ability to restore both the understanding and acceptance of a right relationship between the people of Israel and God Most High. It also acted as a typology for his power and ability to restore and regenerate human life in preparation for the reestablishment of the environment that once existed with the Garden of Eden / garden of God / paradise.

Even though the prophets Isaiah and Jeremiah had foretold of the people of Israel's rejection of their promised

and prophesied messiah, the people of Israel still had the opportunity to choose to accept Jesus Christ as their promised and prophesied messiah. Those that believed Jesus Christ was the promised and prophesied messiah, baptized Jesus Christ (John the Baptist), became his disciples and followers, and they went out into the world so that the message of the arrival of this messiah would spread around the globe.

But for the leaders of the nation of Israel, Jesus Christ was an abhorrent choice for filling the role of messiah. Jesus Christ taught that the personal power that the leaders of Israel had accumulated for themselves utilizing their positions for personal gain, was not what God Most High had envisioned for the leadership of the nation of Israel. Jesus Christ taught that what they had gained for their own personal benefit at the expense of other people, was unacceptable in the kingdom of heaven. The enraged and infuriated leaders of the people of Israel, truly believed that they were justified in rejecting all aspects of Jesus Christ as messiah.

Jesus Christ's response to their rebellion against God Most High's redemption, reconciliation and regeneration plan, included embedding the deeper messages of the kingdom of heaven, into the parables that Jesus told. Jesus Christ even told his disciples that the secrets of heaven were being kept from those who rejected the promised and prophesied messiah.

Jesus Christ identified some of the parables that he told, as reveling the secrets of the kingdom of heaven to those who could see and hear their meaning, while keeping the message hidden from those who would not. The parable of the sower (Matthew 13:14-23), the parable of the weeds (Matthew 13:24-30, 13:36-43), the parables of the mustard seed and yeast (Matthew 13:31-33), the parables of the hidden treasure and the pearl (Matthew 13:44-46), and the parable of the net (Matthew 13:46-52) were some of the parables where Jesus Christ specifically used to point out how the rebellion against God Most High and against the kingdom of heaven, had rendered the leaders of Israel to *become spiritually blind and deaf. The messages of these parables incorporated multiple layers of meaning along with multiple layers of message. But embedded within the parables of Jesus Christ was the recognition and warning against rejecting Jesus Christ as the promised and prophesied messiah.*

The disciples came to Jesus and asked, 'What is your reason for speaking to them in parables?'

Jesus answered them, 'Because to you it has been granted the knowledge of the mysteries of the kingdom of heaven. However, it has not been granted to them.'

'For whoever has, will be given in abundance. Whoever has not, even what that one has will be taken away from that one.'

'Because of this, I speak to them in parables; because seeing they do not see, and hearing they do not hear, nor do they understand.'

'This is the fulfillment of the prophecy of Isaiah which says,

'In hearing you will hear and yet not understand.'
'And in seeing you will see and yet not perceive.'
'The heart of this people has grown dull.'
'And with their ears, they have barely heard.'
'And their eyes, they have closed.'
'Otherwise, they should see with their eyes and hear with their ears.'
'Otherwise, they would understand with their heart and would return, and I will heal them."

'However, you are blessed, for your eyes see and your ears hear. Truly I say to you, that many prophets and righteous longed to see what you see, and did not see it, and to hear what you hear, and did not hear it.'

Matthew 13:10-16 (within the parable of the sower) translated *(Isaiah 6:9-10, (6:11-13, defining the timespan of the diaspora)) (See also: Mark 4:10-12, Luke 8:9-10, etc.)*

Jesus spoke all these things in parables to the crowds, and Jesus did not speak to them without a parable; so that it might be fulfilled what was spoken by the prophet, saying:

'I will open my mouth in parables. I will utter things kept secret from the foundation of the world.' Matthew 13:34-35 translated (*Psalm 78:2*)

Matthew concluded his record of this set of parables with this:

Jesus' rejection at Nazareth

It came to pass, that when Jesus had finished these parables, Jesus withdrew from there. Having come into his own region, he was teaching them in their synagogue so that they were astonished and said, 'Where did this man obtain this wisdom and these miraculous powers? Is this not the son of the carpenter? Is his mother not called Mary? And are his brothers James and Joseph and Simon and Judas? And are all his sisters not with us? From where does this man get all these things?'

And they were offended at him.

But Jesus said to them, 'A prophet is not without honor, except in his own hometown and in his own household.'

<u>And Jesus did not do many miracles there because of their unbelief</u>. Matthew 13:53-58 translated

Rejecting Jesus Christ as the promised and prophesied messiah, causes spiritual blindness and deafness. But it also prevents God Most High's redemption, reclamation and regeneration plan from being able to work in one's life. And without redemption, reclamation and regeneration, one is unable to enter into the perfection of the kingdom of heaven / Garden of Eden / garden of God / paradise.

Rebellion against God Most High's plan removes God Most High's full protection and creates an environment of vulnerability.

During the final week before Jesus Christ's crucifixion, As Jesus approached the city (Jerusalem) and saw it, he wept over it. He said, 'If you had only known today what is needed for peace! But now it is hidden from your eyes. For the days will come upon you that your enemies will build an encampment around you, barricading you. And they will surround you and close you in on every side. And they will level you to the ground and your children within you. They will not leave a stone upon a stone within you. For you did not recognize the season of your visitation.' Luke 19:41-44 translated

In 70 AD, forty years after Jesus Christ made this statement recorded by Luke, Jerusalem Israel was destroyed. The nation of Israel went from being occupied by Roman governance to having the people of Israel being dissolved into the Roman empire. The majority of the people of Israel became undesirable subjects and slaves of the Roman empire. And within the Roman Catholic Church, the people of Israel were viewed with disdain, with the responsibility the crucifixion of Jesus Christ being entirely transferred to them.

The majority of the people of Israel lost their peace, their sight, their security, their freedom, their lives, their sovereignty and their right to rule. And they lost the closeness of God Most High's presence and absolute protection. From that point on, the history of the people of Israel has been a history where the people of Israel have been ruled over, destroyed, and exiled. From 70 AD until 1948, the people of Israel did not have a homeland. Jerusalem Israel has been trampled on by the Gentiles during the times of the Gentiles. (Luke 21:24)

But the greater result of the rection of the people of Israel, was for God Most High to place a veil over their eyes for the duration of the times of the Gentiles (2 Corinthians 3:12-18). The result was that the people of Israel as a whole, have been spiritually blind and deaf for almost two thousand years, without the wisdom to recognize that God Most High was faithful to them and faithfully sent to them the promised and prophesied messiah.

What then? What the people of Israel sought so earnestly they did not obtain. The elect among them did, but the others were hardened, as it is written: 'God gave them a spirit of stupor, eyes that could not see and ears that could not hear, to this very day.'

And David says: 'May their table become a snare and a trap, a stumbling block and a retribution for them.' Romans 11:7-9

God the Creator's knowledge from the time when they all lived together in the Garden of Eden / garden of God / paradise, that the promised and prophesied messiah would be rejected

Consistently, the prophecy of Genesis 3, the message in the stars, the layout of the required feasts of Israel, the message of the prophets, and even Jesus Christ's own teaching, all anticipated two separate events of the coming of the promised and prophesied messiah, into the world. The first coming was described with the depiction of messiah as the Lamb of God. The second coming of Jesus Christ was described with the depiction of messiah as the Lion.

God Most High knew while the people of Israel wandered in the desert, that the people of Israel were stiff necked people who would reject the authentic messiah when God Most High sent messiah to them.

God Most High even acknowledged this condition to Moses.

'I have seen these people,' the Lord said to Moses, 'and they are a stiff-necked people.' Exodus 32:9

God Most High knew five hundred years before Jesus Christ was sent to the people of Israel, that the people of Israel would reject the promised and prophesied messiah.

To the prophet Zechariah (fl. 520 to 480 BC), God Most High provided this message:

'This is what the Lord Almighty said: '...they refused to pay attention. Stubbornly they turned their backs and covered their ears. They made their hearts as hard as flint and would not listen to the law or to the words that the Lord Almighty had sent by the Lord's Spirit through the earlier prophets. So the Lord Almighty was very angry.'

'When I called, they did not listen. So when they called, I would not listen,' says the Lord Almighty. 'I scattered them with a whirlwind among all the nations, where they were strangers. The land they left behind them was so desolate that no one traveled through it. This is how they made the pleasant land desolate.' Zechariah 7:11-14

The diaspora in 70 AD, forty years after the crucifixion and resurrection of Jesus Christ was the result of the people of Israel rejecting messiah. When the people of Israel left the land of Israel, the land of Israel became like a desert. When Mark Twain / Samuel Clemens visited Israel, he noted the desolate condition of the land of Israel (1867).

And the land of Israel remained a desert ... until the people of Israel began to return to the land beginning around 1948.

The story of the people of Israel has yet to reach its full conclusion. God Most High does not forget. God Most High remembers God's covenant promises; promises made to Abram / Abraham, Isaac, Jacob / Israel, Moses, the prophets, etc.

The very next passage reads:

The word of the Lord Almighty came to me. This is what the Lord almighty says: 'I am very jealous for Zion. I am burning with jealousy for her.' This is what the Lord says: 'I will return to Zion and dwell in Jerusalem. Then Jerusalem will be called the Faithful City, and the mountain of the Lord Almighty will be called the Holy Mountain.' Zechariah 8:1-3

God Most High must be faithful to God's covenant promises as a part of God's inherent character of truth. The spiritual blindness and deafness of the people of Israel will not remain forever. In fact, messiah / the Lamb / Jesus Christ will not return until the people of Israel have come to recognize him as their promised and prophesied messiah.

Jesus Christ said, 'Jerusalem, Jerusalem, you who kill the prophets and stone those who have been sent to you. How often I longed to gather your children together, like a hen gathers her chicks under her wings. And you were not willing. Look, your house is left desolate! I say to you, you will not see me again from now until you say, 'Blessed is the one who comes in the name of the Lord." Matthew 23:37-39 translated

Jesus Christ will not return to the people of Israel until they are ready to recognize and receive him as the promised and prophesied messiah.

The dynamics of the relationship of the people of Israel with God Most High, during the span of time between the people of Israel's rejection of Jesus Christ as messiah, and the return of messiah / the Lamb / Jesus Christ to the people of Israel

People change. Over time, people's attitudes change. Each generation chooses what will define their lives and what kind of legacy they will leave. This truth has been confirmed since the time of our first ancestors, the first man and the first woman.

And the dynamics of how God Most High has related to the people of Israel has changed over time. God Most High has related according to how each generation has received and followed the direction of God Most High. The fluid dynamics of their relationship has been documented throughout the biblical record.

Possibly the best understanding of the overall dynamics of the relationship between God Most High and the people of Israel, was communicated by the prophet Hosea. Hosea's entire life was a dramatization of the strife that God Most High experienced in God's continuous relationship with the people of Israel. The first fulfillment of Hosea 13, was set in the context of the rebellion of the northern ten tribes of the divided nation of Israel, as they rejected God Most High and fully embraced their worship of baal.

But the message of Hosea 13 concluded with a promise that the contentious relationship would one day end. It would just require two thousand seven hundred years for the relationship between the people of Israel and God Most High to entirely blossom and ripen.

In Hosea 13, 'Ephraim' was another name for the people of Israel. When the people of Israel acted in a cantankerous manner, God Most High would frequently reference them by another name.

Samaria was the capital city of the northern nation of Israel.

Notice how God Most High's plan for relating to the people of Israel, changed over time.

The Lord said: 'When Ephraim spoke, he exalted himself in Israel. But when he offended himself through worshiping baal, he died.'

'Now they sin more and more, and have made for themselves molded images of silver according to their skill. All of them are the work of their craftsman.'

'They say of them, 'They offer human sacrifice and kiss the calves.'

'Therefore, they will be like the morning cloud and like the early dew that disappears; like chaff blown from a threshing floor, and like smoke from a chimney.'

'But I am the Lord your God. Ever since you left the land of Egypt, you have known no God but me, no savior besides me. I cared for you in the wilderness, in the land of great drought.'

'When they had pasture and they were satisfied, they were satisfied and became proud. And so they forgot me. So I will be like a lion to them; like a leopard by the road, I will lurk. I will meet them like a bear deprived of her cubs, and I will tear open their rib cage. And there I will devour them like a lion. The wild animal will tear them apart.'

'Israel, you are destroyed. But your help is from me.' Hosea 13:1-9 translated

'The guilt of Ephraim is kept on record. His sin is stored up.'

'The sorrows of a woman in childbirth, will come on him. But he is a son without wisdom. When the time arrives, he does not present himself to be born.'

'I will deliver them from the power of sheol / the grave. I will redeem them from death. O death, I will be your plagues! O grave, I will be your destruction!' Hosea 13:12-14b translated

When the people of Israel initially rejected Jesus Christ as the promised and prophesied messiah, the decision was made that Jesus Christ would appeal to the Gentiles for a time. Jesus Christ spoke of another sheep pen that would listen to his voice. But always the plan was to one day merge the two flocks (the believers in messiah from the people of Israel (BC) and the predominately Gentile followers of the Lamb (AD)). (John 10:16)

The times of the Gentiles will come to an end. And at the conclusion of the times of the Gentiles, the people of Israel will receive the fulfillment of all that God Most High initially promised within God's covenant with Abram / Abraham, Isaac, Jacob / Israel, Moses, David, the prophets, etc.

Paul wrote: I do not want you to be ignorant of this mystery, brothers and sisters, so that you may not be conceited. Israel has experienced a hardening in part until the full number of the Gentiles has come in, and in this way all Israel will be saved. As it is written:

'The deliverer will come from Zion. He will turn godlessness away from Jacob. And this is my covenant with them when I take away their sins.'

As far as the gospel is concerned, they are enemies for your sake. But as far as election is concerned, they are loved on account of the patriarchs, for God's gifts and his call are irrevocable. Just as you who were at one time disobedient to God have now received mercy as a result of their disobedience, so they too have now become disobedient in order that they too may now receive mercy as a result of God's mercy to you. Romans 11:25-31

(See also Isaiah 27:9-13, Jeremiah 31:29-40.)

When the time that was designated for the people of Israel to experience spiritual blindness and deafness, has expired, then God Most High has promised that they will receive the full benefits of a healthy and whole relationship with God Most High. They will receive protection, and blessing.

> Then the Lord will appear over them. His arrow will flash like lightning.
> The Lord God will blow the trumpet and will march in the storms of the south.
> And the Lord God will shield them.
> They will destroy and overcome with slingstones.
> They will drink and roar as if with wine.

> They will be filled with blood, like the basins used for sprinkling the corners of the altar.
> The Lord their God will save them on that day, as the flock of his people.
> For they will be like the jewels of a crown, lifted like a banner over the Lord's land.
> What great wealth is theirs, what great beauty!
> Grain will make the young men thrive, and new wine the young women. Zechariah 9:14-17 translated

It has been almost two thousand years after the life of Jesus Christ physically dwelling with the people of Israel. Still the people of Israel continue to reject Jesus Christ as a prophet of God Most High and as their promised and prophesied messiah. They still consider Jesus to have been a blasphemer who was crucified and his body was stolen by his disciples. The people of Israel have certainly experienced an era where God Most High / Yahweh has withdrawn a comprehensive level of favor to them.

Most importantly, there is a direct correlation between faith, and the opportunity and ability that God Most High provides in bringing blessing, understanding, and miraculous activity into one's life. This truth will be especially experienced during the era of the time of Jacob's Trouble by both the people of Israel and the followers of the Lamb / Jesus Christ. Those who have faith in Jesus Christ as the promised and prophesied messiah, will be amazed. Those who do not have faith will be amazing because of their apparent ineptitude.

God Most High will not be able to act fully on behalf of the people of Israel until they do find their faith in Jesus Christ as their promised and prophesied messiah. Only after the people of Israel declare that Jesus Christ is Lord will they be able to experience the miracles and healing that God Most High has stored up for them. (Zechariah 12:10, John 19:33-37)

God Most High determined that with the conclusion of the era of the time of Jacob's Trouble, the people of Israel will finally recognize Jesus Christ as their promised and prophesied messiah, will welcome him, and will experience the full blessing that a right relationship with Jesus Christ brings.

The Times of the Gentiles

It has always been God Most High's plan to include Gentiles in receiving the benefits of the blessing of God Most High and everlasting life. It was the plan beginning with the first man and the first woman. It was the plan with Noah and his family who were considered to be Gentiles. And it was the plan from the time of Abram / Abraham, and beyond.

Abram himself was a Gentile, before God Most High called him to be designated as the next in the lineage of messianic covenant bearer. The covenant of God Most High with Abram / Abraham included God Most High's plan that Abram / Abraham's seed would be a light to the nations. (Luke 3:21-38, etc.) The nation of Israel did not even truly begin until Jacob / Israel had twelve sons, and then the nation of Israel was incubated in the nation of Egypt for four hundred thirty years.

Job of the Old Testament, lived around the same time as Abram / Abraham. Job was a Gentile. And yet the book of Job that detailed the ability of Satan to negatively impact human life, along with God Most High's power, ability and willingness to bring restoration to that destruction, was included as standard teaching among the people of Israel. Job's account demonstrated that God Most High's plan and blessings, were not exclusively designated merely for the people of Israel, and that God Most High's blessings were applicable to all of humanity who depend upon God Most High for redemption, reclamation and regeneration.

Including Gentiles as recipients of the benefits of God Most High's redemption, reconciliation and regeneration plan, has always been the plan of God Most High. And the time after the leaders of Israel and their followers rejected Jesus Christ as the promised and prophesied messiah, began the times of the Gentiles.

Jesus Christ's understanding of the place of Gentiles within God Most High's redemption, reclamation and regeneration plan

Theoretically, having the leaders of the people of Israel, and their followers, reject Jesus Christ as messiah, should have placed God Most High's redemption, reclamation and regeneration plan at risk. If the people of Israel who had been entrusted with carrying the message, did not believe, then who would carry the message?

Originally God Most High's plan for making Israel a nation of priests was to give the people of Israel the opportunity to bring the message of God Most High's redemption, reclamation and regeneration plan to the nations. But when the nation of Israel rejected Jesus Christ as messiah, God Most High placed into effect plan B, reaching the Gentiles without the aid of the nation of Israel.

Jesus said: 'I am the good shepherd. I know my sheep and my sheep know me – just as the Father knows me and I know the Father – and I lay down my life for the sheep. I have other sheep that are not of this sheep pen. I must bring them also. They too will listen to my voice, and there shall be one flock and one shepherd.' John 10:14-16

Jesus said to the people of Israel, 'Have you never read in the scriptures: 'The stone the builders rejected has become the capstone. The Lord has done this, and it is marvelous in our eyes?'' *(Psalm 118:22-23)*

'Therefore, I tell you that the kingdom of God will be taken away from you and given to a people who will produce its fruit. He who falls on this stone will be broken to pieces, but he on whom it falls will be crushed.' Matthew 21:42-44

The 'stone' *was Jesus Christ. When Jesus Christ rose from the dead, he became the capstone to God Most High's six thousand / seven thousand years plan. The resurrection of Jesus Christ is marvelous for all who have eyes to see and to perceive the significance of the resurrection of Jesus Christ, because the path has been laid for all believers in messiah (BC) and all followers of the Lamb (AD) to also be resurrected for new life in the kingdom of God / kingdom of heaven.*

Because the religious leaders of Israel and their followers rejected Jesus Christ as messiah, the kingdom of heaven / kingdom of God was taken from them. During Jesus Christ's earthly ministry, they were not good stewards of what God Most High had entrusted to them. The religious leaders were to be the protectors and providers of the message of God Most High for salvation, for eternal life. Instead, they gave to the people a message of the power of the kingdom of Satan, Inc. / kingdom of man. At the time of the earthly ministry of Jesus Christ, the kingdom of Satan, Inc. / kingdom of man had infiltrated the religious organization of the people of Israel, and hijacked it. The 'stone' *fell upon them and they were essentially crushed, shattered, pulverized without hope of being able to have their pieces reassembled.*

When the religions leaders of the people of Isael and their adherents failed to meet required condition of recognizing the promised and prophesied messiah, they effectively rejected the kingdom of heaven / kingdom of God. God's response was to entrust the message to the Gentiles who were then expected to bear fruit, inviting people from all around the world to believe in Jesus Christ as Lord and to become followers of the Lamb / Jesus Christ.

Whether a person belongs to the people of Israel or is a Gentile, those who fall down before this 'stone' *are broken into pieces. But pieces can be used by God Most High to restored as renewed vessels. And those who refused to fall down before this* 'stone' *can only be crushed, shattered and never able to be repaired.*

Jesus also said: 'The people of Israel will fall by the sword and will be taken as prisoners to all the nations. Jerusalem will be trampled on by the Gentiles until the times of the Gentiles are fulfilled. Luke 21:24

Truly Jerusalem has been trampled on by the Gentiles. But Luke documented that the times of the Gentiles has a purpose that must be fulfilled, and at the end of the times of the Gentiles, Jerusalem will again fully belong to Israel. When Jerusalem again fully belongs to Israel, near the end of the era of the time of Jacob's Trouble, then the times of the Gentiles will be truly fulfilled.

The apostles' understanding of the times of the Gentiles

Jesus Christ continued until his crucifixion, to appeal to the people of Israel to accept him as their promised and prophesied messiah. But the people of Israel crucified Jesus Christ, and then believed the lie that denied

Jesus Christ's resurrection / that Jesus' body was stolen, perpetrated by the religious leaders (Matthew 28:11-15). The crucifixion of Jesus Christ was a clear sign that the majority of the people of Israel were not going to be the conduit for communicating the message concerning God Most High's plan for redemption, reclamation and regeneration.

It was during the era of the early apostolic church that began immediately following Jesus Christ's resurrection and ascension into heaven, that the apostles and early disciples went into communities, preached and taught first in the synagogues to the people of Israel, and then to the Gentiles.

In this transition toward taking the message to the Gentiles, discussion began about the process for Gentiles as they became followers of the Lamb / Jesus Christ, for incorporation into the kingdom of heaven.

When they finished, James spoke up. 'Brothers,' he said, 'listen to me. Simon has described to us how God first intervened to choose a people for his name from the Gentiles. The words of the prophets are in agreement with this, as it is written: 'After this I will return and rebuild David's fallen tent. Its ruins I will rebuild, and I will restore it, that the rest of humanity may seek the Lord, even all the Gentiles who bear my name, says the Lord, who does these things' — things known from long ago.' Acts 15:13-18 (reference to Isaiah 49:6, Amos 9:11-12, and possibly other extrabiblical text)

They understood that for a while, David's tent would be fallen. They understood that there would be a period of time when the people of Israel would temporarily fall away from their relationship with God Most High.

And during this time, Gentiles would be given the opportunity to become followers of the Lamb / Jesus Christ. Gentiles would be entrusted to carry and communicate God Most High's plan for redemption, reclamation and regeneration.

They also understood that God Most High would not forget to rebuild David's fallen tent.

When the people of Israel rejected Jesus Christ as the authentic promised and prophesied messiah, the prophecy from Isaiah was fulfilled (Isaiah 6:9-10).

Paul documented the fulfillment of the Holy Spirit's statement to Isaiah. And then Paul identified that the time had come for the message to be given to the Gentiles to carry.

'The Holy Spirit spoke the truth to your ancestors when the Holy Spirit said, 'Go to this people and say, 'You will be ever hearing but never understanding; you will be ever seeing but never perceiving.' For this people's heart has become calloused. They hardly hear with their ears, and they have closed their eyes. Otherwise, they might see with their eyes, hear with their ears, understand with their hearts and turn, and I would heal them.'

'Therefore, I want you to know that God's salvation has been sent to the Gentiles, and they will listen!' Acts 28:25b-28

Many have embraced replacement theology and use Paul's statement as evidence to support their idea. Replacement theology proposed that because of the rejection of Jesus Christ by the nation of Israel, God Most High abandoned the people of Israel and transferred all favor and prophesy of promises made to the people of Israel, onto the Gentiles.

But, if God Most High were to absolutely abandon the people of Israel and forsake God Most High's covenants with the people of Israel, that would effectively cause God Most High to renege on God's covenant agreements, making God Most High a liar and untrustworthy. If God Most High were to actually be a liar, then there would be no assurance to even the Gentiles that God Most High would be faithful to any covenants, including the covenants that God Most High made with the Gentiles.

If God Most High were to be a liar, then there would be no difference between the gods of other religions and God Most High. And the result of all gods being liars would lead to continuous wars among the gods.

But God Most High is truth... absolute truth. What God Most High has said, God Most High will do. The first six days of creation served as the first proof of this.

Moses identified this absolute truth and faithfulness characteristic of God Most High (Numbers 23:19). The prophets understood God Most High's absolute truth and faithfulness as the foundation for all prophecy (Isaiah 46:11, Malachi 3:6). Paul documented the absolute truth and faithfulness of God Most High in the epistle to the Romans

(Romans 9:5). God Most High is the one God that does not lie (Titus 1:2).

God Most High has not forgotten the people and nation of Israel. God Most High's covenants to the people and nation of Israel must be fulfilled.

The apostles and early disciples understood that the message of God Most High would be entrusted to the Gentiles for a time. But at the conclusion of the times of the Gentiles, God Most High would remove the veil that covers the people of Israel so that they do not understand that Jesus Christ is their promised and prophesied messiah. During the era of the time of Jacob's Trouble, God Most High will cause the people of Israel to recognize Jesus Christ as their promised and prophesied messiah, and restore the relationship between God Most High and the people of Israel.

> Consider Abraham: 'He believed God, and it was credited to Abraham as righteousness.' Understand, then, that those who believe are children of Abraham. The Scripture foresaw that God would justify the Gentiles by faith, and announced the gospel in advance to Abraham: 'All nations will be blessed through you.'
> So those who have faith are blessed along with Abraham, the man of faith. Galatians 3:6-9

> In reading this, then, you will be able to understand my insight into the mystery of Christ, which was not made known to people in other generations as it has now been revealed by the Spirit to God's holy apostles and prophets. This mystery is that through the gospel the Gentiles are heirs together with Israel, members together of one body, and sharers together in the promise in Christ Jesus. Ephesians 3:4-6

The mystery of Christ was that the Gentile followers of the Lamb would join with the authentic believers in messiah from the people of Israel, to become coheirs with Jesus Christ. Together the people of Israel and the Gentiles would become coheirs with Jesus Christ.

There would not be an exclusivity of one group over the other.

> Now that faith has come, we are no longer under the supervision of the law. You are all children of God through faith in Christ Jesus, for all of you who were baptized into Christ have clothed yourselves with Christ. There is neither Jew nor Greek, slave nor free,

male nor female, for you are all one in Christ Jesus. If you belong to Christ, then you are Abraham's seed, and heirs according to the promise. Galatians 3:25-29

Paul stressed that followers of Jesus Christ inherit the benefits of the Abrahamic covenant. And within that message was the identification that God Most High did not forget the covenant made with the people of Israel.

If you confess with your mouth, 'Jesus is Lord,' and believe in your heart that God raised Jesus Christ from the dead, you will be saved. For it is with your heart that you believe and are justified, and it is with your mouth that you confess and are saved.
As the Scripture says, 'Anyone who trusts in Jesus Christ as Lord will never be put to shame.' For there is no difference between Jew and Gentile – the same Lord is Lord of all and richly blesses all who call on the Lord, for 'Everyone who calls on the name of the Lord will be saved.' Romans 10:9-13

During the times of the Gentiles, the people of Israel who have rejected Jesus Christ as the promised and prophesied messiah, have still been bound by the requirements of the Law that were provided through Moses and written in the Torah / Pentateuch / first five books of the Bible.

To fulfill the Law given through Moses and to offer sacrifice for the forgiveness of sin, there was a continual tabernacle or temple in the history of Israel between the time of Moses (1446 BC) until forty years after the crucifixion and resurrection of Jesus Christ (70 AD), with only a seventy year break during the exile (586 to 516 BC) and a three year break following the first abomination of desolation event (167 to 164 BC). The seventy year exile was less than one generation so that the nation of Israel was not cut off entirely from God Most High's provision for forgiveness during that time.

In 70 AD when the 'second temple' was destroyed, the nation of Israel was truly was cut off from access to the forgiveness plan God Most High had presented through the Law given through Moses. With the temple destroyed, the only path for reconciliation with God Most High that was available became recognizing Jesus Christ as the promised and prophesied messiah.

Under the rules of God Most High's Law given through Moses, there can be no forgiveness from God Most High without a blood sacrifice. Rejecting God Most High's messiah and the blood sacrificed by Jesus Christ, and without a temple to offer animal sacrifice, the nation of Israel is currently living in a relationship with God Most High that is without opportunity for forgiveness (unless there is acceptance that Jesus Christ is their promised and prophesied messiah).

Without a temple, there can be no fully functioning altar. Without a fully functioning and consecrated altar, there can be no animal sacrifice. And the altar cannot be effective without a tabernacle or temple.

In December 2018, the newly formed Sanhedrin officially dedicated an altar for animal sacrifice. But the official temple sacrifice must wait until the actual temple has been built and is in place.

Paul, a Jewish rabbi who studied under the top rabbi of his era, the rabbi Gamaliel, experienced a 'come to Jesus' moment (Acts 22). After accepting that Jesus Christ is the promised and prophesied messiah, Paul was able to expand his theological knowledge to include Jesus Christ's new covenant plan for the process of restoring a right relationship with God Most High and to put the covenant of the Law given through Moses as subservient to the new law of grace.

Under the new covenant of grace, the requirement that needs to be met for the forgiveness of sins and the reestablishment of a right relationship with God Most High is no longer animal sacrifice in the tabernacle / temple, but rather a sacrifice that takes place in the heart. The new covenant of grace requires an understanding that Jesus Christ fulfilled the first portion of the Law given through Moses, during Jesus Christ's earthly ministry. And the new covenant of grace requires an allowance for Jesus Christ to fulfill the remaining portion of the Law given through Moses, when he returns. 'For it is with your heart that you believe and are justified…' (Romans 10:10)

When belief in Jesus Christ as the promised and prophesied messiah has been realized in one's heart, that *person has been released from the Law of Moses and the tabernacle / temple system covenant of sacrifice. The transfer has been made from the redemption of the tabernacle / temple sacrifices, to the redemption of the sacrifice that Jesus Christ accomplished in his crucifixion. This truth applies to both the people of Israel and to the Gentiles.*

In this way, the people of Israel who formerly were confined to the requirements of the law are released from the law. The Gentile who previously did not have the opportunity for eternal life because for the Gentile there was no sacrifice, could also receive the benefit of the sacrifice of messiah / the Lamb / Jesus Christ.

*Therefore, '***everyone*** who calls on the name of the Lord will be saved' (Joel 2:32, Acts 2:21, Romans 10:13).*

Israel has experienced a hardening in part until the full number of the Gentiles has come in. And so all Israel will be saved, as it is written: 'The deliverer will come from Zion. The deliverer will return godlessness away from Jacob. And this is my covenant with them when I take away their sins.' Romans 11:25b-27

While Paul identified 'all' of Israel as being saved, the prophets and John the Revelator noted that at the conclusion of the times of the Gentiles, only a remnant of the people of Israel will still be alive, but that portion of the people of Israel that remain, will recognize Jesus Christ as their promised and prophesied messiah.

In the intervening time, during the times of the Gentiles, there is a number that God Most High has set as the minimum number of Gentiles that need to become citizens of the kingdom of heaven, before God Most High's redemption, reclamation and regeneration plan can continue (Revelation 6:11). The era of the times of the Gentiles was specifically included in God Most High's plan for human history, in order for God Most High to fulfill God Most High's ultimate plan for eternity.

At this time, God Most High has not yet disclosed what God Most High's full plan for eternity is. Consequently, we do not have an understanding for why this minimum number of people is required.

The religious leadership of the nation of Israel that rejected Jesus Christ as the promised and prophesied messiah, would have also barred the Gentiles from being accepted into God Most High's redemption, reclamation and regeneration plan. In order for the plan to advance, it was necessary for God Most High to harden the hearts of those who rejected Jesus Christ. Through intensifying the rejection Jesus Christ as the promised and prophesied messiah, among the people of Israel, God Most High protected the opportunity to include the Gentile followers of the Lamb as active participants and citizens of the kingdom of heaven.

Note: the entire chapter of Romans 11 addressed the reasoning of God Most High in offering salvation to the Gentiles. It was initially the responsibility of the people of Israel to take the message of God Most High into the world / the Gentiles. But the people of Israel instead opted to embrace an attitude that the people of Israel were exclusively God Most High's elite and elect, just because they were the descendants of Abraham.

God Most High determined that there would be a minimum number of Gentiles who would believe in Jesus Christ before the future abomination of desolation event could take place (Revelation 6:11). Meeting that required number, means that the times of the Gentiles may soon officially conclude.

Following the future abomination of desolation event, the Gentile followers of the Lamb / Jesus Christ have some work that must be accomplished during the second three and a half years of the era of the time of Jacob's Trouble. What the Gentile followers of the Lamb / Jesus Christ must accomplish cannot be achieved without the power of God's Holy Spirit. What the Gentile followers of the Lamb / Jesus Christ will do with God Most High's empowerment during the second half of the era of the time of Jacob's Trouble will be greater than even the miracles that Jesus Christ performed. This was Jesus Christ's promise communicated to his disciples (John 14:12).

The last of the apostles to be called to be an apostle, was Saul (Hebrew) / Paul (Greek). Saul practiced his Judaism on steroids, murdering the followers of the Lamb / Jesus Christ, until he himself, was personally called by Jesus Christ to become a follower of the Lamb and an apostle.

Paul wrote in his epistle to the Romans:

Accept one another, then, just as Christ accepted you, in order to bring praise to God. For I tell you that Christ has become a servant of the Jews on behalf of God's truth, so that the promises made to the patriarchs might be confirmed and, moreover, that the Gentiles might glorify God for his mercy. As it is written:

'Therefore I will praise you among the Gentiles. I will sing the praises of your name.'

Again, it says, 'Rejoice, you Gentiles, with his people.'

And again, 'Praise the Lord, all you Gentiles. Let all the peoples extol him.'

And again, Isaiah says, 'The Root of Jesse will spring up, one who will arise to rule over the nations. In him the Gentiles will hope.' Romans 15:7-12

Yet I have written you quite boldly on some points to remind you of them again, because of the grace God gave me to be a minister of Christ Jesus to the Gentiles. He gave me the priestly duty of proclaiming the gospel of God, so that the Gentiles might become an offering acceptable to God, sanctified by the Holy Spirit. Romans 15:15-16

(See also: Psalm 2 Samuel 22:50, Psalm 18:49, Deuteronomy 32:43, Psalm 117:1, Isiah 11:10, Isaiah 52:14-15.)

The Father has qualified you to share in the inheritance of the holy ones in the kingdom of light. For God has rescued us from the dominion of darkness and brought us into the kingdom of the Son God loves, in whom we have redemption, the forgiveness of sins. Colossians 1:12b-14

Ultimately, the era of the times of the Gentiles has also been an era of preparation for the Gentiles who await the return of messiah / the Lamb / Jesus Christ who is the light of the world.

And the light of the world can only return as the people of Israel have their veil removed and decide that Jesus Christ is that promised and prophesied light.

The duration of the times of the Gentiles

In preparation for Jesus Christ's first coming, there were multiple larger cultural events that had taken place that made the message among the Gentiles able to spread with efficiency and effectiveness. The Roman Road system had been developed making it a possibility to travel from the city of Rome, to any point in the Roman empire, within three days. The shipping network had developed so that sea travel was also efficient and effective. The influence of the Greek empire, had left its impact upon the world through Hellenization and the adoption of the Greek language, so that people from many nations, experienced elements of a common culture and could share in a common language – Greek. (Today the common language around the world would be recognized as English.) The Romans had developed the precision of crucifixion and had perfected its efficiency and effectiveness. The Romans occupied the land of Israel causing a mixture of Gentiles living amongst the people of Israel, which made the connection between the Israelite community and the Gentile community more culturally effective.

All these dynamics were instrumental in preparing the Gentile world for more effective communication with the people of Israel, and for the Gentile world to receive the message of Jesus Christ's messiahship.

All these dynamics made provision for the early apostles and disciples to be able to enter into any town, go to the synagogue first, and then to the Gentiles, and to communicate the message that the promised and prophesied messiah of Israel, had come and fulfilled his role in order to provide the opportunity for any person who believed in this promised and prophesied messiah, to establish a right relationship with God Most High.

The era of the times of the Gentiles began with the people of Israel rejecting the truth concerning the resurrection of Jesus Christ as the risen promised and prophesied messiah (~30 AD). The times of the Gentiles has continued from that historical point, through today.

The prophet Hosea documented the conclusion for the era of the times of the Gentiles, as taking place when the people of Israel will again be fully received by God Most High.

Come. let us return to the Lord. The Lord has torn us to pieces but the Lord will heal us. The Lord has injured us but the Lord will bind up our wounds. <u>After two days the Lord will revive us</u>. On the third day the Lord will restore us that we may live in the presence of the Lord. Hosea 6:1-2

A 'God day' is a thousand years in human time (Psalm 90:4, 2 Peter 3:8).

This passage from Hosea recognized that the God who brings life, would allow the nation of Israel to lie dormant for approximately two thousand years. But at the end of that approximately two thousand year period, God Most High would again bring life to the nation of Israel.

At the time that God Most High revived Israel through the reestablishment of the nation of Israel (May 14, 1948), the Lord set into motion a new level of relationship with the people of Israel where Israel began the process of reestablishing the conditions necessary for the Lord to live in the complete presence of the people of Israel. When Jesus Christ returns, he will return to the Mount of Olives in Jerusalem Israel. And when Jesus Christ returns, he will return to a full, loving, and in person relationship with the people of Israel. Jesus Christ and the people of Israel will never be separated again.

The Hosea passage was also the pattern for Jesus Christ's death and resurrection. Jesus Christ was the best representative of the people of Israel. But the people of Israel are also truly represented by Jesus Christ. The prophecy of the nation of Israel's two thousand years as a 'dead' nation was the typology for Jesus Christ's time spent in the tomb. On the third day the Lord / Holy Spirit raised Jesus Christ from the dead, restoring Jesus Christ so that he would live in the presence of the God Most High forever.

From the time of Abram / Abraham (2166 to 1991 BC), until the time of Jesus Christ' life and earthly ministry (~4 BC to 30 AD), God Most High prepared the people of Israel for the first arrival of Jesus Christ. From the time of

Abram / Abraham until the birth of Jesus Christ, was approximately two thousand years.

In the same way that God Most High prepared the people of Israel for Jesus Christ's first coming, God Most High has been preparing the world for Jesus Christ's second coming, Jesus Christ's return.

Now technology has developed so that worldwide, people have the ability to communicate with anyone in the world at any time, instantly. Through internet and satellites, television can carry the news from anyplace in the world, in order to publicize the events that will be taking place during the era of the time of Jacob's Trouble. Through air travel and shipping routes, people are able to be in contact with people of various cultures and to conduct global commerce. The common language of the world is English, spoken in almost every nation. The era of the time of Jacob's Trouble, will be a time when the message of Jesus Christ will be able to be spread more effectively than at any other time in history. And when the people of the world will be awed by and wondering about the events of the era of the time of Jacob's Trouble, the followers of the Lamb / Jesus Christ, will be able to share the answers with the same kind of effectiveness that the apostles and early disciples experienced in the early church era as described by the book of Acts.

Communicating that Jesus Christ is the promised and prophesied messiah to all of humanity, has been the purpose for the times of the Gentiles.

Throughout human history, the red dragon / serpent / Satan, Inc.'s plan was that when the people of Israel rejected Jesus Christ as their messiah, then the light of the world would be extinguished. There would be no message taken to the Gentiles. If the red dragon / serpent / Satan, Inc.'s plan of dispersing and annihilating the people of the nation of Israel would have worked, there would have been no remnant of messianic believers for God Most High to have cared about. Not only would the red dragon / serpent / Satan, Inc. have thwarted God Most High's plan for the redemption of Israel, but the red dragon / serpent /

Satan, Inc. would have thwarted God Most High's plan for redeeming the Gentiles.

But throughout human history God Most High always reserves a remnant designated by God Most High as his own and placed under the protection of God Most High. The remnant of believers in Jesus Christ from among the people of Israel, became the first followers of the Lamb / 'Christians.' The first followers of the Lamb / Jesus Christ were successful in carrying the message throughout the world and into time. That message that Jesus Christ is Lord, is still told two thousand years later. That message has reached through time and through miles, to reach to you and me.

The times of the Gentiles officially began at the time of Jesus Christ's ascension into heaven following his crucifixion and resurrection. It was marked by Israel's religious leaders officially rejecting Jesus Christ as their promised and prophesied messiah (Matthew 28:11-15).

Jesus Christ followed up the rejection of the religious and political leaders of the people of Israel of his messiahship, with the instruction to his disciples to go into all the world with the message that God Most High had faithfully sent the promised and prophesied messiah. Jesus Christ left his first followers, with the promise that he was with them forever. To be with his followers forever, meant that Jesus Christ would also be with those who were to be told about him and who would receive him, beginning with the people of Judea, Samaria, and the uttermost parts of the world, ... and to the end of the age. *(Matthew 28:16-20)*

So, when is the 'end of the age?' And when does the times of the Gentiles come to an end?

One possibility is that the times of the Gentiles ends at the beginning of the era of the times of Jacob's Trouble when God Most High's first focus again turned to the people of Israel. Hosea told us that there would be two thousand years before the wounds of Israel would be healed. After the two thousand years of healing for the *people of Israel, then the thousand years of living in the Lord's presence would begin (Hosea 6:1-3).*

(Hosea also told us that the Lord will come like the winter rains and also like the spring rains, describing the two comings of the messiah to dwell with us.)

To believe that the era of the times of the Gentiles ends with the beginning of the era of the times of Jacob's Trouble is to place an end to the care that God Most High has provided for the Gentiles who are followers of the Lamb / Jesus Christ. It is a belief that has as its foundation, another form of replacement theology.

Replacement theology or supersessionism, holds that when the people of Israel rejected God Most High, God Most High rejected the people of Israel and replaced the people of Israel with the Gentile church or the Gentile followers of the Lamb / Jesus Christ, and canceled the covenant agreement that God Most High had with the people of Israel that had begun with God Most High's covenant agreement with Abram / Abraham. The beginning of the era of Jacob's Trouble would then by the same formula, cancel God Most High's covenant agreement with the Gentile followers of the Lamb / Jesus Christ. And the relationship between God Most High and the people of Israel would pick up where it left off two thousand years ago with the people of Israel, but at the expense of God Most High severing the relationship that God established with the Gentiles for the past two thousand years.

But the biblical record consistently presented the fact that God Most High's canceling any covenant agreement is just never going to happen. God Most High will always remember God Most High's covenant both with the people of Israel and with the followers of the Lamb / Jesus Christ, including the Gentile followers of the Lamb / Jesus Christ.

The other possibility for determining the conclusion of the era of the times of the Gentiles, would be to understand that the final portion of the times of the Gentiles will merge with the era of the time of Jacob's Trouble.

There was a transition time between the message of messiah being received by the first people of Israel who believed and were called the first Christians, to the message being received by the Gentiles. This period of history was recognized as the time of the early apostolic church. (See Acts, Revelation 2:1-7.) It would be consistent for the reintegration of the people of Israel into the active portion of God Most High's redemption, reclamation and regeneration plan, to also experience the same kind of overlap, once again incorporating the activity of both the people of Israel and Gentiles.

This kind of activity in dual arenas, would result in both the era of the times of the Gentiles and the era of the time of Jacob's Trouble, ending simultaneously with the arrival of messiah / the Lamb / Jesus Christ. (See Revelation 7 (people of Israel), 14:1-4 (followers of the Lamb / Jesus Christ, 19:11-14 (armies of heaven dressed in fine linen, white and clean – from both the people of Israel and Gentiles).) (Also see John 7:35, Acts 17:16-17, 18:1-4, 19:8-10, 20:17-21, Romans 3:22, 10:12, 1 Corinthians 1:20-24, etc.)

Because God Most High is consistently and continually faithful to God Most High's followers of the Lamb / Jesus Christ, and because Jesus Christ promised to be with us <u>until</u> 'the end of this age,' *it is more probable that the era of the times of the Gentiles will end with the victory of Jesus Christ over all the enemies of what will constitute the kingdom of heaven, including the enemies of the people and nation of Israel and the enemies of the followers of the Lamb / Jesus Christ.*

The Holy Spirit in the Book of Revelation

When God is discussed, usually the focus is on God the Father. When Jesus Christ taught us to pray, Jesus Christ began with, 'Our Father who is in heaven, holy is your name… Your will be done on earth as it is in heaven.' (Matthew 6:9 – translated).

It was the will of the heavenly Father that was able to speak creation into existence. It is the will of the heavenly Father that must be accomplished on earth as it is in heaven.

The second member of the office of God is Jesus Christ, the only begotten Son of God the Father. The rest of us are adopted into the family.

As the second member of the office of God, Jesus Christ was also active in creation (John 1). Nothing that has been created, was created without Jesus Christ. And the second role of Jesus Christ in human history has been to provide the means for God Most High's redemption, reclamation and regeneration plan to be fulfilled.

The third member of the office of God is the Holy Spirit. The Holy Spirit is generally the most forgotten member of the office of God and is almost always listed last when referencing the three. But the Holy Spirit's work is equally as important as the work of God the Father and God the Son / Jesus Christ.

The Holy Spirit was the first member of the office of God that was introduced in the beginning. It was the Holy Spirit who hovered over the face of the deep, that began the entire creative process, even before God spoke (Genesis 1:1). It was the Holy Spirit contending with the hearts and minds of humanity that caused God to determine that the lifespan of humanity should be limited to one hundred twenty years (Genesis 6:1-12). Joseph was recognized as having the spirit of God in him (Genesis 41:37-38). The Holy Spirit's presence with the people of Israel as they wandered in the wilderness for forty years, was demonstrated in the pillar of fire / cloud that served to lead them and to protect them (Exodus 13:21-22, 14:19, 14:24, 33:9-10, Numbers 12:5, 14:14, Deuteronomy 31:15, Nehemiah 9:12-19, Psalm 99:7). It was the Holy Spirit that filled Bezalel son of Uri, who was commissioned to construct the tabernacle (1446 BC) (Exodus 31:1-5, 35:30-33). The elders of the newly formed nation of Israel, were given the Holy Spirit's power (Numbers 11:16-17).

The Holy Spirit was present and active when the Law was given to Moses and the people of Israel as the people of Israel exited Egypt (1446 BC). The Holy Spirit was present and active throughout the nation of Israel's history. The Holy Spirit's presence was displayed in the glory of God Most High in the tabernacle and temple. The Holy Spirit was active in the lives of John the Baptist and Jesus Christ, even causing Jesus Christ to be conceived, and visibly blessing Jesus Christ at his baptism. There was a major outpouring of the Holy Spirit that followed the crucifixion, death, resurrection and ascension of Jesus Christ, on the Day of Pentecost (~30 AD) (Acts 2), that was prophesied to take place by the prophet Joel (Joel 2). After that Day of Pentecost (~30 AD), the Holy Spirit now dwells in the hearts of every believer in Jesus Christ / follower of the Lamb.

The Holy Spirit has been actively speaking to the church throughout the times of the Gentiles (Revelation 2 and 3). But the Holy Spirit has only been heard by those who have the kind of ears that can hear the Holy Spirit.

It is within the description of events that Jesus Christ provided to John the Revelator, that the Holy Spirit's work and future work has been described. And because of humanity's neglect in recognizing the person of the Holy Spirit, the work of the Holy Spirit during the era of the time of Jacob's Trouble, has been frequently rendered to be invisible. Humanity has a tendency to mistakenly equate invisibility with nonexistence. But dismissing the person and work of the Holy Spirit during this era of the time of Jacob's Trouble, would be a huge error.

John the Revelator began his record of events with documenting that he received this vision as a result of the work of the Holy Spirit.

On the Lord's Day I was in the Spirit, and I heard behind me a loud voice like a trumpet, which said: 'Write on a scroll what you see and send it to the seven churches: to Ephesus, Smyrna, Pergamum, Thyatira, Sardis, Philadelphia and Laodicea.' Revelation 1:10-11

Without the Holy Spirit, John the Revelator would not have seen the resurrected and ascended Jesus Christ, nor heard his voice, nor received his instruction to pen the book of Revelation that has communicated so much of God Most High's plan, for us who live during the era of the time of Jacob's Trouble.

It was the Holy Spirit that provided John the Revelator with entrance into the throne room of heaven and made it possible for John the Revelator to see God the Father handing the will of God with the seven seals, to the worthy Lamb / Jesus Christ (Revelation 4:2 (4 and 5)).

During the second half of the era of the time of Jacob's Trouble, there will be a special blessing provided personally by the Holy Spirit, given to those who die because they are followers of the Lamb / Jesus Christ (Revelation 14:13).

During the finale for the era of the time of Jacob's Trouble, the great prostitute / Mystery Babylon the Great!, the scarlet beast with the seven / eight heads, and the beast from the Abyss / eighth king beast, will be the leaders in the work on behalf of the kingdom of Satan, Inc. / kingdom of man. It was the Holy Spirit that made it possible for John the Revelator to see the prophesied work that they will accomplish, and to warn the authentic followers of the Lamb / Jesus Christ, to provide distance from them. (Revelation 12, 13, 17, 18:4, etc.)

As John the Revelator experienced the visions that he received concerning the times of the Gentiles and the era of the time of Jacob's Trouble, the Holy Spirit was recognized as the 'Spirit of prophecy.' *During this era of time, one major role of the Holy Spirit is to bear testimony to the authenticity of Jesus Christ as divine and sovereign. (Revelation 19:10).*

It was the Holy Spirit who also showed John the Revelator the even more distant future, scheduled for over one thousand years from now, at the conclusion of the Thousand Years Reign of Jesus Christ, when the Holy City of Jerusalem will come down out of heaven (Revelation 21:10).

And the biblical record ended with its focus upon the work of the Holy Spirit.

> The Spirit and the bride say, 'Come!' And let the one who hears say, 'Come!' Let the one who is thirsty come; and let the one who wishes take the free gift of the water of life. Revelation 22:17

The followers of the Lamb / Jesus Christ were not instructed to 'come out of' Mystery Babylon the Great! without having a destination to enter into. It is the Holy Spirit that invites the followers of the Lamb / Jesus Christ to enter into everlasting life / to drink from the water of life, and to live for an eternity in the presence of all three members of the office of God. And it is the Holy Spirit that has a portion of responsibility in making this new living condition, a reality.

While the main focus of humanity during the era of the time of Jacob's Trouble, will be upon the work of God Most High with the pouring out of the seven bowls of God Most High's wrath / seven last plagues, etc., and the work of the Lamb / Jesus Christ through his fulfillment of the fall feasts of the seven required feasts and the military defeat of the enemies of God Most High and of the kingdom of heaven, it will be possible to miss recognizing the work of the Holy Spirit.

Misidentifying the work of the Holy Spirit could lead to crucial mistakes for those living during the era of the time of Jacob's Trouble.

The sevenfold Spirit of God

One of the biblical record's descriptions of the Holy Spirit was as the sevenfold Spirit of God.

The prophet Isaiah was the first to document the sevenfold Spirit of God.

> A shoot will come up from the stump of Jesse. From his roots a Branch will bear fruit.
> The Spirit of the Lord will <u>rest on him</u> — the Spirit of <u>wisdom</u> and of <u>understanding</u>, the Spirit of <u>counsel</u> and of <u>might</u>, the Spirit of the <u>knowledge</u> and <u>fear of the Lord</u> — and he will delight in the fear of the Lord. Isaiah 11:1-3a

Isaiah's message described the seven aspects of the Holy Spirit that would characterize the promised and

prophesied messiah's nature, because of the Holy Spirit's relationship with him:
1. Presence ('Spirit of the Lord will rest on him')
2. Wisdom
3. Understanding
4. Counsel
5. Might
6. Knowledge
7. Fear of the Lord

In John the Revelator's record of visions from Jesus Christ, there were four references to the sevenfold Spirit of God.
John, to the seven churches which are in Asia: Grace and peace to you from him who is, and who was, and who is to come; and from the <u>seven spirits</u> which are before God's throne, and from Jesus Christ, who is the faithful witness, the firstborn from the dead and the ruler of the kings of the earth. Revelation 1:4-5a

Jesus said: 'To the angel of the church in Sardis write: These are the words of him who holds the <u>seven spirits of God</u> and the seven stars. I know your works, you have a reputation of being alive, but in reality, you are dead. Wake up! Strengthen what remains and is about to die, for I have found your works unfinished in the sight of my God' Revelation 3:1-2

From John's vision of the throne room of heaven: From the throne came flashes of lightning, rumblings and peals of thunder. In front of the throne, seven lamps were blazing. These are the <u>sevenfold Spirit of God</u>. Revelation 4:5

Also from John's vision of the throne room of heaven: Then I saw a Lamb, looking as if it had been slain, standing at the center of the throne, encircled by the four living creatures and the elders. The Lamb had seven horns and seven eyes, which are the <u>sevenfold Spirit of God</u> sent out into all the earth. Revelation 5:6

The sevenfold Spirit of God has not been fully defined for us. With humanity's finite ability to understand the infinite God, we may have to wait until we see God the Father, God the Son / messiah / the Lamb / Jesus Christ, and the sevenfold Spirit of God / Holy Spirit, face to face, in order to understand the fully nature, depth and identity of all three members of the office of God.

Outline of John's Book of Revelation

The book of Revelation was given to John the apostle, one of Jesus Christ's disciples, the disciple known as the disciple that Jesus loved (John 13:23, 19:26, 20:2, 21:7, 21:20). John the Revelator lived to be an old man and was eventually exiled to the island of Patmos (Revelation 1:9). There, John received a series of visions or possibly one vision that needed to be recorded in parts.

The parts contained within the book of Revelation were not recorded as they will be played out chronologically. There are some events that were documented in chronological order. But in attempting to record the full dynamics of the scheduled events there was difficulty in describing so many actors and their changing roles throughout the flurry of activity in such a short period of time.

Therefore, the vision that John received was broken down by the focus of a particular series of events, such as the seven seals, seven trumpets, seven bowls, the activity of the red dragon / serpent / Satan, Inc. against messiah / the Lamb / Jesus Christ, against the people of Israel and against the followers of the Lamb / Jesus Christ, the activity of the two beasts of Revelation 13 and their fluid frenemy relationship, etc.

But within each of the sets of seven (seals, trumpets and bowls), the commencement of each item will be revealed in order. Every part of the three sets of seven has the potential to overlap with another part of the sets of seven. But the beginning of each item described in the sets of seven, begins in the order that John the Revelator presented them in.

John's Revelation also contained parts that focus upon individuals and their activity upon other individuals or groups. John the Revelator recorded the message with this kind of focus when John presented the two witnesses of Revelation 11, the red dragon / serpent / Satan, Inc. of

Revelation 12, and the two beasts of Revelation 13. These individuals were presented separately, but they will perform their greatest activity in partnership, simultaneously, during the second half of the era of the time of Jacob's Trouble.

The message of the book of Revelation was more focused upon the dynamics of the events and the impact of those events upon heaven, the inhabitants of the earth, the followers of the Lamb / Jesus Christ, and upon earth itself, than having a focus upon absolute chronology. Viewing John's book of Revelation with a strict understanding that the parts of the book of Revelation must unfold with a strict chronology, will not allow a true interpretation and understanding of the events included in this message.

The title of this book in Greek was actually 'Apocalypse of Jesus Christ' / 'Apokalupis 'Iasou Christou' / Ἀποκάλυψις Ἰησοῦ Χριστοῦ.' In common English, this translated as the 'Unveiling by Jesus Christ.' There was a great deal of traditional Jewish marriage protocol within the relationship between God Most High and the 'bride' / followers of the Lamb / Jesus Christ. As the bridegroom offers the covenant vows of the marriage service, the bridegroom removes the veil of his bride. The book of Revelation, given by Jesus Christ, told of Jesus Christ participating in the unveiling of the 'bride' in order to enter into a new level of covenant with her. The book of Revelation serves as the unveiling of the plan for how Jesus Christ will return for his 'bride' / followers of the Lamb / Jesus Christ.

For this reason, the book of Revelation is frequently referred to as 'the unveiling.'

Jesus Christ has been waiting to return for his 'bride' / followers of the Lamb, for almost two thousand years since Jesus Christ ascended into heaven. But the plan for Jesus Christ to redeem and reclaim the people of God Most High from out of the kingdom of Satan, Inc. / kingdom of man, has been advancing for approximately six thousand years of human history. The account of Jesus Christ's plan for returning for the bride / the followers of the Lamb / Jesus Christ, actually began with the first man and first woman as they exited the Garden of Eden / garden of God / paradise (Genesis 3).

For this reason, the biblical record has dropped hints throughout every book of the biblical record concerning the events that must take place with Jesus Christ's return. God Most High's continual hints and typologies demonstrated the excitement that God Most High experiences in the very thought of this future return of Jesus Christ to claim the bride / followers of the Lamb / Jesus Christ.

In the book of Revelation, there are four hundred four verses. Two hundred seventy eight of those verses directly alluded to other parts of the biblical record, primarily from the Old Testament / Tanakh. While the bride / followers of the Lamb / Jesus Christ is generally defined as the authentic followers of the Lamb / Jesus Christ from out of the Gentile church, the fact that most of the allusions contained in the book of Revelation being sourced from the Old Testament / Tanakh, dramatically stressed the point that Jesus Christ's 'bride' must first and primarily include the people of Israel who will choose to become followers of the Lamb / Jesus Christ. John the Revelator's book of Revelation was the account of the events that will also unveil Jesus Christ as messiah, to the people of Israel. When the veil will finally be lifted, the people of Israel will recognize that their promised and prophesied messiah is Jesus Christ, and then they will be willing to say, 'Blessed is the one who comes in the name of the Lord' and enter into a new covenant with the bridegroom / Jesus Christ.

The overall outlined for how Jesus Christ has planned to ready the bride / people of Israel who will receive Jesus Christ, and to ready the followers of the Lamb / Jesus Christ

Chapter 1: Introduction of Jesus Christ, the author of the vision given to John the Revelator.

Chapters 2 and 3: The historical church eras in a timeline from the time of Jesus Christ's ascension into heaven until the return of Jesus Christ to defeat the enemies of God Most High and of the kingdom of heaven, and to fully establish the kingdom of heaven on earth. Each of the seven churches of Asia referenced in Revelation 2 and 3, represented a later historical era predominated with the theology of the cultural theology of that church in Asia during the lifetime of John the Revelator. (Also see Daniel 11:1-35.)

Chapters 4 and 5: The significant events that take place in heaven that prepare heaven for the future events on earth. This was a description of the prelude in heaven to the events of the era of the time of Jacob's Trouble.

Chapter 6: Seven seals – yet another timeline beginning with the Lamb having received the will of God Most High and opening the seals that initiated a series of events that will continue until the return of Jesus Christ to defeat enemies and fully establish the kingdom of heaven on earth.

Chapter 7: the sealing of the 144,000 from the tribes of Israel. This must take place prior to any harm coming to the land and the sea (7:1-3). The second part of chapter 7 concerned the great multitude standing before the throne and in front of the Lamb / Jesus Christ, wearing white robes and holding palm branches. The palm branches were used by people of Israel on lamb selection day just prior to Passover, and represented the presence of the people of Israel.

Chapters 8 and 9: Seven trumpets – trumpets #1-5 – yet another timeline. The timeline of the seven trumpets began with the opening of the seventh seal, during the first half of the era of the time of Jacob's Trouble and the effects of the sounding of the seven trumpets will continue until the return of Jesus Christ to defeat enemies and fully establish the kingdom of heaven on earth.

Chapter 10: The Little Scroll dictated by the seven thunders – the message of the seven thunders was provided between John's record of part a and part b of trumpet #6 / woe #2. But the message will not be understood by humanity until the seventh angel is ready to blow trumpet #7, after the two witnesses have concluded their mission.

Chapter 11: The two witnesses – God Most High's injection into the world as we know it, of two prophets who will seek to communicate God Most High's message to the people of Israel, to humanity, and to the red dragon / serpent / Satan, Inc. The timeline for the two witnesses designated their ministry to take place during the second half of the era of the time of Jacob's Trouble. The two witnesses are part b of trumpet #6 / woe #2. They will witness for three and a half years / 1,260 days. And then they will be assassinated together on the temple mount by the beast from the Abyss. (Revelation 11:1-14, 17:8)

Chapter 11 continued: Trumpet #7 will be sounded but not until trumpet #6 / woe #2 is completed, with the death, resurrection and ascension into heaven of the two witnesses.

Chapters 12 and 13: The introduction of the Allies of the Rebellion; Satan, the red dragon / serpent / Satan, Inc., and the two beasts of Revelation 13. The two beasts of Revelation 13 will serve as the red dragon / serpent / Satan, Inc.'s dynamic duo that will be counterparts to God Most High's two witnesses. Both sides of the conflict, Satan's side and God Most High's side, will be armed with supernatural power.

Chapter 14: Sealing of the 144,000 followers of the Lamb / Jesus Christ.

Chapters 15 and 16: Ordering of the seven bowls of God Most High's wrath / seven last plagues. The pouring out of the seven bowls of God Most High's wrath will be the only time during the era of the time of Jacob's Trouble designated as the time of God's wrath. All other previously scheduled events will be the result of the work of the red dragon / serpent / Satan, Inc. and the opportunity provided to them to advance the kingdom of Satan, Inc. / kingdom of man. The pouring out of the seven bowls of God Most High's wrath / seven last plagues was scheduled to take place during the finale for the era of the time of Jacob's Trouble, the final seventy five days. The end of the timeline for the pouring out of the seven bowls of God Most

High's wrath / seven last plagues coincides with the end of all previous timelines.

Chapters 17 and 18: Events that will lead to the implosion of the global religious community and global governance system.

Chapter 19: Announcement and actual arrival of Jesus Christ to fight the final battle of this age and to defeat the enemies of God Most High and of the kingdom of heaven.

Chapter 20: Description of events that will mark the Thousand Years Reign of Jesus Christ (not included on this chart).

Chapter 21: Description of the future new heaven, new earth, new Jerusalem Israel, and bride of the Lamb / Jesus Christ (not included on this chart).

Chapter 22: Description of the Garden of Eden / garden of God / paradise restored, and the invitation to enter it (not included on this chart).

Messiah / the Lamb / Jesus Christ's Message to the Seven Angels of the Seven Churches in Asia, as a Prophetic Historical Timeline for History between Messiah / the Lamb / Jesus Christ's Ascension into Heaven and His Return

John the Revelator was personally instructed by the resurrected and ascended Jesus Christ to: 'Write, therefore, what you have seen, what is now and what will take place later. The mystery of the seven stars that you saw in my right hand and of the seven golden lampstands is this: The seven stars are the angels of the seven churches, and the seven lampstands are the seven churches.' Revelation 1:19-20

Jesus Christ's message to the angels of the seven churches of Asia, holds multiple layers of meaning depending upon the perspective that the message is approached with. There is of course the simple perspective of the address being written to the first century AD churches. But also contained within the message to the seven churches, was the obvious perspective that this message was being written specifically for those living during the era of the time of Jacob's Trouble.

What was not so obvious in this message, were the other layers of meaning that Jesus Christ sought to convey.

John the Revelator who also wrote the gospel of John. In John's gospel, John recorded Jesus Christ's presentation of the good shepherd (John 10:1-21).
The good shepherd must lead the flock through the gate, and cannot allow others to join the flock by climbing in or by some other method.
The good shepherd calls to the sheep and the sheep listen to his voice and follow him because they know his voice.
Jesus Christ as the good shepherd, laid down his life for the sheep.
In contrast, another type of shepherd is the hired hand that does not own the sheep. When he sees the wolf coming, he abandons the sheep and runs away. He does not care for the sheep.

There are good shepherds who are like Christ who will lay their lives down for the sheep.
There are also shepherds who run away like hired hands allowing the wolves to ravage the sheep. They are shepherds / priests / pastors who hold their positions for the purpose of fleecing the flock so that they can personally profit in wealth or in power or in both wealth and power, often at the expense of the sheep.
Jesus Christ also taught that there are false prophets that will come in sheep's clothing, but inwardly they are ferocious wolves (Matthew 7:15).
Most shepherds / priests / pastors are neither good shepherds nor false prophets / wolves dressed as sheep (Matthew 7:15). Most shepherds / priests / pastors are hired hands who are in the position because it is their career, a job, not even a profession, a paycheck. A hired hand will not protect the sheep from the wolves. They will put truth next to error, and because of error's assigned association with truth, they will designate the error as truth.
There were portions of the message concerning the era of the time of Jacob's Trouble directed not to the 'sheep,'

but to the 'shepherds' / pastors. When studying the biblical presentation of the era of the time of Jacob's Trouble, understanding to whom the message was directed, changes the meaning of the message.

Throughout the ages, the struggle has continued between recognizing the truth of the God of truth, and embracing the agenda proposed by both religious leaders and others, that takes the place of God Most High's agenda. Consequently, what should have always been the church that presents Jesus as Lord, crucified, risen, ascended, and planning to return; has become an organization that may or may not follow God Most High's agenda. The organization that we call 'church' has too often become the organization with man's agenda.

One of the signs of the true church is that the divinity of Jesus Christ is recognized. The only sermon the early church preached had these points: Jesus is Lord. We crucified him. God raised Jesus Christ from the dead. There is no other name under heaven through which we can enter into eternal life. And Jesus Christ is returning to fully establish the kingdom of heaven on earth after purchasing that right through giving his perfect blood.

Jesus Christ is the one and only door. There is no 'back door' into heaven. Jesus Christ is the model of what it is to be the good shepherd. In the moments that this message is lost in the 'church,' the 'church' has committed adultery against the God of the church / Jesus Christ. In the moments that this message is found, the church has returned to their first love. The message of the early church remains the message of God Most High throughout time. But the 'church' leaders will sometimes lose that message. It is imperative that those who choose to be followers of the Lamb / Jesus Christ do not lose this message regardless of who the religious leaders are.

Jesus Christ is the embodiment of divinity of love and of truth. Another sign of the true church is that within the true church, love and truth are present and interwoven together. Without a willingness to love, truth will not be given. Without a willingness to embrace truth when it is given, will prevent love from being manifest in life. Over time, from the historical timeline of the church represented by the church of Ephesus until the historical timeline of the church represented by the church of Laodicea, the rate of the loss of love and truth rises exponentially.

There are blips during the historical timeline when the divinity of Jesus Christ and love and truth are rediscovered. But, the general direction of the curve for recognizing the divinity of Jesus Christ, love and truth follows a downward trajectory. Ultimately this is the message of Jesus Christ to John the Revelator. The message to the modern biblical student is that Jesus Christ remains divine, the author of love, and the source of truth.

At the end of this historical timeline of the church, there will be few true shepherds to pasture the flock. But Jesus Christ does not leave us abandoned.

Jesus said, 'I am the good shepherd; I know my sheep and my sheep know me – just as the Father knows me and I know the Father – and I lay down my life for the sheep.' John 10:14

'My sheep listen to my voice; I know them, and they follow me. I give them eternal life, and they shall never perish. No one will snatch them out of my hand. My Father, who has given them to me, is greater than all. No one can snatch them out of my Father's hand.' John 10:27-29.

When there is no longer a church available where the leader or leaders are good shepherds or shepherds willing to protect the people from the wolves, Jesus Christ reminded us that Jesus Christ is the good shepherd and remains still available to all who are willing to hear his voice.

Jesus Christ's message as a continual historical timeline

There was a period of approximately four hundred years, in between the writings of the prophets of the Old Testament / Tanakh and the arrival of John the Baptist and Jesus Christ of the New Testament. That period of four hundred years was labeled the intertestamental period.

During the intertestamental period, God Most High did not send prophets to the people of Israel and consequently, the intertestamental period became known as a period of God Most High's silence.

The account of time from the beginning of creation, until the prophet Malachi was detailed with every moment of God Most High's interaction with humanity, unbroken. And then abruptly, after the prophet Malachi, nothing more was written.

One interpretation of this phenomenon was that God Most High totally separated God's self from humanity. But that interpretation would not include the Daniel's prophecy of the kings of the north and the kings of the south (Daneil 11:1-35).

Daniel received a vision from God Most High which described the details of the events that would take place concerning the world around the land of Israel, during the intertestamental period. Included in Daniel's historical account were descriptions of the activities of the Ptolemies, the Seleucids, Alexander the Great, and other details including a special marriage. Daniel's account was such an accurate and in-depth description of the events of the intertestamental period that some scholars cannot accept that Daniel recorded his account many years prior to the fulfillment of the events. But, if God Most High has foreknowledge of events, then the vision from God Most High that detailed the events, should be expected to be accurate. (Daniel 11:1-35)

Daniel's vision of the kings of the north and the kings of the south was the chord that made the biblical timeline continuous from the time of Adam until the time of Jesus Christ's first coming.

After the crucifixion, death, resurrection and ascension of messiah / the Lamb / Jesus Christ, the apostles and disciples began their trek of taking the message to Judea, Samaria and the rest of the world. They recorded their experiences in the gospels, the book of Acts and their epistles. But when the apostles finished their writing, the canon of the biblical text was concluded.

The fact that the biblical canon ended with the apostles around 95 AD, could also have been viewed as God Most High becoming silent and distant from humanity.

But the book of Acts began with the arrival of the Holy Spirit who provides a personal connection between God Most High and every follower of the Lamb / Jesus Christ.

In addition, Jesus Christ provided the message to the angels of the seven churches that John the Revelator recorded. The seven churches or cities that were addressed, no longer remain to represent the first century church that was addressed in the message. (Revelation 2 and 3)

So, why include the message to the seven churches of the distant past at the beginning of the book of Revelation, a very forward thinking book? The majority of the book of Revelation was a presentation of what is to come in the future that was far distant from the time that John the Revelator recorded it.

Revelation chapters 2 and 3 served the same function as a historical timeline that was similar to Daniel's timeline of the kings of the north and the kings of the south (Daniel 11:1-35).

The timeline of Jesus Christ's message to the seven churches, covered history from the starting point of the first coming of messiah / the Lamb / Jesus Christ, until Jesus Christ returns. This period of time was also known as the times of the Gentiles.

Jesus Christ's message to the seven churches described the transformation of the church throughout history. The history of the church has been marked by definite and distinct phases. The church has experienced eras where the church has presented various theologies, occupied positions of influence, displayed a wide spectrum of what defines morality and displayed a character that ranges from the holy to the totally deviant, etc. Church history has been filled with spots and blemishes. The message of Revelation 2 and 3 supplied a summation of each era of church history, each era of predominant religious theology, and addressed each era of the church's character.

While the church has been changing throughout the centuries, the red dragon / serpent / Satan, Inc. has not remained idle. The red dragon / serpent / Satan, Inc. has remained active in pursuing the mission of being diametrically opposed to the kingdom of heaven in order to establish another kingdom that is in conflict with the kingdom of heaven. The message to the seven churches displayed the tactics of the red dragon / serpent / Satan, Inc. active within each church era. When one tactic failed to achieve all that the red dragon / serpent / Satan, Inc. desired, then the red dragon / serpent / Satan, Inc. moved on to the next strategy.

The red dragon / serpent / Satan, Inc.'s strategies within the church that Jesus Christ addressed in this message to the seven churches included:
- *displaced allegiance from God Most High to a substitute allegiance established with the red dragon / serpent / Satan, Inc. replacing God Most High's rightful place in their hearts,*
- *persecution and death of the followers of the Lamb / Jesus Christ,*
- *deception through immorality and rewriting God Most High's will,*
- *the merger of baal / mystery / mythology religion with Christianity through an unholy marriage and then the introduction of magic, superstition, suppression of education, subjugation, and objectification to enable the elite and elect to rule and to disqualify those who were wrong gender, wrong skin color, wrong genetic background, wrong race or nationality, wrong bank balance, etc.,*
- *convincing people that Jesus Christ is dead,*
- *fostering internal betrayal, and*
- *convincing people that they have everything they need in material wealth so that they no longer need God Most High, with the substitution of pseudo-science that convinces people that they no longer need God Most High, supplying substitute world leaders to replace the leader God Most High sends, and entirely abandoning Jesus Christ as Lord.*

While the red dragon / serpent / Satan, Inc. has been active in shaping the theology and activity of the church, God Most High has also been active in shaping the life of the church.

The message to the seven churches acts as a message in time that reminds us of God Most High's continual provision, God Most High's continual redemptive activity, God Most High's continual activity in preparing the world for Jesus Christ's return, and God Most High's continual preparation of the world for the full establishment of the kingdom of heaven on earth. Even in the midst of the continual twisting of God Most High's theology provided by the red dragon / serpent / Satan, Inc. within the church over the centuries, God Most High has provided a way of salvation to those who overcome the corrupt theology and manipulation that has transpired over the past two millennium. Even with all of the spots and blemishes of the various eras of the church throughout history. God has said, 'Never will I leave you or forsake you' *(Deuteronomy 31:6, 8; Joshua 1:5).*

The continuity that Daniel 11:1-35 and Revelation 2 and 3 brought to the historical timeline documented God Most High's continual activity, even when God Most High sometimes seemed silent.

The reason for God Most High's seeming to be silent was explained by Jesus Christ during his earthly ministry.

During the week of his crucifixion, Jesus Christ said:
'Listen to another parable: There was a landowner who planted a vineyard. He put a wall around it, dug a winepress in it and built a watchtower. Then he rented the vineyard to some farmers and moved to another place. When the harvest time approached, he sent his servants to the tenants to collect his fruit.'

'The tenants seized his servants; they beat one, killed another, and stoned a third. Then he sent other servants to them, more than the first time, and the tenants treated them the same way. Last of all, he sent his son to them. 'They will respect my son,' he said.'

'But when the tenants saw the son, they said to each other, 'This is the heir. Come, let's kill him and take his inheritance.' So they took him and threw him out of the vineyard and killed him.'

'Therefore, when the owner of the vineyard comes, what will he do to those tenants?'

'He will bring those wretches to a wretched end,' they replied, 'and he will rent the vineyard to other tenants, who will give him his share of the crop at harvest time.'

Jesus said to them, 'Have you never read in the Scriptures: "The stone the builders rejected has become the cornerstone; the Lord has done this, and it is marvelous in our eyes?'

'Therefore, I tell you that the kingdom of God will be taken away from you and given to a people who will produce its fruit. Anyone who falls on this stone will be broken to pieces; anyone on whom it falls will be crushed.'

When the chief priests and the Pharisees heard Jesus' parables, they knew he was talking about them. They looked for a way to arrest him, but they were afraid of the crowd because the people held that he was a prophet. Matthew 21:33-46

Jesus' parable had multiple levels of meaning:
- *Israel is efficient in killing the prophets that God Most High sends.*
- *Jesus Christ is the Son of God.*
- *Jesus has been rejected by Israel.*
- *Jesus understood that he would die as a willing sacrifice.*
- *Jesus is the cornerstone, the point on which the kingdom of God is built.*
- *Even though Israel rejects Jesus as their messiah, God Most High's plan for developing a God - human relationship with the people of the world will not be thwarted.*

But most important of all in this narrative, was the response of the Pharisees. The Pharisees finally recognized Jesus as a prophet of God. Jesus Christ became the final prophet of God sent to Israel.

After Jesus Christ's death, resurrection, and ascension into heaven, Jesus Christ sent the Holy Spirit, and the end of the age of prophets was over. From that year's Pentecost, the Holy Spirit resides in the hearts of every person who is a follower of the Lamb / Jesus Christ. The Holy Spirit communicates to every person who uses their eyes to see and ears to hear, the message of what is true, the message of the kingdom of God, sent directly into minds and hearts without the absolute need for any prophet other than Jesus Christ.

The biblical record demonstrated and documented that God Most High will never be silent; not even during the era of the time of Jacob's Trouble.

When we believe that God Most High is silent, in actuality, we are the ones who are not listening to what God Most High has to say. The message of Jesus Christ to the churches was that for those who have eyes, there is also the ability to see and for those who have ears, there is the ability to hear.

While Daniel the prophet wrote for the people of Israel approximately five hundred years prior to the arrival of the incarnate Jesus Christ, John the Revelator wrote to the followers of the Lamb / Jesus Christ, both Jew and Gentile, approximately one thousand nine hundred years before the second arrival of Jesus Christ. God Most High continues to provide the message to those who will listen.

From the time of creation, through the completion of the era of the time of Jacob's Trouble, God Most High demonstrated that God has been and will continue to be, interactive throughout every moment of human history, even into eternity.

The Lamb / Jesus Christ's message to the seven churches, as a message for the era of the time of Jacob's Trouble

Revelation 2 and 3 covered history and historical content from the time of Jesus Christ's ascension into heaven through the era of the time of Jacob's Trouble. In that respect, the historical record presented in Revelation 2 and 3, still seems out of place in a book whose main focus is on the future.

A careful examination of the message of Revelation 2 and 3, provided details of the dynamics that will exist and the impact that will be experienced with the expression of the scheduled events of the era of the time of Jacob's Trouble.

Jesus Christ included this message to the churches as a key component for visioning for the future. Jesus Christ believes that in order to understand the dynamics of the global religious community and the dynamics of the global *political structure / global governance system during the era of the time of Jacob's Trouble, that it is important to understand the history that prepared the foundational influences for the events that must take place.*

The global religious community / great prostitute / Mystery Babylon the Great! does not just come to us during the era of the time of Jacob's Trouble, from nothing. The global religious community / great prostitute / Mystery Babylon the Great! had its seed sown in the Garden of Eden / garden of God / paradise, six thousand years ago, when the serpent / Satan promised the first woman that if she ate the forbidden fruit from the tree of the knowledge of how to do good and evil, that she would become 'like God.' *Inherent in that agreement was the fruit's ability to release humanity from being shaped by God the Creator, so that humanity could be secretly shaped by the gods of the baal / mystery / mythology religion, under the guise of the promise that humanity would be able to shape the baal / mystery / mythology religion gods.*

With this kind of transfer of power and authority, the global religious community / great prostitute / Mystery Babylon the Great! sought to be a global entity in the antediluvian / preflood world. It almost succeeded. The population of the earth at the time of the flood was estimated to be approximately eight billion people. But at the time of the deluge / flood, only eight were deemed to have not been corrupted with Nephilim genetics and under the influence of the serpent / Satan's religious system. Those eight were rescued in an ark. (Genesis 5-8:17)

The global religious community / great prostitute / Mystery Babylon the Great! of the antediluvian / preflood world, was reinvigorated in the postdiluvian / postflood world. Nimrod and the tower of Babel empire, infiltrated the authentic faith system, and redeveloped the false antediluvian / preflood religion, within one hundred years after Noah and his family left the ark. The global power of the religion of the tower of Babel empire, was thwarted through God Most High dividing language. But even with the division of language, the baal / mystery / mythology religion infected the cultures of the entire world. (Genesis

9:18-29, 10:6-20, 11:1-9) Because of the division of language, the account of the eight people rescued through the ark, has been present in multiple cultural histories.

Throughout multiple millennia, the baal / mystery / mythology religion has continued to grow. At various points in human history, the baal / mystery / mythology religion has seemingly consumed the entire world.

But the baal / mystery / mythology religion known by John the Revelator as the great prostitute / Mystery Babylon the Great! has also experienced some major setbacks.

The deluge / flood in Noah's lifetime was one of the serpent / Satan's alternative religion's greatest setbacks. But Satan's alternative religion recovered from the flood.

The resurrection of Jesus Christ and his ascension into heaven to sit at the right hand of God the Father, was another great setback for the baal / mystery / mythology religion.

The establishment of the 'church' / ecclesia / εκκλεσια / 'called out ones,' filled with people who had chosen to deny rebellion against God Most High and to be followers of the Lamb / Jesus Christ, was another major setback for Mystery Babylon the Great!

And yet the serpent / Satan's fake alternative religion has continued throughout human history to overcome, to grow and to prosper. Every time it has experienced setbacks, it begins again with new vigor, to infiltrate the world, to replace God Most High's authentic faith system with its own system, seeking to establish its fake gods to replace the God of the kingdom of heaven.

During the era of the time of Jacob's Trouble, the global religious community that was a seed germinated with the serpent / Satan's alternative antediluvian religion, will have completely blossomed. What was begun in the Garden of Eden / garden of God p paradise, resulted in the necessity of God Most High cleansing the earth with the deluge / flood. What was reinvigorated with the tower of Babel empire and the establishment of the baal / mystery / mythology religion, will have so fully infiltrated the 'church' / ecclesia / εκκλεσια / 'called out ones' so that God Most High during the era of the time of Jacob's Trouble will send an angel to warn God's people to come out of her (Revelation 18:4-5).

For one hundred and twenty years before the deluge / flood, Noah was a preacher, pleading with the people to embrace righteousness.
Moses was God Most High's instrument in Egypt, when God was battling with the gods of Egypt and demonstrating God Most High's divinity and sovereignty over the gods of Egypt.
Messiah / the Lamb / Jesus Christ laid down his life through his crucifixion and death. And yet, God provided resurrection to messiah / the Lamb / Jesus Christ because he did not meet the qualification of unrighteousness that was necessary for death to be able to have held him.
But the entire history of the church has been invested in blending the messages of the authentic faith system of God Most High with the alternative religion of the serpent / Satan, in the attempt to unite the two opposing kingdoms. For examples, consult church history books like *Christianity Through the Centuries* by Earle E. Cairns.
During the era of the time of Jacob's Trouble, humanity will have reached the ultimate climax in the challenge of determining what is righteousness and what is unrighteousness; who is authentic divine and sovereign God and who the gods are that lacking in power and authority; who is the resurrected promised and prophesied messiah and who are posers whose claims for messiahship are false.
All human history has been a struggle to determine which God or gods, of which kingdom, will be fully established on earth. It will be during the era of the time of Jacob's Trouble, that the final determination will be made.

Jesus Christ's message to the seven churches, served to highlight the challenge of the 'church' / ecclesia / εκκλεσια / 'called out ones,' during the past two millennia, *in making the determination for what defined the promised and prophesied messiah. Defining who Jesus Christ is, also determined what God's response would be.*

Of the seven church eras, four demonstrated a spirit of compromise: Ephesus, Pergamum, Thyatira and Laodicea. The era of the time of Jacob's Trouble exists within the historical timeline of the church of Laodicean theology, with the church having become neither hot nor cold about Jesus Christ, and having thrown Jesus Christ out of their theology and lives (Revelation 3:14-22).

But consistently throughout the history of the church era / times of the Gentiles, there have been and will continue to be a remnant of true followers of the God of the kingdom of heaven. In John the Revelator's record, the remnant of true followers of the Lamb / Jesus Christ, were designated by Jesus Christ as those who overcome or who are victorious.

And in the message to the seven churches, Jesus Christ promised to those who chose to remain in opposition to the kingdom of heaven, some very drastic consequences. But for those who overcome or who are victorious, Jesus Christ has promised invaluable benefits and blessings.

(Note: The message was personalized for each of the seven churches / seven eras of church theology during the history of the times of the Gentiles. But while the message was personalized, it remained one message. The first two church eras, Ephesus and Smyrna, experienced their ending already. But the last five church eras, continued on and are active even when Jesus Christ returns. Therefore, the message to the seven churches, applies to all followers of the Lamb / Jesus Christ, and all inhabitants of the earth, especially during the era of the time of Jacob's Trouble.)

The promises made by Jesus Christ to those who do not overcome or who are not victorious:

1. *They will be tolerant of wickedness and false claims (Revelation 2:2).*
2. *They will have forgotten the love of Jesus Christ (Revelation 2:4).*
3. *They will experience the removal of their lampstand from its place (Revelation 2:5).*

4. *They will experience the painful suffering of the second death (Revelation 2:11). (The 'second death' is scheduled for the conclusion of the Thousand Years Reign of Jesus Christ. The 'first death' was recognized as the spiritual death of the first man when he rebelled against God the Creator, and his physical death that resulted from his spiritual death. For all of the rest of humanity, the first death is recognized when a person's physical body no longer functions.)*
5. *They will forever live the lifestyle of baal sacrifice and sexual immorality (Revelation 2:14, 2:20).*
6. *They will be spiritually starved (without access to the hidden manna) (Revelation 2:17).*
7. *They will experience personal war against Jesus Christ and the sword / words of his mouth (Revelation 2:16).*
8. *They will be devoid of personal identity (Revelation 2:17).*
9. *They will endure intense suffering, the same kind of suffering that will be experienced by the baal / mystery / mythology religion of Jezebel (Revelation 2:22).*
10. *They will live without their false religion because of the death of the false religion that has been a legacy of the baal / mystery / mythology religion (Revelation 2:23).*
11. *They will be unable to leave a legacy (Revelation 2:23).*
12. *They will finally be aware and recognize that Jesus Christ searches hearts and minds, and repays each person according to their deeds (Revelation 2:23).*
13. *They will be repaid according to their deeds (Revelation 2:23).*
14. *They will be relegated to being ruled over by those who have embraced God Most High's authentic faith system (Revelation 2:26-27).*

15. *Their work will remain unfinished. They will not be able to accomplish their personal goals. They will not be complete as a human being. (Revelation 3:2)*
16. *They will be surprised with Jesus Christ's arrival, like a thief, unaware of what time Jesus Christ will come (Revelation 3:3).*
17. *They will be unable to escape living in soiled clothes (Revelation 3:4).*
18. *They will not be able to live in the presence of Jesus Christ (Revelation 3:4).*
19. *They will be left to live life as an unworthy person (Revelation 3:4).*
20. *Their name will be blotted out of the book of life (Revelation 3:5).*
21. *They will be disowned before God the Father and the angels of heaven (Revelation 3:5).*
22. *They will be shut out of the presence of God (Revelation 3:8).*
23. *They will be forced to fall down at the feet and honor the followers of the Lamb / Jesus Christ, and acknowledge that the followers of the Lamb / Jesus Christ, are loved by Jesus Christ (Revelation 3:9).*
24. *They will experience the testing of the hour of trial that will permeate the whole world, as an inhabitant of the earth (Revelation 3:10).*
25. *They will have lost the opportunity to hold onto their crown (Revelation 3:11).*
26. *They will be deprived of the personal identity that God Most High supplies (Revelation 3:12).*
27. *They are disgusting to Jesus Christ and will cause him to vomit them out (Revelation 3:15-16).*
28. *They are wretched, pitiful, poor, blind and naked, all while believing that they are wealthy and in need of nothing (Revelation 3:17).*
29. *They are unable to change their circumstances (Revelation 3:18).*

30. They will remain undisciplined (and be forced to live among the habitually undisciplined) (Revelation 3:19).
31. They will experience a state of continual loneliness and aloneness (Revelation 3:20).
32. They will be ruled instead of ruling (Revelation 3:21).

The promises made by Jesus Christ to those who overcome or who are victorious:
1. They will have the right to eat from the tree of life which is in the paradise of God (Revelation 2:7).
2. Jesus Christ is aware of their affliction and poverty (Revelation 2:9-10).
3. They will experience the richness of the kingdom of heaven (Revelation 2:9).
4. They will live life crowned with their own personal victor's crown (Revelation 2:10).
5. They will be protected from all harm of the second death (Revelation 2:11).
6. They will be given hidden manna (Revelation 2:17).
7. They will receive a white stone with a new secret name (Revelation 2:17).
8. They will have authority over nations (Revelation 2:26).
9. They will be given the morning star (Revelation 2:28).
10. They will have the authority and ability to walk with Jesus Christ, dwelling with Jesus Christ (Revelation 3:4).
11. They will be provided with white attire (Revelation 3:4-5).
12. They will be determined to be worthy and experience worthiness (Revelation 3:4).
13. They are given the assurance that their name will never be blotted out of the book of life (Revelation 3:5).

14. They will be recognized as being associated with Jesus Christ, before God the Father and the angels of the kingdom of heaven (Revelation 3:5).
15. They will be locked into the presence of God, unable to be removed from the presence of God (Revelation 3:8).
16. They will be honored by those who are of the synagogue of Satan, who will be forced to acknowledge that Jesus Christ loves them (Revelation 3:9).
17. They will be protected from the hour of trial that will test the inhabitants of the earth throughout the whole world (Revelation 3:10).
18. They will hold onto their crown (Revelation 3:11).
19. They will become pillars in the temple of God Most High (Revelation 3:12).
20. They will be provided with permanent residence status in the temple of God (Revelation 3:12).
21. The name of God Most High and the name of the city of God Most High / new Jerusalem, will be written upon the person (Revelation 3:12).
22. The new name of Jesus Christ will be written upon the person (Revelation 3:12).
23. They will possess gold refined in the fire. They will be rich. (Revelation 3:18)
24. They will be without shame, well clothed and not naked (Revelation 3:18).
25. They will have eyes to see (Revelation 3:18).
26. They will personally dine with Jesus Christ (Revelation 3:20).
27. They will possess and exercise the right to sit with Jesus Christ on his throne (Revelation 3:21).

Paul wrote to the followers of the Lamb / Jesus Christ,

Do you not know that you yourselves are God's temple and that God's Spirit dwells in your midst? If anyone destroys God's temple, God will destroy that person, for God's temple is sacred, and you together are that temple. 1 Corinthians 3:16-17

For those who are followers of the Lamb / Jesus Christ, the kingdom of heaven has already arrived in their *physical body. They have become sovereign property of the kingdom of heaven, with a form of spiritual diplomatic immunity. To declare war upon those who belong to God Most High, will be remembered by God, as an act of war upon God Most High and upon the kingdom of heaven.*

God the Creator, created each human being to be gifted. Disappointingly, most people do not ever realize all that they were created to be. But Jesus Christ has promised that there will be a day when he will return, and on that day, every believer in messiah (BC) and follower of the Lamb (AD) who has overcome or been victorious, will be able to fully express their giftedness that God the Creator endowed them with.

The role of women as influencers upon the events of the era of the time of Jacob's Trouble

The role of women in the religious cultural arena, has been a hotly contested topic since the first man claimed that it was the first woman's fault for his own rebellion against God the Creator, when the first man defied the instruction that God the Creator personally gave to him, to not eat the fruit of the tree of the knowledge of good and evil (Genesis 3, especially 3:12).

The resulting covenant that God the Creator established with the serpent / Satan, was the promise that messiah would be born without the aid of a man, from a virgin (Genesis 3:14-15). (The seal for that covenant was the fact that snakes could no longer walk. Snakes must slither and eat the dust of the earth.)

One of the key characteristics that defined the alternative religion developed by the red dragon / serpent / Satan, Inc., was that it counterfeited the authentic faith system of God the Creator. One of the counterfeits of the religion of the red dragon / serpent / Satan, Inc. has been the altered presentation of the promise that messiah would be born of a virgin. The altered version of the protoevangelium / first covenanted promise of messiah, became known as the mother child cult. In the mother child cult, the mother of the son was worshiped more highly than the son, because she produced the one that attempted to fill the role of messiah. The mother child cult was prevalent before the deluge / flood, and then reestablished after the deluge / flood through Semiramis, Nimrod and Tammuz. Throughout the subsequent millennia, the mother child cult became a crucial tenet of the multiple forms of the baal / mystery / mythology religion (~2358 BC to today). The mother child cult remains prevalent with us even today and was the foundation for the development of the Roman Catholic Church doctrine of the Blessed Virgin Mary / Our Lady of the Eschaton.

In addition to promising a messiah who would defeat the serpent / Satan's vision for the world, God the Creator also established a new dynamic into the relationship between the serpent / Satan and the first woman - hatred. This new hatred dynamic would be essential in furthering God the Creator's redemption, reclamation and regeneration plan. Without this kind of hatred between the kingdom of Satan, Inc. / kingdom of man and women, the offspring of the woman would not have been crucified which caused his heel to be stricken / bruised. And without this kind of hatred, humanity would not create the environment necessary for messiah to crush the head of the serpent / Satan.

God the Creator said to the serpent: 'And <u>I will put enmity</u> <u>between you and the woman</u>, and between your seed and her seed. Her seed shall bruise your head, and you shall bruise his (her seed's) heel.' Genesis 3:15 translated

Before the first man and first woman ate the fruit of the tree of the knowledge of good and evil, God the Creator had already covenanted with humanity to be fruitful, to increase in number, to fill the earth, to subdue the earth, to rule over the living creatures on earth, etc. (Genesis 1:28-30).

When the first man and first woman defied God the Creator and ate the fruit of the tree of the knowledge of good and evil, it changed the entire relationship between God the Creator and humanity. It necessitated a new covenant to be established between God the Creator and the serpent / Satan, and a new covenant to be established with humanity.

In the very first documented covenant established by God the Creator with the serpent / Satan, God the Creator established enmity / hatred, between the serpent / Satan and the first woman, between the red dragon / serpent / Satan, Inc. and all women, and between the kingdom of Satan, Inc. / kingdom of man and the kingdom of heaven which authentically views women as noninferior.

God the Creator established the dynamic that hatred against women would characterize the kingdom of Satan, Inc. / kingdom of man. As a result of this hatred, the red dragon / serpent / Satan, Inc.'s alternative religion has continually used women as disdainful objects in the pursuit of its mission to fully establish the kingdom of Satan, Inc. / kingdom of man on earth. Part of that mission's strategy has been to dehumanize women throughout all of human history. The red dragon / serpent / Satan, Inc. has historically viewed women as objects without personhood, as wombs to incubate Satan's seed, as sheaths for men's swords ('vagina'), etc. And the kingdom of Satan, Inc. / kingdom of man's agenda has consistently pursued the destruction of the offspring of women, first to prevent the birth of messiah, and then to prevent all of humanity born of women to participate in God the Creator's redemption, reclamation and regeneration plan.

In the antediluvian / preflood era, the red dragon / serpent / Satan, Inc. employed the production of Nephilim as an attempt to adulterate creation and replace authentic humanity as created by God the Creator. In the antediluvian / preflood practice of producing Nephilim, daughters were sold by their families to be wombs for breeding the Nephilim giants. Giving birth to the giant infants, caused great child birth mortality for the women. In exchange for selling their daughters, the families would receive 'secret knowledge' / 'mysteries' (first book of Enoch, Ezekiel 28:4-5, 28:16, 28:28, etc. (Deuteronomy 29:29, Revelation 2:24)).

After the deluge / flood, Nephilim production was reestablished with the establishment of the baal / mystery / mythology religion. And as one of the main characteristics of Nimrod's religion, hatred was again directed against women.

The hatred against women was one factor that influenced God Most High's requirement that the one who sits upon the throne of Israel, must have ten generations of legitimate births (Deuteronomy 23:2 (Genesis 38, Ruth 4:18-22)). The development of the messianic lineage required the respect of the mothers included in the messianic lineage, as messianic lineage bearers.

The kingdom of heaven also recognized women as bearers of the message of the kingdom of heaven. Traditionally in the homes of the people of Israel, the mother ushered in every Sabbath worship, beginning with waving her hands over the candles three times to invite God Most High's presence. Women were present at the crucifixion of Jesus Christ. Women were the first to arrive at the empty tomb that had been reserved to house the body of Jesus Christ, but was empty because of Jesus Christ's resurrection.

Joel prophesied that the Spirit of the Lord is accompanied by women prophesying / preaching (Joel 2:28-29). And in the early church, women did prophesy and preach, and advanced the growth of the early church (Acts 1:14, 2:14-18, 6:2-3a, 16:11-15, 16:40, 17:4, 17:12, 17:34, 18:1-3, 18:18-19, 21:8-9, Romans 16:1-19 (seven of these ten women recognized by Paul, were recognized for their ministry), etc.).

Throughout the centuries, women have protected the church's viability and vitality.

Especially during the era of the Great Awakening, women were the predominate spiritual and religious leaders.

The patriarchal stance that many churches and church leaders who deny the necessity of the role of women in the advancement of the kingdom of heaven, have instead centered their own personal missions upon advancing their own personal power, not advancing the message of messiah / the Lamb / Jesus Christ. They involve themselves in the pursuit of establishing their own little kingdoms and their legacy dies soon after their lives are over.

It was the patriarchal stance of the religious leaders of the people of Israel during the earthly ministry of Jesus Christ, that sought to advance their personal power and authority as exclusive religious leaders. They advanced their own power and authority at the expense of the physical life of Jesus Christ. Those who claim to be Christians are not immune to the same temptation and behavior as the religious leaders of Israel who conspired to crucify messiah / the Lamb / Jesus Christ.

Whether or not a person recognizes the essential role of women in the work of the kingdom of heaven in the past, the prophet Joel and Peter both recognized that the arrival of messiah / the Lamb / Jesus Christ will be accompanied by women assuming the role of prophesying / preaching (Joel 2:28-29, Acts 2:14-18). Consequently, to deny women from answering the call made upon them by God to prophesy and to preach, merely because they are women, would be to provide opposition to the work of God in returning messiah / the Lamb / Jesus Christ to earth in order to fully establish the kingdom of heaven on earth.

The serpent / Satan understood the message of God the Creator that was recorded in Genesis 3:15. And the red dragon / serpent / Satan, Inc. understands the importance of attempting to eliminate the influence of women, in order to advance the cause of the red dragon / serpent / Satan, Inc.'s to overthrow the kingdom of heaven and to fully establish the kingdom of Satan, Inc. / kingdom of man on earth.

Historically, when women who have been true followers of the Lamb have been allowed within the church community to be the leaders that God Most High intended them to be, those church eras have been blessed and the church prospered. When the influence of women as leaders has been removed, those church eras tended to receive higher condemnation.

The red dragon / serpent / Satan, Inc. will continue to maintain its stance of enmity against women until the global religious community that sits upon the foundation of the red dragon / serpent / Satan, Inc. has been finally defeated.

Those who practice a 'picker and chooser' alternative method of Bible study, usually do not read or study the first three chapters of Genesis, nor the last nineteen chapters of John the Revelator's Revelation. Consequently, understanding those particular portions of the biblical record, eludes them. Because they do not fully comprehend the weight of the beginning of human history's story, and because they fail to recognize the biblical record's description of the end of this era of human history, they have no framework to understand the present moment in between or God's work in the process of fully establishing the kingdom of heaven on earth. Because they cannot conceptualize what the fully established kingdom of heaven on earth will look like, they tend to just deny the possibility that messiah / the Lamb / Jesus Christ will return and that the kingdom of heaven will be fully established upon earth.

In the fully established kingdom of heaven, women hold a place of equality with men. And women hold a place of equality especially with Jesus Christ. Even the red dragon / serpent / Satan, Inc. understands this and has supported the development of the Semiramis - Nimrod baal / mystery / mythology religion, which incorporated the mother child cult theology. Historically, the mother child cult has been repackaged multiple times including within the theology of the 'Blessed Virgin Mary' and the reimagined Mary as the new 'Queen of Heaven.'

The red dragon / serpent / Satan, Inc. understands that God Most High will use women in the full establishment of the kingdom of heaven and has been at work since the era of the Garden of Eden / garden of God / paradise to diminish women's effectiveness within the church and in the world.

The practice of ignoring God Most High's proper use of women during the era of the time of Jacob's Trouble will be a 'tell' as to which kingdom one truly supports. Joel's *description of the Day of the Lord, detailed the vital importance of women prophesying / preaching especially in the final days before the return of the promised and prophesied messiah (~800 to 700 BC?) (Joel 2:23-32). And on the Day of Pentecost that followed the crucifixion, death, resurrection and ascension of Jesus Christ, Peter reaffirmed the importance of Joel's message (~30 AD) (Acts 2:16-21).*

Messiah / the Lamb / Jesus Christ's message provided to John the Revelator, using the term 'church' / ecclesia / εκκλεσια / 'called out ones'

After Revelation chapter 3, the term 'church' / ecclesia / εκκλεσια / 'called out ones,' *was used only once throughout the rest of the biblical record. In Revelation chapter 22 Jesus Christ offered the reminder of who he is using the same descriptions of himself that he used in Revelation chapters 2 and 3. Revelation 22 recognized the fulfillment of the promises that were made in Revelation chapters 2 and 3. Revelation 22:16 where Jesus Christ said,* 'I, Jesus, have sent my angel to give you this testimony for the churches. I am the Root and the Offspring of David, and the bright Morning Star.' *was the only other occurrence of use of the term 'church' after Revelation chapters 2 and 3.*

The fact that the term 'church' / ecclesia / εκκλεσια / 'called out ones' *was not used from Revelation chapter 4 to chapter 22, was one reason why some believed that Revelation chapters 2 and 3 do not belong with the rest of the book of Revelation.*

This fact was also utilized to support rapture theology, a theology that claims that the believers in Jesus Christ will be taken out of the world before the events of the era of the time of Jacob's Trouble begins. For rapture theologians, the only acceptable explanation for the missing term 'church,' can be a belief that the 'church' will no longer be in existence and therefore 'church' people will be missing. The explanation that rapture theology offered is that there will be a point in time when Jesus Christ will come to remove Christians to heaven, prior to the glorious coming of Jesus Christ at the conclusion of the era of the time of Jacob's Trouble. For rapture theologians, God Most High is limited in God's ability to protect God Most High's people during the events of the time of Jacob's Trouble. And therefore, church people will need to be taken to heaven in order to avoid experiencing the events of the era of the time of Jacob's Trouble.

But to believe that God the Creator who created everything within the cosmos, would not be mightier than the events of the era of the time of Jacob's Trouble, would be a deception concerning the power of God the Creator. God the Creator has utilized humanity for six thousand years in the plan for redemption, reclamation and regeneration. There was a contiguous lineage from the first man and first woman to the birth of messiah / the Lamb / Jesus Christ. Even Jesus Christ came into the world and experienced the human experience complete with his own crucifixion. And for the past two thousand years, it has been the responsibility of the followers of the Lamb / Jesus Christ, to go into all the world and make disciples (Matthew 28:16-20, Mark 16:15). All aspects of human experience are utilized by God the Creator who remains above the human experience, not at the mercy of human experience. God the Creator has no reason to change that strategy now and not use followers of the Lamb / Jesus Christ during the era of the time of Jacob's Trouble.

Another option for how to interpret the missing term of 'church' / ecclesia / εκκλεσια / 'called out ones,' in the center of John's book of Revelation, would be that near the conclusion of this historical timeline detailed in Revelation 2 and 3, the purpose of the church, which was to express the message that Jesus Christ is the divine and sovereign, promised and prophesied messiah, has been squashed within the church community.

And the biblically defined, divine and sovereign, promised and prophesied messiah, is no longer welcome within the church community, possibly because of the requirements that Jesus Christ placed upon the church. After all, Jesus Christ made some significant demands upon the 'church' in the message to the angels of the seven *churches: do not forsake your first love, repent, do not follow the practices of the Nicolaitans, endure suffering and prison and persecution and remain faithful, do not renounce your faith, refrain from eating food sacrificed to idols, refrain from sexual immorality, repent, do not tolerate the teachings of the baal / mystery / mythology religion, know that messiah / the Lamb / Jesus Christ searches hearts and minds and repays deeds, wake up, strengthen what you have, be finished, dress in the actual white clothes of righteousness, hold on to what you have that you share with Jesus Christ, do not be lukewarm about your relationship with the Lamb / Jesus Christ, realize that you need Jesus Christ, buy gold refined in the fire from Jesus Christ, obtain from Jesus Christ white clothes to wear that will cove shameful nakedness, obtain from Jesus Christ salve to put on eyes so that you can have sight, be rebuked and disciplined, and open the door and allow Jesus Christ to eat with you so that Jesus Christ can allow you to sit on the throne with him.*

The message to the churches in Revelation 2 and 3 was the historical timeline describing the transformation of the church from the time of Jesus Christ's first coming until the end of the times of the Gentiles and the era of the time of Jacob's Trouble. Using that timeline to tell the time that we are living in, currently we have reached the era of the church of Laodicean theology and the era of the time of Jacob's Trouble.

Because the church community as a whole, is no longer dedicated to its original purpose, the term 'church' / ecclesia / εκκλεσια / 'called out ones' *has become obsolete and no longer defines the 'church.'*

Jesus Christ identified the era of the church of Laodicean theology as neither hot nor cold. Jesus Christ spits it out of his mouth / vomits it out.

The era of the church of Laodicean theology has abandoned its first love, has abandoned the word of God Most High, has abandoned the will of God Most High, has abandoned the love of God Most High and has abandoned the telling of God Most High's redemptive plan through Jesus Christ. The era of the church of Laodicean theology has a new focus, the final fulfillment of the serpent / Satan's promise to the first woman that humanity could be 'like God,' *only needing to acknowledge humanity's imaginary sovereignty as real, and completely eliminating the personal recognition of the divinity and sovereignty of God Most High. When humanity recognizes its own imaginary sovereignty as real, there is no reason for Jesus Christ to have been crucified and resurrected.*

In the imaginary bubble of the individual human being divine and sovereign, there is no reason to acknowledge anyone else as being divine and sovereign. And in the imaginary bubble of the individual human being divine and sovereign, there is no room for anyone else to exist in that person's bubble. That is possibly the greatest lie of all, and it begins with lying to one's self and believing the lie that a person can be divine and sovereign without a true relationship with Jesus Christ.

The era of the church of Laodicean theology no longer supports the Lordship of Jesus Christ. The era of the church of Laodicean theology has nothing to offer, except the ability to cause Jesus Christ to want to vomit.

If the church is no longer following the will of God, then what was previously defined using the term 'church' / ecclesia / εκκλεσια / 'called out ones' *no longer has a group of people within the organized religious church structure, that the term 'church' /* ecclesia / εκκλεσια / 'called out ones' *can be applied to.*

During the era of the time of Jacob's Trouble, what was once called 'church' / ecclesia / εκκλεσια / 'called out ones,' *will be divided.*

One division will consist of the global religious community that supports the globalization that will eventually be fully led by the two men John the Revelator identified as the beast of the sea and the beast of the earth (Revelation 13). This division was further referenced as 'the great prostitute.' *The great prostitute uses the power of religion to rule and pursues an agenda that actually is centered on destroying the kingdom of heaven and the people of the kingdom of heaven so that the kingdom of*

Satan, Inc. / kingdom of man may be fully established. John the Revelator's imagery of the great prostitute, depicted her riding the seven / eight headed scarlet beast / the corporate church. (Revelation 12, 13, 17, 18:4)

The other division within the 'church' / ecclesia / εκκλεσια / 'called out ones,' still believes that Jesus Christ is the divine and sovereign, promised and prophesied messiah. Eventually this division of people will experience being pushed out by the first division. And they will be also called by God Most High to exit the corporate church (Revelation 18:4).

People who will continue to protest against the religious and political abuses committed by the global religious community will be people who believe that the new Laodicean era transformation of 'church' is not acceptable. This division of what was once the 'church' is referred to in the rest of the book of Revelation under their new designation as 'followers of the Lamb' / Jesus Christ.

The precedence for using descriptions instead of more common titles was already established in the gospels when not once was the term 'Christian' used with the gospels. It was not until the apostles and disciples had been dispersed throughout the world, that the word 'Christian' was even coined (Acts 11:26). And the term 'Christian' meant referenced 'a follower of Christ.'

Jesus Christ's intention was not to begin a new religion. Jesus Christ intended that people would accept the promised and prophesied messiah of Israel.

The red dragon / serpent / Satan, Inc.'s original mission that began in the Garden of Eden (Genesis 3) to cause division between God the Creator and humanity, and to destroy the image of God Most High created in humanity, is still active and alive today. And during the era of the Laodicean church, the red dragon / serpent / Satan, Inc. has caused religious division within the church community and hijacked the original 'church' as an organization, in order to attempt once again to accomplish the purposes of the red dragon / serpent / Satan, Inc.

During the era of the time of Jacob's Trouble, the mission of this global religious community, will be to attempt to fully establish the 'kingdom of man' using religion, where the understanding will be established;
- that the elite class of humanity understands what God should be and can achieve the divine and sovereign activities of a creative god, causing them to be worthy to conquer (Revelation 6:1-2),
- that the elite class of humanity can rule the people of the earth in the place of what should be God Most High's rule, using a form of mob rule (Revelation 6:3-4),
- that the elite class of humanity can create a better pervasive economy that will control humanity through the availability of food, and will incorporate control over the people of the earth to support the elite class of humanity (Revelation 6:5-6, 18),
- that the elite class of humanity can create a sustainable earth through population control, through controlling humanity using sword, famine and plague, and the wild beasts of the earth, and does not need to appeal to the hearts and minds in order to govern (Revelation 6:7-8),
- that the elite class of humanity believes the best solution to problems is the elimination of its opposition (Revelation 6:9-11), and
- that the elite class of humanity can better govern than God Most High through absolute autocratic control of the population, according to the mores of the two global leaders described by John the Revelator as the beast of the sea and the beast of the earth (Revelation 13, etc.).

The kingdom of Satan, Inc. / kingdom of man will continue to present itself as the best alternative for creating a better kingdom than the kingdom of God Most High / kingdom of heaven. The red dragon / serpent / Satan, Inc. continues to tout the belief that humanity can evolve to be 'like God,' can evolve a better form of *posthuman being, greater than the current form of humanity. The red dragon / serpent / Satan, Inc.'s mission is a revival of the fake promise made in the Garden of Eden / garden of God / paradise, a revival of the antediluvian mission as it was in the days before Noah, a revival of the vision of the tower of Babel empire, and a revival of the dream of the religious leaders of the nation of Israel that crucified messiah / the Lamb / Jesus Christ.*

It would not have been appropriate in the message that Jesus Christ provided to John the Revelator, to lump together those who actively pursue globalization, with those who are authentic followers of the Lamb / Jesus Christ, under the term 'church' / ecclesia / εκκλεσια / 'called out ones' in describing the events that will take place during the era of the time of Jacob's Trouble.

The Lamb / Jesus Christ's message to the angels of the seven churches of Asia, as a reference to the historical work of Jesus Christ and of the church, within the seven thousand years plan of God Most High

God the Creator is more than capable of threading a one dimensional needle. God the Creator is also able to weave a two dimensional piece of fabric. God the Creator is even able to layer material and sew a multidimensional product (literal examples: creation of the cosmos, creation of the Garden of Eden / Garden of God / paradise, creation of living creatures including humanity, even the clothes that God the Creator crafted for Adam and Eve, etc.). Everything that God the Creator has created has multiple dimensions.

Throughout human history, Jesus Christ has been one of the active participants in providing this multidimensional cosmos, complete with its multidimensional history (John 1:1-18, 1:29-34, Romans 1:20, Hebrews 9:16-28, 1 Peter 1:20, Revelation 3:14, 13:8, etc.).

It is within the nature of Jesus Christ to have also provided multiple layers of meaning within his message to the angels of the seven churches.

One layer of the message to the angels of the seven churches was as a direct message of instruction to the actual churches of John the Revelator's lifetime.

Another layer of the message to the angels of the seven churches was as a layout of church history spanning time from Jesus Christ's first coming to Jesus Christ's second coming.

Another layer of the meaning of Revelation chapters 2 and 3 was discovered within this message in the references to the Jewish feasts. One example of this referencing was the hidden manna in the message for Pergamum. The hidden manna was reminiscent of the time when the people of Israel were lead through the wilderness, which was annually commemorated in the feast of tabernacles / feast of booths.

Because all the Jewish feasts described some portion of the story of God Most High's activity with humanity through the person of Jesus Christ, it was appropriate that in this message to the churches contained in Revelation 2 and 3 that Jesus Christ would also reference the required feasts with their message that centered around his first coming to set up the redemption plan and his return when his redemption plan will be fully realized. The connection between Jesus' message and the feasts acted as Jesus Christ's recognition of the history of the people of Israel in making his life and ministry into reality, recognition of his own personal history, a personal signature on the message to the seven churches and validation that the message of the entire book of Revelation is from Jesus Christ.

Correlation between Jesus Christ's message to the churches
(Revelation 2 and 3)
and the required feasts of Israel

Church	Imagery used in the message	Associated feast
Ephesus	First love / bride and bridegroom relationship	Feast of trumpets
Smyrna	Ten days of testing / Ten Days of Awe for	Day of Atonement

	preparation for Yom Kippur	*/ Yom Kippur*
Pergamum	*'I know where you live.' Balaam was unable to give a curse to Israel as they wandered in the wilderness. Hidden manna*	*Feast of tabernacles*
Thyatira	*Deep secrets such as the secret that God would raise from the dead, the one who has eyes like blazing fire... a reference to Jesus Christ begin glorified, and the traitorous acts of Jezebel / religious leaders that placed Jesus on the cross*	*Feast of Passover*
Sardis	*'Wake up' a reference to rising from the dead or near death. Those who experience resurrection are now freshly dressed.*	*Feast of firstfruits*
Philadelphia	*Slander and sin represent leavening. 'I know your deeds.'*	*Feast of Unleavened Bread*
Laodicea	*'The words of the Amen, the faithful and true witness...' The Holy Spirit is the finger of God that writes the Law of Moses on the tablets. The Law of God is used in the act of discipline. The Holy Spirit is the baptizer by fire and is the Spirit of truth that witnesses to the human spirit and writes God's law and truth on the human heart. When Jesus Christ sent the Holy Spirit, Jesus Christ was faithful to his promise.*	*Feast of Pentecost*

The connection of the message to the angels of the seven churches with the required Jewish feasts of Israel also communicated that God Most High's seven thousand years plan was the validation of the continual work annually dramatized with the participation of the require feasts. The message to the angels of the seven churches confirmed the return of messiah / the Lamb / Jesus Christ as a vital part of the divine will of God Most High.

This seven thousand years plan began in the Garden of Eden (Genesis 3). The work of messiah / the Lamb / Jesus Christ was annually dramatized in the required feasts. Messiah / the Lamb / Jesus Christ fulfilled a portion of that plan was fulfilled with his earthly ministry almost two thousand years ago. And messiah / the Lamb / Jesus Christ will return to finish what he began in fulfilling this plan. It is a plan that will lead us to the beginning of eternity.

Jesus Christ's message to the angels of the seven churches, as preparation for the events of the era of the time of Jacob's Trouble and the rest of the book of Revelation

God the Creator provided Enoch, Methuselah, Lamech and Noah with a substantial amount of information concerning the first judgment of the world. The evidence of God's instruction was documented in the first book of Enoch.

God the Creator sufficiently instructed Noah on how to prepare for the deluge / flood. The evidence of the sufficiency of God's instruction to Noah was Noah's building of the ark, surviving the deluge / flood, and humanity's existence today.

God Most High instructed Moses on how to lead the people of Israel out of Egypt, to escape the danger of the Egyptians that desired to annihilate the people of Israel. The evidence of God's instruction was the people of Israel crossing of the Red Sea, Moses' conference on the mountain to receive the Law, the memories of other cultures of the dramatic work of God Most High, the existence of the people of Israel even today, etc. (Joshua 2:8-11, and other culture's documentation of events).

The entire Old Testament / Tanakh presented the history of God Most High's progress in the pursuit of God's redemption, reclamation and regeneration plan. God Most High sought to prepare the people of Israel and the Gentiles for the coming of messiah / the Lamb / Jesus Christ. The wise men who followed the star to find the infant messiah in a manger, John the Baptists, the disciples of Jesus Christ, etc. understood God Most High's instruction concerning the coming of the promised and prophesied messiah.

During the earthly ministry of Jesus Christ, Jesus Christ endeavored to prepare his disciples for Jesus' crucifixion, death and resurrection. The four gospel writers documented Jesus Christ's preparation of his disciples.

But within the biblical record, more attention was given to preparing the believers in messiah (BC), followers of the Lamb (AD) and the inhabitants of the earth for the return of messiah / the Lamb / Jesus Christ, than for any other event in human history. The evidence of that was sprinkled throughout the biblical record, and then was especially concentrated in the records of the Old Testament / Tanakh prophet Daniel and John the Revelator.

Jesus Christ's message to the angels of the seven churches was the beginning of the message that focused specifically upon these last seven years that serve as preparation for the conclusion of this era of human history. It has been an era of six thousand years of humanity being exiled from the Garden of Eden / garden of God / paradise, and of being exiled from dwelling in the full presence of God. The message to the seven churches served as an historical timeline for two thousand of those years. And as the historical connector between Jesus Christ's earthly ministry, until the return of messiah / the Lamb / Jesus Christ, the message to the seven churches demonstrated the further continuity of God Most High's redemption, reclamation and regeneration plan.

Jesus Christ's message to the angels of the seven churches of Asia, were filled with multiple layers of meaning.

The first layer of message was specifically to the seven churches that existed during the lifetime of John the Revelator, and provided instruction on how to relate to Jesus Christ. The message also communicated what Jesus Christ expected from the members of the seven churches.

Another layer to Jesus Christ's message to the seven churches was directed to those members of the church community that were not followers of the Lamb / Jesus Christ. For those, the message to the seven churches acted as a warning.

Another layer of the message to the seven churches was to offer instruction and prophecy that is poignant as preparation for the era of the time of Jacob's Trouble.

This entire era of the time of Jacob's Trouble is a culmination of the results of the events throughout thousands of years of humanity history. Many of those events have been rehearsal events for the time of Jesus Christ's return and the full establishment of the kingdom of heaven on earth. The message to the angels of the seven churches validated that all of human history has been intertwined in preparation for the return of messiah / the Lamb / Jesus Christ and for the full establishment of the kingdom of heaven on earth.

The deeper aspects of the message to the seven churches provided clues to the events that will take place and instructions for the followers of the Lamb / Jesus Christ on how to approach the challenges that will arise during the era of the time of Jacob's Trouble. In this manner, another layer of meaning of the message to the seven churches was to provide a foundational preparation for understanding the rest of the book of Revelation and the activity of God Most High during the era of the time of Jacob's Trouble.

When it is understood how God Most High views the original purpose of the 'church' as the method for carrying the message of the Lordship of Jesus Christ and God Most

High's redemptive plan, and how God Most High views the responsibilities assigned to the followers of the Lamb / Jesus Christ on behalf of the kingdom of heaven, then it can be better understood for why God Most High has actively been setting the stage for the events scheduled to take place during the era of the time of Jacob's Trouble. This future kingdom transition has been such a magnificent undertaking that it has required six thousand years of prepping. The message to the seven churches identified that there is much in our world that must be reconfigured in order for our world to be able to effectively receive the fullness and perfection of the fully established kingdom of heaven on earth.

One of the unique characteristics of the Bible as a whole, is that with God Most High there is an 'already' aspect interwoven into the 'not yet' aspect of what God Most High has planned. With God Most High the past, present and future are mixed. The Lamb / Jesus Christ has already acted, and yet the Lamb / Jesus Christ is preparing to act, and the Lamb / Jesus Christ will act again in the future. But all actions of messiah / the Lamb / Jesus Christ in God's redemptive plan, were determined six thousand years ago in the Garden of Eden / garden of God / paradise.

As God Most High wills it to be done, it has already been accomplished. In the world of sports, we would say that the game has been fixed before the opening play. In the computer world we would say that the world is preparing for a reboot with a new base operating system.

Jesus Christ's message to the angel of the church at Ephesus: early apostolic church – Revelation 2:1-7

Church of Ephesus – church of lost love (See Acts 19:8-12)
Jesus said, 'To the angel of the church of Ephesus, write,

'This is the message from the one holding the seven stars in his right hand, and who walks in the midst of the seven golden lampstands. I know your works, your labor, and your endurance; and that you are not able to tolerate evil ones. You have tested those claiming to be apostles and are not, and have found them to be false / liars. You have persevered and have endured for my name's sake and have not grown weary.'

'But I have this against you, that you have abandoned the love you had at first.'

'Remember therefore, from where you have fallen. Repent, and do the works you did at first. If however, you do not, I am coming to you and I will remove your lampstand out of its place, unless you repent.'

'But you have this, that you hate the practices of the Nicolaitans, which I also hate.'

'To the one having an ear, hear what the Spirit says to the churches. The one who overcomes I will give to eat from the tree of life which is in God's paradise.' Revelation 2:1-7 translated

An apostle was defined as a person who had been a follower of Jesus Christ during his earthly ministry, and then personally witnessed the resurrected messiah / the Lamb / Jesus Christ. The number of apostles was limited, and after their death, there would be no apostles unless Jesus Christ made himself known to them in a manner similar to the way that Jesus Christ made himself known to Saul / Paul (Acts 9).

Jesus Christ recognized that the early apostolic church needed to determine the difference between those who claimed to be apostles of Jesus Christ but were instead false, and those who were authentic apostles of Jesus Christ. Even in the early apostolic church community, false leaders were present.

Note that there was no indication that the church of Ephesus era continued into later history and into the era of the time of Jacob's Trouble.

Historical message:

The apostle Paul, Silas and their companions visited Ephesus.

Apollos was a key leader in the Ephesian church (Acts 19).

The name 'Ephesus' means 'desired.'

The name 'Nicolaitans' was a combination of Nicao (to conquer or overcome, to rule) and Laos (laity, people). This reference to the Nicolaitans referred to the act of religious leaders using their status and position to rule over the general population of the people. The practice of religious leaders ruling over the general population of the people was a characteristic of the various forms of the baal / mystery / mythology religion.

The priestly class would determine what class others would be sorted into and then determine what others' relationships with God Most High would be. Most importantly, they proffered that relationships with God Most High could not be established or accessed without going through them.

While God Most High defined the fully established kingdom of heaven as being a kingdom of priests, God's definition of priest was for the priest to bring people to God Most High, not for the priest to prevent the access of people to God. In God Most High's economy, everyone has personal access to God.

While the sacrificial system of the tabernacle / temple required the priests to exclusively offer the sacrifices, Jesus Christ's crucifixion, death, resurrection and ascension into heaven, completed the old tabernacle / temple system of sacrifice. Jesus Christ assumed the role of priest of the order of Melchizedek, which was a priesthood that surpassed all other priesthoods, having been established with Shem, Noah's middle son. From that point on, Jesus Christ became the only intermediary needed. Jesus Christ provided for every individual to experience direct personal access to the God of the kingdom of heaven through the gift of the individual presence of the Holy Spirit.

Jesus Christ provided an entirely unique model for ministry with a unique paradigm for religion that was different from all other versions of religion. In the paradigm provided through the resurrected Jesus Christ, instead of religious leaders holding elite status and being served, Jesus Christ modeled the expectation that leaders who are followers of the Lamb / Jesus Christ will demonstrate an attitude of servitude toward God Most High and God Most High's law with an attitude of loving God Most High's people and providing service to God's people accordingly. Jesus Christ modeled that flavor of servitude in a variety of ways including washing the feet of the apostles.

In contrast, the Nicolaitans, like the Jewish religious leaders and baal / mystery / mythology religion priests, demonstrated that religious leaders were to be considered elite, elect and powerful. Sin was redefined from those things that displease God Most High to being defined as those things that offended the religious leaders and priests.

Laity were considered to be a separate class from the religious leaders and priests. Laity were deemed unworthy and the proof of their unworthiness laid in the fact that they were not elected to be the religious leaders. The elite and the laity were not to mingle together and touching between the classes was undesirable.

The practice of not touching the unclean, dirty and disgusting laity, meant that the writers of the gospels (Matthew, Mark, Luke and John) that documented Jesus Christ's frequent touching of those that he would heal, were describing a messiah that the Jewish religious leaders would not culturally recognize as being a valid priest of God Most High. (Jesus Christ was a descendant of both Judah (king) and Levi (priest) through his mother Mary (Luke 1:5, 1:26-28, 2:1-20, 2:46, 3:23-38).)

Laity were viewed as people who needed to be ruled by other people. The religious hierarchy of the Nicolaitans lorded over the people and wrote their own divine law that defied God Most High's law and was presented as a substitute for God Most High's law.

The Nicolaitans also were known for their extravagant and deviant sexual practices. The Nicolaitans encourage their adherents to participate in all forms of sexual interaction, without boundaries or restraint.

In step with the practice of encouraging a culture of sexual deviancy, the Nicolaitans also injected themselves in between the person and God. The Nicolaitans determined that to worship God, they needed to dictate rituals including sexual rituals, that their adherents were required to participate in. This kind of religious leadership had the effect of separating the individual from God which caused the individual to lose connection with God who should have been their first love.

In marriage when a third party injected themself into the relationship to displace the person that was covenanted to be the husband or wife, it was called adultery. Adultery was not approved by God Most High because the first love relationship is lost.

In the covenant between God Most High and each individual, when a religious leader (who is always inferior to God Most High) injects their self in between God and the individual, it is also a form of adultery called idolatry. Idolatry and adultery both reflect the abandonment of one's 'first love.' Therefore, the red dragon / serpent / Satan, Inc. has found that physical sexual relationships unblessed by God Most High, are effective at pulling people away from God Most High. When a religious leader violates God Most High's intention by injecting their self into someone else's life in a position that is not theirs to possess, the result is always the loss of 'first love,' with the love relationship being substituted by a power based relationship with one party lording over the other.

At the time of John's writing of this message, it was the practice of the priests of the baal / mystery / mythology religion and the Nicolaitans to insist that they were the gatekeepers to God Most High and that access to God Most High and eternal life were available at their discretion. Whenever a person assumes the authority that belongs to God Most High in another person's life, the result can only lead to that person developing a perverted image of God.

Historical timeline message to the historical era of the church of Ephesus:

As part of the historical timeline of Revelation 2 and 3, the message to the church of Ephesus referred to the era of the apostolic church which was led by the apostles of Jesus Christ / those who became disciples and followers of Jesus Christ during his earthly ministry, and were witnesses to the resurrection of Jesus Christ.

The apostolic church did not allow the theology of the Nicolaitans to prosper. For limiting the spread of the theology of the Nicolaitans during the apostolic church era, the church of the apostolic era was blessed.

*Another idea that was emerged during the era of the apostolic church era was the idea of preterism which is the belief that with Jesus Christ's death and resurrection, all of the prophecies of the Old Testament / Tanakh have been fulfilled. Even Jesus said, '*I have come to fulfill the law.' *Preterists interpreted Jesus' statement as Jesus having indicated that with his first coming, all the prophecy of the Old Testament / Tanakh that ever was intended to be fulfilled, was fulfilled.*

The problem with preterism is that there was more written in the biblical record concerning the second coming of the messiah than there was ever written concerning the messiah's earthly ministry. If God Most High did not intend to fulfill the entire word of God and not have Jesus Christ return in the future, then God Most High would technically be a liar, not authentic, and not dependable.

It is the kingdom of Satan, Inc. / kingdom of man that continually presents the message that God is a liar, inauthentic, and not dependable.

But the kingdom of heaven consistently has proven itself to be truth, authentic and dependable. Truth, authenticity and dependability are characteristics necessary for love to exist and to grow.

The return of messiah / the Lamb / Jesus Christ will establish which kingdom possesses the truth; which kingdom is authentic; and which kingdom is dependable.

Paul wrote to the Thessalonians, 'Concerning the coming of our Lord Jesus Christ and our being gathered to him, we ask you, brothers and sisters, not to become easily unsettled or alarmed by the teaching allegedly from us — whether by a prophecy or by word of mouth or by letter — asserting that the Day of the Lord has already come. Don't let anyone deceive you in any way, for that day will not come until the rebellion occurs and the man of lawlessness is revealed, the man doomed to destruction. He will oppose and will exalt himself over everything that is called God or is worshiped, so that he sets himself up in God's temple, proclaiming himself to be God.' 2 Thessalonians 2:1-4

The message of Jesus Christ to the angel of the church of Ephesus, was a reminder that the followers of the

Lamb / Jesus Christ are to not give up on the fulfillment of the plan of the kingdom of heaven. The biblical record provided great assurance that there is a coming day when the 'lawless one' will rise, and that Jesus Christ will return to fully conquer the lawless one at just the right time, on God Most High's time schedule.

The theology of the historical era of the church of Ephesus in the movement toward the theology of the historical era of the church of Laodicea

The theology of the church of Ephesus / early apostolic church, provided the foundation for all church theology that has followed. The early apostolic church leaders understood and taught that messiah / the Lamb / Jesus Christ would return one day, to fully establish the kingdom of heaven on earth. Even though almost two thousand years have transpired between Jesus Christ's earthly ministry and his return, the early apostolic church understood that the final portion of the transition from the dominance on earth of the kingdom of Satan, Inc. / kingdom of man, to the full establishment of the kingdom of heaven, would take place with a rapidness like a flood.

The early apostolic church era, ended with the death of the apostles. Apostles were men and women who were followers and disciples of Jesus Christ during his earthly ministry, and then became witnesses of the resurrection of Jesus Christ, interacting with the resurrected Jesus Christ. They were a very specific group of people. So, when the apostles died, the early apostolic church era ended.

Beyond laying the foundation for all church theology that followed, the theology of the church of Ephesus did not provide movement toward the theology of the church of Laodicea that is currently active within many churches around the world.

Jesus Christ's message for the era of the time of Jacob's Trouble from the message to the angel of the early apostolic church of Ephesus

During the era of the time of Jacob's Trouble, the general global church community will no longer support God Most High as a focus for worship or as divine and sovereign, nor recognize the divinity and sovereignty of Jesus Christ. One motivation for abandoning devotion to God Most High and messiah / the Lamb / Jesus Christ will be that in loosening the ties to God Most High and to Jesus Christ, a broader audience will be able to be incorporated under the umbrella of the global church and to be able to develop the influence of the larger global religious community, in the pursuit of establishing global governance.

In this pursuit, the global church and the global religious community will encourage various forms of sexual activity as a means of pulling people away from the kingdom of heaven and for bonding people to the kingdom of Satan, Inc. / kingdom of man. Unlicensed sexual activity and sexual religious rites have been used throughout the millennia of human history, for advancing the baal / mystery / mythology religion. Forcing people to practice sexual religious rites was even one of the activities conducted on the temple mount during the first abomination of desolation event (167 BC). And in some portions of the religious community, there has been a long standing historical understanding that having sex with a religious leader / holy man, was to be considered as a holy gift, and not a sin offensive to God Most High.

Jesus Christ's message to the Ephesian church was reminiscent of Jesus Christ's imperative to place the right God and right kingdom in the position of first place. If Jesus Christ is chosen to be one's first love, then the covenant with Jesus Christ results in the goodness and fullness of what God Most High intends to offer.

Worship and sex are images of each other. They both identify to whom you belong, either the one who lawfully and rightly holds the position of God Most High (worship) or spouse (sex); or a third party (idolatry and adultery).

Because idolatry and adultery are images of each other, they both break the covenant agreement that has been made between a person and God (idolatry) or spouse (adultery) in order to inject a third party into the relationship.

Consequently, remembering one's first love / first covenant remains the beginning of what it means to be a follower of the Lamb / Jesus Christ. Remember that God Most High offers allowance for passion. David and Solomon had many wives and concubines. Even Solomon was the son of David with Bathsheba, a relationship that began with adultery and conspiracy to murder. But sex outside of the marriage of one man and one woman acts to push away Jesus Christ as one's first love; and that is what makes sex outside of traditional marriage to be offensive.

The era of the time of Jacob's Trouble will be a time of testing when everyone will be required to declare who will be their God. Who will occupy that space as first love?

Jesus Christ as the creator and giver of life hold authentic dibbs for the position of first love. But most people of the world will choose a third party, the red dragon / serpent / Satan, Inc. and those designated by the red dragon / serpent / Satan, Inc. to lead. And sexual deviancy from the traditionally blessed marriage relationship, will be a tool used to pull people away from what should be their first love.

Jesus Christ's overall message was that sex is not love and love is not sex. Trying to incorporate the perverted sexual ideas that originated with baal / mystery / mythology religions (adultery, forced celibacy, homosexuality, pedophilia, prostitution, etc.), will pervert one's understanding of God and what authentic love actually consists of. In God Most High's understanding of how relationships work, unblessed sexual relationships work to pervert the healthy relationship that God wishes for us to experience with our spouse, and more importantly to pervert the healthy relationship that God Most High wishes to experience with us.

The act of sex was intended by God Most High to be used to bond a husband and wife together in love, as a model for the bond that Jesus Christ / the bridegroom will have with the bride / believers in messiah (BC) and followers of the Lamb (AD). The fullness of the relationship that Jesus Christ desires to have with God's holy people, will only be realized when Jesus Christ returns to earth in person.

The act of sex was intended to foster love and commitment for the benefit of both parties, just as Jesus Christ is concerned with giving us life that is full including an unhindered relationship with God Most High. God Most High did not intend for sex or religion to be used against humanity as power tools for exerting dominance of one person over another. God Most High's definition of healthy relationship does not allow one party to lord over another. And God Most High does not tolerate sex to be used in stealing power that rightfully belongs to someone else, or in using power to steal something that rightfully belongs to someone else. Jesus Christ came to provide an avenue to achieving life that is full, not to advocate for life that is denigrated (John 10:10).

God Most High intended a good marriage to be the model relationship for God Most High's relationship with us. For God Most High, worship and adoration of God Most High is to be a part of a covenant that God makes with us without the outside interference of the church community that pursues globalization or the global religious community. For marriage, sex is to be a part of a covenant that is made with one's spouse and with God Most High who blesses the covenant. In the covenant relationship with God Most High, worship is to be a part of that covenant that bonds the believer in messiah (BC) and the followers of the Lamb (AD) with the promised and prophesied messiah / the Lamb / Jesus Christ, so that God Most High can also bless that covenant.

Jesus Christ's message to the angel of the church of Ephesus, inferred that the church community that will pursue globalization, will encourage sex outside of the traditional marriage covenant and also encourage every form of perverted sexual relationship (forced celibacy, homosexuality, pedophilia, prostitution, etc.). This kind of activity will work to sever healthy relationships between God Most High and people. Because God Most High is the source of all forms of life, the end result of advocating this kind of activity will be the separation of humanity from expressing the full image of God the Creator that was pressed into humanity, in the pursuit of the larger goal of the red dragon / serpent / Satan, Inc. of bringing eternal death to individuals. This was why God Most High provided the instruction to refrain from nontraditional and unblessed sexual relationships.

The red dragon / serpent / Satan, Inc.'s various religious teachings presented that all varieties of sex are good and desirable. Receiving the approval of the 'church' merely eases the red dragon / serpent / Satan, Inc. in its pursuit of advancing the mission and goals of the kingdom of Satan, Inc. / kingdom of man. Uniting the mission of religion with the pursuit of establishing global governance, was employed by Semiramis and Nimrod in the establishment of the tower of Babel empire, and it has been an effective methodology employed throughout human history.

The creation of the first woman from the rib of the first man, was a typology of the relationship that the bride / believers in messiah (BC) and followers of the Lamb (AD) share with the bridegroom / messiah / the Lamb / Jesus Christ. One of the reasons that Jesus Christ can share in this eternal covenant with humanity is that Jesus Christ was present at creation and provided the foundation for the creation of both the first woman and for the bride / believers in messiah (BC) and followers of the Lamb (AD).

In honoring boundaries, Jesus Christ is the bridegroom who refrains from entering where he has not been invited. Once invited to enter into covenant, Jesus Christ determined that there is no room for any interlopers in the relationship. Jesus Christ does not tolerate the stripping away of the essence and value of what humanity was created to be. And Jesus Christ will only bring benefit to those that enter into covenant relationship with him.

The red dragon / serpent / Satan, Inc. uses sexual practices for making a claim upon those who choose to reject Jesus Christ, who do not desire to love God Most High or who do not value the experience of God loving them. The red dragon / serpent / Satan, Inc.'s adherents are those who have lost what should have been their first love - God Most High. They have substituted the red dragon / serpent / Satan, Inc.'s authority and the law of the kingdom of Satan, Inc. / kingdom of man for what should have been the position reserved for God Most High and God's law.

God Most High's intention for God Most High's priests including the priests of the nation of Israel was for God Most High's priests to bring God and people together, without a third party ruling over the 'God - person relationship.' Jesus Christ's message to the angel of the church of Ephesus warned those who choose to overcome that they need to apply distance from those religious leaders who have decided that what they have spoken has equal authority to what God Most High speaks. The red dragon / serpent / Satan, Inc.'s religious leaders have continuously sought to challenge God Most High's authority to be God and to alter what God Most High has said. They have continuously sought to inject themselves between God's holy people and God Most High. They have continuously sought to spiritually, and physically, rule over others.

The message of the angel of the church of Ephesus, as a message for our era, would be to remember that the dedication and adoration of the early apostolic church's message has been lost for our time. The 'church' as an institution has been used frequently for the advancement of political power and religious power in direct opposition to God Most High and to the kingdom of heaven, throughout human history. The traditional church organization has frequently placed religious and political power in the place that should have been occupied by devotion to God Most High the Loving Father, and to Jesus Christ the Son, and to the Holy Spirit. Choosing religious power instead of choosing to lovingly surrender to a loving God Most High will not provide the fulfillment that the human heart seeks, or the protection that humanity needs for experiencing full life. And during the era of the time of

Jacob's Trouble, that protection will become even more crucial for being an overcomer.

Jesus Christ documented in the message to the angel of the church of Ephesus, that during the conclusion of the era of the times of the Gentiles and the era of the time of Jacob's Trouble, the religious leaders have lost their first love. They have dedicated themselves to loving the organization that has given them power. They love the 'church' and the global religious community as a means for achieving the global governance that provides them with power and authority to rule. They have forsaken their love for Jesus Christ who is the foundation of the true church.

It is only when individuals renew their devotion to God Most High as the first object of devotion that there will be a renewal of the authentic love relationship God Most High desires for us to experience.

The only kind of covenant that God Most High makes is eternal. There is no breaking of God Most High's covenants by God Most High.

The marriage covenant between the groom who is Jesus Christ and the bride who is the individual who has chosen to be a follower of the Lamb, is eternal and unbreakable.

And the marriage covenant between the God of Israel and the nation of Israel is also unbreakable. God Most High will continue to recognize the covenant agreement that God Most High has made with Abraham, Isaac and Jacob / Israel even when Israel has forgotten the covenant.

The era of the time of Jacob's Trouble will be used by God Most High to incentivize all of humanity to make a decision concerning whom each individual will enter into covenant with: either Jesus Christ and the kingdom of heaven, or the red dragon / serpent / Satan, Inc. and the kingdom of Satan, Inc. / kingdom of man.

Repentance, turning away from the red dragon / serpent / Satan, Inc. and the red dragon / serpent / Satan,

Inc.'s defiant practices, would allow the lampstand of the church to stay in place. Turning away from the red dragon / serpent / Satan, Inc. allows for a right relationship with God Most High to be established, and most importantly, allow for the exchange from experiencing the abusive and destructive power of the kingdom of Satan, Inc. / kingdom of man, to experiencing God Most High's healthy and life-giving love.

Being a citizen of the kingdom of heaven, of the kingdom of love, means that the restricted access to the tree of life, has been removed. Being a citizen of the kingdom of heaven offers the opportunity to eat from the tree of life and to have a personal place reserved for living the Garden of Eden / garden of God / paradise.

Jesus Christ's message to the angel of the church at Smyrna: persecuted early church – Revelation 2:8-11

Church of Smyrna – persecuted church

Jesus said, 'To the angel of the church of Smyrna, write,

'This is the message from the first and the last, who became dead and came to life. I know your tribulation and poverty – but you are rich; and I know the blasphemy of those claiming themselves to be Jews, and are not. But they are of the synagogue of Satan. Do not fear what you are about to suffer. Behold, the devil is about to throw some of you into prison, so that you might be tested. You will have tribulation for ten days. Be faithful unto death and I will give you the crown of life.'

'To the one having an ear, hear what the Spirit says to the churches. The one who overcomes will not be injured by the second death.' Revelation 2:8-11 translated

There was no indication that the church of Smyrna era continued into the era of the time of Jacob's Trouble.

Both the message to the historical era of the church of Ephesus and to the historical era of the church of Smyrna were addressed as eras when the church consisted of a high percentage of people who had originally practiced Judaism or were descendants of people who practiced Judaism. After the historical era of the church of Smyrna, the composition of the Christian population changed and antisemitism, along with a hatred of all things Jewish, reigned within the church. The antisemitism would be interrupted only during the historical era of the church of Philadelphia.

Historical message:

Smyrna was associated with myrrh. 'Myrrh' was even in the name 'Smyrna' and the modern city's name 'Izmir' which also contains 'myrrh.'

Myrrh has a bitter taste but a sweet smell (Matthew 2:11). So, myrrh was used as a preservative in the process of preparing a body for burial (John 19:39). Myrrh was produced by crushing the plant. The followers of the Lamb / Jesus Christ during the historical era of the church of Smyrna, were also crushed by poverty and persecution.

The early Christian church in Smyrna was probably established by Paul (Acts 19:8-10). Smyrna also had a large Israelite population as a result of the Babylonian deportation of the people of Israel from the land of Judah to Babylon / Asia. The Israelite population was hostile to Christianity and added to the persecution of the Christians. The hatred of Christians by the people of Israel was firmly established and heavily fueled by the persecution that the people of Israel provided against the Christians.

Smyrna was the home of Polycarp (69 to 155 AD), the bishop of Smyrna, who was a disciple of John the Revelator. It was John the Revelator who ordained Polycarp as bishop of the Smyrna church.

When Polycarp was instructed to renounce his faith in Jesus Christ and offer incense and wine as a sacrifice to the emperor, Polycarp replied, 'Eighty six years I have served the Lord and the Lord has never wronged me. How then can I blaspheme my King and Savior?' Polycarp was bound and burned at the stake.

In Polycarp's farewell address he said, 'I bless you Father for judging me worthy of this hour, so that in the company of the martyrs I may share the cup of Christ.'

The Israelite population of Smyrna was especially zealous to see Polycarp dead. They ran to procure fuel for the burning (Eusebius, Ecclesiastical History 4:15). Because Polycarp was martyred on the Sabbath, the Israelite supporters of Polycarp's death would have broken the Sabbath law that commanded that no work was to be accomplished on the Sabbath, by their obtaining the fuel for the burning. This kind of activity and attitude earned the Israelite people of Smyrna to be branded as belonging to the synagogue of Satan.

When the fire refused to burn Polycarp, a Roman guard decided to stab Polycarp to end his life.

Ignatius of Antioch / Ignatius Theophorus (? to c. 108/140) was another disciple of John the Revelator who was chosen to serve as bishop of Antioch. When Ignatius was taken to Rome to be martyred, Ignatius passed through Smyrna. On this trip, Ignatius was allowed to send six letters to nearby churches including a letter to the Smyrnaeans, and one letter to Polycarp.

In Ignatius' letter to the Smyrnaeans, Ignatius warned against the doctrine of Docetism which claimed that Jesus was fully God and his human body was only a semblance of humanity without being truly human. Docetism considered Jesus' human form to be only an illusion. But John the Revelator, an actual disciple of Jesus Christ, had already written in John's gospel, that the Word / Jesus Christ was made flesh and dwelt among us (John 1:14).

If Jesus Christ were not fully human, then his sacrifice would not have been able to have provided a path for humanity to enter into the kingdom of heaven and into eternal life.

Irenaeus (c. 130 to c. 202 AD) was a disciple of Ignatius whose hometown was Smyrna and was raised as a Christian, rather than being a Christian convert as an adult. Irenaeus moved to Lyon becoming the bishop of Lyon at a time when martyrdom was prevalent. Included in Irenaeus' writings was *Against Heresies* which addressed the heresy of Gnosticism / (roughly, salvation through knowledge).

There were several times that the biblical record presented 'ten days' as having special significance.

Daniel and his friends were tested for a literal ten days upon entering Babylon (Daniel 1:12).

Also, during the required fall feasts, there was a ten day period between the feast of trumpets and Day of Atonement / Yom Kippur that was referred to as the ten days of awe, a time for every individual annually to consider whether they would be for or against God Most High. On the Day of Atonement / Yom Kippur, those who choose to make their relationship right with God Most High were sealed by God Most High for blessing during the next year. Those who rejected having a right relationship with God Most High were released from God Most High's blessing.

In the Israelite tradition, each person must decide each year during the ten days of awe, whether or not they would seek God Most High's blessing for the next year. Once the final trumpet was sounded on the Day of Atonement / Yom Kippur, the decision concerning God Most High's blessing was final. The feast of the Day of Atonement / Yom Kippur served as a 'rehearsal' for the Great Judgment Day that will take place at the end of the Thousand Years Reign of Jesus Christ.

The Thousand Years Reign of Jesus Christ will act as a global and historical 'ten days of awe' with each 'day' converted to a hundred years of heaven time. The Great Day of Judgment / the final Day of Atonement / the final Yom Kippur, will determine each individual's eternal residence, either to dwell with God Most High or to be separated from God Most High. Those who reside with God Most High for eternity do not experience the second death. Those who do not reside with God Most High for eternity do experience the second death and everlasting separation from God Most High.

Historical timeline message to the historical era of the church of Smyrna:
As a part of the historical timeline of Revelation 2 and 3, the message to the historical era of the church of Smyrna represented the era of the persecution of the Roman empire against the Christians / followers of the Lamb / Jesus Christ.

There were ten major persecutions of Christians from the time of Nero in 54 AD, until 313 AD. During this era of persecution, it was estimated that approximately five million Christians were martyred.

The tenth persecution / Great Persecution, began in Syrian Antioch, in 299 AD, when the Roman emperors Diocletian (fl. 284 to 305 AD) and Galerius Valerius Maximianus (fl. 305 to 311 AD), took part in a ceremony of sacrifice and divination with the purpose of predicting the future. The haruspices / readers of omens, were repeatedly unable to read the entrails of the sacrificed animals. The imperial household blamed Christians for the failure. In autumn 302 AD, Diocletian believed that forbidding Christians from holding public or government office and from participating in the military, would be enough to appease the gods. But Galerius pushed for the extermination of Christians.

The Great Persecution began with the edict of Diocletian issued on February 24, 303 AD, that called for the termination of Christianity and all Christians. The day before was the feast of the Terminalia for honoring Terminus, the god of boundaries. Other edicts would follow.

One persecuted individual, Peter Cubicularius was stripped and scourged. Salt and vinegar were poured in his wounds and then he was slowly boiled over an open flame. Others were executed, or decapitated, or burned alive. The stated goals of the Great Persecution were to either bring Christians back to traditional religion which was the Roman empire's version of the baal / mystery / mythology religion, or to annihilate Christians and Christianity.

During the Great Persecution of 303-313 AD, the attempt to wipe out Christianity included burning the scriptures, destroying church buildings and imprisoning Christian leaders.

Leaders of the Great Persecution were the Roman emperors Diocletian (fl. 284 to 305 AD) (political leader), Maximian / Herculius / Caesar (285 to 286 AD) Augustus (286 to 305 AD) (fl. 285 to 310 AD) (military leader of the west), Galerius Valerius Maximaianus (fl. 305 to 311 AD) (military leader of the east), and Flavius Valerius Constantius Chlorus / Constantius I of the west (fl. 305 to 306) and father of Constantine the Great / Constantine I.

The next Roman emperor, Constantine the Great / Constantine I (fl. 306 to 337 AD) brought reform to the Roman empire through restructuring government, separating civil and military authorities, combatting inflation through the introduction of the gold coin solidus that standardized currency, reorganizing the military, etc. Constantine I's mother Helena was a practicing Christian.

In 313 AD, ten years after Diocletian began his persecutions, Constantine I / Constantine the Great (fl. 306 to 337 AD) and his colleague Licinius, granted legal liberty to Christians to practice their religion, and through law, the persecutions were ended.

During the historical era of the early Christian church of Smyrna, there were a number of versions of Christianity that emerged, causing extraordinary spiritual upheaval. The early Christians developed a number of divergent compositions of who they believed Jesus Christ to be and how to define Jesus Christ. Alternative gospels were developed like the Gospel of Thomas and the Gospel of Mary Magdalene.

Some of the early Christians of Smyrna questioned the need for clergy or for the development of church doctrine.

Others taught that God could be discovered merely through spiritual search without the foundation of a biblical understanding of the promised and prophesied messiah.

Still others believed that Christianity should be considered to be a mere search for enlightenment following the models of Hinduism and Buddhism, with access to God being a matter found merely within one's self.

Included within the various theologies was the question of the reality of the resurrection of messiah / the Lamb / Jesus Christ, and the suggestion that the resurrection of Jesus Christ might be symbolic instead of authentic.

This era of church history questioned whether God should be envisioned only in masculine form, and suggested that God might be feminine as well.

Because martyrdom for one's faith was heavily prevalent at the time, many questioned if expressions of faith were worth investing in.

The early Christians dared to ask deep questions, that later were suppressed by the leaders of the church. But the theologies and doctrines of the early Christian church that resulted from the suppression of the early Christian church leaders, remained prevalent even today.

The authentic Jesus Christ of the biblical record, repeatedly presented God the Father, God the Son / messiah / the Lamb / Jesus Christ, and God the Holy Spirit, as being divine and sovereign, with the ability and responsibility of shaping, preparing and fitting, each follower of the Lamb / Jesus Christ for everlasting life in the kingdom of heaven.

But within the historical era of the early Christian church of Smyrna, as the early Christians struggled with determining an authentic definition for who Jesus Christ was, they were willing to embrace a Jesus who could be shaped by them.

A god who can be shaped by an individual, can only be as powerful as the individual who shaped the god. The god that is shaped is a god that has been created, not a god who creates.

Depending upon a god who can be shaped by the individual, for one's salvation, is ineffective. A god who can be shaped, cannot have the authority and power to salvage and save an individual. The god that can be shaped by humanity, carries all the defects of what has shaped that god, and is actually a god with no power and authority at all. The god who can be shaped, cannot reshape a human being into something better than what currently exists within that human being.

The church of the historical era of the early Christian church of Smyrna, was predominately shaped by the people who shaped it. Denying God Most High the opportunity to shape the church with an infusion of life, the historical era of the early Christian church of Smyrna experienced martyrdom and died. This established the foundation for the next church era in the historical line, the historical era of the church of Pergamum, to become responsible for carrying the message of Jesus Christ.

The theology of the historical era of the church of Smyrna in the movement toward the theology of the historical era of the church of Laodicea

The theology of the historical era of the church of Smyrna redefined messiah / the Lamb / Jesus Christ in a number of ways that were divergent from the understanding of the promised and prophesied messiah of the Old Testament / Tanakh, and from the understanding of the accounts of the apostles and early disciples of Jesus Christ.

While intertwining multiple definitions for who messiah / the Lamb / Jesus Christ is, seems appealing, in reality there can only be one authentic definition for who Jesus Christ is. And that one definition must be true to the original source of truth, God Most High who communicated that one definition through prophets, who recorded the messages that they received from God Most High.

While the church of the historical era of the early Christian church of Smyrna was martyred and died, its legacy of struggling to find a real definition of who Jesus Christ actually is, continued to pop up throughout history.

The practice of removing the actual person of Jesus Christ from the context of history, and then offering a different definition of who Jesus Christ is, would also be repeated throughout history.

The practice of developing a unique Jesus devoid of the confines of the biblical record, was best utilized by the National Socialist / Nazi Party of Germany during the World War II era. During that time, both the Roman Catholic Church and Adolf Hitler who was a Roman Catholic Church member, presented a Jesus Christ who was Arian instead of Jewish.

The practice of redefining the authentic biblical Jesus Christ, with other images vying to fill the role of the promised and prophesied messiah, will shape the cultural climate during the era of the time of Jacob's Trouble, and will be a key component in establishing the foundation for the rise of the two beasts of Revelation 13. It will be that cultural climate that will cause the church as we have known it, to become the persecutor of its own people. And at that point, the church as we have known it, will essentially be as dead as the martyred church of the historical era of the early Christian church of Smyrna.

Jesus Christ's message for the era of the time of Jacob's Trouble from the message to the angel of the early persecuted church of Smyrna

During the era of the time of Jacob's Trouble there will again be an emphasis by the portion of the church that seeks to establish globalization, and the global religious community, to torture, persecute and kill the followers of the Lamb / Jesus Christ in an attempt to wipe out all followers of the Lamb / Jesus Christ. Bibles will again be burned and become illegal to own. All scriptures will become illegal and substitute scriptures supporting the kingdom of Satan, Inc. / kingdom of man's rule will take their place. Leaders who are followers of the Lamb / Jesus Christ will be imprisoned, persecuted and killed.

The message to the persecuted early Christian church of Smyrna as a direct message for the era of the time of Jacob's Trouble would be one of encouragement in the midst of persecution and suffering.

As a future fulfillment of the prophecy within Jesus Christ's message to the church during the era of the time of Jacob's Trouble, the duration of the imprisonment and persecution of contemporary followers of the Lamb / Jesus Christ may possibly have a literal 'ten days' in its fulfillment.

Another detail of the message to those living during the era of the time of Jacob's Trouble from the message to the persecuted early Christian church of Smyrna, included a definition of a true Jew as not being aligned with Satan. It is interesting that in this message to a Gentile church, there was included a Jewish reference and a designation that some are unauthentic Jews working in the employ of Satan under the guise of purifying their Jewish religion.

This reference could be a message to our era to expect that Israelite leaders may betray the people of Israel and pursue Christians / follower of the Lamb, as well.

During the time of Jesus' ministry on earth, Jesus Christ was accused of slander / blasphemy for claiming to be the Son of God / the promised and prophesied messiah, by the religious leaders of Israel. The message to the early Christian church of Smyrna made it clear that those who have rejected Jesus Christ as the promised and prophesied messiah, are actually the true slanderers / true blasphemers. But God Most High has prophesied that during this time of the era of the time of Jacob's Trouble, the people of Israel will again be given the option to accept or reject Jesus Christ as God Most High's promised and prophesied messiah. The people of Israel will need to decide either to reject Jesus Christ as a slanderer / blasphemer or accept Jesus Christ as the authentic promised and prophesied messiah.

As Jesus Christ was put to the test by the religious leaders of the nation of Israel, so the Jewish people will find that this era of the time of Jacob's Trouble will put them to the test by religious and global leaders. This will be the second chance in history that the people of Israel will have of putting Jesus Christ to the test. During the era of the time of Jacob's Trouble, they will finally decide that Jesus Christ was not slanderous, that God Most High has been faithful to God Most High's promises, and that Jesus Christ has always been the promised messiah. And when the people of Israel have made this decision, God Most High will hear them and save them, and the end of the era of the time of Jacob's Trouble will be near. The nation of Israel will also not experience a 'second death' and will be established forever under the protection of God Most High, from whom they will never again be separated.

Jesus Christ's message to the angel of the church at Pergamum: married church – Revelation 2:12-17

The churches of the historical eras of the church of Ephesus and Smyrna were referenced by Jesus Christ as being dead at the time of Jesus Christ's return.

But Jesus Christ defined the next five historical era churches as being alive and active at the time of his return (Pergamum, Thyatira, Sardis, Philadelphia and Laodicea). Relegating the history of Pergamum, Thyatira, Sardis, Philadelphia and Laodicea into a distant past, without any connection to the development of the church as we near the time of Jesus Christ's return, would be dangerous, and defiant of the message of the biblical record.

The challenges that all the churches of Asia encountered, remain the challenges of all churches and of the followers of the Lamb / Jesus Christ, even today, especially as the time of the return of Jesus Christ becomes closer every day.

<u>Church of Pergamos – church of compromised theology and doctrine</u>

Jesus said, 'To the angel of the church of Pergamos, write,

'This is the message from the one having the sharp two edged sword.'

'I know where you dwell, where the throne of Satan is. And you hold fast to my name. You have not denied faith in me, even in the days of Antipas, who was my witness, my faithful one, who was killed among you, where Satan dwells.'

'But I have a few things against you, because you have some in your presence that hold to the teaching of Balaam, who taught Balak to cast a snare before the people of Israel, to eat things sacrificed to idols and to commit sexual immorality. So you also have some holding to the teaching of the Nicolaitans.'

'Therefore, repent! If you do not repent, I am coming to you with speed, and I will make war against them with the sword of my mouth.'

'To the one having an ear, hear what the Spirit says to the churches. To the one who overcomes, I will give hidden manna. And I will give to that one, a white stone, and on the stone, a new name will be written which no one has known, except the one who receives it.'
Revelation 2:12-17 translated

Historical message:

Understanding the fullness of Jesus Christ's message regarding the historical church of Pergamum, requires understanding the greater historical context of Jesus Christ's message.

The Pergamene kingdom was founded by Philetaerus at the beginning of the third century BC.

Originally, the Pergamene kingdom was part of the Hellenistic Seleucid empire that spawned Antiochus IV Epiphanes who had previously caused the first abomination of desolation of the Israelite temple in 167 BC.

The history of Pergamum itself was important, along with the relationship that the city of Pergamum held with the baal / mystery / mythology religion. Pergamum had become known as the city where Satan had his throne.

The connection between the city of Pergamum and Satan's throne was a result of the relationship that Pergamum held with the baal / mystery / mythology religion that created the environment in which Antipas was martyred. And it was the cultural environment created through the baal / mystery / mythology religion that caused the people of Pergamum to be willing to eat food sacrificed to idols, to commit sexual immorality, and to embrace the teaching of the Nicolaitans.

The followers of the Lamb / Jesus Christ, residing in Pergamum, would have understood that participation in all worship within the baal / mystery / mythology religion would have been offensive to Jesus Christ and to God Most High. And they would have understood the importance of Jesus Christ's promised provision for them as they practiced righteousness and holiness.

Basic information on the city of Pergamum

Among the baal / mystery / mythology gods and goddesses worshiped in Pergamum were Zeus, Athena, Asclepius, Dionysus, and Demeter. The Gigantomachy / Pergamum Altar frieze, displayed an epic battle between the Olympian gods and giants for supremacy over the cosmos.

Pergamum was a wealthy city known during its time of importance, to have the largest library in the world with over two hundred thousand books. A large portion of the library, was given as a gift by Marcus Antonius / Marc Antony (83 BC to 30 BC) to Cleopatra VII Philopator (fl. 51 BC to 30 BC). Reading was vital to the culture of Pergamum, and so when a papyrus shortage occurred, Pergamum became a thriving center of *parchment production (c. 323 BC to...). Pergamum lent its name to 'parchment' (Latin: 'pergamenum,' French: 'parchemin').*

Today Pergamum is known as Bergama.

The name Pergamum comes from two parts: 'per' which in the Greek means 'mixed, different, inappropriate or high in status'; and 'gamos' which translates as 'marriage.' Monogamy, polygamy, bigamy all use the suffix 'gamos.' Pergamum means 'inappropriate marriage,' or 'to be married to power.'

The name Pergamum, prophetically demonstrated the mixed marriage between the authentic faith system of God Most High, and the baal / mystery / mythology religion. Pergamum experienced a merger between Christianity and the gods of the baal / mystery / mythology religion.

The church of Pergamum that existed during the lifetime of John the Revelator, faced the theological challenges that were later incorporated into the development of the historical era of the church of Pergamum that was founded approximately three hundred years later. It was the church that developed approximately three hundred years later, that Jesus Christ directed a deeper layer of meaning from his message.

The historical era of the church of Pergamum was originally and legally founded in 381 AD. But the theology and practices of the historical era of the church of Pergamum has continued into the era of the time of Jacob's Trouble.

Pergamum, the home of the temple of Zeus / seat of Satan and the temple's Gigantomachy

In addition to Pergamum representing unholy marriage, Pergamum was also identified by Jesus Christ as the location of where Satan has his throne, *and* where Satan lives.

The people of Pergamum were known as the 'temple keepers of Asia.' As temple keepers, Pergamum's religious leaders also took on the role of 'gatekeepers to heaven.' Pergamum had three temples dedicated to 1) the worship of the Roman emperor, 2) the goddess Athena, and 3) the Great Altar of Zeus / king of the Greek gods. It seems that all their bases (political, spiritual, and religious) were covered.

Zeus was supposed to have been born in Pergamum. The Great Altar of Zeus was known as the 'throne of Satan.' The 'throne' was a reference to the chair that belonged to the master of the house.

The Pergamum temple of Zeus was excavated quite recently, from 1878 to 1886 AD. The temple of Zeus was then moved to Berlin Germany and restored. In 1902, the temple of Zeus was erected on Berlin's Museum Island. This museum proved to be inadequate so a new museum to house the temple of Zeus was opened in 1930 AD. The exhibit of the temple of Zeus, held Adolph Hitler's interest.

The temple of Zeus was shaped like a giant throne complete with arms / wings, like a seat or throne. Jesus used this reference to recognize that Satan felt at home in Pergamum. Pergamum was Satan, Inc.'s territory.

On the circumference of the temple of Zeus was the Gigantomachy, a set of friezes carved from stone, that depicted the war of gods and giants. The fact that the gods of the baal / mystery / mythology religion were known to make war against each other, was in sharp contrast to the God of heaven where the three members of the office of God share perfect love with each other and also entirely agree with each other.

The development of the college of pontiffs and the sovereign pontiff / Pontifex Maximus

Established around one hundred years after the deluge / flood, the tower of Babel empire was infused with the mission of establishing the baal / mystery / mythology religion as a global entity. Sometime in the history of that pursuit, the formal structure of the Babylonian baal / mystery / mythology religion, established a college of pontiffs, with a sovereign pontiff presiding over the college. This organizational structure was intended to provide separation of the individual from experiencing a direct and personal relationship with God Most High.

The priests of God Most High have always been tasked with bringing the individual and God Most High, closer together. But the priests of the baal / mystery / mythology religion have always been tasked with separating the individual from a personal relationship with God Most High, and placing the person under the authority of the baal / mystery / mythology religion's governance.

The high priest of the baal / mystery / mythology religion was himself considered to be divine and sovereign. As the highest divine entity, the high priest was also recognized as the god of the mysteries and keeper of the secrets of the religion.

In the tower of Babel empire, the first true legitimate god of the mysteries, was the deified Nimrod (Genesis 10:8-11, 11:1-9). The deified Nimrod, as the founder and king of Babylon, was the sovereign pontiff. The tradition of the king of Babylon being surrounded by astrologers, soothsayers and magicians, continued until the Babylonian empire was conquered by Darius of the Medes and the Persians (October 12, 539 BC), during the lifetime of Daniel (Daniel 5:30-31).

When the Babylonian empire was conquered by the Medes and the Persians, the Babylonian priests of the baal / mystery / mythology religion with their degradant and brutal polytheism, were no longer welcome in the Medo Persian empire with its kinder and gentler monotheism. The Babylonian priests relocated to Pergamum, transporting the college of pontiffs and taking their sovereign pontiff with them. In Pergamum, the kings of Pergamum then assumed the role of sovereign pontiffs and filled the governing vacancy left by the last ruler of the Babylonian empire, Belshazzar. Being sovereign over both the remnant of the Babylonian empire and over the college of pontiffs of the baal / mystery / mythology religion, the kings of Pergamum were recognized as the new representatives of the Babylonian god of the mysteries.

'Pontifex Maximus' became the title used in ancient paganism, the baal / mystery / mythology religion, that represented both the role of high priest and the role of supreme sovereign. Later, it was also in Pergamum that the Roman emperor adopted the role of 'Pontifex Maximus' / 'Sovereign Pontiff' / 'Representative of Divinity on Earth,' the high priest of the pagan system of religion.

One of the main methods of the expansion of the Roman empire was to establish Roman colonies in other regions or nations. Those Roman colonies would grow and eventually displace the previously established governments, leading to the region or nation becoming an official part of the Roman empire. The Roman empire's favorite method of expansion and conquering new territory was colonization. Establishing a colony led to the assimilation of Roman empire culture in the region, which led to the region being annexed by the Roman empire. Colonization has remained the favorite method of expansion of the remnant of the Roman empire, the Roman Catholic Church.

In the early history of Rome, the worship of the baal / mystery / mythology religion was suppressed. But a colony of Etruscans who were attached to the baal / mystery / mythology religion, settled in the neighborhood of Rome, exercising a powerful influence over the religious worship of the Romans.

Rome adopted the baal / mystery / mythology religion's already established practice of forming a college of pontiffs with a sovereign pontiff presiding over the college.

Julius Caesar was the first prominent Roman emperor to adopt the title Pontifex Maximus in 63 BC, prior to assuming the position of supreme ruler of the Roman state. In this way, Julius Caesar vested himself with the powers and functions of the ancient Babylonian pontiffs, and in some form became a legitimate successor to Belshazzar.

Julius Caesar also was declared to be Jupiter's incarnation on December 25th, 48 BC in the temple of Jupiter in Alexandria. Emperors who followed Julius Caesar were commonly regarded as gods.

Julius Caesar was also the most prominent emperor to import the baal / mystery / mythology religion from Pergamum to Rome. All the Caesars beginning with Julius Caesar, kept the title of 'Pontifex Maximus' until 378 AD. In 378 AD the bishop of Rome absorbed the title 'Pontifex Maximus' for himself and political leaders no longer used the title. Around the same time, the leadership of the Roman Catholic Church began to view themselves as the continued extension of the Roman empire as the Roman empire slipped into decline.

Pergamum, the city of the serpent god Asclepius, the god of healing

In the Hebrew culture, as the people of Israel wandered through the wilderness after exiting Egypt (1446 to 1406 BC), there was a time when a plague of venomous snakes passed through the camp. Moses was instructed to construct a bronze snake mounted on a cross. Anyone who looked upon the snake, was cured from the plague (Numbers 21:4-9). The bronze snake on the cross in the wilderness, was a typology for the healing power of messiah / the Lamb / Jesus Christ who was later crucified through the work of the serpent / Satan, on a cross.

But in the baal / mystery / mythology religion, the serpent on the cross represented the sun god being worshiped in the form of a serpent.

Pergamum was also known as the city of the serpent. Pergamum was a home for the snake god Asclepius. In non-Israelite cultures, the symbol of the serpent on the cross frequently represented healing and the snake god Asclepius.

In Greek, the name Aesculapius meant 'instructing snake.' The instructing snake also symbolized the enlightening of the souls of humans by the sun.

The name 'Lucifer' means 'shining one.'

The god Saturn and the transfer of the seat of Satan / the baal / mystery / mythology religion, from the Babylonian empire to Pergamum, and then to Rome

Babylon, Pergamum and Rome, shared in their investment in the baal / mystery / mythology religion.

Babylon served as the capital city of the tower of Babel empire.

When Darius the Mede (c. 550 to 486 BC) defeated the Babylonians on October 12, 539 BC, Cyrus the Persian (600 to 530 BC) caused the seat of the baal / mystery / mythology religion to be transported from Babylon to Pergamum. The Medes and the Persians believed in the concept of one god and were monotheists. Monotheistic theology opposed the Babylon's polytheism belief in many gods who were constantly at war with each other. When the city of Babylon was destroyed and the temples of the baal / mystery / mythology religion in Babylon were destroyed, the high priest of Babylon and his approximate three hundred associates, fled taking their sacred vessels and images of their religion, to Pergamum.

The symbol of the serpent already established in Pergamum, acted as a welcome mat to becoming the organizational headquarters of the baal / mystery / mythology religion. The religion that was reinvigorated by Nimrod after the deluge / flood, also incorporated the worship of the serpent in their religious rituals.

Pergamum already served as the home for the temple of Zeus / seat of Satan. With Pergamum hosting the refugee Babylonian baal / mystery / mythology religion priests, Pergamum became the initial religious power center for the Roman empire.

Attalus III (fl. 138 to 133 BC) was the last legitimate king to rule in Pergamum. When Attalus III died, he willed his dominions to the Roman Caesar, believing that if he did not, that Rome would take his kingdom anyway.

Receiving the kingdom of Pergamum, included receiving the title Pontifex Maximus. And from Pergamum, the baal / mystery / mythology religion moved to Rome under the name of the Etruscan Mysteries.

The Pergamum Museum located in Berlin, Germany houses artifacts from the Pergamum era of religious leadership, depicting the fish-god Dagon and goddess Cybele who were god and goddess of the Philistines, the Assyrians, Pergamum and then Rome. The priests of the baal / mystery / mythology religion were known to have worn mitre hats in the shape of the fish, split-toped like a fish's mouth, with a tail representing the fish body and tail, and a fish eye. The mitre of the Roman Catholic Church's pope still follows this fashion today.

The temple of Zeus originally located in Pergamum became the model for Adolf Hitler's Luitpold Arena /Zeppelin tribune in Nuremberg. Using 150 search lights creating the cathedral of light, Hitler connected the temple of Zeus and the Third Reich with the ideal of Hitler's kingdom reaching to heaven.

Throughout most of human history, the planet Saturn was associated with Satan. Archeology of ancient history has repeatedly recognized the planet Satan with its rings, and the association of Saturn as a god within multiple cultures of the baal / mystery / mythology religion.

It was Nimrod who was the first to be recognized as the god Saturn within the Babylonian baal / mystery / mythology religion of the tower of Babel empire, established ~2358 BC.

The Babylonian name satur consists of four letters, STUR. The value of those four letters adds to 666. S - 60, T - 400, U - 6, R - 200. And the name STUR was translated as both Saturn and Satan. Historically, satur / satyr was the goat legged half man - half goat deity headed by Pan (a representation of Satan). The prophet Isaiah identified the wild shaggy goats as belonging to Babylon (Isaiah 13:21).

The etymology of the Babylonian name satur, means 'hidden god' or 'god of mystery.'

The word 'Latin' was derived from the Latin word 'lateo' which means 'lie hid.' The Babylonian word 'lat' also means 'lie hid.' The general meaning of the word 'Latin' was translated to mean 'language of mystery' or 'hidden language.'

In the Egyptian version of the baal / mystery / mythology religion, there was a fish god called 'Latus' that was worshiped.

The Egyptian fish god was also documented in the biblical record, as the Philistine fish god Dagon (Judges 16:23, 1 Samuel 5, 1 Chronicles 10:10, etc.).

Throughout the various cultures, the themes of the baal / mystery / mythology religion remained somewhat consistent, including names or meanings of names, theologies and practices.

The beliefs concerning the God of the kingdom of heaven, held by the people of Israel, understood God to be the deity that transforms the world and transformed the covenant relationship that the God of heaven held with humanity, between the Old Testament / Tanakh and the New Testament.

Following that kind of understanding of the God of heaven, the baal / mystery / mythology religion presented that the god Saturn also having similar power, to transform himself from being the one who lies captive in the darkness of matter, to the deity that was swallowed up in his own creation, and as the god who reverts to his original luminous state through the mystery of transmutation.

The traditional story of the founding of the city of Rome, claimed that Rome was founded by two brothers, Romulus and Remus, on Capitoline hill. Capitoline hill is one of the seven hills of the city of Rome.

Rome became known as Saturnia or the city of Saturn (Latin) / Kronos (Greek) (father of Zeus). It was traditionally known as the location where the great Babylonian god Saturn came to be worshipped. The festival for Saturn / Saturnalia, was celebrated in December. The celebration of the birth of the sun deities was also celebrated on December 25th (Mithra, Krishna (Vishnu), Osiris, Horus, Hercules, Dionysus / Bacchus, Tammuz,

Indra, Buddha, other reincarnations of the child god of the Babylonian religious system, etc.).

Capitoline hill was one of the highest points in the region, a great high place for religion. After the deluge / flood, high places were desired because they represented hope of survival from judgment represented by the deluge / flood.

The historical worship of the god Saturn upon Capitoline hill in Rome, may have been one of factors that appealed to the Babylonian baal / mystery / mythology religion priests as they made their journey as exiles from Babylon when the Medes and the Persians conquered the Babylonian empire (October 12, 539 BC), to Pergamum, and then to Rome (129 BC).

The martyrdom of Antipas in Pergamum

Antipas was the bishop of the Pergamum church, ordained by the Apostle John. One of Antipas' activities that brought attention to him, was his efficiency in casting out demons from individuals.

Sometime during the reign of Nero (fl. 54 to 68), the priests of the baal / mystery / mythology religion went to the Roman governor and complained that the prayers of Antipas were driving their spirits out of the city and hindering the worship of their gods, which thwarted their power, authority and effectiveness as priests, and also threatened their source of income. As punishment, the Roman governor ordered Antipas to offer a sacrifice of wine and incense to a statue of the Roman emperor and to declare that the emperor was 'lord and god.'

Antipas refused.

Antipas was sentenced to death as a martyr in the Altar of Zeus.

Located in Pergamum, on the temple of Zeus, in the midst of the Gigantomachy, was a set of friezes which depicted the battle between the Greek gods and the giants. This was interesting because both the Greek gods and the giants are members of the red dragon / serpent / Satan, Inc. system, and consequently should be allies on the same side.

In the center of the Gigantomachy, at the top of the altar, was a hollow bronze bull designed to place the victim(s) inside and then to be burned with a fire lit under the bull. The bull had an acoustic apparatus that converted the screams of the victim(s) into the sound of a bull.

Antipas was martyred by being burned in the bronze bull altar during the persecutions of Emperor Domitian in 92 AD. Even in the midst of experiencing his death, Antipas died praying for his church.

The creator of the bronze bull, Perillos, was himself almost roasted in his creation. Instead, Perillos was taken out of the burning bull just in time to save his life. Then Perillos was thrown off a hill to his death.

Later, Phalaris who commissioned the bronze bull was actually roasted in it when he was overthrown by Telemachus.

Balaam son of Beor and Balak of Moab – Numbers 22-25 and 31 (between 1446 and 1406 BC)

Balaam son of Beor, was a Gentile prophet who was paid by Balak the king of the Moabites, and paid by the Midianites, to curse the Israelites before they entered into the Promised Land. Balaam repeatedly refused to speak what God Most High did not speak. And Balaam ended up refusing to curse the Israelites.

However, Balaam did instruct Balak and the Moabites on how to sabotage the Israelites by enticing the men of the people of Israel to practice sexual immorality with Moabite women, and to partake in eating food sacrificed to idols.

Part of the seduction process was to invite the inductees to the feasts of the gods of baal and have them participate in the Canaanite fertility rites and regular services of their temples through ritual sex. The Moabites invited the Israelite men to a banquet, paraded their young women in front of the Israelites and seduced them to worship the Baal of Peor and to engage in sex with their women as a ritual act of worship. The Midianites then encouraged the Israelites to marry their women.

God Most High's response was to instruct the Israelites to destroy their fellow Israelites who had *worshiped the Baal of Peor. And then God Most High sent a plague upon the Israelites who had participated in the scheme. God Most High also instructed the Israelites to destroy the Midianites. Balaam died in the battle. The Midianites experienced great loss in the battle. But not one Israelite was lost in the battle against the Midianites, a sign of God Most High's exacting precision.*

This reference from Numbers 22-25 and 31 concerning the negative account of Balaam, acted as a warning to those who conspire to destroy God Most High's people. Those who plot against God Most High's people and who practice immorality will face the double edged sword of Jesus Christ, especially during the era of the time of Jacob's Trouble when this double edged sword's activity will be fully realized.

The double edged sword was a reference to the double edged sword that proceeds from the mouth of Jesus Christ, activated when Jesus Christ returns to fight the final battle of this age. This double edged sword is so precise that the truth of Jesus Christ is able to separate bone and marrow. Jesus Christ's double edged sword is able to set a person free from judgment or to administer judgment.

The Nicolaitans and their work in Pergamum

The antediluvian / preflood world religion and the baal / mystery / mythology religion taught that sex with angels offered a connection to the divine that lead to special knowledge. And having sex with angels generated the supposed greater than human species of Nephilim. By the lifetime of Noah, the predominate human culture had accepted these ideals.

In the antediluvian / preflood era, Noah was a preacher of righteousness. But the religious leaders of the antediluvian / preflood world, operated on an economy that valued power brokering, like the later Nicolaitans.

The Nicolaitans were referred to in the message to the angel of the church of Ephesus, and then referenced again in this portion of the message to the church of Pergamum.

In Ephesus, the church had resisted the manipulation of the Nicolaitans. But in Pergamum the Nicolaitans were successful in establishing their religious rule over the people.

Inherent within the issues that God Most High held against the Nicolaitans was God Most High's disapproval of the Nicolaitans' advocation of sexual immorality and idolatry.

According to Irenaeus in his book Against Heresies, 'The Nicolaitans were the followers of Nicolas who was one of the seven first ordained to the diaconate by the apostles. The Nicolaitans led lives of unrestrained indulgence. They taught indifference to the practice of adultery and to eating food sacrificed to idols.' *Against Heresies* 1:26:3

Epiphanius in Panarion 25:1 recorded that Nicolas had an attractive wife and yet for a time he practiced celibacy as a form of Gnostic worship. There came a point when Nicolas abandoned his position on celibacy and was then noted as saying, 'Unless one copulates every day, he cannot have eternal life.'

Initiation into the red dragon / serpent / Satan, Inc.'s baal / mystery / mythology religion required a sexual experience with a 'temple prostitute' / 'temple priestess' as a seal of one's initiation into membership or as an annual renewal of membership. In a similar manner, the Nicolaitans were known for perverting healthy sexual practices and sexually usurping their authority over those they ruled. In the context of the biblical record, and within the Greek culture of the New Testament, 'usurping one's authority' was always a reference to using one's religious position and authority in order to influence someone to engage in an unblessed sexual relationship. Today's term for usurping one's authority is 'clergy sexual misconduct,' with clergy utilizing their position of religious power, authority or trust, in order to influence others to have sex with the clergy person.

Homosexuality was also used in the red dragon / serpent / Satan, Inc.'s various religious practices and rites.

When Nimrod and Semiramis revived the antediluvian / preflood religion in the form of the baal / mystery / mythology religion, they incorporated similar deviant sexual practices into their system of worship. Homosexual sex with angels was supposed to allow the snake god that resides within a person's spine to awaken and grow.

Because they believed that they would receive a divine blessing, the citizens of the city of Sodom during the time of Abram / Abraham's nephew Lot, sought to have sex with the angels that God Most High had sent to investigate Sodom and Gomorrah. Those that sought to have homosexual sex with God Most High's angels, believed that the act would have been a high and holy act of worship of the gods of the red dragon / serpent / Satan, Inc., and therefore rewarded by those gods (Genesis 19:1-29)

Both before and after the deluge / flood, the Nephilim were the creation of forbidden sex between humans and rebellious angels. All sex not blessed by God Most High has the potential to be used for the power agenda of the kingdom of Satan, Inc. / kingdom of man, including sodomy with angels, sex with angels for the purpose of producing Nephilim, adultery and homosexual sex.

Throughout human history, the 'seed war' that began in the Garden of Eden (Genesis 3) included deviant sexual practices that have been an active influence upon religion. The way a person perceives the act of sex consummates what that person is devoted to.

God Most High understands passion outside of the marriage relationship, and frequently blesses it. But God Most High does not bless sexual acts that are used as rebellion against God Most High's goal of providing full life to human beings.

One's view of sex either demonstrates loyalty to God Most High's relationship structure or it demonstrates loyalty to rebellion against God Most High through a type of sale of one's self or sale of others, a stealing of life and love from one's self or a stealing of life and love from another.

One's perception of the act of sex can represent purity, loyalty, and respect of individuals as treasures of God Most High, belonging to God, and with the blessing of God Most High. Or one's view of sex can demonstrate idolatry, perversion, objectification, subjugation, and domination that seeks only to establish a position of power to be a lord and master over another or to be lorded over.

It is not the act of sex itself that determines how a person views God Most High. The act of sex merely seals what is in one's heart.

What concerns God Most High is the fact that sex in history has been used by both God (to foster love, grow and bond relationships) and also by the red dragon / serpent / Satan, Inc. (to pervert, to trade for power and knowledge, to gain religious power through perversions of sex, to destroy relationships and people, to genetically modify humanity, and as a weapon in the red dragon / serpent / Satan, Inc.'s attempt to takeover heaven).

Idolatry and adultery both reflect a relationship that is broken. Idolatry represents a broken relationship with God Most High. Adultery represents a broken covenant relationship with one's spouse with a marriage covenant that was blessed by God. Therefore, the red dragon / serpent / Satan, Inc. has found that unblessed sexual relationships are effective at breaking covenant relationships and pulling people away from God.

At the time of John's writing of this message, it was the practice of the priests of the baal / mystery / mythology religion and of the Nicolaitans to insist that they were the gatekeepers to God Most High and that access to God Most High and eternal life were available at their discretion or denied at their prerogative. In all their ritual activities, the goal of the Nicolaitans was to inject themselves in between the person and God Most High which would result in separation between God Most High and the person, and leave a larger void for the Nicolaitans themselves to fill while gathering power.

In a sense, the Nicolaitans desired to practice religious rape, forcing themselves upon their congregants.

In the covenant between God Most High and each individual, when a religious leader (who is always inferior to God Most High) injects their self in between God and the individual, they assert their own interests. And it is a form of adultery / idolatry.

And whenever a person assumes the authority that belongs to God Most High in another person's life, the result can only lead to that person developing a perverted image of God Most High. God Most High has always been highly offended by priests that do not present God Most High or the kingdom of heaven, accurately.

Historical timeline message to the historical era of the church of Pergamum:

As a part of the historical timeline of Revelation 2 and 3, the message to the church of Pergamum represented the historical era of the church of Pergamum, as taking place during the era of the later Roman empire.

Eventually, Constantine the Great / Constantine I (fl. 306 to 337 AD), found the pagan Roman culture so abhorrent that Constantine began to recognize Christianity as a preferable solution, and laid the foundation for the establishment of the Roman Catholic Church. With all religion placed under the authority of the Roman empire, the priests of the baal / mystery / mythology religion were forced to adopt Christian language and Christian practices. Priests that formerly were priests within the baal / mystery / mythology religion, became priests for Christianity, almost overnight. In that transition, those same priests continued to maintain many of their old dogma, doctrines, theologies and practices of the baal / mystery / mythology religion, giving them 'Christian names.'

The formerly baal / mystery / mythology religion priests, were not afforded time to study Christian theology or to understand the mission of Christianity in advancing the kingdom of heaven.

In the forced marriage of the baal / mystery / mythology religion with Christianity, many of their baal / mystery / mythology religion dogmas, doctrines, theologies and practices were also 'married' into their new version of Christianity.

In 330 AD Constantine moved the capital of the empire from Rome to Byzantium and renamed the city Constantinople. Around that time, Constantine made a large number of truly impacting reforms. Constantine:

- abolished work on Sunday (not the Sabbath) in order to begin to unite the religious ideals of the baal / mystery / mythology religions and Christianity.
- ceased the gladiator fights.
- made it illegal to kill unwanted children.
- abolished crucifixion as a form of execution.
- repealed the persecution edicts of Diocletian.
- reduced slavery.

Also during this historical era, the Roman emperors increasingly developed an ambition to rule, including an ambition to rule religiously.

On February 27, 380 AD, Theodosius officially merged Christianity with the established baal / mystery / mythology religion in the Edict of Thessalonica. The Roman Catholic Church was founded. The emperor Theodosius, ruler of the political empire, also gained religious authority as the founder of the church of Rome.

With the Edict of Thessalonica, the marriage of the church with the established baal / mystery / mythology religion was complete. But the marriage of the church was also a marriage with the Roman empire, the government. And as the state religion and extension of the government of the Roman empire, the organized church began to rise as its own new ruling body.

During the later historical timeline for the era of Thyatira's theology, the church would complete its transition in fully becoming the ruling church, and would understand itself to be the continuation of the Roman empire with the goal of ruling the world as the Roman empire had once aspired to globally rule. The structure of the Roman Catholic Church continues to maintain its understanding that the Roman Catholic Church was *designed to rule. But the seed for the Roman Catholic Church's transition to becoming the ruling church, was sown with the establishment of the Roman Catholic Church during the historical era of the Pergamum church as defined and documented in Jesus Christ's message to the angel of the church of Pergamum.*

Because of the Edict of Thessalonica (February 27, 380 AD), new religious laws including forced attendance at church services served to disseminate a politically acceptable pseudo theology which assisted in easing he governance of the empire.

Theodosius made Christianity the official state religion, but that also meant that adherents to the baal / mystery / mythology religion were forced to bring their dogmas, doctrines, theologies and practices, under the Christian church umbrella. The church experienced a forced mingling of the authentic faith system of Christianity, with paganism, specifically the baal / mystery / mythology religion known in Rome as Mithraism.

The result was a merging of the church with the world, an unholy union that continues to exist today within the Roman Catholic Church and even within many Protestant churches. The mingling of the baal / mystery / mythology religion, with true faith in Jesus Christ and the practices that please God Most High, will only be able to be fully separated by a sword of the quality of Jesus Christ's double edged sword.

The portion of the historical era of the church of Pergamum that was devoted to the pursuit of the authentic faith system of Christianity, understood that the double edged sword that proceeds from the mouth of God, as a tool that had great meaning and power. The biblical record documented that the word of God was contained within the biblical message. Consequently, there was a portion of the membership of the historical era of the church of Pergamum, that emphasized the importance of living a life that was directed by the message of the biblical record. They concentrated on Bible reading and study, and that focus shaped the ethos of the authentic portion of the church.

This high view of scripture was also accompanied with success in the church's mission of spreading the message of God Most High and changing lives. The ideas of 'the whole Bible for the whole world' and 'all of scripture is God breathed and worthy for instruction,' established a missionary impetus that caused the Roman Catholic Church to experience an extensive influence.

Using the biblical message to advance a chosen agenda, was identified as 'eisegesis.' Eisegesis provides an interpretation that reflects the personal ideas and viewpoints of the interpreter. Eisegesis employs the person speaking in authority over the text. Eisegesis requires the interpreter to inject one's own personal message.

In contrast to eisegesis, there is a bible study method that is recognized as 'exegesis.' Exegesis requires the text to provide its own message. The practice of exegeting a message requires the interpreter to participate in a critical review with the expectation of concluding with an explanation and interpretation of the text in which the text is required to 'do the speaking.' Exegesis requires an understanding of what the speaker intended to communicate to the audience, of who the audience was and how the audience would have received the original message, of what the message is to future audiences, and the authority the speaker held as the speaker provided the message. Exegesis requires the message to come out of the text.

Theologians that embraced the baal / mystery / mythology religion, would have participated in eisegesis of the biblical text. In fact, there were church leaders who dismissed the authenticity of portions of the biblical text because those portions were offensive to their theological sensibilities, or those portions prohibited participation in activities that those church leaders found desirable.

Theologians that embraced the authentic faith system of the kingdom of heaven, desired to hear the message of the God of the kingdom of heaven. They practiced exegeting all of the biblical message in order to obtain an accurate perception of what God was attempting to communicate.

John Wycliffe (c. 1328 to 1384) lived during the historical era of the church of Thyatira which followed the historical era of the church of Pergamum. The historical era of the church of Thyatira experienced the results of the practices of the historical era of the church of Pergamum with both eisegesis and exegesis.

John Wycliffe was an English theologian, biblical translator, Roman Catholic priest, and University of Oxford seminary professor. Wycliffe was rejected by the Roman Catholic Church because he questioned the privileged status of the clergy and because he had translated the Bible into the vernacular language of the people. With the populace being able to read the biblical record in their own language, it made it more difficult for theologians and religious leaders to make false claims that the Bible supported their own interpretations and agendas.

Wycliffe also brought attention to the errancy of the Roman Catholic Church Mass, specifically the doctrine of the transubstantiation of the elements being magically / mysteriously changed from bread and wine into the actual body and blood of Jesus Christ through the words spoken over the elements.

The term 'hocus pocus' originated from 'hoc est corpus meum,' which was Latin for 'this is my body.' 'Hoc est corpus meum' are the words uttered by all Roman Catholic priests during the consecration of the elements as they are elevated. Uttering the words 'hocus pocus' was accepted as a mysterious incantation that could magically transform one element into another.

Cannibalism is the act of physically eating the flesh of another being of the same species. The world 'cannibal' originated as a 'feast of baal' / feast to honor baal, or as a 'priest of baal.' Cannibalism was one of the practices of the Nephilim in the antediluvian / preflood era, that disturbed God the Creator. Cannibalism was one of the practices of the Nephilim that were bred after the deluge / flood. And cannibalism continued throughout human history, sometimes united directly with the worship of baal. For the early Christians, an emphasis was made to not eat the food that was sacrificed to idols, which ritually resembled cannibalism, because it offended God Most High (Ezekiel 16:20, 23:36-39, Acts 15:29, 21:25, 1 Corinthians 8:1-7, Revelation 2:14, 2:20, etc.).

The doctrine of transubstantiation and the practice of cannibalism could only be acceptable if the authentic and complete message of the biblical record, was merged with the dogmas, doctrines, theologies and practices of the baal / mystery / mythology religion.

It was in this context of the unholy marriage of the baal / mystery / mythology religion with authentic Christianity, that allowed theologians like Augustine of Hippo (354 to 430) to conduct eisegesis and introduce the new idea of the Seth Cain interpretation of the origin of the Nephilim. The Seth Cain version of Nephilim proposed that Seth was the son of God because Seth became the messianic lineage bearer. And Augustine presented that it was the daughters of Cain, giving birth to the children sired by Seth, that produced Nephilim. Of course, both Seth and Cain were purely human in their genetics, and so they would not have been able to produce something so genetically mutated as giant Nephilim. Augustine's Seth Cain version of Nephilim production defied the biblical record that documented the origins of the Nephilim as being the offspring of rebellious angels.

It was theologians like Augustine of Hippo who admitted that they had difficulty with the biblical record's documentation of the Thousand Years Reign of Jesus Christ, who sought to develop a more palatable theology, employing obscure biblical passages to promote their own ideologies. Augustine's rationale for this practice was that the book of Revelation mingled both literal and figurative expressions, with only a few plain passages to aid in interpretation. Augustine's solution was to adopt a spiritual interpretation which minimized the prophetic *portion of the book of Revelation, and then to relegate the symbolism of the book to be an application in the moral conflict that each person, and the church, faces. Augustine determined that the book of Revelation was merely mythological fiction, devoid of apocalyptic eschatology. And for Augustine and his supporters, that meant that the return of Jesus Christ to fully establish the kingdom of heaven and to establish the Thousand Years Reign of Jesus Christ, was an impossibility.*

Because of Augustine's position of authority as a bishop within the Roman Catholic Church, Augustine's theology heavily influenced the hierarchy of the Roman Catholic Church of the historical era of the church of Pergamum, to embrace the idea of the Roman Catholic Church's assumption of ruling after the dissolution of the Roman empire proper. The leadership of the Roman Catholic Church adopted the belief that establishment of the kingdom of heaven on earth had been entrusted to the leadership of the Roman Catholic Church. If the Roman Catholic Church were to assume global rule, then the popes would need to become global rulers, which was a mission that appealed to popes, cardinals, archbishops, bishops and even parish priests.

(Note that John the Revelator's description of the two beasts of Revelation 13, documented that they will finally receive the power and authority that they have craved, for a forty two month term, as part of the allowance for the red dragon / serpent / Satan, Inc. to attempt to fully establish the kingdom of Satan, Inc. / kingdom of man on earth.)

Part of the reason that Augustine's ideas were so appealing was the changing political climate of the Roman empire at the time. With the decline of the Roman empire, the Roman Catholic Church's mission to become an extension of the Roman empire provided hope.

Before Constantine I's conversion, the biblical message of the radical freedom that being a follower of Jesus Christ offered, provided profound meaning for those followers of the Lamb / Jesus Christ who had experienced persecuted by pagan society and traditions. Christianity was contrasted with the realities of ancient Roman life that determined that human life seemed insignificant, and therefore worthy of enslavement / imprisonment in a variety of forms. Christianity assigned a value and worth to life that could not be stripped away by enslavement / imprisonment, or even death.

When the Roman empire embraced some of the Christian ideology and made peace with Christianity, the radical freedom of Christianity was no longer considered to be drastically radical. When torture and persecution were no longer threats for Christians, truly devout Christians then needed to search out other methods for filling the void for demonstrating their devoutness. Many went to the desert to live in silent reverence. Others employed other methods and practices to demonstrate their devotion.

In the midst of this cultural transition, Augustine's theology assumed that human beings could not be entrusted to govern themselves because the nature of humanity had become corrupted as the result of Adam's sin. Augustine's theology favored the idea that this state of human depravity could not be overcome by the simplicity of obtaining a redemptive relationship with Jesus Christ. Therefore, a political entity was required to control humanity. And the best choice for that governance was the Roman Catholic Church.

The Roman empire under pagan rule, was considered to be evil, filled with injustice and violence. But with the infusion of Christian ideals, Roman rule could be perceived to be truly just and moral, able to produce moral men and women. And the Roman Catholic Church agreed to step in and fill the role of providing 'guidance' for its subjects / members.

The Donatists provided resistance to Augustinian ideals of using imperial forces to enforce the will of the Roman Catholic Church's hierarchy. Augustine's response was to increasingly force the denial of civil rights, to enact fines and penalties, to exile dissidence, and to physically coerce those who offered opposition. The justification for the church's response to opposition, was the assessment that humanity was ravaged by sin and in need of outside intervention. In this way, the Roman Catholic Church's imposing of secular power was validated and was touted as being essential for human salvation.

Another dynamic that rose from the historical era of the church of Pergamum, was the development of the Roman Catholic Church's version of mystagogy.

Mystagogy was the study of mysteries or the interpretation of mystery.

With an incomplete understanding of the mysteries of the biblical record, especially regarding the role of Jesus Christ as the future King of kings and Lord of lords, the hierarchy of the Roman Catholic Church substituted their own version of mystagogy into their void of understanding.

Leaders in the development of the Roman Catholic Church's mystagogy were Augustine of Hippo, Cyril of Jerusalem, Ambrose of Milan, John of Chrysostom, Maximus the Confessor, and Theodore of Mopsuestia.

Mystagogy education became the final stage of the initiation of adults into the Roman Catholic Church. During this period, the meaning of the sacraments was explained to initiates as if the meaning of the sacraments was a secret. Mystagogy within the Roman Catholic Church, was a similar practice to the rituals of mystery religions where it was intended that the meaning of the initiation rituals would be kept secret from the initiates until they experienced the appropriate stages of initiation.

Within the mystery religions, the initiation of baptism included the initiate being bathed in the actual blood of the animal sacrificed; an experience probably best kept secret from the initiate if the goal was to garner a greater membership in the mystery cult.

The church has always baptized with water, not blood. But the aura of mystery of the mystery religions had its attraction to the early leaders of the Roman Catholic Church.

It is important to remember here, that before 1517 and the Protestant Reformation, all of church history was

Roman Catholic Church history. There is no room for arrogance in denying the effects of Roman Catholic Church history, among those who have chosen to embrace Protestantism.

What hampered the continual utilization of the major teachings of mystagogy within the Roman Catholic Church, was authentic scholarship. With the gradual and limited incorporation of authentic biblical education, there was a gradual intellectual emphasis upon the study of biblically defined Christianity, that influenced the liturgical rites, causing the expression of the sacraments to become more deeply and widely understood within the context of the Christian communal experience. With a greater scholarly understanding of the sacraments, the understanding of mystagogy among Roman Catholic Church theologians began to change. The assumption that the full meaning of the Christian tenets of faith were unknowable, began to be replaced with biblically based intellectual answers. The allegorical understanding of the Christian tenets of faith, were demystified.

In contrast to Christianity's insistence upon truth and full disclosure, the baal / mystery / mythology religion must guard its secrets and must meter the secrets out via trade, in order for the religion to prosper.

One of the great contrasts between the secrecy inherently required in the baal / mystery / mythology religion and the authentic faith system of God Most High, is that the authentic faith system discloses its so called secrets. God the Creator established the six days of creation as the template for the six thousand / seven thousand year plan for redemption, reclamation and regeneration of humanity and the earth - not a secret. God Most High established covenant with Noah, with Abram / Abraham, with Isaac, with Jacob / Israel, with Moses and the people of Israel, with David, with Jesus, etc. - not a secret. The prophets of the Old Testament / Tanakh foretold events that took place, and foretold events that are scheduled to take place specifically during the era of the time of Jacob's Trouble - not secrets. The one thing that the biblical record specifically documented was that the God of heaven is not a mystery! The God of heaven is striving to be made known to all who earnestly seek to know God.

And the God of heaven has a future plan that will fill eternity. It is a plan that requires the participation of every believer in messiah (BC) and every follower of the Lamb (AD), as qualified priests in the kingdom of heaven.

God Most High's intention for God's priests, including the priests of the nation of Israel, is for God's priests to bring God and people together, without a third party ruling over the individual God – person relationship. In Jesus Christ's message to the church of Pergamum, Jesus Christ warns those who choose to overcome, that they need to establish a distance from those religious leaders who have decided that what they have spoken has equal authority to what God Most High speaks.

The red dragon / serpent / Satan, Inc.'s religious leaders throughout history, have sought to challenge God Most High's authority, and to fill the position of God Most High with their own candidates, and to alter what God Most High has said. They have sought to inject themselves between individuals and God Most High, for the purpose of ruling over others.

The practice of lording over others, of employing objectification and stratification within the religious culture, of using celibacy and sex as manipulation and power tools, and of injecting religious leaders between parishioners and their God, etc. was expanded beyond the sect of the Nicolaitans to become standard practices of organized religious structures including the historic Roman Catholic Church as well as other organized religious structures.

But God Most High intends to interact with individuals directly, without outside redefinitions of who God Most High is.

The importance of receiving a new name

In marriage, usually the bride takes a new name. Prophetically, the church was always referenced as the bride belonging to Jesus Christ.

Names are important to God Most High.

Language itself does not have value without names, titles, words, designators, definitive actions, adjectives, subjects, verbs, etc.

During creation, God Most High named the evening / chaos, the morning / order, light / day, darkness / night, sky / heavens, ground / land, waters / seas, each of the stars and a variety of other things. But on the sixth day of creation, humanity was tasked with ruling over the creatures of the earth. With the task of ruling over the creatures of the earth, the first man was also tasked with naming animals and birds, and the living creatures on earth. The first man even named the first woman. Adam named her Eve. (Genesis 1-2).

For the activity of naming things and naming living creatures, to be documented in the record of creation, provided evidence that names hold great importance for God Most High.

The names of the men in the antediluvian / preflood messianic lineage, when connected in order, provided a prophetic message.

One of the main purposes for the construction of the tower of Babel was 'to make a name' for its builders (Genesis 1:4). Making one's 'name' known, was considered essential for keeping the inhabitants of the earth together and under the control of those with important 'names.' The tower of Babel was constructed during the time when the whole world had one language and a common speech.

God Most High responded to the tower of Babel empire by dividing language into seventy languages, corresponding to the seventy grandsons of Noah, giving each grandson's family their own language. (~2358 BC)

Throughout the genealogies of the people of Israel, the names the fathers gave to their children provided identity to the children. Abram was the son of Terah. Terah was the son of Nahor. Etc. (Genesis 11:24-26). And when a man named a child, it was the act of the man accepting the child as his own, even if the child was adopted to be his own as was the case of Joseph accepting Jesus to be his own son (Matthew 1:25).

Receiving a new name is the equivalent of receiving a new identity or relationship. When it was God that provided the new name, the new name represented the covenant relationship that the person then held with their God.

Abram's name was changed by God Most High to Abraham. God Most High changed Sarai's name to Sarah. With the addition of the 'h' in their names, was the addition of the Holy Spirit's mark upon their lives.

God Most High named Isaac before he was born with the name Isaac, because 'Isaac' means 'laughter.' (~2000 BC) (Genesis 17:5, 17:15, 17:19).

Jacob, after wrestling with God, was renamed Israel. The name 'Jacob' meant 'supplanter / deceiver.' The name 'Israel' means 'one who wrestles with God and prevails.' (Genesis 32:28)

All of Jacob's children's names were chosen with unique meaning (Genesis 29:31- 30:23, 35:16-18).

- *Reuben / God has seen my misery / see, a son:* 'It is because the Lord has seen my misery. Surely my husband will love me now.'
- *Simeon / one who hears:* 'Because the Lord heard that I am not loved, the Lord gave me this one too.'
- *Levi / attached:* 'Now at last my husband will become attached to me, because I have borne him three sons.' *The Levites became the priests for the nation of Israel, tasked with 'attaching' humanity with God Most High and God Most High with humanity.*
- *Judah / praise:* 'This time I will praise the Lord.' *The tribe of Judah became tasked with carrying the messianic lineage, intended to bring people from all the nations of the world from that time on, to come to praise the Lord.*
- *Dan / God has vindicated:* 'God has vindicated me. God has listened to my plea and given me a son.' *(Dan was the first son of Bilhah, Rachel's maid.)*
- *Naphtali / my struggle:* 'I have had a great struggle with my sister, and I have won.'
- *Gad / good fortune or a troop:* 'What good fortune!'

- *Asher / happy:* 'How happy I am! The women will call me happy.'
- *Issachar / reward:* 'God has rewarded me for giving my servant to my husband.'
- *Zebulun / honor:* 'God has presented me with a precious gift. This time my husband will treat me with honor, because I have born him six sons.'
- *Dinah: daughter of Jacob and Leah.*
- *Joseph / may God add:* 'God has taken away my disgrace.' 'May the Lord add to me another son.'
- *Benjamin / my right hand: originally named Ben-Oni / son of my trouble by Rachel, and renamed Benjamin / son of my right hand by his father Jacob.*

When the people of the southern tribe of Judah, were taken into exile into Babylon, there were four young people / adolescents who stood out. In Babylon, Ashpenaz the chief official, provided these four young people with new names (Daniel 1:6-7). It was an ancient practice of victors to rename their captives in the attempt to cause their new captives to surrender their old traditions, religions, beliefs, and culture; in order to assimilate into their new society.

Daniel 1:8 recorded 'But Daniel resolved in his heart not to defile himself with the royal food and wine...'

Adolescence is one of the prime times in life to shape or reshape one's worldview, one's character, one's conscience, one's sense of purpose, one's understanding of God Most High, etc. The context of Daniel 1 implied that Daniel was resolved to not accept the mental and cultural makeover that the Babylonian empire intended to accomplish in their new captives.

Hebrew name	Meaning	Babylonian name	Meaning
Daniel	God is my judge / God is judge and the source of justice	Belteshazzar	Keeper of the hidden treasure of Bel / baal or Bel protect his life!

Hananiah	The Lord is gracious to me	Shadrach	You are the servant of the pagan gods; particularly Aku the Sumerian moon god.
Mishael	Like God	Meshach	Like Aku
Azariah	The Lord is my helper	Abednego	Servant of Nebo / Nego / Nebu

In developing spiritual life, there are two choices for direction, to pursue God Most High or to rebel against God Most High. To place one's self in the position to receive blessing from God Most High, then what is rebellious against God, must be removed. Daniel and his friends resolved in their hearts to not just deny what they knew would not please God, but they resolved in their hearts to pursue pleasing God Most High.

And God Most High brought to their relationships with God, the same kind of dedication.

Daniel survived the night in the lion's den.

Shadrach, Meshach, and Abednego survived being thrown into the superheated fiery furnace.

Daniel was lifted to one of the highest positions in the kingdoms of Nebuchadnezzar of the Babylonians and Cyrus of the Medo-Persian empire. The kings of the kingdoms and various kingdoms rise and fall. But Daniel continues for over seventy years.

Jesus Christ renamed Simon / bends with the wind, Peter / rock (Matthew 16:18, Mark 3:16, Luke 6:14, John 1:42).

When a child is named, they receive their identity from their parents. When God the Father, or Jesus Christ the Son provides a person with a name, it is an indicator that they have a direct relationship with God Most High, and that their identity has been recognized by God Most High.

But there will come a time during the middle of the era of the time of Jacob's Trouble when the inhabitants of the earth that have chosen to receive the mark of the beast, will receive a number. Their number will replace their name. Their number will act as their new form of 'identity,' provided by the two beasts of Revelation 13 along with the global religious community, the global governance system and the global economic structure. Their number will be used to strip away any identity that would have caused the person to be unique, any identity that would have designated that person as having been a unique creation of God Most High.

Personal identities and names are a constant reminder of the image of God that was pressed into humanity in the Garden of Eden / garden of God / paradise.
During the era of the time of Jacob's Trouble, personal identities and names will be viewed as the product of God the Creator and of the kingdom of heaven. For the red dragon / serpent / Satan, Inc. to achieve the goals of the kingdom of Satan, Inc. / kingdom of man, personal identity will need to be stripped from individuals. By removing personal identity, the kingdom of Satan, Inc. / kingdom of man will be positioned to better rule the inhabitants of the earth.

It will be the theology of the historical era of the church of Pergamum, that will have established the precedence for the beast of the sea and the global religious community assigning numbers to replace names.
One precedence for this kind of activity took place during World War II when those incarcerated in the National Socialist Party / Nazi camps, were stripped of their names and numbered. And in that activity, the people incarcerated were viewed as not being human, but rather as deplorable animals, stripped of their humanity.

Many people wonder how it could be possible that those who ruled at the time, could view other human beings in this manner. But wondering how, does not remove the fact that it took place. And the biblical record documented that this kind of inhumane treatment, will take place again with the establishment of the mark of the beast(s) system.

What makes a person unique, was, is and always will be, a personal gift of God the Creator. In order to utterly destroy the world created by God the Creator, the red dragon / serpent / Satan, Inc. and the allies of the rebellion, must strip away every possible shred of what God the Creator has uniquely created within humanity that was created in the image of God the Creator.

All of creation itself, sings as the creative artwork of God the Creator, displaying the handiwork of God the Creator, proclaiming that God the Creator is here.

For the followers of the Lamb / messiah / Jesus Christ, it will be important that they remain true to the name of Jesus Christ.

John the Revelator's vision recorded in Revelation 13:16-17, described the beast of the earth as attempting to assign numbers, not names, to every individual on earth, all eight billion of us. The act of assigning numbers to human beings, will be the attempt by the kingdom of Satan, Inc. / kingdom of man, of removing the core of what God the Creator created humanity to be.

When God the Creator created the first man, God the Creator assigned the first man with naming things, and with naming the first woman (Genesis 2:19-20). And then God the Creator used the names that the first man had assigned to them.

To remove names from human beings, will be an act that will attempt to remove the image of God the Creator from humanity. Those who have chosen to live in rebellion against the kingdom of heaven, will accept having the uniqueness that was created in them, stripped away. In receiving their number / mark of the beast(s), they will enter into a system of dehumanization. They will be denied the opportunity to buy or sell according to their own created ability to make decisions.

Once enlisted within the mark of the beast(s) system, the adherents of global governance / kingdom of Satan, Inc. / kingdom of man, will be compelled to obtain food and other necessities of life, under the regulations established by the two beasts of Revelation 13 (Revelation 13, 17, etc.).

The alternative to enlisting in the mark of the beast(s) system, will be to overcome during the era of the time of Jacob's Trouble, and to receive a new name from the second Adam / messiah / the Lamb / Jesus Christ. That new name will be accompanied with a refreshed and full identity, and the fullness of what God the Creator created that individual's life to be.

The theology of the historical era of the church of Pergamum in the movement toward the theology of historical era of the church of Laodicea

The theology of the church of Pergamum laid the foundation for the era of the theology of the church of Laodicea.

The theology of the church of Pergamum became predominate theology in the church during this era of the time of Jacob's Trouble.

The church of historical Pergamum theology, renamed and redefined the Jesus originally described within the biblical record. While redefining Jesus Christ, the church also redefined the role of the church and the tenets of the authentic biblical theology.

Redefining Jesus Christ, devoid of some of his characteristics defined within the biblical record, has become a practice of many modern theologians.

That redefining of Jesus Christ began with Jerome and other leaders within the early Roman Catholic Church.

Jerome translated some of the books of the Bible and then compiled Latin translations of other books of the Bible.

While Jesus Christ and his disciples read and spoke both Hebrew and Greek, understanding the message of the

Old Testament / Tanakh in its original language, the leaders of the Roman Catholic Church did not.

While the Septuagint (Greek translation of the Old Testament / Tanakh original text), was edited by seventy rabbis, the Latin Vulgate translation of the Bible, was only edited by Jerome. While the Septuagint was edited with the motivation to translate truth so as to not offend God Most High, the Latin Vulgate was edited so as to not offend the leadership of the Roman empire.

Redefining anything within the biblical record, leads in a dangerous direction.

The Latin Vulgate translation, complete with its errors and biases, became the official translation of the Roman Catholic Church. And the Roman Catholic Church leadership built upon the Latin Vulgate translation's errors and biases.

In addition, the people of Israel were required to memorize portions of the Old Testament / Tanakh as a rite of passage into spiritual adulthood. The people of Israel were expected to have a familiarity with the biblical record. Reading from the scrolls was a part of their temple / synagogue worship.

But within the Roman Catholic Church, most churches did not even possess a copy of the Bible. And familiarity with what was included within the biblical record was not a requirement or even expected in order to serve as a priest / religious leader within the church and community. In fact, there were times in the history of the Roman Catholic Church when reading portions of the Bible, or the Bible in its entirety, was forbidden by the church hierarchy.

The low view of biblical authority that was prevalent during the historical era of the church of Pergamum's theology, has again become prevalent within most churches during the era of the time of Jacob's Trouble. The church religious leaders have again adopted a low view of biblical authority in espousing the various cultural theologies that defy the message of the biblical record.

Religious church leaders preach against revival and outpourings of the Holy Spirit and against any focus upon the Holy Spirit, while the Holy Spirit grows contentious about the condition of the spirits of humanity (Genesis 3:6, Revelation 14:13, etc.) The thought among these religious leaders is that maybe if the presence and work of the Holy Spirit today is denied, the Holy Spirit might just go away and leave us alone in our own pursuit of attaining personal power.

But the Holy Spirit remains a vital participant in the work that will be achieved during the era of the time of Jacob's Trouble, working in communicating the message of God to people, and in writing fresh messages upon the hearts of humanity (the prophets of the Old Testament / Tanakh who wrote under the inspiration of the Holy Spirit, Joel 2:28-29, Matthew 3:11-16, 12:31-32, 28:19, Mark 1:8-12, 3:23-29, 13:11, Luke 3:16, 3:22, Luke 4:14-18, 10:21, 11:13, 12:10-12, John 1:32-33, 3:5-8, 3:34, 4:23-24, 6:63, 7:39, 14:15-26, 16:13-15, 20:22, Acts 1, 2, (the entire book of Acts), Romans 1:4, 2:29, 5:5, 7:6, 8 (especially 8:16), 14:17, 15:13-30, 1 Corinthians 2:6-15, 3:1, 3:16, 6:11, 6:19, 12, 14, 2 Corinthians 1:21-22, 3:3, 3:6-11, 3:17-18, 6:3-6f, 11:3-4, 13:14, Galatians 3:3-5, 3:14, 4:6, 5:5, 5:13-25, 6:1, 6:8, Ephesians 1:13, 1:17, 2:18-22, 3:2-6, 3:16, 4:3-4, <u>4:30</u>, 5:18-19, 6:12-18, Philippians 2:1-4, Colossians 3:16, 1 Thessalonians 1:2-6, 4:8, <u>5:19</u>, 2 Thessalonians 2:13, 1 Timothy 3:16, 4:1, 2 Timothy 1:7, 1:14, Titus 3:3-7, Hebrews 2:4, 3:7-11, 4:4-6, 9:6-8, 9:14, 10:28-29, 1 Peter 1:1-2, 1:10-12, 2:1-2, 3:18, 4:14, 2 Peter 1:21, 1 John 3:24, 4:13, 5:7-8, Jude 1:17-21, Revelation 1:10, 2, 3, 4, 14:13, 17:3, 19:10, 21:10, 22:17, etc.) (These should be enough passages to begin to assist in addressing those who deny the work of the Holy Spirit through their one or two verses that have been selectively pluck from the biblical record.)

Without the Holy Spirit, Jesus Christ would not have been resurrected from death (Romans 8:11-13, 1 Peter 3:18).

The message of the Holy Spirit cannot be heard by those that deny the work of the Holy Spirit.

If Jesus Christ needed the Holy Spirit in order to accomplish his work during his earthly ministry, and to be resurrected from death, why do church leaders need to be so arrogant as to believe that they should accomplish their work for the kingdom of heaven, without the guidance and power of one of the members of the sovereign and divine office of God? It does not make sense to effectively baptize people in the name of the Father and the name of the Son and the name of the Holy Spirit, and then deny the importance and work of the Holy Spirit.

The picker and chooser Bible study method, and the denial of the work of the Holy Spirit, were just two points on which the theology of the historical era of the church of Pergamum, transcended into our day. Denying that all of scripture is God breathed / Holy Spirit inspired, and worthy for instruction (2 Timothy 3:16), leads to the path of removing essential portions of the biblical message.

It is like having a map of the state of Pennsylvania, with holes in it, so that the navigator does not know where the intersections are for giving direction.

Ultimately the biblical message serves to place people in the path that allows God Most High to pour out protection and blessing upon them. Without the fullness of that message, a person will be left to the work of the evil one (Matthew 6:13, 13:19, 13:38, John 17:15, Ephesians 6:16, 2 Thessalonians 3:3, 1 John 2:13-14, 3:12, 5:18-19).

The church of Pergamum theology dangerously adapted the church to fit the culture, instead of the church influencing the culture to adapt to the requirements of the kingdom of heaven and to be righteous.

Mariology in conflict with the eschatological plan of God the Father, messiah / the Lamb / Jesus Christ / God the Son, and God the Holy Spirit

Whenever the biblical record has not been recognized as the Holy Spirit inspired message of God Most High (2 Timothy 3:16), then the process of substituting variant dogmas, doctrines, theologies and practices, into the authentic faith system, becomes an acceptable practice.

Historically practiced within the kingdom of Pergamum (282 to 133 / 129 BC), was the worship of Semiramis as the 'Queen of heaven.' She was worshiped in Pergamum as Aphrodite (Greek) and was featured on the Gigantomachy frieze on the temple of Zeus, as she fought other gods. In Pergamum, Aphrodite (Greek) would have been the goddess known in other cultures as Sammuramat (Assyria), Atargatis (Syria), Ishtar / Inanna (Babylonia), Astarte (near east), etc.

Semiramis / Aphrodite (Greek), as the Queen of heaven, was carried to Pergamum, and then into the Roman empire through the priests of the Babylonian baal / mystery / mythology religion.

The name Pergamum itself means unholy marriage. The theology of the church of Pergamum faced the marriage of variant dogmas, doctrines, theologies and practices, with the authentic faith system of the kingdom of heaven.

When the Roman empire forced Christianity to become the official religion of the empire, the priests of the baal / mystery / mythology religion were compelled to become priests in the new Christian religion. However, the new priests forced into Christianity, retained many of their baal / mystery / mythology religion dogmas, doctrines, theologies and practices. And just as the Babylonian Semiramis / Queen of heaven, was adapted to the Greek culture in the formation of Aphrodite, Aphrodite was adapted to the new Christian culture in Rome through the formation of the doctrine of the Blessed Virgin Mary / Queen of heaven.

The mother-child cult that was so firmly established by Semiramis and her sons, was applied to Mary and Jesus, and required that Mary no longer remain a mere human mother of Jesus. Between Semiramis and her sons, Semiramis held the greater share of 'divine' genetics. Consequently, in Christian art, the Christian version frequently depicted Mary as being greater or larger than Jesus.

With actual copies of the Bible being a scarcity, there was little challenge made to the biblical Mary being interchanged with the new doctrine of the Blessed Virgin Mary / Queen of heaven. There were very few who could offer an authentic theological correction to any religious theology that the priests of the new religion presented.

The same kind of biblical illiteracy of the historical era of the church of Pergamum, exists today. And the same situation where religious leaders use religion to push their own personal agendas upon their biblically illiterate followers, also exists today.

The theology of the historical era of the church of Pergamum, developed the Blessed Virgin Mary to serve as an alternative to the biblical Mary. The Roman Catholic Church presented:
1. Mary as the theotokos / mother of God - which required Mary to be divine instead of a fully human needing salvation like all other fully human beings (Council of Ephesus (431)).
2. Mary's perpetual virginity - which required Mary to not have consummated her marriage with Joseph, which would have rendered Jesus' birth to have the status of illegitimate and would have caused Jesus Christ to have been unable to assume the throne of Israel / throne of God Most High (early Roman Catholic Church / Council of the Lateran (649)) (Deuteronomy 23:2). This dogma also denied the existence of Jesus Christ's brothers and sisters, including Jesus' brother James who became the head of the church in Jerusalem and Jesus' brother Jude who authored the book of Jude in the biblical record.
3. Mary as the one who was immaculately conceived - which substituted the biblical record's conception of Jesus Christ by the Holy Spirit, with the imagined baal / mystery / mythology religion's immaculate conception of Mary / Semiramis (Council of Trent (1545 / 1563), Pius IX on December 8, 1954, etc.). It was the dogma of Mary's immaculate conception that defied Mary's own need for a savior (Luke 1:46-55).
4. The assumption of Mary into heaven (Council of Chalcedon (450), Pius XII on November 1, 1950, etc.) - which eliminated the need for the

ascension of Jesus Christ into heaven to sit at the right hand of God the Father (Mark 16:19, Luke 22:69, Acts 2:33, 5:31, 7:55-56, Romans 8:34, 2 Corinthians 6:7, Colossians 3:1, Hebrews 1:3, 1:13, 10:12, 12:2, 1 Peter 3:22, Revelation 4, 5). But the biblical record documented that it was the resurrected Jesus Christ who ascended into heaven forty days after his crucifixion, death and resurrection (Acts 1:1-11) (~30 AD). And the biblical record provided no evidence to support the assumption of Mary into heaven. Jesus Christ ascended into heaven as a sign of divine power. The dogma of Mary's assumption into heaven, merely elevated Mary in her power within the hierarchy of heaven because of her assumed divine motherhood.

5. Mary as the New Eve / Our Lady of the Eschaton (especially ~1700) – which substituted the necessity of the return of messiah / the Lamb / Jesus Christ to defeat the enemies of God Most High and to fully establish the kingdom of heaven on earth, with Mary / the New Eve / Our Lady of the Eschaton, substituting for Jesus Christ as the new leader of God's armies, and the one to lead in the full establishment of the Roman Catholic Church's version of the kingdom of heaven, on earth.

In the Latin Vulgate translation of the Bible (compiled by Jerome (382)), Genesis 3:15 was translated to reflect that the woman would provide the offspring whose heel would be bruised (Jesus Christ through crucifixion); and that a woman would also be the one to avenge her offspring's injury by crushing the head of the offspring of the serpent. The Latin Vulgate's alteration of the original text, continued in subsequent Roman Catholic translations of the Bible, until just recently.

But it was the Latin Vulgate's mistranslation of Genesis 3:15, that served to be considered as an endorsement of the development of the theology of the

Blessed Virgin Mary as Our Lady of the Eschaton, where the Blessed Virgin Mary would become the ultimate savior, instead of messiah / the Lamb / Jesus Christ. Following the biblical idea that Jesus filled the role as the second Adam, the Blessed Virgin Mary also became known as the New Eve.

In this altered scenario, the New Eve / Our Lady of the Eschaton would have the authority to establish her kingdom, according to her desires, and honor those who have so faithfully prayed to her throughout the centuries.

During the era of the time of Jacob's Trouble, if it were to be the Blessed Virgin Mary who will come to defeat the enemies of the kingdom, and the biblical record documented that in fact it will be Jesus Christ who will come to defeat the enemies of the kingdom of heaven, then the Blessed Virgin Mary / the New Eve / Our Lady of the Eschaton and Jesus Christ, must fight on two different sides and for two different kingdoms.

Substituting the New Eve / Our Lady of the Eschaton, in the place of messiah / the Lamb / Jesus Christ in the final battle, also allowed for the substitution of the Blessed Virgin Mary being the authority designated to rule during the Thousand Years Reign. Removing Jesus Christ from being the ruler during the Thousand Years Reign of Jesus Christ, served to advance the hierarchy of the Roman Catholic Church to proceed in their mission of finally establishing the Roman empire as the global kingdom via the Roman Catholic Church, and establishing the leader of the Roman Catholic Church as the global leader.

In this way, substantial alterations to authentic biblical theology were founded within the theology of the historical era of the church of Pergamum. And those ideas still serve to guide and direct the hierarchy of the Roman Catholic Church. In the pursuit of establishing global rule, the Roman Catholic Church finally achieved the election of a Jesuit to the papal office. The Society of Jesus / Jesuits were founded with the mission of eventually establishing global papal rule.

During the first half of the era of the time of Jacob's Trouble, the global religious community will unify under the direction of the beast of the sea / false prophet / eighth king beast. It will be essential that during the formation of the global religious community, that the Roman Catholic Church, along with other church denominations and other religions, will come to reside under the umbrella of the Roman Catholic Church leadership. Other church denominations and other religions of the world, will need to find a consensus on the importance of establishing global religious rule, and will need to find a consensus on the doctrines concerning the identity and authority of Mary. During the era of the time of Jacob's Trouble, the Roman Catholic Church doctrine of the New Eve / Our Lady of the Eschaton and the Blessed Virgin Mary's role as the true savior of the world, will be fully tested.

    Because all forms of religion that serve as alternatives to the authentic faith system, were derived from the antediluvian / preflood version of the baal / mystery / mythology religion, the definition of who Mary is, will be required to maintain a connection to the original story of Semiramis. And the biblical definition of Mary will need to be relaxed.

    In Roman Catholic Church theology, Mary as the theotokos / mother of God, required Mary to be considered to be divine, similar to Semiramis' assumed divinity.

    The baal / mystery / mythology religion's version of 'Mary' will continue to describe the mother of God as divine, while the biblical Mary understood her own need for a savior just like the rest of humanity (Luke 1:46-55).

    Mary filling the position as the mother of God, would have been a source for Jesus' divinity, potentially placing the Mary above Jesus Christ in the hierarchy of heaven. For those who continue to invest themselves in the baal / mystery / mythology religion, Mary as the mother of God follows the typology of Semiramis the mother of Nimrod and Tammuz, which serves as an acceptable merger of religious belief. In the baal / mystery /

mythology religion, Nimrod and Tammuz were subservient to their mother's divinity. If the relationship of Semiramis, Nimrod and Tammuz served as a typology for the relationship of Mary and Jesus, then the omnipotence of Jesus Christ would be negated, rendering Jesus to be able to be defeated after the manner of the defeat of Semiramis' son Nimrod / Amraphel (Genesis 14).

The baal / mystery / mythology religion's version of 'Mary' will continue to describe the mother of God as divine, while the biblical Mary understood her own need for a savior just like the rest of humanity (Luke 1:46-55).

The divine Mary was deemed to be worthy of receiving worship, worship that properly belongs to God the Father, messiah / the Lamb / Jesus Christ / God the Son, and God the Holy Spirit. But the biblical Mary worshiped the God of heaven (Luke 1:46-55).

In Roman Catholic Church theology, the Blessed Virgin Mary remained a perpetual virgin, complete with a story where Mary's perpetual virginity was reinstated immediately after the birth of Jesus Christ.

The major problem with the doctrine of the Blessed Virgin Mary was that perpetual virginity required that Mary's marriage to Joseph would not have been consummated. Without a consummated marriage, Jesus' birth would have been rendered to have been illegitimate and would have invalidated Jesus Christ's authority to sit upon David's throne in Israel (Deuteronomy 23:2). This circumstance if true, would have created a void for the identity of who should fill the throne in Israel during the Thousand Years Reign of Jesus Christ.

In Roman Catholic Church theology, it was Mary who was immaculately conceived, not Jesus Christ. In Roman Catholic Church theology, the Blessed Virgin Mary's immaculate conception would have rendered Mary to be divine, part goddess, similar to the understanding of the constitution of Semiramis.

In the Roman Catholic Church version, Mary's son / Jesus, had an earthly father.

In the biblical description of the conception of Jesus Christ, it was Jesus Christ who was conceived by the Holy Spirit, in the womb of the fully human Mary, after Mary had consented to God's plan. (Luke 1:26-38).

As the global religious community coagulates, it will be important to maintain the story of the immaculate conception of the Blessed Virgin Mary, because it mimics the conception of Semiramis of the baal / mystery / mythology religion, whose father was a rebellious angel.

More importantly, the alternate version of Jesus having a semidivine mother would have negated the fully human origin that the promised and prophesied messiah was required to have in order to be the acceptable sacrifice through his crucifixion. If Jesus Christ were an inferior sacrifice, then he would not have been able to be rendered to be the worthy Lamb that opens the seven seals on the will of God Most High (Revelation 4 and 5).

In addition, it was recorded in the will of God Most High that it would be messiah / the Lamb / Jesus Christ, and not the Blessed Virgin Mary / the New Eve / Our Lady of the Eschaton, who would return to defeat the enemies of God Most High and of the kingdom of heaven. And the biblical record repeatedly presented that it would be messiah the Lamb / Jesus Christ who would fully establish the kingdom of heaven on earth and sit on the throne in Israel as the global ruler.

Another belief that defies the biblical record, held by the hierarchy of the Roman Catholic Church has been the belief that Jesus Christ was not resurrected.

Matthew documented that the religious leaders of Israel paid the Roman guard to spread the story that Jesus's disciples stole his body and hid it (Matthew 28:11-14).

The hierarchy of the Roman Catholic Church has historically also agreed with that story. The Roman Catholic Church official explanation that was offered to explain Jesus' disciples' walking and talking with the resurrected Jesus Christ, was to present the disciples as being so emotionally distraught that they imagined a resurrected Jesus Christ.

Without an authentic resurrected Jesus Christ, the authenticity of Jesus Christ's ascension into heaven was also be dismissed. Without Jesus Christ's ascension into heaven, the depiction of the Lamb / Jesus Christ receiving the will of God Most High in the throne room of heaven (Revelation 4 and 5), was also rendered to be invalid by the hierarchy of the Roman Catholic Church.

This left open the alternative story to develop, of the assumption of Mary into heaven. Having found the designated tomb of Mary to be empty, the conclusion was made that the dead body of Mary was taken into heaven. With the Blessed Virgin Mary's residing in heaven through her assumption, the Blessed Virgin Mary could be considered to be seated next to God Most High instead of Jesus Christ. The Blessed Virgin Mary could be recognized as filling the role of heavenly intercessor, in contrast to the biblical role that Jesus Christ fills as an advocate for all followers of the Lamb / Jesus Christ.

It is the biblical role of advocate that Jesus Christ fills exclusively, that allows the recognition of Jesus Christ as the way and the truth and the life, the gatekeeper for whom is allowed to come to God the Father (John 14:6).

The biblical record was clear that there are only two ways to approach God the Father; through Jesus Christ with Jesus Christ as the advocate who offers a friendship with God the Father, or as an enemy willing to battle God the Father. During the era of the time of Jacob's Trouble, it will be essential that Jesus Christ be presented as the one who determines who will approach God the Father with a right relationship as friend.

The baal / mystery / mythology religion's genius has always been to take what God Most High has planned and twist the message so that in the end, instead of God Most High being the victor, it will be the red dragon / serpent / Satan, Inc. who wins.

The astrological message of the zodiac, was a twisted version of the Way of Salvation / message in the stars / Mazzaroth. In the astrological message of the zodiac, the red dragon / serpent / Satan, Inc. wins through *establishing rule over humanity via the stars / angels / gods and goddesses.*

But in the Way of Salvation / message in the stars / Mazzaroth, the promised and prophesied messiah / Jesus Christ is the victor.

After six thousand years of twisting the authentic faith system, the futility of the twisted message will be finally demonstrated during the era of the time of Jacob's Trouble. With the opening of the first seal and the release of the white horse and its rider (Revelation 6:1-2), the global religious community will be allowed to be temporarily established globally on earth. Through the work of the global religious community, the kingdom of Satan, Inc. / kingdom of man will also be allowed the attempt to be fully established on earth. But the global religious community will be only a twisting of what is authentic. The global religious community, with its rider on a white horse (Revelation 6:1-2), will only be a fake copy of the kingdom of heaven with its rider on a white horse / Jesus Christ who will fully establish the authentic kingdom of heaven on earth (Revelation 19:11-21).

The theology of the church of Pergamum established the practice of fake copying; placing the names, titles, ideas of their baal / mystery / mythology religion into places and onto the people, that belonged to the authentic faith system. During the era of the time of Jacob's Trouble, that practice of producing facsimiles will continue, until Jesus Christ proves himself to be the true King of kings and Lord of lords (1 Corinthians 6:13-16, Revelation 17:14, 19:11-16).

The problem with facsimiles is they are not authentic.

Other aspects of the historically developed doctrines of Mariology within the hierarchy of the Roman Catholic Church, and their conflicts with authentic biblical theology

There was much documentation within the hierarchy of the Roman Catholic Church concerning the growth and development of the doctrines of Mariology. In the development of Marian theology, there were some significant main phases.

Phase one was to view the biblical record as having presented Mary as the actual type of church, prefiguring the church.

But the biblical record clearly defined that Mary was not the church, and her womb did not give birth to the church. Mary was a human being.

Phase two consisted of certain church fathers providing an elucidating and clarifying role to Mary. Mary was declared Theotokos / mother of God. While the biblical record presented Mary as merely a human woman who gave birth to messiah / Jesus Christ, the term 'Theotokos' / 'mother of God' elevated Mary's position to imply that Mary was herself divine and was essential to providing divinity to the nonbiblical, redefined Jesus the Christ. (Realistically, if Mary were a Theotokos / mother of God, then Jesus Christ would not have been able to meet the required criteria of being fully human along with being fully divine. Even Paul insisted that Jesus was 'born of woman' Galatians 4:4) It took Roman Catholic Church fathers over four hundred years to determine how to fully incorporate Theotokos / mother of God theology into Roman Catholic Church Christology; to be able to express their invented theology as coherent, consistent and logical.

The third phase was described clearly in Bernard of Clairvaux's writings on Mary which considered Mary as a stand-alone person, distinct from the church. With the presentation of Mary not personally needing the redemption of Jesus Christ, the idea of Mary's piety was amplified. Around 1050, the Hail Mary prayer was developed. By 1218, the *Salve Regina* / 'Hail Holy Queen,' a Marian hymn, was already incorporated into the daily worship of the Cistercians. Throughout the centuries, the amplification of Mary's piety continued to be amplified, culminating in the development of Mary as having been immaculately conceived, a decision made official by Pius IX in *Ineffabilis Deus* (1854). Mary was declared to be the Immaculate Virgin free from all stain of original sin, and exalted by the Lord as Queen over all things, a decision made official by Pius XII in *Munificentissimus Deus* (1950). Mary was also declared to have experienced bodily assumption instead of death, also a decision made official by Pius XII in the same *Munificentissimus Deus* (1950).

But the biblical record offered Mary's own very human genealogy which served as evidence that Mary was not immaculately conceived (Luke 3:23). Mary's father was Heli, a descendant of Nathan, Solomon's third son. Mary herself was merely a woman, not intrinsically divine.

The fourth phase was historically associated with the Protestant Reformation era, beginning with the Lutheran tradition. It was the Protestant Reformation that provided an authenticity check to the Roman Catholic Church's elevation of Mary as divine. When the Protestant Reformation insisted that the biblical record held higher authority than the words of the Roman Catholic Church's hierarchy, then Mary as Theotokos / mother of God, and Mary as having received intrinsic divinity through her supposed immaculate conception, was scrutinized. A hostile environment was developed concerning the non-biblically defined Mary.

The fifth phase in the development of Mariology was set in contemporary thought within the Roman Catholic Church. Mary became interlinked with the actual Roman Catholic Church. This interlinking of the Roman Catholic Church and Mary consisted of three aspects.

The first aspect of contemporary thought related to Vatican II's Constitution of the Church, *Lumen Gentium* / 'Light of the Nations' (November 21, 1964), promulgated by Paul VI, in which John XXIII's desire for a refined, scriptural Mariology renewed Mary's role in the development of Christology and ecclesiology (Christology / understanding of Jesus Christ and ecclesiology / the understanding of the church in theology and in the act of salvation). Mary again became a type of the church, indivisibly linked with the Roman Catholic Church. Mary became a required conduit for understanding the Roman Catholic Church, with the church required as a conduit for understanding Mary's authority and power. Mary and the Roman Catholic Church became inextricably linked. The Roman Catholic Church essentially assumed ownership of Mary and Mary became a figure that stands with the Roman Catholic Church, that can no longer stand alone as a simple woman who mothered the human infant Jesus.

(Note that the Roman Catholic Church's proposed role of Mary, was the same kind of relationship that Semiramis held with the baal / mystery / mythology religion of the tower of Babel empire after the deluge / flood. Semiramis was recognized as the original postdiluvian / postflood world's 'Queen of Heaven.')

The *Lumen Gentium* / 'Light of the Nations' (November 21, 1964) chapter 8, addressed the place of Mary within the Roman Catholic Church's theological structure. Ecumenicalism was also discussed in relation to the topic of Mary. The conclusion was that any church that decided to unite with the Roman Catholic Church would be required to also recognize the special veneration of Mary as the Blessed Virgin Mary, Theotokos / Mother of God, and the Mystery of Christ and the Roman Catholic Church.

The 'Mystery of Christ and the Roman Catholic Church' was a reference to acknowledging the Roman Catholic Church's view that when Jesus Christ's body was stolen or when Jesus Christ was considered to be ascended into heaven, that Jesus Christ had left the church, relinquishing to the Roman Catholic Church, all responsibility and authority on earth for the kingdom of heaven. The paradigm held by the hierarchy of the Roman Catholic Church was that the Roman Catholic Church assumed full control over decisions concerning who should be included in the kingdom of heaven, and who should be excluded.

In contrast to this developed theology, the biblical record was clear that entrance into the kingdom of heaven was, is and always will be, determined by Jesus Christ and the Holy Spirit alone. But previous popes have declared that their decisions hold more authority than the biblical record. And traditional Roman Catholic Church groups have officially considered the *Lumen Gentium* / 'Light of the Nations' (November 21, 1964) document to demark when the Roman Catholic Church irrevocably fell into this heresy.

This interlinking of the redefined Mary and the Roman Catholic Church required a redefinition of the biblically presented trinity. The ecclesiastical / church theme of trinity became represented by the relationship of Christ, the Blessed Virgin Mary, and the Roman Catholic Church. In this theology, without the redefined Mary, Jesus Christ would not have been able to have been given life. Without this redefined Mary, the Roman Catholic Church could not have existed. Because of this redefined Mary's faith, Christ and the Roman Catholic Church have their 'being.'

The second aspect of contemporary thought related to the redefined Mary, concerned the transmission of Mariology throughout the 'Christian community' / various Christian denominations. Since the Roman Catholic Church's Vatican II Council, and the institution of the ecumenical movement, the emphasis has been on engaging in ecumenical dialogue with a desired objective to agree on common ground on the theology of Mary among the various Christian denominations. In 1967, the Ecumenical Society for the Blessed Virgin Mary was formed in order to assist in dialogue for developing and disseminating Marian theology.

The third aspect of contemporary thought related to the development of feminist theology. There was this sense that by raising Mary's status to 'the Blessed Virgin Mary,' that Mary in a way, absorbed the value of all other women and simultaneously created a negative status within the Christian community for the value of all other women. There was this understanding, that because the Roman Catholic Church pays homage to Mary and worships Mary as divine, that it is not necessary to recognize or value all other women as equals with men.

In contrast to the rationalization for the justification of the exclusion of women within the Roman Catholic Church hierarchy, is the feminist theology that focuses upon Mary's worth as being reason for actually recognizing the value of the contributions of women to the Roman Catholic Church as more than merely shrine priestesses.

In contrast to Mary as the typology for church, as Theotokos, as immaculately conceived, as experiencing bodily assumption, as being wholly divine, as being the Blessed Virgin Mary, Queen of Heaven; the biblical message presented an entirely different portrayal of Mary the mother of the fully human, fully divine infant Jesus.

According to the biblical record, Mary was approached by God Most High's angel to request of her to be used for the incarnation of Jesus Christ. If Mary had been immaculately conceived, there would have been no need to request Mary's consent to take part. Mary would have been designated and predestined prior to her own birth for the role.

The actual conception of Jesus Christ, required the work of all three persons of the trinity. The Holy Spirit, provided the conception of Jesus Christ. The Holy Spirit provided the conception through the power and will of God Most High. And Jesus Christ emptied himself of the power of his heavenly divinity in order to become fully human. While Mary was the receptacle of God's plan, the relationship that was established was not divinity with divinity, but rather divinity (God the Father, Son and Holy Spirit) with humanity (Mary). If Mary were divine, the relationship of divinity with humanity would not have been able to have been established, and this would have rendered Jesus Christ's sacrifice through crucifixion, as the 'second Adam,' to have been void and ineffectual for the redemption of humanity.

Jesus Christ's own instruction to the apostles was 'All authority in heaven and on earth has been given to me. Therefore, go and make disciples of all nations, baptizing them in the name of the Father and of the Son and of the Holy Spirit, and teaching them to obey everything I have commanded you. And surely, I am with you always, to the very end of the age.' Matthew 28:18-20

Authority was given to Jesus Christ, not to Mary. The names to baptize with are the name of the Father, the name of the Son and the name of the Holy Spirit; not the name of Mary. It is Jesus Christ who is with us always, to the very end of the age; not Mary.

Throughout history beginning with the Protestant Reformation, the various Christian denominations have pointed out that the original biblical message emphasized Mary as a mere human who needed the redemption brought through her son Jesus Christ, just as much as every other human being on earth and throughout her life, Mary needed redemption just like every other human being (Luke 1:46-49).

During the historical era of the church of Laodicea, the presentation of Mary will continue to develop so that the Blessed Virgin Mary will become the Illuminator of the fullness of Christian faith and theology. The emphasis will be focused upon Mary as a combination of a partially biblically described Mary with the image of Mary developed through Roman Catholic Church tradition. In this way, Mary will be able to be presented through the ecumenical movement, appealing to various historically Christian denominations; and to other religions that tolerate the presentation of the diminished divinity and sovereignty of messiah / the Lamb / Jesus Christ. In this way, the redefined Mary will be able to be in relationship with all religions.

It will be an important achievement to develop phraseology / language / terms that can define Illuminator Mary in such a way as to be palatable to the various Christian denominations, while still urging Christian denominations to receive the doctrine and theology of Mariology.

The Roman Catholic Church was founded in the fourth century using this kind of merger / marriage of baal / mystery / mythology religion with Christianity through the development of a common phraseology / language / use of terms that was able to mean different things to different people. The Roman Catholic Church will be able to draw upon their distant past experience, to impact the world once again with a religion of facsimiles of authentic personalities.

Jesus 'the Christ' theology

A result and response to the demotion of Jesus Christ from his position as the divine and sovereign savior of the world, was the development of the theology of Jesus as 'the Christ.' In 'the Christ' theology, the actual biblical and archeologically documented life of Jesus Christ, was denied. And all subsequent accounts of the factual Jesus Christ, were rendered as false. In 'the Christ' theology, the divinity and authority of Jesus Christ was rendered to be fable.

Those who embraced the theology of 'the Christ,' claimed that the historical physical human being of Jesus, did not exist. And they claimed that the biblical Jesus Christ did not found Christianity.

In the newly defined 'the Christ' theology, the idea of the actual existence of a historical Jesus Christ was replaced with a caricatured Jesus created from the minds of the twelve men plus Paul, who conspired together to present a mythological personality that would credibly act as a facsimile for the people of Israel to fulfill their expectations of the biblical messiah. Using religious syncretism / the blending of two or more religious belief systems, along with mythological components, it was supposed that the gospel writers produced an individual comprised of the characteristics they felt were important for a mythological god to possess.

The purpose in developing the story of 'the Christ,' was to provide a story that portrayed a messianic fulfillment to the prophecies of the Old Testament / Tanakh. According to those who have embraced the narrative of 'the Christ,' the entire biblical account of the life, crucifixion, death, resurrection, and ascension into heaven, lived only in the minds of this committee who developed the story line.

In the presentation of 'the Christ' myth theory / Jesus myth theory / Jesus mythicism / Jesus ahistoricity theory, the biblical record's documentation of Jesus was considered to be a piece of mythology, and afactual. The crucifixion, death, and resurrection of Jesus then became merely the pivotal point in the climax of an enticing story line. The mythological ascension of Jesus Christ into heaven, explained Jesus Christ's absence from us, and the fact that Jesus Christ does not reside in a grave, then was able to be translated as the explanation and 'proof' that Jesus Christ never really existed.

    If Jesus Christ were in fact, a mythological being that never really existed, then there would be no reason to believe that Jesus Christ will return. If Jesus Christ never really existed and will not return to hold the inhabitants of the earth accountable, then there would be no reason to teach about Jesus Christ as presented by the biblical authors. If Jesus Christ never really existed, will not return to hold the inhabitants of the earth accountable, and lives only in the minds of the biblical authors, then the message of Jesus Christ and of the rest of the biblical message can be altered and revised to fit modern day sensibilities and feelings. If Jesus Christ never really existed, will not return to hold the inhabitants of the earth accountable, lives only in the minds of the biblical authors, and humanity has the right and responsibility to revise the biblical message to meet modern day sensibilities and feelings, then humanity also has the right and responsibility to become 'like God,' and in agreement with the new definition of redefining 'God,' humanity should provide a ruling class of humanity to rule over the nonruling class of humanity.

    Just as the Scribes, Pharisees, teachers of the Law, etc. rejected the biblical Jesus Christ because, as true high priest and ruler of the kingdom of heaven, Jesus Christ would have taken away the power, authority and wealth of the Jewish religious leaders; modern day religious leaders have found the biblical Jesus Christ to be an equal threat to their power and wealth. For modern day religious leaders, 'the Christ' has become the more appealing alternative over the original biblical Jesus Christ that fills the role as authentic God, with the power to rule.

    The pseudo theological / pseudo mythicism thought, was also supported in theory with the evidence of mythemes. Mythemes were the fundamental generic unit of narrative from which a variety of myths were constructed. Mythemes were why the mythological stories could stay relatively the same while the settings, characters, and names could be changed, but the outcome would be somewhat the same. Because the first three gospel writers told the story of Jesus Christ from their own perspective, but with the same kind of outline, those who support demythologizing the biblical record, categorized the gospels as having been developed from the same kind of mytheme originally utilized to promote the baal / mystery / mythology religion. They denied that three individual men could possibly have written their gospels from their own personal experience with a real living physical human being, Jesus Christ.

Beginning in the nineteenth century, (during the historical era of the theology of the Philadelphia church) pseudo theologians advanced the idea of a mythological Christ and developed critical methods for demythologizing the original biblical Jesus Christ. Demythologization replaced events described as miracles, with an understanding that those events were best described as myths. Demythologization viewed the parables that Jesus taught as messages that described the kingdom of heaven, as mythological entertainment.

The biblical record that was traditionally viewed as God Most High's instruction book on how to relate to God Most High and on how to live life in this world, became redefined through demythologization as merely a story with ideas and suggestions for experimentation in one's own life. But the biblical record certainly did not provide appropriate instruction to follow, or provide models to follow for living life.

For those who chose to interpret the biblical message through demythologization, Jesus was trapped as a first century Israelite who offered principles, teachings, and concepts that cannot be applied to any other time period in history, or in the lives of other people.

For those engaged in attempting to demythologizing the biblical record, the assumption that the actual person of Jesus Christ needed to be classified as a myth, effectively *invalidated the hope of the second portion of the work of Jesus Christ / the return of Jesus Christ. If Jesus Christ did not exist as an actual physical human being to accomplish the first part of the responsibilities in God Most High's redemption, reclamation and regeneration plan, then there would be no actual physical Jesus Christ to complete the second portion by returning and physically defeating the enemies of God Most High and of the kingdom of heaven. There would be no hope for the fully established kingdom of heaven on earth and no Thousand Years Reign of Jesus Christ.*

Message for the era of the time of Jacob's Trouble from the message to the angel of the married church of Pergamum

Jesus said in the message to the church of Pergamum, 'Repent therefore! Otherwise, I will soon come to you and will fight against them with the sword of my mouth.' *The fact that Jesus is not scheduled to come with the double edged sword from his mouth until the end of the era of the time of Jacob's Trouble, means that this church represented by Pergamum / the global religious community, with the Roman Catholic Church as its foundation, will continue to exist until the end of the era of the time of Jacob's Trouble.*

The first two of the seven churches in Jesus' message have dissolved within history. But, the last five churches of the historical timeline beginning with the Pergamum era church will continue until Jesus Christ returns. The culmination of the combination of the last five historical timeline churches will crescendo with activity until Jesus Christ returns. Their ripples will grow to become tsunamis.

Notice also that Jesus says, '…I will soon come to you and will fight against them…' *It is as if Jesus Christ is assuring us that even though we may be members of an apostate church during the era of the time of Jacob's Trouble, that Jesus Christ will still come on behalf of individuals who seek Jesus Christ and fight against those who continue to hold onto the worship of the baal / mystery / mythology religion.*

Just as the goal of the baal / mystery / mythology religion attempted to deceive and to substitute the myth for the truth, the global religious community will attempt to substitute their myth for the truth. The leaders of the global religious community believe that because they have married and merged their substitute theology into the original church system and have grown power for over fourteen hundred years, they will be able to transform their role as spiritual guides into finally being able to fully rule the people as political leaders also.

The global religious community will rewrite divine law so that practice of immorality will become legal and the cultural norm. The practice of God Most High's authentic morality will be viewed as nonsensical.

The global religious community will teach that God is non-existent and therefore unable to act. Therefore, they will present the global religious community as a solution to fill the world's leadership void created by a missing God.

While the global religious community will provide each individual with a new number the 'mark of the beast' (Revelation 13:17, 14:11, 16:2, 19:20, 20:4), Jesus Christ offers to provide a new name. The promise of a new name, which only the one who receives it will know, is a promise of an identity that is provided by God Most High, not a government issued number that serves to strip a person of their identity. It will be reminiscent of Hitler's numbering of the victims of the Nazis. The global religious community can only offer their 'numerical identity, and not an identity provided as an offer of acceptance into the world's religious kingdom / the kingdom of Satan, Inc / kingdom of man.

The identity provided by the two beasts of Revelation 13, along with the identity that Jesus Christ offers, both have the power to change people. The red dragon / serpent / Satan, Inc.'s identity will have the power to change a person so that the receiver of the red dragon / serpent / Satan, Inc.'s identity will find a place within a power system that views humanity as disposable. The God given identity will change the receiver into becoming all that God Most High had originally created that person to be. The question is, 'How do you want to be changed?'

Note that the red dragon / serpent / Satan, Inc.'s religious kingdom is a kingdom of works, of power, and of forced rituals that must be practiced as a condition of acceptance within a pyramid scheme structure. The mark of the beast(s) is designed to destroy the image of God created within humans. The mark of the beast(s) system will substitute a relationship with Jesus, for a relationship with the two beasts of Revelation 13. The global religious community will force adherents to worship representatives of the red dragon / serpent / Satan, Inc. and ultimately Satan himself, who rejects the premise that you are worthy to be loved simply because you were created in God's image. Noncompliance in worshiping the leadership of the kingdom of Satan, Inc / kingdom of man will result in an immediate death sentenced which will be executed in moments after being decided.

In contrast, the kingdom of heaven is the kingdom of faith and love. The kingdom of heaven provides a covenant and a God who loves, a covenant that cannot be broken. Noncompliance with worshiping Jesus Christ does not lead to immediate punishment by death.

This act of God Most High in providing identity also acts as a form of sealing God's people. The new name that God provides will tell of your relationship with God. With God Most High's act of naming you, you are identified and sealed as belonging to God Most High and God Most High as belonging to you. Those who are not sealed by God Most High will experience substantial events of torture during the era of the time of Jacob's Trouble.

The message that Jesus Christ wants us to remember is that those who practice morality and encourage the practice of morality, those who act as true followers of the Lamb / Jesus Christ will be provided added benefit during the era of the time of Jacob's Trouble including hidden provisions and deeper understanding.

Jesus Christ's message for the era of the time of Jacob's Trouble from the message to the angel of the married church of Pergamum

The historical era of the church of Pergamum was the first of the seven churches that was indicated in Jesus Christ's message, to exist until the return of messiah / the Lamb / Jesus Christ.

In addition, the historical era of the church of Pergamum / early Roman Catholic Church, established a solid foundation for the historical era of the church of Laodicea to set aside any recognition of the divinity and sovereignty of messiah / the Lamb / Jesus Christ.

Jesus Christ's message for the era of the time of Jacob's Trouble to the church, was that the followers of the Lamb / Jesus Christ need to recognize:

- *the power of the truth concerning the authority of Jesus Christ's authentic message (the double edged sword),*
- *the power of the throne of Satan as something to be cautious about,*
- *the importance of not renouncing faith in Jesus Christ, even when experiencing persecution, and*
- *to refrain from sexual immorality because it is a gateway to being enticed to participate in the mission of the kingdom of Satan, Inc. / kingdom of man, to separate humanity from any chance of experiencing a right relationship with God Most High.*

Jesus Christ's message to the angel of the church at Thyatira: ruling church – Revelation 2:18-29

<u>Church of Thyatira – daughter church of corruption (See Acts 16:11-15)</u>

Jesus said, 'To the angel of the church of Thyatira, write,

'This is the message from the Son of God, the one who has eyes like a flame of fire and his feet like burnished bronze.'

'I know your works, and love, and faith, and service, and your perseverance. And your last works are greater than your first works.'

'But I have this against you. You tolerate the woman Jezebel, the one calling herself a prophetess, who teaches and misleads my servants to commit sexual immorality and to eat things sacrificed to idols. I have given her time to repent of her sexual immorality, and she is not willing to repent of her sexual immorality. Behold, I will cast her into a sickbed, and those committing adultery with her into great tribulation, unless they repent of her deeds. And her children, I will kill with death. And all the churches will know that I am the one searching the affections and hearts. And I will give to each of you, according to your works.'

'To you however, and to the rest in Thyatira, I say, as many as do not have this teaching, who have not known the depths of Satan, as they say, 'I will not cast any other burden upon you. But hold fast to what you have until I come.''

'To the one who overcomes and keeps my works until the end, I will give that one the authority over the nations, and that one will shepherd them with power over the nations: 'He will shepherd them with a rod of iron, as the vessels of the potter are broken in pieces.' Just as I have received from my father. And I will give to that one the morning star.'

'To the one having an ear, hear what the Spirit says to the churches.' Revelation 2:18-29 translated

Note that Jesus Christ's message to the era of the church of Thyatira had a provision that Jesus Christ expected the historical era of the church of Thyatira, to hold onto what they have until Jesus Christ comes. This expectation implied that the historical era of the church of Thyatira will continue until the end of the era of the time of Jacob's Trouble.

To understand Jesus Christ's message to the church of Thyatiran theology during the era of the time of Jacob's Trouble, requires understanding the history of Jezebel, and her influence upon Ahab the king of the northern kingdom of Israel / northern ten tribes.

The biblical record documented that, there was never anyone like Ahab, who sold himself to do evil in the eyes of the Lord, urged on by Jezebel his wife. 1 Kings 21:25

Jezebel was the daughter of the king of Sidon, Ethbaal. Sidon was located in modern day Lebanon. Her father, Ethbaal of Sidon, was the high priest of the Babylonian mysteries in the Zidionite kingdom.

Jezebel was married to the king of the northern ten tribes of Israel of the divided kingdom of Israel. Jezebel's religion was the Zidionite kingdom's version of the baal / mystery / mythology religion. Her husband, Ahab, an Israelite, should have been practicing the authentic faith

system of the worship of the Lord. Instead, Ahab adopted the religion that Jezebel practiced.

Jezebel did not comprehend a difference between her religious power and her political power. Consequently, Jezebel paid her priests and priestess out of the treasury of government of the northern kingdom of Israel. And Jezebel also acquired revenue by having people killed and seizing their property.

Jezebel was also known for her eye makeup and her arrangement of her hair, even in preparation for her execution (2 Kings 9:30). Jezebel was very concerned with her outward appearance. So, in Jesus Christ's message to the seven churches, this message that referenced Jezebel, also referenced the obsession that the church has with possessing art, architecture, music, etc., for the purpose of providing a good appearance instead of holding greater concern for the issues of the day.

The nature of Jezebel, the obsession with outward appearances, the perpetuation of false prophesying to advance one's personal agenda of power collection, the advancement of sexual immorality, the eating of food sacrificed to idols, the perpetuating of Satan's so-called deep secrets, etc., continued to be foci throughout most of church history, of many churches. They were all behaviors that Jezebel enticed her husband Ahab to practice, or that she practiced.

Ahab's name means love. Many churches have practiced these divisive practices in the name of love. But these practices are not loving.

The behaviors that Jesus Christ referenced, distract those who seek to be overcomers from truly being able to focus upon the full development of their own personal relationships with Jesus Christ.

Historical message:
During the lifetime of the apostles, Paul and Silas were instructed by the Holy Spirit to baptize, educate and commission Lydia of Thyatira (Acts 16:8-15). Lydia was appointed by Paul as the senior clergy leader who developed the establishment of the churches in Thyatira.

The city of Thyatira has held multiple names; Pelopia, Euhippia, Semiramis, Thyatira and today is known as the city of Akhissar.

The character of the couples Semiramis and Nimrod, and Jezebel and Ahab, set both power couples on a course to indiscriminately rule. Both of their reigns were defined by immoral practices. The baal / mystery / mythology religion was the only religion practiced originally practiced in this city. For these reasons, 'Semiramis' became a name worthy to be placed upon this city.

The name of the city was changed from 'Semiramis' to Thyatira when the Seleucid king Seleucus I Nicator (fl. 305 to 281 BC) was in the city in 290 BC. At that time, Seleucus I Nicator first heard of the birth of his daughter. The name 'Thyatira' means 'daughter.'

The city was also the home of a temple to Apollo, the sun god. Understanding the connection to Tammuz, the son of Nimrod the first postdiluvian / postflood baal god, and of Semiramis, to his Greek counterpart Apollo also known as the son of a god; Jesus Christ introduced himself to the church of Thyatira as the true Son of God.

The name Jezebel / Izevel (Hebrew) means 'where is the exalted one?' / 'where is the prince?' Traditionally this question was asked in the ritual worship of baal. The name also came to mean unmarried, idolater, and adulterer. The fact that Jesus Christ's message included the name of the woman who was the main teacher of idolatry in the northern kingdom of Israel, and that her name was Jezebel, intentionally referenced the Old Testament / Tanakh queen of the northern nation of the ten tribes of Israel Jezebel, who married the kingdom of Israel's king Ahab.

In order to be employable in the city of Thyatira, it was a requirement to belong to a guild. A requirement for belonging to a guild was to also worship the gods or goddesses chosen by the guild, which included participating in the sexual rituals of the temples to the gods or goddesses, sacrificing food to idols, and participating in the public sexual orgia. The public sexual orgia were defined as involving at least five members in the sex party and involved group sex. Some of the public orgia involved the castration of priests in a frenzied trance. The primary goal of the orgia was to achieve an ecstatic union between the celebrant and the gods or goddesses.

One of the major industries in Thyatira was metallurgy / iron working. Iron working was one of the forbidden knowledges originally taught by the rebellious angels to humanity in the exchange of families giving their daughters for the production of Nephilim. Note that during the Thousand Years Reign of Jesus Christ, the swords will be beaten into plowshares and warfare will not be taught anymore (Isaiah 2:4, Joel 3:10, Micah 4:3).

The environment of Thyatira included the sexual immorality modeled after the antediluvian / preflood world, the emphasis on learning military warfare for financial gain, the use of the baal / mystery / mythology religion secretism (especially with the Eleusinian Mysteries), for expanding disfunction within the community and world, and other 'deep things of Satan.' The secret societies of the Thyatiran culture created an environment where their version of Jezebel's teaching was able to thrive.

Thyatira's link to Semiramis and Nimrod

Semiramis was the product of a rebellious angel father and a human mother, following the recipe for how to make Nephilim. Semiramis became the wife and mother of Nimrod. Nimrod was Cush's son, Ham's grandson and Noah's great grandson (Genesis 10:8). Nimrod ruled as a rebel against God Most High beginning soon after the deluge / flood. Semiramis produced sons Nimrod and Tammuz, in an effort to fulfill the prophecy concerning the coming messiah originally promised to the first man and first woman in the Garden of Eden / garden of God / paradise (Genesis 3:15). Semiramis began the postdiluvian / postflood mother-child cult.

Ham's sons understood that within the prophecy given to Adam and Eve and to their messianic lineage was an immaculate conception. So Ham's descendants; Nimrod, Semiramis and Tammuz; were the product of their own version of the Immaculate Conception. Having a rebellious angel ancestor made them Nephilim / demigods. All three believed that they were gods in human form. Nimrod, Semiramis and Tammuz were an unholy trinity.

    In the antediluvian / preflood era, humanity had been willing to participate in altering genetic makeup, to create new species, including a species that was part human – part 'divine,' through the mating of humanity with the rebellious angels. Details of the activities of the antediluvian / preflood era were documented in the first book of Enoch, the book of Jasher, other ancient writings and in biblical references throughout the Bible. In the biblical account, only Noah, his three sons and their wives remained 'pure' in their genetics / generation. (The original Hebrew text clarified this.) This purity qualified Noah and his family to be preserved on the ark during the flood.

    According to ancient tradition as provided in the book of Jasher and other sources, after the deluge / flood, Ham along with his sons Canaan and Cush, were distraught because they lost their old acquaintances from before the flood. Out of this sense of loss of relationship with their ancestors and friends, and their sense of indignation against God Most High for judging the world, they reinitiated the antediluvian religion complete with worship of their deceased friends who were now dead Nephilim and dead Nephilim offspring. The spirits of the dead Nephilim and Nephilim offspring are 'demons.'

    The deluge / flood had been God Most High's response to the original antediluvian / preflood Nephilim issue. Because of the devastation of the earth and its creatures that the Nephilim produced, God Most High did not desire the production of Nephilim to continue after the deluge / flood. Through the deluge / flood God destroyed the existing Nephilim at that time, and imitated the shortened the lifespan of humanity (Genesis 6-8).

But during the time immediately after the deluge / flood, while lifespans were transitioning from a thousand years to one hundred twenty years, the red dragon / serpent / Satan, Inc. once again enticed humanity to participate in Nephilim production.

After the deluge / flood, during the transition time of decreasing lifespan, Ham, Canaan and Cush reintroduced the mating of rebellious angels with humanity producing Semiramis, Nimrod and other offspring that became nations of Nephilim. The Nephilim were reintroduced into the world for the purpose of gaining power for the purpose of ruling over the rest of humanity, and for advancing the red dragon / serpent / Satan, Inc.'s initial plan to storm the highest heaven and depose God Most High (Isaiah 14).

The Nephilim in the postdiluvian / postflood world were usually referred to as 'giants,' known for having six toes, six fingers, and a double set of teeth that were useful for devouring things (1 Enoch, 2 Samuel 21). They were also tall. The biblical Goliath who was killed by David, and his four brothers were the best known Nephilim in the postdiluvian / postflood world, after the notorious Nimrod (1 Samuel 17, 21:9, 22:10, 2 Samuel 21:19, 1 Chronicles 20:5).

The original Nephilim power family in the post flood world, Nimrod with his wife / mother Semiramis led in the construction of the tower of Babel empire as a tool for assisting in achieving the purposes of the red dragon / serpent / Satan, Inc. Semiramis and Nimrod established themselves as religious leaders and world rulers; the original power couple of the ancient postdiluvian / postflood world.

The name 'babel' means 'gate of bel.' Nimrod, Semiramis and the red dragon / serpent / Satan, Inc. empowered the building of the tower of Babel and were established as the gate keepers for contacting the gods. The tower of Babel was also designed to provide an escape for the elite and elect in the event of another worldwide flood.

God Most High's response to the tower of Babel was to confuse and divide the language in order to hinder the achievement of the red dragon / serpent / Satan, Inc.'s goal which would have again destroyed God Most High's creation on earth while pursuing the establishment of the kingdom of Satan, Inc. / kingdom of man. Because of the division of language, construction on the tower of Babel was unable to be finished. Because of the division of language, after culture was divided into seventy cultures, the foundational story of Nimrod and Semiramis was established throughout the ancient cultures. The names in the stories have been changed due to the division of language, but the foundational story remains the same.

    The European Union building architecture was inspired by the tower of Babel and the tower of Babel empire. The European Union building was designed to appear unfinished to symbolize that humanity is still evolving and has not finished its work yet.

    Throughout the postdiluvian / postflood world, Semiramis was worshiped and adored by those who supported the power structure that Nimrod and Semiramis had established. Semiramis was the first in the postdiluvian / postflood world to be titled 'Queen of Heaven.' Jeremiah referred to the queen of heaven as the object of worship that provoked God Most High to anger and corrective action with the people of Israel who worshiped her. (Jeremiah 7:18, 44:17-25)

    Semiramis set herself up as a goddess claiming that she was immaculately conceived. Because the moon went through a twenty eight day cycle, she claimed that she had come down from the moon in a giant moon egg that fell into the Euphrates River at sunrise at the time of the first full moon after the spring equinox, on a Sunday. Semiramis' day of the year was known as 'Easter.' Semiramis was also known as Ishtar / Easter / Ashtoreth. She was often represented by the two dimensional eight pointed star or the three dimensional sixteen pointed star. Her moon egg became known as 'Ishtar's egg.' Because Semiramis had her own version of immaculate conception, Semiramis also became known as the fertility goddess and became associated with the fertile rabbit. The tradition was established to make rolls on Easter Sunday in the shape of the bull's horns to represent the baal / mystery /

mythology religion or crescents to represent the moon that was worshiped in the baal / mystery / mythology religion.

The ancient Greek historian, Diodorus Siculus, reported that when Nimrod was killed, Queen Semiramis erected a one hundred thirty foot obelisk in Babylon, for the worship of the sun and as a phallus representation of Nimrod, whom she claimed was the sun deity. The obelisk was copied throughout the world as a symbol of the Semiramis - Nimrod baal / mystery / mythology religion.

Nineveh (modern Mosul, Iraq) was known as the 'city of Nimrod.'

Nimrod in ancient art, would sometimes be depicted with the halo to represent his deification. The halo continued to be an element in art throughout the centuries, as a recognition of assigned divinity.

When Semiramis gave birth to her son, Tammuz / Horus, she declared that she had been visited by the spirit of Nimrod who had left her pregnant with the baby. She claimed that Tammuz / Horus was Nimrod reincarnated. Because Tammuz was presented as the reincarnation of Nimrod, the stories of Nimrod and Tammuz were frequently intermingled, with Nimrod and Tammuz being interchanged or substituting for each other in the various storylines.

Tammuz was killed by a wild pig. For the forty days prior to the anniversary of the death of Tammuz, Semiramis proclaimed a time of mourning. In the Roman Catholic tradition, this forty day period of mourning coincided with the season of Lent.

Ezekiel 8:14-17 expressed his dismay at the women weeping for Tammuz. This ritual of mourning involved ritual prostitution in a rite in which they mourned the death of Tammuz who in mythology was resurrected to new life because of the effectiveness of the ritual of mourning. Ezekiel reported that the increase of the worship of Tammuz was accompanied with an increase in rape, murder and violence.

The Babylonian account of Tammuz's uniqueness and supposed divinity, presented Tammuz as dying at the winter solstice, December 22nd, and then being resurrected as the days became longer. The celebration of the burning of a yule log honored Tammuz's death. 'Yule' meant 'infant.' The morning after the yule log was burnt, the yule log was replaced by a decorated tree honoring Tammuz's resurrection. Jeremiah referenced this celebration (Jeremiah 10: 1-5). After Tammuz's death, Semiramis claimed that when Tammuz was killed, some of his blood fell on the stump of an evergreen tree and that she saw a full grown evergreen tree spring out of the roots of the tree stump, symbolizing the springing forth of new life for Tammuz. The evergreen tree became sacred by the blood of Tammuz.

In the Hebrew calendar, the fourth month of the ecclesiastical year / tenth month of the civil year, took its name from Tammuz.

Throughout the ancient baal / mystery / mythology religious system, Semiramis was depicted as the woman crowned with stars, or with the halo of the sun. And Semiramis was frequently portrayed either with a child or riding a beast. Through the wordship of Semiramis, Semiramis would appeal to her resurrected son to find favor with the 'gods.'

Throughout the various cultures, Nimrod was depicted as wearing a halo that represented the sun and generally was portrayed as a giant, frequently seated upon a throne.

In Babylon and on the plain of Shinar (modern Iraq), the unholy trio was known as; Nimrod with the title of baal, Semiramis with the title 'Queen of Heaven,' and Tammuz as the 'son of god' that was falsely claimed to have died and then been resurrected.

In Egypt the trio was known as Osiris, Isis and Horus. The horoscope was named in honor of Horus.

Throughout other cultures the unholy trio held other aliases. The stories underwent variations even within the same cultures, and throughout history. But the core of the stories remained the same: There were multiple gods and goddesses. The main gods and goddesses were closely related or married. There were illicit sexual relationships. And there was a deified son born with a special birth.

Comparison of the names of Semiramis, Nimrod and Tammuz among various ancient cultures

Region	Male	Female	Son
Babylon and the plain of Shinar	Nimrod / Ninus / Markuk / Apkallu	Semiramis / Rhea /Ishtar Zarpanit	Tammuz / Ninyas / Mardon
Phoenicia /Sidonia	Baal / Malik / Kronos	Astarte / Ashtart	Bacchus
Assyria	Ninus / Assur	Beltis / Ishtar	Dumuzi / Hercules
Philistia	(Oannes is fish-god father) Dagon / Fish / Dagan	Belatu / Lady / Shala / Ishara	Hadad
Ammon	Molech / Moloch / Milcom	Ashtoreth	
Moab	Chemosh / Malik	Ishtar / Asthor-Chemosh	Mesha
Canaan / Phoenician	Molech / Moloch / Milcom / Baal	Ashtart / Ashtoreth	
Persia	Ahura-Mazda	Anahita / Venus	Mithras / Mitra / Mithra / Meitros / Mihr / Mehr / Meher / Aries /

			Mars / Sol Invictus
Greece	Helios / Apollo / Zeus	Aphrodite / Hera	Dionysius
Rome	Jupiter	Cybele / Diana / Juno / Magna Mater	Sol Invictus / Mithras / Attis
Egypt	Osiris	Isis / Hathor	Horus
North Africa	Baal-hamon	Tanith / Tanit	
Arabia	Athtar	Venus	
Phrygia	Attis	Cybele	Deoius
Kassite	Ninurta		Murudash
Europe	Zeus	Europa / Astarte	King Minos
India	Vishnu	Isi / Devaki	Iswara / Krishna
Scandinavia	Odin	Frig / Freyda	Blader

(Sources: Bible, Jewish Encyclopedia, Wikipedia and other scholarly sources)

Nimrod and Semiramis fully understood the power of religion as a tool for controlling people and establishing their political rule. They used their religion as a main tool for building their political empire. Nimrod filled the position as the first baal god with Semiramis as the first Ishtar goddess and cohort to baal.

As demigods / Nephilim they physically possessed the personal strength and height to be imposing to individuals. The Nephilim at the time of the lives of Semiramis, Nimrod and Tammuz, were estimated to have been ten to thirty feet tall and were estimated to have consumed over twelve thousand calories a day, about four times what a human would consume.

Nephilim devoured resources including the consumption of humans. That 'fee fi fo fum, I smell the blood of an Englishman, be he alive or be he dead, I'll grind his bones to make my bread' from Jack and the Beanstalk, may have a more ancient historic foundation than being merely a children's fable.

To further accomplish the goal of achieving human genocide, the religion of Nimrod and Semiramis incorporated human sacrifice including infant and child sacrifice. Sacrificing a child also had the additional benefit of cutting off that child's future offspring and limiting the number of future potential citizens of the kingdom of heaven.

The appeal for producing Nephilim came with the promise of the red dragon / serpent / Satan, Inc. to provide secret / hidden / divine knowledge to those who would trade for it, or offer their daughters as mates in exchange for the 'secret knowledge' (1 Enoch, Ezekiel 28:16). This hidden knowledge was marketed to humanity as secret knowledge and mystery knowledge. So, the resulting religion was referred to as 'mystery religion.' Nephilim were also genetically modified to be able to better communicate with the 'divine' / the rebellious angels, which aided their ability to have access to that 'forbidden knowledge.'

In the antediluvian / preflood world, the hidden knowledge provided by the rebellious angels prescribed methods for destroying God Most High's creation and especially God Most High's creation as displayed in humanity that fully bears God Most High's image. If God Most High had not acted to cut off the red dragon / serpent / Satan, Inc.'s plan of destruction, God Most High's created world would not have survived. In fact, in Noah's era, only eight people could be found who had not had their image of God corrupted.

When God Most High decided before the deluge / flood to limit the lifespan of humanity to one hundred twenty years (Genesis 6:3) it was a decision that seemed to be in opposition to the larger character of God Most High who created and sustains life. But in order to ensure the life of humanity as it was created in the image of God, God Most High needed to limit the ability of the Nephilim to destroy. That meant limiting the Nephilim's ability to exist. By shortening the survival of the life of humanity, the ability to produce the more physically fragile Nephilim was also limited. Eventually around the lifetime of Abram / Abraham, direct Nephilim production was no longer possible. But the production of offspring from Nephilim was not able to be extinguished until long after the antediluvian / preflood version of the baal / mystery / mythology religion was reestablished.

One of the areas of hidden knowledge resourced by the rebellious angels was military technology. The sword of Goliath (~ 1000 BC), a giant / Nephilim descendant, was produced with iron that was forged to be stronger than what any of the peoples living at that time were able to produce. The knowledge for how to produce this strengthened iron had been given by the rebellious angels through the Nephilim / giants. With this strengthened iron, the Philistines / Nephilim / giants were able to terrorize at will. The Philistine military superiority was why the account of David (God Most High's representative) killing Goliath (the red dragon / serpent / Satan, Inc.'s representative) with a stone (representing messiah as rock) was such a powerful typology for the people of Israel and continues to be a powerful account even for this time, for the era of the time for Jacob's Trouble.

The religion established by Nimrod and Semiramis incorporated their special knowledge from 'the gods' / rebellious angels. Out of their knowledge obtained from the rebellious angels, they developed magic, ritual prostitution, and a counterfeit mother-child cult as the red dragon / serpent / Satan, Inc.'s attempt to produce God Most High's promised and prophesied messiah from a virgin. Their technological knowledge sourced by the rebellious angels, provided the opportunity to convince the populace that they were like gods. With their special knowledge, advanced technology, superior weaponry for making war, *gigantic physical presence, the doctrine of reincarnation, etc., they were able to develop domineering, tyrannical governments. (first book of Enoch and biblical references)*

With Nimrod and Semiramis, the original message in the stars / The Way of Salvation / Mazzaroth that was taught to Adam and Eve, was given a new twist in meaning. The twisted message no longer told of God Most High's redemptive plan of salvation. The astrological story of the zodiac was created. But in the story of the zodiac, it was the red dragon / serpent / Satan, Inc. who is the victor instead of the king of the kingdom of heaven.

The Nephilim demigoddess Semiramis was notorious for her fantastic sexual affairs. Because Semiramis was the product of forbidden union between the rebellious angels and humanity, the baal / mystery / mythology religious worship would include sexual rites, frequently with hallucinogens. Initiation into the baal / mystery / mythology religion required a sexual initiation rite to be performed with an official temple priest or priestess. In some versions of the baal / mystery / mythology religion, adherents were required to annually renew their membership and 'give up their god or give up their chastity.'

Because the gods / rebellious angels were constantly in a struggle to determine their hierarchy of dominance within the rebellious angel community, adherents to the baal / mystery / mythology religion would need to invest in multiple gods and goddesses in order to ensure that they would be in a proper relationship with at least one of the gods or goddesses in power for the moment. This also necessitated that adherents to the baal / mystery / mythology religion were required to visit multiple temples that represented the gods or goddesses of choice for the individual.

Sex between a temple authority and an initiate was intended to mimic the red dragon / serpent / Satan, Inc.'s 'divine' invasion into humanity through the activities of the rebellious angels. The sexual rites of worship were performed in an entirely unholy manner. This theology continues today with some religious leaders even in mainline churches who openly express their rationale for their own personal activity of clergy sexual misconduct, with their personal statements that claim that the victim should feel honored that they had a relationship with a 'holy representative of god' and therefore the clergy act was actually to be considered to be a gift and not to be viewed as misconduct.

The act of the sexual merging of the red dragon / serpent / Satan, Inc.'s representative / temple priests and priestesses, with the initiate, had many goals. One goal was meant to genetically displace the image of God Most High that was created in each human individual. Ritualistic sex venerated Nephilim as a superior species greater than humanity. Ritualistic sex was intended to honor and recognize the authority of the rebellious angels to genetically alter humanity and eliminate the image of God the Creator inherent within created humanity.

Nephilim cannot hold a theological claim for living an eternity with God Most High because the Nephilim were the product of rebellion against God Most High. Nephilim were the offspring of rebellious angels instead of the genetically pure offspring of human beings, and because of their adulterated genealogy, Nephilim were denied entrance into the kingdom of heaven. This was one reason why sexual immorality was so heavily linked with idolatry, and why sexual immorality has been utilized in advancing rebellion against God Most High.

Another goal of temple ritual sex was to displace humanity's opportunity to be worthy to hold dominion over the earth. If humanity could be proven to be unworthy to God Most High to hold dominion over the earth, then the rebellious angels would have proven that humanity could not be trusted to exercise the dominion over the earth that God the Creator had assigned to humanity (Genesis 2). That was why the Lamb being worthy to receive the seven sealed will of God Most High was so crucial in cosmic history (Revelation 4 and 5).

Nephilim will never be able to be classified as 'children of God.' Genetically modifying humanity with the seed of the rebellious angels and producing Nephilim / 'children born of rebellion' meant that for every Nephilim child born, a human child was displaced, which meant less contenders for the throne of the kingdom of heaven.

The effect of sexual dominance upon the populace was, to make humanity seem unworthy to rule in the eyes of God Most High, to make people more vulnerable to needing to be ruled, and also to create an environment where people were more easily ruled. Those who are easily ruled tend to not rise to become rulers themselves.

By creating Nephilim, the red dragon / serpent / Satan, Inc. produced beings whose only alternative was to maintain their allegiance to the kingdom of Satan, Inc. / kingdom of man. Because Nephilim had no opportunity to even live in the kingdom of heaven, the Nephilim had every reason to support the mission and goals of the kingdom of Satan, Inc. / kingdom of man. Being denied entrance into the kingdom of heaven also prohibited the Nephilim from any opportunity to be authorized by God Most High to rule or to share the throne assigned to Jesus Christ.

Among humanity, temple ritual sexual activity was also intended to disqualify human individuals from being able to rule in the kingdom of heaven.

In Jesus Christ's message to John the Revelator, recorded as the book of Revelation, Jesus Christ promised humanity that those who overcome will be able to sit on the throne with Jesus Christ (Revelation 2:26-27, 20:1-6, etc.) For the red dragon / serpent / Satan, Inc. to make advancement in the goal of Satan being the occupant of the throne of God Most High, it became vitally important to disqualify humanity, all of humanity including messiah / the Lamb / Jesus Christ, from being able to regain their authority to rule and to sit on the throne that was assigned to humanity in the Garden of Eden / garden of God / paradise. Temple ritual sexual activity provided the opportunity for eliminating human individuals as contenders to share the throne with Jesus Christ.

In all the places where the baal / mystery / mythology religion thrived, male and female prostitution also thrived. In Thyatira, religious prostitution was *prevalent even as Christianity was introduced.* The emerging Thyatira church, during the lifetime of John the Revelator, still initially held onto Thyatira's cultural practices of the baal / mystery / mythology religion, endorsed by the sexual worship rites, as a necessary step to their religion's definition of eternal life. The priests and priestesses exercised the authority to determine if the member of the temple community met the qualifications for entrance into their version of heaven. This was another reason why God Most High deems it inappropriate to use forced sexual relationships for religious purposes and for manipulation of others.

Within the Thyatiran community, the people were taught and seduced to commit sexual immorality as an offering to the only gods they knew. Eventually, they attempted to incorporate their sexual immorality into the worship of Jesus Christ and the kingdom of heaven.

Throughout human history, great tyrannical leaders have incorporated religion into their plans because religion and theology, when altered to aid the purposes of leaders, aids in making people more docile and less rebellious to being ruled. Historically, that dynamic was especially true when religion included a physically sexual element.

God Most High intended for sex to be a powerful bonding experience for growing love between a husband and a wife, not between a rebellious angel and a person or between people without a commitment to God Most High and to each other. Without God Most High's love and blessing to influence sexual experiences, the acts of sex merely become manipulation, accompanied with various degrees of spiritual, religious, psychological, and physical violence. Sex unblessed by God Most High, is a highly effective tool for the red dragon / serpent / Satan, Inc.

For the adherents to the kingdom of Satan, Inc. / kingdom of man, participating in sex with the gods / rebellious angels or sex with the demigods / Nephilim was considered to bring blessing and be the venue for receiving additional hidden knowledge and blessing. It was this understanding that drove the people of Sodom to seek out the angels who were spying out the city in order to participate in ritual sex (Genesis 19).

When the city of Thyatira took on the name 'Semiramis' and erected temples to honor her baal / mystery / mythology religion, the city also endorsed and practiced the rites and rituals of the religion of Semiramis and Nimrod, and embraced the history of the baal / mystery / mythology religion.

Thyatira's link to Jezebel and Ahab

From around 874 to 853 BC, the queen of the northern kingdom of Israel, Jezebel, was the wife of the Israelite king of the northern ten tribes of Israel, Ahab, during the divided kingdom era. Jezebel was the daughter of the king of Sidon, Ethbaal. Sidon was located in modern day Lebanon. Ethbaal of Sidon was the high priest of the Babylonian mysteries in the Zidionite kingdom.

Just as Jezebel represented everything that was unholy, Ahab as the king of the northern kingdom of Israel in covenant with God Most High, was supposed to represent what was holy. Ahab's background was Judaism and Ahab was intended to represent the holiness of the God of Israel, and of the nation that was intended to be comprised of the holy priests for God Most High. The marriage of Ahab and Jezebel was a merger of what was intended to be most holy, with what was most definitely unholy (1 Kings 16:29-34).

The offspring of this mixed marriage and the attempted merger of the baal / mystery / mythology religion of Jezebel, with the authentic faith system that was Ahab's heritage, was the practice of idolatry amongst the people that were intended to be God's holy people.

Jezebel forced upon the Israelites the worship of the god baal and the goddess Ashtoreth / 'Queen of Heaven' (Jeremiah 44:17, 18, 25). Jezebel made immorality and idolatry official policy for the Israelite society. Prostitution of young girls was included. Jezebel and Ahab also encouraged and practiced human sacrifice including child and infant sacrifice.

Ahab, acting as a most unholy king, warranted a response by God Most High to send a most holy prophet. This was where Elijah entered the scene. 1 Kings 17 through 21 documented Elijah's multiple encounters with Ahab and Jezebel. Out of Ahab and Jezebel's hatred for Elijah's God and God Most High's prophets, Ahab and Jezebel declared Elijah an enemy of the state and even put out a contract for Elijah's death.

Elijah finally challenged Ahab, Jezebel, and eight hundred fifty of their favorite baal and Ashtoreth priests on Mount Carmel in an altar challenge. Elijah's God won. (1 Kings 18)

At the end of Elijah's work on earth for that era of time, Elijah was taken alive into heaven (2 Kings 2:1-18). It was made apparent that Elijah the prophet will return (Malachi 4:5). A place is set annually at the Seder / Passover table to remind the people of Israel that Elijah will return.

When Elijah does return, there will be a new spirit of Jezebel to greet him (Revelation 11:1-14). But Elijah is already experienced in confronting Jezebel's baal / mystery / mythology religion.

Ahab and Jezebel mastered evil and supplied future tyrannical political and religious leaders with models from their own activities.

The story of Naboth's vineyard (1 Kings 21) became a model for the Roman Catholic Church Inquisitions.

The account of Naboth's vineyard began with King Ahab's sulking over not being able to possess Naboth's vineyard, for use as a vegetable garden. Because of Ahab's pouting, Jezebel set about obtaining the vineyard for Ahab.

Note that the Jezreel Valley is also known as the Valley of Megiddo, where the final battle of this age against the city of Jerusalem, will be staged. The location of Naboth's vineyard in the Jezreel Valley, is known.

Jezebel wrote letters in Ahab's name, placed his seal on them and sent them to the elders and nobles who lived in Naboth's city with him. In those letters she wrote:

'Proclaim a day of fasting and seat Naboth in a prominent place among the people. But seat two scoundrels opposite him and have them bring charges that he has cursed both God and the king. Then take Naboth out and stone him to death.'

So, the elders and nobles who lived in Naboth's city did as Jezebel directed in the letters she had written to them. They proclaimed a fast and seated Naboth in a prominent place among the people.

Then two scoundrels came and sat opposite him and brought charges against Naboth before the people, saying, 'Naboth has cursed both God and the king.' So, they took him outside the city and stoned him to death. Then they sent word to Jezebel: 'Naboth has been stoned to death.'

As soon as Jezebel heard that Naboth had been stoned to death, she said to Ahab, 'Get up and take possession of the vineyard of Naboth the Jezreelite that he refused to sell you. He is no longer alive, but dead.' When Ahab heard that Naboth was dead, he got up and went down to take possession of Naboth's vineyard. 1 Kings 21:8-16

The Law God Most High gave through Moses required two witnesses in order to validate any claim. But the two scoundrels were false witnesses. Naboth's experience would act as a model for how the red dragon / serpent / Satan, Inc. would accomplish the crucifixion of Jesus Christ, placing two false witnesses around Jesus Christ and using them to condemn Jesus Christ in the court of the Sanhedrin that was located in Jerusalem Israel.

The account of Naboth's vineyard included;
1) *false accusation,*
2) *false witnesses,*
3) *torture and death of victim and heirs, and*
4) *confiscation of property.*

Along with Naboth, all Naboth's heirs were also destroyed so that they could not make an inheritance claim upon the vineyard. In that way, the deed for the vineyard was free to be acquired.

The final battle of this age will be an attempt to annihilate all the people of Israel with the goal of cutting off any claim of inheritance in the covenant of God Most High to make the people of Israel a nation of priests.

Jezebel's swift confiscation of property became the model that the Roman Catholic Church used for its Inquisitions (~1184 to ~1814, with the Congregation for the

Doctrine of Faith awaiting the revival of Inquisition). The Roman Catholic Church Inquisitions were great fund raisers for the Church. The Inquisitor would begin with false accusations, seek out and bribe false witnesses, torture and kill the 'heretics' along with their heirs, and most importantly, they would confiscate their property. The process of Inquisition became a great source for generating revenue for the hierarchy of the Roman Catholic Church.

The Roman Catholic Church Inquisitions were conceived and directed by monarchs and popes, involving diabolic tortures that were consistently improved upon in order to make them more excruciating. Maximizing the pain also eased the extraction of a confession or recantation of the alleged heresies, that were mostly manufactured accusations.

Since the establishment of Inquisitions, there continues to be no confession of culpability on the part of the Roman Catholic Church, nor any attempt made to pay penance, nor any recompense made for the property that was stolen through the Inquisitions. It has been estimated that historically there were approximately eighty 'Vicars of Christ' / Inquisitors who supervised or insisted upon the application of the Inquisitions.

The model that the Roman Catholic Church used for its Inquisitions became the model for Adolf Hitler's Nazi Germany.

During the era of the time of Jacob's Trouble, the Inquisition will again be a model used by the two beasts of Revelation 13 in their plot to establish global governance. They will utilize the methods of the Inquisition to redistribute wealth, to depopulate the world, and to gain greater political power and favor.

God Most High responded to Ahab and Jezebel with containing Ahab and Jezebel's evil. Ahab and Jezebel were so notoriously evil that God Most High initiated a campaign to have all seventy of Ahab's male descendants killed. Instead of God Most High's heirs being annihilated, Ahab and Jezebel's heirs were killed. (2 Kings 9-10)

An added note: Later, Ahab himself died on the property that was once Naboth's, in accordance with the prophecy from the Lord.

Historical timeline message to the historical era of the church of Thyatira:
The historical era of the church of Thyatira was distinguished as being separated from the historical era of the church of Pergamum. And yet, the two historical eras were inextricably linked with the description of their relationship as being parent and daughter.

The challenge of determining the 'birthdate' for the historical era of the church of Thyatira
When does a daughter become a daughter? Does that happen with conception, or birth, or when the relationship is cemented in the heart of the child, or…? And the lives of the parents always overlap the life of the daughter.

In fact, the lives of the later five historical eras of the church, share overlap. All five of the latter historical eras of the church, were noted by Jesus Christ, as continuing until he returns.

Pinning down the exact date for when the historical era of the church of Thyatira began, is difficult.

There were several dates that were options for when the transition was made on the historical church era timeline, between the historical era of the church of Pergamum and the historical era of the church of Thyatira.

Dates for consideration:
- *476, when Romulus Augustus (fl. 475 to 476), the last of the western Roman emperors, died. His kingdom was divided with Odoacer reigning over a region of Italy and Syagrius reigning over the region of Soissons / northern Gaul, south of the Franks.*
- *588, when the Constantinopolitan synod determined that the patriarch of Constantinople be granted the title of 'Universal Bishop.'*

Justinian declared himself to be a theologian, uniting the roles of ruler and religious leader. Theodora persecuted the enemies of the church, bringing unification of the empire with the unification of the church. The seventh day Sabbath became illegal. Justinian changed the times and the laws (Novellae XLVI and coins).

- *590, when Gregory I became Patriarch of Rome (590 to 604). Gregory I conducted political and military campaigns for the conversion of pagan peoples to Roman Catholicism and established papal supremacy for western civilization.*
- *606, when the Roman empire experienced a crisis in monarchy. In 606, the Eastern Roman emperor Flavius Phocas (fl. 602 to 610), experienced a crisis in his monarchy. Phocas decreed in 606, that the 'head of all churches,' should be titled 'Universal Bishop.' Phocas issued a decree that aided in the significant advancement of papal primacy / authority of the pope over episcopal sees, and papal supremacy / full, supreme and universal power over the whole church, a power to always be exercised unhindered. With the challenge against the papal office, Boniface III (fl. c. 606 to 607) declared that the Roman pontiff was the head of the church.*
- *800, when Charlemagne / Charles I (747 to 814) was coronated as the first Holy Roman Emperor. In crowning Charlemagne to be Holy Roman Emperor, Leo III (fl. 795 to 816) exhibited the right of the papal office to establish superiority over Europe by holding authority over the office of Holy Roman Emperor.*
- *1054, when the Roman Catholic Church of the east experienced schism from the Roman Catholic Church of the west, and the eastern branch became the Orthodox Church. The Orthodox Church's relationship to the Roman*

Catholic Church resembled a mother - daughter relationship.
- 1088, when Urban II (fl. 1088 to 1099) raised the level of the supremacy of the papal office, transforming the relationship between the Roman Catholic Church and monarchs.
- Etc.

The Dark Ages / Middle Ages / medieval period of Europe began around the time of Emperor Justinian and his wife Theodora. In 537 AD, the cathedral Hagia Sophia in Constantinople, commissioned by the Byzantine emperor Justinian and Theodora, was completed. In 538 AD, seeking to establish his future, Justinian declared himself to no longer be a soldier, but a theologian, combining the civil leadership obligation with a religious leadership obligation.

It became Justinian's vision to build the kingdom of God on earth. While Justinian had outlawed cults, Justinian also infiltrated the religious domain with his own theology and began the process of the transformation of the church. As the church further transformed into the state religion, the Roman Catholic Church was able to leave behind its spiritual responsibility of connecting individuals with God Most High, in order to pursue political and military power to rule and control people, governments, and world events. With Justinian, the Roman Catholic Church's religious leaders' thirst for power was given the blessing of the state.

Charles Martel / Charles the Hammer, duke and prince of the Franks (fl. 718 to 741), was known as leading the victors of the Battle of Tours in 732, defeating the Umayyad Caliphate / Muslims, and retaking territory lost to the Muslims.

Pepin the Short, king of the Franks (fl. 751 to 768), was the younger son of Charles Martel / Charles the Hammer. When the Roman Catholic Church was threatened by the Lombards, Pepin's first major act as king was to restore the property seized from the Roman Catholic Church. Pepin the Short also confirmed the *papacy's establishment of the papal states and the temporal reign of the papacy, in essence making the pope a king.*

When the office of the pope that had been recognized as a spiritual ruler, began to also be recognized as the office of a temporal ruler, the popes would govern lands and people (like kings do), the popes would have armies (like kings do), the popes would side for or against nations (like kings do), the popes would declare war (like kings do), etc. The papacy became a mixture of religious authority and political authority. This environment would later lead to popes declaring themselves as kings. During the era of the time of Jacob's Trouble, the two beasts of Revelation 13 will declare themselves to be a kind of 'king of kings.'

Charlemagne / Charles the Great / Charles I (April 2, 748 – January 28, 814), was the son of Pepin the Short, king of the Franks, king of the Lombards, and finally Holy Roman Emperor. Charlemagne continued his father's policy of supporting the rule of the papacy and became the protector of the papacy. Charlemagne removed the Lombards from power in northern Italy and lead an incursion into Muslim Spain, reclaiming Spain for Roman Catholic Church's Christianity.

Charlemagne / Charles the Great / Charles I practiced the Christianizing of those he conquered, by threating death to those who did not convert.

It was during the reign of Charlemagne that the papacy was also significantly challenged. Leo III (fl. 795 to 816) was captured and taken prisoner by the relatives of a previous pope, with Charlemagne's men rescuing him. As a reward, and also to form a military allegiance with Charlemagne's vast political and powerful influence, Leo III established the office of Holy Roman Emperor and crowned Charlemagne as the first to hold the office (December 25, 800).

Charlemagne was called the 'Father of Europe' because he united parts of Europe that had never been under Frankish or Roman rule. Charlemagne used the circumstances to claim that he was the 'renewer of the Roman empire.' As the Holy Roman Emperor, Charlemagne instilled the idea that the emperor was entitled to the obedience of Christendom.

With Leo III's establishment of the office of Holy Roman Emperor, the spiritual and temporal realms were considered to be united. While the two offices of the papacy and of the Holy Roman Emperor were both considered to be supreme over the other, they worked in a symbiotic relationship to support each other. Charlemagne and Leo III's symbiotic relationship will be mirrored by the relationship that the two beasts of Revelation 13 will share.

Over the centuries of the disintegration of the Roman empire, a void in European political leadership was created that the papacy of the Roman Catholic Church sought to fill. The Roman Catholic Church began to be regarded as 'the universal church,' an idea that the Roman Catholic Church should be the only church, and that the papacy of the Roman Catholic Church should rule the world with the same kind of vision of the Roman empire (Imperium Christianum / Christian empire). Just as the inhabitants of the Roman empire had been united by a common Roman citizenship, the vision developed in the Roman Catholic Church for the people to be united by a common religion. The Roman Church believed that it would unite religion and government, and spread this model throughout the world as the universal church.

Another option for establishing the date for the fulfillment of the establishment of the historical era of the church of Thyatira on the historical timeline, was the birth of the Orthodox Church, and the segmented Roman Catholic Church, through the schism / division of 1054.

In 1054 the Roman Catholic Church was divided into five sees / regions, three considered to be in the west, two considered to be in the east. The schism was the culmination of centuries of theological and political differences between eastern (Greek) and western (Roman / Latin) Christianity. Prominent theological issues included understanding the position of the Holy Spirit, and whether leavened or unleavened bread should be used in the Eucharist / sacrament of holy communion. The prominent political issue concerned the bishop of Rome / pope's claim to universal jurisdiction, and the place of the see of Constantinople in relationship to the other sees.

In 1053, the pressures had climaxed. The Greek / eastern churches located in southern Italy, were required to conform to Latin / western practices, or face the threat of closure.

In retaliation, the patriarch (role similar to the bishop of Rome / pope) Michael I Cerularius of Constantinople (fl. 1043 to 1059) ordered the closure of all Latin churches in Constantinople.

In 1054, the legates sent by the bishop of Rome / pope, Leo IX (fl. 1049 to 1054), travelled to Constantinople in order to deny Michael I Cerularius the title of ecumenical patriarch and to insist that Cerularius recognize the pope's claim to be the head of all churches. There were also governmental politics that applied pressure to the situation at the time.

But when the patriarch Michael I Cerularius refused to accept the demand, the leader of the papal legates excommunicated Cerularius from the church (and from eternal life in the kingdom of heaven).

In response, Cerularius excommunicated the papal legates from the church (and from eternal life in the kingdom of heaven).

From this interaction, the church of the east and the church of the west split, maintaining doctrinal, theological and political differences. Both sides accused the other of committing heresy and of having initiated the schism.

Reconciliation was made more difficult with the western church's Crusades, the eastern church's Massacre of the Latins in 1182, the western church's retaliation with the Sacking of Thessalonica in 1185, the western church's capture and pillaging of Constantinople in 1204, etc. The primary motivation behind this conflict was not to fulfill the biblical definition of church, but to establish supremacy and governance.

In 1965, Paul VI (fl. 1963 to 1978), nullified the previous actions of the persons involved in the schism of 1054, initiating the potential reunion of the Eastern Orthodox Church (along with the Oriental Orthodox churches and the Church of the East), with the western Roman Catholic Church.

Throughout the centuries the Roman Catholic Church went through a series of transformations. One of those transformational eras was marked by the change in the view of the papacy within the Roman Catholic Church. By the time of Urban II (fl. 1088 to 1099), the higher leadership of the Roman Catholic Church came to view the papacy as gaining greater and greater supremacy.

The Roman Catholic Church had substantially lost its moral compass by the time of the papal reign of Urban II (fl. 1088 to 1099). It was Urban II who launched the Crusades in 1095. The act of declaring war against Jerusalem Israel, was an act that fully established the papacy and the Roman Catholic Church as a kind of rising 'nation' in its own right.

Throughout Roman Catholic Church history, the Roman Catholic Church has experienced eras when its leadership has been devoid of an understanding of a responsibility to operate under the authority of the teachings of Jesus Christ who 'called out' his followers from the culture of the world. During those historical eras, the leadership of the Roman Catholic Church's first focus became establishing global governance.

It was the establishment of the Roman Catholic Church's political / temporal position in the world, that would set the trajectory for the development of the papacy's position and activity that will take place during the era of the time of Jacob's Trouble. Near the end of the era of the time of Jacob's Trouble, the two beasts of Revelation 13 will rise and proclaim themselves as sovereign over all other kings and rulers of the earth.

The historical era of the church of Pergamum / unholy marriage, developed the religious leadership aspect of the Roman Catholic Church, incorporating the elements of the baal / mystery / mythology religion. The historical era of the church of Thyatira / daughter, developed the political aspirations of the Roman Catholic Church, incorporating the aspiration of establishing global governance.

As the Roman empire dissolved and somewhat disintegrated into the world, the Roman Catholic Church hierarchy defined the mission of the Roman Catholic Church as filling the void of empire building.

Popes would accomplish this mission through a variety of methods. The role of Holy Roman Emperor was established. Military alliances between popes and kings would be established. Popes would influence monarchies and the marriages of monarchs. Biblical authority was repressed for a variety of reasons including the fact that the biblical message proclaimed that the kingdom of heaven, will not be able to be replaced with a version of the Roman empire. The biblical message also proclaimed that each individual possessed power endowed to them by God the Creator, and this fact worked at a cross purpose to the goal of the Roman Catholic Church's pursuit of amassing that individual power, in order to rule.

The theology of the historical era of the church of Thyatira in the movement toward the theology of the historical era of the church of Laodicea

There were multiple ways in which the church during the Dark Ages / Middle Ages / medieval period established the foundation for the theology and culture of the church during the historical era of the church of Laodicea and the era of the time of Jacob's Trouble.

The dogmas, doctrines, theologies and practices established by the historical era of the church of Thyatira, advanced the work of the baal / mystery / mythology religion that was intertwined within the church beginning with the Roman Catholic Church becoming the official church of the Roman empire. With this unholy union, the dogmas, doctrines, theologies and practices of the Roman Catholic Church became a support for the advancement of the kingdom of Satan, Inc. / kingdom of man.

In addition, the Roman Catholic Church actively repressed the owning, translating into one's language, reading, studying, and disseminating of the Bible. Without access to the biblical message to provide direction and correction to theology and practices, the church set a course direction that was slightly off course for arriving at the correct understanding of the return of messiah / the Lamb / Jesus Christ and the process of fully establishing the kingdom of heaven on earth.

The Roman Catholic Church also embarked upon kingdom building under the assumption that messiah / the Lamb / Jesus Christ was not going to fully establish the kingdom of heaven on earth.

There were other ways in which the church of the Dark Ages / Middle Ages / medieval period advanced the progress of the church toward its arrival at its prevalent culture of the historical era of the church of Laodicean theology. But these were the most significant ways in which the church of the historical era of the church of Thyatira contributed to that movement.

The dogmas, doctrines, theologies and practices of the historical era of the church of Thyatira, that distinguished it from other historical eras

The history of the original city of Thyatira that existed during the lifetime of John the Revelator, provided a great deal of prophetic information concerning the subsequent historical era of the church of Thyatira. And the message of Jesus Christ concerning the church of the original city of Thyatira laid the foundation for what the historical era of church of Thyatira represented in the historical timeline message.

The portion of Jesus Christ's message to the angel of the church of Thyatira was the fourth portion of the message to the angels of the seven churches. This message was placed in the middle of the seven.

On this historical timeline, Thyatira represented the historical church era of the Dark Ages / Middle Ages / medieval period of Europe, which was a middle point in the two thousand years of church history leading up to the era of the time of Jacob's Trouble.

One of the main truths concerning the church during the Dark Ages / Middle Ages / medieval period of Europe was that the Roman Catholic Church, which encompassed all church at the time, strove to rule Europe. At that time, the Roman Catholic Church hierarchy believed itself to have been entrusted by Jesus Christ to establish the kingdom of heaven on earth, because Jesus Christ had left that part of his mission unfulfilled at the time of his crucifixion and death. And the Roman Catholic Church hierarchy believed itself to have been entrusted with continuing the mission of the Roman empire to establish global rule, during the dissolution of the Roman empire.

'Darkness' indicated ignorance and error. 'Light' was associated with 'knowledge and authenticity or accuracy.

The Dark Ages were called dark because wherever the Roman Catholic Church cast its shadow, it was dark, devoid of light. Access to education was restricted by the Roman Catholic Church hierarchy, and the education that was allowed and available, was stilted toward supporting the Roman Catholic Church's dogmas, doctrines, theologies and practices, instead of supporting the truth of authentic science. Even reading or studying the biblical record was restricted.

While Christianity had elevated the status of women, during the Dark Ages / Middle Ages / medieval period, the Roman Catholic Church had instituted some practices that deflated the status of women.

The Roman Catholic Church supported feudalism because it was easier to control a few lords who lorded over the populace, than it was to control the populace without lords. Even the Roman Catholic Church engaged in feudalism.

The Roman Catholic Church was also a prevalent land owner. During the Dark Ages / Middle Ages / medieval period, the Roman Catholic Church became the greatest property owner in western Europe. The Roman

Catholic Church owned about a third of the land of western Europe, and for the church, land ownership was tax free, while all others paid their taxes primarily to the church. Monks would have the opportunity to choose to pursue living in the vast wealth of the church or taking a vow of poverty. So groups like the Franciscans, who embraced life lived in poverty, posed a threat to the church that amassed vast amounts of private property and employed serfs to amass vast amounts of wealth.

Papal taxation developed with extraordinary rapidity and complexity under John XXII (fl. 1316 to 1334). The Roman Catholic Church exploited its spiritual authority for fiscal goals, accumulating massive wealth, property, gold and art; and then built buildings to house it all. The Roman Catholic Church's hoarding of wealth, through religious manipulation, and at the expense of the people, was part of the motivation for the Protestant Reformation.

Accompanying the resultant excessive clerical wealth, was lax clerical morality, which further encased the direction set by the Roman Catholic Church and further added to the 'darkness.'

Even now, it has been estimated that the Roman Catholic Church controls around 177 million acres of land around the world.

When discussing any church organization, it is important to remember the difference between the church's religious leadership and the people who were or are ruled by the that church's leadership. Jeremiah 51:45 and Revelation 18:4 made it clear when God Most High provides the warning, 'Come out of her, my people,' that there will still be some members of every church who still belong to God Most High. They will be the people whom the direction to 'Come out of her, my people,' will be addressed to.

In every church there can be found some of God Most High's people residing within the church for two reasons. It has always been the practice of God Most High to preserve a remnant. And when the followers of the

Lamb / Jesus Christ are present, Jesus Christ is also present along with the Holy Spirit, to keep that community alive.

When God Most High's 'remnant' in a church no longer exists in that church denomination or church community, then there is no longer anyone for God Most High and particularly the Holy Spirit, to connect with within that religious community. Without the Holy Spirit's connection, there is no opportunity for the Holy Spirit to infuse life into the religious community. Therefore, a church community without followers of the Lamb / Jesus Christ connected through the Holy Spirit, withers and dies.

Also note that the composition of a religious community is frequently not represented by the religious organizational leadership. In the case of the kings of the unified nation of Israel, and after Solomon, the kings of the divided nation of Israel, there were various times when the kings, or the priests, or the prophets would represent the religious climate of the people of Israel. But there were other times when a king or priest or prophet would experience a different type of relationship with God Most High, than the type of relationship that the mass of the people would have.

Throughout human history, in most instances, the government has represented the majority view of the populace. But all forms of government and governmental exercises, have their dissenters.

During Jesus Christ's earthly ministry, there were both people devoted to God Most High (Mary, Joseph, Zechariah, Elizabeth, Simeon and Anna in the temple, John the Baptist, the twelve disciples / apostles, the followers of Jesus Christ, Mary, Martha, Lazarus, Nicodemus and Gamaliel of the Sanhedrin, Joseph of Arimathea, etc.) and dissenters against God Most High (Ananias, Caiaphas and other members of the Sanhedrin, scribes, Pharisees, teachers of the Law, etc.).

It has been the nature of the life cycles of God Most High's religious groups and nations to begin as a movement, totally dedicated to the mission and goals of what they defined to be pure and holy; then to grow to a level where organization was required for the benefit of the community. Once a high level of organization was achieved, the organization became susceptible and ripe for infiltrators who did not share the original mission and goals of the initial group. The dissenters, or sometimes it has been the next generation, found the opportunity for obtaining power to alter the mission to be too great an enticement to refuse.

Power seekers manage to find ways to rise to the tops of organizations. This phenomenon within the lifecycle of organizations was true for the nation of Israel, for governments throughout history, in family dynamics, in religious communities, etc. And this phenomenon continues to be at work even today.

Consequently, the theology of the historical era of the church of Laodicea, the final portion of the message to the angels of the seven churches, will also have its compass set on exercising power instead of remembering the original mission of the church that Jesus Christ established of communicating the news of God Most High's redemption, reclamation and regeneration plan. The historical era of the church of Thyatira will have established the foundation for fully integrating power and governance into religion. But it will be the historical era of the church of Laodicea that will accomplish what the historical era of the church of Thyatira began, and will eventually assume authority over all church organizational hierarchies.

Too often religious organizational leadership has not been comprised of God Most High's holy people. The religious organizational leadership that does not follow the Lamb / Jesus Christ will eventually deny the divinity and sovereignty of Jesus Christ, the Jesus Christ that founded the church originally. Too often the religious leadership will cause or allow the practice of the baal / mystery / mythology religion in some form to infiltrate the church community and hierarchical structure.

It was Ham, one of the eight people who exited Noah's ark, who resuscitated the antediluvian / preflood religion, and his sons who reestablished it in Babylon and *the tower of Babel empire. The Babylonian religion, originally reestablished in Babylon, has never left us, just as God Most High has never left us. Jesus Christ referred to it as 'Mystery Babylon the Great!' in the message that Jesus Christ provided to John the Revelator (Revelation 17, 18).*

Mystery Babylon requires secrecy in order to accomplish its purpose of infiltrating what God Most High designated as holy. This mission of secretly overtaking what God Most High has designated should be holy, has been the goal of secret societies both within church communities and outside of traditional church communities. The kingdom of Satan, Inc. / kingdom of man thrives on secret societies.

In contrast, Jesus Christ said, 'This is the verdict, that the light has come into the world, and the people loved darkness rather than the light, because their deeds were evil. Everyone who practices evil, hates the light and does not come to the light, so that their deeds will not be exposed. But the one who practices truth comes to the light so that it may been seen plainly that what they have done has been done in the sight of God.' John 3:19-21 translated

Jesus directed this message to Nicodemus, a member of the Sanhedrin.

It would be the Sanhedrin's secret court that would illegally place Jesus on trial and conspire to have Jesus crucified. But there was no documentation that Nicodemus supported the action.

The era represented by the historical era of the church of Thyatira was an era when the church sought to merge both church and state, to combine religious power with political power to gain a greater level of power to rule. In this way, the historical era of the church of Thyatira became the ruling church.

It was the Roman Catholic Church that merged with state, and became its own religious-political entity. The church lost its official mission which was to unite people with Jesus Christ as Lord. Instead, the Roman Catholic Church gathered the power and even the military might, to act like its own empire. The Roman Catholic Church ruled the monarchies of Europe, establishing monarchies and dissolving monarchies. But the Roman Catholic Church also became an arm of government and finally became an acting unique government. The Roman Catholic Church ruled the people through forced conversions, forced baptisms, and with forced memberships in the Roman Catholic Church. The Roman Catholic Church also ruled the people through tax and financial incentives or consequences.

As the red dragon / serpent / Satan, Inc. pursued its infiltration into the highest levels of power within the Roman Catholic Church (and all church denominations), the Roman Catholic Church has throughout its history, overtly and covertly, made political agreements with various governments, participated in political intrigue, aligned itself with world leaders, participated in politics of wars, influenced world leaders, etc. for the benefit of the Roman Catholic Church. Historically, the organization of the Roman Catholic Church even drew political / national boundaries and actively participated in empire building. Using the threat of the excommunication of monarchs, and actually excommunicating monarchs, the Roman Catholic Church placed monarchs of their own choosing upon thrones.

All of this resulted in people becoming leaders within the Roman Catholic Church for personal financial, political, and power gain.

With the change in the motivation to become a leader in the Roman Catholic Church, moving away from dedication to Jesus Christ and to the kingdom of heaven, the new replacement motivation centered around accruing greater financial, political, and power gain. Policies and activities were decided based on how much revenue would be brought in. The leaders of the Roman Catholic Church began to believe that they were the head of the church instead of Jesus Christ. The leaders adopted being called, 'papa,' which later became 'pope.' Because the Roman Catholic Church had transformed into more of a political system than a church, there was one 'papa' / 'pope' who believed that he should be head of all the other churches.

Siricius (fl. 384 to 399 AD) had established papal authority and commanded celibacy for priests (386 AD) which was the first decree on the subject. But the biblical record recognized the forbidding of people to marry as an act that was opposed to God Most High's will (1 Timothy 4:3).

As time continued, the successive popes participated in greater and greater evils including bribery, gross sexual immorality, fratricide, murder, etc.

Leo I (fl. 440 to 461) decided who would be cast into hell and who would be eligible for citizenship in heaven.

Popes adopted the title 'Vicar of Christ,' which implied that the pope possessed the same power and authority that Jesus Christ had over the church. The term actually means 'in the place of Christ,' and when translated into Greek literally means 'antichrist.' The first pope to have the title applied to him was Gelasius I (fl. 492 to 496).

Gregory I (fl. 590 to 640) asserted the doctrine of Petrine supremacy, defining the pope to hold a position assigned by God Most High that was equal to that of the apostle Peter. Holding Petrine supremacy meant that, at least in the mind of the pope, that the pope held universal authority over all Christian churches.

The Roman Catholic Church is vastly different from the apostolic church / church of the historical era of the church of Ephesus, or the persecuted church of the historical era of the church of Smyrna. Those churches were intent upon placing as their primary mission, the connection of the worshiper with God and God with the worshiper. They were even willing to be persecuted and martyred for pursuing the primary mission established by Jesus Christ.

But during the era of the time of Jacob's Trouble the Roman Catholic Church hierarchy will have exhausted its patience upon focusing any attention on honoring the divinity and sovereignty of God Most High. The Roman Catholic Church hierarchy will again embrace a manipulative and militant style of operation, and utilize their supposed relationship with God Most High merely as a tool for manipulating the world's religious culture and political systems, to achieve its own purposes.

The practice of the Roman Catholic Church's hierarchy of placing its own power over benefiting God Most High's people, and of seeking to rule the entire world, will continue to be practiced until Jesus Christ returns and the global religious community self-destructs, putting an end to it (Revelation chapters 17 to 19).

No other entity has historically tortured and killed more people, especially people who have professed to being followers of the Lamb / Jesus Christ, than the Roman Catholic Church. The Roman Catholic Church has truly drunken the wine of the blood of the holy ones (Revelation 17:6).

Throughout the history of the Roman Catholic Church, the stated motivation for the 'works' of the Roman Catholic Church has been to achieve its goal of ruling the world. With Byzantine / Western Roman Emperor Justinian and Theodora, the Roman Catholic Church received the government's blessing, and its path for the pursuit of world power and domination was 'birthed.'

The historical era of the church of Thyatira commonly known as the 'Dark Ages' was also termed the 'Devil's Millennium' or the Church's 'dark night of the soul.' The Dark Ages / Middle Ages / medieval period was a period ushered in by the fall of the Roman empire and ushered out by the Renaissance and Protestant Reformation. This era of history lasted for over a thousand years, with plenty of time for the leadership of the Roman Catholic Church to repent.

The Dark Ages / Middle Ages / medieval period was marked by a lack of literature and cultural achievements due to religious and governmental power induced poverty, ignorance and oppression. The Roman Catholic Church supported poverty, ignorance, and oppression along with feudalism, elitism, and election. Poverty, ignorance, oppression, feudalism, elitism, and election are social instruments that create an environment where the populace is more easily dominated. The saying is, 'the Dark

Ages were only dark where the Roman Catholic Church covered the light.'

During the Dark Ages / Middle Ages / medieval period, the powerful Roman Catholic Church endorsed and encouraged the practice of alchemy, magic and sorcery among monks, priests, physicians, surgeons, midwives, folk healers, and diviners. They would use charms, potions, leeching, herbal remedies, and the activity of casting spells. The use of magic and sorcery placed those who practiced magical sorcery at risk for assault from the demons that they sought to control and use for their own purposes. And just as magic could be used for achieving a positive publicity result, magic could also be used to curse crops, animals, and people.

It was during this era that the Roman Catholic Church developed seven sacraments, the rites of; baptism, confirmation, extreme unction, mass, ordination, penance, and marriage. The Roman Catholic Church of the Dark Ages / Middle Ages / medieval period, provided these seven sacraments with an accompanying magical application.

For instance, during a baptism, a certain ceremony and prayer were performed to exorcise the child of any demonic spirits arising from the sin of conception and childbirth.

During the rite of communion, the bread and the wine were believed to be actually changed into the real body and blood of Jesus through transubstantiation, a belief that continues today. The mass was designed to be a rite honoring the dead with the belief that the dead still have the active ability to influence the living, as precedented by the spirits of the dead Nephilim / demons. 'Christi's mass' / Christmas is technically an activity that honors a dead Jesus. Masses were led in Latin, which created a magical, mystical, mythological atmosphere to worship and allowed the Roman Catholic Church to worship whomever they desired without the populace that did not speak Latin, being able to recognize what was said or the true allegiance of those leading in worship. One of Martin Luther's largest contentions was that during Latin *ceremonies, the scriptures and the accompanying activities, held too close of a resemblance to magical incantations.*

The mass is the continual sacrifice of Jesus Christ, believing that the priest transubstantiates the elements of bread and wine, into the actual body and blood of Jesus Christ. It is a statement that says that Jesus Christ's death has not been a sufficient and complete sacrifice and therefore Jesus Christ needs to be sacrificed again and again. (Hebrews 7:27, 9:26-28, 10:1-18)

The mass denies Jesus Christ's declaration made while he was on the cross when Jesus said, 'It is finished!'

The biblical record clearly documented that Jesus Christ's sacrifice on the cross was the complete sacrifice that never needed to be repeated again.

Unlike the other high priests, Jesus Christ does not need to offer sacrifices day after day, first for his own sins, and then for the sins of the people. Jesus Christ sacrificed for their sins once for all when he offered himself. For the law appoints as high priests men in all their weakness; but the oath, which came after the law, appointed the Son, who has been made perfect forever. Hebrews 7:27-28

For Christ did not enter a sanctuary made with human hands that was only a copy of the true one; he entered heaven itself, now to appear for us in God's presence. Nor did he enter heaven to offer himself again and again, the way the high priest enters the Most Holy Place every year with blood that is not his own. Otherwise, Christ would have had to suffer many times since the creation of the world. But he has appeared once for all at the culmination of the ages to do away with sin by the sacrifice of himself. Just as people are destined to die once, and after that to face judgment, so Christ was sacrificed once to take away the sins of many; and he will appear a second time, not to bear sin, but to bring salvation to those who are waiting for him. Hebrews 9:24-28

Day after day every priest stands and performs his religious duties. Again and again, he offers the same sacrifices, which can never take away sins. But when this priest, Jesus Christ, had offered for all time one sacrifice for sins, he sat down at the right hand of God, and since that time he waits for his enemies to be made his footstool. For by one sacrifice, he has made perfect forever those who are being made holy.

The Holy Spirit also testifies to us about this. First, he says: 'This is the covenant I will make with them after that time, says the Lord. I will put my laws in their hearts, and I will write them on their minds.' Then he adds: 'Their sins and lawless acts I will remember no more.'

And where these have been forgiven, sacrifice for sin is no longer necessary. Hebrews 10:11-18

Jesus said the bread of the communion service represented his broken body. The Roman Catholic Church mass placed the bread that was intended to represent the body of Christ, into the monstrance designed to honor the sun god. In Roman Catholic Church theology, by causing the bread to repeatedly become the body of Christ in the offering of the mass, the Roman Catholic Church was willing to break the body of Christ continually and then to symbolically and effectively offer it as a sacrifice to the sun god.

The communion wine which was intended to represent the blood of Christ and was given for the forgiveness of sin, is withheld from church members. In withholding the communion wine from church members, the Roman Catholic Church also symbolically withholds the forgiveness of sin that comes from Jesus Christ sacrifice of blood.

The Roman Catholic Church has designed their own system for forgiveness, determining who meets their criteria for entrance into heaven and who does not. Because the Roman Catholic Church believes that the hierarchy of the Roman Catholic Church holds the keys to the kingdom of heaven, they also believe that they are gatekeepers to both heaven and hell. But Jesus Christ pointed out in his teaching that only God Most High can forgive sins... and God Most High determines who will enter into heaven and who will not... and God Most High determined that Jesus Christ was the only way to approach God the Father.

The theology of the Roman Catholic Church mass denies Jesus Christ's divinity and sovereignty and authority as the supreme priest of God Most High that is able and willing to take away the sins of the world. The Roman Catholic Church's mass denies Jesus Christ's resurrection into a glorious and unable to be killed again body, and Jesus Christ's ascension into heaven to assume the throne of God Most High. The Roman Catholic Church's mass denies Jesus Christ's plan to return to defeat the enemies of God Most High and of the kingdom of heaven, and to make his enemies his footstool. And the Roman Catholic Church's mass denies that God Most High's plan is to perfect those God Most High will make holy.

Those who are holy do not need to be ruled. The manipulative power of reminding a holy person of their sin, when their sin has been forgiven by God Most High and disposed of, is void, impotent, pointless, and only serves to provide vain religious manipulation for the purpose of obtaining greater power that does not rightfully belong to those who would be rulers.

The Roman Catholic Church embraced magical like practices like 'churching,' where a woman was kept indoors, dressed in white on white linen, and prevented from looking at the ground for a month after she had given birth. This was to prevent her impurities from corrupting the world around her.

Necromancy (nekros, 'dead', and manteia, 'divination') is the practice of communicating with the dead, especially for predicting the future. While the Roman Catholic Church leadership practiced Necromancy especially during the Dark Ages / Middle Ages / medieval period, necromancy was a violation of God Most High's Law.

After the deluge / flood, beginning with Ham's lineage and the reestablishment of the antediluvian religion, the baal / mystery / mythology religion, people would pray to their 'ancestors' and to those they had lost in the flood. They would actually use the demons who are dead Nephilim spirits trapped in an earthly abode, for communicating with dead ancestors. Ancestor worship and demon worship developed into communicating with the dead and with rebellious angels. After the deluge / flood, reestablished communication with the rebellious angels led to the reestablishment of Nephilim production until after a few centuries of transition time for the world's environment to change so that the shortened lifespan could take effect to extinguish the possibility of *further first generation Nephilim production and human genetic modification.*

When the first king of Israel, Saul, had realized that the Spirit of God had departed from him, Saul practiced communication with the dead. Saul went to the witch of Endor and implored her to provide him contact with the prophet Samuel (1 Samuel 28:3-25.). God Most High had forbidden communication with the dead as part of the Law given to Moses and the people of Israel (Deuteronomy 18:9-13) (1446 BC). So Saul knew that communicating with the deceased Samuel was not going to be tolerated by the God of Israel.

Necromancy was founded on the belief that the soul survives after death with a new possession of superior knowledge. The souls of the dead can then be contacted at the right time and under the right conditions with the right rituals. The rituals for contacting the dead would include the blood sacrifice of animals and even of people, usually around a fire pit at night. (This was a unique twist to sitting around a campfire.) Some practitioners would consume corpses or rotten juice and food as a part of the rituals. Ancestor worship and necromancy were practiced as an expression of the baal / mystery / mythology religion.

The Dark Ages / Middle Ages / medieval period was an era when the belief was fostered that members of the clergy derived special benefits from being a link between earth and heaven. This further inspired a holy and untouchable aspect to be applied to unstandardized religious doctrines, practices, and the magic arts as well as to the Roman Catholic Clergymen themselves.

Medieval practitioners believed they could accomplish three things with necromancy: will manipulation, illusions, and knowledge:

- *Will manipulation affects the mind and will of another person, animal, or spirit. Demons are summoned to cause various afflictions on others, to drive them mad, to inflame them to love or hatred, to gain their favor, or to constrain them to do or not do some deed.*

- *Illusions involve reanimation of the dead or the conjuring of food, entertainment, or a mode of transportation.*
- *Knowledge is allegedly discovered when demons or rebellious angels provide information about various things. This might involve gaining new technology or knowledge identifying criminals, finding items, or revealing future events.*

The Law of Moses (~1446 BC) forbid the practice of necromancy and made it punishable by death (Leviticus 19:31, 20:6, 20:27, Deuteronomy 18:14, 1 Samuel 28:7-9). But the practice was unofficially and covertly reinvigorated by the Roman Catholic Church during the Dark Ages / Middle Ages / medieval period (~538 to 1517 AD).

Another practice that developed during the Dark Ages / Middle Ages / medieval period was the 'veneration of the holy ones.'

The Bible defined a saint as anyone who has decided to believe that Jesus is Lord, that we crucified him, and that God raised him from the dead (book of Acts).

But the Roman Catholic Church defines a saint not according to what a person believes about Jesus Christ, but according to the work that a person has accomplished, especially for advancing the purposes of the Roman Catholic Church. A saint then became a person who had been particularly 'holy in life,' with 'holiness' being defined by the work and gifts given to the Roman Catholic Church.

Those who were qualified to be holy ones according to the Roman Catholic Church's definition, maintained a special position of privilege after they died which marked them worthy to pray to for requesting assistance. This special assistance could be harnessed through the use of a talisman / amulet / holy relic that has been imbued with the spirit and power of that particular saint.

During this Dark Ages / Middle Ages / medieval period, religious ritual murder was practiced even within 'Christian' communities.

During the Dark Ages / Middle Ages / medieval period of history, quality education was rare and was generally reserved for those that the Roman Catholic Church deemed worthy to receive it; mainly the wealthy and powerful who were willing to share their wealth and power for advancing the interests of the Roman Catholic Church. Unbiased education was nearly non-existent. Books were rare and copies of the Bible were even more rare. Most priests had very limited access to Bibles. If a large community actually possessed a Bible, it was generally chained to the church entrance. Illiteracy was great. For many the only biblical instruction came in the pictures of the church's stained glass windows. Even church worship was led in a foreign language. Religious leaders were not well prepared or trained to understand and embrace true Christianity. This environment meant that aspiring religious leaders were able to apply their cultic practices as Christian representatives without accountability to what defined authentic Christianity.

Also, the Roman Catholic Church teaches that lending assistance in the afterlife, is Mary the mother of God. Semiramis was the first after the flood to be titled 'Queen of Heaven.' The Roman Catholic Church also bestowed upon Mary the mother of God this title of 'Queen of Heaven,' beginning in the Dark Ages / Middle Ages / medieval period of human history.

In the same manner that Semiramis as the Queen of Heaven, united the early postdiluvian / postflood world, titling the Blessed Virgin Mary as 'Queen of Heaven' unified those goddesses who had held the 'Queen of Heaven' title throughout history between Semiramis and the Blessed Virgin Mary. It was an act that served to further unite Mithraism, a sect of the baal / mystery / mythology religions, with Christianity within the church.

Semiramis was a Nephilim with a rebellious angel father and a human mother. Semiramis was also the demigod mother of both Nimrod and Tammuz. Both Nimrod and Tammuz fulfilled the role as the blessed son born of a mother with a unique birth. Depending upon the culture, either Nimrod or Tammuz became the red dragon / serpent / Satan, Inc.'s pseudo messianic fulfillment for the post flood world of the Genesis 3:15 prophecy.

Through the merger of the early Christian church with the baal / mystery / mythology religion primarily known as Mithraism, the Roman Catholic Church produced a theological reinvention of Mary the handmaiden of the Lord, so that she became 'the Blessed Virgin Mary.' In the Roman Catholic Church reinvention of Mary, it was no longer Jesus Christ who was immaculately conceived. The Blessed Virgin Mary became the one who was immaculately conceived with a human mother and a god as her father.

The familiar language of Mithraism, the Roman empire's version of the baal / mystery / mythology religion, accommodated the repackaging of the biblically defined Mary, into the Queen of Heaven / Blessed Virgin Mary. In that process, Jesus Christ was also redefined to possess a similar character to the character of the son Tammuz. Because the reimagined Blessed Virgin Mary became the Queen of Heaven who now was defined as immaculately conceived, the Blessed Virgin Mary version could know no sin. The reimagined Blessed Virgin Mary / Queen of Heaven now gave birth to only one child, Jesus, and then regained her virginity after his birth. The repackaged Jesus was now effectively able to be theologically killed without the possibility of being able to rise from the dead. In this way, Jesus would be able to remain on the crucifix, and be able to be the sacrifice continually offered in mass with the bread and wine continually transubstantiated into the actual body and blood of Jesus.

But the biblical account of Jesus' birth, life, death, and resurrection does not read the same as the Dark Ages / Middle Ages / medieval period version produced by the Roman Catholic Church. Without an educated clergy or educated laity, the Roman Catholic Church's version of history and theology would continue unchallenged.

The founders of the colonies in the Americas and the founders of the nation of the United States understood the *importance of education and made provision for every citizen to be able to receive education as a defense against poor theology (~1600 to present).*

The multiple accounts of Jesus Christ's birth in the biblical record presented Jesus Christ as the one who was immaculately conceived, who had God Most High as his father, who lived the sinless life, etc. The biblical account of Jesus Christ presented Jesus as having brothers and sisters through his mother Mary. For example, James the brother of Jesus became the leader of the Jerusalem Church during the era of the Apostolic church. (Matthew 12:46-47, 13:55-56 – brothers: James, Joseph, Simon and Judas, and more than one sister, Mark 3:31-32, 6:3, Luke 8:19-20, John 2:12, 7:1-10, Acts 12:17, 1 Corinthians 9:5, Galatians 1:18-19, Jude 1:1)

The theological repackaging of Christianity, complete with the incorporation of the old familiar rites, rituals and practices of the baal / mystery / mythology religion, was an easy sell to the uneducated populace and uneducated religious leaders. Using the new labels of Christianity, applied to the established Mithraism / baal / mystery religion, the Roman Catholic Church leadership was able to continue many of their old practices under the new labeling, utilizing Christian language.

The Roman Catholic Church also instituted several doctrines that were simply fund raisers designed to enrich the coffers of the Roman Catholic Church, while creating fear in order to maintain their authority and to insure the dominance of the Roman Catholic Church over the populace.

Among the Roman Catholic Church's fundraisers was the doctrine of purgatory. Purgatory became the place where the souls of people go after death to wait until the living prays them out or purchases their release through payment made to the Roman Catholic Church's coffers. Purgatory is a place of suffering where the souls of sinners reside while they are waiting for their sins to be expiated so that they can go to heaven.

The doctrine of purgatory is contrary to the biblical forgiveness of sins that Jesus Christ provides and is free for those who receive the invitation to be set free from their sin. Jesus Christ promised the thief on the cross next to Jesus' cross, that he would be with Jesus Christ in paradise yet that very day, without passing through purgatory (Luke 23:43).

The Roman Catholic Church developed within the doctrine that many years in purgatory are necessary for the cleansing and purifying of sins in preparation for heaven, insuring a steady stream of income for the Roman Catholic Church.

Because the biblical Mary had been reimagined by the Roman Catholic Church as having been immaculately conceived and having lived a sinless life, the Blessed Virgin Mary was now in a unique place to assist souls in purgatory. Through prayer to the Blessed Virgin Mary, the Blessed Virgin Mary could be influenced to give aid to souls when she visited purgatory on the special feast days of Mary and on Saturdays, similar to how one visits a person in jail.

Purgatory invokes fear. Fear causes people to be more easily dominated. An uneducated populace is without resources to be able to know any different theology than what the Roman Catholic Church offered to them. To this day, and even during the era of the time of Jacob's Trouble, the Roman Catholic Church will continue its doctrine of purgatory and continue to use fear of an eternity in hell as a motivator for allegiance to the church.

In contrast, the God of the kingdom of heaven, has been defined as pure love. Pure love is about casting out fear. Purgatory and the fear associated with it, could never meet the criteria for being utilized by the kingdom of heaven.

Also, the Roman Catholic Church developed the payment of indulgences to the Roman Catholic Church. An indulgence came with a paper certificate that was documentation of a promise that the time a soul spent in purgatory would be shortened. The sale of an indulgence reasoned that a person could purchase salvation from the

Church with earthly funds and that the church held the ultimate decision concerning one's eternal address.

The Roman Catholic Church's definition of the salvation process is also mirrored in the baal / mystery / mythology religion hieroglyphs of Egypt where the deceased's heart was placed on one side of the scale, a feather was placed on the other, the priest placed his hand under the heart to lift up the heart, and with the priest's other hand the priest received the bribe. Then one's heart could be judged to be 'as light as a feather' and acceptable for a positive afterlife.

Forgiveness of sins for a member of the Roman Catholic Church, could be accomplished with a donation to the Church, and accepted by a priest. With the Church's program of indulgences, God Most High was no longer needed to forgive sins.

Another selling point for indulgences was that a person could purchase an indulgence for one's self or for someone else dead or alive.

But the sale of indulgences was one of the practices heavily protested during the Protestant Reformation, by laity who finally possessed and read the Bible, translated into their own language.

With the institution of the sacrament of penance and reconciliation, the Roman Catholic Church fully assumed the authority to forgive sins. Within Judaism and the early church, only God could forgive sins. When Jesus Christ forgave sins, Jesus was accused of blasphemy by the Israelite religious leaders because only God can forgive sins. While Jesus Christ instructed his followers to confess sin to God Most High, the Roman Catholic Church taught that confession to the priest and performing the subsequent acts of penance were required for reconciliation with God and with the community of the church. The Roman Catholic Church taught that a person needs to be in a right relationship with the church as a prerequisite for being eligible to enter heaven. Only if the priest, bishop, cardinal or pope granted forgiveness, then the church member could be absolved from their sin and avoid the condemnation of hell.

People with unconfessed sin were not allowed to receive communion. Theologically, to not be allowed to receive communion was the Roman Catholic Church's equivalent of being barred from entrance into heaven. People with unconfessed mortal sins or who remained under some form of censure at their death were not allowed a Roman Catholic funeral mass and burial rites.

In contrast, the biblical Jesus Christ forgave sins upon request. Sometimes Jesus forgave sins without the request even having to have been made. Jesus Christ and the apostles even taught that Jesus Christ's crucifixion and resurrection paid the debt for all sin, in full. Jesus said that forgiveness is available merely upon a simple request... to him and only him.

But for the Roman Catholic Church penance required payment for sin in the form of self-abasement, mortification of the body (fasting, abstinence, pious kneeling, wearing sackcloth, flagellation, etc.), an act of devotion or sorrow, a financial transaction to the church, etc. While the purpose of Jesus Christ's work was to alleviate suffering, penance required it. Ultimately the purpose of penance was to once again use an individual's inherent power, as a tool to rule them.

The Roman Catholic Church also experienced an era of pornocracy known as the Rule of the Prostitutes or the Rule of the Harlots. This specific era was entitled Saeculum obscurum / 'Dark Age' (904 to 964 AD).

The era of pornocracy began in 904 AD with the installation of Sergius III (fl. 904-911 AD) as pope. Sergius III was completely under the control of a beautiful woman named Theodora who was married to a Roman consul Theophylactus. Theodora's fifteen year old daughter Marozia became the concubine of Sergius III.

Anastasius III (fl. 911-913 AD) followed Sergius III and was considered to potentially be the son of Sergius III.

John X (fl. 914-928 AD) was a lover of Theodora and was an appointed pope rather than having been elected. Marozia smothered him to death.

Stephen VII (fl. 928-931 AD) was elected to be pope, with the support of Marozia until her own son John was ready to assume the position.

John XI (fl. 931-935 AD) was the son of Marozia and Sergius III.

John XII (fl. 955-963 AD) was the grandson of Marozia. John XII was known for violating virgins and widows. He lived with his father's mistress. John XII was so immoral that the Basilica of Rome / Lateran Palace was said to have been converted into a brothel during his reign. John XII's other offenses were also very immoral and colorful. John XII was killed in the act of adultery by the woman's enraged husband.

The era of pornocracy ended with John XII in 963 AD.

Following the era of the Rule of the Harlots, the papacy continued questionable and immoral practices.

John XIII (fl. 965-972) was Marozia's nephew, the son of her younger sister Theodora.

Benedict VII (fl. 974-983) was the grandson of Marozia.

Benedict VIII (fl. 1012-1024) and John XIX (fl. 1024-1032) were the great grandsons of Marozia. Benedict VIII (fl. 1012-1024 AD) and John XIX (fl. 1024-1033) purchased the office of the papacy through open bribery.

Benedict IX (fl. 1032-1044, 1045, 1047-1048) was the great great grandson of Marozia. Benedict IX was made papal ruler three times during his lifetime. Benedict IX was made pope as a twelve year old boy. Other accounts say he was twenty. Benedict IX's papacy was arranged with a money bargain through the powerful families that ruled Rome. Benedict IX committed murders and adulteries even during the day. He robbed people on the graves of martyrs. The latter part of the reign of Benedict IX (1045-1046 AD), was challenged during the last year of his reign, with two other rivals for the office; Gregory VI (fl. 1045-1046 AD) and Sylvester III (fl. 1045-1046AD).

Finally, Clement II (fl. 1046-1047 AD) was appointed pope by the king of Germany Henry III (fl. 1028 to 1056) in an attempt to end the purchasing of the papacy, the fornication, and the adultery. Clement II then crowned Henry III the Holy Roman Emperor.

In an attempt to keep revenue flowing into Roman Catholic Church, it became important to limit education so that education was available to only a select few who were chosen by the church to receive education. Those educated were frequently chosen because of their family's financial or political influence that would aid the church. In this way, the Roman Catholic Church became the retailer of education. Even to the select chosen few, education consisted of what the Roman Catholic Church decided to present.

Prevention of education was accompanied with prevention of access to the Bible. During the Dark Ages / Middle Ages / medieval period, a Bible was time consuming to copy and extremely costly, costing about a year's wages. Bibles were rare and if a church was fortunate enough to possess a copy, it was frequently chained to the church building. Consequently, the populace was unaware that the Bible holds many injunctions against the practices that the Roman Catholic Church had developed in the name of the same God who prohibited those practices.

A populace that is not able to have access to the Bible or to be able to read the Bible is less likely to discover what the Bible says. Stained glass window pictures were developed to tell the 'important' biblical stories.

The Roman Catholic Church fostered the distance between the people and the Bible. Some of the decisions regarding the Roman Catholic Church's stance on sharing the Bible with the laity included:

The Decree of the Council of Toulouse (1229 C.E.): 'We prohibit also that the laity should be permitted to have the books of the Old or New Testament; but we most strictly forbid their having any translation of these books.'

Not only were the laity not permitted to possess the Old or New Testaments, they were also forbidden to have them as translations in their own language.

The Ruling of the Council of Tarragona of 1234 C.E.:
'No one may possess the books of the Old and New Testaments in the Romance language, and if anyone possesses them, he must turn them over to the local bishop within eight days after promulgation of this decree, so that they may be burned...'

Pause for a moment... The Roman Catholic Church actually practiced the forced burning of the Bible in order to prevent their people from reading it.

The practice of celibacy is similar to the practice of the priests of Cybele, a sect of the baal / mystery / mythology religion. The priests of Cybele were all castrated in a religious ritual. The ascetics in the Roman Catholic Church viewed this ritual castration as an act that symbolized the renunciation of the body and its passions.

Hippolytus documented the ascetic sect in the early church, their practices and their connection to Cybele worship. Ascetics would either live as if they were castrated or literally remove their genitals.

The act of castration also deprived a person of their offspring. Women priestesses of Cybele would also renounce marriage and reproduction.

The worship of Cybele included parents offering their children as human sacrifice, cutting off their offspring.

Another purpose of refraining from marriage and reproduction was to gain special knowledge 'gnosis' which was considered to be available from the gods / rebellious angels and their offspring / Nephilim / demons. The special knowledge / mystery knowledge / false teaching, and the various practices associated with this special knowledge were equated with the practice of magic arts or divination (1 Timothy 2, 5).

November 18, 1302, Boniface VIII (fl. 1294 to 1303) published the papal bull Unam sanctam / The One Holy. The papal bull sought to establish dogmatic propositions on the unity of the Roman Catholic Church including, the necessity of belonging to the Roman Catholic Church in order to receive everlasting salvation, the position of the pope as the supreme head of the Roman Catholic Church and therefore head of all churches, the requirement of submission to the pope in order to belong to the church and to attain salvation, the higher position of the spiritual in comparison with the secular order, etc.

Boniface VIII's papal bull remained a foundational document for Roman Catholic Church theology.

While Jesus Christ's goal is to perfect individuals and provide for humanity, the opportunity to obtain friendship with God, the Roman Catholic Church's goal was to remind the laity of their unworthiness and convince them that they are unforgivable so that the only way they may obtain heaven is through the manipulative process determined by the Roman Catholic Church. With this context, the practices of the Roman Catholic Church throughout the Dark Ages / Middle Ages / medieval period caused the earthly pope and the Roman Catholic Church to gain increasingly greater power.

Some of the teachings and practices that have pagan origins, which were ripened and incorporated into the Roman Catholic Church:

- *the pope as the vicar of Christ, taking the place of Christ on earth / antichrist (Greek),*
- *images and relics became holy,*
- *use of holy water to bless someone or something,*
- *canonization of dead holy ones,*
- *celibacy of the priesthood,*
- *prayer beads / rosary for counting prayers said to the Blessed Virgin Mary,*
- *inquisitions,*
- *sale of indulgences,*
- *transubstantiation (communion elements are transformed into the actual body and blood of Jesus Christ as part of the sacrifice during the Mass),*

- *forbidding access of the laity to the wine cup during communion and consequently controlling forgiveness of sins,*
- *adoration of the wafer (which is circular in shape, to honor the sun god),*
- *restriction of the Bible and biblical education to laity,*
- *doctrine of purgatory decreed,*
- *doctrine of seven sacraments affirmed as having mystical / magical characteristics,*
- *church tradition elevated to hold equal or greater authority than the Bible,*
- *apocryphal books added to the holy canon, the Bible,*
- *immaculate conception of Mary declared,*
- *infallibility of the pope declared,*
- *assumption of the Blessed Virgin Mary,*
- *Mary proclaimed the Mother of the Church,*
- *etc.*

The repression of biblical authority and its impact upon human history to aid in the development of human culture during the era of the time of Jacob's Trouble

In accentuating the movement of the Roman Catholic Church toward its goal of ruling over the world, the Roman Catholic Church adopted the practice of insisting that the Roman Catholic Church magisterium be the sole interpreter of the biblical message. Intrinsic within this practice was the prohibition against freedom of conscience which is required for the total suppression of basic human rights.

Throughout its history, the Roman Catholic Church has suppressed the authentic biblical message. For example, Jerome compiled the Latin translations of the various books of the Bible, into the Latin Vulgate, which was edited to be acceptable to the Roman empire, suppressing portions of the actual biblical message deemed to be offensive. Throughout the centuries, until after the crowning of Charlemagne as the first Holy Roman Emperor (800), copies of the Bible were rare.

Priests were elected to office by their local communities, based upon popularity and not based upon the priests' quality of understanding upon the God of the Bible.

In 1215, Innocent III (fl. 1198 to 1216), annulled the Magna Carta and issued a law commanding that 'they shall be seized for trial and penalties, who engage in the translation of the sacred volumes, or who hold secret conventicles, or who assume the office of preaching without the authority of their superiors; against whom process shall be commenced, without any permission of appeal.' J.P. Callender, *Illustrations of Popery* 1838, p. 387.

Innocent III 'declared that as by the old law, the beast touching the holy mount was to be stoned to death, so simple and uneducated men were not to touch the Bible or venture to preach its doctrines.' Schaff, *History of the Christian Church*, VI, p. 723.

In 1229, the Council of Toulouse forbade the laity to possess or read the vernacular translations of the Bible (Allix, Ecclesiastical History, II, p. 213). Each parish assigned a search team of one priest and two or three others, who would search each home to find the forbidden Bibles.

The Roman Catholic Church's Inquisitions also determined that Bible reading and Bible possession were authentic offenses.

Leo X (fl. 1513 to 1521) determined in the fifth Lateran Council (1513 to 1517) that no one should be allowed to print any book or writing without a previous examination by the papal vicar and master of the sacred palace in Rome.

The Council of Trent (1546) determined that restrictions should be placed upon translations of the Bible into languages such as German, Spanish and English, and forbade people to read the Bible without a license from a Roman Catholic bishop or inquisitor. It was also unlawful for anyone to print, sell or have in their possession, a Bible, without a license.

Following the Council of Trent decision, Clement VIII (fl. 1592 to 1605) then forbade licenses be granted for reading the Bible under any conditions.

Benedict XIV (fl. 1740 to 1758) confirmed the Council of Trent's proclamations against Bible translations.

Pius VII (fl. 1800 to 1823) considered the distribution of the Bible to be an undermining of religion, 'a pestilence,' in need of remedy, a practice to be abolished, and 'a defilement of the faith, eminently dangerous to souls.'

Leo XII (fl. 1823 to 1829) issued a papal bull *Quid divina sapiential / what divine wisdom* on May 3, 1824 and stated 'If the sacred scriptures be everywhere indiscriminately published, more evil than advantage will arise thence, on account of the rashness of men.' Leo XII included the Bible in the *Index of Prohibited Books*.

Gregory XVI (fl. 1831 to 1846) forbade the free distribution of the Bible (May 8, 1844).

Pius IX (fl. 1846 to 1878), was pope as the region of Italy was unified into the current nation of Italy. It was at that time that the Roman Catholic Church lost possession of its properties and the pope became prisoner on Vatican Hill. Pius IX also presided over the First Vatican Council (1870) that declared the doctrine of papal infallibility which authorized popes' declarations to be assumed to be greater than the declarations of scripture.

Pius IX determined that Bible societies that distributed Bibles were 'renewing the crafts of the ancient heretics,' by distributing to 'all kinds of men, even the least instructed, gratuitously and at immense expense, copies of vast numbers of the books of the Sacred Scriptures translated against the holiest rules of the Church into various vulgar tongues...'

In the absence of biblical guidance, much of the apostolic tradition was redefined by the Roman Catholic Church to support the hierarchy's stance on several issues. This redefinition of the early apostolic church was deliberately manufactured fraud. Counterfeit doctrines became so interwoven into Roman Catholic Church practice that even where the ruse was exposed, the hierarchy of the Roman Catholic Church during its entire history, has refrained from returning to the authentic base established with the early apostolic church. Pius IX (fl. 1846 to 1878) used this fraudulent history to build his case for establishing papal infallibility as an official dogma at the First Vatican Council (1869 to 1870 / 1960).

Papal infallibility was the dogma established, at the same time that the nation of Italy was experiencing its *unification. Papal infallibility decreed that the pope is infallible when he decrees a teaching on faith or morals that is recognized by the universal church to be true, or when he ratifies the work of a church council.*

But what the 'universal church' determined to be true, still remains able to be interpreted with a diversity of interpretations.

Translators of the biblical text into the common language of the people, and their supporters, were persecuted, tortured and killed, with their translations forbidden to be read (i.e., Peter Waldo (c. 1140 to c. 1205), John Wycliffe (c. 1328 to 1384), John Huss / Jan Huss (c. 1369 to 1415), William Tyndale (c. 1494 to 1536), Martin Luther (1483 to 1546), Patrick Hamilton (c. 1504 to 1528), Louis de Berquin (c. 1490 to 1529), Pierre Chapot (to 1546), etc.

The Roman Catholic Church's stance on forbidding Bible distribution, possession and reading was not relaxed until the Second Vatican Council (1962 to 1965). One of the outcomes of the Second Vatican Council (1962 to 1965) was the development of the Code of Canon Law, which lifted some of the past oppressive practices, but maintained the dominance of the teachings of church representatives over the authority of the biblical record.

'Christ's faithful, conscious of their own responsibility, are bound by Christian obedience to follow what the sacred pastors, as representatives of Christ, declare as teachers of the faith or determine as leaders of the Church.' Cannon 212 §1.

Currently, there are many Protestant church denominations that have joined with the Roman Catholic Church hierarchy in sharing the opinion that the Bible is anathema. After the pattern of the Roman Catholic Church, some churches have determined that only portions of the biblical text should be read or considered to be valid. Some churches have reinterpreted biblical information in order to fit into personal agendas. Some churches have determined that all biblical text is worthy to be ignored.

But the apostles taught that the entire composition of the biblical text needs to be incorporated, in order to arrive at an appropriate and right theology.

In the presence of God and of Christ Jesus, who will judge the living and the dead, and in view of his appearing and his kingdom, I give you this charge: Preach the word. Be prepared in season and out of season. Correct, rebuke and encourage — with great patience and careful instruction.

For the time will come when people will not put up with sound doctrine. Instead, to suit their own desires, they will gather around them a great number of teachers to say what their itching ears want to hear. They will turn their ears away from the truth and turn aside to myths.

But you, keep your head in all situations, endure hardship, do the work of an evangelist, discharge all the duties of your ministry. 2 Timothy 4:1-5

The Bible was never as important as it is today. The Bible has never been better distributed and available than it is today. And the biblical message has never been more vital and applicable than it will be during the era of the time of Jacob's Trouble. The entire biblical message points to the full establishment of the kingdom of heaven on earth that will be fully realized at the conclusion of the era of the time of Jacob's Trouble. And the entire biblical record provided a plethora of details for what will take place during the era of the time of Jacob's Trouble to bring the transition of kingdoms into a reality.

During the era of the time of Jacob's Trouble, distributing, possessing and reading the Bible may again become illegal, and a validation for the future version of Inquisition to practice martyring those who believe in the biblical message. It may be that the implementation of the mark of the beast(s) system will incorporate the repression of the Bible (Revelation 13:14-18). And the reason for the Bible's illegality will be because the biblical record identified methods for opposing the nefarious plan of the red dragon / serpent / Satan, Inc. for annihilating all of humanity.

Jesus said, 'If those days had not been shortened, no one would have survived. But because of the elect, the days will be shortened.' Matthew 24:22 translated *(Mark 13:20)*

Papal kingdom building and its foundation for the global religious community during the era of the time of Jacob's Trouble

Possibly the best examples of the influence of papal kingdom building took place after the spark of the Protestant Reformation had been ignited on October 31, 1517. A series of events took place that pitted the power of the papal office of the Roman Catholic Church, against those who protested the power of the Roman Catholic Church to hold reign.

Some dramatic examples of the conflict between the power of nations and the power of the Roman Catholic Church, took place in France and in England, with the influence of Spain.

Even though the events took place after the historical era of the church of Thyatira was ebbing, they were just some of the events that demonstrated the heart of the Roman Catholic Church's determination to expand its empire and to hold rule over the kings of the earth (Revelation 17:18).

In France:

Leo X (fl. 1513 to 1521) / Giovanni di Lorenzo de' Medici, arranged the marriage of Lorenzo de' Medici who was the Duke of Urbino, and Madeleine de La Tour d'Auvergne as part of the alliance between Leo X and the king of France Francis I (fl. 1515 to 1547), against the Holy Roman Emperor Maximilian I (fl. 1508 to 1519) from Portugal. Lorenzo and Madeleine became the parents of Catherine de' Medici.

Catherine de' Medici (1519 to 1589) / Caterina Maria Romula de' Medici, was born a Florentine Italian into the powerful and wealthy Medici family. Catherine's marriage was arranged by her uncle who was pope, Clement VII (fl. 1523 to 1534) / Giulio di Giuliano de' Medici. Her marriage to the king of France, Henry II (fl. 1547 to 1559) took place in 1533 when they were both fourteen years old. As Queen consort and later as Queen mother, Catherine de' Medici reigned in France (fl. 1547 to 1563). Catherine became the mother of the French kings Francis II, Charles IX and

Henry III. During her tenure, Catherine held powerful influence over the political life of France.

As the Protestant Reformation gained popularity, the severely Roman Catholic Catherine de' Medici conflicted with the Huguenots / French Protestants living generally in eastern France.

Catherine de' Medici and her son Charles IX (fl. 1560 to 1574), arranged for the marriage of their Roman Catholic daughter and sister Margaret of Valois, to the Protestant Henry of Navarre who would later reign as king of France.

Henry Navarre / Henry IV (France) / Henry III (Navarre) (fl. 1589 to 1610) was known as Good King Henry and Henry the Great.

The wedding took place in Paris on August 18, 1572 on the parvis in front of Notre Dame Cathedral. Five days later, the St. Bartholomew's Day massacre began. Several thousand Protestants had come to Paris for Henry's wedding, and they became the first victims of Charles IX and the Catholic League. Henry himself narrowly escaped death with the aid of his wife Margaret, under the promise to convert to Catholicism. Henry then became a prisoner of the French court until he escaped in 1576.

The St. Bartholomew's Day massacre expanded into the countryside and the slaughter continued for several weeks. Estimates of five to thirty thousand people were massacred. The Huguenot political movement was crippled by the loss of many of its prominent aristocratic leaders. But the event 'printed upon Protestant minds the indelible conviction that Catholicism was a bloody and treacherous religion.' Henry Chadwick and G. R. Evans, *Atlas of the Christian church,* Macmillan, 1987.

In England:

The Wars of the Roses (1455 to 1487) / civil wars, were fought to determine control over the English throne. The House of Lancaster (represented by the red rose) and the House of York (represented by the white rose) finally ended their dispute when Henry VII of the House of Lancaster married Elizabeth of York, merging the two families into the House of Tudor. The House of Tudor also had a rose, red on the outside, white in the center.

Henry VII (fl. 1485 to 1509) and Elizabeth of York had seven children. Of their children, Henry VIII became king of England, Margaret became Queen of Scotland, and Mary briefly became Queen of France.

When Henry VIII (fl. 1509 to 1547) was not able to produce a male heir through his first marriage to Catherine of Aragon (m. 1509 to 1533), Henry VIII sought to obtain an annulment of their marriage. While divorces and annulments of most people were granted through the governments of which the divorcees were citizens, the divorces and annulments of the marriages of monarchs were granted through the papal office of the Roman Catholic Church with the permission of the pope.

Catherine's Spanish nephew, Charles V (1500 to 1558), had inherited domains from all four of his grandparents, making him possibly the most powerful man in Europe at the time. Charles V was Lord of the Netherlands and Duke of Burgundy (1506 to 1555), king of Spain (Castile and Aragon (1516 to 1556)), Archduke of Austria (1519 to 1521), and Holy Roman Emperor (Germany and Italy (1519 to 1556)). Charles V's childhood tutor, Adrian of Utrecht / Adrian VI (fl. 1522 to 1523) went on to become pope for twenty months, following Leo X (fl. 1513 to 1521) and preceding Clement VII (fl. 1523 to 1534).

Charles V was opposed to the annulment of the marriage of his aunt Catherine from Henry VIII. And because Charles V provided military support to the papal office, Clement VII (fl. 1523 to 1534) refused to grant an annulment of their marriage. The inability for Henry VIII to obtain a legal separation from Catherine, fueled the advancement of the establishment of Protestantism in England.

The Roman Catholic Church's influence in the lives of the monarchs of France, England and Spain, and in the lives of the citizens of Florence, was merely an example of the influence that the Roman Catholic Church exercised around the world.

The power and authority that the Roman Catholic Church exercised at the beginning of the Protestant Reformation (1517f) was extensive and global. A substantial Roman Catholic Church presence was established on the continent of South America.

With the formation of the Society of Jesus / Jesuits (1540 to present), the development of the Roman Catholic Church's Inquisitions was advanced to new levels. Jesuits became personal confessors to monarchs and people of power in most nations. The Society of Jesus / Jesuits developed a great spy network (supplying the OSS / CIA (World War II) with much information). The Society of Jesus / Jesuits also established colleges and universities tasked with teaching Jesuit ideals. And the Vatican formally established its interstellar research which advances evolutionary theory as a replacement for creation theology.

The understanding that developed in the North American colonies that preceded the establishment of the United States as a nation, was that there should be a distinction between the power of the church as a ruling body and the power of the government of the people, by the people and for the people. In the colonies, filled with colonists that sought to flee the religious tyranny of the Old World and the Protestant Reformation wars, it was difficult to image that nations would abdicate so much power to the Roman Catholic Church.

On a personal note, my ancestors were established in the colony of New Amsterdam by 1600. Their genealogical history stated that the motivation for moving to America was, 'to flee the religious tyranny of the Old World.'

While members of the Roman Catholic Church opposed the advancement of Adolf Hitler during World War II (1938 to 1945), the Vatican's Cardinal Secretary of State Eugenio Pacelli (later Pius XII (f. 1939 to 1958)) negotiated the Reichskonkordat (concordat between the Roman Catholic Church and the German Reich, 1933), on behalf of Pius XI (fl. 1922 to 1939).

The global influence that the Roman Catholic Church held during the sixteenth century, was put on pause through the work of the Protestant Reformation.

However, as the Protestant Reformation lost its vision and dedication to the authentic faith system as established in the full biblical record, the opportunity for the Roman empire's mission of establishing global dominance, will again be invigorated through the hierarchy of the Roman Catholic Church.

Understanding history as a series of events that have been woven together to impact the future, provides a methodology for understanding the scheduled events of prophecy.

Prophecy is future history that has not taken place yet.

Riding on a Ferris wheel provides a different perspective of the landscape below, with every second providing a unique depiction of the space.

Every second looking out of the window of a moving airplane, provides a different perspective.

In the six thousand years of human history, every moment has provided a new understanding to how God Most High acts. And understanding why God Most High has specifically acted in the past, provides understanding for the purpose and goals of the scheduled events of the era of the time of Jacob's Trouble.

The church was once recognized as one church, the Roman Catholic Church. The hierarchy of the Roman Catholic Church continues to hold the paradigm that all churches that have been daughtered out of the Roman Catholic Church, will come together again under Roman Catholic Church rule. And the hierarchy of the Roman Catholic Church continues to pursue its mission through the Society of Jesus / Jesuits, of establishing global papal rule over all peoples, multitudes, nations and languages (Revelation 17, 13). Toward this goal, the current pope Francis (fl. 2013 to present) continues to raise the Vatican's diplomatic clout.

As the scheduled events of the era of the time of Jacob's Trouble occur, the foundation that was laid by the theology of the historical era of the church of Thyatira, will continue to exert its influence upon history and prophecy.

Preparatory work during the historical era of the church of Thyatira for the Renaissance, Protestant Reformation, and the historical era of the church of Sardis

During the Dark Ages / Middle Ages / medieval period, for a person living in a region where the Roman Catholic Church reigned, to choose to not participate in the rituals of the Roman Catholic Church, resulted in significant consequences. To resist or refrain from the practice of indulgences, penance, sacraments, etc. meant possibly being accused of being a heretic. Those accused of heresy, would be met with torture, death, or worse, excommunication which meant there would be no opportunity to enter heaven.

During the Dark Ages / Middle Ages / medieval period, ignorance, superstition, fear, etc., overrode the opportunity to pursue biblical knowledge, truth, love, etc.

The power of the papacy would repeatedly cycle through waves of increasing and decreasing power during the millennium of the Dark Ages / Middle Ages / medieval period. Always the Roman Catholic Church remained focused on the act of exerting power as having precedence over the activity of caring for people.

But occasionally during the Dark Ages / Middle Ages / medieval period, there was injected into the history of the Roman Catholic Church, some who brought reform.

On December 25, 800 AD, Charlemagne / Charles the Great, king of the Franks and the Lombards, became the first to be crowned 'Holy Roman Emperor.' The Holy Roman Emperor was neither holy nor Roman.

In the crowning of Charlemagne as Holy Roman Emperor, there was a transfer of a segment of power from centering on the Roman empire to resting with the Germans. The leopard beast with its four heads described in Daniel 7, began its next phase of prophecy fulfillment. Each of the leopard beast's four heads represented an era of reign. The third reign, third reich, was lived out with the rise and reign of Adolph Hitler, prior to and during World War II.

Using the position of Holy Roman Emperor, Charlemagne brought some corrective measures to the Roman Catholic Church. Charlemagne was opposed to the use of magic. Charlemagne declared that all who practiced sorcery or divination would become slaves to the Church and that all those who sacrificed to the devil or to the Germanic gods would be executed. This decision marked the beginning of the decline in the use of baal / mystery / mythology religious practices, but not their extinction within the church. It is amazing that Charlemagne, with his limited reading and writing ability, would have the insight to understand the destructiveness of the magical arts and other similar rites and rituals.

Charlemagne also sponsored the copying of biblical and theological manuscripts and made them available to local churches. Charlemagne brought reforms and integrity to government and to trade, requiring government officials and merchants to give accounts for their work. Charlemagne initiated educational reform and encouraged education to be made available throughout his kingdom and to all classes of people. Many believe that it is because of the foundational work of Charlemagne that the Renaissance became a possibility.

Charlemagne's dark side was expressed in his missionary work. Charlemagne enlarged the church by forcibly conquering people and then coercing them to either make a commitment to the Roman Catholic Church or to go and meet their god immediately. Charlemagne's bloody methods for church growth were completely alien to the true gospel of Jesus Christ. But students of church history also must wonder if the church would have survived without Charlemagne.

John Wycliffe, Oxford professor and theologian, was the first to translate the New Testament into English (1380 AD) to '...help Christian men to study the Gospel in that tongue in which they know best Christ's sentence.' For this 'heresy' Wycliffe was posthumously condemned by Arundel, the archbishop of Canterbury. By the Council's decree 'Wycliffe's bones were exhumed and publicly burned and the ashes were thrown into the Swift River.'

Martin Luther, a German Augustinian priest, had begun translating the Bible into German.
In 1517 AD, the 'evils' of the Roman Catholic Church had become so great that the protests for reformation became organized in the Protestant Reformation.

William Tyndale translated the Bible into English (1536 AD). Tyndale accomplished his translation in an era when the Roman Catholic Church forbid owning or reading the Bible in order to control and restrict the teachings and to enhance their own power and importance of the Roman Catholic Church. Tyndale was burned at the stake.
John Wycliffe, William Tyndale and others were sowing the seeds for the coming reformation of theological teaching.

Around 1517 the Protestant Reformation became a movement to be addressed. The Bible was translated into the languages that the people spoke and was copied with the printing press. When the people read this new literature, the people discovered the liberties that the Roman Catholic Church religious leaders had taken to use religion to manipulate and to abusively rule over people.
The Protestant Reformation consisted of people who eventually left the Roman Catholic Church to join other movements and church denominations. Immediately after the Protestant Reformation formally began (~October 31, 1517), the Counter Reformation was seeded within the Roman Catholic Church.
The Counter Reformation initiated the opportunity for more theological diversity to exist within the Roman Catholic Church.
Some remained devoted to the theology of the Blessed Virgin Mary as the Queen of Heaven and other dogmas, doctrines, theologies and practices that were not

advocated by the biblical record. Some remained devoted to magic, sorcery, or the occult.

But the counter reformation caused some within the Roman Catholic Church, to became devoted to scriptural authority, recognizing the divinity and lordship of Jesus Christ in a way that was similar to the view of many Protestants.

The resulting theological upheaval provided an opportunity for all to reevaluate Roman Catholic Church dogmas, doctrines, theologies and practices, what constituted the way of salvation, and the path to dynamic and effective relationship with God.

Jesus Christ's message for the era of the time of Jacob's Trouble from the message to the angel of the ruling church of Thyatira

Because the Roman Catholic Church was formed with the merging of two theological rivers, elements of both true authentic Christianity as well as the baal / mystery / mythology religion have survived throughout history within the Roman Catholic Church.

From the time of the edict of Thessalonica on February 27, 380 AD, throughout history to today, parishioners can find elements of both the baal / mystery / mythology of the ancient past, as well as the biblical presentation of authentic Christian faith, merged into the church's teachings.

But, from the Roman Catholic Church perspective, the Dark Ages / Middle Ages / medieval period was not considered dark. The rationale of the modern Roman Catholic Church is to view the church of the Dark Ages / Middle Ages / medieval period as an era where the Roman Catholic Church stepped in where there did not seem to be any rule, to provide leadership. They supplied order and a hierarchical structure to the uneducated and unworthy masses, assessing the uneducated and unworthy masses with the value that the Roman Catholic Church deemed they should have.

During the era of the time of Jacob's Trouble, the global religious community founded upon the history of the Roman Catholic Church, will again step in with the offer to *rule the uneducated and unworthy masses of people, along with the educated masses of people.*

Jesus Christ's message to those who have true faith as followers of the Lamb / Jesus Christ, within the historical timeline church of Thyatira was to 'hold onto what you have until I come.' *Jesus communicated that there is something that remains even within the Roman Catholic Church and all churches, that remains worthy for Jesus Christ to return for. There are still those within the Roman Catholic Church who maintain a true faith in Jesus Christ as messiah.*

But Jesus Christ's message to those that continue to embrace the aspects of the baal / mystery / mythology religion, inherent within the constitution of the Roman Catholic Church and other churches, was not pleasant.
That portion of the church that developed the dogmas, doctrines, theologies and practices established with the church of the Dark Ages / Middle Ages / medieval period, severely fell short of meeting Jesus Christ's expectations.
From Revelation 2:18-29, Jesus Christ said: 'But I have this against you. You tolerate the woman Jezebel, the one calling herself a prophetess, …' Revelation 2:20a translated
Jesus Christ determined that there is no difference between the practices of Jezebel and the practices of those who claim to be prophets in the historical era of the church of Thyatiran theology. In the same way that Jezebel fostered the practices of the baal / mystery / mythology religion in Israel, the religious leaders of the Roman Catholic Church fostered the practices of the baal / mystery / mythology religion for infiltration into the church.
Jesus said: '…By her teaching she misleads my servants into sexual immorality and the eating of food sacrificed to idols.' Revelation 2:20b
Jesus Christ's reference to sexual immorality was both a literal and symbolic assessment of the historical era of the church of Thyatira. Not only have the religious leaders of the Roman Catholic Church and many

subsequent churches, practiced and taught sexual immorality as good and wholesome activity, they continue to practice sexual immorality even today. Even more significantly, Jesus Christ's concern also included those upon whom the teaching and practice of spiritual immorality was used against, those Jesus Christ called his servants, those who belong to Jesus Christ.

During the era of the time of Jacob's Trouble, the Roman Catholic Church, along with other churches, will continue to loosen its stance on supporting God Most High's rules for appropriate sexual activity. They will engage in the many horrific practices that Jezebel fostered in the northern nation of Israel.

Jesus said: 'I have given her time to repent of her immorality, but she is unwilling. So, I will cast her on a bed of suffering, and I will make those who commit adultery with her suffer intensely, unless they repent of her ways.' Revelation 20:21

During the era of the time of Jacob's Trouble, the Roman Catholic Church, along with other churches, will attempt to compel the inhabitants of the earth, the people of Israel and the followers of the Lamb / Jesus Christ to engage in the form of worship modeled by Semiramis and Jezebel, including the compulsory worship of the image of the beast of the sea. (Revelation 12, 13, etc.)

Jesus Christ provided the Roman Catholic Church with time to repent. If the Protestant Reformation was the wakeup call provided by God Most High to the Roman Catholic Church, then the Roman Catholic Church has had over five hundred years to repent.

Instead, the historical trend has been for the Roman Catholic Church to double its efforts in its already established track of rebelling against the requirements of God Most High as documented in the biblical record. The Roman Catholic Church just continued to repeatedly repackage itself, in preparation for its final great era of activity, scheduled for the era of the time of Jacob's Trouble.

When Jesus Christ said, 'And her children, I will kill with death.' Revelation 2:23a translated

'Her children' *were the Roman Catholic Church's societies and orders, and those Protestant churches that will return to the Roman Catholic Church umbrella and will embrace the traditions of the baal / mystery / mythology religion remaining within the Roman Catholic Church practice.*

Jesus Christ determined that those that follow their practices, will be stricken dead.

Jesus said: 'Then all the churches will know that I am the One who searches hearts and minds, and I will repay each of you according to your deeds.' Revelation 2:23b

While the papal office claimed the title 'Vicar of Christ' and believed that the pope is ultimately the head of every church throughout the world regardless of the church's connection or disconnection with Rome, Jesus Christ was clear that it is Jesus Christ who is the only One who possesses the power and ability to search hearts and minds. Jesus Christ is determined to exercise his power and ability and to search hearts and minds.

Contrary to the belief of religious leaders, Jesus Christ has the power and will to act, to rectify, to avenge. Jesus Christ will repay each person according to the kingdom choice they have invested in.

In the economy of the Roman Catholic Church and various other churches, righteousness is determined by one's 'deeds' / 'works.' But Jesus Christ employed a different economy and based righteousness upon one's love and faith.

Jesus Christ determined that the economy that one employs will be the economy that one will be judged by. Concerning the Roman Catholic Church and various other churches, Jesus Christ determined that the standard that will be employed to judge them will be the same standard of 'deeds' / 'works.' They will receive their repayment, paid 'according to deeds' *because they rejected the manner in which Jesus Christ extends forgiveness.*

Jesus Christ also recognized the power of religious organizations to carry individuals to places that they did

not desire or deserve to go. For example, Jesus Christ was taken to the cross by the Israelite religious ruling organization, the Sanhedrin. So, Jesus Christ's message of encouragement for those swept into the power of the religious organization against their will, was a message that communicated Jesus Christ's determination to bring a glorious response to those who overcome the coercion and destruction of the church, church communities, and the world.

'To you however, and to the rest in Thyatira, I say, as many as do not have this teaching, who have not known the depths of Satan, as they say, 'I will not cast any other burden upon you. But hold fast to what you have until I come."

'To the one who overcomes and keeps my works until the end, I will give that one the authority over the nations, and that one will shepherd them with power over the nations: 'He will shepherd them with a rod of iron, as the vessels of the potter are broken in pieces.' Just as I have received from my father. And I will give to that one the morning star.'

'To the one having an ear, hear what the Spirit says to the churches.' Revelation 2:24-29 translated

Jesus Christ's message to the angel of the church of Thyatira, identified that within the Roman Catholic Church and other similar churches, there remains those who can and should reject the teachings of Jezebel, Satan's so called deep secrets, etc. For those that remain faithful to following the Lamb / Jesus Christ, Jesus Christ recognized that their struggle, their burden has been enough to bear. Within the Roman Catholic Church and other similar churches, the followers of the Lamb / Jesus Christ, only need to hold on to what they have until Jesus Christ returns. (Revelation 2:24-25)

John the Revelator understood in Jesus Christ's message to the angels of the seven churches, that Jesus Christ foretold the status and character of each historical era of the church in the historical timeline beginning from the time of Jesus Christ's ascension into heaven, until Jesus Christ's return (Revelation 2, 3).

Jesus Christ's message as a whole, was directed to all churches, with sections of the message specifically directed to the specific eras of church history.

Jesus Christ's message to the angels of the seven churches demonstrated that the historical eras represented by the last five of the seven churches, would experience a comingling together in time, with coexistence and overlap. The followers of the Lamb / Jesus Christ, in the last five of the churches, were given the direction to overcome, to be victorious, <u>until Jesus Christ returns</u>. This fact indicated that all the last five of the seven historical church eras, will extend until the time when Jesus Christ returns.

The continuation of the historical eras of the churches until Jesus Christ returns, was also a model for the opening of the seven seals whose dynamics will share interaction and overlap in their events. (Revelation 6, etc.)

This overlap in time for the historical eras of the churches, also recognized the influence that the predominate theology of each historical era, would have upon the theologies of the other historical eras. A specific example was the legacy of the historical era of the church of Pergamum, that was extended to the daughter / historical era of the church of Thyatira.

The Roman Catholic Church will become the foundation for the global religious community. Currently, the Roman Catholic Church is active in its initiative to welcome back Protestant churches, 'the daughters' of 'Jezebel' that are willing to concede to the theologies and power structure of the Roman Catholic Church. Not only are Protestant churches being encouraged to reunite with the Roman Catholic Church, but the current pope, Francis, and the Vatican are forming relationships with a host of other religious organizations and various other religions. The ultimate goal is to forge a worldwide religious organization that incorporates the entire world and world population using religion as glue, and to establish an even greater and more powerful Roman Catholic Church / global religious community. With this centralized power base, the global religious community will attempt to finally realize the Roman Catholic Church's dream of being able to govern the world under papal rule. Establishing papal rule is one of the goals of both the hierarchy of the Roman Catholic Church and the Jesuits who take the vow during their initiation into the Jesuit Order / Society of Jesus, to pursue and destroy Protestants and others they consider to be heretics. The current pope, Francis, is the Roman Catholic Church's first Jesuit pope. This is the optimal arrangement for pursuing the full establishment of the ultimate power kingdom.

Satan offered the opportunity to Jesus Christ, to hold leadership in the kingdom of Satan, Inc. / kingdom of man, when Satan tempted Jesus Christ in the wilderness at the very beginning of Jesus Christ's earthly ministry (Matthew 4:1-11, Luke 4:1-13, Hebrews 4:15). To accept Satan's offer would have necessitated Jesus Christ abandoning the love economy of the kingdom of heaven, forever. Jesus Christ turned down Satan's offer to be a ruler in the kingdom of Satan, Inc. / kingdom of man.

But the two beasts of Revelation 13, have already accepted Satan's offer to be rulers in his kingdom of Satan, Inc. / kingdom of man (Revelation 12, 13, etc.). And the two beasts of Revelation 13 will both rule using their religious backgrounds as a launching point.

National boundaries limit nations to regions. But religion transcends national boundaries. And the Roman Catholic Church has been established and colonized in almost every nation of the world, making the Roman Catholic Church the natural foundation for the rise of the global religious community / great prostitute / Mystery Babylon the Great!, for supporting the influence of the Jewish religion upon the temple mount and among the people of Israel, for the rise of the two beasts of Revelation 13, 17, etc., for the establishment of global governance, for the installation of the global economic structure, and for the tyrannical influence of the global cultural theoterrorism movement.

Jesus Christ's message to the angels of the churches of Asia documented that all church communities have shared in laying a foundation for the dynamics necessary for the events of the era of the time of Jacob's Trouble to occur. That included the historical era church of Thyatira.

    Long before 1500 AD, Europe had been Christianized. But that did not make most aspects of European worldview align with the biblical understanding of Christianity. Portions of the biblical view of authentic Christianity, were buried under Europe's pre-Christian paganism previously established by the Greco-Roman cosmological worldview and the Islamic fatalism. In medieval Christendom, fear, worship of the spirits, demigods, and other miscellaneous elements of the baal / mystery / mythology religion continued in the form of fear of spirits, prayers to the holy ones and angels, idol worship and iconography, etc. Rebellious angels accept and crave worship. Holy angels do not.

    John the Revelator described the global religious community and the beast of the sea / false prophet / eighth king beast that is the head of the global religious community, throughout the book of Revelation, but especially in Revelation 17. The global religious community / great prostitute, sits upon the beast with the seven / eight heads. The seven heads with seven crowns, were first depicted by John the Revelator, in association with the red dragon / serpent / Satan, Inc. in Revelation 12. The descriptions of the seven heads associated with the red dragon / serpent / Satan (Revelation 12), and the beast of the sea (Revelation 13) and the scarlet beast (Revelation 17), identified the beast of the sea / beast from the Abyss / eighth king beast as definitely belonging to the kingdom of Satan, Inc. / kingdom of man, and a leader of the enemies of God Most High and of the kingdom of heaven.

    During the era of the time of Jacob's Trouble, it will be the red dragon / serpent / Satan, Inc. that will empower both beasts of Revelation 13, and consequently provide direction to the global religious community and the global governance system.

    In Revelation 17, the vision that John the Revelator received included the description of the great prostitute (baal / mystery / mythology religion), that sat upon the *scarlet beast with the seven / eight heads (Roman Catholic Church and other churches aligned with the Roman Catholic Church).*

In that description, the great prostitute was also titled 'Mystery Babylon the Great! the mother of prostitutes and of the abominations of the earth.'

The 'mother of prostitutes' must have daughters without legitimate fathers. This mother is also the mother of the abominations of the earth.

The first man / Adam, named the first woman / Eve because she was the mother of all living humanity.

But the great prostitute / mother of prostitutes and of the abominations of the earth, Jesus Christ holds responsible for all abominations throughout history.

The Roman Catholic Church has not existed throughout history. But, antediluvian / preflood version of the baal / mystery / mythology religion that began in the Garden of Eden with the eating of the fruit of the tree of the knowledge of good and evil (mystery knowledge), grew during the antediluvian / preflood era and was reinitiated after the deluge / flood with Ham, Canaan, Cush and Nimrod. It was this baal / mystery / mythology religion that has infiltrated and will finally completely overcome the leadership of the Roman Catholic Church and what will be the core and foundational theology for the global religious community. During the era of the time of Jacob's Trouble, God Most High will have nothing left to say to her except,

> Then I heard another voice from heaven say:
> "Come out of her, my people,' so that you will not share in her sins, so that you will not receive any of her plagues. For her sins are piled up to heaven, and God has remembered her crimes.' Revelation 18:4-5 translated

While the Roman Catholic Church has been the receptacle for housing authentic Christianity since 380 AD, the Roman Catholic Church has also harbored the dogmas, doctrines, theologies and practices of baal / mystery / mythology religion. And for allowing the offenses that have resulted from harboring the baal / mystery /

mythology religion, God Most High has remembered her crimes.

As the date for the return of messiah / the Lamb / Jesus Christ draws closer in time, the Roman Catholic Church's dogmas, doctrines, theologies and practices have drawn the hierarchy of the Roman Catholic Church closer to the kingdom of Satan, Inc. / kingdom of man.

A part of the Second Vatican Council's legislation was to develop a constitution for the Roman Catholic Church. A part of that legislation, the Lumen Gentium / 'Light of the Nations' (November 21, 1964), was fully focused on reiterating that the opportunity for people to enter heaven, according to the Roman Catholic Church, is not possible unless individuals become members of the Roman Catholic Church. Through baptism into the Roman Catholic Church, the initiate places themselves under the rule of the Roman Catholic Church (not under the authority of the God of heaven). By adopting the doctrine that the Roman Catholic Church controls entrance into heaven, the Roman Catholic Church assumes the role of also controlling earth and continues to pursue the goal of total world domination.

During the era of the time of Jacob's Trouble the questions being decided will be, 'Who will rule the earth? Who will have authority over the nations? Which kingdom will be more powerful and able to be fully established? Which God will be supreme? Which kingdom will be everlasting?'

While the global religious community itself will be unable to be reconciled with God Most High, the global religious community will continue to have authentic followers of the Lamb / Jesus Christ within its organization even until just a few weeks before Jesus Christ returns. It may be that the global religious community will practice its abominations until the coming of Jesus Christ.

In Jesus Christ's revelation provided to John the Revelator, Jesus Christ described the attitude of the great prostitute / Mystery Babylon the Great! And then Jesus Christ depicted the destruction of the great prostitute /

Mystery Babylon the Great! on the day of the final battle of this age.

> 'As much as she has glorified herself and lived in luxury; give to her as much torment and misery, because in her heart she says,'
> > "I sit as a queen, and I am never a widow. I will never mourn."
>
> 'Therefore, in one day her plagues will overtake her. Death, mourning and famine. She will be consumed by fire, because mighty is the Lord God who judges her.'
> Revelation 18:7-8 translated

The woman who rides the scarlet beast with the seven / eight heads, was referred to as 'the harlot' because she was not a bride. She was never betrothed to the bridegroom / messiah / the Lamb / Jesus Christ. She never entered into a marriage covenant relationship with Jesus Christ.

And she can never be a widow because she was never betrothed or married.

She holds not claim upon any throne. And yet she believes that she is the queen of her kingdom. Because she has no covenant relationship with Jesus Christ, she will not be sharing the throne with Jesus Christ. Consequently, her kingdom cannot be the kingdom of heaven. Her kingdom can only be the kingdom of Satan, Inc. / kingdom of man.

Because Jesus Christ will be returning to fully establish the kingdom of heaven on earth, Jesus Christ will be defeating her kingdom, the kingdom of Satan, Inc. / kingdom of man. So, just before Jesus Christ returns, it will seem as if the great prostitute / Mystery Babylon the Great! will have finally established her kingdom, and she will seem to have finally attained the status of queen. But when Jesus Christ defeats her kingdom, her short lived reign as queen will be over.

When Jesus Christ fully establishes his kingdom on earth, there will be no place for the great prostitute except to be thrown out. The woman who rides this beast will not be invited to the wedding feast known as the 'wedding supper of the Lamb.'

Jesus Christ's message to the angel of the church at Sardis: reformation church – Revelation 3:1-6

Church of Sardis – incomplete and unfinished church

Jesus said, 'To the angel of the church of Sardis, write,

'This is the message from the one having the seven Spirits of God, and the seven stars.'

'I know your deeds, that you have the characterization that you are alive. But you are dead.'

'Be watching and strengthen the things that remain, which are about to die. For I have not found your works to be completed in the sight of my God. Therefore, remember what you have received and heard. Keep it and repent. Therefore, if you do not watch, I will come like a thief and you will not know at what hour I will come upon you.'

'But you have a few people in Sardis who have not soiled their garments. They will walk with me in white, because they are worthy.'

'The one who overcomes, will be clothed in white garments. And I will not blot out that one's name from the book of life. And I will confess the name of the one who overcomes, before my Father and before my Father's angels.'

'To the one having an ear, hear what the Spirit says to the churches.' Revelation 3:1-6 translated

Jesus Christ desired that the church of Sardis will wake up, before it is too late. And Jesus Christ promised that if they do not awaken, then Jesus Christ's coming will be to them like a thief in the night.

This type of message implied that the church representing the historical era of the church of Sardis will continue until the end of the era of the time of Jacob's Trouble. It must be present in order to be asleep, or awake, when Jesus Christ returns.

Historical message:

Sardis was known for its gold that would wash down from the mountains around the city. Sardis was also known for the coins they minted out of their gold.

Sardis used the legend of Midas to explain their gold. The Sardis legend claimed that Midas came upon a drunken satyr named Silenus who had passed out in his garden. Silenus was believed to be the foster father of the god Dionysus. Midas was kind to Silenus and returned him to the safety of Dionysus in Lydia. As a reward, Dionysus offered Midas his choice of rewards. Midas chose to have everything that he touched turned into gold, but soon discovered that gold is difficult to eat. Realizing that turning things into gold was really a curse, Midas prayed to Dionysus for release. Dionysus' instruction was for Midas to bathe in the Pactolus River. When Midas touched the river, his power passed into the river and the river sands changed into gold.

The city of Sardis was built on the edge of a mountain with three sides guarded by nearly vertical walls that dropped fifteen hundred feet into the valley. The Pactolus River ran along its one open access. The citizens of Sardis believed that the city was impregnatable. Because of their confidence they rarely posted guards on the three sides with the mountain slope.

Yet Sardis was conquered twice.

Around 547 BC, King Croesus of Lydia sent representatives from Sardis to the oracle at Delphi in what is now Greece, in order to gain advice concerning the Persians. The oracle told Croesus, 'If you went to war, a great empire will be destroyed.' Croesus was encouraged and attacked the Persians. The Persian king, Cyrus, forced Croesus to retreat to the city of Sardis.

Cyrus of Persia then attempted a frontal attack that failed. Cyrus offered a reward to any of his soldiers who could solve the problem. Later that night, after watching a soldier of Sardis climb down into a crevice in order to retrieve a helmet, Cyrus sent Persian soldiers up the same crevice and entered the sleeping city like a thief.

The oracle was correct, a great empire was destroyed. But the empire that was destroyed was of Croesus.

Cyrus, king of the Persians, was also the king responsible for releasing the Israelites from their exile so that they could return and reestablish the nation of Israel.

Later, in 215 BC, Antiochus III / Antiochus the Great captured Sardis in a similar way, while the city of Sardis ignored its previous history.

Sardis was a city with an aloof attitude toward finishing projects, both for their protection and in their building projects. Sardis was a wealthy city with a number of uncompleted projects including the temple dedicated to the worship of Artemis / Cybele. Around 27 BC Sardis unsuccessfully attempted to establish Asia's first temple to Caesar Augustus. It was not until 5 BC that Sardis was able to establish their local temple to Augustus; twenty two years after the project began.

Note that ancient temples tended to be about one thousand to two thousand square feet. They were small buildings in comparison to modern structures.

Sardis was a city that was alive, but did not grow or achieve or flourish. They were known for having difficulty in finishing what they would start.

Historical timeline message to the historical era of the church of Sardis:

The name 'Sardis' means 'the escaping one' or 'those who come out.' During the Reformation Period of church history, those who protested the abuses of the Roman Catholic Church and its adulterated theology, 'escaped' from the traditional religious organization. They became known as 'Protestants.'

This is one of those places in the storyline where the reader must understand the distinctions between the Roman Catholic Church, the Protestant churches, and the Roman Catholic Church Counter Reformation as three very different movements, in order to understand the message.

The Roman Catholic Church was the result of the unholy marriage of the faith system of God Most High, with the baal / mystery / mythology religion. There have always been found within the Roman Catholic Church, people who have been authentic followers of the Lamb / Jesus Christ, along with those who have embraced some form of the baal / mystery / mythology religion. Elements of both camps have been on display within the Roman Catholic Church, throughout the centuries.

For example, in Saint Peter's Basilica, there are elements of the baal / mystery / mythology religion throughout the basilica; the sixteen pointed star, the marble statue of Mary holding the crucified Jesus with Mary being enlarged in relationship to the body of Jesus, the halos on the various personages, the crucifix that depicts a dead Jesus still on the cross, etc.

But also in Saint Peter's Basilica are the words of Jesus Christ engraved around the entire circumference of the inside of the basilica, the dove that represents the Holy Spirit, the images of the apostles who preached that Jesus Christ is Lord and we crucified him and God raised him from the dead, etc.

The Protestants that represented the historical era of the church of Sardis, began their protest against the reign of baal / mystery / mythology religion apostasy. But the first Protestants, including John Calvin, Henry VIII (fl. 1509 to 1547) of England, etc., while rejecting the aspects of the baal / mystery / mythology religion, sought to form and shape their new version of church, after their own images. They substituted the authority of the papal office, with their own authority. John Calvin continued to view the leaders of the church as having ecclesiastical authority as representatives of God Most High, merely because they held their religious offices. Henry VIII determined that the ruler of England should be head of the Church of England, in the stead of the pope.

While the early Protestants came out of the Roman Catholic Church, they remained surrounded by paganism, idolatry, and antisemitism. They failed to stand spiritually out in the midst of the darkness. They had the form of religion, but not the full devotion for what makes faith in Jesus Christ, alive.

The theologies of the churches of Pergamum (mixed theology), Thyatira (ruling church / 'daughter'), and Sardis (reformation remix of mixed theology and the daughter of mixed theology), have not left us. They will continue and eventually allow and support the rise of the global religious community / great prostitute that will be shaped by these traditional, historical, politically motivated theologies, that continue the practice of rebellion against God Most High and against Jesus Christ.

Seeded and antagonized by the Roman Catholic Church

In the historical timeline of Revelation 2 and 3, the theology of the church of Sardis was seeded by the theology of the Roman Catholic Church after the Dark Ages / Middle Ages / medieval period.

The historical era of the church of Sardis in the historical timeline, was reactionary to the Roman Catholic Church. And at the same time, the historical era of the church of Sardis, incorporated much of the Roman Catholic Church's dogmas, doctrines, theologies and practices.

The historical era of the church of Sardis on the historical timeline was the church that resulted in the early Protestant Reformation. The spark that was considered to be the beginning of the Protestant Reformation was when the Augustinian priest Martin Luther nailed his letter to the pope, with 95 protests, to the church door in Wittenberg Germany (October 31, 1517).

Approximately two centuries later, a part of the Reformed tradition would embrace the theology of the church of Philadelphia and the Great Awakening / Evangelical Revival.

The Protestant Reformation initially shed many of the elements of the baal / mystery / mythology religion supported by the hierarchy of the Roman Catholic Church.

While the hierarchy of the Roman Catholic Church diminished the truth of the resurrection of Jesus Christ, the Reformation stressed that Jesus Christ had been resurrected and needed to be removed from the crucifix. In the theology of the hierarchy of the Roman Catholic Church, without the resurrection of Jesus Christ, there could be no ascension into heaven of Jesus Christ. Jesus Christ's ascension into heaven is necessary in order for Jesus Christ to ascend to the throne of God Most High, and then to return to earth as the King of kings and Lord of lords (Acts 1:1-11, etc.). In contrast to Roman Catholic Church theology, the Reformers stressed the divine and sovereign kingship and lordship of Jesus Christ.

The Roman Catholic Church hierarchy denied the authority of Jesus Christ to be the only source of salvation.

If Jesus Christ is dead, then there is no Jesus Christ to forgive sins or to act as the gatekeeper for heaven. Popes and priests sought to fill the role of the absent and dead Jesus Christ, assuming the power to forgive sin and to serve as the gatekeepers for determining who should be included and who should be excommunicate from the kingdom of heaven. But the Reformers rejected this nonbiblical theology. Instead, the Reformers stressed that Jesus Christ was the member of the office of God that every person must first be accountable to. (John 14:6, etc.)

The Roman Catholic Church hierarchy understood that if Jesus Christ is not currently in heaven, then Jesus Christ must remain dead and there can be no return of Jesus Christ. The Roman Catholic Church denied Jesus Christ's ability and power to return to defeat the enemies of God Most High and of the kingdom of heaven, and to fully establish the kingdom of heaven on earth. The hierarchy of the Roman Catholic Church rendered their still dead Jesus Christ as unable to return, and not able to fully establish the kingdom of heaven on earth, and not capable of ruling. If Jesus Christ does not establish his rule and fully establish the kingdom of heaven on earth, then the power of the teaching of the Roman Catholic Church's global papal rule can remain in place with the hierarchy of the religious leaders and the authority of the pope intact.

But there were some theological areas where the Reformed tradition fell short in making their theological corrections.

While the Reformers stressed the biblical approach to soteriology (means and process of salvation), they also embraced some of the doctrine of predestination into their repertoire of theology. Reformed theology negated the importance of developing a personal relationship with God. Instead, Reformed theology stressed that a person was considered by God Most High to either be included in or excluded out of the kingdom of heaven, purely upon the arbitrary decision of God Most High without the influence of the choice that a person made. Developing a personal relationship with God was a nice idea, but the reality according to the Reformed tradition, was that every person was already predestined to either heaven or hell. And men were more predestined to heaven than women. Rich men were more predestined to heaven than poor men. Men who held positions of power and authority were more predestined to heaven than serfs, etc.

In the Reformed tradition, the role of the church was redefined without the emphasis of extending the message of salvation to all with the understanding that people could truly choose heaven or hell for themselves. The role of the church was to allow those people who had already been predestined to heaven, to find God, and to employ God's power to further the goals of God, especially in the lives of rich powerful men. And for the church to shun those that the church leadership determined were not worthy to receive salvation in the kingdom of heaven.

The Reformed tradition baulked at the Roman Catholic Church practice of excommunication. But Reformed tradition also assumed authority over the determination of what defined worthiness for entrance into the kingdom of heaven.

In Reformed tradition, a person could live a life of evil and still end up in heaven. Or a person could live a saintly life and honor God Most High and still end up in hell. In Reformed theology, predestination meant that when each person is awakened after death, they will be greeted with either 'Surprise! You are in heaven!' or 'Surprise! You are in hell!'

With this kind of unpredictable outcome, then the whole nature and reason for the crucifixion, death, resurrection and ascension of Jesus Christ, took on an entirely different meaning than the definition of Jesus Christ's work that was presented in the biblical record.

The ecclesiastical authority within the church, was another doctrine and practice that the Reformed tradition adopted from the Roman Catholic Church hierarchy.

Within the Reformed tradition, communities would develop laws that required church attendance and that required certain behaviors while a person attended church. There were many other mandatory rules within the

Reformed tradition that had no connection with the biblical message. The Reformed tradition embraced their own version of the absolute hierarchical rule of the Roman Catholic Church, and then added their own twist to it.

The example of ecclesiastical authority established by the Roman Catholic Church, had resulted in the Roman Catholic Church having maximized its power grip in Europe, at the end of the Dark Ages / Middle Ages / medieval period. It has been estimated that the Roman Catholic Church at one point, possessed or had control of approximately one third of the lands of Europe.

To influence world politics, the Roman Catholic Church had established the position of Holy Roman Emperor on December 25th, 800 AD. On that day, Leo III (fl. 795 to 816) coronated Charlemagne / Charles the Great / king of the Franks and the Lombards (747 to 814), as the first Holy Roman Emperor in the old Saint Peter's Basilica in Rome. This act reflected the Roman Catholic Church view that the Roman Catholic Church could rule the nations and that the nations could use the religious organization of the church to advanced their rule and control the populace.

Leo X (1513 to 1521) forbade the courts in every country to try anyone for a crime after that person had received absolution from the Roman Catholic Church and had made their payment of the set fee designated for that particular offense. Any judge who attempted to circumvent this dictate was excommunicated from membership in the Roman Catholic Church (and therefore from the opportunity to enter into the kingdom of heaven).

The Medieval Inquisition began in 1184 for the purpose of suppressing heresy / ideas that opposed the theology, authority, power, and wealth gathering of the Roman Catholic Church.

The Spanish Inquisition in Spain and all of Spain's colonies and territories, began in 1478, by Ferdinand II of Aragon and Isabella I of Castile. The purpose of the Spanish Inquisition was to identify heretics, to force conversions, and to confiscate the property of heretics in the effort to stop the spread of heresy and opposition to the rule of the

Roman Catholic Church. The truer purpose was to eliminate the people of Israel and the Muslims from the Spanish society. In 1492, Columbus of Portugal, sailed to 'discover' a new world. North America later became the refuge for those who sought to 'flee the religious tyranny of the Old World.'

Paul IV (fl. 1555 to 1559) formally established the office and role of inquisitor. Paul IV was an unrivaled torturer and persecutor of Christians and Jews. Paul IV quarreled constantly, even with the kings Charles V of Spain (1500 to 1558) and Charles V's son Philip II (1527 to 1598), the only two friends of the papacy at the time. Paul IV's personal mission was 'to tread under foot kings and emperors.' In the papal bull *Cum ex Apostolatus Officio / by virtue of the apostolic office* (February 15, 1559), Paul IV declared that the pope, specifically Paul IV, held unlimited power, including the power over nations and kingdoms, as judge of all men, and unable to be judged by anyone. With this kind of power, Paul IV also declared that he was authorized to take anyone's possessions without needing to observe legal process. Any resistance was met with excommunication, loss of title or rank, with their own lives and possessions placed in a position to be taken.

Sixtus V (fl. 1585 to 1590) rewrote the Bible in order to justify the adoption of his own unique ideas. Sixtus V declared that he held religious and civil jurisdiction over all kings and princes and that he could appoint or dismiss anyone at any time according to his own pleasure, including monarchs and emperors. The Roman Catholic Church traditionally taught that to be excommunicated from church membership, was the equivalent of being banished from eternal life and the kingdom of heaven, the equivalent of being sentenced to an eternity in hell. Excommunication has always been a most effective manipulative tool for the papal office and for the Roman Catholic Church in maintaining the power of their rule.

Clement XI (fl. 1700 to 1721), in his 1715 bull *In Coena Domini*, excommunicated all who would not obey the pope or who refused to pay their portion assessed by the Roman Catholic Church. Clement XI's bull also declared that the *pope held supreme authority over all people including monarchs in their secular and religious affairs. Popes that succeeded Clement XI reconfirmed this dogma and the dogma has never been rescinded by the Roman Catholic Church.*

As the Reformed tradition developed, it adopted the same high view of ecclesiastical authority that was established by the dogmas, doctrines, theologies and practices of the hierarchy of the Roman Catholic Church. But the Reformed tradition did not allow for the same level of grace that had been exercised by the Roman Catholic Church.

Both hierarchies of the Roman Catholic Church and the Reformed tradition, believed themselves to be infallible and impenetrable.

The Reformed tradition began with a high and lofty vision of what they needed to accomplish. But without a deep dependance upon the development of a personal relationship with God Most High, or a full return to an understanding of the biblical message, their mission remained shaped by their ecclesiastical leadership that enjoyed the power of ruling that continued to supersede their dedication to pursue a full return to being a living and thriving church community with a living and thriving core theology.

Jesus Christ's response was, 'I know your deeds, that you have the characterization that you are alive. But you are dead.'
'Be watching and strengthen the things that remain, which are about to die. For I have not found your works to be completed in the sight of my God.' Revelation 3:1b-2 translated

One of the distinctive theologies that established from Reformed tradition theology, was the development of Rapture theology. Rapture theology stresses that Jesus Christ will come like a thief in the night because Christians must remain unaware of the timing of the return of messiah / the Lamb / Jesus Christ. Somehow, nineteen hundred years ago, Jesus knew that Rapture theology would become a reality.

And Jesus Christ said this: 'Therefore, remember what you have received and heard. Keep it and repent. Therefore, if you do not watch, I will come like a thief and you will not know at what hour I will come upon you.' Revelation 3:3 translated

And yet, the historical era of the church of Sardis accomplished great things for advancing the kingdom of heaven on earth. Their deeds, their martyrdom, etc., worked to advance the mission of the kingdom of heaven on earth. Their protests against the elements of the baal / mystery / mythology religion that were retained by the Roman Catholic Church, served to provide a purification of sorts, to the total understanding of the authentic mission of the church.

But the historical era of the church of Sardis / Reformed tradition, was still assessed by Jesus Christ to be dead. Their works were merely a façade or a veneer over their stated mission. Ultimately, instead of completing the task of working to fully establish the kingdom of heaven, they worked to establish their own personal kingdoms, utilizing the church to accomplish their personal agendas. Repentance / asking Jesus Christ to forgive sin, loving others, etc. became less important than meeting the requirements established by the ecclesiastical hierarchy of the Reformed tradition church.

They observed ecclesiastical law, at the expense of honoring the authority and desires of the Holy Spirit. And that practice of denying the importance of the work of the Holy Spirit, remains active within the Reformed tradition even until this present time.

Without the work of the divine and sovereign Holy Spirit, there cannot be life.

The only assessment that Jesus Christ could offer to the historical era of the church of Sardis / Reformed tradition, was an impending certification of death, if they insisted upon remaining steeped in their humanly developed tradition, and asleep to the deeper mission of messiah / the Lamb / Jesus Christ.

Paul wrote:

Love does no harm to a neighbor. Therefore, love is the fulfillment of the law.

And do this, understanding the present time: The hour has already come for you to wake up from your slumber, because our salvation is nearer now than when we first believed. The night is nearly over. The day is almost here. So let us put aside the deeds of darkness and put on the armor of light. Let us behave decently, as in the daytime, not in carousing and drunkenness, not in sexual immorality and debauchery, not in dissension and jealousy. Rather, clothe yourselves with the Lord Jesus Christ, and do not think about how to gratify the desires of the flesh. Romans 13:10-14

Seeded by the protestors against the Roman Catholic Church

By 1517 and the beginning of the Protestant Reformation, the seat of the Holy Roman Emperor was occupied by the King of Spain / Charles V (1500 to 1558), who was nephew of Katherine of Aragon, Queen of England (1485 to 1536 / fl. 1509 to 1533) (daughter of Ferdinand II of Aragon and Isabella I of Castile), and was nephew-in-law of England's King Henry VIII (1491 to 1547 / fl. 1509 to 1547). All these monarchs were Roman Catholic, except in the case of Henry VIII. Even Henry VIII began life as a member and supporter of the Roman Catholic Church. It was a result of the interrelational conflict of these monarchs, that the Protestant Reformation began to take place in England.

But, the seeds of reformation had already begun forming long before Henry VIII, during the Dark Ages / Middle Ages / medieval period as a response to the unbridled and unaccountable power of the Roman Catholic Church and popes. The seeds of reformation were sown among those who did not accept Satan's so-called deep secrets. The seeds of reformation were sown and grew during the prime time in the life of the historical era of the church of Thyatira. But those seeds of reformation did not fully germinate until the historical timeline of the era of the church of Sardis.

John Wycliffe (1320s to 1384), a seminary professor at the University of Oxford, and others began sowing the seeds of reformation two hundred years before the 'spark' of the reformation that occurred when Martin Luther attached his Ninety five Theses to the door of the church in Wittenberg, Germany. Wycliffe completed a translation of the Bible from the Latin Vulgate into Middle English by

1384. Wycliffe attacked the privileged status of the religious leaders and priests, and the luxury and ceremonies of the local parishes of the Roman Catholic Church. Wycliffe also supported secular authority to be separate and superior to the spiritual authority of the church, which would have freed people from abuses of the Roman Catholic Church. Wycliffe was opposed to the veneration of holy ones, the sacraments as defined by the Roman Catholic Church, the masses held for the dead, monasticism, the papacy, etc. Wycliffe believed and taught that the Bible should be the center of Christianity instead of the dictates of the papacy and the practices of the Roman Catholic Church. May 4, 1415, a hundred years before the Protestant Reformation 'spark,' the Roman Catholic Church became incensed with Wycliffe's teachings, declared him a heretic, dug up his body, burned his dead body, and cast the ashes into the River Swift a tributary to the River Avon in England.

John Huss / Johannes Hus (1369 to 1415), a Czech Catholic priest and rector of the Charles University in Prague, spoke out against indulgences. Huss was burned at the stake on July 6, 1415.

In 1492, Spain expelled the Jews. Christopher Columbus sailed, exploring the world for a new trade route, and a safe haven for the religiously oppressed of Spain. Just twenty five years after Columbus sailed to the Americas, the seeds of protests and reformation germinated.

Martin Luther (1483 to 1546), a German professor of theology and Augustinian monk, lectured on various books of the Bible. The more Luther studied and lectured from the original biblical text; the more Luther became disturbed by the abuses of the Roman Catholic Church. Luther proposed an academic discussion on the practice and efficacy of indulgences in his Ninety-five Theses that he nailed to the door of the All Holy Ones' Church in Wittenberg, Germany on October 31, 1517.

Three of Luther's works published in 1520 were 'To the Christian Nobility of the German Nation,' 'On the Babylonian Captivity of the Church,' and 'On the Freedom of a Christian.'

The pope and the Roman Catholic Church hierarchy did not appreciate Luther's theology nor the fact that Luther's work was printed and distributed. As a professor, Luther translated books of the Bible into German and used his German translation of the Bible to teach Bible study classes.

Luther determined there were five _solas_ that comprised the foundation for Christianity:
1. The Bible _alone_ is our highest authority.
2. We are saved through faith _alone_ in Jesus Christ and not through the forgiveness of priests and popes.
3. We are saved as a result of God's grace _alone_ and not through rituals or rites.
4. Jesus Christ _alone_ is our Lord, Savior, and King.
5. We live for the glory of God _alone_. This sola stands in opposition to the veneration of the Blessed Virgin Mary and Queen of Heaven.

In April 1521, the Roman Catholic Church put Luther on trial as a heretic before the Diet of Worms. King Charles V of Spain who was conveniently also the Holy Roman Emperor, presided over the trial.

Meanwhile back in England, King Charles' aunt, Catherine of Aragon, Queen of England, was opposing the annulment that King Henry VIII was demanding because Catherine had not produced a male heir. At that time, royal marriages required the pope to approve both the marriages and divorces of royalty. Henry VIII encountered opposition for his divorce from Catherine, from the pope who depended upon the power and authority of the Holy Roman Emperor in order to maintain his position of power as pope. The Holy Roman Emperor was the king of Spain, Charles V, who was also the nephew of Catherine. There would be no divorce or annulment decree issued from the papal office. In response, Henry VIII declared himself head of the church in England. In 1534, the English Church separated from Rome. And the Protestant Reformation officially arrived in England.

The Great Bible (1539) became the authorized Bible translation of the newly formed Church of England. But during the reign of Mary I of England (fl. 1553 to 1558), who was Roman Catholic like her mother Catherine of Aragon, a number of Protestant scholars fled from England to Geneva Switzerland.

Also during the reign of Mary I, William Whittingham supervised the translation of the Bile now known as the Geneva Bible / Breeches Bible (first published c. NT - 1557 / entire Bible 1560). Other collaborators in this work were Myles Coverdale, Christopher Goodman, Anthony Gilby, Thomas Sampson and William Cole. The Geneva Bible was the first complete English version of the Bible to be translated from the original languages of Hebrew, Aramaic and Greek.

The Geneva Bible / Breeches Bible was the English Bible translation used by subsequent Protestant Reformation leaders like Oliver Cromwell, John Knox John Donne, etc. And the Geneva was the translation of the Bible used by William Shakespeare. The Geneva Bible continued to be the translation used during the reign of Elizabeth I (fl. 1558 to 1603). It was also used by many English dissenters. And the Geneva Bible was carried to America on the Mayflower.

It was James I (fl. 1603 to 1625) who commissioned the King James Version translation.

The Geneva Bible was the first version of the Bible to be mechanically printed, mass produced and made available directly to the general public. Included with the Geneva Bible, were a variety of scriptural study guides and aids ('apparatus'), which provided cross referencing of relevant verses, maps, tables, illustrations, and indices.

Once people began reading the Bible in their own language and they possessed their own personal copy of the Bible that they could reference at their own discretion, people realized that what the Roman Catholic Church taught and what the Bible taught, could not be reconciled.

Wars ensued all over Europe as a result of the laity seeking escape from power and authority of the Roman Catholic Church. The Roman Catholic Church's war against the heretics that dared to seek escape, lasted for decades. The 'Christian' on 'Christian' violence caused an estimated sixteen to fifty million deaths.

The Protestant Reformation rejected most of the doctrines and practices that had infiltrated the Roman Catholic Church through the incorporation of the baal / mystery / mythology religion. In Protestant churches, Mary returned from being the imitation of Semiramis, Queen of Heaven of the baal / mystery / mythology religion, to being Jesus' mom as portrayed in the biblical record. Protestants took Jesus Christ off the cross, allowed Jesus Christ to have risen from the dead and allowed Jesus Christ to have ascended to the throne in heaven.

The original Reformed tradition was not able to reconcile their predestination theology with the complete biblical understanding of the necessity of the crucifixion, death, resurrection, and ascension of Jesus Christ. So even though Jesus Christ was taken off the cross and allowed to ascend into heaven, the effect and meaning of Jesus Christ's death and ascension were essentially theologically nullified. At least the Roman Catholic Church understood that Jesus Christ's sacrificial death had a meaning that connected the individual to heaven.

But the Protestant Reformation was successful in bringing other reforms that provided the seeds for the historical timeline church of Philadelphia's theology to begin to develop.

With the translation of the biblical message into a readable language for the common people, a newly educated laity quickly discovered that the doctrines and theology of Christianity through the Roman Catholic Church had been infected with the baal / mystery / mythology religion. The newly educated laity became keenly aware of the adulteration and oppression that the Roman Catholic Church had brought to Christianity. The abuse of power by the Roman Catholic Church became another impetus for the Protestant Reformation.

The Protestant Reformation's origins began in scripture. But, the political landscape of nations and royalty soon adopted the theology of the Protestant Reformation because it allowed monarchs and nations to separate from the Roman Catholic Church and its domination. The Protestant churches embraced the reconnection with the Bible and early Christian thought, but at the same time, kings and queens were not willing to sacrifice their power as divinely appointed monarchs through the historically understood 'divine right of kings.' The reforms of the Protestant Reformation offered monarchs and nations freedom from the Roman Catholic Church. But monarchs and national leaders were not willing to relinquish their own power and embrace the tenets and theology of the original true Christianity.

The influence of monarchs unwilling to relinquish their power and authority, influenced the Reformed tradition churches to also be unwilling to entirely embrace the dictates and full theology of the biblical record. The early Protestant churches were not willing to relinquish their ecclesiastical power that had its precedent in the Dark Ages / Middle Ages / medieval period of the Roman Catholic Church.

The early Protestant churches had a reputation of being alive, but still remained dead.

The effect of the Protestant Reformation upon the Roman Catholic Church, and the Counter Reformation

The Protestant Reformation acted as a wakeup call to the Roman Catholic Church. But the Protestant Reformation failed to wake up the religious leaders and papacy of the Roman Catholic Church to anything other than their loss of control. The papal office remained occupied by men who were politically cunning enough to arrive at the chair of the papacy, but not wise enough to realize that if Jesus Christ did indeed rise from the dead, then it is Jesus Christ who is the true sovereign.

The pressure inside of the Roman Catholic Church from those who remained members of the Roman Catholic Church but understood the wisdom of the Protestant Reformation, caused the Roman Catholic Church to *respond through the introduction of the Counter Reformation.*

In 1540, the Catholic priest Ignatius Loyola and six of his buddies founded the Society of Jesus / Jesuit Order. Publicly, the Society of Jesus / Jesuits were missionaries sent out to create schools, colleges, and seminaries that would teach social programs that favored the theological and political position of the Roman Catholic Church. The Jesuits gave to the poor. The Jesuits established settlements like St. Ignace, Michigan that was named after Ignatius by Father Jacques Marquette. The Jesuits established colleges such as Boston College, Fordham University, Georgetown University, Gonzaga University, the Loyola Universities, Regis University, University of Detroit Mercy, etc.

To compete with the Protestant Reformation's movement to make education available to all people, the Jesuit schools were developed for educating people, specifically Roman Catholics, with an adherence to the Roman Catholic Church's dogmas, doctrines, theologies and practices.

The Jesuits provided a positive public persona but privately they were the secret military arm of the pope accomplishing work that publicly and politically, the pope did not want to be directly connected with.

Privately, the Jesuits took a special vow of obedience to the pope, completed discrete assignments for the pope, and became the secret military arm of the pope. Even though the Society's name presented a society dedicated to Jesus, the Jesuits were consecrated under the patronage of the 'Blessed Virgin Mary,' complete with connection to Semiramis and Jezebel's baal / mystery / mythology religion.

An additional incentive for dedication to the papal office for the Jesuits was the financial gain they received. In the pursuit of caring for the interests of the papal office, the Jesuits also acquired wealth and power for the order.

The three great rules of the code of the Jesuits are:
1) the end justifies the means;
2) it is safe to do anything if it be probably right, even if it is more probably wrong, and

3) given the right intention, one may ignore the moral character in order to give license to act in a seemingly impossible task.

These three great rules of the code of the Jesuits effectively gave license to the Jesuits for any activity that they decided to undertake. These three great rules of the code of the Jesuits are dramatically estranged from any semblance to the Law given to Moses or to authentic biblical teaching.

Once the 'Society of Jesus' / the Jesuits was organized, the goal given to the Jesuits by the pope, was to defeat Protestantism and regain papal rule. To accomplish this goal, the Jesuits became known for their deception, spying, infiltration, assassination, and revolution. The nature of the activities of the Jesuits became widely known.

President Abraham Lincoln viewed the Jesuits as a great enemy.

Francesco Borgia, Third Jesuit Superior General said, 'We came in like lambs and will rule like wolves. We shall be expelled like dogs and return like eagles.'

During the era of WWII, even Hitler was influenced by the Jesuit tactics.

'I learned much from the Order of the Jesuits… Until now, there has never been anything more grandiose, on the earth, than the hierarchical organization of the Catholic Church. I transferred much of this organization into my own party.' Adolf Hitler

The Roman Catholic Church viewed and will continue to view all Protestants and non-Catholics as heretics.

The Oath of the Jesuits requires the inductee to promise 'when opportunity presents, to make and wage relentless war secretly or openly, against all heretics, Protestants, and Liberals, as I am directed to; extirpate them from the face of the earth; and that I will spare neither age, sex, or condition, and that I will hang, burn, waste, boil, flay, strangle, and bury alive those infamous heretics; rip up the stomachs and wombs of the women, and crush their infants' heads against the wall in order to annihilate their execrable race. That when the same cannot be done openly, I will secretly use the poisonous cup, the strangulating cords, the steels of the poniard, or the leaden bullets …' *The oath continues and includes an oath of allegiance to the pope.*

Even with the Counter Reformation, the Roman Catholic Church continued to advance their power, feudalism, serfdom, etc. The religious leadership of the Roman Catholic Church during the Counter Reformation continued any practice that assisted the Roman Catholic Church in maintaining its power and papal authority.

The Protestant Reformation branch known as the Anabaptist movement included Calvinism and the Reformed tradition.

The Anabaptist movement of Protestantism, while rejecting the massive power and rule of the Roman Catholic Church, still practiced holding onto the authority and power to religiously rule people that had been firmly established over the previous thousand years by the Roman Catholic church.

The Anabaptist movement of Calvinism and the Reformed tradition maintained some of the doctrines and theologies of the baal / mystery / mythology religion that had been a part of the Roman Catholic Church teachings. The doctrine of predestination which espouses that before the foundation of the world, God Most High had predestined every person that would be created, for their eternal destination, without any opportunity for the person to make the decision for their self either for or against the kingdom of heaven. With predestination, each individual would be surprised when they died, to discover the destination that God Most High had selected for them, either heaven or hell.

But the biblical record documented that when God Most High placed the first man and the first woman in the Garden of Eden / garden of God / paradise, they were already citizens of the kingdom of heaven / citizens of the Garden of Eden / garden of God / paradise. It was the decisions that the first man and first woman made, that caused them to be exiled from the kingdom of heaven / Garden of Eden / garden of God / paradise.

The biblical record clearly documented that every person has been given the opportunity to make choices about their future, and that each of us must choose who will be our God, and that God Most High respects and honors each individual person's choice.

But embracing the theology of free choice as a substitute for the theology of predestination, would have caused the Anabaptist movement and Reformed tradition to need to relinquish their control over the people. They were just not willing to go that far.

The historical timeline and the historical era of the church of Sardis / Reformed tradition's incomplete theology

Some of the main leaders in the Protestant Reformation movement were Martin Luther (Germany - Augustinian priest), John Calvin / Jehan Cauvin (France / Switzerland - humanist lawyer), Menno Simons (Friesland / Netherlands - Roman Catholic priest, founder of the Mennonites), and Ulrich Zwingli (Switzerland - Roman Catholic priest and humanist).

Jesus Christ's indictment against the historical era of the church of Sardis / Reformed tradition, was that it held incomplete theology.

'I know your deeds, that you have the characterization that you are alive. But you are dead.'

'Be watching and strengthen the things that remain, which are about to die. For I have not found your works to be completed in the sight of my God. Therefore, remember what you have received and heard. Keep it and repent. Therefore, if you do not watch, I will come like a thief and you will not know at what hour I will come upon you.' Revelation 3:1b-3 translated

The Anabaptist / Reformed tradition doctrine of predestination, espoused that citizenship in the kingdom of heaven was determined by God Most High alone without the recognition of any consent or dissent of the person, and the person is helpless to change God Most High's decision. Even the church and one's relationship to the church, could not change God Most High's decision concerning a person's eternal destination.

Having espoused the doctrine of predestination, there was no longer any deep need for recognizing a risen Jesus Christ, nor the authority and power of Jesus Christ to forgive sins. There was no longer any need to focus upon the deeper meaning of the crucifixion, death, resurrection and ascension of Jesus Christ. There was no longer any *need to deeply focus upon Jesus Christ's return to earth to fight a final battle against the enemies of God Most High and of the kingdom of heaven. With predestination, all decisions were already made before the foundation of the world.*

This conceptualization of god required that God Most High operate out of power devoid of deep love for humanity. The Reformed tradition theology of predestination meant that God so loved the world, but not necessarily all the people in it. The Son came so that the world might be saved, but not necessarily all those who choose to follow the Son. The Son has rejected some in spite of their choice to repent of their sins.

In contrast, the biblical record documented:

'For God so loved the world, that God gave the one and only begotten Son, so that everyone who believes in him should not perish but should have eternal life. For God did not send his Son into the world that he should judge the world, but so that the world might be saved through him.'

'The one who believes on him is not judged. But the one that does not believe on him, has already been judged, because he has not believed in the name of the only begotten Son of God.' John 3:16-18 translated

The doctrine of predestination presented a god whose best days took place before the creation of the world, and before the creation of the first man and first woman, during the time when the rules concerning predestination were written.

But reality is that the only 'god' whose best days took place before the creation of the first man and first woman, was Satan. And the only 'god' who predestined humanity to an eternal life in their kingdom, was Satan, Inc.

In contrast to Reformation theology, the biblical message that began six thousand years ago, continues to promote that God Most High's best days are yet to come. God Most High's plan for the future is to conclusively defeat God Most High's enemies, celebrate with the followers of the Lamb / Jesus Christ, and to see the full establishment of the kingdom of heaven on earth, with a culture that fully encompasses the character of a loving God. God Most High's motivation for accomplishing all of this, remains God Most High's determination to have a personal relationship with whomever has decided of their own accord, to become a follower of the Lamb / Jesus Christ.

Other Protestant denominations that were birthed by the Protestant Reformation also maintained similar views of the superiority of church authority. Consequently, they also were unable to fully embrace the theology that originally gave true power to the apostolic and early Christian church. Their reformation process remains unfinished.

The Protestant Reformation was also unable to finish its work in reforming the Roman Catholic Church or in presenting a truly unadulterated Christianity to people.

The churches of the Protestant Reformation made great gains in recapturing the tenets of authentic Christianity. But they still held onto many theologies and doctrines that had corrupted the practice of Christianity. And those theologies and doctrines prevented the Protestant Reformation from completing the work.

The theology of the historical era of the church of Sardis in the movement toward the theology of the historical era of the church of Laodicea

Unfortunately, the incomplete theology of the historical timeline Sardis church remains with us even today. Predestination theology is alive and well; which renders Jesus Christ's resurrection to life nonessential. Predestination theology also leaves undefined who the enemies of God Most High and of the kingdom of heaven. Having an undefined enemy works to thwart Jesus Christ's return to defeat the enemies of God Most High and of the kingdom of heaven.

In addition to predestination theology, the era of the church of Sardis / Reformed tradition's replacement theology is alive and well, a theology that declared that God Most High abandoned God's covenant with the people of Israel and has replaced the church as the new recipient of the blessings once promised to the people of Israel. Etc.

While there have been and always will be some who have not soiled their garments, within the historical era of the church of Sardis, the majority of the adherents of Reformed theology continue to practice the dictates of a false ecclesiastical hierarchy, passing judgment upon those who are in fact, followers of the Lamb / Jesus Christ and who have allowed the Holy Spirit to guide and direct.

Many in the Reformed tradition camp continue to claim that there is only one true and authentic Bible, the King James Version. Some even claim that Jesus Christ spoke in King James' English and that the original biblical texts written in Hebrew, Aramaic and Greek, are fakes. They practice biblical proof texting / taking a verse or verses out of context and developing an alternate theology using the now isolated verse(s) to support their own personal idea.

What is more amazing is that many people discard their own personal abilities to process thought, and then blindly follow the direction of the self-proclaimed ecclesiastical leaders.

The unwillingness and inability of the Reformed tradition to wake up, to strengthen what remains, to finish their deeds according to God, to remember what they received and heard, to repent, to recognize that messiah / the Lamb / Jesus Christ will indeed return according to all of the prophecies documented within the biblical record, to walk with Jesus Christ through the power of the connection that the Holy Spirit provides to every follower of the Lamb / Jesus Christ; has impacted the church as a whole to also hold an unnatural distance with messiah / the Lamb / Jesus Christ. Propagating that distance, has contributed to the historical era of the church of Laodicean theology to be able to cast Jesus Christ outside of the church entirely.

The natural outcome of Reformed theology was the diminishment of the authority and power of Jesus Christ saving work, and the rejection of the work of the Holy Spirit. Wherever there is a denial of the recognition of the authority and power of Jesus Christ and a denial of the recognition of the Holy Spirit and the Holy Spirit's work, God Most High's will during the era of the time of Jacob's Trouble, will not be realized. (See the parables of Matthew 25 and the other kingdom parables.)

In recent history, the importance of giving the message of who Jesus Christ is, of what the kingdom of heaven is, of how to become a citizen of the kingdom of heaven, etc., has been lost. Somewhere in culture, the incorrect assumption was made and proliferated that if a person was born into a Christian family or into a Christian church or into a Christian nation, that the person was automatically predestined to be a Christian and therefore a citizen of the kingdom of heaven. Consequently, these latest generations do not understand the importance of personally making a decision to become followers of the Lamb / Jesus Christ. This has led to Jesus Christ being disgusted and nauseated with the modern church culture, and the biblical Jesus Christ no longer being welcome in any form inside of the modern church culture. (Revelation 3:14-20).

The influence of the historical era of the church of Sardis / Reformed tradition, upon the historical era of the church of Laodicea and the era of the time of Jacob's Trouble

The Reformed tradition began its work with the rejection of the Roman Catholic Church's Mariology and the 'marriage' of church and state. But it did not finish its work. Instead, the Reformed tradition substituted the development of its own power and hierarchy to fill that space. The ecclesiastical arrogance of the Reformed tradition will impact those who embraced the Reformed tradition, by allowing them to remain asleep, unable to be impacted by the fullness of biblical authority and to waken to the full biblical message.

The Reformed tradition's practice of also holding ecclesiastical authority as sovereign over biblical authority, through the practice of supporting theologies that were not supported by the full biblical record, will continue to cause those that follow the established theologies of the original Reformed tradition, to continue to miss the full biblical message. They will miss the warning signs of the thief that is about to approach during their sleep.

'Therefore, remember what you have received and heard. Keep it and repent. Therefore, if you do not watch, I will come like a

thief and you will not know at what hour I will come upon you.'
Revelation 3:3 translated

In the list of Reformed tradition theologies that do not adhere to the theology presented in the full biblical record were:
- *Ecclesiastical authority as supreme over the God of the kingdom of heaven's authority.*
- *The rejection of the full work of the Holy Spirit.*
- *The evaluation of an individual's wealth, power and gender as the method for assessing one's status in relationship with God Most High.*
- *Seeking to prevent the parousia / the return of messiah / the Lamb / Jesus Christ, as documented within the biblical record.*
- *The development and insistence upon rapture theology as a replacement for the biblical schedule of eschatological events.*
- *The rejection of Israel as the nation in covenant with God Most High and replacement theology.*
- *Etc.*

These theologies negated portions of the full message of the biblical record, and these theologies impacted the church into the future and the church as a whole. The theologies developed through the Reformed tradition, fostered the development of the theology of the historical era of the church of Laodicean theology.

Ecclesiastical authority as supreme over biblical authority and the authority of the God of the kingdom of heaven.

The Reformed tradition was a protest against the iron hand of the Roman Catholic Church's authority. But in the Reformed tradition, the iron hand of the Roman Catholic Church's authority was merely replaced with the iron hand of the newly formed Reformed tradition.

The Reformed tradition eliminated the rule of the pope, but replaced papal rule with the rule of the newly formed ecclesiastical hierarchy of the Reformed tradition churches.

One of the impetuses of the Protestant Reformation era was a push toward a better translation of the biblical message, but only as it was translated through Jerome's Latin Vulgate which was produced to please the Roman empire. The better translations of the day were also produced to please those who commissioned them. (Dedication to accurately translating the text from the original language, was sparse and not a major concern until the era of the Great Awakening / Evangelical Revival / Holiness Movement (~1730 to 1900s).)

In the midst of the various translations of the Bible, the Geneva Bible / Breeches Bible (Genesis 3:7) (1557) rose as the most accurate text of the time and became the version that fostered the theology of the colonists in America that provided democracy in the formation of the United States. The Geneva Bible gave rise to the Great Awakening in the colonies (and the Evangelical Revival in Britain), which fostered the rise of the historical era of the church of Philadelphia and its theology, that would come later.

But for the followers of the Reformed tradition, the Geneva Bible supported too much freedom in religious thought, and not enough support for ecclesiastical authority. It has always been a tenet of the old Reformed tradition movement to offer some religious freedom from Roman Catholicism while maintaining the church's hierarchical control over the people that the church wishes to rule.

The King James Version of the Bible (1611) was commissioned by James VI of Scotland / James I of England (Scotland fl. 1567 to 1625, England fl. 1603 to 1625). Consequently, statements that would have been offensive to the rule of the monarchy were removed. In this way, the King James Version became a means for reestablishing the authority of the church hierarchy over parishioners / laity, while still allowing for the denunciation of some the tenets that were the result of the Roman Catholic Church's embrace of the baal / mystery / mythology religion.

Holding onto the tenet that the church's hierarchy held the religious authority to rule over the people, resulted in a theology that had the reputation of being alive, but in fact was asleep and dead. The historical era of the church of Sardis / Reformation movement theology was unfinished. It would be the theology of the era of the Great Awakening / Evangelical Revival that would finish what the original Reformers had begun.

During the era of the Great Awakening / Evangelical Revival / Holiness Movement (~1730 to 1900s), the Reformed tradition in America did for a time embrace the theology of the Great Awakening. But around 1830, the Reformed tradition returned to its original sixteenth century heritage and again sought to establish ecclesiastical rule over the laity, confining the Holy Spirit to prevent the Holy Spirit in providing leadership. (Note that the Civil War in the United States began thirty years later.)

Rejection of the full work of the Holy Spirit

The Reformed tradition eliminated in their theological composition, Mariology, the canonization of holy ones, and the idolatry that is inherent within the Roman Catholic Church.

But the Reformed tradition also eliminated in their theology, the Holy Spirit as the voice of God Most High that rules the hearts and minds of individuals.

Jesus Christ addressed the historical timeline church of Sardis as the one 'who holds the seven spirits of God and the seven stars.' (Revelation 3:1)

The Old Testament / Tanakh prophet Isaiah defined the seven spirits of God (Isaiah 11:2) as:
- the Spirit of the Lord
- the Spirit of wisdom
- the Spirit of understanding
- the Spirit of counsel
- the Spirit of might
- the Spirit of knowledge
- the Spirit of the fear of the Lord

When Jesus Christ addressed the angel of the church of Sardis, as the one who holds the seven spirits of God, it was Jesus Christ's recognition of his own personal relationship with the Holy Spirit. It was also a recognition that without the Holy Spirit, Jesus Christ could not accomplish the fullness of his work in God Most High's redemption, reclamation and regeneration plan.

When Jesus Christ presented himself to the church of Sardis, making reference to his relationship with the Holy Spirit, it was a message to the historical era of the church of Sardis that they had rejected the work of the Holy Spirit, and that they needed to turn that around / repent from their rejection of the work of the Holy Spirit. Jesus Christ tasked the historical era of the church of Sardis with developing their relationship with the work of the Holy Spirit.

Without the recognition of the full work of the Holy Spirit in the Reformed tradition theology, there can be no complete understanding of the God of the kingdom of heaven. And without a complete understanding of the God of the kingdom of heaven, an understanding of the process of messiah / the Lamb / Jesus Christ fully establishing the kingdom of heaven on earth, will be illusive.

Assessment of wealth, power and gender in determining worth to God Most High

Another dogmatic idea held by the Reformed tradition in its catalog of theology, was the idea that the sign of God Most High's blessing, took the form of having wealth, position and maleness, bestowed upon God Most High's chosen elect. In this way, the elite were considered to be the elect. And because those that possessed wealth, power and were of the dominant gender, also were the source of financial support for the church, this dogmatic idea became predominant within the Reformed tradition.

The Reformed tradition utilized the biblical message for support of this dogmatic idea. God Most High had blessed Abram / Abraham with wealth and military strength. Isaac with blessed with success with agriculture. And Jacob / Israel was blessed with children and gained wealth from working for his father-in-law Laban.

But Jacob / Israel, the son of Isaac and grandson of Abram / Abraham, also lived during the massive famine that so hampered the wealth of Jacob / Israel and his twelve sons, that Jacob / Israel relocated his family into Egypt (1876 BC). The famine had wiped out the family's means of income and their wealth. And yet Jacob / Israel and his family, continued to be identified as being chosen and blessed by God Most High, even during the years of enslavement that the people of Israel experienced. For the following four hundred thirty years after the people of Israel first relocated to Egypt, God Most High never removed God's hand of protection from the people of Israel. And then God Most High led that same group of chosen and elect people out of Egypt, during the era of their enslavement (1446 BC).

The idea that God Most High's blessing upon a person could be identified by the amount of wealth and power that a man wielded, was denied by rest of the biblical message.

A traditional Jewish prayer was, 'Blessed are you, Lord, our God, ruler of the universe who has not created me a woman.'

Paul responded to this kind of thinking with 'There is neither Jew nor Gentile, neither slave nor free, nor is there male and female, for you are all one in Christ Jesus.' Galatians 3:28

The pursuit of money, sex and power, was an integral part of the baal / mystery / mythology religion from its beginning. It was Satan who was accused of being the master of trade (Ezekiel 28:5). And the practice of trading is necessary in the pursuit of money, sex and power.

In contrast, the fruit of the Holy Spirit, provided to those who are truly God Most High's elect, is love, joy, peace, patience, kindness, goodness, faithfulness, gentleness and self-control (Galatians 5:22-23). None of the fruit of the Holy Spirit is dependent upon one's economic evaluation, gender or social standing.

Challenging the biblical record's parousia / the return of messiah / the Lamb / Jesus Christ

Because most of the original Reformed tradition theology was developed by former Roman Catholic Church priests, it was natural for the original Reformed tradition theology to still maintain its links to the Roman Catholic Church theology. A clear separation of the mixture of authentic biblical theology from the baal / mystery / mythology religion, would require over a century of refinement.

The hierarchy of the Roman Catholic Church believed that Jesus Christ had not finished his mission in fully establishing the kingdom of heaven on earth during his earthly ministry, and that Jesus Christ had entrusted the hierarchy of the Roman Catholic Church to establish their version of the full establishment of the kingdom of heaven on earth, and that the further dissemination of the Roman empire's mission to globally control the earth.

Major portions of the belief system of the hierarchy of the Roman Catholic Church, were adopted by the original leaders of the Reformed tradition. And with that adoption, the idea was also incorporated of the denial of the return of messiah / the Lamb / Jesus Christ.

The study of hermeneutics developed, with a slant toward maintaining past accepted theologies. Preterism was strengthened within the Reformed tradition community. (Preterism is the belief that soon after Jesus Christ was resurrected and ascended into heaven, that God Most High discontinued fulfilling the prophecies of the Bible that Jesus Christ had left 'unfinished' with his earthly ministry.)

Calvinism for example, taught that God Most High does not truly love everyone. If this idea were true, then God Most High would not be able to be described as love (1 John 4:8, 4:16). The God of the Reformed tradition made unchangeable decisions long ago. Calvin's version of Jesus Christ was that Jesus Christ did not die so that there would be a day when the sins of the whole world would be washed away or covered. Calvin's version of Jesus Christ's death only applied to the elect. (See 1 John 2:2, 3.)

But the God described within the biblical record constantly interacts with humanity, wooing humanity because of his core nature of love, to make the decision to join in the movement to fully establish the kingdom of heaven on earth.

Because the God of the original Reformed tradition was so very arbitrary, there was no room for the *allowance that Jesus Christ would return to fully establish a kingdom on earth that would look vastly different from the kingdoms that each leader deeply committed to the Reformed tradition, would create. Reformed tradition leaders may acknowledge the biblical record's mention of the return of Jesus Christ. But their theology does not allow them to fully accept the biblical record's description of Jesus Christ's return or the biblical record's description of the fully established kingdom of heaven on earth.*

It was called the Reformed tradition because it was a reformation of already existing Roman Catholic Church dogmas, doctrines, theologies and practices. But approaching a mission of moving closer to the authentic faith system defined in the biblical record, does not require passing through the detour of the dogmas, doctrines, theologies and practices of the Roman Catholic Church. That trip can be made merely by resourcing the actual biblical record.

Rapture theology

Rapture theology was the development of the Reformed tradition. Because of the Roman Catholic Church's stance that ecclesiastical authority trumped the biblical message, the Reformed tradition developed and proliferated their version of dispensationalism and rapture theology.

Rapture theology presents the idea that Jesus Christ will return to collect the elite and elect prior to, or during, the era of the time of Jacob's Trouble, as a protection of the elite and elect from the expression of God Most High's wrath. This (secret?) return of Jesus Christ would take place prior to the glorious return of Jesus Christ when he comes to defeat the enemies of God Most High and of the kingdom of heaven.

Rapture theology requires some assumptions to be true.

One erroneous assumption of rapture theology is that the God of the kingdom of heaven, who created the heavens and the earth and whose word is powerful enough to speak light, heaven, earth, etc. into existence, and whose word is sharp enough to divide bone and marrow, would not be able to protect God Most High's elite and elect without removing them from events on earth.

Except for Noah's ark, which was a judgment and a baptism of the earth, God Most High has not utilized the strategy of protecting people from God Most High's wrath by taking them temporarily to heaven.

And there is no biblical evidence that Jesus Christ has been scheduled to return twice.

The fact that rapture theologians cannot agree upon when this rapture should take place in the scenario of events scheduled for the era of the time of Jacob's Trouble, should also be a clue that a rapture of God's elite and elect is not a probability.

Another erroneous assumption of rapture theology is that during the era of the time of Jacob's Trouble, the followers of the Lamb / Jesus Christ will not have any responsibility.

But John the Revelator specifically described some of the activities that the followers of the Lamb / Jesus Christ will be responsible for during this time.

Another erroneous assumption of rapture theology is that God Most High's nature is able to experience periods of discontinuity. For rapture theology to even be a 'thing,' God Most High must discontinue God's love for the people of the world during the time that the elite and elect are temporarily raptured into heaven.

If God Most High's personality, nature and character were able to be suspended for even a brief period of time, then the questions must be raised as to whether God Most High would suspend God's loving nature at other times, and what would keep God Most High from suspending God Most High's nature indefinitely.

Rapture theologians utilize Jesus Christ's description of his return as an event that will take place instantaneously, in their support of rapture theology.

Jesus said, 'Understand this, if the master of the house had known at what time of night the thief was coming, he would have watched, and not have allowed his house to be broken into. You also must be ready, because the Son of Man will come at an hour you do not expect him.' Matthew 24:43-44 translated *(Luke 12:39)*.

Interpreted with a rapture theology mindset, Jesus Christ's teaching of coming as a thief in the night, supported rapture theology and the idea that God's elite and elect do not need to be concerned about waking up.

But the message that Jesus Christ provided to the church of the angel of Sardis expressly stressed the importance of the historical era of the church of Sardis, to wake up.

To the angel of the church of Sardis, write,

'This is the message from the one having the seven Spirits of God, and the seven stars.'

'I know your deeds, that you have the characterization that you are alive. But you are dead.'

'Be watching and strengthen the things that remain, which are about to die. For I have not found your works to be completed in the sight of my God. Therefore, remember what you have received and heard. Keep it and repent. Therefore, if you do not watch, I will come like a thief and you will not know at what hour I will come upon you.' Revelation 3:1-3 translated

During Jesus Christ's earthly ministry, the instruction that Jesus provided that defined his coming to be like a thief in the night, was immediately followed by the parable of the ten virgins / church people (Matthew 25:1-13).

In the parable that Jesus Christ told, there were ten virgins / members of the church / ecclesia, who were waiting for the bridegroom. But only five of the virgins / members of the church / ecclesia, came prepared with oil to wait during the night for the bridegroom's arrival. The prepared five had oil and were actually taken by the bridegroom. But the five that were unprepared, had expected the bridegroom to come early, before the night came. When the bridegroom did not come early, when they expected the bridegroom to come, and it became night, they discovered that they were without oil, needing oil if they were to meet the bridegroom.

During the time that the bridegroom tarried, the unprepared five needed to go into town to buy their oil and were no longer present nor where they were supposed

to be for the bridegroom to even find them. When they realized their error, it was too late.

The five that were unprepared were left outside of the bridal chamber, where there is 'weeping and gnashing of teeth.'

Embracing rapture theology, is spiritually and eternally dangerous.

The rejection of Israel as the nation in covenant with God Most High / replacement theology

Because the Reformed tradition embraced a theology of God Most High only extending favor to those that God Most High loves for the moment, the Reformed tradition developed the idea that God Most High had abandoned forever, the people and nation of Israel, and that God Most High no longer was obligated to fulfill the covenant that God Most High established with Abram / Abraham, Isaac, Jacob / Israel, Moses and the people of Israel, David, etc.

In place of fulfilling the covenant that God Most High established with the people of Israel, the Reformed tradition taught that the church / ecclesia now filled the position of being the recipient of the fulfillment of God Most High's covenant. Because the church / ecclesia replaced the people of Israel, this was called 'replacement theology.'

The reality is that a true and authentic God cannot experience any point of discontinuity. A true and authentic God's promises must be fulfilled. Therefore, the covenant agreement that God Most High made with the people of Israel, must also be fulfilled.

The biblical message presented a God who is love and loves. Surely the God of the biblical record has enough love for both Jews and Gentiles, to be motivated to fulfill the covenant agreement made with the people of Israel, and to also care for the Gentile followers of the Lamb / Jesus Christ.

The infiltration of incomplete theologies / unfinished work, into the church in preparation for the era of the time of Jacob's Trouble

The main scheme of the red dragon / serpent / Satan, Inc. was to infiltrate, divide, and conquer what authoritatively belonged to, belongs to, and will belong to, God Most High. The main schemes of the red dragon / serpent / Satan, Inc. was to colonize, convert, and control. Throughout human history, colonizing, converting, and controlling groups of people or even nations, has been an effective and successful method of bringing change and acquiring property for the infiltrator. Infiltration, division, and conquest / colonization, conversion, and coercion, are currently being used with finesse during this era of the time of Jacob's Trouble.

The culture that humanity lives in, has become accustomed to the schemes of the red dragon / serpent / Satan, Inc. Essentially our world culture has the effect of lulling the followers of the Lamb / Jesus Christ, into accepting the infiltration of the red dragon / serpent / Satan, Inc.

In the message that Jesus Christ communicated to the angel of the church of Sardis, Jesus Christ implored the historical era of the church of Sardis to 'Wake up! Strengthen what remains and is about to die...' (Revelation 3:2).

During the revelation of the seventh trumpet / woe #3 / seven bowls / seven last plagues, after the sixth bowl / sixth last plague was poured out, Jesus Christ reiterated the fact that, 'Look, I come like a thief! Blessed is the one who stays awake and remains clothed, so as not to go naked and be shamefully exposed.' Revelation 16:15.

Reiterating this message at that point in the vision given to John the Revelator, was yet another indicator that Jesus Christ's coming will not include a rapture either before or during the era of the time of Jacob's Trouble.

Jesus Christ's message for the era of the time of Jacob's Trouble from the message to the angel of the reformation church of Sardis

Jesus said: 'To the angel of the church of Sardis, write,

'This is the message from the one having the seven Spirits of God, and the seven stars.'

'I know your deeds, that you have the characterization that you are alive. But you are dead.'

'Be watching and strengthen the things that remain, which are about to die. For I have not found your works to be completed in the sight of my God. Therefore, remember what you have received and heard. Keep it and repent. Therefore, if you do not watch, I will come like a thief and you will not know at what hour I will come upon you.' Revelation 3:1-3 translated

While Protestants protested the very aspects of the Roman Catholic Church that messiah / the Lamb / Jesus Christ identified as offensive in the message given to the angels of the seven churches (Revelation 2 and 3), in many ways the early Protestants further increased and enhanced their theological drift that was founded upon the errant portion of the Roman Catholic Church's dogmas, doctrines, theologies and practices.

The biblical message documented points from which conclusions can be made. But theological drift begins with errant conclusions and then creates further conclusions that are not in agreement with the overall message of the biblical record.

Too often in Reformed theology, the importance of biblical commentary study supersedes authentic biblical study. And Jesus Christ determined that the practice of injecting one's own agenda into theology, and then imposing one's agenda over the agenda of God Most High, is offensive.

One of the theological improvements that the early Protestant Reformers brought was the realization that within every Roman Catholic Church mass, was the symbolic sacrifice of Jesus, again and again and again. But the biblical record documented that Jesus Christ needed to be sacrificed only once for all time (Hebrews 7:27, 9:26-28, 10:1-10). Messiah / the Lamb / Jesus Christ's one time sacrifice that took place with the feast of Passover around 30 AD, was sufficient to be able to cover all sin for six thousand / seven thousand years.

But the early Protestant Reformers failed to complete their theological realization and to understand

the full meaning and value of messiah / the Lamb / Jesus Christ's sacrifice. When the full meaning and value of Jesus Christ's sacrifice is not recognized, then the benefits of his sacrifice cannot be fully realized. Without the full covering of Jesus Christ's sacrifice, reliance for relationship with God reverts to one's works. And one's works can never be sufficient for entrance into the kingdom of heaven.

While the early Protestant Reformers preached against the insufficiencies in the dogmas, doctrines, theologies and practices of the Roman Catholic Church, their own personal lives and some of the theologies that they developed, fell short of being fully aligned with the authentic biblical message.

Churches and organizations have a life cycle. Over time, leadership changes. Rules change. Values change. Words and their meanings change.

The Protestant church lifecycle will eventually lead some Protestant churches back to their roots of the Roman Catholic Church.

During the era of the time of Jacob's Trouble, this will give the Roman Catholic Church and those Protestant churches that reunite with the Roman Catholic Church a sense of security from the deep history of the Roman Catholic Church and its endurance through time, a sense of impregnability. The Roman Catholic Church will again believe that they are autonomously sovereign and do not need to be accountable to God Most High.

Francis, who concurrently holds both the position of pope and leader of the Jesuits, provided leadership for the Roman Catholic Church to return to the Roman Catholic Church's belief in its own autonomy, and its supposed sovereignty over the biblical record, over Jesus Christ's version of the fully established kingdom of heaven on earth, and over all churches of the world. The Protestant churches that return to the Roman Catholic Church umbrella, have also chosen to pursue and support this path.

With Francis, once again in history, religious power and political power will seek to be combined in a single office for the purpose of advancing global papal rule. And

Protestant churches that embrace this kind of globalization of religion, will be sleepwalking into the very religious culture and environment that was once so repulsive that it initiated protestation.

Once again individuals will be faced with the question of who will be deified and who will be defied. Will it be the global religious community or will it be God Most High? Both the global religious community and God Most High will possess great power. It is an important and dangerous time in history. Each of us must choose carefully which kingdom we will support.

As the time of Jesus Christ's return draws closer, Jesus Christ's message to the historical era of the church of Sardis, acts like an alarm clock intended to wake up the individual so they are prepared for the activities of the day. Jesus Christ's message also encourages renewal to the basic truth of the importance of allegiance to Jesus Christ and of faith in God Most High. Refusing to not wake up will mean that Jesus Christ's coming will be a surprise, just as a thief uses the element of surprise to gain advantage in the pursuit of the thief's mission.

The further implication of Jesus Christ's message was that if one is awake, then one will be prepared for Jesus Christ's coming. The followers of the Lamb / Jesus Christ are expected to be watching. Jesus Christ expects the followers of the Lamb / Jesus Christ to be prepared. Even the Israelites needed to prepare for the Exodus out of Egypt, and the ten plagues served as their wake up call in their preparation to leave. The era of the time of Jacob's Trouble will require people to be prepared for the events of this era.

Jesus Christ's message was also directed for the time when there will be concerted effort to blot out the people of God by the two beasts of Revelation 13 and the organizations that they provide leadership for. The campaign of the global religious community, will be to once again convey the false message that the global religious leaders possess the keys to the gates of heaven and hell, that they have the authority to reward those who are willing to embrace their authority and willing to *incorporate the practices of the baal / mystery / mythology religion into their lives, that they are able to excommunicate individuals who do not comply with their regime from their version of the kingdom of heaven, that they are justified in killing those who do not meet their worship requirements, and that they have the authority and are vindicated in blotting out the names of those who are truly followers of God Most High from the book of life.*

While God Most High's people may feel forgotten, God's people will in reality never be blotted out of the book of life. In reality, God's people hold a position worthy of being announced before God Most High and God's angels; a position that Satan, the rebellious angels and their adherents, no longer hold.

God the Creator told Noah years before the deluge / flood to build an ark. God the Creator told Noah seven days prior to the deluge / flood's arrival that it was time to enter the ark.

God Most High told Moses and the people of Israel how to prepare for Passover.

God Most High told the prophets where and when to anticipate the arrival of the promised and prophesied messiah, in preparation for the era of Jesus Christ's earthly ministry. Jesus Christ attempted to prepare his disciples for his crucifixion, death and resurrection and still they did not understand. But Jesus Christ did endeavor to prepare them.

To those who are listening to God, there is an awareness of what to prepare for and when.

Jesus said to the historical era of the church of Sardis, 'But if you do not wake up, I will come like a thief, and you will not know at what time I will come to you.'

Paul wrote, However, you brothers and sisters, are not in darkness so that the day will surprise you like a thief. For all of you are descendants of the light. We do not belong to the night or to the darkness. 1 Thessalonians 5:4 translated

For those who are diligent in the things of God, those who desire to be awake, the coming of Jesus Christ will not be a surprise. For the authentic followers of the Lamb / Jesus Christ, the return of Jesus Christ will be anticipated

and greeted, as a bride fully prepared to meet her bridegroom.

Jesus Christ's message to the angel of the church at Philadelphia: holiness church – Revelation 3:7-13

Jesus Christ's message to the church at Philadelphia was unique from the rest of the message to the angels of the seven churches.

First, the message to the church of Philadelphia did not contain an admonition for correction. The message directed to the other six churches, began with a description of what needed to be corrected. But directions for correction were not included for the church of Philadelphia. They obviously had found their first love (Ephesus), understood the meaning and reality of resurrection (Smyrna), did not embrace the elements of the baal / mystery / mythology religion (Pergamum), did not embrace teachings devoted to other gods or idols or the pursuit of idol worship / idolatry or the pursuit of sexual immorality (Thyatira), did not pursue righteousness as a result of their own works and were willing to personally repent and personally walk with Jesus Christ (Sardis), and they did not adulterate the message of the kingdom of heaven to allow themselves to believe that they were rich and clothed and could see while they were poor and naked and blind and repulsed by the presence of Jesus Christ (Laodicea).

Second, the message to the church of Philadelphia was a message centered upon bringing comfort to the hearts of the members of the church of Philadelphia. While the rest of the message to the seven churches identified the consequences of decisions made for or against the expectations of Jesus Christ, the message to the church of Philadelphia took the approach of reaching deeper into the relationship that Jesus Christ seeks to establish with every follower of the Lamb / Jesus Christ. And that message began with identifying that the followers of the Lamb / Jesus Christ, in Philadelphia would be greeted with an open door. And it was not just an open door. It was an open door that no one can shut, not with apathy (Ephesus) or martyrdom (Smyrna), or other religions' ideas (Pergamum), or other pursuits (Thyatira), or false legalism (Sardis), or narcistic self-pursuits (Laodicea).

The relationship between God the Creator and humanity was created to be unblemished and uninhibited. The church of Philadelphia grasped that understanding of what God Most High intended. And with that understanding, the door of the kingdom of heaven was flung open to them and they were welcomed with joy and open arms and jubilant greetings and wonderful anticipation and the opportunity to experience the fullness of authentic love.

The heart is the one part of the body that we naturally protect from injury. We guard what we eat, where we go, what we do, in order to protect the physical aspect of our hearts. We guard what enters into the mind, in order to protect the spiritual aspect of our hearts. We guard who we let into our lives, in order to protect the emotional aspect of our hearts.

But for the church of Philadelphia, the safeguards have been removed. The hearts of the followers of the Lamb / Jesus Christ, are able to freely connect with the heart of God; without fear, without barriers, without encumbrances.

Isaiah documented that being greeted with an open door, was the goal of God Most High for humanity, and that it would only be possible with the presence of messiah / son of David.

'In that day I will summon my servant, Eliakim ('God establishes') son of Hilkiah ('portion of Yahweh' / 'portion of the Lord'). I will clothe him with your robe and fasten your sash around him and hand your authority over to him. He will be a father to those who live in Jerusalem and to the people of Judah. I will place on his shoulder the key to the house of David. What he opens no one can shut, and what he shuts no one can open.'

'I will drive him like a peg into a firm place. He will become a seat / throne of honor for the house of his father. All the glory of his family will hang on him. Its offspring and offshoots — all its lesser vessels, from the bowls to all the jars.'

'In that day,' declares the Lord Almighty, 'the peg driven into the firm place will give way. It will be sheared off and will fall, and the load hanging on it will be cut down.' The Lord has spoken. Isaiah 22:20-25

Living within earth's broken cultural environment, we can only imagine the fullness of the relationship that God Most High has desired to share with the believers in messiah (BC) and the followers of the Lamb (AD). But for the those living during the time of Eliakim son of Hilkiah, and for those living in Philadelphia, they had glimpses of the beauty and majesty and glory and wonderfulness of that relationship.

For those followers of the Lamb / Jesus Christ, living in the historical timeline of the era of the church of Philadelphia, they were able to capture those same kind of glimpses of an unincumbered relationship with God Most High.

<u>Church of Philadelphia – church of love and faithfulness</u>
Jesus said, 'To the angel of the church of Philadelphia, write,
'This is the message from the Holy One, the True One, having the key of David, the one who opens and no one will shut, and who shuts and no one opens.'

'I know your deeds. Behold I have set before you a door that has been opened, which no one is able to shut. You have little power, and yet you have kept my word and you have not denied my name. Behold, I give those from the synagogue of Satan, those who declared themselves to be Jews and who are not, but lie – behold I will make them come and worship before your feet and they will know that I have loved you. Because you have kept my word of patient endurance, I will also keep you out of the hour of trial that is about to come upon the whole inhabited world, that will test those dwelling upon the earth.'

'I am coming with speed. Hold fast to what you have so that no one may take your crown.'

'The one who overcomes, I will make a pillar in the temple of my God, and that one will not go out anymore. I will write upon that one the name of my God and the name of the city of my God, the new Jerusalem coming down out of heaven from my God, and my new name.'

'To the one having an ear, hear what the Spirit says to the churches.' Revelation 3:7-13 translated

Note Jesus Christ's words of encouragement to the church of Philadelphia were, 'I will also keep you from the hour of trial that is going to come on the whole world to test the inhabitants of the earth.' *and* 'I am coming soon.'

Being kept from the hour of trial implied that the church of the historical era of the church of Philadelphia needs to be prepared to meet the test of the inhabitants of the earth and that the church of Philadelphian theology will receive support from Jesus Christ to meet the challenges of that time, through to the return of Jesus Christ and to the end of the era of the time of Jacob's Trouble.

Historical message:
The name 'Philadelphia' was from the Greek 'phileo' which means 'beloved' or 'dear' and 'adelphos' which means 'brother.'

Philadelphia was founded by Eumenes the king of Pergamum or Attalus his brother. King Attalus was so devoted to his brother that he was called by his brother 'Philadelphous' which meant 'one who loves his brother.' The city took on this character from its name.

Philadelphia was located on an area that has volcanic activity and earthquakes. In 17 AD Philadelphia was destroyed by an earthquake. Other cities also were devasted by earthquakes at the time. Sardis fared worse than Philadelphia. But Philadelphia experienced severe aftershocks, traumatizing the population.

Rome allowed Philadelphia to not pay taxes for five years. Once the city was rebuilt by Tiberius, the citizens temporarily renamed the city 'Neocaesarea' which meant 'new city of Caesar' in honor of Rome's favor. Under the reign of Vespasian (fl. 69 to 79 AD), the city changed its name to Flavia. But by the lifetime of the apostle John, the city was again named Philadelphia.

Philadelphia was close to the borders of three regions and became the gateway to the cultures of other nations. Philadelphia culturally acted like an open door.

During the era of the apostolic church, the Jewish people were exempted from having to pledge allegiance to the Roman emperor as god. The requirement for exemption in emperor worship was to have your name written in the synagogue record. But the followers of Jesus Christ, who believed that Jesus Christ was the promised and prophesied messiah, discovered that they were no longer accepted in the synagogues and their names were stricken from the synagogue record. The synagogue doors were shut to them leaving even the Jewish Christians vulnerable to persecution when they denied giving allegiance to the Roman emperor.

The city of Philadelphia remained a Roman town until 1379 when it finally was ruled by the Turks. Today, the city of Alasehir / 'city of God' occupies the original site of the old city of Philadelphia.

Historical timeline message to the historical era of the church of Philadelphia:

The message to angel of the church of Philadelphia, was nestled into the context of the entire history of the church that laid the foundation for the historical era of the church of Philadelphia.

Near the beginning of church history, the historical era of the church of Pergamum established the Roman Catholic Church, and presented the mixture of the theology that was entrusted to Peter, the apostles and the rest of the disciples of Jesus Christ, with the baal / mystery / mythology religion theology. The church of the historical era of the church of Pergamum, had themselves flung open the doors of the kingdom of heaven, attempting to channel all religion into fitting within the narrow passage provided by Jesus Christ.

The theology of the church of Pergamum mothered the church of Thyatira.

The historical era of the church of Thyatira, established the foundation for historical era of the church of Sardis, and presented a theology that the pope and Roman Catholic Church religious leaders Peter had assigned all responsibility of church leadership to the hierarchy of the Roman Catholic Church. Through the sacrament of extreme unction / last rites, and with the authority to excommunicate members of the Roman Catholic Church, the Roman Catholic Church had determined that Roman Catholic priests were the authorized gatekeepers for heaven. And the Roman

Catholic Church was the ruling church that endorsed feudalism.

The historical era of the church of Sardis, represented the church that came out of the era of the early Protestant Reformation. The theology of the Reformed tradition, presented the salvation plan of God Most High as having already been predetermined, predestined, with the eternal destiny of every individual having been preestablished prior to their conception. The feudalism that marked the historical era of the church of Thyatira, complete with the hierarchy of monarchs, barons, lords, dukes, etc., supported this supposition and worked as a device for keeping the masses of people under the governance of the elite and the elect. Unfortunately, the Reformed tradition applied this element of feudal governance to its theology. The Reformed tradition presented the idea that while God Most High is the one who determines who is considered elected for heaven, it is the church leaders who decide what the rules for the entrance to heaven are. Wealthy are more elected than the poor. Men are more elected than women. Some races are more elected than other races. Older is more elected than youth. Those who support the system of rules of the church are more elected than those who rebel against their onerous ecclesiastical rule. Etc. As the Reformed tradition formed, it became a system of law without the presence of grace or mercy, and was devoid of allowing any heart to heart type of relationship between God Most High and humanity.

Within this historical context, Jesus Christ introduced himself in addressing the historical era of the church of Philadelphia, as the one who holds the key of David, with the power to open and shut the door of heaven. Jesus Christ reassured the historical era of the church of Philadelphia that it is not the church or its religious leaders who determine who is eligible for passing through heaven's doors. It is in fact Jesus Christ who makes that determination. And that determination is based upon the condition of the heart to heart relationship that a person has with God Most High.

Following the message to the historical era of the church of Philadelphia, came the message to the historical era of the church of Laodicea. In that message, Jesus Christ was found locked out of the church, and forced to knock on the door of individuals in order to be accepted in. Only in the message to the historical era of the church of Philadelphia, did Jesus discuss the church's doorway to heaven with positive results.

In the historical timeline of the history of the church, the historical era of the church of Philadelphia was positioned in the historical era that was termed the 'Great Awakening' in the American colonies, and the 'Evangelical Revival' in Britain. Some have called this era the missionary movement because of its missionary emphasis. As the Great Awakening / Evangelical Revival developed, it became known as the 'Holiness Movement.' This era was known for its focus upon developing holiness of the heart. The missionary emphasis invested in taking the message that Jesus Christ is Lord and desires to have his heart known, into the entire world. The missionary movement that began in the mid-1700s, sought to reach people in every area of the earth began in the mid-1700s.

The seeds for the Great Awakening / Evangelical Revival / Holiness Movement actually began with the Protestant Reformation (c. 1517) and the printing press. The Protestant Reformation supplied the foundational theological emphasis upon the importance of understanding the biblical message. The printing press provided the opportunity for Bibles to be published in the languages of the peoples, and to be able to be purchased at a reasonable price so that now every person could afford to own their own copy of the Bible. But it was the activity of the people of the era of the Great Awakening / Evangelical Revival / Holiness Movement who became active in reading and studying the word of God, that allowed that message to touch their hearts and influenced them to act.

With the mass distribution of the Bible, written in the languages that the people spoke, the Bible was now able to be read by everyone and memorized. People were now able to be ruled by the Ten Commandments and God Most High's law instead of being ruled by their dependence upon the religious leaders with the power of the organized church's hierarchy, and the religious dogmas, doctrines, theologies and practices that were sometimes in opposition against the message of the biblical record.

Because each individual was now allowed and expected to explore God Most High through a personal biblical understanding without the filters of the church or religious leaders, the depth of understanding concerning God became deep. Individuals were now allowed and encouraged to become 'seekers of the truth.'

As a part of the historical timeline of Revelation 2 and 3, the church of Philadelphia represented the church during the era of the Great Awakening / Evangelical Revival / Holiness Movement. During this time, the Roman Catholic Church was under heavy Society of Jesus / Jesuit influence. As an alternative to the heavy oppression of the Society of Jesus / Jesuit influence, Protestant churches experienced a great amount of influence around the world. The theology of the Great Awakening / Evangelical Revival / Holiness Movement heavily influenced the world with the message of Jesus Christ and his love, with its focus upon the supremacy of biblical authority over ecclesiastical authority. The Great Awakening / Evangelical Revival / Holiness Movement became the foundation for democratic and republic governments around the world, including the founding of the United States of America.

The theology of the Great Awakening / Evangelical Revival / Holiness Movement influenced the founders of the United States who were intent upon including religious freedom in the newly formed government. The founders of the United States professed their faith in God Most High and would publicly and in their writings describe their relationship with God. The first amendment of the United States' Constitution reads, 'congress shall make no law respecting the establishment of religion, or prohibiting the free exercise thereof; or abridging the freedom of speech, or of the press; or the right of the people peaceably to assemble, and to petition the Government for a redress of grievances.' The founders of the United States took care to separate the power of the church from the power of the state so that neither should rule over each other nor join forces in order to rule over people. And they shared that ideal because of the cultural and spiritual climate established with the Great Awakening / Evangelical Revival / Holiness Movement.

The theology of the historical era of the church of Philadelphia reintroduced the lost early church theology, that true religion requires hearts and minds of individuals to be devoted to God Most High first, family second, church and government afterward. In the theology of the Great Awakening / Evangelical Revival / Holiness Movement, the practice of obligatory rites and rituals, or of meeting some kind of religious organization requirement, did not ensure a right standing with God Most High, or justification, or righteousness, or salvation, or regeneration, or entrance into the kingdom of heaven. A right relationship with God Most High, etc., was totally dependent upon one's relationship with Jesus Christ.

Christian Perfection / Entire Sanctification is a theological doctrine of the Great Awakening / Evangelical Revival / Holiness Movement. Christian Perfection / Entire Sanctification is the belief that a true follower of the Lamb / Jesus Christ is so devoted to God that their heart can experience a 'perfection' where they love God and love the people of God so devotedly that there is no room in the heart for the desire for sinning or rebelling against God. Amongst the holiness preachers, John Wesley offered sermons and wrote *A Plain Account of Christian Perfection* to better explain the doctrine of Christian Perfection / Entire Sanctification, which is primarily an exposition of Paul's book of Romans and the teaching of Jesus Christ.

The Great Awakening / Evangelical Revival / Holiness Movement presented Jesus Christ as resurrected, alive and currently dwelling in heaven with a purpose that would require his return to fully establish the kingdom of heaven on earth. Jesus Christ was presented as Sovereign King over all rulers of the earth. Jesus Christ was presented as Righteous Judge who is active, alive, all knowing and most just. Jesus Christ was presented as Loving God who seeks to be in a personal relationship with each individual without any governmental structure or religious organization interfering.

Ultimately the historical era of the church of Philadelphia was focused on the importance of each person being responsible for 'working out their salvation,' and developing their own personal relationship with God. Practicing some rite or ritual dictated by a religious organization no longer 'worked' for covering sin. Being a member of the community of the elite and elect no longer allowed a person's sin to be automatically excused. Being born with specific 'acceptable' parentage was no longer the standard for automatic acceptance or rejection for church membership or heaven's reception requirement. Each person was expected to prepare to stand before God Most High, stripped naked of bank account, holdings, property, possessions, titles, and position.

The historical era of the church of Philadelphia brought an understanding of God Most High that recognized the significance of God's love and recognized God's love as an essential foundation for the full establishment of the kingdom of heaven. The kingdom of heaven was now able to be defined with a king whose economy base is not power, but love, and a kingdom that trades in the economy of love. A God of perfect love seeks to live in a kingdom where perfect love is the motivation for decisions and for living. A God of perfect love is the kind of God who creates creatures with the capacity to love. A God of perfect love is the kind of God who loves so deeply that God is willing to go to any lengths in order to be surrounded by a humanity that also loves perfectly. Christian Perfection / Entire Sanctification takes place when a person is so filled with the love of God in one's heart that sin is expelled and holiness replaces all sin.

The doctrine of Christian Perfection / Entire Sanctification and the understanding that God Most High's kingdom economy is love, not power, meant that the impact that religion should have on society is not as a ruling organization but rather as a haven where people are safe to develop relationship with a loving God, where people are influenced to love God, and where people practice caring for others. True Christianity influences people to discard the power economy of the kingdom of Satan, Inc. / kingdom of man and exchange it for a love economy where the love of God becomes the supreme motivation for actions.

This biblical message of the God who authors love was able to spread across the colonies and the territories that became the United States. But it also transformed England and the positions of the upper classes in English society. With this new perspective, the biblical message spread throughout the world.

The resulting freedom from church tyranny resulted in the disintegration of the rigid class structure of rich and poor / lord and servant / master and slave / male and female. Now there was the opportunity for a middle class. The disintegration of rigid class structure meant that everyone now had equal opportunity to access God Most High and heaven, not based on status assigned by religious leaders.

The theology of the historical era of the church of Philadelphia in the movement toward the theology of the historical era of the church of Laodicea

The historical timeline era of the church of Philadelphia / Great Awakening / Evangelical Revival, was commended by Jesus Christ for its deeds, its strength, its emphasis upon the entire authentic biblical message, its refusal to deny the name of Jesus Christ, its determination to withstand the pressure of previous church oppressive theology, and its endurance.

While the theology of the era of the Great Awakening / Evangelical Revival was commended for its advancement of the kingdom of heaven, it was also an era that influenced the movement toward the theology of the church of Laodicea.

During the era of the time of the historical era of the church of Sardis, the Reformed tradition embraced the King James Version of the Bible, commissioned by the king of England, James I and VI (fl. 1603 to 1625), who produced a version of the Bible that conformed to the ideas of the leadership of the ecclesia and reflected favorably upon the episcopal structure of the Church of England. The Reformed tradition advocated a focus upon the law of the kingdom of heaven, and the trust that God Most High placed on ecclesiastical authority to determine how that law should be metered out.

But the people of the historical era of the church of Philadelphia, the Great Awakening / Evangelical Revival, more heavily relied upon the Geneva Bible, that was translated without regard to the pressures of the ecclesiological hierarchy. Instead of seeking to support the establishment of church law, the Geneva Bible translation and other earlier English translations, sought to support the authentic message of the kingdom of heaven contained within the original text of the biblical record. And that message was one of a love affair between God Most High and the followers of the Lamb / Jesus Christ. Instead of picking and choosing which passages of the biblical text should be focused upon (and which should be neglected) to maintain ecclesiastical order, the rally cry was 'the whole Bible for the whole world.' Law was to be tempered by the purpose of the law; and that purpose was that the hearts of God Most High and individuals, would meet, and then thrive together.

The problem that the historical eras of the previous churches had with the theology of historical era of the church of Philadelphia was that love forgives easily.

During the era Great Awakening / Evangelical Revival, its greatest strength was also its greatest weakness. Sharing a love that easily forgives, also allowed those who claimed to have experienced the deepest love of God, but who did not, to infiltrate the church that was founded upon love, and to establish their ideas of ecclesiastical legalism. Those that infiltrated also established their own ideas of the rules of Christianity.

And establishing church community based on a love that easily forgives, allowed those who desired to abandon the biblical rules of Christianity, to also infiltrate the church and become leaders. This was termed antinomianism theology.

Both the ecclesiastical legalism that crept back into church theology at one extreme, and the idea of redefining Christianity without rules at the other theological extreme, eventually worked to establish the theological culture of the historical timeline era of the church of Laodicea where the church is neither hot nor cold, and nauseating.

If the theology of the era of the Great Awakening / Evangelical Revival would have more actively insisted upon religious leaders having a personal working relationship with Jesus Christ instead of allowing ecclesiastical legalism to worm its way back into church culture, and antinomianism to be expressed within the ecclesia, the era of the Great Awakening / Evangelical Revival would have been able to stand up to the foes against the kingdom of heaven, residing within the church.

And if the theology of the era of the Great Awakening / Evangelical Revival would have more actively insisted upon religious leaders having a dedication to the biblical authority of the entire biblical text, instead of allowing love to be the guide, then the era of the Great Awakening / Evangelical Revival would have been able to confront the consistent redefining of religion that is currently underway within the modern church culture.

The Reformed theology ecclesiastical legalism focused upon elevating law over love and the loving work of the Holy Spirit.

The post Christian church community culture focuses upon elevating personal agendas over God Most High's authentic law, love, and the cleansing work of the Holy Spirit.

It was the allowances made by the church of the era of the Great Awakening / Evangelical Revival to again embrace the tenets of Reformed theology and to adopt antinomianism theology, that allowed for the development of the theology of the historical era of the church of Laodicea.

Jesus Christ's message for the era of the time of Jacob's Trouble from the message to the angel of the holiness church of Philadelphia

One of the teachings within the message to the church of Philadelphia was that even Jesus Christ himself has a new name. The importance of Jesus Christ having a new name was reiterated with the description of the return of Jesus Christ as documented by John the Revelator. (Revelation 3:12, 19:11-16) In fact, in John the Revelator's book of Revelation, 'name' ins some form, was referenced thirty times.

Names have meaning… and power. Not only does Jesus Christ have a new name, but to those who overcome, Jesus Christ is willing to place that name onto the followers of the Lamb / Jesus Christ, sharing the power of his new name. As the era of the time of Jacob's Trouble advances, Jesus Christ's message conveys a sense of urgency. Followers of the Lamb / Jesus Christ are not allowed to be passive participants within a corrupt church structure. Followers of the Lamb/ Jesus Christ have been instructed to be prepared for the return of Jesus Christ. During the era of the time of Jacob's Trouble, it is not merely the true holy ones in heaven and the heavenly beings who act. On earth, the followers of the Lamb / Jesus Christ also have been given responsibilities and instructions. And because the church represented by the theology of the era of the Philadelphia church will observe God Most High's activity transpiring quickly, the followers of the lamb / Jesus Christ also must be prepared to act quickly.

The message of the feast of Yom Kippur / Day of Atonement was that the Day of Atonement following the return of messiah, will be the day designated in the six thousand years of human history, for 'closing the books' as to whom will reside in heaven and whom will not reside in heaven. The one who authentically holds the keys to the kingdom of heaven has the authority to determine who enters and who does not enter. Once the door on heaven is shut, there is no opportunity to sneak in via a window or a hole in the roof or a tunnel underground or any other opening. The era of the time of Jacob's Trouble will conclude with shutting the door to the Garden of Eden /

garden of God / paradise / kingdom of heaven, against those who have chosen to not be believers in messiah (BC) or followers of the Lamb (AD).

But those who are opposed to God Most High and the kingdom of heaven will continue to insist that there are other ways to enter into heaven and that they can still rise with their own power, to displace God Most High and negate the rules of the kingdom of heaven, because they believe they are good enough for heaven without a need to concede to the rules of heaven living. They believe that they are entitled to bring their rebellion into a perfected kingdom of heaven and to spread rebellion against God Most High's kingdom all over again. Those opposed to the leadership of God Most High will unite with the global governance system to become adherents of the kingdom of Satan, Inc. / kingdom of man under the guise that their kingdom choice is actually heaven and living under the rules of the kingdom God Most High is actually hellish.

The era of the time of Jacob's Trouble will be a time when desperation will seek to reign. Those who truly believe that Jesus Christ is Lord, that we crucified him, that God raised Jesus from the dead, and that Jesus Christ is returning to claim what is his, will no longer be welcomed in most churches. The doors to churches and synagogues will again be closed to those who believe that Jesus Christ is the promised and prophesied messiah. It will seem as if there is no strength left for the true followers of the Lamb / Jesus Christ / God's holy people.

The red dragon / serpent / Satan, Inc.'s kingdom will appear to have the win in the bag. Worldwide, people will be ready to capitulate to the two beasts of Revelation 13, and the kingdom of the red dragon / serpent / Satan, Inc. / kingdom of man.

The kingdom of the red dragon / serpent / Satan, Inc. / kingdom of man will provide a new global government issued identity and the promise of a new eternal virtual type residence.

And Jesus Christ offered to the true followers of the Lamb / Jesus Christ, throughout the various church ages, the opportunity to overcome / to be victorious, and to receive their eternal identity, related to the name of Jesus Christ, complete with a position of importance in the fully established kingdom of heaven on earth. (Revelation 2, 3, 20, 21, 22, etc.)

The era of the time of Jacob's Trouble will possibly be the most important era in human history for the purpose of compelling humanity to make their final decision concerning their choice of which kingdom they will invest in for their eternal residence.

The global religious community and global governance system empowered by the red dragon / serpent / Satan, Inc., is about establishing power, and therefore giving out 'crowns,' Jesus Christ reminded us that each individual determines which crown they will hold on to; the 'crown' offered by the two beasts of Revelation 13 and the kingdom of Satan, Inc. / kingdom of man; or the crown that Jesus Christ offers to those whose loyalty is with God (Revelation 2:10, 3:11).

The two beasts of Revelation 13 and the kingdom of Satan, Inc. / kingdom of man will actively assign people inventory numbers and new virtual type identities that will cause them to be indentured to the kingdom of Satan, Inc. / kingdom of man. They will also assign people new locations to live and develop new cultures, redefining community identities.

But Jesus Christ offers to the followers of the Lamb / Jesus Christ, the opportunity to share God's name, and to receive their own new name, assigned by God Most High and Jesus Christ. Jesus Christ offers to the followers of the Lamb / Jesus Christ the opportunity to be regenerated with the full image of God that we were created to possess. Jesus Christ offers to every follower of the Lamb / Jesus Christ their own personal new identity that is the validation that God Most High is faithful to allow us to become all and everything that we were created to be, unfettered by the limitations of sin and to live in an environment that is sinless. Jesus Christ also provided the additional promise that this new eternal residence will have the provision of living in a face to face friendship relationship with God Most High.

In the context of the Bible as a whole, the crown that the two beasts of Revelation 13 and the kingdom of Satan, Inc. / kingdom of man offers is a symbol and tool of bondage. Satan once offered a crown to Jesus who rejected it. The only crown that the two beasts of Revelation 13 can offer is a victor's crown, the symbol of dominance. Satan is the one who dreams of rising to the top, of ascending to the most high place. Satan cannot rise to 'the top' without placing everyone else on 'the bottom.' (See Isaiah 14:4-23, Ezekiel 28:1-19, etc.)

In contrast, the crown that Jesus Christ offers is a symbol and tool of freedom. Jesus Christ has promised the followers of Lamb, the opportunity to be joint heirs with him, to share a seat on the throne that he inherited through the will of God Most High, and to occupy that seat next to Jesus Christ for eternity. The crown that Jesus Christ offers is a crown that demonstrates the position one has as an heir, in a familiar relationship with God.

The message to our era, to the era of the time of Jacob's Trouble was that in this battle of the kingdoms to determine which kingdom will be fully established for eternity, there is an intrinsic battle to determine which economic system is more powerful; the economic system of power without love that is the foundation for the kingdom of Satan, Inc. / kingdom of man, or the economic system of love that is greater than power that the kingdom of heaven utilizes.

The kingdom of Satan, Inc. / the kingdom of man cannot conceive that love, true love, God Most High's love can be strong enough to stand against the power structure of Satan's dream. Satan never understood that the path to the throne of heaven is the path of love, not power. This lack in understanding was why the red dragon / serpent / Satan, Inc. believed that they could crucify the promised and prophesied messiah and that he would remain dead.

With the love economy of the kingdom of heaven, the throne of heaven is a throne that is shared with whom God desires to share it with. The throne of God Most High cannot be taken from God Most High. God Most High lovingly chose to share the throne with the Lamb / Jesus

Christ, and Jesus Christ lovingly chose to share his throne with the believers in messiah (BC) and the followers of the Lamb (AD). The throne of God Most High, like love, must be given. It cannot be forcibly stolen.

Satan and the red dragon / serpent / Satan, Inc.'s arsenal against humanity contains the act of deception / lying, in order to convince humanity that their kingdom is superior. The greatest lie of all is the lie that says God Most High does not love you, and that you have not been created in God's image and therefore you are not already like God Most High and consequently you are unlovable. The lie continues with teaching that love itself is weak and has no power.

And yet it is when we are the weakest, when strength has departed, that we quit flailing and we assume a position where we can be rescued. When we are weakest, we are in a condition to receive an infusion of love and be strengthened with the full force of love.

When Jesus Christ said, 'I will make them come and fall down at your feet and acknowledge that I have loved you,' Jesus Christ promised that there is more blessing to come for the church that lives out the theology of the historical timeline era of Philadelphia.

Those whom God loves, God Most High will protect or avenge. The biblical message described this character of God beginning with the book of Genesis and without wavering, reiterated God Most High's protecting and avenging character all the way through to the end of the book of Revelation.

All human history began with God the Creator's love for the first man and first woman, that was tampered with and interfered with in the Garden of Eden. God the Creator fell in love with them and could not walk away. God the Creator fell in love with their offspring just because they belonged to Adam and Eve. God so loved the world, Adam, Eve, and their offspring, that God the Creator developed the plan to gain loving humanity back and to completely infuse them with the perfection and love they were created to experience.

All of God Most High's true message documented God's love; the six thousand years of human history lived away from the face of God, the interaction of the red dragon / serpent / Satan, Inc. in this world, God's acts of salvation and planning along the way. All of God Most High's true message documented God's unbreakable, unfathomable, unrelenting love for humanity, the creature that God was willing to press God the Creator's image into.

Even after six thousand years, the red dragon / serpent / Satan, Inc. who does not possess the image of God Most High, still cannot understand this kind of love, cannot be the recipient of this kind of love, and remains jealous of it.

When we respond to God's love with rebellion, we remove ourselves from God Most High's opportunity to bless us, to protect us, to embrace us.

But when we respond to God Most High's love with love returned to God, we secure a place for ourselves in God's own heart. In that place, destruction cannot touch us. Because God Most High is everlasting, ageless, uninfluenced by time, space, etc., there is no power that is sufficient enough to destroy or bind God or to be able to touch what abides inside God's heart. Understanding God Most High's love for us and responding to God's love with love for God causes us to be 'perfect' in God's eyes. The act of experiencing God's perfect love that causes us to love God perfectly was called 'Christian Perfection.' This is the power of God that can be extended to exist between any two beings or people. This is what the church of the historical timeline of Philadelphia embraces.

Evil still must do its thing, be allowed 'out of the box' in order for God Most High to clean up the mess. Evil may still bring death to some of God's people during the era of the time of Jacob's Trouble. But God's love will most certainly avenge what will be temporarily taken.

God's promise is, 'I will restore to you the years that were eaten – the swarming locust, the crawling locust, and the consuming locust, and the chewing locust – My great army which I sent among you.' Joel 2:25. translated

Along with the 'locusts' that regularly devour, during the era of the time of Jacob's Trouble there will also be literal scorpion locusts of the red dragon / serpent / Satan, Inc.'s creation that will come and bring destruction (Revelation 9:1-12).

More importantly, God Most High's love for us means that Jesus Christ is able to promise, 'I will also keep you from the hour of trial that is going to come on the whole world to test the inhabitants of the earth.'

This verse can also be translated, 'I will also keep you through the hour of trial…'

Both translations guaranteed that for those who love God Most High, God carries them deep in God's heart. Both translations guaranteed that those who love God will have a unique and special purpose for their life during the era of the time of Jacob's Trouble. And both translations guaranteed that we do not travel this historical era of the time of Jacob's Trouble alone. Even though Jesus Christ is physically unseen and working in heaven, Jesus Christ is also working on earth, providing God's people with a canopy of protection keeping them safe from the red dragon / serpent / Satan, Inc.

Jesus Christ's message to the angel of the church at Laodicea: antagonistic apostate church – Revelation 3:14-22

Church of Laodicea – lukewarm and distasteful church (See Colossians 2:1-5)

Jesus said, 'To the angel of the church of Laodicea, write,

'This is the message from the Amen, the faithful and true witness, the beginning of God's creation.'

'I know your works and that you are neither cold nor are you hot. Oh, that you were cold or hot! So because you are lukewarm, and neither hot nor cold, I am about to vomit you out of my mouth. For you say, 'I am rich and I have made myself rich, and there is nothing that I need.' And you do not realize / remember / appreciate that you are wretched / afflicted and miserable and poor and blind and naked. I recommend that you buy gold from me that has been refined by fire wo that you may be rich, and white garments so that you may be clothed and might not be shamed by the exposure of your nakedness, and eye salve to anoint your eyes so that you may see.'

'As many as I love as friends, I rebuke and discipline. Therefore, be zealous and repent.'

'Behold, I stand at the door and knock. If anyone should hear my voice and open the door, then I will come in to that one and dine with that one, and that one with me.'

'The one who overcomes, I allow to sit with me on my throne, as I also overcame and sat down with my Father on my Father's throne.'

'To the one having an ear, hear what the Spirit says to the churches.' Revelation 3:14-22 translated

Jesus Christ presented himself as present during the church of Laodicean era.

But Jesus Christ is no longer in the church. In the message to the angel of the church of Laodicea, Jesus Christ is located outside, expelled from the church.

Now Jesus Christ presents himself to the individual and waits for the individual to discover Jesus Christ, despite the church having exiled him.

True to his promises, Jesus Christ remains present and available even until the end of the age / the end of the era of the time of Jacob's Trouble.

Historical message:

Laodicea was known for its production of eye salve. Laodicea hosted a medical school with famous physicians. Two of Laodicea's physicians were featured on coins. Laodicea was a world leader in healthcare.

Laodicea was also known for its production of fine black wool which was quite rare. Through the production and sale of their rare, luxurious black wool and specialty clothes, Laodicea had become wealthy.

Wealth creates a false feeling of independence. Wealth allows people to believe that they no longer need to be accountable to others, to family, to society, to God, etc. The residents of Laodicea took pride in their wealth and believed that their self-sufficiency negated a need for God. But, one characteristic of wealth is that wealth is able to be removed from a person or a city or an organization and therefore cannot be a true defining characteristic of a person or a group of people. Wealth is a temporary phenomenon. Wealth can only be a cover.

Laodicea also had a water problem. One nearby town had hot springs. Another nearby town had cold, clear water. But Laodicea was stuck with tepid, mineral laden water. Not hot. Not cold. It was the kind of water that

people did not desire to drink, water that initiated the urge to vomit.

The theology of Laodicea was neither hot nor cold. During the time of Antiochus the Great / Antiochus III, two thousand Israelite families were transported to Phrygia from Babylonia. Consequently, many Laodiceans possessed Jewish heritage. The Jewish people of Laodicea were known for having little compassion for others outside of their Jewish community.

Because of their wealth, the population of Laodicea frequently did not even recognize a need for religion, or for a relationship with God. Laodicea seemed to not possess any religious fervor or clarity. Spiritual life in Laodicea was set aside in the pursuit of health and wealth.

Historical timeline message to the historical era of the church of Laodicea:

The seventeenth century saw the development of four main factions of theological thought. There were those who remained loyal to the pope and to the hierarchy of the Roman Catholic Church / the papists (Thyatira). There were those who found their escape route into Protestantism, rejecting just enough of Roman Catholicism to experience freedom, but holding onto enough of Catholicism to still feel comfortable in their traditions / the reformers (Sardis). There were those who embraced the Lordship of Jesus Christ, who devoted themselves to being followers of the Lamb / Jesus Christ and finding friendship with God / the believers (Philadelphia). But, during the seventeenth century, the seeds were also being sown for what would blossom in the nineteenth, twentieth, and twenty first centuries; a religion founded upon the work of Christianity, that would not acknowledge the divinity and sovereignty of God Most High and of Jesus Christ, and that relied upon altered laws of science for the ultimate purpose of establishing the kingdom of man, the ecumenical theologies of humanism, the evolutionary theory promulgated by the pseudo scientists of scientism, and the dismissal of the authority of the biblical record (Laodicea).

'Laodicea' means 'people' from 'laos' and 'right judicial verdict' from 'dike' / 'dicea.'

The entomology of the name offered multiple interpretations.

One option for interpretation was 'the people judge,' as in the people have judged Jesus Christ to not be the promised and prophesied messiah worthy to be the divine and sovereign ruler of the cosmos.

Another option for interpretation was 'the people are judged' as in Jesus Christ has judged the people to have rebelled and fallen short of God's expectation.

As Jesus Christ addressed the historical era of the church of Laodicea, Jesus Christ made it clear that he is the ruler of creation.

To the angel of the church of Laodicea, write,
'This is the message from the Amen, the faithful and true witness, the beginning of God's creation.' Revelation 3:14 translated

(The gospel of John introduced Jesus Christ, validating that Jesus Christ was present and active at the beginning of the creation process (John 1:1-18). The early Christians also understood that Jesus Christ was active in creation (1 Corinthians 8:6, Colossians 1:16, Hebrews 1:2).)

Being the ruler of creation has two parts. First, God the Father, Son and Holy Spirit created the world. Second, Jesus Christ has the authority and power to rule over creation. As ruler of creation, Jesus Christ asserted that it is the Creator who has the authority to judge, to rule, to determine who is 'in' and who is 'out,' and who will share in ruling with God.

'Here I am! I stand at the door and knock. If anyone hears my voice and opens the door, I will come in and eat with that person, and they with me.'
'To the one who is victorious, I will give the right to sit with me on my throne, just as I was victorious and sat down with my Father on his throne.' Revelation 3:20-21

The church of the historical era of the church of Laodicea rejected both the authority and power of Jesus Christ to rule and rejected the authorship of God the Creator when God created the world. Both tenets of the denial of creation and the denial of the divinity and sovereignty of the God of the kingdom of heaven, were also the foundation of both baal / mystery / mythology religion and of evolutionary theory. And both evolutionary theory and the baal / mystery / mythology religion claimed that there is no effective, functional and powerful God of heaven, and that the world was not created.

The idea that God the Creator did not create the world, was propagated as a necessary tenet of the baal / mystery / mythology religion in order to allow a created being / Satan to have a chance to take the throne of God. If God the Creator was indeed a real entity, then the created gods made from silver, gold, wood, plastic, electronics, etc. and the stories that support them, would be ineffectual, which would drastically hamper the religion business for apostate priests and for those who marketed idols and other religious trinkets. If humanity could produce its own gods, then humanity would be able to prove humanity's superiority to the gods and would in effect become like God. Having taken God Most High's place as gods, humanity would conceivably be able to rule themselves.

(Note that in this past six thousand years of human experience, humanity has yet to successfully rule independent of God Most High.)

The tower of Babel was germinated from the idea that humanity could ascend to heaven and take over the throne of God. If humanity could accomplish reaching heaven and taking the throne, then humanity should also be able to obtain the mysteries of heaven. Once the mysteries were obtained, then the holder of the mysteries / God Most High would conceivably become obsolete. The baal / mystery / mythology religion embraced the idea that there were those who possessed superior genetics as sons of the gods and because of their genetics, were able to receive the knowledge of the mysteries of heaven. The superior humanoid type specimens became the kingdom of Satan, Inc. / kingdom of man's new 'elect.'

Evolutionary theory shared some of the same foundational characteristics of the baal / mystery / mythology religion, including the belief that some people possess superior genetics, and that some races of people have evolved to be better than other races, and that some people are more valuable because of their possession of wealth, and that some people are more endowed to be rulers over others, etc.

During the era of the time of Jacob's Trouble, the offer will be made by the kingdom of Satan, Inc. / kingdom of man for humans to be fully evolved / transformed into 'better beings' / demigods who may not even be able to be defined as humans.

Currently, clergy from various denominations are able to fill pulpits of other denominations without ever understanding the distinctives or history of the denominational pulpit they fill. There is no longer a theological standard of belief based upon biblical theology that must be met. Each denomination has its unique history of how it discovered the love and greatness of Jesus Christ in the midst of opposition and oppression. But that history has now been ignored in church denominations. The passion that motivated that history has died. The theological distinctives within various church denominations, has disappeared. And the passion for discovering Jesus Christ afresh and new, has fizzled. For the most part, the 'church' has become merely another social organization led by people who filter out those who carry a passion for Jesus Christ and the biblical message within their hearts. Jesus Christ is now outside. His voice is no longer heard by the church. His voice is now heard only by individuals.

Jesus Christ's message to the historical church era of Laodicea was addressed to 'the church **of**' Laodicea. The rest of Jesus Christ's message to the churches followed the formula of being addressed to 'the church _in_...' It was another indication that what Jesus Christ recognized as the true composition of the church, the presence of people who are followers of the Lamb / Jesus Christ, is predominately minimized within the recognized body that bears the name 'church' during the era of the time of Jacob's Trouble.

The historical timeline era of the church of Laodicea where they have eyes to see and ears to hear, but refuse to perceive, also coincides with the end of the times of the

Gentiles. It is appropriate that the times of the Gentiles comes to a close when the majority of the leaders of the church have become blind to the fact that when Jesus Christ has been eliminated from the church, that the entire foundation for the church is also removed. The Gentile church defined without Jesus Christ, is no longer functional for the kingdom of heaven, just as the nation of Israel became no longer functional for the kingdom of heaven when the majority of the people of Israel rejected Jesus as messiah around 30 AD.

When the nation of Israel rejected Jesus Christ, they became blind to an understanding of Jesus Christ as their messiah and have lived in that blindness for almost two thousand years. When the era of the church of Laodicea models itself after the theology of the religious leaders, who during Jesus Christ's earthly ministry, rejected the divinity of Jesus Christ as messiah, they too will become blind to Jesus Christ's invitation to experience salvation.

The church without the divinity of Jesus Christ is like salt that has lost its flavor (Matthew 5:13-16, Mark 9:50, Luke 14:34).

It is as if the church of this historical era of the church of Laodicean theology, has built a new tower of Babel, only this time instead of making the tower out of bricks, this tower was constructed as a theological tower built with the belief that if humanity can build its structure of ideas high enough, then humanity will have the power it needs to override the kingdom of heaven, and this time succeed in replacing the kingdom of heaven with the kingdom of man.

The act of replacing God Most High as the highest sovereign would mean that humanity would have achieved 'god' status and fulfilled the Genesis 3 promise of the red dragon / serpent / Satan, Inc. made to Adam and Eve.

But the biblical record documented that the kingdom of Satan, Inc. / kingdom of man possesses some fatal flaws in their structure of ideas. Like a game of Jinga, their blocks will fall.

Laying the foundation for the global religious community – the great prostitute of Revelation 17

The incident between the first woman, first man, serpent and God the Creator, in that took place in the Garden of Eden / garden of God / paradise, laid the foundation for the religion of the rebellion, and all its variations throughout human history (Genesis 3).

After the deluge / flood, the antediluvian / preflood religion of rebellion against God the Creator, was reestablished as the baal / mystery / mythology religion (Genesis 10:18-29, 11).

The rest of the biblical record documented that throughout human history, the foundation has been laid for the religious organization that will be predominate in influencing the cultural climate that will exist prior to the return of messiah / the Lamb / Jesus Christ.

Prophetically, the global religious organization was described by John the Revelator, in Revelation 17 and 18 as the great prostitute / woman who is carried by the scarlet beast / Mystery Babylon the Great! the mother of prostitutes and of the abominations of the earth / rider of the eighth king beast / queen / great city that rules over the kings of the earth. No one title adequately described her. And each description of the global religious organization, identified another aspect of its character, activity, relationships, motivation, etc.

Throughout human history, there have been several dogmas, doctrines, theologies and practices that have coalesced to manufacture the final form that the great prostitute / apostate religion will take during the era of the time of Jacob's Trouble. But predominate in the defining of the great prostitute / apostate religion, will be the development and dependance of evolutionary theory and ideas extrapolated from evolutionary theory, as evolutionary theory seeks to fully replace the biblical record of creation, and the progress of the ecumenical movement that will continue to permeate its influence throughout the world.

Scientism's modern evolutionary theory and its support from the church

Throughout history, seeds were planted that would grow to become the historical timeline era of the church of Laodicean theology. But during the era of the Protestant Reformation (1517f), some of those planted seeds experienced some substantial growth.

In 1660, the organization named 'President, Council and Fellows of the Royal Society of London for Improving Natural Knowledge' was formed with a royal charter issued by the king of England, Scotland, and Whales, Charles II (fl. 1660 to 1685). It is commonly known as the Royal Society of London or the Royal Society.

Charles II was a Protestant with Catholic parents and a catholic brother, James II.

The established purpose of the Royal Society was to disseminate propaganda that would assist the ruling class in providing governance in the midst of the religious controversy and religious civil wars that England, Scotland and Whales experienced. Depending upon the power and authority of the Roman Catholic Church to support monarchy had proven to be a less than dependable strategy. And the Protestants of the Reformed Tradition did not provide an appealing alternative. New strategies for ruling the masses needed to be developed.

The solution of the ruling class of the 1660s and afterward, was to advance in removing God Most High from science and society. The reasoning was that if God Most High were eliminated from God's role as divine and sovereign, then the elite and elect ruling class would be able to fill the position of supreme authority, provide better governance than governance dependent upon a recognition of God Most High, and provide a more easily governed society.

The Royal Society of London provided two main solutions:

- an alternative theory of origins / evolutionary theory that eliminated God the Creator as the actor in creation, that abolished the need for God the Creator to be divine and sovereign, and

- *an alternative version and definition of science / scientism that denied the authentic nature of the created universe, and created a void for humanity to claim its authority in controlling the earth and its environment.*

Historically, members of the Royal Society included: Erasmus Darwin, Charles Darwin, the Huxleys, the Wedgwoods, even Stephen Hawking, Charles III, William, and others.

Evolutionary theory and scientism offered themselves as a strategy for aiding in the ruling of the masses. Evolutionary theory and scientism found a nurturing womb within the Royal Society. Religion entered an era of embracing a newly defined 'greater truth' and science began its departure from truth. It was the reinitiation of an earlier version of the baal / mystery / mythology religion when the baal religion introduced its evolutionary fish god Dagon that had evolved into a man, and the mystery religions supplied their 'secret explanations' for climatic phenomena.

In the 1830s, Charles Lyell published *The Principles of Geology* in which he argued that the present state of the earth's surface had been brought about by a long and gradual development. The chalk cliffs of Dover contained the remains of sea creatures which had been deposited over many centuries. It was claimed that the fossils found there dated back to an uncalculatable time.

Denying the actual natural process for the formation of fossils which requires that an organism be trapped in a short period of time with some catastrophic event such as a flood, Lyell instead based his hypothesis on the idea that organisms will fossilize over time. Embracing the idea that organisms take long periods of time to fossilize requires setting aside the natural law of entropy which basically says that dead things rot, not fossilize, over time. Science has not been able to replicate the fossilization process using time.

Lyell walked in the powerful circles of people who believed their own notions as a man of substantial societal status, should triumph over actual scientific and natural laws and because of the power of the membership of the Royal Society, Lyell's scientism ideas were taught as scientific fact.

Erasmus Darwin, provided the seeds of modern evolutionary theory and advanced his ideas through his grandsons, and through his book *Zoonomia*, 1794. Erasmus placed in writing the idea that all living organisms originated from one common ancestor and denied that various organisms were created to be unique from one another with each organism reproducing 'its own kind' (Genesis 1).

Erasmus Darwin instilled his ideas in his descendants including the idea that some people possess superior genetics that cause them to be of higher intelligence and possess superior physical attributes. The Darwin and Wedgwood families (of Wedgwood pottery and china) believed that genetics, and family money, should not be shared outside of the family.

To keep the genetics, and the money, within the family, the Darwin and Wedgwood families practiced marrying cousins. Josiah Wedgwood I, grandfather of Charles Darwin, had married his third cousin Sarah Wedgwood. Susannah Wedgwood, the daughter of Josiah I and Sarah, married Robert Darwin the son of Erasmus Darwin and father of Charles Darwin. Charles Darwin married his first cousin Emma Wedgwood who was also the granddaughter of Josiah I and Sarah Wedgwood. Charles Darwin's sister, Caroline Darwin, married Emma's brother and Caroline's first cousin, Josiah Wedgwood III. Etc.

The internal family inheritance of Wedgwood wealth created by Charles Robert Darwin's grandfathers gave Charles Darwin the leisure time to casually attend college, and to formulate his own ideas for advancing the theory of evolution.

Erasmus' grandson Charles Robert Darwin studied medicine at Edinburgh and theology at Cambridge, but was not successful at either discipline. Charles Darwin finally garnered enough classes to graduate with a degree in Natural Science from Cambridge. Charles Darwin published his book, *On the Origin of Species by Means of Natural Selection for the Preservation of Favored Races in the Struggle for Life* (Yes, this was the actual title of his book), in 1859. The influence of his family's high social standing, assisted in popularizing the theory of evolution that his grandfather and his grandfather's contemporaries had introduced to him. Charles Darwin's opinions were formed many years prior to his 'scientific discoveries' that took place during his cruise on the Beagle. Instead of a God Most High who created the world in six days and created humanity to bear God Most High's image, Charles Darwin taught that humanity was the result of a world encased in a vast power struggle were only the fittest survive, become wealthy and rise to rule.

One of Charles Darwin and Emma Wedgwood Darwin's beliefs was that they possessed superior genes and needed to keep their genetics undiluted. But most of the ten children of Charles and Emma Darwin, either died in childhood or did not have children. Only George, Francis, and Horace produced children.

Ironically, when Charles Darwin died, as one of the men who sought to eliminate God Most High, Darwin was buried in Westminster Abbey, a place where people who have faith in God are interned. Residing in a plot in Westminster Abbey was considered to be a declaration by the church that one was destined for heaven.

(Note: After questions arose concerning the authenticity of the Peking Man fossil record, the fossils that were interpreted to support evolutionary theory, disappeared in 1941.)

Thomas Henry Huxley, another member of the Royal Society, advanced Charles Darwin's ideas on the theory of evolution. Thomas Henry Huxley took on the challenge of defending the ideas of evolutionary theory with Bishop Wilberforce of Oxford and evolutionary theory furthered its competition with Christianity and Judaism to explain the origins of humanity.

Huxley also coined the term 'agnosticism' as a way to express that with evolutionary theory we do not know. In Greek 'a' (α) means 'against' and 'ginosko' (γινοσκο) is 'to know.' Technically 'agnosticism' means we 'cannot know.' But being an agnostic did not keep Thomas Huxley from claiming to know his version of the world history of the origins of life without God as the acting force.

Thomas Huxley's grandsons included Aldous Huxley the author of Brave New World and Doors of Perception, Julian Huxley the evolutionist and first director of UNESCO / United Nations Educational, Scientific, and Cultural Organization; and Andrew Huxley the Nobel Laureate and physiologist. The Huxleys believed that their Brave New World will be realized through scientific dictatorship.

'I suppose the reason why we leapt at the Origin of Species was that the idea of God interfered with our sexual mores.' *Sir Julian Huxley offered when asked in a television interview why the scientific community had so unexpectedly engaged in the opportunity of embracing Darwin's ideas.*

Aldous Huxley presented in his book Brave New World, a future where humans are no longer born, but cloned and hatched in incubators to create a worldwide slave state where people are taught to enjoy servitude beginning with their 'birth.'

Aldous Huxley spoke in support on the topic of ultimate revolution and the engineering of society for the purpose of controlling society through a series of techniques and the control of the mind. 'If you are going to control any population for any length of time, you must have some measure of consent. It's exceedingly difficult to see how pure terrorism can function indefinitely. It can function for a fairly long time, but I think sooner or later you have to bring in an element of persuasion, an element of getting people to consent to what is happening to them.' UC Berkeley 1962

'In my fable of *Brave New World*, the dictators had added science to the list and thus were able to enforce their authority by manipulating the bodies of embryos, the reflexes of infants and the minds of children and adults. And, instead of merely talking about miracles and hinting symbolically at mysteries, they were able, by means of drugs, to give their subjects the direct experience of mysteries and miracles – to transform mere faith into ecstatic knowledge. The older dictators fell because they could never supply their subjects with enough bread, enough circuses, enough miracles and mysteries. Nor did they possess a really effective system of mind-manipulation. In the past, free-thinkers and revolutionaries were often the products of the most piously orthodox education. This is not surprising. The methods employed by orthodox educators were and still are extremely inefficient. Under a scientific dictator, education will really work – with the result that most men and women will grow up to love their servitude and will never dream of revolution. There seems to be no good reason why a thoroughly scientific dictatorship should ever be overthrown.' Aldous Huxley, *Brave New World Revisited*, Section XII, 1958.

Julian Huxley was a prominent advocate of eugenics, the science of improving a human population by controlled breeding to increase the occurrence of desirable heritable characteristics. The practices of forced reproductive sterilization and abortion of babies are some of the practices of eugenics.

Developed largely by Sir Francis Galton who was a half cousin of Charles Darwin, as a method of improving the human race, eugenics fell into disfavor only after the Nazis used the Eugenics Society of America organization as a model for some of the pogroms of Nazi Germany. After World War II, the Eugenics Society of America underwent a name change for public relations purposes to become Planned Parenthood.

Julian Huxley in his book The Vital Importance of Eugenics, argued that the principal goal of eugenics in the short term was that mentally defective individuals should cease having children. Huxley supported the prohibition of marriage of the unfit, segregation of institutions containing degenerative individuals, sterilization of the unfit, and other ideas that would limit the population of 'undesirables.'

Society and the United Nations were assigned the task of determining the definition of 'undesirable' and it is conceivable that the definition of 'undesirable' will come to include those who do not agree with the principles of the global religious organization or the global governance system.

After becoming the first Director General of the United Nations Educational, Scientific and Cultural Organization, in 1945 Julian Huxley wrote *UNESCO: Its Purpose and its Philosophy*. In this work, Huxley proposed that international peace and security, collaboration among the nations, and human welfare could only be accomplished if individuals pursued the most desirable direction in human evolution. While most people recognize 'desirable direction' as a positive term, UNESCO uses the term to refer to activity such as the extermination of massive numbers of people.

In 1945, around the time of the formation of UNESCO, the world had just concluded WWII, a war that would not have been able to have been worldwide in scope without substantial support of Nazi ideas including eugenics.

Julian Huxley was also attributed to have coined the term 'transhumanism' in a book called *New Bottles for New Wine*. I believe in transhumanism: once there are enough people who can truly say that, the human species will be on the threshold of a new kind of existence, as different from ours as ours is from that of Peking Man. It will at last be consciously fulfilling its real destiny.' Julian Huxley, '*Transhumanism*' New Bottles for New Wine, pp 13-17. London: Chatto & Windus, 1957.

'Transhumanism' is the belief or theory that the human race can evolve beyond its current physical and mental limitations, especially by means of science and technology. Transhumanism is frequently abbreviated as H+ or h+.

While transhumanism is predominately presented as a philanthropic endeavor to aid in increasing the ability of humans, the ulterior motive of the Royal Society that birthed and nurtured the concept of transhumanism, is to cause the ruled classes to be better able to be ruled by the ruling class.

During the era of the 'birth' of evolutionary theory, Christian leaders addressed evolutionary theory with various responses. Some believed evolutionary theory as a monstrous error. Other Christian leaders favored evolutionary theory and sought to merge this new pseudo-

science with religion. Christian leaders who embraced evolutionary theory would even preach in support of the theory and in support of eugenics.

Leaders like Friedrich Nietzsche, Karl Marx, and the Nazis took advantage of the new thought that God Most High was either dead or never existed. They used the opportunity to advance their own agendas and developed their own religious ideas. After all, without a supreme and sovereign God Most High, there was no one to be accountable to. Hitler even dreamed of establishing the Third Reich that would reign over the world for a thousand years. 'Truth' was redefined according to the definition determined by the rulers of the world and 'scientists' became the new carriers of 'truth.'

Before the Royal Society, authentic science / the study of natural phenomena, and authentic biblical theology / the study of God, were inseparable. Before the development of evolutionary theory, true science and biblical theology were merged as one and had supported each other. True science and biblical theology validated each other.

After 1660, both true science and biblical theology were eliminated precisely because they supported and validated each other. After the formation of the Royal Society, the development of evolutionary theory and the embracing of evolutionary theory, the adoption of the new 'science' became contradictory to biblical theology and denied the biblical archeology that supports the biblical record.

Since the historical timeline era of the church of Sardis / Protestant Reformation, the Roman Catholic Church has built upon the foundation of evolutionary theory and developed the Vatican observatory with its Society of Jesus / Jesuit leadership (1540f). With the Royal Society's presentation of evolutionary theory, the Roman Catholic Church has taken substantial measures to merge the 'new science' with religion. The Roman Catholic Church continues to embrace theologies and doctrines that will aid in achieving their goal of achieving global papal rule.

Pierre Teilhard de Chardin (May 1, 1881 - April 10, 1955) was a French Jesuit priest with a vision for bringing the *Brave New World* into reality. As a paleontologist and geologist, Teilhard de Chardin had joined the 1912 original dig team with Arthur Smith Woodward and Charles Dawson at the site where the fossil record of the Piltdown Man was 'discovered.' Piltdown Man was considered to be evolutionary theory's missing link between ape and man, and touted as scientific archeological evidence of the veracity of evolutionary theory. After the human-like skull was discovered, more bones and artifacts were also discovered at the same site and assumed to be connected to the same individual. Woodward assigned a 500,000 years date to Piltdown Man, which assumed that bones that old would not have dissolved and would be able to be found intact.

In 1953, the Piltdown Man was determined to have been a fraudulent hoax. The mandible was altered. Some of the teeth were from an orangutan. And those bones were deliberately combined with the cranium of a modern human.

But there were forty one years between Piltdown Man's discovery and the revelation that Piltdown Man was a hoax. During that time evolutionists advanced their position of power, promoting their scientism as authentic science in the scientific field. Teilhard de Chardin has been accused of having directly participated in the Piltdown Man hoax and may have been the main person to have assembled Piltdown Man.

Later, Teilhard de Chardin also participated in the discovery of Peking Man (1929-1934). Peking Man was supposed to be an example of evolutionary theory's homo erectus species. Discovered in China, Peking Man was supposed to have been 750,000 years old. Other bones discovered in the same cave area were estimated to be between 500,000 and 300,000 years old. Pierre Teilhard de Chardin had assumed responsibility over the study of the fossils in 1934. After questions were raised about the authenticity of Peking Man, the Peking Man fossils disappeared in 1941.

Pierre Teilhard de Chardin had a consistent history of integrity issues. And yet, Pierre Teilhard de Chardin was one of the sculptors of modern evolutionary theory as well as the current theological stance of the hierarchy of the modern day Roman Catholic Church. Teilhard de Chardin, a Jesuit priest in the Roman Catholic Church, continued the advancement of the Jesuit Vatican Observatory's pursuit of developing a substitute theology for creationism. As an influential Jesuit priest in the Roman Catholic Church, Teilhard de Chardin was instrumental of the global dissemination of evolutionary theory throughout educational systems, beginning with Roman Catholic schools and Jesuit Universities.

Pierre Teilhard de Chardin also embraced the Jesuit vision of the Roman Catholic Church as both the spiritual and temporal ruling body with the pope as a supreme global leader. Pierre Teilhard de Chardin believed that 'science' / scientism could add a power boost to the Jesuit goal of global papal rule. Teilhard de Chardin was determined that there should be a merger of evolutionary theory 'science' and religion.

It was the kind of theological vision provided by Pierre Teilhard de Chardin that influenced the Roman Catholic Church's Second Vatican Council (1962 to 1965).

When John XXIII (fl. 1958 to 1963) decided in 1962 to hold the first session of the Second Ecumenical Council of the Vatican, it presented the opportunity to reshape the Roman Catholic stance on how the Roman Catholic Church interacted with the world and to set the Roman Catholic Church on a different theological course for the future. Joseph Ratzinger who would be elected to the papal office as Benedict XVI (fl. 2005 to 2013), shared Pierre Teilhard de Chardin's theological vision and was one of the organizers of the Second Vatican Council (1962 to 1965). The adjusted course moved the Roman Catholic Church toward the achievements of electing a Jesuit pope as the Roman Catholic Church pursues establishing global papal rule. The Roman Catholic Church embraced ecumenism as an opportunity to reincorporate the 'separated brethren' of the various church denominations, under the umbrella of the Roman Catholic Church as it expands its ruling domain.

Pierre Teilhard de Chardin also recognized that the world would not agree to global Roman Catholic Church rule or global governance without the world reaching a crisis point.

It is in the nature of the process of change, that humans are not motivated to change or to accept change until they reach a point of crisis where the cost of change is more economical than remaining on their more comfortable current path. It was Teilhard de Chardin's goal that the Roman Catholic Church and the elite world leaders would be ready when that world crisis point arrived, to supply a religion based global governance system to meet the challenge of change. In fact, Teilhard de Chardin and other world thinkers believe that the time for reaching the necessary crisis point should be hastened.

Teilhard de Chardin coined the term 'Omega Point' to describe a spiritual belief that everything in the universe is fated to spiral towards as a final point of divine unification. In the midst of this point of divine unification, Teilhard's 'science' / scientism and religion would merge. Using borrowed language, and with a unique definition of 'Christ,' Teilhard de Chardin argued that the Omega Point resembled the Christian Christ who draws all things into himself. Because Jesus Christ described himself three times in the book of Revelation as 'the Alpha and Omega, the beginning and the end,' Teilhard de Chardin believed that naming this conflict point the 'Omega Point' was applicable.

Note that the biblical record did not separate authentic science and the authentic faith system of God Most High. Instead, the biblical approach was that authentic science validated the authentic faith system of God Most High. And the authentic faith system of God Most High validated authentic science.

Note that it was the baal / mystery / mythology religion that invented the concept of secret mysteries that explained climate phenomena with a religious explanation. It was the priests of the mystery religions that profited from disclosing the secret mysteries with their scientism explanations.

While Jesus Christ draws all things to himself in order **to bring life**, Teilhard de Chardin and others believed that the purpose for congealing all things was to establish a greater ability **to bring governance** to the world through the establishment of the 'kingdom of man.' In the 'kingdom of man,' humanity selects their rulers and solves the problems of humanity. The 'kingdom of man' defies the need for Jesus Christ to provide instruction or to rule. The 'kingdom of man' would very much resemble Adolph Hitler's vision for world domination. Instead of the standard of the kingdom of heaven where every person is a treasure, the 'kingdom of man' would find it necessary to eliminate the 'undesirables,' removing them from the reproductive population and decreasing the tax of unproductive life upon the planet.

While Teilhard de Chardin and his supporters of great thinkers have sought to rule over humanity, Jesus Christ's vision is that all of humanity in the kingdom of heaven will share the throne with Jesus Christ, and that each person is 'desirable' to the loving god Most High.

It is ironic that Teilhard de Chardin, who took pride in his 'scientific' explanations that eliminated God Most High and any possibility of God's existence (using manufactured evidence), would contradict himself and use Jesus Christ / God in his argument for the development of the 'Omega Point.' If the divinity of Jesus Christ is nonexistent, then how could Jesus Christ draw all things to him and how could he be the Alpha and Omega? More importantly, if Jesus Christ as God and as a participant in the work of creation is nonexistent, then any argument based upon a nonexistent God should also hold nonexistent weight. But, when truth is a relative concept under the control of 'scientists' instead of an absolute reality, contradictions to truth are irrelevant.

Frank Jennings Tipler (1947 – present) further expanded the idea of the Omega Point. Tipler's Omega Point is realized in the ultimate future when the universe reverses its expansion and contracts / collapses. To explain the possibility of the occurrence of an Omega Point that is based upon defying God's natural laws, Tipler believes that at some point, our constantly expanding universe must change direction. For the laws of physics to be consistent through this reversal transition from expansion to contraction, Tipler believes that the laws of physics will experience a point when they are suspended. How the laws of physics will be suspended, and how they will come out of suspension, have yet to be determined. At the point where the change from expansion to contraction takes place is what Tipler called the Omega Point. Tipler's Omega Point is vastly different from Teilhard de Chardin's Omega Point, but Tipler believes that they should be discussed together.

Tipler's Omega Point is omniscient, knowing everything that is to be known; omnipotent, having harnessed all the power of the universe; and omnipresent, transcending through all space, even contracting / collapsing space. In essence, Tipler's Omega Point is 'god' without actually being an entity, and processes thought without a mind to contain thought. Tipler's Omega Point will have the capability and willingness to save us all. Tipler's Omega Point is able to bring each of us back into existence as a computer type simulation causing each of us to be reborn or resurrected as virtual beings. While Tipler erases the character and power of God to resurrect actual human life, Tipler does connect this activity as being similar to the work of the angels. Note that Tipler has no explanation for the creation or origins of angels, nor an eschatology concerning the ability of the angels to transcend and survive Tipler's Omega Point and the accompanying suspension of physical laws.

Tipler described his envisioned cosmology in *The Physics of Immortality*, 1994. Immortality is able to be achieved when somehow humanity is able to evolve to be able to provide intelligent information-processing. Once the existence of intelligent information-processing has been established in the universe, the universe will never die out.

This idea seems to cause humanity to be irrelevant. But Tipler believes that for there to be logic in the existence of the universe, the universe must contain observers, otherwise there would be no one to state whether the universe exits or does not exist. For Tipler, if the universe were to die with no more observers, then the universe would no longer exit. Tipler has no explanation for how the observers will survive when his version of the universe dies. Nor does Tipler explain the importance for the universe to continue to exist beyond being something for virtual humanity to observe.

What Tipler promises to transpire when the Omega Point has been achieved is humanity being transformed and changed so that the evolved beings that take the place of humans, no longer resemble humanity. They will be virtual humans, uploaded into a computer type entity, human spots and blemishes removed along with the essence of what it means to be and individual human being.

Building on Huxley's transhumanism idea, Tipler's transhumanism supports all forms of technology to improve human beings. Called h+ or human+ by its supporters, transhumanism is a movement for replacing all parts of a human individual including spiritual and religious beliefs. The movement is comprised of more than what is portrayed in movies. Body 2.0 will be designed to have better eyes, more flexibility, better memories, etc. Genetic structure will be altered to prevent aging and death. The resulting creature will be so vastly different from what we know as 'human' that it will be classified as a new species.

The purpose of transhumanism is to provide a hive mind of drugged and physically altered workers who are willing to obey the instructions of a dictator so that the world will find the order and the 'world peace' that it seeks. Or is that the order that the final world ruler seeks?

Body 2.0 will also be connected to the 'brain net' that will install a computer link to a global hive net within the brain that is similar to the current internet.

Contrary to how it is being presented as being disjointed from religion, transhumanism does have a very religious component and will be a part of the mark of the beast(s) system of the two beasts of Revelation 13.

Creating a better species to replace humanity is not a new idea. The activity of creating creatures superior to God Most High's creation was the mission of the red dragon / serpent / Satan, Inc. beginning in the antediluvian world. It was the impetus of the creation of Nephilim and chimera.

The definition of a 'superior' human being contains an allegiance to the kingdom of Satan, In. / kingdom of man. After failing to genocide the first man and first woman with the poison fruit of the tree of the knowledge of good and evil deception, Satan decided to alter humanity, how it thinks and how it is genetically constructed. In the antediluvian / preflood world the red dragon / serpent / Satan, Inc. was so successful in distorting and destroying God the Creator's creation, that the only humanity that remained worthy of redemption boarded an ark for a yearlong ocean cruise. Only eight people and the animals selected by God Most High went onboard and survived the deluge / flood. The deluge / flood was God the Creator's response to the red dragon / serpent / Satan, Inc.'s attempt to alter and destroy God's creation. God the Creator also responded by binding the rebellious angels that were directly responsible for the alteration of God the Creator's creation. The rebellious angel leaders and masterminds remain bound, awaiting future punishment as referenced in the first book of Enoch, other ancient cultural works, and biblical references including the book of Revelation.

Pierre Teilhard de Chardin envisioned the establishment of the kingdom of man and the use of the Omega Point crisis to usher it in. Frank Jennings Tipler redefined the Omega Point and envisioned a pseudo-scientific explanation for how the natural world would respond.

The Huxleys and others have installed the pursuit of transhumanism into the United Nations. The Roman

Catholic Church has offered to be the foundation for establishing the global religious community that will be active in the events of the era of the time of Jacob's Trouble. All these dynamics combined to create the environment of the historical timeline era church of Laodicea, a church that rejects the divinity of Jesus Christ and the fact that the image of God was pressed into humanity by God as Creator of the world.

The work of the Second Vatican Council of the Roman Catholic Church (1962 to 1965) was also assimilated into the workings of the United Nations. The United Nations major initiative of Agenda 21 was enhanced with Agenda 2030 (initiated September 2015 and blessed by Francis on September 23, 2017).

Negating the authenticity of the divinity and sovereignty of Jesus Christ left the historical era of the Laodicean church as an era filled with 'happy Christians' with a happy theology, accepting only what sounds superficially happy and rejecting what God Most High defined as the way to find true happiness. Already the church's membership is 'drugged' so they will enjoy their enslavement. The church no longer communicates the wonder and richness of a working relationship between Jesus Christ and the human person.

Relationships require giving and taking in order to reach new depths of experience. Relationships require giving love and taking on a lifestyle of living a life guided by the rules of the relationship. Making a relationship work is not 'happy thought.' Functional relationships are work.

Within most churches today, there is no longer a focus upon Jesus Christ and what Jesus Christ's life, death and resurrection were about. Frequently, Jesus Christ's name is used only to advance a thought that aids in human agendas, or in maintaining control over people, or in fund raising. There is a new defiance in churches, of God Most High's rules, God's law, God's message, etc. as contained in the biblical record. There is a skepticism taught concerning the actual existence of God Most High, and even the existence of God Most High's promised heaven. There is no longer a focus upon the importance of becoming a citizen of the kingdom of heaven or upon what citizenship in the kingdom of heaven demands. Jesus Christ's instruction to repent from sin is now ignored. It has become the assessment of the modern church to assume the role of judge over God Most High, and to judge God Most High as too judgmental to be allotted the authority to judge. God Most High is no longer accredited with the authority to ask us not to sin because the concept of a sovereign God Most High no longer exists. The instruction to 'take up your cross daily' is now ignored. Today in churches, the sacrament of communion that Jesus Christ instituted to do in remembrance of Jesus Christ, is now offered without any remembrance of Jesus Christ and with the arrogance of religious leaders who no longer need to pray over the elements, or to even acknowledge that God Most High wishes to commune with us.

Around 1936, the Protestant churches lost significant fervor for embracing Jesus Christ as Lord and turned their attention to ecumenicity. Integration or ecumenism places a higher value on arriving at consensus rather than maintaining authentic theology. Ecumenicity operates on the idea that if we all agree, or at least the religious leaders all agree, then the church has the authority to redefine sin, salvation, what Christianity consists of, etc. Interdenominational cooperation means that theological distinctives that previously fueled the passion of churches in their missions, are now displaced with an attitude that theological distinctiveness could be sacrificed in order to embrace 'cooperation,' 'world peace,' and shared good feeling. Ecumenicity is vital to the development of the global religious community.

The exchange took place of sacrificing authentic theology that might be considered offensive, in favor of a 'gaining new friends' theology. The argument for Jesus Christ being the only way to salvation became offensive. Modern theologians do not spend time seeking to understand the heart of God Most High, and therefore they have a list of unanswered questions.

- *How could a loving God not welcome everyone into heaven and still be a loving God?*
- *How dare God judge what an individual does, as sin?*
- *How can a God who is so great, not allow each individual to express their self freely without restraint or accountability, no matter who they hurt or injure in the process of exercising free expression?*
- *What kind of heaven is God Most High preparing that insists upon absolute perfection of its citizens?*
- *Why would God Most High insist upon valuing each human being so much that God would insist upon offering each individual who chooses Jesus Christ to be their God, nothing less than perfection?*
- *Why would God Most High want to give unworthy broken humanity the opportunity to be perfected and live with God for an eternity?*
- *If God Most High can forgive humanity why can't God forgive rebellious angels and allow them to live with God for eternity and remake the earth and heaven after their own image?*

The concepts, ideas and facts of the kingdom of heaven have been assessed to be offensive to anyone who does not hold a clear perception of the entire plan of God Most High. Because many religious leaders deny God Most High's entire plan for salvation and its necessity, large hunks of the biblical message have been removed from the modern church's teaching.

This new theology of the modern church created an opportunity for the red dragon / serpent / Satan, Inc. to take the next step in reshaping the Roman Catholic Church and its ecumenical relationship with churches worldwide. The office of the papacy has always viewed the pope as ruler of all churches of the world. But with ecumenism, that vision was able to take another step closer to becoming a reality.

When Jesus Christ's teachings about heaven have been deemed to be offensive, it leaves the world as a spiritual desert, a place where people are unable to find refreshment for their spiritual thirst. People thirst for a spiritual connection to the God who loves them so much that God is not willing to settle for anything less than an eternity of perfectly loving bliss. People thirst for spiritual connection to the God who has created them, who knows the desires of their hearts and has the power and determination to supply what they need to have the desires of the hearts realized and to experience full life.

When the modern church adopted the decentralization / demythologization method of Bible study, it ensured that the practice of picking and choosing from the biblical record also removed the authority and power and absolutely perfect love of God Most High. People are no longer certain to find the spiritual nourishment that they seek, in the contemporary church.

The historical timeline era of the church of Laodicea rejected God Most High's definition of full life and embraced 'life' that has been redefined by the kingdom of man / kingdom of Satan, Inc. The establishment of the kingdom of man / kingdom of Satan, Inc. seeks to fulfill the goals that Satan established in the Garden of Eden, that were reinitiated through Semiramis and Nimrod with the reestablishment of the antediluvian / preflood religion as baal / mystery / mythology religion and the building the tower of Babel, that was continued through Satan's work to place Jesus on the cross, etc.

According to the biblical record, the preparation for the crisis point / Omega Point, will begin at a midpoint for the era of the time of Jacob's Trouble (Daniel 9:26b-27, 12:11-12, Revelation 13:14-18).

When the world arrives at the crisis point, the 'Omega Point,' required for the red dragon / serpent / Satan, Inc. to usher in the kingdom of man and fully establish the kingdom of Satan, Inc., the red dragon / serpent / Satan, Inc. will have finally and effectively *declared God Most High to be not just merely dead, but really, really, really dead.*

But the biblical record identified the global crisis point as the final battle of this age / battle of Yom Kippur / Day of Atonement, that will take place after Jesus Christ returns. It will be the day when the red dragon / serpent / Satan, Inc. will attempt to fully establish the kingdom of Satan, Inc. / kingdom of man on earth and in heaven. But the biblical record also identified that the adherents to the kingdom of Satan, Inc. / kingdom of man will fail, be defeated and the survivors will be incarcerated.

The ecumenical movement as a precursor for the global religious community / great prostitute of Revelation 17

Evolutionary theory was a replacement for creation theology, that was adopted and further developed by the church. The ecumenical movement provided the ability of apostate dogmas, doctrines and theologies, to infiltrate all churches and also to infiltrate all forms of religious practice.

The Greek word for 'world' is oikumene / οικυμενε from which the word 'ecumenical' has been derived. 'Ecumenism' means 'the whole inhabited world.' Like the Roman empire that sought to, and has successfully 'inhabited the whole world,' the goal of the ecumenical movement has been to inhabit the whole world providing a unity of local congregations within a worldwide communion or network, and developing a single global religion.

With a foundation of the Roman Catholic Church, and her 'daughters,' there has been a worldwide movement to merge again all Christian religious flavors with the utopian idea that a consensus could be achieved where one theology, with one doctrinal standard could rule. Even the Counter Reformation and the formation of the Society of Jesus / Jesuits (1540), did not recognize the Protestant Reformation as forming separated churches. Within the teaching and vows of the Society of Jesus / Jesuits, the Protestants were referenced as 'separated brethren,' with the implication that one day that separation would be mended as the separated brethren returned to their place under the authority of the Roman Catholic Church. The perspective of the hierarchy of the Roman Catholic Church has maintained that Protestants may have excommunicated themselves from membership in the Roman Catholic Church, but not from the ultimate sovereignty of the Roman Catholic Church.

With the formation of the Roman Catholic Church being the merger of Christianity and the baal / mystery / mythology religion that was endemic within the Roman empire (Pergamum, 380 AD), the ecumenical movement is also comfortable with the inclusion of all religion dwelling under Roman Catholic Church rule.

It is essential for the red dragon / serpent / Satan, Inc., during the era of the time of Jacob's Trouble, to unite Christian denominations and all religion, in order to establish the beast of the sea / false prophet / eighth king beast as the supreme leader of the global religious community. It will require the united efforts of the two beasts of Revelation 13, to garner the power available within the world. And garnering the support of humanity will be necessary in the pursuit of attempting to storm heaven and dethrone God Most High. In the process of pursuing this enormous mission, the beast of the sea / false prophet / beast from the Abyss / eighth king beast will not be able to divide attention among the dissension of Protestant denominations, or of other religions.

Various ecumenical movement historical events

In more recent history, the ecumenical movement became formalized into established organizations. Among Protestant denominations, there have been several historical events that have worked to mend the separation between the Roman Catholic Church and Protestant denominations.

In the Conferences of Reunion in Bonn held in 1874 and 1875, that were convened by Dollinger who represented the Old Catholic theologians, the Old Catholic theologians dedicated themselves to a reunion of the denominations. Representatives of the Orthodox, Anglican and Lutheran churches were also invited.

The 1910 Edinburgh Missionary Conference was the result of the work of the Young Men's Christian Association / YMCA (1844), the Young Women's Christian Association / YWCA (1855), the World Student Christian Federation / WSCF (1895) and the Federal Council of Churches / FCC (1908). The Methodist layperson John R. Mott (former staff member of the YMCA and General Secretary of WSCF (1910)), provided leadership in the World Mission Conference. The World Mission Conference marked the largest Protestant gathering at that point in history, with the expressed purpose of working across denominational lines, in order to advance world missions. The Edinburgh Missionary Conference became the predecessor to the National Council of Churches USA.

After the first World War, the Faith and Order movement was led by Charles Henry Brent, and the Life and Work movement was led by Nathan Soderblom. In the 1930s, the tradition of celebrating World Communion Sunday was established to focus on the ecumenical ties established in the Presbyterian Church and several other denominations.

While the ecumenical movement began before World War I, the first meeting of the World Council of Churches took place in 1948 in Amsterdam with the theme of 'Man's Disorder and God's Design.' The focus of the World Council of Churches was to address the damage created by World War II. With the foundation of the World Council of Churches, the themes of the world ecumenical movement resembled the same themes publicly supported by the United Nations: peace with justice, helping all those in need / redistribution of wealth and controlling the ruled class, etc.

It is interesting that the World Council of Churches was formed in 1948, the same year that Israel was recognized as a nation.

The National Council of Churches was organized in 1950.

The Joint Declaration by the Council of the Lutheran World Federation was presented June 16, 1998 and its response from the Roman Catholic Church was provided June 25, 1998.

The Coexist Foundation is another organization that seeks to increase ecumenism throughout the world.

'Churches Uniting in Christ,' was organized in 2002. Etc.

Within the Roman Catholic Church of recent years, there was an increased focus upon ecumenicalism.

Pius XI (fl. 1922 to 1939) stated in 1928 that the only means by which the world Christian community was to return to faith (as defined by the Roman Catholic Church), was to return to Roman Catholic worship. Pius XI stated that the 'One true Church' was the Roman Catholic denomination. But the Roman Catholic Church did not attend the 1948 organizational meeting of the World Council of Churches and members of the Roman Catholic Church were barred from attending World Council of Churches conferences.

In 1958, John XXIII (fl. 1958 to 1963) reversed this stance. John XXIII met with the Archbishop of Canterbury (senior bishop of the Church of England / Anglican), Geoffrey Fisher, the first meeting between a pope and an Archbishop of Canterbury in six hundred years. One result of the new initiative, was the development of the Secretariat for Promoting Christian Unity established within the Roman Catholic Church.

With the Second Vatican Council, the Unitatis Redintegratino documentation was approved that officially recognized the ecumenical initiative of the Roman Catholic Church. Within the document, the term 'heretics' was replaced with 'separated brethren.' The blame for the schism between the Roman Catholic Church and the Protestant movement now declared that both Roman Catholic and non-Roman Catholic element were responsible. Non Roman Catholics were to be recognized for their contributions to overall Christian belief.

In 1961, Roman Catholic Church members attended the World Council of Churches conference in Delhi, signifying publicly, the embrace of the interdenominational relations documented through the initiatives of Vatican II.

The World Council of Churches currently is a fellowship of around three hundred fifty member denominations of churches. Some of the denominations included in their membership are various churches from the denominations of the Orthodox, Anglican, Assyrian, Baptist, Evangelical, Lutheran, Mennonite, Methodist, Moravian, Old-Catholic, Pentecostal, Presbyterian, Reformed, Disciples of Christ, and Friends (Quakers).

Interdenominational ministries associated with the World Council of Churches include the American Bible Society, Boys' Brigade, Church World Service, Cru / Campus Crusade for Christ, Girls' Brigade, Pentecostal Charismatic Peace Fellowship, People of Praise, Sabeel Ecumenical Liberation Theology Center, Student Christian Movement (Britain), Week of Prayer for Christian Unity, World Communion Sunday, and World Student Christian Federation.

The Roman Catholic Church is not a member of the World Council of Churches, but has worked closely with the Council for more than three decades. The Pontifical Council for Promoting Christian Unity also nominates twelve members to the World Council of Churches' Faith and Order Commission as full members.

Various Moravian Church provinces are members of the World Council of Churches, the Lutheran World Federation, National Council of Churches, and a variety of other church councils. Moravian Church provinces also hold agreements with the Church of England, Evangelical Lutheran Church in America, the Episcopal Church (September 2010), Presbyterians, etc.

The Episcopal Church is currently engaged in dialogue with the Churches Uniting in Christ, the Eastern Orthodox Church, the Roman Catholic Church, the Presbyterian Church USA, the United Methodist Church, the Reformed Episcopal Church, and the Anglican Province of America.

The World Council of Churches has frequently displayed its adversarial position toward the state of Israel through activities and through publications that criticize Israel. The destruction of Jewish religious sites has gone unrecognized by the World Council of Churches, while complaints are consistently made concerning alleged crimes against Christian sites in Israel.

Israel itself remains distanced from the World Council of Churches.

In August 2001, the World Council of Churches called for an international boycott on goods produced in Israeli settlements.

One of the key aspects of the culture of the historical timeline church of Thyatira was the requirement to worship the pagan deities as a part of belonging to the guilds. Each guild had its own god or set of gods. Within society, belonging to a guild was a requirement in order to practice one's craft. People of the time were not 'employed.' A person had to have their own craft.

As human history continues to unroll toward the era of the time of Jacob's Trouble, there will come a time when people will not be able to 'buy, sell, or trade,' without participating in the mark of the beast(s) religious, political, economic, and social system (Revelation 13:14-18). Instead of belonging to a local community guild, there will be one global guild, requiring mandatory membership and participation. This global structure will be the fruit of the mission of the ecumenical movement, that will be fully ripened during the era of the time of Jacob's Trouble.

The employment of the picker and chooser Bible study method in the development of the theology of the historical era of the church of Laodicea

Jesus Christ's introduction to the angel of the church of Laodicea began with Jesus Christ presenting himself as 'the faithful and true witness.'

To the angel of the church of Laodicea, write,

'This is the message from the Amen, the faithful and true witness, the beginning of God's creation.' Revelation 3:14 translated

And yet, modern leaders of churches around the world insist that portions of the biblical record are unfaithful and untrue and therefore Jesus Christ cannot be faithful or true.

The largest problem with the picker and chooser Bible study method is that it ultimately leads to the worship of the first being who advocated that humanity could pick and choose what to believe about God the Creator, and to pick and choose which instructions to follow that God the Creator issued.

In the Garden of Eden / garden of God / paradise, the serpent / Satan's words to the first woman were: 'Did God really say, 'You must not eat from any tree in the garden'?' Genesis 3:1c. *And in that moment, the serpent / Satan introduced the false idea that what God the Creator said, was open to debate and was able to be dismissed. The end result of dismissing what God the Creator said was the exile of humanity from dwelling in a face to face relationship with God the Creator and exile from the Garden of Eden / garden of God / paradise.*

The real danger of the picker and chooser Bible study method is that it leads to elimination from entrance into the kingdom of heaven. Jesus taught, 'Not everyone who says to me, 'Lord, Lord,' will enter the kingdom of heaven, but only the one who does the will of my Father who is in heaven. Many will say to me on that day, 'Lord, Lord, did we not prophesy in your name and in your name drive out demons and, in your name, perform many miracles?' Then I will tell them plainly, 'I never knew you. Away from me, you evildoers!' Matthew 7:21-23

Jesus Christ also messaged the angel of the church of Laodicea with this:
'I know your works and that you are neither cold nor are you hot. Oh, that you were cold or hot! So because you are lukewarm, and neither hot nor cold, I am about to vomit you out of my mouth.' Revelation 3:15-16 translated

Along with noting the historical era of the church of Laodicea's lack of relationship with Jesus Christ, Jesus noted their lack of awareness of their situation. Jesus noted the authentic poverty, the shameful nakedness and the

blindness of the church during the era of the time of Jacob's Trouble. (Revelation 3:14-22)

In most recent history, the hierarchy of the modern church approached the biblical record as unfaithful and untrue. Their approach has been to claim that the biblical record needs to be decentralized and demythologized. The layers of the onion need to be peeled away to arrive at what an individual is willing to embrace as truth, tossing the offensive portions away. In the church of our era, the Bible is no longer the authoritative word of God. If the Bible is no longer the word of God, then religious leaders can use 'picker and chooser' Bible study methods to pick and choose from the Bible what will advance their own agendas.

The biblical record told of a God of Creation that remains determined to not give up on Garden of Eden / garden of God / paradise living becoming a reality on earth. In Garden of Eden living there is no blaming of others, no positioning of one party to be artificially lifted above another.

Consequently, to accomplish the goal of establishing the kingdom of Satan, Inc. / kingdom of man, the authority of the Bible must be destroyed, if not through the burning of the book physically, or the separation of the people from the book, then by the adulteration of the message of the Bible through religious leaders who pick and choose which passages should be rendered as valid.

For most leaders in the modern church, the Bible as a whole is now considered to be an impotent, ancient, mythological, novel epic, to be read aside the Greek classics as entertainment.

Jesus Christ's message to the angel of the church of Laodicea also documented the need for repentance.

'As many as I love as friends, I rebuke and discipline. Therefore, be zealous and repent.' Revelation 3:19 translated

Determining that God Most High is unsovereign, impotent and inactive, and then rendering the biblical

record as unfaithful and inaccurate, yields a new definition for sin.

God Most High defined sin in the biblical record as those deeds that offend God Most High.

But without a sovereign, omnipotent and active God, there can be no accountability, rendering God's word to also be unsovereign, impotent and inactive.

Without a faithful and true book to define sin, then the biblical definition of sin can be dispensed with and sin can be redefined. Sin then becomes whatever offends the person(s) at the top of the hierarchy.

Evolutionary theory defines sin as merely the remnant of animal instinct within humanity.

But the authentic God Most High defined sin as those acts that seek to injure the creation that God loves.

As the church hierarchy successfully adopted new definitions of sin, the church lost its connection with any definition of biblical righteousness. Jesus Christ was banished beyond the walls, doors, and windows of the church and was left outside knocking in hope that there will still be a few individuals who would hear and respond. The church effectively became just another social club. Instead of encouraging members to shed those things that once offended the biblical God, church members were encouraged to bring their offenses into the church community and spread their offenses to others. The Bible documented that sex outside of marriage or homosexual activity or participating in pedophilia, places people in a position that renders God unable to bless them. But statements can be heard in the church like this one that was shared at one church denomination's annual conference: 'We should not criminalize adults having sex with children. Sex is a pleasurable activity, even for children. We should not deny children sexual experiences just because they are the wrong age.'

No longer able to address sin as defined by the Bible, the church adopted the new standard of 'good conduct.' Good conduct is merely activity deemed suitable by each generation as proper conduct for society. Therefore, the ends justify the means and any behavior is acceptable in order to arrive at the desired goal. People and relationships are disposable. War can be used to determine who the fittest are for survival, who consequently are also the most righteous. Peace is determined to be finding agreement with whomever wields the most power and authority. Ethics and morals are determined by the elite and the elect, the power brokers in the world according to their sensibilities. Poverty and starvation are used for the purpose of causing the populace to be more easily governed, used for redistributing wealth to the ruling class, and for advancing the cause of the world reaching 'sustainability' according to the definition of the elite and elect.

The picker and chooser Bible study method currently employed by many church leaders, eliminates the portions of the biblical message that are deemed offensive. But the picker and chooser Bible study method also renders the promises of the biblical message to be unreliable.

World War II and the Holocaust / holy burning of 1938 to 1945, as a typology for the historical era of the church of Laodicea

There have been Jewish theologians that believed that the people of Israel must endure two events of the era of the time of Jacob's Trouble, because Jacob / Israel had two wives, Leah and Rachel. World War II's Holocaust / holy burning, was the first event. Therefore, according to these Jewish theologians, the people of Israel must endure a second era of the time of Jacob's Trouble.

If this era of the time of Jacob's Trouble were laid upon the foundational blueprint of the Holocaust / holy burning of 1938 to 1945, then it becomes important to review the world cultural dynamics that existed from 1938 to 1945, in order to better understand the cultural dynamics of the actual era of the time of Jacob's Trouble that will culminate with the full establishment of the kingdom of heaven on earth.

Out of a review of World War II culture, arises some questions that may be helpful to consider in understanding the world cultural dynamics that will exist during these final days of this age.

In performing the autopsy of what went into creating a culture that could foster the Holocaust, questions need to be asked, like:

- *How was it that advanced and highly cultured nations like Germany, Italy, etc., could develop ideals like national socialism / Nazi, and fascism, so quickly and easily, and then allow those ideals to become so pervasive in society and in government?*
- *How could parties that were so radical, rise with such dramatic suddenness and with little serious resistance to assume control of governments?*
- *How could Adolf Hitler and Benito Mussolini accomplish building an alliance with the Roman Catholic Church and other church denominations, that supported the plans of the leaders of the Axis Powers of World War II? And why did churches continue to support those plans during World War II?*
- *How did so many people come to blame the Jews for their issues, when the Jewish population was merely a fraction of the total population of Europe?*
- *Why did so many European citizens fail to perceive the potentially disastrous consequences of the violent, racist, murderous and destructive nature of the cultural movement of the time?*
- *Why have many German citizens, and other Europeans, continued to deny the facts of the Holocaust and failed to perceive the opportunity for similar events of the Holocaust, to be repeated?*

Characteristics of the cultural climate that developed to lay the foundation for the events of World War II, will also be characteristics of the cultural climate necessary for the scheduled events of the era of the time of Jacob's Trouble to transpire.

The same 'church' that failed to act during World War II, will also fail to act during the era of the time of

Jacob's Trouble, on behalf of the kingdom of heaven. Instead, organized church leadership has already sown the seeds of aligning themselves to support the globalization of religion, of governance, of economics and of culture. This globalization will be necessary in the red dragon / serpent / Satan, Inc.'s attempt to fully establish the kingdom of Satan, Inc. / kingdom of man on earth.

'False messiahs and false prophets, will arise; and they will provide great signs and wonders to intentionally mislead, if possible, even the elect.' Matthew 24:24 / Mark 13:22 translated

The religious right that believes that they have been entrusted to hold purity in religion, will be purchased with the temptation of power and position in the new world order. They will refuse to act to prevent the advancement of the kingdom of Satan, Inc. / kingdom of man. Their hotness for actual righteousness, will not be hot enough.

The irreligious left who believes that they have been empowered to open the gates of heaven, against the will of God Most High, will be purchased with the delusion of power and position, to believe that they have absolute freedom from being accountable to God Most High and God's law. They will willingly advance the kingdom of Satan, Inc. / kingdom of man, believing that it is the kingdom of Satan, Inc. / kingdom of man that holds the true solutions and wisdom for the problems of humanity.

During the era of the time of Jacob's Trouble, both the religious right and the irreligious left, have rejected the promised and prophesied messiah / the Lamb / Jesus Christ as defined in the biblical record. They have invented their own forms of Jesus Christ, made in their own images. The religious right and the irreligious left, will find common ground for uniting, around their hatred and rejection of the biblical messiah / the Lamb / Jesus Christ. It will be this cultural religious environment that will provide the context for making the scheduled events of the era of the time of Jacob's Trouble possible.

But for those who have chosen to give their allegiance, not to the church, but to the Lamb / Jesus Christ, they are those who have heard Jesus Christ

knocking at their door and opened their door to allow Jesus Christ to come in. They are those who have overcome.

The movement of Jesus Christ's foci from nations to individuals, and from churches to individuals

Humanity began life living with God the Creator, in the Garden of Eden / garden of God / paradise. During that time, life and human culture, centered around God the Creator walking and talking, face to face, with the first man and the first woman as individuals. God the Creator's dialogue was unique to each individual. And each individual's dialogue with God the Creator, was also unique. This fact was demonstrated in the first three chapters of Genesis. Even the dialogue that God the Creator held with the serpent / Satan, was unique for the serpent / Satan. God spoke with Cain individually, and Enoch, and Noah, and Abram / Abraham, and Isaac, and Jacob / Israel, etc.

God the Creator has always focused on individuals first, not nations or organizations, or churches as a whole single entity.

After the deluge / flood, it was Nimrod who first sought to organize humanity, to place humanity under the power and authority of Nimrod's kingdom for the purpose of providing global governance under Nimrod's rule. Nimrod attempted to create an empire that he would rule over, replacing God Most High as the divine and sovereign ruler. And Nimrod attempted to interrupt the relationships that God Most High desired to hold with individuals.

The very nature of seeking to rule over others is a defiance of the unique relationships that God Most High desires to have with each unique human being. In Nimrod's act of establishing his kingdom, Nimrod sought to take the place of God Most High, to embrace and foster the spirit of antichrist. And by attempting to replace God Most High in the lives of individuals, Nimrod advanced the idea that God Most High could be eliminated, from the God – human relationship, from being the divine and sovereign ruler of the universe, and from existence.

But the God of the kingdom of heaven still met with individuals. The God of the kingdom of heaven met and individually covenanted with Abram / Abraham. And then with Isaac. And then with Jacob / Israel.

Only after the nation of Israel had been formed, did the God of the kingdom of heaven covenant with the nation of Israel. And the God of the kingdom of heaven did that through individual men: Moses, Aaron and the seventy elders of Israel.

The God of the kingdom of heaven came to individual prophets. And then the prophets communicated God Most High's message to the people of Israel.

Jesus Christ chose twelve individuals to be his initial main core of followers. And then Jesus Christ developed his relationship with each disciple individually, understanding each disciple's character, nature, belief system, etc., and addressing them as individuals. It was out of the personal relationship that Jesus Christ held with each of his disciples, that the church began to form.

It was because Jesus Christ held a unique relationship with each of his disciples, that meant that when one disciple betrayed Jesus (Judas), the entire group of disciples were still able to carry the message of Jesus Christ. Each disciple with a personal relationship with Jesus Christ has the ability to carry Jesus Christ and the mission of Jesus Christ, in their hearts, minds and lives.

While the God of the kingdom of heaven has been noted to be the God of nations, the God of the kingdom of heaven was and is, first the God of the individual human heart. The God of the kingdom of heaven has certainly used nations, temples and synagogues, and churches throughout the centuries. But first, the God of the kingdom of heaven requires holding a functional relationship with individuals.

During the era of the time of Jacob's Trouble, the dichotomy of the view held by the church and the view held by the followers of the Lamb / Jesus Christ, will demonstrate the division of thought concerning the kingdom of Satan, Inc. / kingdom of man's desire to establish global rule over humanity in the name of God, and the belief of the God of the kingdom of heaven to reach and connect individually with the hearts and minds of those who are followers of the Lamb / Jesus Christ.

That division of thought will be dramatically demonstrated for the people of Israel, when two thirds will be killed and only one third who decide to enter into a personal functional relationship with Jesus Christ, recognizing him as their promised and prophesied messiah, will remain alive (Zechariah 13:8).

That division of thought will be dramatically demonstrated for the followers of the Lamb / Jesus Christ, when a voice from heaven will proclaim, 'Come out of her, my people.' Revelation 18:4b, and will call the followers of the Lamb / Jesus Christ to leave the church that once held a loving and functional relationship with Jesus Christ.

But that division of thought was also reflected in the entire message of Jesus Christ to the church of the historical era of Laodicean church theology.

For the church of the historical era of the church of Laodicea, there is an apathy about the very human and very individual Jesus Christ. Currently, the majority of the modern church is filled with people who are not hot for Jesus Christ. They do not love what Jesus Christ loves. They do not hate what Jesus Christ hates. They are also not cold against Jesus Christ, utilizing those characteristics of Jesus Christ that they find appealing, in the advance of their own pursuits.

Historically it has been typical for church leadership to pursue the development of their own personal kingdoms and to pursue their own personal agendas. It became rare to find ecclesiastical leadership that embraces the theology of the authentic faith system or the theology of the historical era of the church of Philadelphia, where developing a personal functional and loving relationship with Jesus Christ is the goal.

Those who embrace the theology that God Most High is the God who requires a functional and loving relationship with individual human beings, are under attack from the rest of the church community. Individual human beings who believe that a functional and loving *personal relationship with Jesus Christ is the only requirement for entrance into the kingdom of heaven, can be found in all churches of all denominations. But during this historical era of the church of Laodicean theology, the true followers of the Lamb / Jesus Christ will be under attack in all churches of all denominations.*

Consequently, in the message to the historical era of the church of Laodicea, Jesus Christ did not address the church as an organization. In this portion of the message to the seven churches, Jesus Christ stands outside of the church, outside the door. The door that Jesus Christ knocks on, is the door to the individual.

Jesus Christ recognized the fact that the church will no longer provide a home for those individual human beings who pursue a functional and loving personal relationship with Jesus Christ. In the message provided to John the Revelator, from chapter 4 to chapter 22 (22:16), those individual human beings that hold a functional and loving personal relationship with Jesus Christ, were designated as 'followers of the Lamb.' They were not referenced as 'church members' or even 'Christians.'

Somehow, the church during the era of the time of Jacob's Trouble has come to be defined as containing more enemies of God Most High and of the kingdom of heaven, then friends. But God Most High, still knocks on the doors of every individual human heart, waiting for the individual to open the door and allow Jesus Christ to come in.

In Psalm 118 it was written that God Most High still does God's best and most important work, with the individual human being. And in allowing God Most High to enter through the individual's door, the opportunity is provided for the individual to pass through God Most High's gates of righteousness.

> The voice of rejoicing and salvation sound in the tents of the righteous.
> The right hand of the Lord acts valiantly.
> The Lord's right hand is raised in triumph!
> The Lord's right hand has struck powerfully / done mighty things / acts valiantly!

> I will not die. But I will live and declare the works of the Lord.
> The Lord has disciplined me / corrected me severely.
> But the Lord has not given me over to death.
> Open the gates of righteousness.
> I will go through them and will praise / thank the Lord.
> This is the gate of the Lord through which the righteous will enter.
> I will praise you for you have answered me, and you have become my salvation.
> The stone that the builders rejected, has become the chief cornerstone.
> This was the Lord's doing.
> It is marvelous in our eyes. Psalm 118:15-23 translated

Jesus Christ is that cornerstone that the stone builders / apostate Jewish religion and apostate church, rejected. Jesus Christ came to seek and to save the lost, not to seek and to save the church and its organizational structure established for the purpose of establishing global governance.

The established organizational structured church recognizes humanity as a glob of interchangeable personalities whose identities need to eliminated and their names removed. The established organizational structured church views the personal identities that God the Creator invested God's self to create, as needing to be eliminated and the remaining individual glob redefined as an assigned number.

But Jesus Christ continues to recognize each and every human being as being a unique created individual whose worth has been measured by God Most High to be as immeasurable as the omnipotence of the God of the kingdom of heaven. You are as valuable to the God of the kingdom of heaven as the value that the God of the kingdom of heaven has determined for God's self. For God so loved the world, that God was willing to trade God's self in order for you to have the eternal life that the God of heaven possesses (John 3:16f). The promise of Jesus Christ is that every follower of the Lamb / Jesus Christ will receive a new name, named by our heavenly Father and Jesus Christ the Father's Son. Receiving a new name authenticates the fact that the God of the kingdom of heaven places value upon the one who has received their unique individual name, and that the God of the kingdom of heaven holds a personal relationship with that individual.

Jesus Christ personally makes his appeal to you to covenant with God Most High, just as God Most High personally appealed to Enoch, Noah, Abram / Abraham, Isaac, Jacob / Israel, Joseph, Moses, David, the prophets of God Most High, etc. Each of the people whose lives were documented in the biblical text, were provided with the opportunity to accept the invitation to personally covenant with God Most High, or to reject personal covenant with God Most High. Before God Most High is the God of nations, God Most High must be the God of those who have chosen to accept the invitation to personally covenant with God Most High.

In this era when the culture of the church community is led by self-described rulers, Jesus Christ still appeals to you the individual, to allow Jesus Christ to fully rule in every individual's personal home, on the inside of the door of every individual's personal being.

Jesus Christ's message for the era of the time of Jacob's Trouble from the message to the angel of the antagonistic apostate church of Laodicea, and the message to the followers of the Lamb / Jesus Christ:

In the message to the historical timeline era church of Laodicean theology, Jesus Christ's message to the antagonistic apostate church displayed a separation from Jesus Christ's message to those who overcome / the followers of the Lamb. Jesus Christ informed the antagonistic apostate church that they made him nauseated, and caused him to vomit them out.

Because the antagonistic apostate church no longer has eyes to see or ears to hear, this message actually acted to set aside the antagonistic apostate church, in order to directly appeal to the remaining followers of the Lamb / Jesus Christ.

The message to the overcomers / followers of the Lamb, concerning the antagonistic apostate church

During the era of the time of Jacob's Trouble, those who are true followers of the Lamb / Jesus Christ, will experience the church as no longer being a safe haven for authentic biblical theology, or a place to find support for believing in the importance of preparing for the return of messiah / the Lamb / Jesus Christ. There may be hidden pockets of true followers of the Lamb / Jesus Christ, found within the church community (Revelation 18:4b). But the hierarchy of churches have predominately succumbed to the enticement of the insidious and covert plan of the red dragon / serpent / Satan, Inc. to infiltrate and seize the very church community that Jesus Christ had intended to be dedicated to himself.

The cultural climate will become reminiscent of the era of World War II and other eras of excessive conflict, when dissidents were forced to go underground, in order to provide resistance against evil.

'The days are coming,' declares the Sovereign Lord, 'when I will send a famine through the land – not a famine of food or a thirst for water, but a famine of hearing the words of the Lord. Men will stagger from sea to sea and wander from north to east, searching for the word of the Lord, but they will not find it.'
'In that day, the lovely young women and strong young men will faint because of thirst.' Amos 8:11-13

Amos predated and prevalidated Jesus Christ's message to the angel of the church of Laodicea. During this era of the time of Jacob's Trouble, the religious leaders will no longer speak for the Lord. But this is an era when more than ever, people will long to hear about the Lord and what the Lord has planned for humanity. But the global religious community will no longer be a primary source for people to learn about whom God the Father is or whom Jesus Christ the Son is or whom the Holy Spirit is or the work that the Holy Spirit will do.

The day of your watchmen has come, the day God visits you. Now is the time of their confusion. Do not trust a neighbor. Put no confidence in a friend. Even with her who lies in your embrace be careful of your words. For a son dishonors his father, a daughter rises up against her mother, a daughter-in-law against her mother-in-law —

a man's enemies are the members of his own household. But as for me, I watch in hope for the Lord, I wait for God my Savior. My God will hear me. Micah 7:4b-7

Micah described the atmosphere of human relationships set within the context of the day when God visits.

Nazi Germany would reward family members that turned in other family members who were a threat to the Third Reich. The promise of biblical prophecy was that this practice and other detestable practices will be revived and enhanced during this era of the time of Jacob's Trouble.

Jesus said, 'All this I have told you so that you will not fall away. They will put you out of the synagogue. In fact, the time is coming when anyone who kills you will think they are offering a service to God. They will do such things because they have not known the Father or me. I have told you this, so that when their time comes you will remember that I warned you about them. I did not tell you this from the beginning because I was with you.' John 16:1-4

During this era of the time of Jacob's Trouble, the religious leaders will present themselves as speaking for God Most High and they will expel those who truly believe in Yahweh and Yeshua / Yeshua Christ. The synagogue, and the church, will no longer represent God the Father or Jesus Christ the Son or honor the Holy Spirit of God. Those who are followers of the Lamb / Jesus Christ and those Israelites with true faith that God will be faithful to send the promised and prophesied messiah, will no longer be welcome in the majority of synagogues or churches.

Paul wrote, 'For the time will come when people will not put up with sound doctrine. Instead, to suit their own desires, they will gather around them a great number of teachers to say what their itching ears want to hear. They will turn their ears away from the truth and turn aside to myths.'

'But you, keep your head in all situations, endure hardship, do the work of an evangelist, discharge all the duties of your ministry.' 2 Timothy 4:3-5

The prophets of the Old Testament / Tanakh, Jesus Christ, and the apostles, all documented that this time in human history would come, when the antagonistic apostate church would provide an ingenuine message. The time that they spoke of, was during the era of the time of Jacob's Trouble. (Revelation 12:13-17)

At the core of baal / mystery / mythology religion, and at the core of the doctrine of predestination, and at the core of the theory of evolution, is the principle that there exists among individuals, characteristics that are beyond our control, that are genetically prearranged to determine either one's ability to be among the elite and elect or to be merely one who is only able to be ruled over. Within the various theological traditions, markers have been identified for determining if someone is of the elite and elect class. The elite and elect have greater wealth or power or position or special knowledge or are better at 'negotiating' than the masses. These qualities cause them to be qualified to rule over others less qualified, less superior in their genetics, less wealthy, less positioned, less knowledgeable, less capable.

The mission of the red dragon / serpent / Satan, Inc. has been to bring into reality the kingdom of man / kingdom of Satan, Inc., and to use the elite and elect class of society to accomplish the reality of this vision.

The dream of fully establishing the kingdom of Satan, Inc. / kingdom of man, devoid of all aspects of the kingdom of heaven on earth, was the vision of Satan when the serpent / Satan convinced the first woman and first man to eat from the tree of the knowledge of good and evil. And in eating the fruit, the first man and first woman made themselves available to accomplish the work of Satan, Inc.

In response to the first man and the first woman's violation of God Most High's instruction, instead of allowing the immediate annihilation of the first man and first woman, God delayed Satan's strategy of total human genocide by giving the plan for redemption to the first man and first woman (Genesis 3).

The dream of establishing the kingdom of Satan, Inc. / kingdom of man was the vision of those who created Nephilim before and after the deluge / flood. God Most

High ended that strategy by shortening the lifespan of humanity.

The dream of establishing the kingdom of Satan, Inc. / kingdom of man was the vision behind the construction of the tower of Babel as a connection to the gods and a center for education for the baal / mystery / mythology religion. God Most High delayed the tower of Babel strategy from becoming a reality with the division of language.

The dream of establishing the kingdom of Satan, Inc. / kingdom of man was the vision that was offered to Jesus Christ when Satan tempted him with the position of supreme ruler of the nations, if only Jesus would place Satan above him. Jesus eliminated that strategy by choosing not to accept Satan's invitation to be a traitor to God the Creator's vision of the kingdom of heaven. Jesus Christ instead, accepted God Most High's invitation to rule and went to his crucifixion (Psalm 2:6-9, Isaiah 9:6-7, Daniel 2:44, 7:13-14, etc.).

The dream of establishing a global ruling organization was the vision of the Roman Catholic Church and was almost achieved during the Dark Ages / Middle Ages / medieval period. God Most High delayed that strategy from becoming a reality using plagues and removing the Roman Catholic Church as the gatekeeper for education. While the Roman Catholic Church attempted to deny people from hearing God speak through the limitation of access to the Bible and limitation of access to the Bible in common languages, God Most High inspired people to translate and print the Bible, and to educate people to read and understand the Bible.

Because of the biblical record, we have been given glimpses of what God Most High's kingdom of heaven looks like. The kingdom of heaven on earth experience began with a lush garden where humanity did not labor. Food was ready to be picked without toil. Health was perfect without illness or death. Originally, relationships were void of power struggles, manipulation, deception, etc. In God's kingdom of heaven originally established in the Garden of Eden / garden of God / paradise on earth, humanity walked and talked with God face-to-face as friends. The power structure between the lower status of humanity and the sovereignty of God the Creator, was blurred to non-existence because love is so very strong that love overshadows the differences in the levels of power held by God and by humanity. Fruit was large. Life was large. Humanity held large and deep insights and an understanding that lit up life.

When the kingdom of heaven will be restored and regenerated on earth with the Thousand Years Reign of Jesus Christ, the large living of the Garden of Eden / garden of God / paradise will also be restored and regenerated. Being restored and regenerated requires that what will be restored and regenerated must first have existed once before in the past, and therefore can exist again in the future.

We also know what the kingdom of Satan, Inc. / kingdom of man will look like if the red dragon / serpent / Satan, Inc. were to be successful in fully establishing the kingdom of Satan, Inc. / kingdom of man on earth. As the kingdom of Satan, Inc. / kingdom of man strives to achieve its goal of total global domination, humanity's understanding of the full meaning of the kingdom of heaven will grow dim and continue to be veiled. The struggle for producing food will become more laborious. False rationales that call for depopulation and the genocide of humanity will increase. Serfdom, feudalism, tyranny, slavery and sexual slavery will all rise. Deceit, dishonesty, disrespect and death will continue to permeate throughout the culture of the inhabitants of the earth. The inhabitants of the earth will continue to be distanced from the God who created humanity and who is the author of love, until all love among them will be extinguished and the absolute power and rule of the red dragon / serpent / Satan, Inc. has been fully established among them.

The mission of establishing the kingdom of Satan, Inc. / kingdom of man will require utilizing every avenue available in order to have a chance for success. During the historical timeline era of the church of Laodicea, the dream of establishing the kingdom of Satan, Inc. / kingdom of man will blossom into full bloom. The entity of the general church that once opposed Satan, Inc., will become Satan, Inc.'s advocate. What was once the church will no longer allow Jesus Christ's voice to be heard. The antagonistic apostate church will assist in establishing the kingdom of Satan, Inc. / kingdom of man.

There will need to be a religious leader who is powerful enough and powerfully placed enough, to give the illusion and convince the people that he speaks for God, with special knowledge, power, etc. The new global religious leader / beast of the sea / false prophet / beast from the Abyss / eighth king beast will need to be able to seem to defy death in order to convince people that the laws of nature can truly be suspended in order to offer a 'resurrected' life to those who worship him. This religious leader will be the first to experience this new form of 'resurrection' as an imitation of Jesus Christ's resurrection and as a pseudo fulfillment of the feast of firstfruits.

There will also need to be a political leader who is able to lead governments as a supreme political leader, to govern even the 'kings' of the earth as a pseudo 'King of kings' in order to convince people of his supremacy. This pseudo 'King of kings' will need to perform miraculous works in order to convince people of his superiority. The global political leader / little horn / beast of the earth / final world ruler will need to perform deeds that mimic the grandeur and scale of Moses, Elijah, and Jesus Christ.

Together these two leaders will need to prove to humanity that they possess the power over life and death. They will need to prove to humanity that they possess the power over physical life and afterlife. They will need to provide a method for transforming human life, a method for achieving transhumanism in order to succeed in establishing the kingdom of Satan, Inc. / kingdom of man and to provide activity that mimics God's activity as an authentication that humanity can actually be 'like God.' They will need to develop a storyline that justifies the elimination of the Creator God.

These two leaders will need the organizational system of the global religious community and the support of the global governance system to achieve their goals. (Revelation 13, etc.)

To accomplish these goals, the red dragon / serpent / Satan, Inc. has needed to fully infiltrate the church / the body of Jesus Christ, and the church leadership of the Roman Catholic Church and the Protestant churches / the daughters of the Roman Catholic Church, and the church of our modern era, in order to unite them in the goal of rejecting the biblical Jesus Christ as the promised and prophesied messiah.

Biblical eschatology defined perfection coming into this world only by the direct intervention of God Most High, as the return of Jesus Christ.

Evolutionary theory and biblical eisegesis replaced the entrance of Jesus Christ and the perfection and righteousness that Jesus Christ brings, with a view of a world that is being increasingly 'improved' by human effort. Humanity and the kingdom of Satan, Inc. / kingdom of man will perceive itself as wealthy, providing food, providing health care, providing technology, providing governance, etc. Humanity no longer needs God's provision. Because humanity is determined to be no longer guilty of original sin, there is no longer any need for repentance or for Jesus Christ as Savior.

But wealth is a temporary phenomenon. Wealth can only be a cover.

And health not infused by the Creator, is fleeting.

Jesus Christ made the statement to the angel of the church of Laodicea:

'For you say, 'I am rich and I have made myself rich, and there is nothing that I need.' And you do not realize / remember / appreciate that you are wretched / afflicted and miserable and poor and blind and naked. I recommend that you buy gold from me that has been refined by fire wo that you may be rich, and white garments so that you may be clothed and might not be shamed by the exposure of your nakedness, and eye salve to anoint your eyes so that you may see.' Revelation 3:17-18 translated

Proverbs 7 provided a diorama for depicting the dynamics of the relationship between the church and the unsuspecting. In prophecy, women represented religious *entities. In this diorama, the prostitute represented the antagonistic apostate church and religion.*

I saw among the simple, I noticed among the young men, a youth who had no sense.

He was going down the street near her corner, walking along in the direction of her house at twilight, as the day was fading, as the dark of night set in.

Then out came a woman to meet him, dressed like a prostitute and with crafty intent. (She is unruly and defiant, her feet never stay at home: now in the street, now in the squares, at every corner she lurks.)

She took hold of him and kissed him and with a brazen face she said: 'Today I fulfilled my vows, and I have food from my fellowship offering at home. So, I came out to meet you. I looked for you and have found you! I have covered my bed with colored linens from Egypt. I have perfumed my bed with myrrh, aloes and cinnamon. Come, let us drink deeply of love till morning. Let us enjoy ourselves with love!'

'My husband is not at home. He has gone on a long journey. He took his purse filled with money and will not be home till full moon.'

With persuasive words she led him astray. She seduced him with her smooth talk.

All at once he followed her like an ox going to the slaughter, like a deer stepping into a noose until an arrow pierces his liver, like a bird darting into a snare, little knowing it will cost him his life.

Now then, my sons, listen to me. Pay attention to what I say.

Do not let your heart turn to her ways or stray into her paths.

Many are the victims she has brought down. Her slain are a mighty throng. Her house is a highway to the grave, leading down to the chambers of death. Proverbs 7:7-27

The goal of the organized and institutionalized church of today, is to make people feel loved, but not loved with the genuine love of God Most High. 'My husband is not at home.'

Her goal seems very pure. She incorporates the use of myrrh (life and death), aloe (healing), and cinnamon (anointing). She appears to have everything that is necessary to be an authentic religious entity. But she is not whole in her relationship with God Most High.

The true mission of the authentic church, is not to make a person feel loved, but to teach how to love and worship God Most High. Out of learning how to authentically love and worship God Most High, comes the recognition of the genuine love of God Most High and the feeling of authentically being loved by God.

Why invest in a church where God the Father, God the Son / messiah / the Lamb / Jesus Christ, and God the Holy Spirit, are not present? They are the beings who author authentic love. They are the beings who hold the true authority and power over all that transpires in the cosmos.

The husband of the antagonistic apostate church, is not coming back. The antagonistic apostate church expelled the authentic God of the biblical record, from their home. The antagonistic apostate church does not believe that the biblical description of the return of messiah / the Lamb / Jesus Christ, is authentic, and that his return is imminent. And if messiah / the Lamb / Jesus Christ does not return, then the mission of fully establishing the kingdom of heaven can be substituted with their mission of fully establishing the kingdom of their desires.

Many religious leaders have redefined the path for entering into the kingdom of heaven / Garden of Eden / garden of God / paradise. Their path bypasses messiah / the Lamb / Jesus Christ as the way to find entrance. (John 14:6).

They have preached that what the human soul searches for, can be found by following them, investing in their dogmas, doctrines, theologies and practices. And then they redefined what the authentic biblical record has documented, as incomplete or as lies.

Religious leaders who have been entrusted to teach truth and to prevent manipulation, have become the major manipulators.

For the time will come when people will not put up with sound doctrine. Instead, to suit their own desires, they will gather around them a great number of teachers to say what their itching ears want to hear. They will turn their ears away from the truth and turn aside to myths. 2 Timothy 4:3-4

The leaders of the early church also understood that among the Gentiles who received the message of Jesus Christ as Lord, there would come a time when the church would no longer teach the message of the authentic faith system. Religious leaders entrusted with communicating the message of messiah / the Lamb / Jesus Christ, would *substitute a new message that would be more palatable to the ears and be exchanged for the truth.*

Within this religious culture established during the era of the time of Jacob's Trouble, the theology of the lukewarm church of Laodicea will become so prevalent, that the followers of the Lamb / Jesus Christ will feel as if they have been exiled from the church, in the same manner that Jesus Christ has been exiled from the church.

One theologian that is a follower of the Lamb / Jesus Christ, identified the problem of the religious leadership, as 'Christophobia.'

It will be within this religious cultural climate that during the second half of the era of the time of Jacob's Trouble, the mark of the beast(s) system will be implemented throughout the world. The mark of the beast(s) system will control trade and commerce throughout the world, under the guise that their antagonistic religious answers to human and environmental problems, are best. John the Revelator's vision, promised that humanity will not be allowed to buy or sell, without the mark of the beast(s) implanted in our right hand or forehead. The money and wealth that each of us has accumulated, will no longer hold its value. One's personal possessions will be commandeered to be placed into the central global financial system, and utilized 'for the common good.' The mark of the beast(s) system will determine each individual's value and will supply each individual's needs according to the level of value the mark of the beast(s) system has determined that the individual should have.

Relationship with God Most High, being dependent upon God Most High pouring out blessings through family and community, will all be replaced with the individual relating directly with the image of the beast of the sea / false prophet / beast from the Abyss / eighth king beast / holy father.

But also during the era of the time of Jacob's Trouble, Jesus Christ will continue to offer himself as an alternative to the antagonistic apostate church community. Jesus Christ is willing to enter wherever the door is opened to him. Jesus Christ is willing to establish relationship directly with every individual who accepts his invitation to become a follower of the Lamb / Jesus Christ.

Jesus Christ encourages those living during the era of the time of Jacob's Trouble to consider him as the best investment. Being authentically and truly wealthy, is only available through Jesus Christ.

The role of the antagonistic apostate church as it supports the red dragon / serpent / Satan, Inc. in the attempt to fully establish the kingdom of Satan, Inc. / kingdom of man, on earth

In Jesus Christ's message to the seven angels of the seven churches, Jesus identified that before his return, the first two eras of churches would be deceased, and the other five church eras would continue until his return.

During the era of the time of Jacob's Trouble, the historical era of the church of Laodicean theology will be recognized as antagonistic and apostate, with no reason for redemption. But other historical era churches will join in the apostasy.

The antagonistic apostate church will have changed sides in this cosmic conflict, from having supported the church's one foundation of Jesus Christ, to now being antagonistic against God Most High and predominately supporting the red dragon / serpent / Satan, Inc. (Revelation 12, 13, 17, 18 and 19). The apostate church has come to serve as the place where the baal / mystery / mythology religion has found a comfortable place to nestle itself. And with that theological shift, the apostate church became aligned with the unholy trinity who together will work in concert to challenge the divinity, sovereignty, authority and power of Jesus Christ.

The apostate church has supported this alliance:
1. through offering an alternative ending to what God the Father, Jesus Christ the Son and the Holy Spirit have started,
2. through providing a lesser standard for truth and a greater appreciation and acceptance of

lies and manipulation in the pursuit of personal agendas, and

3. *through the church's attempts to claim authority over all of creation, and to claim authority over the climate of the earth, and to claim authority over all of heaven and all of earth, as well as earth's inhabitants.*

When God is no longer defined by the Bible, the concept of 'god' can no longer be defined by characteristics like 'love,' or 'truth,' or 'righteousness,' or 'creator,' or 'sovereign,' or...

During the era of the time of Jacob's Trouble the antagonistic apostate portion of the church with Laodicean theology will come to fully support the unholy trinity with the goal of fully establishing the kingdom of Satan, Inc. / kingdom of man. This portion of the church, with Laodicean theology, will provide for the development of the global religious community / great prostitute / Mystery Babylon the Great!

During this era the various church denominations and all forms of other religion, will be pressured to join the ecumenical global religious community. Other forms of religion abandoned the God of the biblical record, millennia ago. And to varying degrees, the various church denominations have abandoned their responsibility to prepare for the return of messiah / the Lamb / Jesus Christ.

Many of today's religious leaders teach that in the pantheon of gods, because it cannot be known which of the many gods is currently supreme, it is important for humanity to invest in the worship of all the many gods. This has become a teaching disseminated even throughout churches.

In this modern church era, the authority of the biblical record has been consistently assaulted and diminished. For many, the message of the biblical record has been considered to be too personally demanding to be totally accepted. The biblical message of the unacceptability of antisemitism, elitism, racism, sexism, agism, idolatry, lying, murder, theft, destruction of others *and their property, etc., has rendered the full biblical message to be too weighty to be accepted as authoritative.*

The Bible described one absolute God who first covenanted with the people of Israel, to be the nation to provide the world with the promised and prophesied messiah, who would fulfill God Most High's redemption, reclamation and regeneration plan, and fully establish the kingdom of heaven on earth. But the antagonistic apostate church determined that the promised and prophesied messiah was offensive, too militaristic, too violent, too demanding, and incapable of fully establishing the kingdom of heaven on earth.

For all these reasons, the biblical message became too onerous for many religious leaders and church members today. They have eyes to see and ears to hear, but do not perceive the greatness and glory and perfection of God Most High and of the kingdom of heaven.

As a result, the modern church has predominately relegated the Bible as a historical mythological novel epic, where the message of the Bible can be picked at for its choicest parts, in the manner of birds of prey feasting on carrion. In many churches, biblical study has been consigned to decentralizing and demythologizing the biblical record, pealing back the layers of the message to arrive at those parts that are unoffensive to the individual. With an open mind, the new standard for Bible study became what can be designated as a biblical message translated 'by' man instead of 'for' humanity.

During the era of the time of Jacob's Trouble, there will again be times when it will be important to religious leaders that the laity not read or study or interpret the Bible for themselves. For in the Bible is laid out the plan of God as God Most High deals with the opposition; the rebellion that is the practice of the church as it distracts people from understanding or being in relationship with authentic God, Jesus Christ. The Bible tells of the plan of the red dragon / serpent / Satan, Inc.'s deception in providing substitutes for the promised and prophesied messiah of God Most High's original plan. The Bible tells of God's enemy's plan for attempting to achieve total world domination and of God Most High's plan to defeat it. Most of all, the Bible documented the defeat of the kingdom of Satan, Inc. / kingdom of man.

During the era of the time of Jacob's Trouble it will again be illegal to own, read or study the Bible and biblical literature.

The relationship between the historical era of the church of Laodicea and Jesus Christ has become so strained, that the connection has reached the point of being non-existent. In the era of the historical era of the church of Laodicea, the biblical Jesus Christ cannot be found within the hearts of many within the organized church. It is like a game of hide and seek where no one is seeking Jesus Christ and Jesus Christ finally must reveal himself. Jesus Christ's message is, 'Here I am! I am at the door, outside, where you put me. You cannot even hear me. I am nonexistent to you.' Jesus Christ stands outside the church that was founded on his work, with his having no way to enter in. Jesus Christ is left to knock and must wait for the invitation to enter.

Jesus Christ no longer addressed his plea to the church. Now Jesus Christ makes his plea to the individual. Jesus Christ now says, 'If <u>anyone</u> hears my voice...' Jesus Christ knows that the church hierarchy, religious leaders, and those who are blindly loyal to the power of the church organization instead of to Jesus Christ, can no longer hear.

Jesus Christ offers no commendation to the church of the era of Laodicea. The church of Laodicea has grown so wealthy and self-sufficient that Jesus Christ will not be appealing to the church. The church determined that it no longer needs Jesus Christ or God Most High's guidance.

During the era of the time of Jacob's Trouble, what once was called the 'church' is so distant from what Jesus Christ envisioned that it causes Jesus Christ to vomit it out.

Humanity has acted upon its determination to attempt to 'storm the gates' of heaven with their own power, to destroy the God of the actual kingdom of heaven. And the antagonistic apostate church will be leaders in this initiative (Revelation 12, 13, 17, 18, and 19).

Messiah / the Lamb / Jesus Christ's role during the historical era of the church of Laodicean theology / era of the time of Jacob's Trouble

The historical dynamics within the cultural religious community, have culminated to create a church environment that is afraid to be the church that Jesus Christ intended the church to be. It has been defined as an era of Christophobia. The historical era of the church of Laodicea is not the first time the church has lost its way. But it will be the last.

Jesus Christ addressed the church of Laodicea as 'the great Amen.' The term 'amen' means that this is the end of the discussion and that as it is in heaven so it shall be on earth. There is nothing left to argue. Negotiations have ceased. The one with the power to make the final decision has done so. The covenant agreement has been signed.

Jesus Christ addressed the church of Laodicea as 'the faithful and true witness.' It was a reminder that Jesus Christ will definitely complete all that Jesus has said he would do, faithfully. It was a statement that Jesus Christ is the standard for truth. All truth is to be measured against Jesus Christ. What cannot stand next to Jesus Christ cannot be true. What cannot stand next to Jesus Christ must be untrue and on the opposite side of the door from Jesus Christ.

Jesus Christ addressed the historical era for the church of Laodicea as the one holding the role of 'the ruler of God's creation.' Not only is Jesus Christ the ruler, but God Most High has created and has determined that it should be Jesus Christ who will be the ruler of God's creation.

What once was the 'church' is now divided into those who have chosen to embrace the vision of the red dragon / serpent / Satan, Inc. on one side; and on the other side are those who are authentic followers of the Lamb / Jesus Christ.

Within the modern church, on one side there are those who have eyes to see and ears to hear, and yet they do not perceive.

And finding no place to continue within the church, there are those who have purchased gold refined by fire, white clothes to cover nakedness and eye salve so they can see. Even the first man and first woman recognized their nakedness and adorned themselves with the clothes God the Creator made for them.

There are those who remain undisciplined, that refuse to leave their determination to destroy God Most High's creation, to rule over others with power, and to accomplish their destructive and tyrannical goals under the guise of 'saving the planet' and 'establishing world peace.'

On the other side of the division are those who know that a perfect kingdom of heaven requires citizens that are disciplined, who repent, who turn away from destruction and power. They are able to find friendship with God Most High. And instead of seeking to rule over God Most High or God's people, they are able to sit down and eat together with God as friends who share a meal.

In ancient times, at the conclusion of the battle, a meal was shared among the victors. The conquered did not eat with the victorious. And the meal was a symbol that the battle had been won. Those who ate together were the rulers.

What was once the 'church' founded upon the mission of Jesus Christ, now consists of the global religious community that was referred to in the rest of the book of Revelation as 'the great prostitute.' The great prostitute uses the power of religion and pursues an agenda that actually is centered on destroying the kingdom of heaven and the people of the kingdom of heaven. So, the imagery of the great prostitute was of her riding the scarlet beast with the seven / eight heads that represented the modern church. The message of the prophetic imagery was that the red dragon / serpent / Satan, Inc. with its baal / mystery / mythology religion, has so infiltrated the organized church structure and so distorted the message of God Most High that what was once the church dedicated to its relationship with Jesus Christ, is now unrecognizable as the bride of Jesus Christ. No longer is the 'church,' as represented by the global religious community, in connection with Jesus Christ. A bride 'unites' with the groom. A bride does not seek to destroy the groom. No longer is this antagonistic apostate 'church' waiting for the return of the bridegroom / Jesus Christ.

During the era of the time of Jacob's Trouble, those who continue to await the coming of the bridegroom / Jesus Christ, those who seek to overcome, those who continue to believe that God Most High is alive and immortal, that God Most High is sovereign, that God Most High is able, capable and determined to fully establish the kingdom of heaven on earth with the return of God's messiah / Jesus Christ; those people were referred to with a new title. From the point of Revelation chapter 4 through the rest of the book of Revelation, they were referred to as the 'followers of the Lamb' / Jesus Christ.

The red dragon / serpent / Satan, Inc. has pursued the genocide of humanity since the beginning of human life in the Garden of Eden / garden of God / paradise. The red dragon / serpent / Satan, Inc.'s mission to destroy the image of God the Creator created in humanity is still active and alive today. During the era of the Laodicean church, the red dragon / serpent / Satan, Inc. has hijacked the 'church' in order to accomplish this and other purposes.

But messiah / the Lamb / Jesus Christ will not allow the red dragon / serpent / Satan, Inc. to succeed. And those who remain followers of the Lamb / Jesus Christ to the end will join him in the victory feast.

The Attempt to Disconnect the Message of the Lamb / Jesus Christ Given to the Angels of the Seven Churches, From the Rest of the Message Given Through John the Revelator as Recorded in the Book of Revelation

There exists within the circles of religious academia, a desire to separate Revelation 2 and 3 from the last nineteen chapters of the book of Revelation. This portion of religious academia portrayed Revelation 2 and 3 as having no influence upon the rest of John the Revelator's book of Revelation.

But understanding the full, multilayered message of Revelation 2 and 3 remains essential for understanding the full, multilayered message of the rest of the vision that Jesus Christ provided to John the Revelator and that was recorded in the book of Revelation.

Without understanding the many layers of the message of Jesus Christ to the angels of the seven churches, there cannot be an adequate understanding of the reasoning and motivation behind the scheduled events that will be played out on a cosmic scale, during the era of the time of Jacob's Trouble.

Without understanding the history of the journey that has led humanity to this place where God Most High must decisively act, there can be no deep understanding of the corrective action that God Most High will be instituting in order to change the trajectory of the cosmos, and avert absolute and total destruction of what God has created and cherishes.

Jesus Christ described the eminent danger of the era of the time of Jacob's Trouble this way: 'If those days had not been shortened, no one would have survived. But because of the elect, the days will be shortened.' Matthew 24:22 / Mark 13:20 translated

The world's modern cultures have conditioned the thinking of humanity to believe that the spiritual dynamics that exist within the world, are either nonexistent or impotent, and therefore can be ignored.

The world's modern academics have taught that the history of God Most High's past interactions with humanity, are ancient history and have no significant influence upon the present or the future. Hence the necessity for the Lamb / Jesus Christ to introduce himself as 'the one who was, is, and is to come.' (Revelation 1:4, 1:8, 4:8)

And the instruction that has resulted from the religious community has been to separate their pupils from understanding the true events and the deep implications of this cosmic conflict that will be played out during the era of the time of Jacob's Trouble.

Religious, governmental, economic and social leaders all play this mind game together, of dismissing the *factuality of the biblical record that outlined what was, is and what is to come. They have disconnected the past, from the present and the future, as if that disconnection actually can exist. And then they have sought to discard the past as if obliterating the past can change the trajectory of the present and the future.*

Jesus Christ's message to the angels of the seven churches, was not a thread to the past that can easily be snipped. The true and deep and ultimate message that Jesus Christ sent, consisted of seven bundles of thick and strong steel cables with the ability to hold the weight of all the rest of the message of the book of Revelation that is suspended from it.

A Message 'Hidden in Plain Sight' From Paul to the Followers of the Lamb / Jesus Christ Who Live During the Era of the Time of Jacob's Trouble

Paul understood that a great deal of understanding of the kingdom of heaven, would be lost as the kingdom of Satan, Inc. / kingdom of man gained a greater authority among humanity on earth. Encrypted within Paul's letter to the Colossians, Paul was able to send a message to the 'future' followers of the Lamb / Jesus Christ in Laodicea.

I want you to know how great a struggle I am having for you and for those at Laodicea. Many of you have not seen me face to face and in the flesh. My goal is that you may be encouraged in your hearts and knit together in love, so that you may have all of the riches of the full assurance of understanding the knowledge of the mystery of God, which is Christ, in whom are all the hidden treasures of wisdom and knowledge. This I tell you so that no one might delude you by persuasive speech.

If truly indeed in the flesh I am absent from you, yet in spirit I am with you, rejoicing and seeing your good order and the firmness of your faith in Christ. Colossians 2:1-5 translated

Be careful of anyone who would take you captive through philosophy and empty deceit, according to the tradition of men, according to the principles of the world and not according to Christ. For in Christ dwells all the fullness of the deity, embodied in human form, and you are complete in Christ who is the head of all rule and authority. Through Christ you also were circumcised with the circumcision not performed by human hands. Your whole bodily self, ruled by the flesh, was put off when you were circumcised by Christ, having been buried with Christ in baptism, in which you were also raised with Christ through your faith in the working of God, who raised Christ from out of the dead.

When you were dead in your trespasses and in the uncircumcision of your flesh, God made you alive together with Christ, having forgiven us in all our transgressions, having blotted out the transgressions that were handwritten against us in the decrees which were against us, that condemned us. Christ has taken it out of the way, having nailed it to the cross. Having disarmed the rules and authorities, Christ made a show of them in public, having triumphed over them through Christ's crucifixion.

Therefore, do not let anyone judge you regarding what you eat or drink, or regarding a feast or a New Moon or Sabbaths which are a shadow of the things to come. However, their reality is found in the body of Christ. Do not allow anyone who delights in false humility and the worship of the angels, disqualify you. The one who promotes false humility and the worship of angels, vainly details what he has seen, puffing up with idle notions by their unspiritual mind and not holding fast to the head from whom all the body is connected by the supplied joints and ligaments, and being knit together; a body that increases with the increase of God.

If you have died with Christ away from the principles of the world, why do you still submit to the decrees of the world as if you still belonged to the world? 'You should not handle! You should not taste! You should not touch!' They are decrees which deal with things destined to decay with their use, according to the commandments and teachings derived from men. Indeed, they have the appearance of wisdom in self-imposed worship and humility and in the harsh treatment of the body. But they are certainly not of honor in restraining sensual indulgence. Colossians 2:8-23 translated

Paul understood that the principalities and powers of this world will continue to offer useless and false philosophies that will have the ability to capture human hearts. The principalities and powers of this world will have the appearance of wisdom because they will address the concerns of the earth that affect the human body. But the rules over the body that are contrived by the systems of the world, will always be ineffective in substantially impacting the human head, heart and soul; areas that are governed by the principalities, powers and authority of the spiritual dimension.

Paul's message is about messiah / the Lamb / Jesus Christ disarming all principalities and powers that seek to rule over the physical earth and the human body. Jesus Christ has made a public example of them, and has

celebrated a triumph over them through his crucifixion, death, resurrection and ascension into heaven. All that God Most High accomplishes on earth is contingent upon God being the one who forgives sins because of the work of Jesus Christ's crucifixion, death, resurrection and ascension into heaven.

We live in the world of two dueling kingdoms. Eating the fruit of the tree of the knowledge of good and evil allowed the kingdom of evil to enter into the kingdom of good. The current world that we experience, with the 'kingdoms of this world,' are in constant struggle with the kingdom of heaven (message of the Old Testament / Tanakh prophets, and all of Jesus Christ's teaching).

What God Most High has been and will be able to accomplish for God's holy people, has only been able to be accomplished because of the forgiveness of sins. The work of Jesus Christ has been the merger of God Most High's redemptive plan, God Most High's forgiveness of sin, and God Most High's activity on earth.

The exodus from Egypt, the crossing of the Red Sea as an escape for the people of Israel, the defeat of the Egyptian army / the enemies of God Most High, the establishment of the ancient nation of Israel, the production of messiah / the Lamb / Jesus Christ as God dwelling in human form, etc. were all illustrations of this merger of the types of activities accomplished through God Most High on earth. Different people would focus their perspectives on various elements. But from God Most High's perspective, they were all essential in God Most High's overall plan. Each portion of God Most High's activity has acted to provide more pieces of the puzzle of how God Most High acts throughout human history to bring humanity and the earth to the place where the Garden of Eden / garden of God / paradise can be restored on earth.

The events of the era of the time of Jacob's Trouble and the return of messiah / the Lamb / Jesus Christ to fully establish the kingdom of heaven on earth, remains just another piece put into its proper place in the puzzle, *another of God Most High's mighty acts, with its foundation upon all other previous mighty acts of God Most High. All of God Most High's activity, including the personal activity that God Most High accomplishes within every human individual who becomes a follower of the Lamb / Jesus Christ, acts as essential interconnected pieces of this overall cosmic plan.*

Because of the complexity of this plan that will have required six thousand / seven thousand years of human history, God Most High's plan remains a plan hidden in plain sight, and unrevealed to all who remain in rebellion against God Most High and against the kingdom of heaven.

Jesus Christ's message to those who will experience life during the era of the time of Jacob's Trouble

Revelation 2 and 3 presented a prophecy directly from Jesus Christ who stands in the midst of the church ages throughout time until Jesus Christ returns to fully establish the kingdom of heaven on earth. Jesus Christ identified for John the Revelator and for us, that there will be a number of church ages which today translated into the language of the various theologies of the various historical church denominations.

While the beast of the sea / false prophet / beast from the Abyss / eighth king beast is intent upon fostering a global religious community, Jesus Christ made it clear that the church denominations or the world's various religions coming together into one global religious community, is not supported by God Most High and by Jesus Christ. The seven lampstands had seven lights, not one large light (Revelation 1:12, 1:20, 2:1).

Throughout the biblical message, when a woman was referred to as a prophetic image, there was a corresponding relationship either as the nation that birthed the messiah, or as a bride of the messiah, or as a prostitute without a husband. When the prophetic woman was a 'virgin,' it usually referenced either the nation that birthed the messiah or the bride of the messiah / church.

In Revelation 17, the woman was described as the great prostitute that rides the beast. The prostitute of Revelation 17 was a reference to the apostate church and all other incorporated religion, that the global religious community will become. The great prostitute does not have messiah as a husband because she will not enter into that covenantal marriage relationship with Jesus Christ. The prostitute commits 'adultery' against Jesus Christ because the church that the great prostitute sits upon, was betrothed to Jesus Christ, and yet has chosen to give allegiance to the red dragon / serpent / Satan, Inc.

Revelation chapters 2 and 3 were the last time in the biblical record, that the term 'church' was used until 'church' was used in the description of the Thousand Years Reign of Jesus Christ and of eternity. During the historical era of the church of Laodicea, Jesus Christ has been expelled from what was once the church and the 'church' is no longer betrothed to Jesus Christ.

After the message to the angels of the seven churches (Revelation 2, 3), Jesus Christ and John the Revelator no longer referenced the church. Humanity was designated as either the followers of the Lamb / Jesus Christ, or the inhabitants of the earth. The followers of the Lamb / Jesus Christ were also recognized as the bride of Jesus Christ. The inhabitants of the earth were recognized as comprising the great prostitute that rides the scarlet beast with the seven heads and ten horns, whose dedication is to the red dragon / serpent / Satan, Inc. (Revelation 12, 13, 17, etc.)

The goal of the unholy trinity of the red dragon / serpent / Satan, Inc. with the two beasts of Revelation 13, is to gain total global domination and to fully establish the kingdom of Satan, Inc. / kingdom of man on earth and in heaven. This has been Satan's goal from the beginning (Genesis 3). The goal of Satan has always been to ascend to the throne of God Most High. But to accomplish this goal, Satan must have the power to unseat God Most High. Satan believes that with the amassed power of the inhabitants of the earth, he has that power. The era of the time of Jacob's Trouble will be the test to determine if Satan is correct.

In the goal of ruling heaven and fully establishing the kingdom of Satan, Inc. / kingdom of man on earth, the red dragon / serpent / Satan, Inc. must destroy the followers of the Lamb / Jesus Christ along with God's people defined as the Israelites. God Most High has covenanted with the people of Israel so that the people of Israel will become a nation of priests for God Most High. God Most High has covenanted with the followers of the Lamb to join Jesus Christ on the throne to rule during the Thousand Years Reign of Jesus Christ. Both the people of Israel and the followers of the Lamb / Jesus Christ have their own kind of loyalty to God Most High and as such are enemies of the kingdom of Satan, Inc. / kingdom of man.

Peter wrote, 'But you are a chosen people, a royal priesthood, a holy nation, God's special possession, that you may declare the praises of God who called you out of darkness into God's wonderful light.' 1 Peter 2:9

The plan of God Most High is to make the people of God who were believers in messiah (BC) or who became followers of the Lamb (AD) to be both royal / kings and priests. Traditionally in the era of the Old Testament / Tanakh, a person was either a king or a priest, not both. But during the Thousand Years Reign of Jesus Christ, God Most High determined that all chosen people will be royal / kings, and priests.

Consequently, throughout Israel's history, the red dragon / serpent / Satan, Inc. has been instrumental in urging the people of Israel to reject Jesus Christ as their promised and prophesied messiah. In addition, the red dragon / serpent / Satan, Inc. has infiltrated the 'church' in order to address the threat the followers of the Lamb/ Jesus Christ present to the kingdom of Satan, Inc. / kingdom of man. What was once the 'church,' dedicated to the Lordship of Jesus Christ will become a full-fledged total enemy of Jesus Christ. What was once the church that recognized the foundation that Israel provided for the coming of Jesus Christ, will now seek to 'wipe Israel off the map.'

When Israel rejected Jesus Christ as their promised and prophesied messiah, they demanded that the followers of the Lamb / Jesus Christ leave the nation of Israel, and that they take their Tanakh (Old Testament) along with their new messages of covenant (New Testament) with them. As a consequence, God Most High sent the nation of Israel into the world where they then spent the next one thousand eight hundred seventy eight years without a homeland, and living a life that was blind to the fact that God Most High had fulfilled God's promise to send to them their messiah.

While church religious leaders used to welcome people into the church, we now live in the era where gatekeepers of the church escort those who love Jesus Christ to the door and ask them to step outside with their Jesus Christ. The gatekeepers request that as the followers of the Lamb / Jesus Christ leave, that they take their Bibles with them.

During the era of the time of Jacob's Trouble, the roles of the 'church' and of Israel will be reversed. It will be the 'church' / global religious community that will reject Jesus Christ. And it will be Israel that finally has their veil lifted so that they do realize that Jesus Christ is their promised and prophesied messiah.

Prior to the era of the time of Jacob's Trouble, Revelation 12 described two celestial events followed by war in heaven led by the angel Michael and his angels. Daniel 12 also documented the angel Michael leading in this heavenly war. We do not have access to the details of the events of heaven or the exact timing of the events of heaven. But we do have knowledge of the events taking place on earth.

With the fulfillment of Revelation 12:1-4, the timer has been set in heaven.

With the fulfillment of Daniel's prophesied seven year covenant agreement / peace treaty with Israel, the timer was set on earth. (Abraham Accords, September 15, 2020)

The red dragon / serpent / Satan, Inc. is aware that the time is short and has determined that the goal is that every individual must either join the kingdom of Satan, Inc. / kingdom of man, or be eliminated.

The red dragon / serpent / Satan, Inc. enticed a third of the angels of heaven and the majority of people throughout history on earth, to join in this plan. During the era of the time of Jacob's Trouble, they will add the 'church' to their arsenal and unite all apostate religion to supporting the mission of fully establishing the kingdom of Satan, Inc. / kingdom of man on earth.

During the era of the time of Jacob's Trouble, the red dragon / serpent / Satan, Inc. will provide its own version of a messianic king in the form of the little horn / eleventh king / final horn on the shaggy goat / prince who is to come / king that will exalt himself / beast of the earth / final world ruler who will lead the world to global governance.

Together, the two beasts of Revelation 13 and apostate religion will create a cultural sense that through the kingdom of Satan, Inc. / kingdom of man, all problems can be solved, all needs will be provided for, people will no longer need God Most High or need to meet God Most High's requirements, their version of virtual eternal life will be awesome and also the most that people can hope for. And while slavery in all forms will be increasing, the kingdom of Satan, Inc. / kingdom of man will present itself as the source for true freedom.

The only requirement for receiving all of what the kingdom of Satan, Inc. / kingdom of man has to offer is to bow down to worship the image of the beast of the sea / false prophet / eighth king beast (and relinquish one's first love, the tree of life and paradise - Ephesus, relinquish one's crown of life, eternal life - Smyrna, relinquish one's faith system, hidden manna / hidden spiritual nourishment, identity, and personhood - Pergamum, relinquish one's true knowledge, personal authority, and relationship with true God - Thyatira, relinquish one's security, position, and righteousness - Sardis, relinquish one's personal relationship with Jesus Christ, being loved by God Most High, protection provided by God, personal identity, and character - Philadelphia, and relinquish one's true wealth, health, insight, and fellowship with God - Laodicea).

In reality, the kingdom of Satan, Inc. / kingdom of man will provide for its adherents, wretchedness, pitifulness, poverty, blindness, a number in the place of one's identity, and nakedness; because that is all that slavery allows a person to inherit.

Deception, infiltration, and counterfeiting remain the best tools in Satan's toolbox. Satan mastered the art of deception in the Garden of Eden / garden of God / paradise, with the first man and first woman. Through the red dragon / serpent / Stan, Inc.'s deception, the 'church' that was once betrothed to the bridegroom / Jesus Christ, has abandoned the promised marriage covenant relationship. Through the red dragon / serpent / Satan, Inc.'s infiltration into the 'church,' the great prostitute / Mystery Babylon the Great! has been able to reach full maturity and be ready to rule the earth. Through counterfeiting God Most High's promised and prophesied messiah with the little horn / eleventh king / king that will exalt himself / beast of the earth / final world ruler, the rule of the kingdom of Satan, Inc. / kingdom of man will become a reality, or rather a near reality, before the return of Jesus Christ.

There are those who concluded that because the word 'church' / ecclesia / ekklesia was not used after chapter 3 in the book of Revelation (until Revelation 22:16), that the church will no longer exist during the era of the time of Jacob's Trouble. The claim was that the discontinuation of the use of the term 'church,' was evidence for a 'rapture,' where the followers of the Lamb / Jesus Christ were to be removed from experiencing the scheduled events of the era of the time of Jacob's Trouble.

However, what John the Revelator documented in Revelation chapters 4 through 19, designated three groups present during the era of the time of Jacob's Trouble:
1. the followers of the Lamb / Jesus Christ,

2. the people who are citizens of the nation of Israel that will finally conclude that Jesus Christ is the promised messiah sent by God Most High, and
3. the inhabitants of the earth that comprise the religious and idolatrous prostitute that rides the beast / global religious community / Mystery Babylon the Great!

The last 19 chapters of the book of Revelation display a very active group of followers of the Lamb / Jesus Christ. Just as Noah's family that cruised on the ark had a responsibility to tell their children and their children's children of God's mighty acts; and just as those who left Egypt and passed between the water walls of the Red Sea had a responsibility to tell their children and their children's children of God's mighty acts; and just as those who witnessed the resurrection of Jesus Christ had a responsibility to tell their children and their children's children of God's mighty acts; those of us who experience this era of the time of Jacob's Trouble will have a responsibility to tell our children and our children's children of the power of a God who can bring people through the worst that the red dragon / serpent / Satan, Inc. can devise and attempt to accomplish. For six thousand years, God has used deliverers, not escapists. This is the time when the followers of the Lamb must begin our occupation of becoming true priests, fostering the relationship between the true God Most High and people.

The groups that will not realize a good outcome will be those who decided to deny the divinity and power of Jesus Christ, either as God Most High's chosen people of Israel, or as people who have claimed to be followers of the Lamb but who deny their responsibilities, or as inhabitants of the earth who refuse to recognize their need to repent and turn to Jesus Christ. They will worship the image of the beast of the sea and receive the mark of the beast(s) that is the seal of belonging to the kingdom of Satan, Inc. / kingdom of man. And with receiving the mark of the beast(s), they will irrevocably list themselves as citizens of the kingdom of Satan, Inc. / kingdom of man.

Near the end of the era of the time of Jacob's Trouble, the events of Revelation 18:4-8, will be fulfilled. There will be a time when a voice will come out of heaven and instruct the followers of the Lamb / Jesus Christ:

> "Come out of her, my people,' so that you will not share in her sins, so that you will not receive any of her plagues. For her sins are piled up to heaven, and God has remembered her crimes.' Revelation 18:4-5 translated

This will be an instruction to the followers of the Lamb / Jesus Christ to leave the theological prostitution of the global religious community / great prostitute / Mystery Babylon the Great! and to not look back. Jesus Christ will 'harvest' every follower of the Lamb / Jesus Christ that remains within what was once the church, before the apostate church succumbs entirely to the red dragon / serpent / Satan, Inc. (Revelation 14:14-16, 18).

'Amen' means 'so be it,' or 'this is a certainty.' In the context of theology, 'amen' means 'it is established on earth as it has been established in heaven.'

Near the end of the era of Jacob's Trouble, coinciding with the feast of trumpets and the ten days of awe, there will be a time of final decision making. It will be a time for each individual to give their final answer. Is Jesus Christ the promised and prophesied messiah sent by God Most High to be the true Lord of the world, the true King of kings? Or are the two beasts of Revelation 13, the divine and sovereign leaders that will be fully installed to be global rulers and the determiners of each individual's destiny? Each individual must choose between the kingdom of heaven or the kingdom of Satan, Inc. / kingdom of man.

Jesus Christ presented himself to the angel of the church of Laodicea as the Amen (Revelation 3:14). It was a statement that Jesus Christ will be the means for establishing on earth what has been established in heaven. The entire biblical record validated that Jesus Christ and his kingdom will win; and that the promise of what has been established in heaven being established on earth, will be fulfilled.

God Most High's Covenant with the Righteous, and with the Survivors of this Final Battle that Will Take Place with the Return of Messiah / the Lamb / Jesus Christ and the Full Establishment of the Kingdom of Heaven on Earth

Throughout human history before the incarnate life of messiah / the Lamb / Jesus Christ, God Most High made covenants beginning with the serpent / Satan / Lucifer and the first woman (Genesis 3:15). Also included in the group that God Most High initially established covenant with, were those included in the covenant messianic lineage, and specifically, Enoch, Methuselah, Noah and humanity (c. 2342 BC), Abram / Abraham, Isaac, Jacob / Israel, Moses and the people of Israel (1446 BC), David, etc.

The incarnate messiah / the Lamb / Jesus Christ lived his earthly life in full covenant with God the Father and the Holy Spirit. The resurrection of messiah / the Lamb / Jesus Christ, became the evidence that the covenant that God Most High made with all these people, and with humanity, was valid.

After messiah / the Lamb / Jesus Christ was crucified, died, resurrected and ascended into heaven, he sent the Holy Spirit to seal the covenant with all throughout the world who would become followers of the Lamb / Jesus Christ and would enter into covenant with God Most High.

To seal these covenants, God Most High used water and circumcision. God Most High used a deluge / flood, passing through the Red Sea, crossing the Jordan River, etc. as baptismal sealings of God Most High's people. God Most High also sealed covenant through the ritual of eighth day circumcision. And after the resurrection of Jesus Christ, baptism and the presence of the Holy Spirit in the lives of the followers of the Lamb / Jesus Christ, became the seals for God Most High's covenant. (Acts 2, 2 Corinthians 1:21-22, Ephesians 1:13, 4:30, etc.)

During the era of the time of Jacob's Trouble God Most High will employ a special sealing process for the people who God Most High has established covenant with.

Only some of the details of this sealing process have been revealed through the biblical record.

Jesus Christ disclosed to John the Revelator, that there would be three distinct sealings that must take place during the beginning of the era of the time of Jacob's Trouble.

- 144,000 people of Israel will be sealed (Revelation 7:1-8).
- 144,000 followers of the Lamb / Jesus Christ will be sealed (Revelation 14:1-5). Together these 288,000 of God Most High's people will be selected and sealed for the purpose of standing on Mount Zion with Jesus Christ when he returns at the conclusion of the era of the time of Jacob's Trouble.
- All of God Most High's holy people will also be sealed (Revelation 9:4, 9:20-21).

The general sealing of all of God Most's holy people will provide protection to those sealed, from experiencing specific events that will generally fall upon the inhabitants of the earth through the work of the red dragon / serpent / Satan, Inc. (Revelation 9:4, 9:20-21). Those sealed by God Most High have been promised protection from the outpouring of God Most High's wrath during the final days of the era of the time of Jacob's Trouble.

The pouring out of the wrath of God Most High will take place during the pouring out of the seven bowls / seven last plagues of God Most High's wrath, scheduled to take place after the two witnesses have been assassinated, have died, have been resurrected and have ascended into heaven (Revelation 11:14). Daniel defined this period as lasting a maximum of seventy five days (Daniel 12:11-12 – 1335 days, minus the 1260 days designated for the ministry of the two witnesses – Revelation 11:1-14).

I saw in heaven another great and marvelous sign: seven angels with the seven last plagues – last, because with them God's wrath is completed. Revelation 15:1 translated

Then one of the four living creatures gave to the seven angels seven bowls filled with the wrath of God, who lives for ever and ever. Revelation 15:7

Then I heard a loud voice from the temple saying to the seven angels, 'Go, pour out the seven bowls of God's wrath on the earth.' Revelation 16:1

And the angel swung his sickle to the earth, and gathered the vine of the earth, and cast them into the great winepress of the wrath of God. Revelation 14:19 translated

The great city (Rome) was split into three parts, and the cities of the nations, fell. Babylon the great was remembered before God, to give her the cup of the wine of the fury of God's wrath. Revelation 16:19 translated

There is only one way to receive God Most High's seal and protection from experiencing the wrath of God Most High.

Jesus said, 'Whoever believes in the Son has eternal life, but whoever rejects the Son will not see life, for God's wrath remains on them.' John 3:36

The wrath of God is being revealed from heaven against all the godlessness and wickedness of people, who suppress the truth by their wickedness. Romans 1:18

But because of your stubbornness and your unrepentant heart, you are storing up wrath against yourself for the day of God's wrath, when God's righteous judgment will be revealed. Romans 2:5

Put to death, therefore, whatever belongs to your earthly nature: sexual immorality, impurity, lust, evil desires and greed, which is idolatry. Because of these, the wrath of God is coming. Colossians 3:5-6

Once a person has turned away from their sin, requested forgiveness from God and have accepted Jesus Christ as divine and sovereign God, sins are washed away. And with the sin's removal, the need to experience God Most High's wrath is also removed.

Since we have now been justified by Jesus Christ's blood, how much more shall we be saved from God's wrath through Jesus Christ! Romans 5:9

God's holy people are those who, because of the covering of the perfect sacrificial blood of messiah / the Lamb / Jesus Christ, have been made to be worthy of receiving the covenant sealing of God Most High. Because they are covered by the perfect sacrificial blood of the one who is most worthy, they too share in the benefits of Jesus Christ's worthiness. They are covenantally sealed, and they are protected from the outpouring of the wrath of God Most High.

With every additional provision added to the covenant that began with the serpent / Satan / Lucifer and the first woman in the Garden of Eden / garden of God / paradise, God Must High has built on the foundation of the previous addition to the covenant. Not one of the provisions of God Most High's covenant can be removed and still have the entire covenant make sense. The lineage of covenant agreements that God Most High made with people in the past, cannot be separated even from this covenant action that God Most High has established for the era of the time of Jacob's Trouble, in sealing God's people. The lineage of covenant that began with the serpent / Satan and the first woman, extends like a chain, to the followers of the Lamb / Jesus Christ who live during this era of the time of Jacob's Trouble.

God Most High's covenant continues... and God Most High's promises continue... to this very point in human history and every point throughout eternity.

www.ingramcontent.com/pod-product-compliance
Lightning Source LLC
Chambersburg PA
CBHW071957150426
43194CB00008B/900